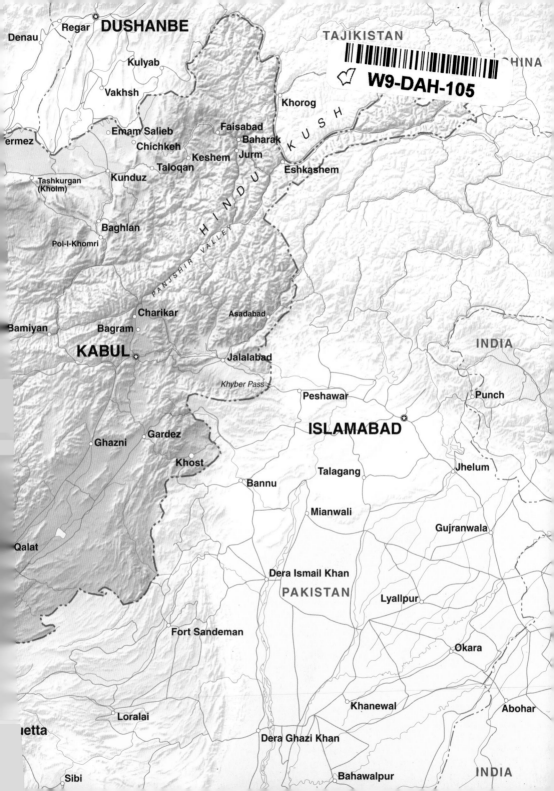

FOREWORD
His Excellency Hamid Karzai
President of the Islamic Republic of Afghanistan

In the Name of God, Most Gracious, Most Merciful

Few lands are as beautiful or as rich in tradition as Afghanistan. It has played host to some of the most famous names in world history: Alexander the Great, Genghis Khan, Tamerlane, and the Emperor Babur. It was, in former times, a meeting point of East and West, the home of the greatest Kingdoms of the Silk Road, legendary for their wealth and their culture; later, it became the cradle of some of the most magnificent cities of Islamic civilization, celebrated for their arts and architecture, philosophers and poets.

With the help of the international community, Afghanistan is emerging from the shadows of the last twenty years, and retaking its place as a respected member of the fellowship of nations. As peace returns with the establishment of democracy and the rule of law, visitors are beginning to re-discover the wonders of Afghanistan. Travellers are now returning to see the snow-capped mountains and fertile valleys of the Hindu Kush; the northern plains, the Amu Darya (Oxus) and Balkh, 'Mother of all cities'; the wondrous scenery, the rivers and glaciers of the Wakhan Corridor and the 'Roof of the World'. Others may come to see the Burial Gardens in Kabul of the Emperor Babur, or the Kabul Museum, which has survived with many of its wondrous treasures intact.

Whether you wish to learn more about the history, society and culture of Afghanistan, or if you intend to travel here as a visitor, you will find in this book a full introduction to Afghanistan's natural beauty, rich heritage and cultural diversity, along with the practical information which a traveller might require.

I hope we will soon have the pleasure of welcoming you to Afghanistan; I can promise that the Afghan people will receive you with the heartfelt hospitality for which they have always been renowned.

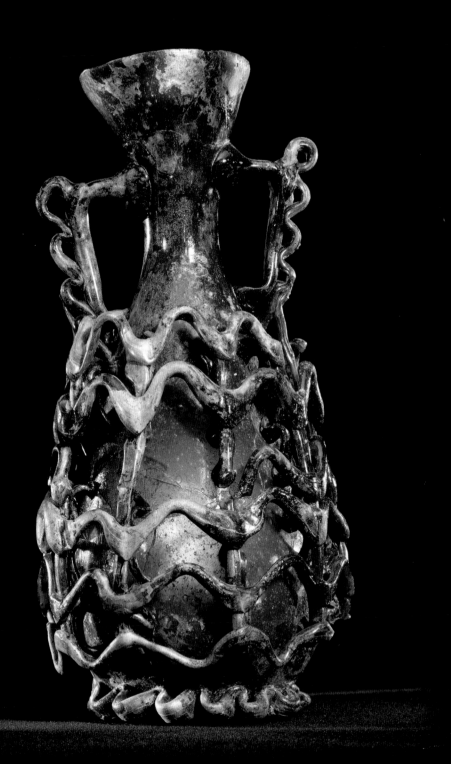

AFGHANISTAN:
A COMPANION AND GUIDE

AFGHANISTAN:
A COMPANION AND GUIDE

BIJAN OMRANI AND MATTHEW LEEMING
INTRODUCTION BY ELIZABETH CHATWIN

Odyssey Books & Guides

ODYSSEY BOOKS & GUIDES

Distribution in the USA by
W.W. Norton & Company, Inc.,
500 Fifth Avenue, New York, NY 10110, USA
Tel: 800-233-4830; Fax: 800-458-6515
www.wwnorton.com

Distribution in the UK and Europe by
Cordee Books and Maps, 3a De Montfort St.,
Leicester, UK, LE1 7HD, UK
Tel: 0116-254-3579: Fax: 0116-247-1176
www.cordee.co.uk

Afghanistan: A Companion Guide © 2005 Airphoto International Ltd.
Odyssey Books & Guides is a division of Airphoto International Ltd.
903, Seaview Commercial Building, 21–24 Connaught Road West, Sheung Wan, Hong Kong
Tel: (852) 2856 3896; Fax: (852) 2565 8004; E-mail: sales@odysseypublications.com

ISBN: 962-217-746-8 Library of Congress Catalog Card Number has been requested.

Grateful acknowledgment is made to the following:
Photography/illustrations courtesy of **Bodleian Library, University of Oxford** 76, 456, 469, 484, 512, 590, 629, 636; **Gary W. Bowersox** 200, 201; **British Library** 74, 124, 371, 374; **Estate of Robert Byron** 334; **Anthony Cassidy** 35, 243; **Elizabeth Chatwin** 15; **Yolande Crowe** 39, 44, 45, 56, 103, 110, 191, 205, 209, 246, 260, 272, 276, 282 (bottom), 285, 286 (top), 287, 288, 293, 298, 365, 380–1, 385, 386, 416, 417, 419, 421, 422, 432, 433, 434 (top), 444, 449, 450 (bottom), 451, 458, 460, 465; 558, 559, 562, 563, 600; **Courtauld Institute/Conway Library** 318; **Veronica Doubleday** 649, 650, 652, 653, 654; **Dupaigne** 233; **Egyptian Museum, Cairo** 134; **Duncan Grossart** 131, 143, 152, 158, 163, 165, 166, 167, 169, 171, 295, 574, 646; **Musée Guimet** 6, 115, 188, 189, 190, 258, 259, 486; **Frank Holt** MBE/**Mrs Anne Holt** 19, 208, 221, 222, 305, 345, 357, 397, 413, 546; **Benedict Jenks** 87, 112, 186, 197, 213, 216, 224, 306, 328, 336, 340, 343, 350, 353, 405, 412, 415, 418, 420 (top), 424, 428, 604, 612, 613, 710; **Edgar Knobloch** 368, 434 (bottom), 436, 474, 475, 477, 478, 479, 480, 481; **Matthew Leeming** 21; **Metropolitan Museum of Art** 369, 567; **Roland & Sabrina Michaud (Woodfin Camp)** 84, 149, 151, 172–3, 240, 253, 254, 256, 263, 267, 274, 291, 300, 310–1, 324, 348, 383, 493, 495, 503, 509; **Mateo & Luna Paiva** 233, 492, 523, 768; **Parsons** 177, 178, 180, 181, 182, 183, 184 (top); **Pitt Rivers Museum** 96, 98, 146, 160, 494, 535, 536, 537, 538, 540, 550, 557, 575, 713; **Private Collection** 184 (bottom), 526, 530, 578; **Jonathan Renouf** 757; **Royal Collection** 120, 137; **Royal Geographical Society (RGS)** 18, 118, 248; **Royal Society of Asian Affairs (RSAA/Ken Walton)** 73, 79, 138, 140, 438, 490, 497, 500, 501, 506, 516, 634, 639; **Collection of Prince Sadruddin Aga Khan** 446; **V. Sarianidi** 8, 48, 237, 657; **Smithsonian Institution, Washington D.C.** 64; **Spink and Sons Ltd** 302, 303, 531; **Tate Gallery** 642; **Topkapi Palace Museum Library, Istanbul** 372, 373; **Jonathan Tucker** 525, 527; **Bill Woodburn** 4–5, 31, 43, 49, 51, 58, 59, 60, 95, 193,

236, 265, 268–9, 271, 281, 282 (top), 284, 286 (bottom), 289, 314, 316–7, 321, 322, 326–7, 330, 331, 332, 338, 351, 356, 376, 384, 388, 390–1, 392, 399, 400, 407, 410, 420 (bottom), 423, 426, 427, 430, 450 (top), 459, 462, 464, 466, 570–1, 583, 586, 587, 643, 644; **Michael Yamashita (Woodfin Camp)** 2–3, 16–7, 89, 123, 129, 139, 155, 217, 253, 254, 257.

122–6, 203–5, 483–4, 513, from *Afghanistan of the Afghans*, by Sirdar Ikbal Ali Shah, courtesy of Tahir Shah; 132–3, from *Nasir Khusraw, the Ruby of Badakhshan*, by Alice C. Hunsberger; 177–83 from *The Carpets of Afghanistan* by Richard Parsons, courtesy of the Estate of Richard Parsons; 193–9, 204–6, 398–403, 571–3, 573–6, from *Legendes et Coutumes Afghanes* by R.P. Hackin and A.A. Kohzad; 200–2, from *The Gem Hunter*, by Gary Bowersox, courtesy of the author; 206–8, from *Afghanistan, Land of the High Flags*, by Roseanne Klass; 208–211, from *A Short Walk in the Hindu Kush*, Eric Newby/Vogue, ©The Conde Nast Publications Ltd; 211–7, from *Afghanistan Weighs Heavy on My Heart*, by Mark Buser and Gail Ann Broadhead; 218–221, from *Ils ont Assassiné Massoud*, by Jean-Marie Pontaut and Marc Epstein, by courtesy of Marc Epstein; 238–9, 243–4, from the *Shahnameh* of Firdousi, translated by Reuben Levy; 270–2, 289–90, 385–7, 451–2, 457–9, from *The Road to Oxiana*, by Robert Byron, by courtesy of Lucy Byron; 317–20, from *Intimate Conversations*, by Ansari of Herat, translated by W.M. Thackston, by courtesy of the translator; 323–4, 325–6, from *Habibu's-siyar* by Khwandamir, translated by W.M. Thackston, by courtesy of the translator; 337–9, from *A Century of Princes*, translated by W.M. Thackston, by courtesy of the translator; 334–5, from *The Sewing Circles of Herat*, by Christina Lamb, by courtesy of the author; 387, from *Light Garden of the Angel King*, by Peter Levi; 390–6, from *The Valley of Bamiyan*, by Nancy Hatch Dupree, by courtesy of the author; 409–10, from *The Hazaras of Afghanistan*, by Sayed Askar Mousavi; 594–6, from *Spies behind the Pillars, Bandits at the Pass*, by Kathleen Trautman; 597–600, from *Beyond Khyber Pass*, by Lowell Thomas.

Front cover photography: Michael Yamashita
Other cover photography: Bill Woodburn and Yolande Crowe

Managing Editor: Bijan Omrani
Editor: Patrick Booz
Cover Design: Alex Ng Kin Man
Design: Au Yeung Chui Kwai

Maps: Mark Stroud
Production by Twin Age Ltd, Hong Kong
E-mail: twinage@netvigator.com
Printed in Hong Kong

(pp.2–3) *Enroute to Baharak, Badakhshan, NE Afghanistan* [M. Yamashita]
(pp.4–5) *One of the lakes at Band-i-Amir. Minerals give the intense colour to the water.*
      [B. Woodburn]
(p.6) *Two-Handed Glass Vase, Bagram, 2nd century* AD [Musée Guimet]
(p.8) *Detail of gold from the Kushan burial hoard of Tillya-Tepe, 2nd century* AD
      [V. Sarianidi]

INTRODUCTION

In the summer of 1969 my husband went on an expedition to Afghanistan with Peter Levi. Peter, a scholar, writer and poet, was going to look at the traces of the Greek satrapies and kingdoms from over two-thousand years ago, and Bruce was going partly because he loved the country and partly to do some journeys he was unable to complete on his first ventures. He asked me to join them after two months; he thought I might not like the country.

I was smitten. Afghanistan has been my yardstick ever since for judging every country I go to—beauty of landscape, of people, of hospitality.

In those days, before the boutiques and restaurants in Kabul's Chicken Street, we ate kebabs and nan bread in the *chaikhanas* (teahouses). I remember a serving of kebabs cost less than a stamp for a letter to England. The poorest people, who couldn't afford meat, were served the gravy from stew, into which they dipped their nan. This was recognized as the most nourishing bread in the world by some international survey group. Coarse and bitter when it got cold, it was full of protein, I'm sure. When warm it was delicious, and certainly filled the stomach.

We were regarded with polite curiosity wherever we went, as soon as we got out off the hippy trail. Sadly, Bruce only spoke enough Dari—the form of Persian spoken in Afghanistan—to make basic requests, so we couldn't have complicated conversations. I learned on a later trip that many educated Afghans had gone to the Lycée and spoke fluent French.

That first trip began with Bruce getting us a taxi to go over the Salang Pass north of Kabul. I remember him shouting at the driver not to turn the engine off. Such drivers liked to free-wheel down the mountains to save petrol, but this practice was incredibly dangerous. They had no sense of danger, or if they did, they liked the thrill.

We went as far as Kunduz, where we bought a white felt tent hanging, appliquéd with Kirghiz designs in red and blue cotton, and some kilims, those marvellous flat-woven carpets. Somewhere I acquired two horsehair fly-whisks. They were a far cry from the jade and ivory handled objects one sees in museums, but these were their ancestors.

From Kunduz we took a Russian jeep for Badakhshan; this was the end of the tarmac, and the dust came at us in clouds. Never have I been so uncomfortable in my life, but the landscape was staggering—riverbeds with monolithic walls, wonderful colours in the rocks and cliffs, beautiful valleys, silver poplars everywhere along the irrigation channels. These last were sometimes four feet deep, and I bathed in them at night if there was no one around. But it was not a crowded country.

In a village in Badakhshan we stayed in a resthouse and were asked by the local headman to come to dinner. He had already sent us some food as a welcome. There was an American family of two doctors, with their three children, who had been working for the Peace Corps—we all went up the path along a rushing stream to his compound. There in the garden was a platform covered with dhurries, then a lovely carpet from Yarkand on top, and bolsters for us to lean on. With the sound of water, the full moon, his favourite grey horse tethered nearby, and platters of delicious pilau, it was a Persian miniature come alive. The doctors spoke some Dari, and they told us the host complained he could no longer get carpets from Yarkhand since the Chinese had closed the border with Xinjiang (Sinkiang). The only trade going on along this road was lapis lazuli. The ancient mines were not many days away.

We met a lorry from France going downhill from Badakhshan. The French driver had brought wine in cartons for a mountaineering expedition in the Pamirs —a litre per man per day—*mais c'est la morale*! That would have made life perfect, I thought. And the next time I came to Afghanistan, there *was* perfection: good wine, made near Kabul by two Italians. Grapes are native to the country, and the choice of fruits in the local bazaars was enormous. What to take? The grapes—large red, long white, small, purple, black, green, seedless, endless! The melons of Afghanistan are the best in the world, and I see why Emperor Babur complained in India that there were no decent ones. The largest, reddest pomegranates, marvelous peaches —you could live on fruit.

In the spring the vineyards were suddenly full of rosy pink tulips. Called *gul-i-lala*, they were the first sign of spring, as snowdrops are here in Europe. Little boys ran through the streets of Kabul, selling bunches of them. The species is *Tulipa clusiana*, but these varied tremendously in size and shape. I thought they were the most exciting flowers I had ever seen. And overall—and everywhere—the spring was hugely exciting! The silver poplar bark became incandescent as the sap rose. The bare hills grew a pale green fuzz of grass, and almond blossoms glowed in the mud-brick villages. I could hardly sit still for all the colour, as we drove on and on and finally out of the Hindu Kush.

This time as we stopped in Kunduz, locals told us that the final of the *buzkashi* was being played that day. The two great rivals—Mazar-i-Sharif and Kunduz—were going to meet on the plain outside town. So we drove to the site, and were, I believe, the only people in a vehicle. We climbed onto the 5th-century burial mounds of the White Huns (Hephthalites) to keep out of the way of the horses.

Buzkashi is the fiercest game in the world, a wild melee during which horsemen struggle and fight to carry the *buz*—a headless goat, but sometimes a calf—to a scoring area. Although the riders apparently have teams, each man is out for himself, and if he wins, his individual victory brings credit to the town he comes from. The men are big and incredibly strong. The horses are stallions taught to fight; they don't play until about seven years old.

I later saw a more formal version, which took place in a stadium for some special occasion. The only remarkable thing was the good behaviour of about 40 stallions, who were kept waiting in a line for over an hour for a VIP.

In Kunduz, there were no boundaries as far as the horizon. The horsemen disappeared into the distance as they chased the man carrying the *buz*. Bets were taken by a bookie, who circulated among the mounted spectators. Eventually the players, fighting all the time, swept back to the crowd. A good time was had by all.

In those early days, we took whatever transport was going our way. We rode in the back of a truck carrying lumps of raw rock salt. We drove all night in a Russian jeep, which Bruce negotiated from Herat to Lashkhari Bazaar. There was a *chaikhana* where the walls had naive paintings of the building of the road—it was quite new then. Everywhere men had red-legged fighting partridges in cloth-covered, bell-shaped cages, or fighting quails, which they handled constantly. They believed they could strengthen the birds' legs by holding them on their knees and lifting them up and down. The loser of the fight got eaten. The men also bought and sold quails by the sound of their calls. In a darkened room they kept a crowd of calling birds, and buyers chose the ones they liked most—not by seeing the

quails, but by the sounds they made, rather like rippling water.

The Afghanis fought all kinds of animals, from quails to camels. It was a Friday occupation, and one friend discouraged us from going to watch because of the blood.

I would love to think that lots of these things still go on. This guidebook is a great sign of optimism for Afghanistan. I do hear good news from people who have been recently. Matthew Leeming, one of the authors, has seen things I've not known about, and I envy his discoveries and anyone who gets to follow them up. Afghanistan—it is a most wonderful country.

Elizabeth Chatwin, Oxfordshire 2005

(Following pages) *Harvesting wheat, near Saat, Badakhshan [M. Yamashita]*

Bala Murghab, Badghis, NW Afghanistan: the Winter Camp of the Afghan Boundary Commission, by T.H. Holdich, 1885 [RGS]

Editor's Note

Although we hope this book will be of use and interest to scholars, it is primarily directed towards those with no broad acquaintance either of Afghanistan or its languages. As a result, we have decided to avoid the cumbrous and somewhat intimidating scholarly treatment and transliteration of names and foreign words. Instead, we have chosen to use the versions that are most readily recognizable and familiar to a general audience. In a work such as this, where a great deal of unfamiliar information is being presented, the most important considerations must be clarity and ease of understanding. But even here, consistency and uniformity have not always been possible either. Two main authors and numerous contributors, using widely varying source materials, have written the many chapters and sections of this book, and differences of word choice and spelling are an inevitable part of such a large effort. Still, there should be no genuine problems or confusion, even as the reader encounters the great many new terms, words, names and usages from the complex and fascinating land of Afghanistan.

Patrick Booz,

Wolfson College, Oxford, January 2005

Fortified village in the Ghorband Valley [F. Holt]

This book is dedicated to
the land and people of Afghanistan

ACKNOWLEDGMENTS—MATTHEW LEEMING

I must first thank two people: Radek Sikorski who introduced me to Afghanistan —his courageous travels during the 1980s' jihad made it much more his place than mine—and the intrepid and remarkable Charlotte Harford, who first took me there. Boris Johnson first published something I had written about Afghanistan in *The Spectator*; and in Oxford, Robin Lane Fox and Craig Raine took concrete steps to make me become a writer; and two other dons, Tom Braun and John Eidinow, encouraged me in my Alexander research. And it was a Cambridge don, Dr John Sayer, whose lectures originally put the idea of going to Afghanistan into my teenage head, an idea that took 12 years to become a reality.

This book started as a set of notes I wrote for James Cecil in 2002 to give him an idea of what to see outside the capital when he was working in Kabul. Unexpectedly, these notes turned into a commission thanks to the publisher Magnus Bartlett. In London, thanks are due to HE the Ambassador Wali Massoud, Dr Abdul Wahab and Dr Said Zeweri, whose enthusiasm got the project going; also Mrs Noushin Farzam and Colonel Muslim Hayat at the Afghan Embassy; in Warsaw, HE the Ambassador Ahmed Zia Massoud, now vice-president of Afghanistan, whose kind invitation took me back to Afghanistan after many years away, during those fateful months of August and September 2001. And thanks to those people who shared their enthusiasm for Afghanistan with me and whose example kept me going when my energy flagged: above all, the late Sir Wilfred Thesiger K.B.E., D.S.O.; his friend, biographer and travel-book expert, Alex Maitland; Sandy and Eleanor Gall, the Countess Jellicoe, Andrea Busfield, Justin Marozzi, Elizabeth Chatwin, Robert Oakeshott, Major-General Charles Vyvyan and his wife Elizabeth; Colin Thubron, Tahir Shah, and Christina Lamb who kindly waived their copyrights to allow sections of their (or their relatives') books to be reprinted.

Haji Safit Mir, Chief Guide of the Afghan Tourist Organisation, Ajar Valley, 2004 [M. Leeming]

In France, to Jean-Jacques and Elizabeth Brondeau and their delightful children for a very productive month writing in their beautiful house; in Paris, Professor Paul Bernard, the excavator of Ai Khanoum; and Baron Eric de Rothschild, who shared with me his father's diaries of hunting in the Pamirs and the Ajar Valley in the 1960s.

In Afghanistan, above all, to my dear friend Gary Bowersox—without whom my career as an independent Afghan traveller would have been still-born—and his friend and guide Khudai Akbary, who took me under his wing and round Badakhshan and the Panjshir in 2001—a journey with more consequences than we ever imagined at the time—and to my close friend and colleague Muqim Jamshady for more help than I can possibly catalogue over the past few years.

Heartfelt thanks in Kabul to Peter Jouvenal and all the staff of the Gandamack Lodge; Haidar Jailani, Catherine McMullen and all the staff of the Kabul Lodge; Mobin Jamshady, Haji Safit Mir—the most famous guide in Afghanistan—Fateh Mohammed, Dr Hamra, the late Mirwais Sadiq—son of Amir Ismael Khan—Minister of Tourism when this book was conceived, who was then appallingly murdered in Herat in 2004, Deputy Minister Captain Jahed Azimi, Deputy Minister Raz Mohammed Alami, Mohammed Farhad Pirzad, Minister Bismillah Bismillah, Mirwais's successor as Minister of Tourism, Dr Abdullah Abdullah, the Foreign Minister, his colleague the late Farhad Ahad, Fateh Mohammed Shehzai, head of the cultural section at the Ministry of Foreign Affairs and this book's Afghan godfather, Dr Sayeed Makhdood Raheen, the Minister of Culture; Daud Akbary, who took me to the Pamirs in 2002; Fiona Gall and her husband Philippe Bonhoure; Deborah Dunham and Satish Nanda at Bagh-i-Babur; Brendan Cassar and Nancy Dupree at SPACH, P.P. Verghese at Standard Chartered Bank, Engineer Nawaz, who cashed cheques for me; at Kabul University, Professors Waissi and Shindandi, who introduced me to Persian poetry—and their thanks also to Philip Blackwell, of the famous Oxford booksellers—who re-stocked the university's library, burned by the Taliban; at the Gandamack and Kabul Lodges, Anthony Fitzherbert, Christian Struwe, Xabier Melan, Ilene Prusher and Jake Sutton for congenial, erudite and amusing company and good advice; Jamie Astill,

Liz Sly and Catherine Philp for late-night poetry readings; Roland Besenval at DAFA; Prince Nadir Naim and Jonathan Ledgard, who re-discovered the Ajar Valley and shared it with me; the King's shikari there, Mir Abdul; in Kunduz, General Daud (whose personal bravery on the road to Faisabad held back the Taliban attack in November 2000, and whose failure would have had unimaginable consequences for the West a year later).

In Jalalabad, again to Andrea Busfield, Haji Zahir, son of the famous mujihad and vice president Haji Qadir, Zalmay Abdul Haq and Professor Richard Strand.

In Bamiyan, Peter Maxwell—also my neighbour in England—who was the UN proconsul running Bamiyan, for his excellent hospitality; Professor Kazuya Yamaouchi, Mr Nawaz at the Bamiyan Hotel, and the unforgettable beauty of the star of *Kandahar,* Niloufa Pazira, with whom I was lucky enough to share the hotel.

In Herat, above all (speaking for Radek and Charlotte, too) to our close and long-time friend Dr Yusuf Qawam, whose introduction to the most distinguished living commander from the jihad, Haji Amir Ismael Khan, led to enormous hospitality and courtesy being extended to me in his city; there also, to Syed Ismael, Abdul Qadir Hakimi and Abdul Baqri, Director of Transport.

Also to my long-suffering travelling companions over the years, above all, Charlotte Harford, James Baldwin, Peter Lowes, Benedict Jenks—who cashed cheques for me—Lesley Scoular and Wendy le Tissier, the latter two both veterans of Afghanistan's golden age who shared their memories with me, for some very happy journeys.

And to the memory of the great mujahedin commander, Ahmed Shah Massoud, a man to whom Churchill's magnificent epitaph on Orde Wingate equally applies: *"There was a man of genius, who might well have become a man of destiny,"* and, above all, the endless and unstinting hospitality of the many, many Afghan people who had never before met me and who I, sadly, will probably never meet again, who killed their sheep to feed me and let me sleep in the best rooms in their houses. It appears that their country's dreadful martyrdom has now run its course and everyone who loves this place must hope that the improvement will continue—*in the name of Allah, the Compassionate, the Merciful.*

But, above all, to my mother, without whom—I can genuinely say—this book would never have been written.

ACKNOWLEDGEMENTS—BIJAN OMRANI

A great deal of my research was done at the Indian Institute Library, Oxford. My thanks there are due to Dr Gillian Evison, Dr Simon Lawson, Dr Colin Wakefield, Mrs Emma Mathieson, Mrs Helen Topsfield, Mrs Kalpane Pant, Ralf Kramer and also especially to Emma Blake, without whose help I would have got stuck many times over on texts in Persian, Pashto, and Hindi. Also in Oxford I would like to thank Jocelyne Dudding of the Pitt-Rivers Museum Photographic Collection for her patient work with me on the photographs of Sir Wilfred Thesiger, Vivien Bradley of the Bodleian Library, and Dr Tom MacFaul.

In London, the assistance of the Royal Society for Asian Affairs—both its library and the expertise of its members—was invaluable. Here, I should particularly like to thank the Society's secretary, Mr Norman Cameron, for his unstinting support; also Hugh Leach OBE, Mrs Merilyn Hywel-Jones, Brigadier Bill Woodburn and his wife Ingrid, Joan Hall CBE, and Ken Walton, the Society's photographer; Pauline Hubner of the Royal Geographical Society helped us also in the quest for pictures, as did Dr Lindi Grant and Geoffrey Fisher of the Conway Library. At the British Museum, I would also like to thank the curator of the Asia section, Dr Robert Knox, as well as his colleagues, for lending their expertise.

Others who supplied assistance at various times include: James Knox; Setitia Simmonds and Lucy Byron (who has generously permitted us to reproduce sections from the works of her late brother); Mrs Anne Holt, (who has generously allowed us to reproduce her late husband's drawings); Alex Maitland; Dr Muhammad Isa Waley of the British Library; Elizabeth Winter OBE of the British Agencies Afghanistan Group; John Koh and Paul Barthaud of Spink; Miffy Evans; Chang Tsong-zung; David Tang OBE; Maxwell C. Lovell-Hoare, Robert J. Finnis and

Jennifer Mordue; Anne Lesage; Bernard Dupaigne of the Musée Guimet; Dr Victor and Veronica Sarianidi; Mateo and Luna Pavia; Lucette Boulnois; Pierre and Micheline Centlivres; Bruce Wannell; Mohammed Yasin of Tribal Rugs Ltd, Hong Kong; Wong How Man; and Christopher C. Burt.

Thanks also to Nancy Hatch Dupree—author of the last authoritative guidebook to Afghanistan to appear before the Soviet invasion—for her permission to reproduce an excerpt from her Bamiyan guide, and also for her more general words of encouragement. I would also like to register my gratitude to all of the academic contributors to this volume for their hard work and the great help that they have variously rendered.

In Hong Kong, I would like to thank the staff of Odyssey who have helped me with this project—Magnus and Margarita Bartlett, Helen Northey, Cecilia Lee and Gary Ng—and also of Twin Age Ltd—Li Suk Woon, Au Yeung Chui Kwai and Tony Tang. Also my tailors, Bonnie and Johnnie Yuen, of Central Market.

My especial thanks to my editor, Paddy Booz, who worked through the Christmas holidays to prepare the manuscript; my friends at home and in Oxford, who kept me diverted after long days in the library with judicious administerings of *witte port*; to James Breen, who first engendered my interest in travel literature; and finally to my parents for their patient and enduring support.

PUBLISHER'S ACKNOWLEDGEMENT

Apart from every one of those already mentioned above, we have received immense support, encouragement and generosity from others whose names we may have inadvertently overlooked. So that we may rectify such omissions of attributions, permissions, and heartfelt thanks, we hope those thus left out in this first edition will identify themselves or be identified by their respective representatives before we prepare the next edition. In the meantime my gratitude goes foremost to Anthony Baynes, late of Minster Lovell, Oxfordshire, without whose generosity this book would have taken infinitely longer to bring to press.

—Magnus Bartlett

CONTENTS

Marco Polo, Hsuen-Tsang, the love story of Farhad and Shirin, accounts of the Badakhshi and Wakhani Ismailis by Wood and Olufsen; the poetry of Nasir Khusraw, Ismaili mystic and exile; remains of Zoroastrianism under Islam; mining for lapis lazuli and rubies, and the golden fleece; the Kirghiz nomads; Lake Zorkul and the question of the source of the Oxus.

Alexander the Great founds Bagram and marches through Panjshir, finding the rock of Prometheus; the Greek Philosopher Apollonius of Tyana walks over the mountains to India; the Afghan legend of Bagram, and other folk tales; silver mining and emerald hunting; the paradise of the Panjshir—Rosanne Klass; Newby's meeting with Thesiger; Mujahedin—a Russian soldier's account; the life and death of Ahmed Shah Massoud, Lion of the Panjshir.

The legendary invasion by Ninus, King of Babylon, and Queen Semiramis; Zoroaster, King Goshtasp and the Gathas; Firdousi and the *Shahnameh*—Sohrab and Rustam; the adventures of Alexander and the marriage of Roxane; the Graeco-Bactrian Kingdom and the site of Ai Khanoum; Buddhist foundations under the Kushan Empire; The Poetess Rabi'a Qozdari; Visits of the travellers, Ibn Battuta and Marco Polo; the Uzbeks and Buzkashi; the modern remains—Robert Byron.

Foundation legends from Harawi's History; Alexander passing through Herat (Alexandria Ariana); story of the Mosque and the Fire Temple under the Tahirids; the love of Nasr ibn Ahmad for Herat; geographers' accounts—Ibn Hawqal and Yaqut al-Hamawi; Ansari's poetry and Gazargah—accounts and inscriptions, Bruce Chatwin; the disaster of Genghis Khan—history of the sieges by Khwandamir; the Timurid renaissance—architecture, the Musalla of Gawhar Shad, poetry of Arifi of Herat, Jami's *Lawa'ih*, writings and apologia of Sultan Husayn Bayqara, the visit of Babur and the wine party; Herat in the 19th century—Charles Masson; the Persian Siege of 1838 and the hero, Lt Pottinger; Christina Lamb describes women's education under the Taliban.

Accounts of early Buddhist travellers, the Great Buddhas and the Silk Route; the Islamic conquest; the devastation by Genghis Khan and the legend of Shahr-i-Gholghola; geology and folk stories of Mir Ali—the Dragon of the Red Valley; the Hazaras, accounts and folk poetry.

First mentions of Ghazni in late Greek epics; Chinese travellers; accounts from Ferishta and Juzjani of Subuktigin and Sultan Mahmud's Ghaznavid Empire; Patronage of Firdousi and his satire of Mahmud; Ghaznavid architecture; the poetry of Sana'i; Towers of Victory; Babur's visit; the karaiz underground canals; the British siege in the First Afghan War and the visit of its army of retribution—story of the Gates of Somnath.

Legends of Alexander; Buddhist inscriptions and Asoka; mythical history of the Pushtuns—the lost tribe of Israel; the Durrani and Ghilzai tribes, nomads and farmers; the hill tribes, and a war dance; Pushtunwali, honour code; monuments of Babur; Khushal Khan Khattak,

Special Topics:

Maps:

AFGHANISTAN—A BRIEF HISTORY

It is not difficult to be confused by the history of Afghanistan. To one approaching the subject for the first time, there is presented the most extraordinary and varied panoply of peoples, religions, dynasties; conquerors who appear seemingly from nowhere; empires that from insignificant beginnings sweep over and subdue territories of unimaginable magnitude, before ebbing away and dissolving with equal rapidity; cities that oscillate between the heights of prosperity and the depths of utter ruination; and a diversity of cultures in which can be discerned influences from as far afield as Ancient Rome, Greece, Arabia, Iran, Central Asia, India and China.

It is perhaps sensible, therefore, before launching into a bare recitation of the historical facts, to expose the simple pattern which lies beneath them. The land now known as Afghanistan has always been—and continues to be—the cockpit of three great civilisations: the Persian to the west, the Central Asian to the north, and the Indian to the southeast. Until recently, the Afghan territories were apportioned between these three powers in varying measures according to their strength; it was only thanks to their coincident decadence in the 18th century of our era that the indigenous tribes in the south—the Pushtuns—were able to rise up and carve out their own empire, which evolved into Afghanistan as we know it today. (Although Afghanistan did not exist as an entity until this period in the 18th century, I use the term throughout the book for the sake of convenience to refer to the lands that fall within its present borders.)

Nonetheless, the established pattern of history was not broken, and despite its independence Afghanistan continued to find itself, even until now, a theatre for conflict and external interference. Afghanistan is cursed and blessed by its geography. Its central location has allowed it little peace, but in those periods of peace its position as—using the word of Arnold Toynbee—a "roundabout" of cultures has caused it to bring forth the greatest achievements in every sphere of human endeavour.

The Walls of Balkh [B. Woodburn]

The Aryan tribes of Central Asia are thought to have been the first participants in this great cycle of invasions. Crossing the River Oxus in several waves after 1500 BC, they encountered a native population of no little wealth and sophistication. Not only had there already been by that time, for more than a thousand years, the domestication of animals, agricultural cultivation of the land, and settlements in small villages and urban conurbations; great administrative and religious centres at Dashly near Balkh and Mundigak near Kandahar oversaw an international trade in such commodities as lapis lazuli and tin, with economic connections stretching from Mesopotamia in the west to the Indus Valley in the east. The Aryans, moving south, are believed to have sojourned for a time in the plains around Balkh and the fertile valley of the Hari Rud River, before splitting into two branches: one to move westwards along the Iranian plateau, the other to continue southeast towards Mundigak, before passing through the Bolan Pass to settle permanently in the north of India. It is with the original Aryan presence in Balkh around 1400 BC (although

some scholars place the date as late as the 6th century BC) that the preacher and religious reformer Zoroaster (Zardusht, Zarathustra) is generally associated. Proclaiming the supreme deity Ahura Mazda, and His rewards for those who pursue "good thoughts, good words, good deeds", Zoroaster's doctrines as enshrined in the *Avesta* went on to furnish, centuries later, the state religion for the Persian Empire, the descendants of the western branch of the Aryan migrants.

It is with the Persian Empire that the lands of Afghanistan first enter the annals of recorded history. The Greek writer Herodotus declares that Cyrus the Great (r. 550–529 BC) of the Achaemenian dynasty "… subjected the upper regions [of Asia], conquering every nation, and suffering not one to pass". Beyond this, he gives no further detail. However, a trilingual rock inscription at Bisutun not only confirms Herodotus' statement, but also goes on to inform us that, amongst other countries, Cyrus was able to capture the districts of Ariana, Gandhara, Arachosia and Bactria—respectively known to us as Herat, the Kabul Valley, Kandahar and Balkh (or more properly, Afghan Turkestan). Cyrus' successor, Darius the Great (r. 521–485 BC), fought further campaigns throughout these areas in the first years of his reign to confirm the Persian hegemony. Having suppressed any lingering dissent, he designated these districts, along with Drangiana (Seistan) and Sattagydai (the Hazarajat, central Afghanistan), as satrapies of his empire, ruled in his name by deputies, or satraps, responsible for raising a monetary tribute and a military levy. Indeed, native troops from all of these territories accompanied the following king, Xerxes, on his invasion of Greece in 480 BC. In Herodotus, we catch the faintest glimpses of the Bactrian soldiers wearing caps, "armed with their native cane bows and short spears", or the fighters from Ariana, carrying "Median bows", under the command of "Hydarnes' son, Sisamnes".

These satrapies remained under the control of the Achaemenian dynasty until the advent of Alexander the Great. Alexander's father, King Philip of Macedonia, had by 338 BC established his city as the leading power in Greece and, having attained this position, decided to launch an invasion of Persia. However, by reason of his assassination, the responsibility for this project devolved to his 20-year-old son.

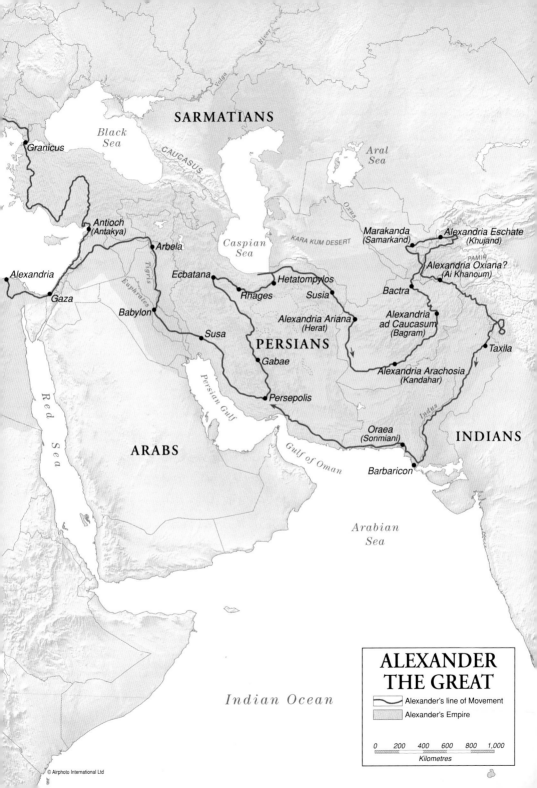

SARMATIANS

Black Sea

● Granicus

Volga River

CAUCASUS

Aral Sea

● Antioch
(Antakya)

● Arbela

Caspian Sea

KARA KUM DESERT

● Ecbatana

Oxus

Marakanda
(Samarkand) ●

Alexandria Eschate
(Khujand) ●

PAMIR

● Alexandria
Alexandria ●
Gaza ●

Euphrates
Tigris

● Babylon

● Susa

● Rhages

● Hetatompylos

● Susia

Alexandria Ariana
(Herat) ●

● Bactra

Alexandria Oxiana?
(Ai Khanoum) ●

Alexandria
ad Caucasum
(Bagram) ●

● Taxila

PERSIANS

● Gabae

Red Sea

Persian Gulf

● Persepolis

Alexandria Arachosia
(Kandahar) ●

Indus

ARABS

Oraea
(Sonmiani) ●

INDIANS

Gulf of Oman

Barbaricon ●

Arabian Sea

Indian Ocean

┌─────────────────────────────────┐
│ **ALEXANDER**   │
│ **THE GREAT**   │
│ ⌇⌇⌇ Alexander's line of Movement │
│ ▒▒▒ Alexander's Empire   │
│   │
│ 0 200 400 600 800 1,000   │
│ ▬▬▬▬▬▬▬▬▬▬▬▬▬▬▬▬▬▬▬▬▬   │
│ *Kilometres*   │
└─────────────────────────────────┘

© Airphoto International Ltd

Despite his age, Alexander was not unqualified for such a task; he had received his education at the hands of Aristotle himself, and had already shown his martial prowess against the armies of the Thebans and Athenians at the battle of Chaeronea. Therefore, after crossing the Hellespont in the spring of 334 BC at the head of 30,000 infantry and 5,000 elite cavalry, Alexander, within the course of three years, not only conquered the cities of Asia Minor, the Levant, Egypt and Mesopotamia, but he also defeated the Persian armies, many times greater than his own, in three major battles, and, after the last of these, Gaugamela (331 BC), was able to march into the very capital and home citadel of the Achaemenians, Persepolis itself. It seemed to many that at this point the campaign was over. However, after it was announced that the defeated king, Darius III, had sent his family east through the Caspian gates towards Afghanistan and intended to raise another army there to fight the Macedonians, Alexander decided to act. After selecting Ecbatana (modern-day Hamadan) as a forward base, and garrisoning it with 6,000 men, he set out in pursuit of the fleeing monarch. Yet, in the midst of the chase, news came that Darius had fallen victim to the treachery of his courtiers. Bessus, the Satrap of Bactria, conspiring with Darius' other officers, arranged the king's murder, after which he himself assumed the title of Artaxerxes V and hurried to his native satrapy to raise an army in order to support his claim to the Persian throne.

Alexander was dismayed to find Darius' body outside Damghan, covered in fresh wounds and abandoned in a wagon. Angered at Bessus' dereliction of duty to his master, Alexander resumed his course eastwards, strengthened in his determination not only to subdue the Afghan and Transoxianan satrapies, but also to punish Bessus in particular for his betrayal. Proceeding on his way, Alexander received the submission of various Persian nobles, including Satibarzanes, the Satrap of Ariana, and even various companies of Greek mercenaries who had been fighting for the Achaemenians. Having entered Afghanistan, he further acted to portray himself as the rightful leader of Asia by the assumption of Persian dress and court customs—a move that dismayed his Macedonian companions, who found the luxury of the barbarians debilitating and their vestments effeminate. Despite the unhappiness this caused amongst his troops (the historian Diodorus of Sicily

Medes and Persians, from the reliefs at Persepolis, Iran, 5th–4th centuries BC. The Median trousers are clearly visible. [A. Cassidy]

implies that Alexander was sensible to draw the line at wearing trousers, which the westerners considered particularly unmanly), he pressed on towards Bactria, leaving a small number of representatives in Artacoana (Herat), the capital of Ariana.

It was after he had moved out of the vicinity of Artacoana that Alexander encountered his first difficulty. Satibarzanes, judging that Alexander's forces were at a safe distance, rebelled, killing the Macedonian representatives and declaring his support for Bessus. Alexander reacted as soon as he learnt of the crisis: a detachment under the generals Erigyius and Caranus was ordered to make a forced march back to Artacoana to put down the revolt. Their sudden appearance outside the city took the rebel satrap thoroughly by surprise, and, after an immediate battle, they were able to regain control of the territory. However, not fully reassured by this victory, Alexander decided to change his strategy. Instead of heading northeast straight

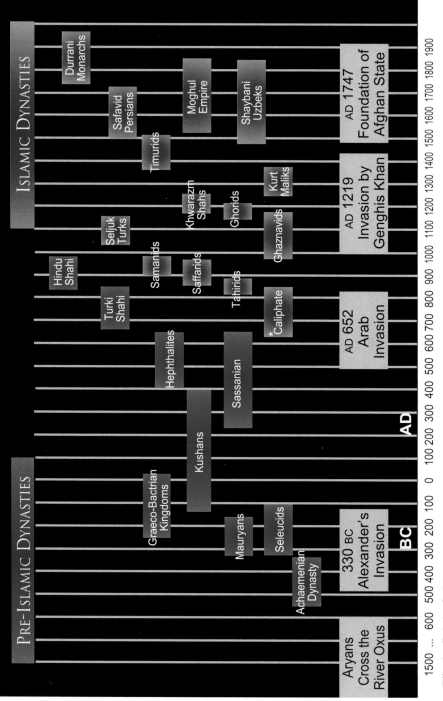

Afghanistan Timeline

Pre-Islamic Dynasties

Islamic Dynasties

Aryans Cross the River Oxus

Achaemenian Dynasty

330 BC Alexander's Invasion

Mauryans

Seleucids

Graeco-Bactrian Kingdoms

Kushans

Sassanian

Hephthalites

AD 652 Arab Invasion

Turki Shahi

Hindu Shahi

*Caliphate

Tahirids

Saffarids

Samands

Seljuk Turks

Ghaznavids

Ghorids

Khwarazm Shahs

Kurt Maliks

AD 1219 Invasion by Genghis Khan

Timurids

Safavid Persians

Moghul Empire

Shaybani Uzbeks

Durrani Monarchs

AD 1747 Foundation of Afghan State

1500 ... 600 500 400 300 200 100 0 100 200 300 400 500 600 700 800 900 1000 1100 1200 1300 1400 1500 1600 1700 1800 1900

BC

AD

* Effective Rule by Caliphate

towards Bessus in Bactria, he decided to turn south; this would allow him to secure and garrison the cities towards his rear when it came to the eventual confrontation with his rival for the empire. Accordingly, he occupied Prophthasia (Farah), defeated Barsaentes, satrap of Drangiana (Seistan) and co-conspirator against Darius, and established a fortified colony at Alexandria Arachosia (probably Kandahar).

When it seemed that the threat in this area had been extinguished, Alexander began to journey northwards in the direction of Bactria. It was at this point, as they crossed the Paropanisadae mountain range between Kandahar and Kabul, that his army began to suffer unaccustomed privations. Quintus Curtius describes the original inhabitants of the place as "a wild people, uncivilised even for barbarians"; the deep snow and the land tough with ice had "hardened [their] very nature". Nonetheless, they had never seen strangers in their country before, and, terrified by their appearance, the natives "brought them everything they possessed, begging them only to spare their lives". Nevertheless, Alexander's troops were struck down with starvation, frostbite and blindness from the cold and snow. According to the historian, Alexander had to exert himself to the utmost, moving amongst the soldiers, supporting those who were weak and aiding those who were unable to go on through exhaustion. At length, he was able to lead them to the more temperate plains around the Kabul River, where, after establishing another fortified garrison —Alexandria-ad-Caucasum (Bagram)—he halted the advance, allowing them time to recuperate.

In the meantime, Bessus had managed to collect a force of 8,000 Bactrian horsemen. One final obstacle, the Hindu Kush (which the Macedonians mistakenly thought to be the Caucasus), remained to protect him from Alexander. Assuming that the invaders would take the easiest route across the mountains—by way of the Ghorband valley and Bamiyan—Bessus devoted his energies to a scorched earth policy throughout the vicinity, destroying food stocks and ravaging the land. Alexander, however, did not behave as Bessus had expected. Setting off from Bagram in the spring of 329 BC, he led his troops across the mountains by way of the more difficult Khawak Pass in a mere 17 days—a remarkable achievement, given that the passage at 11,600 feet was still virtually icebound, yielding very little in the way of food or supplies for the army in transit. Alexander's column finally debouched into the Bactrian plains around Drapsaca (Kunduz). Bessus' horsemen, astonished to see the Macedonians appearing at their rear with such swiftness, feared that they would meet the same fate as the Persian army of Darius. To save themselves, they deserted, leaving Bessus no other option but to flee over the River Oxus to take refuge with the Soghdians. Believing that it would be almost impossible for Alexander to take his men across the river, he decided that he would be able to use the area to muster fresh support for a renewed attack.

Yet, once again, he was confounded. After securing the major cities of Bactria without a struggle, Alexander marched his army across the inhospitable deserts of Afghan Turkestan up to the very banks of the river. Lacking timber for the construction of boats, and finding the ground unsuitable for the building of a bridge, Alexander ordered his men to take the skins that they used as tents, stuff them with straw, and sew them shut. These they were able to use for buoyancy, and the Oxus was traversed without delay. The Soghdian chiefs, not eager to enter into any military confrontation, tendered their submission to him and yielded up the custody of Bessus. The rebel satrap, who had failed in his hopes to foment a revolt against the Macedonians, ended his career in an ignominious fashion. Alexander, condemning him for his treachery, ordered his ears and nose to be cut off after the local fashion, and then that he be sent to Ecbatana for execution before an assembly of Persian nobles—though whether by impalement, shooting by arrows or crucifixion, the historians do not agree.

Alexander spent the next two years campaigning in Transoxiana, attempting, without uniform success, to subdue the local tribes. After making his way beyond Marcanda (Samarkand) and establishing a city—Alexandria Eschata (Khujend)—near the Jaxartes (Sir Darya), he returned to Bactria. Having increased his forces by recruitment from amongst the local population, he re-crossed the Hindu Kush, and,

Mountains and Bridge, Pech Valley, Nuristan, 1971 [Y. Crowe]

meditating an invasion of India, reached Bagram in the spring of 327 BC. A short pause was made whilst the army prepared for this undertaking, after which they set off, following the Panjshir River to its confluence with the Kabul River, and then on to Jalalabad. Here, the force was divided in two. Alexander sent the main column through the Khyber Pass, whilst he himself, with a small detachment, went northeast to pacify the tribes in the Kunar Valley. It was in this almost inaccessible region, now known as Nuristan, that he discovered a city named Nysa, which its inhabitants claimed to be a foundation of the wine god Dionysus. Overjoyed to find ivy and grapevines growing around the settlement—the only place, it seems, that these plants were to be found in this part of Asia—he and his men took the opportunity to celebrate the Bacchic mysteries in praise of the deity before setting out again on their way. Leaving Afghanistan, Alexander rejoined the main body of the Macedonian army in the Swat Valley, leading them on via Taxila to the River Hydaspes (Jhelum), where, in 326 BC, they fought and overcame the Indian king Porus.

Alexander's reaction to this hard-won victory was different to that of his men. Whereas he took it as the signal to proceed to the valley of the Ganges, the soldiers, worn out by the endless fighting and suffering in the monsoon rains, declared that they would go no further: their only wish was to return to Greece and enjoy the fruits of the conquests they had already made. In the end, Alexander had no option but to acquiesce to their desires. He led them south to the coast, and then, turning west, began the march back to their homeland. He was, however, never to complete the journey. Reaching Babylon in 323 BC, he was struck by an attack of what historians generally believe to have been malarial fever, and died suddenly after a short illness at the age of 32.

The vast empire that Alexander had built was by no means ready for his departure. He left, on his death, no legitimate son, and no agreed rules for the succession to his throne. A period of some disorder was to follow. The Macedonian royal family was annihilated by internecine feuds. Some 3,000 Greek soldiers stationed in Bactria attempted to march home, but were prevented from doing so by the Median satrap, Pithon, and then put to death by the orders of Perdiccas, one of Alexander's leading officers. After ten years of strife, however, one of Alexander's younger generals, Seleucus, began to emerge as a leading power in the region. In 312 BC, he set out from Babylon, and, after mounting a nine-year long campaign throughout Asia as far as the Jaxartes, his authority in the east was close to undisputed.

It was in the south of Afghanistan that he found himself unable to impose his rule. By 302 BC, the kingdoms in the north of India had come together under the protection of the great conqueror Chandragupta, founder of the Mauryan dynasty; now united, their increasing influence threatened to weaken Seleucus' grasp over the southeastern corner of his empire. At first, Seleucus was inclined to launch an expedition against them, but on further consideration decided that such a course of action would not be militarily viable. Instead, he chose to negotiate a peace. At length, he agreed to hand over to Mauryan control the Afghan territories south of the Hindu Kush, in return for 500 war-elephants and a substantial quantity of gold.

GRAECO-BACTRIAN, SELEUCID & MAURYAN EMPIRES 250 BC

Greeco-Bactrian Empire
Seleucid Empire
Mauyran Empire

0   200   400   600   800   1,000
Kilometres

© Airphoto International Ltd

To complete the accord, a daughter of the Macedonian general was given in marriage to Chandragupta, and a Greek embassy maintained at his capital city, Pataliputra (Patna). Thus, at the beginning of the 3rd century BC, the northern regions of Afghanistan such as Bactria remained under the government of Seleucus, administered, as was the case during Persian times, by local satraps; the south, by contrast, looked towards India. This arrangement, thanks to the greatest king of the Mauryan dynasty, Asoka (273–232 BC), was to leave a lasting impression. Asoka, who started his career as a somewhat bloodthirsty empire builder (even by the standards of the time), underwent around 250 BC what may best be described as a Damascene conversion. Seized with guilt over the great suffering his wars of conquest were causing throughout India, he embraced Buddhism and spent the rest of his life attempting to propagate his belief throughout his wide dominions. To house relics of the Buddha, thousands of monuments (stupas) were built, many of which are still visible in Afghanistan today; monasteries were founded; missionaries were sent out. More remarkable, inscriptions were found in the ruins of Old Kandahar exhorting the citizens to a life of piety and humility; the language of these inscriptions—Greek and Aramaic—bears witness not only to the continuing presence of Westerners many years after Alexander's invasion, but also suggests that the city must have borne witness to the most extraordinary miscegenation of European and Eastern culture.

The rest of Asoka's reign passed in peace and prosperity. However, although he was able to leave an unparalleled spiritual legacy—in the words of Sir Percy Sykes "it was due to his influence that Buddhism was transformed from a local Indian sect into one of the world's great religions"—the same was not the case in the temporal sphere. Soon after his death, the Mauryan Empire began to disintegrate, and the last representative of its royal dynasty was eventually killed in 185 BC.

As for the Afghan lands north of the Hindu Kush, it is unfortunate for this and following periods that literary records are particularly scarce. Archaeological and numismatic finds provide us with some data, but, rather predictably, the lack of hard evidence has led to a surfeit of conjecture and scholarly controversy. The most plausible account at present is that Seleucus' descendants—the Seleucids—kept

Pillaster bases at Surkh Kotal, a Kushan royal dynastic temple, from the 2nd century AD. *The Greek influence is clearly apparent. [B. Woodburn]*

hold of Bactria, but that around 250 BC the satraps charged with its government on their behalf began to behave autonomously. A shadowy king, Diodotus, appears as the first ruler of a breakaway Graeco-Bactrian state, and, despite the best efforts of the Seleucids to take the territory back under their sovereignty, the new kingdom was able to maintain its independence.

The Graeco-Bactrian Kingdom is perhaps one of the greatest curiosities of the ancient world. In the midst of the Central Asian steppe, surrounded by nomads, at least a year's solid march from the Mediterranean—from which no Greek ever liked to be distant—colonies of settlers attempted to recreate the existence they had previously enjoyed on the shores of the Aegean. A recently excavated Graeco-

Bactrian city near Ai Khanoum on the River Oxus shows how tenaciously the new inhabitants adhered to the old ways of life. Despite being 2,000 miles east of Greece, no institution of the Hellenic *polis* was absent, whether the main street, the market-place, the gymnasium or the theatre; wine and olive oil were consumed; papyrus rolls of Aristotelian philosophy and Attic drama were preserved; craftsmen and stonemasons—although betraying some vestiges of Iranian influence—made Corinthian capitals and statues of Heracles and Hermes; and, across the walls of a *heroön* (shrine) dedicated to Kineas, the founder of the city, were engraved oracular maxims from the very heart of the Greek world—the temple of Apollo at Delphi.

This new independent kingdom was not to be of long duration. Although it was able for a time to control the lands north of the Oxus and, after the fall of the Mauryan empire in 185 BC, to establish its power on the other side of the Hindu Kush in the south of Afghanistan, it was undermined by a series of civil wars and nomadic invasions. Since the middle of the 3rd century BC, Central Asia had been a ferment

of tribal migrations ultimately set in train by the Chin (Qin) dynasty's unification of China. By 150 BC, these displacements began seriously to affect the Graeco-Bactrian state. At around this time, the Sakae people—the likely forebears of today's Pushtuns—made their way across the region to settle in the southern part of Seistan; following them around 130 BC came the Yueh-chih, who, under the leadership of the Kushan clan, overthrew the Greek rulers and eventually set up their own empire in the heart of the Bactrian plains.

Painted glass found at Bagram,
Kabul Museum, 1976 [Y. Crowe]

Nancy Dupree says of the Kushans, not without justification, that "they wrote one of history's most brilliant and exciting chapters in Afghanistan". Not long after their move into the region of Bactria, the traveller Chang Kien (Zhang Qian) made contact with them on behalf of the Han Emperor of China, which contributed significantly to the establishment of the Silk Road. By the time of the dynasty's greatest monarch, King Kanishka (c. AD 128), the Kushan Empire stretched from northwestern India to the Aral Sea to Kashgar and Yarkand, and found itself the sole conduit for the most expensive luxury goods from every corner of the known world. Excavations at the summer capital of Kapisa (Bagram) bear testament to the fabulous wealth accumulated by the Kushans on account of their international trade. Intricate carved ivories from India were discovered in great quantity, as well as Chinese lacquerwork, Roman and Greek bronzes and reliefs, glass from Alexandria and jewellery from every nation. Under Kanishka's reign, the flowering in prosperity and commerce went hand in hand with a renaissance in religion. Although the king himself was probably a Zoroastrian (the recent unearthing of a temple complex at Surkh Kotal suggests a combination of fire worship and a royal family cult), he presided over the evolution of the  school of Mahayana Buddhism. This doctrine, also known as the "Greater Vehicle", recast the Buddha as being ever-present and universal, rather than just a past and venerable sage. The earlier taboos, which only allowed the Buddha to be depicted in art by way of symbols, were reversed; it was now licit, and even encouraged, for each and every event of the Buddha's miraculous life to be portrayed, with a particular emphasis being laid on the contemplation of his transcendent humanity. Missionaries began to carry the message of the revivified religion along the trade routes to China and beyond. Buddhist craftsmen, seeking a fresh artistic language

Buddhist fresco, Kabul Museum, Kabul, 1971 [Y. Crowe]

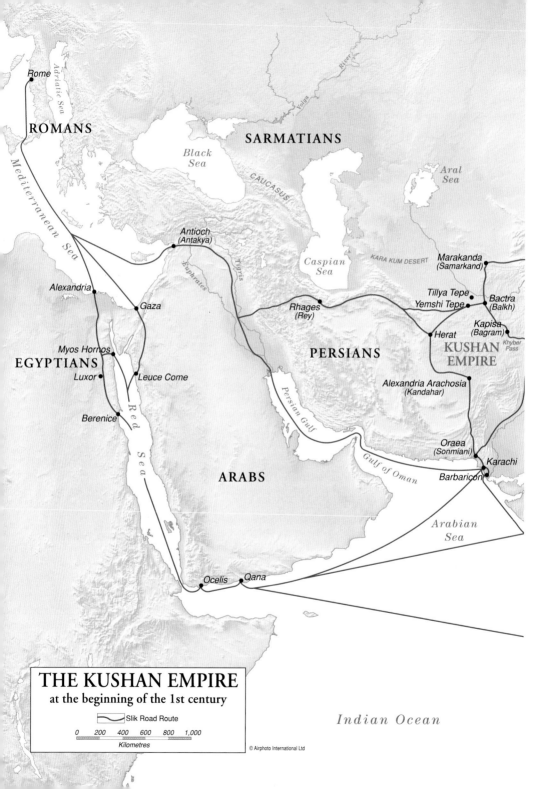

Rome

Adriatic Sea

ROMANS

Mediterranean Sea

SARMATIANS

*Black
Sea*

CAUCASUS

Volga River

*Aral
Sea*

Antioch
(Antakya)

Euphrates

Tigris

*Caspian
Sea*

KARA KUM DESERT

Marakanda
(Samarkand)

Alexandria

Gaza

Rhages
(Rey)

Tillya Tepe
Yemshi Tepe

Bactra
(Balkh)

Kapisa
(Bagram)

Herat

*Khyber
Pass*

**KUSHAN
EMPIRE**

Myos Hornos

EGYPTIANS

Luxor

Leuce Come

PERSIANS

Alexandria Arachosia
(Kandahar)

Persian Gulf

Berenice

*Red
Sea*

Oraea
(Sonmiani)

Gulf of Oman

Karachi

Barbaricon

ARABS

*Arabian
Sea*

Ocelis Qana

Indian Ocean

THE KUSHAN EMPIRE
at the beginning of the 1st century

⌒ Slik Road Route

0   200   400   600   800   1,000
Kilometres

© Airphoto International Ltd

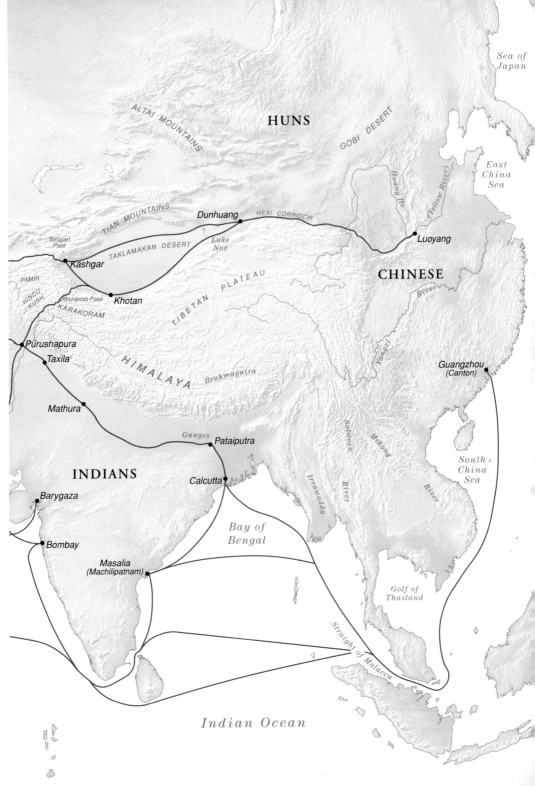

Sea of Japan

ALTAI MOUNTAINS

HUNS

GOBI DESERT

East China Sea

TIAN MOUNTAINS

Dunhuang

HEXI CORRIDOR

Haung He (Yellow River)

Luoyang

Torugart Pass

TAKLAMAKAN DESERT

Lake Nor

Kashgar

PAMIR

TIBETAN PLATEAU

CHINESE

River

HINDU KUSH

Khunjerab Pass

Khotan

KARAKORAM

Purushapura

Taxila

HIMALAYA

Brahmaputra

Yangzi

Guangzhou (Canton)

Mathura

Ganges

Pataiputra

Salween River

Mekong River

INDIANS

Calcutta

Barygaza

South China Sea

Bombay

Bay of Bengal

Masalia (Machilipatnam)

Irrawaddy River

Golf of Thailand

Straight of Malacca

Indian Ocean

to respond to the evolving ideas of their faith, began to draw from every available source, and, mixing together Indian, Persian and even Graeco-Bactrian traditions, gave birth to the art of Gandhara. Countless sculptures and reliefs in this striking new style, an amalgam of Eastern and Western motifs, have been found throughout Afghanistan; to this period of artistic experimentation, we owe, more than anything else, the genesis of the familiar figure of the Buddha.

For all of its brilliance, the Kushan Empire was not immune from the pattern that had been established by its predecessors. The Roman Empire and the Han dynasty of China began, by the end of the 2nd century AD, to falter; as a consequence, international trade went into decline and the revenue generated for the Kushans by the Silk Road began to shrink. Perhaps as a result of this, the Kushan Empire in Afghanistan broke up into a set of petty kingdoms ruled by Kushan princes, no longer answerable to a single sovereign. These new fragmentary states made an easy prey for external powers, and Persia, now resurgent under the Sassanian dynasty, was not reluctant to exploit the turmoil on its eastern border. By around AD 250— although the exact details of the process whereby this took place are still unclear— the Kushan princedoms had acknowledged the suzerainty of the Sassanians, and Afghanistan again came to be under the control of the Persians.

It is worthwhile to note that, over the last ten years, a considerable number of manuscripts dating from this period have been discovered. Work is currently in progress to decipher and translate these (they are written in the ancient language of Bactria, cognate with Persian), and once this academic labour is completed a great deal more light should be shed on this indistinct and hazy period of Afghan history.

(Above) *Goat, from the Kushan hoard of Tillya-Tepe [V. Sarianidi]*
(Right) *General view of the Bamiyan Valley, 1972. In the distance on the left centre, the Large Buddha, and on the far right, the Small Buddha. [B. Woodburn]*

After 150 years of relatively peaceful Sassanian rule, another invasion from the north was to throw Afghanistan into chaos. At the beginning of the 5th century AD, a central Asian tribe known as the Hephthalites, or White Huns, began to migrate from the vicinity of the Aral Sea and, having crossed the Oxus, wrested Bactria and Khurasan from the Persians. Although a desperate effort made by Bahram Gur, the Shah of Persia, managed to prevent them from penetrating any further into the heartlands of his empire, he was unable to stop them from waxing in strength. Within a hundred years, the Hephthalites had displaced all of the Kushan vassal princes, taken over the rest of Afghanistan and found themselves in a position to mount attacks on northwestern India. From what we know of them, it is clear that the Hephthalites made an unhappy contrast to their predecessors; they attacked Buddhist monasteries, destroyed buildings and works of art, massacred the local populations and eventually blotted out an extraordinary culture that could trace its roots directly back to Ancient Greece. The Buddhist traveller Hsuen-Tsang (Xuan Zang), passing through the Kabul River valley in AD 630, briefly summarised the catastrophe which had befallen the whole country: "There are a million Buddhist

monasteries which are in ruins and deserted. They are overgrown with weeds and constitute a mournful solitude."

At the beginning of the 7th century, the Persians made an alliance with various Turkish tribes in Central Asia. Launching simultaneous attacks against the Hephthalite Empire—the Turks in Transoxiana and the Persians in Afghanistan—they were able to bring an end to their dominance. Like the Kushans who came before them, Hephthalite princes, some of them now Buddhist, ruled the lands north of the Hindu Kush as subjects of the Persian Empire. However, an independent Indian dynasty, the Turkishahis, emerged in the south of the county, maintaining a Buddho-Hindu state that embraced the cities of Kabul, Kandahar and Ghazni.

This new settlement of affairs was to endure only briefly. The Sassanian Empire by this time had become deeply enfeebled by its perennial feuding with the Byzantines. The Arabs, in contrast, united by the preaching of Mohammed and his proclamation of a new faith—Islam—were a power in the ascendant. A year after the Prophet's death in AD 632, the Arab armies attacked and comprehensively defeated the Sassanians at Al-Hafar near the borders of modern-day Kuwait. Realising that they were in a position to exploit the weakness of the Persians, they launched a full-scale campaign against them, and after two major battles— Khadesiya in 637 and Nehavend in 642—were able to annex all the provinces of Persia (aside from Tabaristan) up to the borders of Afghanistan. Nonetheless, the new Islamic Empire was not content with its extirpation of the Sassanian dynasty and the possession of regions it had already subjugated: in 652, the governor of Basra, Abdullah ibn Amir, ordered an Islamic expedition under the general Abd-al Rahman to proceed eastwards against the principalities of Afghanistan.

They found the invasion by no means an easy affair. In the south, they stationed a garrison in the region of Seistan, but were unable to unseat the Turkishahis of Kabul (despite, for a brief spell, capturing their king). In the north, they took Nishapur, received the submission of Herat and went on to capture Balkh; nevertheless, the occupation was dogged by unrest on the part of the natives and, after one serious revolt against Arab rule in the latter city, the Zoroastrian shrine of

*Remains of the No-i-Gumbad Mosque (the Mosque of the Nine Domes) near Balkh,
from the period of Samanid rule, c.10th century AD. [B. Woodburn]*

Nowbahar was razed to the ground in retaliation. At length, aside from occasional rebellions, the provinces of Khurasan and Afghan Turkestan were subdued and, standing under the umbrella of the caliphate, were used as bases from which to launch further Islamic missions against the kingdoms of Transoxiana and Central Asia.

It is difficult to comment on the rate at which conversions were effected to Islam in Afghanistan; studies on this subject in other areas such as Muslim Spain could not be repeated in Afghanistan for the want of detailed and accurate data. Using as evidence the scraps of information left to us by contemporary historians and geographers, it would be reasonable to conjecture that it was a steady process, taking place over hundreds of years. Herat and Balkh are known to have been centres for Nestorian Christianity; in the former, we learn from a 10th-century traveller, Ibn Hawqal, that a "church for Christians" was still to be seen in his time. At the same moment, Kabul was divided between "Muslims, Jews, and idolaters [Hindus]", and the central region of Ghor was an "Infidel land", although populated by some Muslims. The 12th century writer Yaqut al-Hamawi describes a major Zoroastrian fire-temple in Seistan and alludes to idolaters in the Hindu Kush; of the latter, some in the valleys of modern-day Nuristan were not to accept the faith until the end of the 19th century.

Like the empires that came before, the caliphate was to find it impossible to maintain its authority over the outlying provinces. Sheer size (at its zenith, reaching from Spain to Transoxiana) and bloody internal feuds over the possession of leadership hampered its ability to project power far beyond the central districts. The consequence for Afghanistan was the appearance of a quite bewildering succession of local Islamic dynasties ruling "in the name of the caliph"—but, of course, independently—which would rise, vie for position and territory with other similar enterprises, flourish for a time and then break down. The first of these, the Tahirid, founded by an Arab chieftain named Tahir "the Ambidextrous", seized control of Khurasan in 822. Not long afterwards in Seistan, Yakub bin Lais, an itinerant fanatic nicknamed "Saffar" (copper) from his father's trade of a copper-smith, took command of the local garrison and began on a career of conquest. Having attacked the Buddhist kingdoms in Kabul and Bamiyan, he went on to capture Herat, Kerman and Shiraz, and replace the Tahirids in 872 with his own Saffarid dynasty. Determined to force the Caliph to acknowledge his legitimacy, in 875 he marched against the capital Baghdad but was beaten back, and died three years later whilst trying to raise a new army. Yakub's brother Amr followed as head of the Saffarid house, but he in his turn was opposed by another eminent family, the Samanids. Starting from a base in Transoxiana, they fought against and defeated Amr, secured Balkh and Khurasan, and established their own empire which, within 50 years, came to embrace the whole of Afghanistan, and Persia as far as the vicinity of Baghdad.

The Samanids chose Bokhara for their capital. Although they embellished it greatly with fine architecture and made it a place of resort for some of the leading scholars of their time, its distant position in Transoxiana led to it experiencing the same problem as the caliphate itself: how to keep adequate control over the far-off provinces. Unrest in the Saffarid heartlands of Seistan was endemic, and the Samanid grip over the rest of Afghanistan was not by any means certain. As a result, the Samanid leaders increasingly turned to the local Turkish tribesmen for help, employing them as *mamluks*, or "slave soldiers", and using them to enforce the Samanid hegemony. Needless to say, the strategy backfired. It was as difficult to maintain their obedience as it was that of the original populations. By 961, one of the mamluk generals, Alptigin, governor of Nishapur, had rebelled with his force of 7,000 men, fought off all attempts by the central government to suppress the revolt and taken the southern fortress city of Ghazni as his stronghold.

At first, the rulers in Bokhara protested at this usurpation of their power in Afghanistan. Yet, as the forces under Alptigin and his successors grew in strength, they found it convenient to recognise them as "governors" of Ghazni, although they acted with full autonomy. In 976, one of Alptigin's sons-in-law, Subuktagin, assumed his position as ruler and launched a series of military campaigns to extend his sphere of influence; it was thanks to one of these that Kabul's Indian kings were finally defeated and that the city, by 988, was brought into the house of Islam. Six years later, at the request of the weak Samanid leader Nuh II, Subuktagin sent his eldest son Mahmud into Khurasan to expel a number of rebels and heretics; that province, including the city of Herat, also fell under their dominion. By the time that Mahmud had succeeded his father in 998, not only was he the de facto ruler of Afghanistan, but it had become clear the Samanid empire in Transoxiana was on the verge of collapse. Mahmud therefore decided to apply for legitimacy not to Bokhara, but rather to the Caliph himself in Baghdad. Al-Kadir Billah, who then held that office, responded favourably to his petition, bestowing on him a robe of honour and the title *Yamin-ad-Daulah*, or "Right Arm of the State". Thus Mahmud, now officially independent from the Samanids, could call himself the founder of a new empire, and a new dynasty—the Ghaznavids.

It would not be unjust to say that Mahmud the Great was a paradigmatic Afghan ruler: both an aggressive but brilliant martial leader and discerning patron of the arts. He led his troops against the remainder of the Samanid lands and Persia; most

Tabriz

Caspian Sea

Aral Sea

CAUCASUS

Volga River

Oxus

KARA KUM DESERT

Samarkand

ALTAI MOUNTAINS

TIAN MOUNTAINS

TAKLAMAKAN DESERT

Rey

Nishapur

Balkh

PAMIR

HINDU KUSH

KARAKORAM

Baghdad

Tigris

Euphrates

Isfahan

Herat

Kabul

Ghazni

HIMALAYA

Kandahar

Indus

GHAZNAVID EMPIRE

Ganges

Pataiputra

Persian Gulf

Gulf of Oman

Sonmiani

Karachi

Calcutta

Arabian Sea

Bay of Bengal

Indian Ocean

GHAZNAVID EMPIRE
AD 1030

| | Ghaznavid Empire |
| | Ghorid Empire |

0   200   400   600   800   1,000
Kilometres

© Airphoto International Ltd

notably of all, he launched 17 expeditions into India, capturing great swathes of territory for his empire, destroying idols and carrying off masses of booty (in that country, he is not remembered fondly). With the spoils and new-found revenues brought back from the east, he adorned Ghazni and his other cities with fine new buildings and was able to support a host of scholars, historians and poets, the most prominent amongst them being Firdousi, author of the Iranian national epic, the *Shahnameh*, or Book of Kings.

Mahmud died in 1030; in accordance with historical precedent, his empire, touching the Ganges in the east and the Caspian in the west, began to crumble round the edges. In India, the Ghaznavid governors periodically withheld taxes from the central treasury and agitated for revolt. In the north, along the course of the Oxus, another migrating Central Asian horde, the Seljuk Turks, began to pose a new threat. By 1040, they had gathered sufficient strength to defeat Mahmud's son, Masud, at the Battle of Dandanqan and seize Balkh, Herat and the whole of Khurasan. Ghazni itself was to continue as a great capital and centre of Persian culture for the next 100 years, but the military capabilities of the Ghaznavids were worn down by internecine strife and disputes over the succession. In 1118, after four years of near anarchy, one of the leadership contenders, Bahram, secured the throne with the help of a force sent by the Seljuk ruler, in return for acknowledging himself as one their vassals; as a result, the independence of the Ghaznavid monarchy came to an end. Their empire, however, persisted until the middle of the century, at which point they fell into conflict with the Shansabani chiefs in the mountain stronghold of Ghor, near Herat. In 1149, after a bitter struggle and a number of battles, the Ghorid forces under Ala-ud-Din swept into Ghazni and left the magnificent city as a ruin—a deed which earned Ala-ud-Din the title of *Jahan Suz*, or "World-burner". King Bahram fled to the Ghaznavid possessions still held in India, but the Ghorids pursued him, absorbing his own territory as they went. By 1186, the Ghorids had made themselves the masters of Afghanistan, capturing not only all of the Ghaznavid land in India, but also the Seljuk lands in Khurasan and the city of Herat. Yet it will be no surprise to the reader that the new Ghorid Empire quickly went the way of the Ghaznavid. In the north, the Khwarazm-Shahs, who had

ruled the Transoxianan land of Khwarazm as vassals of the Seljuks, began to grow in prominence. As soon as the Ghorid chiefs began to squabble with each other for primacy, the Khwarazm-Shahs started to make their way across the Oxus and, by 1215, swallowed up Afghanistan and the empire of the Ghorids. Their freshly-won hold over Central Asia was only to last for another five years; the whole merry-go-round of empires was to be brought to a sudden halt by the appearance of one man —Genghis Khan.

In the pasture lands north of China between Lake Baikal and the Gobi Desert dwelt a people known as the Mongols. This group of nomads was not, in early times, well regarded. The Europeans and the Arabs referred to them as "Tartars" and "Tata" respectively—alluding to the Latin word *Tartarus*, or "hell"; the Chinese considered them to be uncivilised and barbarian. Nonetheless, whatever they lacked in civilised refinement, they made up for in warlike prowess. In the second half of the 12th century, Yesügei Khan, the leader of a confederation of 40,000 Mongol families, began a series of attacks against the Jin dynasty. Although China suffered considerably in the course of this rebellion, Yesügei himself was killed, and in 1175 his 13-year-old son Temuchin—known to us as Genghis Khan—succeeded to his place. At such a tender age, he found it almost impossible to command the obedience of his subordinates, but, after many difficulties, thanks to "his genius, his valour, and his strong personality" as Sykes puts it, he rose greatly in the esteem of his fellows. In 1206, having lead his faction to victory over several rival groupings, a *kuriltay*, or grand council of the Mongol chiefs was assembled; here, Temuchin was acclaimed with the title of *Genghis Khan*, or "the Very Mighty Khan", and recognised as their overall leader.

In the following years, Genghis continued to fight against the Jin dynasty, capturing large areas of northern China and, by 1218, the provinces of Central Asia contiguous to the dominions of the Khwarazm-Shahs. At this point, Genghis sent an embassy, seeking to establish political and commercial relations between the Mongols and the Khwarazm-Shahs; yet the Khwarazm ruler Muhammad, fearing that the proposal would lead to his own subordination, refused to acquiesce.

The Minaret of Bahram Shah, 12th century AD, Ghazni, 1967 [Y. Crowe]

Although perhaps not the best course of action, it was at least understandable. However, his next move—the arrest of a train of Mongol merchants as spies, their summary execution and the confiscation of their goods—can only be classed as foolish; it gave Genghis the pretext he required to lead an attack against him. Thus, in 1219, Juji, the eldest son of Genghis, marched out with the Mongol forces, and, in an engagement near Osh, utterly routed Muhammad's superior army of 200,000 men. Unnerved by this, the Khwarazm Shah decided to fall back on his cities in Transoxiana, hoping either that they could be defended, or that if taken, the Mongols would be happy with whatever booty they could seize and return back whence they came. He was to be further disappointed. The Mongols captured Bokhara, Samarkand and the Khwarazm capital of Urganj; the men (aside from the artisans) were massacred or taken for use as sword-blunters, the women and children enslaved and the cities themselves sacked. Muhammad, in despair, fled to

(Above) *Watchtowers in the ruins of Shahr-i-Gholghola, Bamiyan;*
(right) *Shahr-i-Zohak, or the Red City, at the head of the Bamiyan Valley. In the 12th–13th centuries* AD, *during the time of the Ghorid kings and the Khwarazm-Shahs, this dramatic fortress protected the eastern entrance to the valley.* [B. Woodburn]

the shore of the Caspian where he died, and Genghis turned his men south to continue the campaign in Afghanistan.

Genghis' pursuit of utter desolation can be put down to three causes. The Mongols were pagan and would remain so for several generations; not sharing the faith of the Muslims whom they were attacking, their violence was not at all mollified by a sense of religious fellowship. By destroying cities as he went and wiping out the total population, Genghis prevented his lines of communication from being cut and insured against strong-points being taken against him in the rear. Moreover, by depopulating the country and, hence, bringing organised agriculture to a standstill, he hoped to allow the fields to degenerate into nomadic pastureland, suitable for the flocks and herds that followed the Mongol army. This whole policy he carried over the Oxus. Balkh, Merv and Nishapur were razed to the ground. Herat was initially spared, but after the Khwarazm Shah's son Jalal-ud-Din made a stand against the Mongols at Ghazni, inflicting a serious reverse, Herat was destroyed in retaliation (1222). According to the historian Khwandamir, 40 people

Part of the Citadel of Herat [B. Woodburn]

survived of a population of 1.2 million, and the massacre took seven days to accomplish. Genghis went on to pursue Jalal-ud-Din as far as the Indus, and attempted to capture Multan before eventually turning back, and, by way of Kabul and Badakhshan, he made his way back home.

Genghis died in his native land in 1227. Louis Dupree says of him that he "was the atom bomb of his day", and that "western Asia still bears the scars, still suffers from the economic impact". Certainly, Balkh—the Mother of All Cities—and Bamiyan never recovered. The ruins of irrigation systems Genghis destroyed are still visible, and a greater part of the agricultural land that he wasted remains desert to this time. Of Afghanistan, for over 100 years after his invasion, there is little to report. Herat, on account of its place on the trade routes and fertile location near the Hari Rud River, was able to regain its former eminence relatively rapidly; granted in 1245 by the Mongols to a dynasty known as the Kurt Maliks—a scion of the Shansabani chiefs of Ghor—it was, with good government, able to flourish. However, much of the rest of Afghanistan, whose cities, as the Arab traveller Ibn Battuta tells us, had been reduced to little more than villages, was ruled over by petty princes and local strongmen of whom not much can be said. The one small boon to come from the conquest was the imposition of a *Pax Mongolica* throughout the East and the consequent reopening of trade routes: through the devastation wrought by Genghis was Marco Polo able to make his way to China.

It was, of course, impossible that this state of weakness and disunity could continue indefinitely; such conditions were ideal for ambitious warlords who desired to carve out new kingdoms for themselves. In the end, it was a descendant of Genghis who succeeded in exploiting the disorder for the sake of empire-building; his name was Timur. Known to the West as Tamerlane (a knee deformity earned him the nickname *lenk* or "lame" —hence his usual sobriquet of "Timurlenk" or "Tamerlane"), he was an outstanding product of the chaos of his age. A member of the Turcoman Barlas tribe, he was born in Kesh (modern-day Shahr-i-Sabz) near Samarkand in 1336. Having come of age, he was noted both for his courage, determination and ability to formulate strategy; putting all of these talents to use in a period of complex civil strife, he was able to bolster himself in the eyes of Tughluq Temür Khan, the governor of Mongolistan, and thus to secure in 1361 the governorship of his home city. However, veiled threats from Tughluq's son, and court intrigues at Samarkand, made Timur's position almost untenable. Deciding to flee, he was joined by his brother-in-law, Amir Husayn, and, reaching Seistan, they spent several years wandering the south of Afghanistan as mercenaries and freebooters. However, tiring of this precarious existence, they rallied a number of tribes to their standard and began to march north. Overcoming Tughluq's army in Kunduz, and inflicting further defeats on his son, they were able to capture Kesh and eventually Samarkand. But with the growth of their power came friction between them, and, breaking off the alliance, each began to fight the other for overall control of this nascent empire. Eventually, by 1369, Timur was able to capture Amir Husayn's stronghold in Balkh, and, after the execution of his former colleague, all the local princes came to make their pledges of loyalty.

After this point, Timur was to spend the rest of his life on campaign. When he had subdued Khwarazm and the rest of Transoxiana, like his predecessors he turned towards Afghanistan. The Kurt Maliks, knowing that they had little chance of making a stand against such a force, decided in 1381 to yield up Herat. Despite their free surrender, Timur somewhat unjustly put the city to plunder, but soon realising the strategic and economic importance of the place, gave orders for it to be restored. This done, he carried on south past Kabul to Seistan, the scene of his earlier life, where he rooted out his previous masters and rivals and utterly destroyed the capital of the area, Zaranj, which has never yet been rebuilt.

Black
Sea

CAUCASUS

Aral
Sea

TIAN MOUNTAINS

Baku

Caspian
Sea

Oxus

KARA KUM DESERT

Bishkek

Tashkent

Samarkand

Kashgar

TAKLAMAKAN DESERT

Dushanbe

PAMIR

HINDU KUSH

KARAKORAM

Tehran

Tigris

Baghdad

Nishapur

Mashhad

Balkh

Mazar-i-Sharif

Euphrates

Isfahan

Herat

Kabul

Peshawar

HIMALAYA

Ahvaz

Kandahar

Lahore

Persian Gulf

Kerman

Delhi

Indus

Ganges

Gulf of Oman

Sukkur

Sonmiani
Karachi

Arabian
Sea

Indian Ocean

Bombay

TIMURID EMPIRE
AD 1400

0 200 400 600 800 1,000
Kilometres

© Airphoto International Ltd

With Afghanistan now added to his domain, he went on to wage further wars of conquest throughout the east and west, from Georgia, Armenia and Persia to India as far as Dehli—all of which fall outside the scope of this account. On his death in 1404 (his departure interrupting a planned invasion of China), he left a giant empire, but his skill in government and consolidation not being equal to his abilities on the battlefield, it did not long outlive him. He filled regional governorships with the members of his family, but this was no help to the empire's stability; indeed, fratricidal disputes were constantly to undermine the empire right up to its end (1506). However, his achievements were also considerable. He was able to secure the freedom and safety of travellers and trade caravans; not only did he receive an embassy from Henry III, King of Castile, but also, 10 years after his death, were a number of diplomatic visits exchanged between Herat and the Ming Emperor of China. In the field of culture, although he himself did not have the opportunity to enjoy a full education, he was a great supporter of the arts in every respect, patronising poets, painters, calligraphers and great works of public architecture. Their work was encouraged by his "Mongol tolerance", particularly in matters of religion. Although a Sunni Muslim, he allowed and, to a great extent, encouraged various manifestations of faith—Sufi mysticism, dervishes, local saints' cults— which were frowned upon by the more orthodox. The tenets of Islamic *shari'a* law were often combined with or subordinated to the Mongolian *yasa*, or law of the steppes, and, perhaps more surprisingly, the followers of Shiism were kept under his protection.

Although his successors were not able to maintain the unity of his empire, by the pursuance of these policies of tolerance they were able to bring about perhaps the most magnificent age that Islam ever saw. During the more peaceful periods, when the empire was not rent by family feuds over power, Timur's son Ulugh Beg, Viceroy of Samarkand until 1447, beautified the city and—for his personal use— built an astronomical observatory; his observations of the stars were acknowledged to be pioneering, and the data he collated was even published in Oxford as late as 1650. In Herat, which Shah Rukh (1404–47)—the son of Timur who managed to win his throne—declared the capital of the empire, writers and artists began to

congregate. Building work on palaces, gardens, religious houses and mosques went on apace, particularly at the instigation of Shah Rukh's wife, Gawhar Shad, known as the *Biqlis*, or "Queen of Sheba", of her time. After disturbances during the middle of the 1400s, this pattern was resumed under the more settled reign of the new emperor, Husayn Bayqara (1468–1506), to whose patronage we owe Mirkhwand, the historian, Bizhad, the miniaturist, and the great mystic writer Jami. The court vizier, Mir Ali Shir Nawai, was a groundbreaking exponent of literary Turki, and Husayn Bayqara himself was a capable writer of devotional poetry.

Herat was unquestionably the cultural capital of Islam at the end of the 15th century, but by then the Timurid house had become decadent. To the west, the Persians were beginning to rally behind the new Safavid dynasty, and in Transoxiana, the Uzbeks were conspicuous as a new and growing power. In Herat, by contrast, Husayn Bayqara's sons were squabbling over the succession and none of them were at all versed in the arts of war. Most of their days, it seems, were spent at inebriated parties, in which, according to accounts, poetry would be recited and servants would perform "obscene drunken tricks" for the amusement of the guests. After the death of Husayn in 1506, it became obvious that his sons were incapable of defending the city, and thus Herat was taken by the Uzbeks in 1507 and then by the Persian Safavids just three years later. The city was despoiled by the Uzbeks and neglected by the Persians, and, as a result, the Timurid Renaissance unhappily was brought to a close.

One character to emerge from the disintegration of the Timurid empire whose career was to have a considerable bearing on the future of Afghanistan was Zahir-ud-Din Muhammad, better known by his nickname of Babur ("Tiger"). This descendant of both Genghis Khan and Timur is perhaps best known through his extraordinary memoirs, the *Baburnama*, which show him to have been a hugely congenial spirit, equally interested in war, wine and gardening; however, it is with his conquests at the beginning of the 16th century that we must here primarily concern ourselves.

Dance of the Dervishes, Herat, attributed to Bihzad,
late 15th century [Smithsonian Institution, Washington D.C.]

In 1494, Babur, at the age of 12, succeeded his father to the throne of the Transoxianan principate of Ferghana. It was not, on the face of it, the most propitious moment to do so. His Timurid cousins, who held various petty fiefdoms throughout the region, were somewhat self-indulgently competing with each other for primacy; at the same moment, the Uzbeks' increasing strength put the very survival of their whole number in doubt. Nevertheless, Babur, in spite of his tender age, threw himself into the fighting with gusto. In 1497, still only 15, he led an army into Samarkand, then held by his cousin Baisungur, but lost it not long after, being unable to feed his men. He repeated the feat three years later, but in the general confusion again had it seized from him by the Uzbeks, along with his native Ferghana. After failing in several attempts to drive them out, he instead turned to Afghanistan, and, in 1504, with an army and a considerable amount of good fortune, captured Kabul from an usurper named Zunnum Arghun.

Not long after this unexpected success, he was summoned by Husayn Bayqara to support the remains of the Timurid empire, but only reached its capital of Herat after his death (1506). Finding his two decadent sons squabbling with each other, and, as he put it "strangers to war, strategy, equipment, bold fight and endeavour", he pledged to lead an expedition against the Uzbeks on their behalf, but his offer went unaccepted and the fate of Herat was sealed. Instead, he returned to Kabul and, in 1507, briefly took Kandahar also from Zunnum Arghun. Three years later, when the Safavids had wrested Herat from the Uzbeks and killed their chief, Shaybani Khan, Babur saw that he had an opportunity to regain power in Ferghana. However, having marched north and skirmished several times against them, he was defeated conclusively at the battle of Ghazdavan in 1512, and reluctantly had to abandon the idea of winning back a kingdom in Transoxiana. Nonetheless, his ambition to possess wider dominions was still fierce and he realised that the one place where this might still be fulfilled was in the opposite direction: India. He did not much care for the country, preferring the cooler climate of Kabul, but after 1519 he began to launch annual raids across the Indus. When, in 1522, Babur had secured his rear by re-occupying Kandahar, he redoubled his efforts against the Lodi dynasty of India, and, after the Battle of Panipat (1526), was able to claim the throne of Dehli: the Mohgul Empire of India had been founded. Babur was to rule for another four years until his passing in 1530; after his death, his body was taken back to Kabul and interred in a garden that he himself had planted.

One should pause at this moment to take stock of the situation. By the 16th century, the land of Afghanistan was divided into three parts. The north was held by the Uzbeks, the west by the Safavid Persians and the southeast by the Moghuls. The Moghuls always held Kabul, the Persians always held Herat, but Kandahar would be contested between them, finally falling to the Persians for good in 1648. The Moghuls would from time to time attack the Uzbeks, but apart from occasionally moving into the province of Badakhshan, they were never able fully to establish their authority north of the Hindu Kush. It is with the territories disposed thus that the stage is set for the emergence of the modern nation of Afghanistan.

Brief mention has already been made of the Pushtuns—the putative descendants of the Sakae migrants of the 2nd century BC who inhabit the south of the country from the Iranian border to the northwestern regions of present-day Pakistan. It is to their two principal tribes—the Abdali, who then lived around Herat, and the Ghilzai, who then possessed Kandahar—that Afghanistan owes its appearance as a state. And although the Abdali were eventually to be its masters, it was the Ghilzai who were responsible for starting the way towards it. At the beginning of the 18th century, the Persians sent a Georgian nobleman, Gurgin Khan, to act as governor of Kandahar. Immediately suspicious that the Ghilzai were plotting some sort of conspiracy with the Moghuls, in 1704 he started a fierce program of repression, strenuously crushing any sign of tribal dissent and sending the chief of the tribe, Mir Wais, as a prisoner to the Persian court in Isfahan. Thinking that he had matters under control, he was not a little surprised to find Mir Wais returned to Kandahar a short time later, invested with robes of honour. Mir Wais had not only been able to persuade the foolish Persian Shah that nothing was amiss, he had also had ample opportunity to observe the decadence of the Safavid regime and came to realise that they would be quite unable to defend themselves were a proper rebellion to be

CAUCASUS

Aral Sea

ALTAI MOUNTAINS

Volga River

UZBEKS

• Bishkek

Oxus

KARA KUM DESERT

• Tashkent

TIAN MOUNTAINS

• Samarkand

TAKLAMAKAN DESERT

• Tabriz

Caspian Sea

• Dushanbe

PAMIR

• Tehran

• Nishapur

HINDU KUSH

KARAKORAM

• Baghdad

• Balkh

• Isfahan

SAFAVID PERSIANS

• Herat

• Kabul

• Peshawar

HIMALAYA

Persian Gulf

• Kandahar

Area of greatest confrontation

• Delhi

• Bam

Gulf of Oman

Indus

Ganges

• Sonmiani
• Karachi

• Calcutta

MUGHALS

Arabian Sea

Bay of Bengal

Indian Ocean

SOUTH-CENTRAL ASIA
SITUATION AD 1650

Uzbeks

Mughals

Safavid Persians

| 0 | 200 | 400 | 600 | 800 | 1,000 |

Kilometres

© Airphoto International Ltd

organised. Having bided his time, in April 1709 he arranged for Gurgin Khan and his Persian entourage to be assassinated and the citadel to be taken over by his own forces. Although the Persians sent an army against the city in revolt, they were unable to regain control. The Ghilzai began to assert their authority in the district around Kandahar, and the Abdali in Herat, also perceiving the weakness, staged a similar action, expelling the Safavids and declaring themselves an independent principality.

Mir Wais died in 1715, and his 18-year-old son, Mir Mahmud, stepped into his place. Leading a Ghilzai force, he first compelled the Abdali Pushtuns in Herat to submit to him—for there was no great love between the Abdali and the Ghilzai—and then, making his way into Persia, raided the city of Kerman and laid siege to Isfahan. After six months, the city capitulated and Mahmud declared himself the new Shah of Persia. However, after committing a series of atrocities—including the execution of nearly all the remaining members of the Safavid family—he lapsed into insanity and was himself executed by his cousin Ashraf, who assumed his position.

The Ghilzai reign over Persia was to be short. The last Safavid claimant to the throne, Tahmasp II, fell into the hands of a Turcoman adventurer, Nadir Quli Beg, who happened to possess a private army. With their aid, and that of a detachment of Abdali warriors, Nadir, acting as Tahmasp's general, managed to defeat the Ghilzais at Mehmandost in 1730 and place Tahmasp back on the Persian throne as a puppet ruler. But after a number of disagreements over policy, Tahmasp was deposed and Nadir established himself as Shah.

Nadir Shah was to spend most of his reign staging expeditions for plunder. Setting out from Persia, he captured Kandhar from the Ghilzais, ordered them to be resettled around Herat and allowed his Abdali allies to take up residence in the area of the city. After this, he marched against the Moghuls, sacked Dehli in 1739 —capturing, amongst other things, the Koh-i-Noor diamond—and later went on to raid Bokhara, Samarkand and Khiva.

The foundation of the Afghan state was to come with the death of Nadir Shah, beheaded by his own officers during the course of a mutiny in 1747. The Abdali warriors who travelled with him, fearing that they would be turned on by the Persians, fled back to Kandahar, where, in order to consider what to do in the midst of the anarchy, a tribal council was convened. On considering the facts, they came to realise that the situation was extremely favourable. Persia and Moghul India were in a condition of extreme enfeeblement. The power of the Ghilzais had been exhausted by their adventure in Persia and their fight with Nadir Shah, whereas they themselves had a large number of fighting men at their disposal and even Nadir's treasure caravan, which had earlier fallen into their hands. They concluded that, if they were able to unite behind one leader—for the Abdali suffered from internal as well as external feuds—they would be able to set up their own empire and, for the first time in history, be independent of the yoke of a foreign imperium.

The two major sub-groups of the Abdali were in contention for the leadership —the Popalzai and the Barakzai—but in the end, one Ahmad Khan Saddozai of the Popalzai, who had commanded the Abdali contingent under Nadir Shah, was chosen by universal consent. Crowned with a garland woven from ears of wheat, Ahmad Shah was acclaimed by the council as king and *Dur-i-Durran* or "Pearl of Pearls". The Abdali tribe was accordingly renamed the "Durrani", and the Afghan empire— "Afghan" being another name for "Pushtun"—was brought into existence.

It should be stressed that, at the moment of his coronation, Ahmad Shah Durrani could only lay claim to the southern areas where the Pushtuns dwelt. Only by a process of conquest was he able to bring different peoples—who regarded and often continue to regard themselves as essentially different from the Pushtuns / Afghans —under his authority, and hence build up the state of Afghanistan roughly as we know it today. Having subdued the Ghilzai, he took Herat, Mashhad and Nishapur from the Persians. Turning east, he attacked Kabul, Dehli and Lahore, annexing all the land west of the Indus, and later Kashmir; his wars against the Moghuls and the Hindu Mahrattas allowed the rise of Sikh power in the Punjab and ultimately paved the way for the British to win their place in India. In the north, he secured the area between the Hindu Kush and the Oxus, bringing Uzbeks, Tajiks and Turcomans under his control; his hold over these areas was secured when the Amir of Bokhara

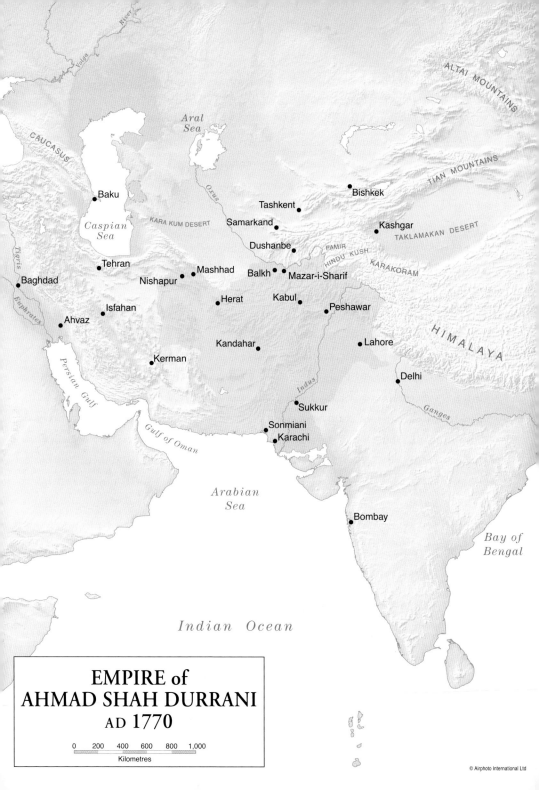

Volga *River*

ALTAI MOUNTAINS

CAUCASUS

*Aral
Sea*

Oxus

*Caspian
Sea*

● Baku

KARA KUM DESERT

Tashkent ●

● Bishkek

TIAN MOUNTAINS

Samarkand ●

Kashgar ●

TAKLAMAKAN DESERT

Dushanbe ●

PAMIR

Tigris

Euphrates

● Baghdad

● Tehran

Nishapur ● Mashhad ●

Balkh ● ● Mazar-i-Sharif

HINDU KUSH

KARAKORAM

● Isfahan

Herat ●

Kabul ●

● Peshawar

HIMALAYA

● Ahvaz

*Persian
Gulf*

Kerman ●

Kandahar ●

● Lahore

Indus

● Delhi

Ganges

Gulf of Oman

Sukkur ●

Sonmiani ●
● Karachi

*Arabian
Sea*

● Bombay

*Bay of
Bengal*

Indian   Ocean

EMPIRE of
AHMAD SHAH DURRANI
AD 1770

0 200 400 600 800 1,000
Kilometres

© Airphoto International Ltd

agreed to recognise the Oxus as the border between their respective domains. To the south, his new empire was only bounded by the shores of the Arabian Sea.

Ahmad Shah died in 1772 at the age of 50. As had occurred several times before in the history of the region, the inheritance of the father was squandered by the sons; in other words, the empire that he had striven to build began to disintegrate. Part of the blame, it must be conceded, should be laid at his feet. Although he stood firmly in the tradition of the literate fighter—in periods of peace, he would write Pashto verse with a mystical slant—he did nothing to organise a proper government or consolidate his possessions. Nevertheless, the kings who followed him did nothing to rectify the deficiency, and as time went on his family gave itself up to some of the most brutal infighting that anyone had ever seen. Within ten years of Ahmad Shah's death, the Afghan empire had lost much of Khurasan, Balkh and the northern steppes, Kashmir, Sind and Sistan. By 1818, when his dynasty finally tore itself apart, many of his male descendants had been killed; three shahs had been deposed, of whom one had been blinded, one sought refuge as a pensioner of the British and one sought refuge in Herat, which he proceeded to rule as a body independent of the Afghan state. After eight years of civil war, another branch of the Durranis under Dost Mohammed Khan was able to take the crown. Yet his authority scarcely extended outside of Kabul and Ghazni, and a number of his brothers and half-brothers held on to regional governorships, even intriguing with external powers against him if they thought it would bring them any advantage.

This period also marked the rise of European involvement in Central Asia. With the onset of the 19th century, Britain moved to become the paramount power in India. In 1807, the Treaty of Tilsit confirmed Franco-Russian influence in Persia, and even raised the possibility of an attack on the British possessions by way of Afghanistan. The danger of this receded with French defeats on the battlefields of Europe, but when Russia overcame Persia in 1828, the new treaty of Turkmanchai made the Qajar Shahs (who had taken over after the death of Nadir Shah) virtually subservient to their northern rivals: once more, a Russian invasion of British India by way of Persia had become a theoretical possibility. In response, Britain began to

A Durrani Pushtun Villager, 1809, by R.M. Grindlay [RSAA]

A Dooraunee Villager with his Arms.

seek an alliance with Afghanistan, taking Dost Mohammed under their sphere to prevent him from falling prey to Russian influence. This should have been an easy policy to pursue; Dost Mohammed's position was weak, and he would readily have supported the British had they offered him even the simplest assistance to shore up his authority, or regain some of the lost Afghan territories. Having failed to do this, however, the British interpreted his reluctance to comply with their diplomatic requests as hostility. When rumours began to circulate of a Russian agent in Kabul bearing letters from the Tsar in Moscow, the British envoys were withdrawn, and instead, an invasion was planned. Misled into believing that Shah Shuja—the ex-king who was living as a guest of the British at Ludhiana—was still popular in Afghanistan, the Governor-General Lord Auckland decided to re-install him on the Afghan throne by force. Accordingly, in October 1838, the British government in India published a document known as the Simla Manifesto—recently described by the diplomat and historian Sir Martin Ewans as "a patently dishonest piece of propaganda"—alleging that Dost Mohammed was plotting to aid Russia in an attack on the India frontier, and claiming that Shah Shuja would be quickly welcomed back and supported by the Afghan people. Thus, on the basis of this flawed and untrue statement, a British force, along with a number of Afghan detachments and the half-hearted support of the Sikhs of the Punjab, set off a short while later to "restore" Shah Shuja as a puppet of the British government. The First Afghan War was underway.

The military objective was easily achieved: Dost Mohammed was deposed and eventually captured, and Shah Shuja was proclaimed king. It became immediately apparent, however, that there was little enthusiasm for him amongst the public, and the British, who had intended soon after to withdraw, realised that they would have to stay in the country to protect him. Despite their miscalculation, the news in 1839 that the Russians had attempted to capture the Central Asian Khanate of Khiva seemed ultimately to confirm their fears and justify their actions. Yet with their

Four Portrait Heads of Afghan Leaders, *1841, By Emily Eden. The four noblemen, Dost Mohammed (later to be ruler of Afghanistan), Haider Khan (Governor of Ghazni), Mohammed Akram Khan and Abdul Ghani Khan, were all held captive by the British in Ludhiana in the early 1840s. [British Library]*

SKETCHES
IN
AFGHAUNISTAN,
BY
JAS. ATKINSON, ESQ.

Louis Haghe, del.

Beloochees in the Bolan Pass.

minds on the more distant dangers, they failed to take account of those at home. By the end of 1841, discontent had grown with Shah Shuja and the British in Kabul to such an extent that a revolt broke out, and one of the British political agents, Sir Alexander Burnes, was murdered by a mob. The disorder could have been contained with prompt action, but the British military in the country had become sclerotic thanks to personal rivalries between commanding officers, and the riot was able to turn into a fully-fledged uprising. More dithering by the top brass led to the loss of the food stores and treasury, and by January 1842 the army of occupation had no alternative but to abandon the city. An agreement was reached to allow the British to retreat in safety, but partly from mismanagement of remaining supplies, lack of order, freezing weather and relentless guerrilla attacks by Ghilzai tribesmen, all but a handful of the 16,500 troops—British and Indian—and camp followers had been killed in the mountain passes before they could come to Jalalabad.

The British were without hesitation in sending an "Army of Retribution" to "re-establish [their] military reputation by the infliction of some signal and decisive blow on the Afghans". This ended up being the recovery of prisoners, an attack on the rebels at Istalif north of Kabul and the somewhat wanton destruction of the Kabul Bazaar. But, in essence, little could be salvaged from the disaster. As the historian Sir John Kaye wrote in 1850, "It was, in principle and in act, an unrighteous usurpation… Instead of strengthening the Afghans, we have weakened them. Instead of making them our friends, we have made them our implacable foes." It was a piece of good fortune that Dost Mohammed, who was released and returned to the Afghan throne, came to admire the British whilst in captivity. Eventually, he agreed to accept various forms of military aid from the British, and even refrained from taking advantage of the Indian Mutiny in 1857 to launch attacks on them across the Indus. The rest of his time was spent in attempting to reunify the country. He was able to establish his authority over Kandahar in 1855, Balkh and Afghan Turkestan in 1857 and Herat in 1863, but not long after his death in that same year,

Frontispiece of Sketches in Afghauntsian, *1842, by James Atkinson. Collections of drawings made by British officers present during the occupation in the 1840s were some of the first images of Afghanistan to reach a wider audience in Europe. [Bodleian]*

his work began to unravel; and, although his son Sher Ali attempted to govern with the support of the British, his reign was often interrupted by the re-emergence of familial strife.

At the same time, the Russians were beginning to succeed in their long-cherished aim of expanding into Central Asia, occupying Tashkent in 1867, Samarkand in 1868 and Bokhara in 1869; Kokand followed suit in 1871 and Khiva succumbed in 1878. This encroachment did nothing to make the British feel easy about the safety of their Indian possessions and, in spite of the previous catastrophe, many began to advocate the so-called "forward policy": the annexation of the Afghan lands south of Herat and the Hindu Kush to act as a defence for their imperial holdings. The refusal of Sher Ali in 1878 to receive a British mission whilst at the same time agreeing to meet an unexpected Russian delegation was seized upon as a pretext. At the end of that year, British troops began to move into the southeast of the country, and the Second Afghan War was underway.

Unable adequately to defend himself, Sher Ali fled to the north of the country, hoping there to receive some sort of assistance from the Russians. However, in this he was disappointed. With no way out of his predicament, he died, exhausted and disheartened, in Mazar-i-Sharif in February 1879. Nevertheless, his son, Yakub Khan, went forward to meet the British, and was able to bring hostilities to an end by signing a treaty agreeing to the permanent residence of a British representative in Kabul and delegating the responsibility for foreign affairs to the British Government. Yet history—as is its usual custom in Afghanistan—repeated itself. There was immediate anger at the renewed British interference and, within three months of their arrival, the British agent and his entourage—following the example of Sir Alexander Burnes 40 years previously—were massacred. Britain immediately reacted by occupying Kabul and assuming control of the Kabul government, whilst Yakub Khan gave up the throne. The general population was by no means amenable to this new situation and, by constant unrest, made it clear to the British that their position was untenable. At the same moment, one of Dost Mohammed grandsons, Abdur Rahman, who had been in exile in Samarkand for the previous ten years,

Riflemen of the Afghan Army, 1857 [RSAA]

Captⁿ P. S Lumsden, del^t

M & N Hanhart, lith,

THE KINGS OWN JAZAILCHIS.

Published by Smith, Elder & C° 65, Cornhill, London. 1862.

sensing that he might be in a position to bid for power, made his return. He was known to be an energetic and capable tribal leader and, as he moved south through Badakhshan collecting troops to support his cause, the British could think of no other way out of the crisis than to give him the crown. Overcoming their misgivings that Russian influence would follow in his wake, the British handed Kabul to him in August 1880, and began their withdrawal. They were not, however, able to leave the country without delay. One of Yakub Khan's brothers, Ayub Khan, had also declared himself the sovereign, defeated a British brigade at Maiwand near Kandahar and besieged the British garrison stationed in the city. Making a forced march from Kabul, a relief column was able to arrive within 23 days, and, in one of the most remarkable actions of the war, beat back and dispersed the forces of the rebel king. At length, the British army finally left Afghanistan in April 1881.

Many of the British Government's fears about the appointment of Abdur Rahman turned out to be unfounded. Thanks to a Russian incursion and land grab in the northwest of the country—the Pandjeh Crisis of 1885—he turned to the British for help, accepting their aid in return for allowing them to control Afghan foreign policy, as they had wished all along. In imitation of his more capable predecessors, he set to work unifying the country under strong central authority, putting down other members of his family who attempted to challenge him for the throne and crushing rebellions by the Ghilzai in 1886 and the Hazaras in 1891. To secure the northeast against Russian attack, in 1895 he subdued the ancient pagan communities living in the Kafiristan region, stationing troops in the distant valleys and forcibly converting the native population to Islam—a feat that even Timur was unable to accomplish. In order to tame the power of the clergy, he insisted that his sovereignty was of divine right, and that he himself constituted the supreme religious authority in the country. Saying of the mullahs that "[their] tyranny and cruelty… was unbearable", he enacted measures to bring them under state control, including compulsory examinations to test their religious knowledge. Believing the tribal chiefs to be an equal menace, he began a program of forced migration – for example, moving various Pushtun groups north of the Hindu Kush—in order that, away from their accustomed homelands, they would be less capable of fomenting revolts. His reign is also notable for the various boundary commissions charged with demarcating the Afghan borders. One result of their work was the unpopular Durand line, laid down in 1893, dividing Afghanistan from the British Indian Empire, but also falling through the midst of Pushtun tribal territories, an act which would, in the following century, go on to cause considerable difficulties.

One of Abdur Rahman's final achievements was to bequeath the throne to his son, Habibullah, without any dispute over the succession. Habibullah began to rectify his father's one great omission—the failure to develop the country—and he initiated a number of projects, including the construction of factories, hydro-electric plants and road-building schemes. Some schools, based on foreign models, were also founded and made available to the upper class elite. Despite internal dissent, he confirmed the right of the British to administer Afghanistan's foreign policy, but refused to acknowledge an Anglo-Russian convention of 1907 that officially designated Afghanistan as a buffer state, unhappy at not being involved in the initial negotiations. As time went on, it became increasingly difficult to adhere to his treaty obligations: a considerable part of the population, which favoured modernisation, but also anti-imperialism and pan-Islamism, began to agitate against the British. In 1915, in the midst of the First World War, they rallied to a Turco-German delegation which arrived in Kabul, calling for a jihad on British India. Habibullah was, on the surface, sympathetic to their request, but managed to avoid launching any actual hostilities, as a consequence of which he was accused of betraying both the nation and Islam; his loyalty to the British led to his assassination in February 1919.

His son, Amanullah, who was very much under the influence of the modernising pan-Islamists, succeeded Habibullah to the throne. His immediate goal was full and formal independence from the British; his way of achieving this was, on 3 May 1919, to launch an unprovoked attack on British India in the region of the Khyber Pass. The British, after the conclusion of the First World War, had no appetite for any further fighting, yet, equally, the Afghans had no appetite for the aerial bombardments unleashed against Jalalabad and Kabul—a new means of combat to which they had not yet been introduced. This, the Third Afghan War, was brought to an end by a ceasefire called on 3 June 1919; a peace treaty signed two months later finally granted Afghanistan full independence in both its internal as well as external affairs. The British were willing to grant this concession in view of the chaos enfolding Russia after the revolution, reckoning that they were too enfeebled to pose any further threat to India. Amanullah promptly set out to accelerate the country's modernisation program. Being one of the first Afghan monarchs to travel extensively in Europe, he was in a position to compare the development of Afghanistan with that of other states and, as a result, pressed for a series of wide-reaching changes. Treaties were signed with the Soviet Union, Turkey, Britain, France and Italy; the latter three set up a number of new schools and colleges. Constitutional and judicial reforms proposed the move to a secular state and judicial system. Women were encouraged to remove the veil and the citizens of Kabul were ordered to wear Western clothing.

Many of the conservative vested interests did not take at all kindly to Amanullah's reforms, which challenged their grip on power. The common people also, unsettled by the pace of change, were unhappy with the behaviour of the king. Discontent eventually exploded in 1928 in the form of a revolution; Amanullah escaped to live as an exile in Italy until his death in 1960, and an illiterate Tajik known as Bacha Saqao, or "son of the water-carrier", for a few anarchic months seized hold of the throne. However, one of Amanullah's distant relatives, Nadir Khan, a general who had fought in the Third Afghan War, was able to raise an army, depose the usurper and gain the throne for himself.

Nadir continued the program of development started by Amanullah, whilst appeasing the people by a return to orthodox Islamic law and customs, cloaked in the façade of a constitutional democracy. In spite of this, there was still opposition to his rule, and after a reign of just four years he was assassinated in 1933 by a student in Kabul. His brothers acted quickly to avert a crisis and, ensuring the accession of his 19-year-old son, Zahir Shah, banded together to act as de facto regents.

Afghanistan's relations with the outside world continued to burgeon under their leadership; membership of the League of Nations came in 1934, followed by a treaty with the United States two years later. They continued the policy of non-alignment throughout the Second World War, despite receiving considerable sums of development aid from the Axis powers and playing host to a substantial German presence in the capital throughout the length of the conflict.

With the end of the war came British decolonisation and, in 1947, the partition of British India into the modern states of India and Pakistan. During this process, Afghanistan began vociferously to challenge the validity of the Durand Line. Pointing out that it split the Pushtun lands, they called for the tribesmen on the Pakistani side of the line to be allowed a plebiscite, giving them the option of forming an independent state—"Pushtunistan"—which the Afghans eventually hoped to absorb. Appealing abroad for support on this issue, they were disappointed not to receive any help from the United States; the Americans had formed an anti-communist alliance with Pakistan and were not inclined to interfere in the affair to Pakistan's detriment. Consequently, the Afghans turned to the USSR. The United States was content to allow this, thinking it unlikely that Afghanistan would ever fall into Soviet hands, and unimportant enough to matter even if it did. The Afghans, moreover, thought that a Soviet alliance would be safe, for they believed communism would be a system of little interest in such a conservative country and unlikely to penetrate it, even were the Russians to become a significant presence. Thus, Soviet technicians began to fill the country, undertaking road-building, irrigation and airport construction projects. Settlement programs were started for the nomad population. A five-year plan was promulgated in 1956, Afghan army officers were taken for training in the Soviet Union and military aid began to arrive in large quantities from the Eastern bloc countries. The United States, at length growing uneasy at the tide of Russian money flowing into Afghanistan, began to match their investments. For a time, the curious situation prevailed of two superpower rivals attempting to curry favour with the same regime: the Soviet projects primarily took place in the north, the American in the south, and the Kabul government was left

to tread a careful line between the two, whilst nevertheless rejoicing in the influx of foreign capital.

Towards the end of 1960, the Pushtunistan issue again flared up, with a number of serious consequences. The Afghans made a series of small-scale attacks into Pakistani territory, which were all repulsed with the help of Pakistani Pushtuns. Pakistan reacted moderately with the closure of consulates in Jalalabad and Kandahar; the Afghans' response was the full-scale breaking of diplomatic relations and the complete closure of the Afghan–Pakistan border. Afghanistan was thrown further into the arms of the Soviets, having no alternative but to import many basic goods from the USSR. With no other communication links to the rest of the world, trade suffered severely and the economy went into decline. By the end of 1962, with inflation rising steeply, it became clear that the state of affairs could not continue; in March 1963, the Prime Minister, Mohammed Daoud—also the king's uncle— handed in his resignation and a series of reforms were announced.

There followed a ten-year long experiment in genuine representative democracy, with an elected bicameral parliament, the formation of political parties and liberalisation of the press. Yet the new system was hampered by the lukewarm support of the king and the propensity of the new legislature to paralysis and inaction. The economy continued to falter and in 1973, after a rapid succession of prime ministers, Mohammed Daoud, aided by left-leaning sympathisers in the army, effected a coup whilst Zahir Shah was out of the country. Declaring a republic, he assumed the offices of president and prime minister and proceeded to govern with the help of a high-ranking committee drawn from the military. However, contrary to expectations, he endeavoured to reduce the level of Soviet influence in the country and began negotiations with nations such as Iran, India, and even the US for monetary and developmental assistance. Dismayed at this behaviour, the army led another coup on 27 April 1978, and an overtly Soviet-backed regime led by the People's Democratic Party of Afghanistan came to power under Nur Muhammad Taraki, sometime editor of a communist periodical entitled *Khalq* ("The Masses").

Pushtuns in Paktia Province, which is bordered by the Durand Line [R. & S. Michaud]

It was the intention of the new government to reform the country utterly along Marxist lines, but they rapidly fell into disagreement amongst themselves over the speed of the changes. Before long, the extremist wing prevailed, and year zero-style changes were decreed almost at once. These included the redistribution of land without compensation, the abolition of usury, immediate modernisation of marriage customs, a drive towards universal literacy and education for both sexes based on a Marxist curriculum. The result was not only immediate chaos in the agricultural sector, with one-third of all cultivable land falling out of use, but also a welling-up of resentment amongst a majority of the people, who regarded the reforms as un-Islamic. This anger finally broke through the surface in March 1979 with an uprising in Herat. Russians, communists and government officials were tortured and murdered as the government itself strove to regain control of the city with tanks and helicopter strikes. Twenty-thousand Heratis are thought to have died as a result, and a rebel guerrilla army under a former army officer, Ismail Khan, came into being.

The Russians were dismayed at the turn of events in Afghanistan. Fearing that communism would be seen to fail there, they tried to persuade the Afghan government to slow the pace of reform. They failed to do so, however, and the disorder escalated. At the beginning of September, Taraki was killed in a struggle with his deputy, Hafizullah Amin, at which point the Soviets decided to move their own troops into the country and install their own moderate candidate, Babrak Karmal, as president. The Soviet intervention immediately met with widespread international condemnation, and within Afghanistan itself a jihad was declared, with the Soviet forces and the remainder of the Afghan army ranged against rebel army units and mujahedin guerrilla fighters. As the conflict intensified, huge numbers of refugees made their way out of the country. By 1981, estimates indicate that 1.7 million had fled to Pakistan and 400,000 to Iran; within three years, this had grown to 3.5 million in the former and 1.5 million in the latter. Much of the displacement came through the sheer ferocity of the war and the tactics employed by the Soviet army. Finding themselves only able to control the urban centres, and incapable of facing the mujahedin in the difficult rural terrain, they sent armoured

Abandoned Soviet tank, Panjshir Valley, 2004 [B. Jenks]

columns supported by aircraft and artillery to destroy and depopulate the villages in the countryside where they believed their opponents to be hiding: in essence, a scorched earth policy. Nonetheless, these armoured columns were particularly vulnerable to ambush and, as the war continued, fresh waves of mujahedin, led by such notable leaders as Ahmed Shah Massoud, emerged from camps in Pakistan to continue the struggle; these were backed by large tranches of financial and military aid from the US, Saudi Arabia, Iran and China. In 1985, the new Russian president Mikhail Gorbachev, conscious of the increasing discontent amongst his own people at the human and economic costs of the war, started to search for a means of withdrawal. In addition, US-made Stinger missiles began to appear on the battlefield. These made it near impossible for Soviet aircraft to operate with any degree of safety, and it became increasingly clear that the war was, for them, unwinnable.

In the next year, 1986, Babrak Karmal was replaced as Afghan President by Mohammed Najibullah, a former head of the secret police, and Gorbachev signalled his intention to pull out Soviet troops with a token withdrawal of 8,000 men. It was not, however, until 1988, after protracted negotiations with the US, which were concluded with the signing of the "Geneva Accords", that the process was completed and the Soviet Army retreated north back across the Oxus. Nevertheless, fighting continued between Najibullah's government and the various mujahedin factions until 1992, when the US and USSR agreed to cease their financial and military backing for the warring parties. The loss of Russian support spelt the end of Najibullah's presidency, which came to an end with his resignation on 18 March. Yet his departure failed to bring an end to the fighting, as the mujahedin factions began to dispute over the allocation of posts in a new government. The leading Pushtun commander, Gulbuddin Hekmatyar, objected to non-Pushtuns holding prominent roles in the new administration. In particular, his ire fell against Abdul Rashid Dostum, the Uzbek leader, as well as Ahmed Shah Massoud and Burhanuddin Rabbani, who were both Tajiks. After the fall of Najibullah, Kabul fell into the hands of an alliance of the Tajik and Uzbek commanders, and Hekmatyar, refusing attempts at conciliation, began to bombard the city at random. From this, a wider

Commander Massoud with his officers at prayer [M. Yamashita]

and more complex civil war broke out between the ethnic factions. General anarchy and hardship severely affected not just the rural communities, but also the urban populations, who had not suffered to the same degree in the previous conflict.

At this time, other nations, notably Pakistan, began to grow restless. They were eager to open up road transport links to the Central Asian states and, if possible, to find some way of taking control of the Afghan government. Pakistan feared the prospect of war with India over the disputed territory of Kashmir and wanted to keep a hold over Afghanistan as a hinterland in the event of any conflict. Accordingly, the Pakistani Secret Intelligence Service (SIS) began to support a new faction called the *Taliban*, or "Students". Using young men drawn from the madrassahs, or Koranic schools, primarily from the North-West Frontier Province, this movement, led by a petty village cleric, Mullah Mohammed Omar, went on to score a rapid series of victories. Kandahar was taken in November 1994; Herat was wrested from

Ismail Khan in September 1995; and Massoud was forced to retreat from Kabul in September 1996. Fighting raged also throughout Afghan Turkestan, and Mazar-i Sharif changed hands between Dostum and the Taliban on at least two occasions. Under Massoud, an anti-Taliban grouping known as the Northern Alliance was able to maintain a stronghold in the Panjshir Valley and the northeast, but much of the rest of the country remained under the grip of the Taliban.

At first, this new movement was welcomed by many. The warlords and local commanders whom they replaced were acting with extreme lawlessness, and the Taliban were able to give the population, for the first time in years, a semblance of peace and order. However, the soldiers of this new movement—in the main Afghan Pushtuns who had grown up in Pakistan as war refugees—had little understanding of the history and traditions of their own nation and, indeed, only a slight knowledge of the whole body of Islamic scholarship and philosophy. Raised in the single-sex madrassahs, encouraged to understand the Koran literally, they promulgated a regime of extreme Puritanism mixed with Pushtun tribal law, entirely out of sympathy with the nature of the country at large. The educational and medical systems broke down thanks to their proscription against women being allowed to work or learn; their "breaking of idols" in the Kabul museum is well-known, along with the destruction of the Buddhist statues of Bamiyan in March 2001; their decrees against television, shaving, kite-flying and other such activities also received much prominence in the international media. Famine spread after earthquakes in 1998, on account of their refusal of humanitarian aid organisations to operate freely; their patent disregard for the welfare of the people brought about huge anger. More than this, their hosting of foreign Islamist terror organisations, particularly al-Qaeda under Osama bin Laden, caused equal resentment both within and without the country. Their tolerance of the activities of these bodies—including their training of militants for attacks not only on the United States, but also Central Asia, Russia, China and Iran—was, however, eventually to lead to their downfall. In 1998, after bomb attacks on US embassies in Africa, President Clinton ordered a number of Cruise missile strikes against al-Qaeda bases in Afghanistan—an action that turned out to be ineffectual. Three years later, after the suicide attacks on New York and Washington, the Americans demanded that the Taliban close down the terrorist training camps and hand over al-Qaeda's leading members for trial. Their failure to do so brought about US and British action against the Taliban regime in conjunction with the Northern Alliance forces, and by 7 December 2001, the last major Taliban stronghold—Kandahar—was abandoned.

Shortly before this, the remaining factions of the mujahedin met in Bonn and agreed terms for an interim government—a process made more difficult with the loss of the Northern Alliance leader Massoud to al-Qaeda suicide bombers on 9 September 2001. Yet, by the end of the year, a leading Pushtun, Hamid Karzai, was declared President, along with a 30-member interim government. International peacekeeping forces were drafted in and military operations continued to take place particularly along the border with Pakistan, behind which remnants of the Taliban had retreated hoping to regroup. Tortuous programs for re-stabilisation and re-unification, including the disarmament of warlords, the training of a new national army and development initiatives, were steadily advanced. In the midst of this, work was begun on a new moderate Islamic constitution. After long and difficult discussions, a Loya Jirga, or "Grand Tribal Council", was presented with a draft document calling for a new government by a strong elected president and a legislature run on the principles of a representative democracy. This they eventually agreed to accept as the country's new constitution on 4 January 2004. Despite the continuing threats of the Taliban, government agencies successfully compiled an electoral register by September of that same year. Suffrage was granted to all Afghans over the age of 18, male and female; 10.5 million were placed on the electoral roll, 41% of that figure being women. A presidential poll took place on 9 October that same year with a field of 18 candidates (including one woman, Dr Masooda Jalal); Hamid Karzai, gaining 55% of the vote, was eventually declared the elected President and sworn in at a ceremony in Kabul on 7 December 2004.

CHRONOLOGY OF 20TH CENTURY AFGHAN HISTORY

1901 Habibullah, son of Abdur Rahman, accedes peacefully to throne

1907 Visit of Habibullah to India

1911 Pan-Islamic nationalist Mahmud Beg Tarzi establishes first intellectual periodical, *Seraj-ul-Akhbar*

1914 First World War: Habibullah remains neutral in face of call for Pan-Islamist Jihad against British

1919 **February**: Habibullah assassinated; son Amanullah takes throne

May: Attack on British India; Third Afghan War

June: End of war after British aerial bombing of Kabul and Jalalabad

August: Peace treaty allows Afghanistan independence from British in conduct of foreign policy

1921 Treaties with USSR and Turkey

1923 Pushtun tribal revolts near Khost due to Amanullah's reforms

Establishment of *Délégation Archéologique Française en Afghanistan* (DAFA)

1925 Soviet troops occupy Utra Tagai island on Oxus

1926 Non-aggression treaty with USSR; Soviets withdraw from Utra Tagai

1927 Amanullah departs on world tour

1928 Amanullah promulgates further far-reaching westernising reforms

Queen Soraya appears unveiled in public

November: serious uprisings near Jalalabad and Kabul

1929 **January**: Amanullah abdicates; brother Inayatullah King for three days before abdicating Tajik warlord Bacha Saqao takes throne in Kabul

July: General Nadir Khan (descendant of Dost Mohammed) returns to Afghanistan and defeats Bacha Saqao; is declared King.

Many of Amanullah's reforms rescinded

1932 Foundation of Kabul University

1933 Nadir Assassinated; 19 year old son Zahir Shah assumes throne, with his uncles as regents

1936 US representative to Tehran visits Kabul

1939 Second World War; Afghanistan remains neutral

1942 Diplomatic relations established with US

1944 Alliance with China

1946 Afghanistan joins the UN

1947 British withdrawal from India/Pakistan; tension with Pakistan over Durand Line

1950 Treaty of friendship with India

1951 Agreement with US for economic development

1952 Inauguration of Helmand Dam project

Discovery of oil fields near Sheberghan

1955 Border incidents and riots in Kabul over Pushtunistan question

1956 Inauguration of Five-Year Plan with Soviet aid

1959 Abolition of requirement to wear veil

US President Eisenhower visits Kabul

1960 Salang Highway and tunnel started with Soviet aid

1961 Borders close with Pakistan in Pushtunistan flare-up; economic crisis

1962 Second Five-Year Plan

1963 Kabul–Kandahar Highway constructed with US aid

February: Crisis trade protocol with USSR

March: New administration formed with Mohammed Yusuf

Resolution of Pushtunistan conflict and re-opening of borders

1964 Opening of Salang Highway

Inauguration of Democratic constitution with bi-cameral parliament

1965 Democratic elections, including female suffrage

Yusuf resigns; Prime Minister Mohammed Maiwandwal

Communist Nur Mohammed Taraki founds People's Democratic Party of Afghanistan (PDPA)

1966 First female cabinet Minister, Kubra Nurzai

Communist periodical, *Khalq*, founded by Taraki; later supressed

1967 Maiwandwal resigns through ill-health; Nur Ahmad Etemadi becomes Prime Minister

Inauguration of Supreme Court

PDPA breaks into '*Khalq*' faction under Taraki, and '*Parcham*' under Babrak Karmal

1969 Disturbances at Kabul University

Second Parliamentary election

1971 Afghanistan hit by severe drought and famine

Etemadi resigns after deadlock in legislature; Abdul Zahir becomes Prime Minister

1972 Abdul Zahir resigns after continuing difficulties in government; technocrat Musa Shafiq appointed Prime Minister

1973 Mohammed Daoud effects coup with help of *Khalq*
and *Parcham*
1976 Aid programs agreed with USSR, China and Iran
Daoud marginalizes leftists in government
1977 Daoud's policies criticised by Soviet President
Brezhnev
1978 **April**: Daoud murdered in coup engineered by
Khalq and *Parcham*
New President Taraki inaugurates 'Year Zero'
Style reforms
1979 **March**: Anti-government uprisings in Herat
September: Taraki murdered by deputy
Hafizullah Amin
December: Amin killed in Soviet-backed coup
Moderate Babrak Karmal becomes President
Soviet troops move 'by invitation' into Afghanistan
1980 Jihad fought against Soviet troops throughout
Afghanistan
Refugees begin to flee into Pakistan and Iran
1981 Afghan government army heavily depleted by
desertions
Resistance groups begin to evolve, based in refugee
camps
Continuous UN mediation efforts begin
1982 CIA funding reaches Afghan Mujahedin via Pakistan
government
1983 UN efforts to negotiate withdrawal continue
unsuccessful
1984 Soviet troops in heavy fighting around Panjshir
Valley
1986 US-made Stinger Missiles reach Mujahedin
Soviet President Gorbachev announces token troop
withdrawal
Karmal replaced as Afghan leader by Secret Service
chief, Mohammed Najibullah
1987 Fighting intensifies throughout country
USSR announces plans for withdrawal of troops
1988 Signature of Geneva Accords. Russians begin to
withdraw.
1989 Russian withdrawal complete.
Civil war continues between Communist
government and mujahedin rebels
1991 US and USSR cease supplies of arms to both sides
1992 **April**: Mujahedin enter Kabul; Najibullah
government falls
June: New government formed under Tajik
Burhanuddin Rabbani

Factional fighting erupts between mujahedin
factions
1993 Fighting continues between Pushtun leader,
Gulbuddin Hekmatyar, and Rabbani
1994 Bombardment of Kabul by Hekmatyar
Emergence of Taliban
1995 Herat falls to Taliban
1996 Kabul falls to Taliban
1997 Taliban takes control of most of Northern
Afghanistan
Resistance to Taliban concentrated in NE/Panjshir
Valley
Taliban is recognised as legitimate government by
Saudi Arabia and Pakistan
1998 **February**: Thousands die in earthquakes in NE
Afghanistan
August: US missile strikes on Taliban/Al-Qaeda
bases in retaliation for terrorist attacks on US
embassies in Africa
1999 Imposition of UN sanctions on Afghanistan
2001 **March**: Bamiyan Buddhas destroyed
September: anti-Taliban Leader Ahmed Shah
Massoud murdered
Terrorist attacks on US
October: US begins attack on Taliban
December: Fall of Kandahar, final stronghold of
Taliban
Hamid Karzai declared leader of interim government
2002 Peacekeeping force (ISAF) drafted into Afghanistan
April: Ex-King Zahir Shah returns from exile in
Italy, but makes no claim to throne
June: Karzai chosen as interim President by Loya
Jirga
2003 Nato takes control of security in Kabul
Work proceeds on disarmament of militias and
establishment of national army
Occasional minor attacks by Taliban remnants
2004 **January**: New constitution adopted for
democratic Islamic republic
August: Electoral roll prepared, with universal
suffrage
October: Presidential election, undisrupted
despite Taliban threats
December: Hamid Karzai sworn in as elected
President
2005 Parliamentary elections scheduled for Summer

TRAVEL OVERVIEW: GENERAL ADVICE FOR TRAVELLERS

SECURITY

When you tell people that you are going on holiday to Afghanistan the response is one of incredulity, sometimes tempered by admiration. In fact, most of the country is perfectly safe to travel in. The province of Badakhshan, Afghanistan's most remote and beautiful area, has been safe since the end of the Russian occupation in 1989. This is the area that will become one of the world's most desirable travel destinations. No security problems have been reported there since the fall of the Taliban in 2001. The same is true of the Hazarajat area in central Afghanistan and the northern cities.

The war fought between the Northern Alliance and the Taliban was basically a civil war—the Pashto speaking south againt the Persian speaking north. This has always been the ethnic faultline that has plagued Afghanistan since the time of Abdur Rahman in the 19th century.

In practical terms for travellers' security, this has meant that the Pushtun heartlands are strictly off-limits. Gardez, Ghazni and Kandahar should not be attempted. Taliban and possibly al-Qaeda remnants come across the border from Pakistan on butcher-and-bolt raids, targeting Afghans involved in the election process and any foreigners they can lay their hands on. It appears that this strategy to undermine the democratic process has been a complete failure and I believe we will see security and stability spreading from the north and central parts of the country to the south.

Official security advice, regularly updated, can be found at the US State Department website (travel.state.gov/travel/afghanistan.html); at the Foreign Office website in London (www.fco.gov.uk); and at the Australian Department for Foreign Affairs and Trade (www.smartraveller.gov.au).

In the Ghorband Valley, on the road between Bamiyan and Kabul via the Shibar Pass. [B. Woodburn]

SECURITY IN KABUL

Since the fall of the Taliban, there have been a number of bombs in Kabul. One must remember, though, that Kabul is a city of several million people and that the percentage chance of being a victim is tiny. But the election of 2004 passed off without any violence in Kabul, despite the Taliban's bloodcurdling threat that they could deploy 200 suicide bombers, and this reinforces the perception that they are now a spent force.

It is sensible, though, to heed any warnings being put out by ANSO (Afghanistan NGO Security Office) and to travel with an English-speaking driver within the city.

SECURITY IN THE NORTH AND BADAKHSHAN

There have been incidents reported in Herat and Mazar-i-Sharif, between rival warlords, but on the whole foreigners have been able to travel there without much danger. Bamiyan and Badakhshan, the two areas most interesting for travellers, have had no incidents.

Road sign in the Khyber Pass, c. 1920 [Holmes]

However, it is sensible to take the precaution of not travelling at night because robbery is always a possibility.

MINES

Afghanistan is one of the most heavily mined countries in the world. Appallingly, one gets used to seeing men and children missing limbs, and one of the best charities in the country is the Sandy Gall Afghanistan Appeal, which runs workshops that produce artificial limbs. Progress in de-mining has been good—for example, between 2002 and 2004 the Shomali plain, the large fertile area to the north of Kabul where most of the battles for the city started, has been completely cleared. Herat, heavily mined by the Russians and the mujahedin during the war, has also been cleared. Many demobilised soldiers are trained as mine-clearers and earn a good wage.

But in areas where mines are still present you should be careful. Such areas are easy to spot; minefields are marked with white and red stones. Again, Badakhshan is completely clear—it was never a battleground during the civil war.

GETTING THERE BY AIR

Air links are improving all the time, and the days are long gone when one arrived on a Red Cross flight at bomb-damaged landing strips. Below is a summary of flights to Kabul, the capital.

1. Ariana Afghan Airlines, the country's flag carrier, flies in three times a week from Dubai. However, this airline has a reputation for unreliability and baggage loss.

2. Kam Air (www.flykamair.com) also flies three times a week from Dubai.

Both these flights leave from Dubai's little-known and unglamorous Terminal Two. On arriving, you should immediately check in with the Ariana or Kam Air representative, with your luggage tags. These are scanned and your baggage is routed onto the Kabul flight. Surprisingly the system works very well and on a tour group in August 2004, only one bag of over 30 went missing on the Kam Air flight.

3. Ariana is now also flying one flight a week from Frankfurt in conjunction with the Portugese Air Luxor, using modern A330-300 aircraft. There is a possibility that this may increase to two flights a week. See www.flyariana.com

4. Kam Air is also planning to run flights from Dusseldorf, Istanbul, and Almaty.

5. British Mediterranean Airways (part of British Airways) run an excellent service three times a week to Baku, capital of Azerbaijan. You can then connect with the Azeri Airlines' flight to Kabul. This requires an eight-hour overnight stopover on the way out (which can be spent on a Thermarest in the deserted airport), and a longer 16-hour overnight stop on the way back. A visa to enter Azerbaijan is available at the airport for US$30, and Baku is a lovely town, well worth exploring. A night in a hotel makes it quite comfortable.

6. Pakistan International Airways (PIA) fly regularly to Kabul from Islamabad.

7. Swiss Skies are scheduling direct flights from Paris to Kabul. The airline claims to 'specialise in providing safe, secure, reliable and efficient air transport to challenging destinations'. See www.swissskies.com

GETTING THERE BY LAND

The most dramatic way to enter Afghanistan is through the Khyber Pass, starting at Peshawar in Pakistan. The entire drive to Kabul, via Jalalabad, takes about eight hours. In Peshawar, you need to get a police permit to enter the border area—a condition strictly enforced. The indispensable Shuja Uddin, manager of Green's Hotel in Peshawar—that legendary hang-out of spies and journalists—is the man to consult on this and he can arrange transport, often with an Afghan trader returning to Kabul. On the trip through the pass itself, you are accompanied by a soldier of the Khyber Rifles. You can get a taxi from Peshawar to Torkhum, the border town, where you walk across the border, your luggage carried by a porter, and either hire another taxi there or make arrangements to be met by a car. Afghan Logistics (see below) are excellent at this.

The historical resonances here, the number of invaders that have crossed this pass, from the Aryans and Alexander the Great to Lord Roberts and the British Army of the Indus in 1878, make this an unforgettable experience. There is a train from Peshawar as far as Landi Kotal near the start of the Khyber Pass, but beyond here, on the pass itself, erosion has washed away the soil, leaving the rails hanging in space next to the road. Only the tunnels are in perfect condition, a testament to the engineering skills of the British who built the railway in the 1920s.

Trainline in the Khyber Pass, c. 1920 [Holmes]

A number of other passes cross into Afghanistan from Pakistan. These are technically closed to foreigners, although the Boroghil Pass, between Gilgit and Boroghil (see section on the Wakhan, p. 168), was used by a few foreigners in 2004.

The most exciting, though arduous route, is from Chitral over the 14,800 foot Dorah Pass. This three-day journey by horse takes you to Skarzer, a village close to the lapis lazuli mines of the Blue Mountain. This route has been used for millenia by traders bringing lapis out of Afghanistan, and you will see caravans of donkeys loaded down with blue stone. It was also the main supply route used by Ahmed Shah Massoud during the war against the Russians. When I used this in 2001, it was technically closed to foreigners but I was given no trouble entering Pakistan. The other way round, though, was a bit more tricky and involved sneaking round the Pakistani border posts at night. Security on the Pakistani side has become much tighter, but there are reports that if a foreigner simply turns up at the Pakistani border post from the Afghan side, they will be let in.

The other main land route into Afghanistan involves crossing the Oxus from Termez in Uzbekistan, using the bridge across which Soviet tanks poured in 1979, the grotesquely-named Friendship Bridge. In theory, an Uzbek and an Afghan visa are all you need to cross.

Visas and Documents
Remember to bring with you: passport, 2 extra passport photos, photocopies of passport and relevant visa pages, flight ticket, flight itinerary, proof of insurance.

You need a visa to enter Afghanistan and the authorities now require a letter of invitation from Afghanistan to establish your bona fides. Certain tour groups—Travel Afghanistan is one—have a special arrangement with the Afghan embassy in London that avoids this requirement. The embassy now needs three days to process the application.

In London, a single-entry tourist visa costs £30. The Afghan embassy is at 31 Prince's Gate, London SW7, tel. (44) 207 589 8891. The form is downloadable from the internet at www.afghanembassy.co.uk/html/consulate.html

In the US, the Afghan embassy is at 2341 Wyoming Avenue, Washington, DC 20008, telephone (1) 202 483 6410.

Their website is www.embassyofafghanistan.org

In Australia, the Afghan embassy is at P.O. Box 155, Deakin West, Canberra, ACT 2600, tel. (61) 2 6282 7322.

Their website is www.afghanembassy.net.

EMBASSIES IN KABUL

The British Embassy—sadly not the famous one near the Intercontinental, where the "best housed man in Asia" (the British ambassador) lived—is now at Karte Parwan, PO Box 334, Kabul. Satellite tel. 873 762 854 939.

US Embassy, The Great Massoud Road, Kabul, tel. (00 93) (2) 230 0436

A new US Embassy is being built on a titanic scale and will reputedly have an underground link to a shopping mall, hotel and restaurant. It is opposite ISAF, near the Great Massoud roundabout.

BUSINESS IN AFGHANISTAN

Kabul is booming with the influx of money from international donors. Its mineral wealth means that Afghanistan is potentially a rich country and in the old days it exported a good deal of dried fruit. Local entrepreneurs are rebuilding this industry.

The following organizations may be able to help people wanting to do business in Afghanistan:

Afghan-American Chamber of Commerce, 9293 Old Keene Mill Road, Burke, VA 22015, USA.

Telephone 703 440 4000. Website: www.a-acc.org

The Afghanistan-America Foundation (www.afghanistanamericafoundation.org) is led by Congressman Don Ritter and raises funds for, and co-ordinates, reconstruction.

GETTING AROUND

In the good old days of the 1960s and 1970s, tourists travelled everywhere by bus. These routes—operated by the Millie Bus Company—are starting again and are noted in the guide sections of this book at the end of each chapter, where applicable.

Although there is a programme of resurfacing the roads—principally, so far, the route northwards through the Salang Tunnel and the Kabul-Kandahar highway—the roads in Afghanistan are terrible. In river valleys they are often simply the bottom of the river bed. This makes road travel arduous (and even experienced Third-World travellers are shocked by their journeys) and requires a reliable four-wheel-drive vehicle. The word reliable is to be stressed. Many Afghan cars are not and are prone to irretrievable breakdown in the most inconvenient places (when fording a river, for example). Make enquiries about the firm that is hiring you the car, and don't necessarily take the cheapest offer. Afghan Logistics are to be recommended; also the Afghan Tourist Organisation (ATO).

BY AIR

Internal flights link the major cities, and travellers who can provide accreditation from NGOs can use the Pactec air service.

It is a personal opinion—but one I believe soundly based on evidence—that Kam is preferable for internal flights to Ariana, even though Kam use Russian Antonov 24s.

When arranging Kam or Ariana tickets, the actual flight coupons are only issued the day before the flight leaves. You can make a booking and pay for the tickets before—make sure you see your name being put on the flight manifest in the office and get a receipt.

Kam Air fly to Herat daily and Faisabad twice a week

Ariana Airlines fly to Herat, Mazar-i-Sahrif, Faisabad, Herat, Kandahar and Jalalabad when they feel like it.

TOUR OPERATORS AND TRAVEL AGENCIES

Few tour operators have actually run trips to Afghanistan. The first to do so was Live Travel, 120 Hounslow Road, Twickenham TW2 7HB, UK; tel. 44 208 894 6104; www.live-travel.com.

Overland specialist Geoff Hann, who ran buses from England to Kabul in the 1970s, has also taken a party: Hinterland Travel, 12 The Enterdent, Godstone, Surrey RH9 8EG, UK; tel. 44 1883 743584.

The company that has run most tours recently is Travel Afghanistan—an Anglo-Afghan joint venture: in England, Travel Afghanistan, Unit 4 Townmead Business Centre, William Morris Way, London SW6 2SZ, UK; tel. 44 20 7736 3968. Email: info@travelafghanistan.co.uk. In Afghanistan, at the Kabul Lodge, Passport Lane, Kabul; tel. 0702 77408, satellite tel. 00 88 216 2116 4294. Tours are offered to Bamiyan, Ajar, Herat, and in Badakhshan, trekking in the Wakhan Corridor and to Lake Shiva.

Abercrombie & Kent Hong Kong Ltd. also run tours, 19th Floor, Tesbury Centre, 28 Queen's Road East, Wanchai, Hong Kong; tel. 852 2865 7818, fax. 852 2866 0556. Email: pmacleod@abercrombiekent.com.hk.

In London, Abdul Karim at the Afghan Travel Centre provides an excellent service and encyclopeadic knowledge of flights to Afghanistan. He can issue Kam Air tickets in London.

Afghan Travel Centre, 107 Great Portland Street, London W1W 6QG, UK; tel. 44 207 580 7000.

In the US, veteran Afghan traveller Gary Bowersox takes parties to Afghanistan. He has over 30 years of experience travelling and organising expeditions in the country. He can be contacted by email: mrgary77@aol.com; his fascinating website is www.gems-afghan.com. Two other operators are running a small number of tours which either visit or pass through Afghanistan: Geographic Expeditions, 1008 General Kennedy Avenue, PO Box 29902, San Francisco, CA 94129-0902; tel. 415 922 0448; www.geoex.com. Distant Horizons, 350 Elm Avenue, Long Beach, CA 90802; tel. 800 333 1240; www.distant-horizons.com.

In Canada, Sayed Hashemi is the general sales agent for Ariana Airlines, Unit 203, Harvard Square, 801 Mohawk Avenue Road West, Hamilton, Ontario L9C 6C2, Canada; tel. 905 389 099 or toll-free 866 330 3431; email canada@flyariana.com

In Afghanistan, the leading supplier of vehicles and translators to journalists and aid workers is Afghan Logistics, run by the indefatigable Muqim Jamshady. They have a huge fleet of cars, from a 50-seat bus to air-conditioned Toyota Corollas and are invariably punctual and reliable. Their website is www.afghan-logistics.com; tel. 0702 77408/ 0793 91462 or via satellite tel. 882 162 1164 294; email: muqim@afghan-logistics.com

The government service is the Afghan Tourist Organisation, with an office at the airport and its headquarters outside the airport; tel. 0702 76378.

ITINERARIES

This book is organised around various regions, sites and journeys. However, the main tourist destinations may be set out briefly.

1. The Panjshir Valley with the option of trekking round the mountain Mir Samir (see p. 222). The Panjshir's nearness to Kabul and astonishing natural beauty made it the first destination for travellers when Afghanistan was on the tourist map.

Camel, Kunduz, 1975 [Y. Crowe]

It is still a wonderfully beautiful and fertile valley, a half-day journey from Kabul.

2. Bamiyan and Band-i-Amir (see p. 411). The monstrous destruction of the famous giant Buddhas and the frescoed caves has made this a less interesting destination. But there are a number of other sites nearby worth visiting, and Band-i-Amir still ranks as one of the great natural wonders of the world.

3. The Ajar Valley, the old royal hunting grounds, is a one-day journey north of Bamiyan (see p. 425).

4. Herat, though badly damaged and modernised, is still one of the legendary cities of Central Asia.

5. *The Road to Balkh*, the title of a 1970 guidebook by the great Nancy Dupree, takes in all the northern cities and now includes the sites of some spectacular archaeological sites, including Tillya Tepe and Balkh, where Greek remains were discovered in 2002, plus Mazar-i-Sharif and some beautiful towns, like Taloqan.

6. The jewel in the crown of Afghanistan's tourist attractions is the province of Badakhshan. Untouched by war and untroubled ever since, it contains the mighty Wakhan Corridor, the source of the Oxus and the summer grazing grounds of the Kuchi nomads at Lake Shiva, plus the Blue Mountain—the ancient world's only source of lapis lazuli. This area may well become the world's ultimate trekking destination, displacing Nepal, Tibet and Bhutan.

CLIMATE

North of the Hindu Kush, the summers are torrid. Travel here is best during the spring and fall. The high summer is the time for visiting the mountain areas, especially the Wakhan. Even at the height of summer it can freeze in such areas, and winter in the mountains (and this includes Kabul) can be very cold. The south of the country, though, has an Indian climate. The royal family used to decamp to Jalalabad, where the climate is pleasantly warm in winter.

Health

You must consult your doctor on this. The northern parts of the country do have malaria. Rabies is not unknown. Hepatitis is a risk from unpeeled fruit and unhygienic food preparation. The high passes of Badakhshan can cause altitude sickness, though doctors can prescribe acetalzolamide to be taken to help acclimatisation. Dexamethasone, for acute oedema (caused by the most severe form of altitude sickness), can be bought in Kabul. It must be emphasised, though, that a person suffering from altitude sickness *must* be taken down to a lower altitude as soon as possible. Drugs only mask the symptoms.

Medications are inexpensive and readily available in Kabul, without a prescription; consider taking the following:

Anti-diarrhoea pills: Imodium or Flagyl.

Anti-headache pills: Aspirin or paracetemol, not ibuprofen as it masks altitude sickness.

Stomach antibiotic: Ciprofloxacin, etc.

Broad-spectrum antibiotic.

Do not bring sleeping pills. They are a respiratory depressant.

Take plenty of oral rehydration salts to counteract the dehydration of the climate and diarrhoea.

Water should only be drunk if it is boiled or treated with the addition of iodine or chlorine tablets. Bottled water is available in the towns, but the staple drink is tea (*chai*).

Clothing and Equipment

Men should, on no account, wear shorts. Afghans find bare legs offensive. Technically, men's arms should be covered, but I have never encountered any objection to short-sleeved shirts. Women should cover their hair with a scarf and also cover their arms.

The most comfortable clothing for the Afghan summer is undoubtedly the shalwar kameez, which is a long shirt and a pair of baggy trousers. Made of light cotton, the outfit is easily washed daily—something very necessary in the heat and dust of an Afghan summer.

For luggage, consider two options: a 60 litre rucksack into which you put all your possessions; or a 40 litre rucksack and a small duffle bag. In addition you should take a small day-pack into which you can put your camera, reading material, water bottle and sunscreen. This bag can double as hand luggage on airplane flights.

It is essential that you can carry your entire luggage, usually for short distances, without the aid of a porter.

There are limited opportunities to have clothes washed in Kabul, Bamiyan and Herat. Plan to take robust clothes that you don't mind subjecting to washing by locals.

Cotton shirts: make sure you have a selection of short and long sleeves, and have adequate sun protection if you choose collarless shirts.

Cotton sun hat or a cotton headscarf.

Socks: take as many as you can get away with; clean socks are a definite luxury.

Cotton underwear (see above).

Trousers: 2 or 3 pairs cotton or modern synthetic long trekking trousers; 2 light-weight and one mid-weight for evenings or rainy days in Bamiyan or Ajar. No shorts (unseemly) or jeans (hard to dry if they get wet). Optional: wind/waterproof trousers.

Sandals or flip-flops for showering or toilets in hotels.

Bathing suit/swimming costume (you never know).

Jackets, tops: 2 or 3 fleece jackets or tops; choose differing weights and make sure that you can wear them in combination on top of each other.

Wind/waterproof jacket: if you have a Gore-Tex "wind stopper" jacket that is showerproof this will be the only "outer" that you need.

Boots: a pair of sturdy top-quality trekking boots ("broken-in"). You can get away with trainers, but boots provide support and protection.

Shoes: lightweight running shoes or slip-ons for city wear. Afghans take off their shoes and these save time for visits to mosques and museums or homes.

Equipment

Gloves: warm poly-thermal gloves (optional).

Head torch: consider an LED one that uses less power, provides more light and lasts for a long time; with extra battery.

Sunglasses: for eyeglass wearers, prescription dark glasses are best; extra prescription glasses, contact lenses etc; if you are a contact lens wearer you may have problems with hard lenses in the very dry and dusty environment. Don't forget a small travel mirror.

Water bottle: 1 or 1.5 litre bottle (Sigg brand is good), and iodine or chlorine tablets.

Lip suncream and skin suncream (minimum factor 25); skin blister repair kit.

Toothpaste/toothbrush.

Liquid soap/1 small towel.

Wet-wipes or baby-wipes in flat pack: for cleaning hands before and after meals and for cleaning feet and intimate areas when showers and baths are not available (carry a 72-pack with clothes, and 24-packs in day-pack).

Hygiene supplies.

Earplugs.

Small roll of repair tape and sewing kit.

Cigarette lighter or small box matches.

Small multi-purpose knife: do not carry in hand luggage when you check in for flights.

Alarm clock/watch.

A goose-down (duvet) sleeping bag; this might be too warm on hot nights but will keep you warm in Ajar and other mountain areas. Goose down is lighter and packs smaller than synthetics.

Inflatable foam mattress (Thermarest) or closed cell foam kari-mat.

MONEY

The national currency is the afghani, always knows as afs. There are (at time of writing) about 50 afs to US$1. The best rate of exchange can be had in the Kabul money bazaar. In most places, US dollars are accepted as an alternative to afs, though the change will normally be given in afs. Surprisingly little difference exists in the exchange rate between Kabul and the provinces. The Afghan money markets are incredibly efficient.

Bring US dollars in cash, and also credit cards (with photocopies), traveller's cheques etc.

In Kabul, Standard Chartered Bank in Wazir Akbar Khan has an ATM that accepts Visa and will soon accept Mastercard.

If you need to transfer money almost anywhere in Afghanistan or even the world, you can use the *hawala* system, which for efficiency and speed beats anything that Western banks have ever come up with. Under this system, you give money—or give a Western cheque to a money broker—and immediately the funds are available through his counterparty. You simply ring the person to whom you wish to transfer the money, give him the transaction's code number, and the money is immediately available. The system is a nightmare to the CIA because terrorists can use it to transfer any amount of money anywhere in the world and leave no paper or computer trail.

I have always used Javad and Brothers. Engineer Nawaz's number is 0702 79641 and his shop is no 67 on the first floor at Kabul Sarai Shahzada. He has offices in Herat and Peshawar. In Herat his office is in 24–25 Khurasan Market, tel. 0704 01516.

Photography

Afghanistan is certainly among the most spectacularly photogenic countries in the world. Bring camera and film, or if a digital camera, plenty of memory; you may not be able to charge a digital camera for several days at a time, so have spare batteries etc.

Extra film is easily bought in Kabul and the major cities.

Communications

Satellite phones

For trekking and independent travel, a satellite phone is a must. The cheapest option is an Iridium phone. In Britain they may be hired from a number of companies, including:

Hire4Lower, 35 Camborne Road, Southfields, London, SW18 4BH tel: (44) 208 870 0558

Mobell Communications Ltd., The Winding House, Walkers Rise, Rugeley Road, Hednesford, Staffordshire, WS12 0QU UK

The land-line telephones in Afghanistan are very bad. Most people in Kabul and other major cities rely on mobile phones, which work remarkably well. There are two systems: AWCC (Afghan Wireless Communication Corporation) and Roshan. Debate rages amongst Kabulis as to which is the best. Both networks are GSM, which means that European phones will work, though you will be paying international rates for calls within Afghanistan. Better to buy a Roshan or an AWCC chip for your phone at a cost of $50 or a complete handset at a cost of about $100. Top-up pay-as-you-go cards are available from shops all over Kabul. Chips can be bought in Kabul from the Roshan shop in Wazir Akbar Khan or AWCC ones at the main post office.

Shopping

Afghanistan is a shopper's paradise. Kabul's shopping centre for classic Afghan products is Chicken Street in Shahr-i-Naw. This is the place to find rugs, fur coats, clothes of various types, jewellery and lapis lazuli.

Beautiful rugs can be bought all over Kabul, but especially in Chicken Street. There is one rug shop that stands out: Nomad. Found here are beautiful modern designs made in the traditional way with earth-toned vegetable-dyed wool. The owner has a contract to supply Liberty's, but they do not seem significantly cheaper in Kabul than London – a 6 x 10-foot rug with an attractive geometric square pattern sells for $950; also traditional designed carpets: a large antique one sells for $1,750. Nomad is located just before the UNICA guesthouse; tel 0702 296878.

Another favourite shop is Parsa, a women's cooperative that makes and sells the most beautiful scarves. It is located off the Darulaman Road, next to Pizza Express and opposite a Federal Express office.

The ancient world's only source of lapis was in Afghanistan (see p. 134), and some of the carvers here are outstanding. Emeralds (from the Panjshir Valley) and rubies—as good as the best Burmese and Colombian stones—can be bought in Chicken Street, but if you want to buy a good gem it is certainly more sensible to purchase it from a reputable dealer. The best dealer is in the US: Geo Vision Inc.

They can ship all over the world and can be contacted via their website: www.gems-afghan.com

One of my favourite Afghan products is the *chapan*, the striped silk coat that President Hamid Karzai wears. I have seen some truly beautiful embroidered antique ones in Chicken Street and in Istalif. Thicker, padded ones are used in winter. *Chapans* have already begun to make an appearance on the catwalks at haute couture shows.

Other clothing products are made from fur, including mink, wolf and fox; also pakul hats, made from felted wool.

Consider bringing an additional locking duffle bag, with lock, to transport carpets or other souvenirs.

ELECTRICITY

Electricity is supplied at 220 volts 50 hertz. The supply in Kabul is intermittent at best, and good guesthouses and hotels have their own generators. Voltage fluctuations are a real problem for computer users, making a voltage-smoothing transformer a necessity. Plugs are European style two-pin.

MEDIA

Kabul's two English-language newspapers, the *Kabul Times* and the *Kabul Weekly*, can be bought from children in the street and in traffic jams, of which the city has plenty. The children also sell maps, magazines and books. Of the last two categories the best are the Bradt *Kabul Mini Guide* and *Kabul Scene* magazine, both the creation of the remarkable Dominic Medley, and the children keep half the cover price. *Kabul Scene* is written by foreign journalists who love Afghanistan. It is paid for and printed by the advertisers and will keep you up to date with Kabul's rapidly changing hotel and restaurant scene. Also, see the online version of the Bradt Guide, www.kabulguide.net, and Paul Clammer's www.kabulcaravan.com site, run by the author of the Afghanistan section in Lonely Planet's *Central Asia* guide.

Vegetable covered market, Kunduz, 1975 [Y. Crowe]

The *Asian Age* newspaper and *The Economist* are often available from street vendors.

The BBC World Service is available on 89 FM. A plethora of local-language stations is emerging, many supported by foreign donors.

The Afghanistan Foreign Press Association meets on the first Thursday of every month at the Gandamack Lodge; these gatherings provide an opportunity to find out what is going on.

TIME DIFFERENCE

Afghanistan, one of the few countries in the world to have a half-hour time adjustment, is four-and-a-half hours ahead of G.M.T.

FOOD AND DRINK

Afghan food can be excellent, but the country's terrible poverty means that the fare is generally very simple. Outside the main cities, a meal tends to be a bowl of greasy rice and mutton or a sort of pillau. This is supplemented with bean or mutton stew and large circles of *nan* bread. One quickly becomes very tired of it.

More interesting is the Kabuli pillau (rice livened up with shredded carrots and raisins) and kebabs. Don't buy these off the street as they often lead to appalling dysentery. Dumplings stuffed with spicy mince, known as *mantu*, are found at more ambitious restaurants and can be excellent. Afghan ice cream is, in the highlands, made from snow and has a taste all of its own.

Tea (*chai*) is the staple drink all over the country and, having been boiled, is always safe to drink. There are two varieties: green (*chai sabst*) and black (*chai siah*). Black is similar to the English variety and, in the more superior establishments, comes with milk and sugar.

HOLIDAYS

New Year (*Nao-Ruz*)	21 March
Islamic Revolution Day	28 April
Labour Day	1 May
Martyrs' and Disabled Day	4 May

| Independence Day | 19 August[1] |
| Massoud Day | 9 September[2] |

RELIGIOUS HOLIDAYS

The major religious holiday is Ramadan. It currently falls in October and November, though its precise start depends on observation of the new moon by specialist mullahs in Mecca. Muslims must fast between dawn and dusk for one lunar month (29 days), so working hours are cut back to a minimum. Most people are very bad tempered by the early afternoon and getting anything done is more difficult than usual. It is compensated for by *iftar,* the meal at dusk, which breaks the fast. The final day sees a massive celebration known as Eid-ul-Ramzan (Eid-ul-Fitri).

Owner of a kebab stall, Bamiyan, 2004 [B. Jenks]

OTHER RELIGIOUS HOLIDAYS

Arafa	10 February
Eid-ul-Asha	11-13 February
Ashura	13 March[3]
Eid-ul-Nabi	14 May

BEHAVIOUR, CUSTOMS AND CULTURE

Afghanistan is a deeply Muslim culture and visitors must respect this. Some Europeans living in the country join the Afghans in keeping the Ramadan fast.

The most striking aspect, to a secular Western visitor, is the comparative absence of women. In the street many are covered with the burqa. If you are invited to dinner at an Afghan house (and you almost certainly will be), you will be struck by the complete invisibility of women. Meals are taken in the front room and the food and drink is brought in either by children or an unmistakeably female arm appearing round a curtain.

Western women in such circumstances are treated as honorary men and will eat with the men, although they will also be able to visit the women in their part of the house, which can be a fascinating experience, although most Afghan women do not speak English.

Afghans eat with their right hands, digging into a pile of rice and squeezing it into a ball. Most Westerners find this difficult and the feel of the grease on one's palm unpleasant. Afghans will always provide a spoon as a concession to this disability. Meals are eaten sitting cross-legged on the floor, on cushions round the edge of the room, and this position can be uncomfortable to those who have not spent their lives practicing it. The arrival of the food is usually signalled by a child unrolling a length of oilcloth on the central carpet, which acts as a tablecloth. In more devout households, the eldest man or a haji (if one is present) will utter thanks to Allah at the end of the meal.

If you are travelling, expect to make regular stops for the drivers to pray at set times prescribed by Islam. Also, you should remove your shoes before entering houses, as well as mosques.

MAPS

The best relief map available of Afghanistan is the Afghan Cartographic Survey's 1:1,000,000 map, available in Kabul from Shah M Bookstore. In the UK, Stanfords sell the Nelles relief map of Afghanistan and the National Geographic map, readily available in America and by ordering, is also good. For travel in the Wakhan corridor, the best map available is the Survey of Pakistan Hunza map, sheet number N.J.—43/SW.

[1]Afghans have inflicted so many defeats on foreign invaders—three on the British alone—that there are many possible days for this celebration. This one commemorates the end of the Third Afghan War against the British in 1919. It was a potty little war that ended with what some might characterise as a draw rather than a victory.

[2]The anniversary of the fatal suicide bomb attack by two al-Qaeda members on the greatest mujahedin general, Ahmed Shah Massoud, in September 2001; this was very probably the signal for the attacks two days later in New York and Washington, DC.

[3]This commemmorates the death of the Prophet's son-in-law, Ali, at the battle of Qerbala (AD 640). It is the occasion of a huge gathering at his reputed tomb in Mazar-i-Sharif, with extraordinary scenes of grief and young men flagellating themselves and cutting their scalps with knives.

Stylized Boar's Head, Bamiyan, 6th century AD *[Musée Guimet]*

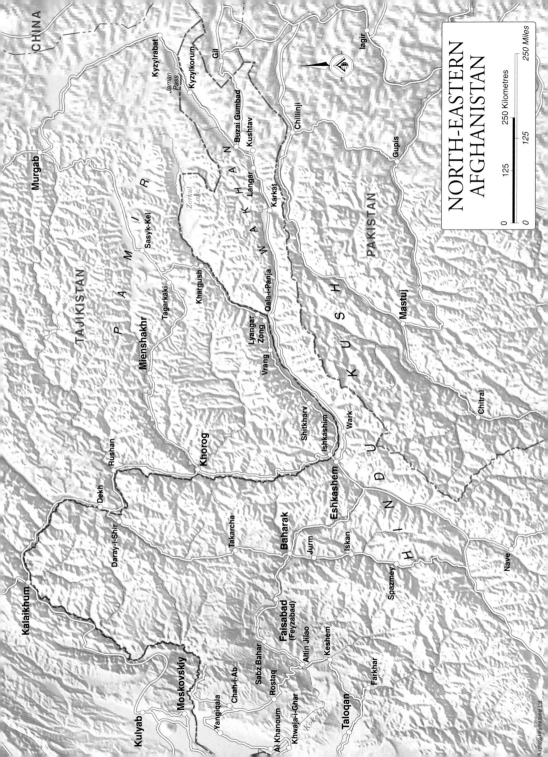

NORTH-EASTERN
AFGHANISTAN

250 Kilometres

250 Miles

0   125   250

0   125   250

CHINA

Kyzylrabat

Jarman Pass

Kyzylkorum

Gil

Buzai Gumbad

Kushtav

Iagir

Chillnji

Langar

Karkat

Gupis

W A K H A N

Murgab

Sasyk-Kel

Zorkul Lake

P A M I R

Tagarkaki

Khargush

Qala-i-Panja

TAJIKISTAN

Mienshakhr

Lyangar
Zong

Vrang

K U S H

Mastuj

Rushan

Khorog

Shitkharv

Ishkashim

Wark

PAKISTAN

Chitral

Dekh

Takarcha

Baharak

Eshkashem

D   U

Daray-i-Shir

Jurm

Iskan

H

Nave

Kalaikhum

Spazmey

Moskovskiy

Sabz Bahar

Rostaq

Faisabad
(Feyzabad)

Keshem

Kulyab

Yangiqala

Chah-i-Ab

Altin Jilao

Farkhar

Ai-Khanoum

Khwaja-i-Ghar

Kokch

Taloqan

A Journey to the Source of the Oxus: Badakhshan, the Wakhan Corridor and the High Pamirs

Aside from Matthew Arnold's famous poem *Sohrab and Rustum*, there can be few better evocations of the romance of the River Oxus than that written by Lord Curzon, the sometime Viceroy of India :

> "To myself the Oxus, that great parent stream of humanity, which has equally impressed the imagination of Greek and Arab, of Chinese and Tartar, and which, from a period over three thousand years ago, has successively figured in the literature of the Sanskrit Puranas, the Alexandrian historians, and the Arab geographers, has always similarly appealed. Descending from the hidden 'Roof of the World', its waters tell of forgotten peoples, and whisper secrets of unknown lands. They are believed to have rocked the cradle of our race."

There is no exaggeration in what Curzon says. It is the Oxus that the original Aryan tribes are thought to have crossed around 2,000 years before Christ, making their way towards northwestern India and Iran; the Oxus, along with the Jaxartes to the north, which, according to the Zoroastrian *Avesta*, bounded the lands of Paradise; the Oxus, which marked the boundary between the legendary kingdoms of Iran and Turan, forming a backdrop to the most dramatic episodes of the Iranian national epic, the *Shahnameh*; and the Oxus, which Alexander the Great crossed in pursuit of the rebel Bessus on his quest to dominate the whole of Asia.

The Oxus, or Amu Darya as it is now known, has never ceased to play a role in the allotment and partitioning of empires. In the 19th century, as the Russians and British vied for power and authority in Central Asia—playing the so-called "Great Game"—the Oxus came to be set as the final line of demarcation between their spheres of influence. After the Russian encroachment into Tashkent in 1868 and Khiva in 1873, an agreement was reached whereby "the line of the Oxus... will form the northern boundary of Badakhshan province of Afghanistan throughout its extent..." Moreover, the Russians assented to "raise no objection to the material,

Horse-drawn ferry at Kilif on the Oxus, c. 1885, by T.H. Holdich [RGS]

moral and financial influence of the British government over... Afghanistan", in essence confirming the country as a buffer state and client of the British, and the Oxus as the watershed of their control.

Needless to say, this agreement placed a great strain on the geographers and cartographers of the time. The course of the upper reaches of the river was still little-understood—one British minister, Lord Salisbury, described the affair as "drawing lines upon maps where no human foot has ever trod"—and the lack of certain knowledge combined with political necessity acted as a great incentive for explorers to search out the Wakhan and Great Pamir region, to discover for certain the true source of the River Oxus.

Any journey to the source of the Oxus starting in Afghanistan must necessarily pass through the province of Badakhshan, where the Oxus, on account of its five tributaries, is known as the *Ab Panj*, or "Five Rivers". The region, generally speaking, appears for much of its history to have behaved autonomously, even when under the nominal rule of external powers; true control belonged to whatever local chiefs (or *mirs*) happened by chance to become prevalent. It is known to have been a part of the Persian Achaemenid Empire from the 6th century BC, and after Alexander's conquest to have devolved to the Graeco-Bactrian Empire. Afterwards, to a certain extent, it fell under Chinese influence; indeed, one of the first accounts of the area comes from the Chinese Buddhist traveller Hsuen-Tsang (Xuan Zang) in AD 644:

> "This kingdom is an old territory of the Tu-ho-lo country; it is about 2000 *li* [650 miles] in circuit, and the capital, which is placed on the side of a mountain precipice, is some six or seven *li* [2miles] in circuit. It is intersected with mountains and valleys, a vast expanse of sand and stone stretches over it; the soil is fit for the growth of beans and wheat; it produces an abundance of grapes, the khamil peach, and plums. The climate is very cold. The men are naturally fierce and hasty; their customs are ill-regulated; they have no knowledge of letters or the arts; their appearance is low and ignoble; they wear mostly garments of wool. There are three or four *sangharamas* [centres of Buddhist fellowship], with very few followers. The king is of an honest and sincere

disposition. He has deep faith in the three precious objects [three jewels] of worship."

Genghis Khan invaded the area in 1220, causing it some damage, but nevertheless re-opening the silk trading routes, which had beforehand been closed for some time. One famous traveller who took advantage of this new freedom of movement was Marco Polo, who paused in Badakhshan in around 1272, whilst recovering from an illness:

"Badshan is a province inhabited by people who worship Mahomet, and have a peculiar language. It forms a very great kingdom, and the royalty is hereditary. All those of royal blood are descended from King Alexander and the daughter of King Darius, who was lord of the vast empire of Persia. And all these kings call themselves in the Saracen tongue Zulcarnian, which is as much to say Alexander, and this out of regard for Alexander the Great.

"It is in this province that those fine and valuable gems the Balas Rubies are found. They are got in certain rocks among the mountains, and in the search for them people dig great caves underground, just as is done by miners for silver. There is but one special mountain that produces them, and it is

The Timur Ruby Necklace. The great stone in the centre, mined in Badakhshan, once belonged to the Emperor Timur (Tamerlane); Persian inscriptions visible on the stone record this fact, along with the names of its later owners. © Reserved, the Royal Collection

called Syghinan. The stones are dug on the king's account, and no-one else dares dig in that mountain on pain of forfeiture of life as well as goods; nor may anyone carry the stones out of the kingdom. But the king amasses them all, and sends them to other kings when he had tribute to render, or when he desires to offer a friendly present; and such only as he pleases he causes to be sold. Thus he acts in order to keep the balas at a high value; for if he were to allow everybody to dig, they would extract so many that the world would be glutted with them, and they would cease to bear any value. Hence it is that he allows so few to be taken out, and is so strict in the matter.

"There is also in the same country another mountain, in which azure is found; 'tis the finest in the world, and is got in a vein like silver. There are also other mountains which contain a great amount of silver ore, so that the country is a very rich one; but it is also (it must be said) a very cold one. It produces numbers of excellent horses, remarkable for their speed. They are not shod at all, although constantly used in mountainous country, and on very bad roads.

"The mountains of this country also supply Saker Falcons of excellent flight, and plenty of Lanners likewise. Beasts and birds for the chase there are in great abundance. Good wheat is grown, and also barley without husk. They have no olive oil, but make oil from sesame, and also from walnuts.

"Those mountains are so lofty that it is a hard day's work, from morning till evening, to get to the top of them. On getting up, you find an extensive plain, with great abundance of grass and trees, and copious springs of pure water running down through rocks and ravines. In those brooks are found trout and many other fish of dainty kinds; and the air in those regions is so pure, and residence there so healthful, that when the men who dwell below in the towns, and in the valleys and plains, find themselves attacked by any kind of fever or other ailment that may hap, they lose no time in going to the hills and after abiding there two or three days, they quite recover their health through the excellence of that air.

"In this kingdom there are many strait and perilous passes, so difficult to force that the people have no fear of invasion. Their towns and villages also are on lofty hills, and in very strong positions. They are excellent archers, and much given to the chase; indeed, most of them are dependent for clothing on the skins of beasts, for stuffs are very dear among them. The great ladies, however, are arrayed in stuffs, and I will tell you the style of their dress. They all wear drawers made of cotton cloth, and into the making of these some will put 60, 80, or even 100 ells [one ell equals six hand breadths] of stuff. This they do to make themselves look large in the hips, for the men of those parts think that to be a great beauty in a woman."

Twenty-five miles (40 km) beyond the present-day regional capital of Faisabad, walking eastwards towards the source of the Oxus, lies the town of Baharak, which once also served as the capital of Badakhshan. In the centre of the Baharak Valley is a *jui*, or irrigation canal, situated at the foot of a small hill. This hill is known as the Mountain of Shirin-o-Farhad; according to a legend, first recorded by the 12th century poet Nizami, the canal was dug as a work of devotion by a stone-cutter, Farhad, for Shirin, Queen of Armenia. Many folk versions of the tale of unfulfilled love are still in circulation; this example was recorded in the early 20th century by Sirdar Ali Ikbal Shah, in *Afghanistan of the Afghans*:

"There was a brave man named Farhad, who loved a Princess named Shirin, but the Princess did not love him. Farhad tried in vain to gain access to the love-cell of Shirin's heart, but no-one would dare betray the fact that a stone-cutter loved a lady of royal blood. Farhad, in despair, would go to the mountains and spend whole days without food, playing on his flute sweet music in praise of Shirin. At last people thought to devise a plan to acquaint the Princess of the stone-cutter's love. She saw him once, and love which lived in his bosom also began to breathe in hers. But she dared not open her lips before her father— for how could a mean labourer aspire to win the hand of a princess?

It was not long, however, before the King himself heard some rumour of this extraordinary change of sentiment. He was naturally indignant at the discovery, but as he had no other child than Shirin, and Shirin was also pining away with love, he proposed to his daughter that her lover, being of common birth, must accomplish a task such as no man may be able to do, and then—and only then— might he be recommended to his favour. The task which he skilfully suggested was that Shirin should ask her lover to dig a canal in the rocky land among the hills. The canal must be six lances in width and three lances deep and forty miles long!

Faisabad, aerial view [M. Yamashita]

The Death of Farhad, attributed to Bihzad, from Khamsah *of Nizami, Herat, 1494.*
[British Library]

The Princess had to convey her father's decision to Farhad, who forthwith shouldered his spade and started off to the hills to commence the gigantic task. He worked hard and broke the stones for years. He would start his work early in the morning when it was yet dark and never ceased from his labour till, owing to darkness, no man could see one yard on each side.

Shirin secretly visited him and watched the hard-working Farhad, who forthwith shouldered his spade sleeping with his spade under his head, his body stretched on the bed of stones. She noticed, with all the pride of a lover, that he cut her figure in the rocks every six yards, and she would sigh and return without his knowing.

Farhad worked for years and cut his canal; all was in readiness but his task was not yet finished, for he had to dig a well in the rocky beds of the mountains and sprout a fountain from which the canal should receive its perpetual supply. He was half-way through, and would probably have completed it, when the King consulted his courtiers and sought their advice. His artifice had failed. Farhad had not perished in the attempt, and if all the conditions were fulfilled, as soon seemed likely, his daughter must go to him in marriage. The Viziers suggested that an old woman should be sent to Farhad to tell him that Shirin was dead; then, perhaps, Farhad would become disheartened and leave off the work.

It was an ignoble trick, but it promised success and the King agreed to try it. So an old woman went to Farhad and wept and cried till words choked her; the stone-cutter asked her the cause of her bereavement.

'I weep for a deceased,' she said, 'and for you.'

'For a deceased and for me?' asked the surprised Farhad. 'And how do you explain it?'

'Well, my brave man,' said the pretender, sobbing, 'you have worked so well, and for such a long time too, but you have laboured in vain, for the object of your devotion is dead.'

'What!' cried the bewildered man, 'Shirin dead?'

Such was his grief that he cut his head with the sharp spade and died under the carved image of his beloved. The only liquid that streamed into the canal was his own blood. When Shirin heard this she fled in great sorrow to the mountains where her wronged lover lay; it is said that she inflicted a wound in her own head at the precise spot where Farhad had struck himself, and with the same sharp edge of the spade which was stained with her lover's gore. No water ever flows into the canal, but the two lovers are entombed in one and the same grave."

A little way south of Baharak is the town of Jurm. Lieutenant John Wood, who in 1838 made a famous and pioneering journey to what he considered to be the source of the Oxus, stayed with a Badakhshi family in Jurm, and fully recorded his impressions.

"We took up our abode with Hussain, our former host, who, though at first suspicious of his guests, became ere long our warm friend and almost constant companion. It is customary in these countries for relations to live in the same hamlet, often to the number of six to eight families. An outer wall surrounds this little knot of friends, within which each family has its separate dwelling-house, stable, and cattle-shed; and a number of such hamlets form a *kishlak*, or village. In Hussain's homestead were four houses, one of which had been vacant ever since its former inmates perished in the earthquake of 1832. This was now our abode. The style of building does not differ throughout the country, and our quarters at Jerm [Jurm] may be taken as a fair specimen of them all. The site is the slope of a hill, and a rivulet is usually not many paces from the door. Its course is here and there impeded by large, whitened boulders, glassy-smooth from the constant action of running water; while its banks are shaded by a few gnarled walnut trees, and the lawn adjoining planted in regular lines with the mulberry. Down in the bottom of the valley, where the rivulet falls into the larger stream, lie the scanty corn-lands of the community. The mountains rise immediately behind the village, and their distant summits retain their snowy covering throughout the greater portion of the year. An enclosure is formed by running a dry-stone wall round a space proportioned to the size and wealth of the family. The space this enclosed is divided into compartments, the best of which form the dwelling-houses, whilst the others hold the stock. These latter compartments are usually sunk two feet under ground, while the floors of the rooms for the family are elevated a foot or more above it: flat roofs extend over the whole. In the dwelling-house the smoke escapes by a hole in the middle of the top of the roof, to which is fitted a wooden frame, to stop up the aperture when snow is falling. The rafters are lathed above, and then covered with a thick coat of mud. If the room be large its roof is supported by four stout pillars, forming a square, in the middle of the apartment, within which the floor is considerably lower than in the other parts, and the benches thus formed are either strewed with straw or carpeted with felts, and form the seats and bed-places of the family. The walls of the house are of considerable thickness: they are smoothly plastered inside with mud, and have a similar though rougher coating without. Where the slope of the hill is considerable the enclosing wall is omitted, and the upper row of houses are then entered over the roofs of the lower. Niches are left in the sides of the wall, and in these are placed many of the household utensils.

"The custom of relations grouping together has its advantages, but they are not unmixed. Many of the sorrows of the poor are thus alleviated by the kindness of friends: the closeness of their intercourse adds to their mutual sympathy; and when death occurs, the consolation which the afflicted survivors receive from those near around them is great indeed. But to the newly-married couple the benefits derived from this arrangement are frequently very dearly purchased; and the temper of the poor bride, it is to be feared, is often permanently *damaged* by the trials she has to undergo at the hands of a cross-grained mother-in-law. Thus it often happens that the bitterest enemies are inmates of the same house. Were I to venture an opinion on so *very delicate* a subject, it would be in favour of a separate establishment for all newly-married people; but in these barren Alpine lands it is poverty which renders it necessary thus to congregate together...

"The vessels for holding water are made from the fir-tree, and those for containing flour from the red willow; the latter are circular and hooped. Earthenware is scarce, though in some families very pretty china bowls are to be met with. The bread is baked upon a stone girdle; the lamp is of the same material, and its shape is nearly that of a shoe... Besides the lamp a very convenient light is obtained from a reed called '*luz*,' about an inch in circumference. It is pasted round with bruised hemp-seed, and bunches, thus prepared, are to be found in every house, suspended generally from the rafters over head. When it is wished to extinguish the burning reed, a circle of the bark is peeled off, and the flame, when it reaches that spot, expires of itself. Throughout Badakhshan I remarked a great disinclination to extinguish a light by blowing upon it with the breath."

The reluctance of the inhabitants of Badakhshan and the Wakhan to extinguish flames was noticed by many travellers throughout the 19th century. Their deep-rooted conviction that blowing out a lighted taper would bring bad luck is generally accepted to be a remnant of fire-worship and Zoroastrianism, which was the prevalent religion there before the advent of Islam. One visitor to the Wakhan in the 1890s, Olaf Olufsen, examined the phenomenon closely, drawing parallels between surviving superstitions and Zoroastrian (or Avestan) practice.

"Their chief god is called Allah, as in Islamic religion, or Khoda, but they also have one Almasdé, which is probably a corruption of Ormuzd (Ahura Mazda), who is not, as in the old Iranian faith, the creator of the world, but has here degenerated into an evil spirit, who lives in the rivers, into the eddies of which he tries to draw bathing or swimming men. Sometimes he will go into the stables at night and amuse himself by disturbing the horses and donkeys or by pulling hairs out of their tails and manes.

"The whole world was created by Allah or Khoda—the heavens in 45 days; the water in 60; the earth in 75; the trees in 30; the cattle in 80; and, at last, man in 75 days. This corresponds exactly with the time that Ahura Mazda took for the creation.

"The world is made of fire, earth, water, and wind, and these four elements are given to man to make use of. The Mazdak sect of the old Iranian religion held that everything had developed itself out of fire, earth, and water, and to this later on was added wind.

"The sky is of silver, and the stars of cut glass; each man has his own star ('zöthroog'), and when a person dies a shooting star is seen. (In the Iranian faith the sky is of bright steel or silver, and both good and evil stars are found.) There are several skies, one above another—the uppermost sky ('asman') is of silver; and there Khoda (God) lives. In the earth lives the devil ('Shaitan') with all his brood; but there is besides a kind of between-world, the air, which is full of spirits, whereof some seem to be quite useless for man, and the rest to be evil spirits. In the main features this is the old Iranian faith also. The spirits of the air are male and female, and it is one of the female spirits that tries to contract the throats of sleeping people and so produces snoring. Another rides on

Wardui River, on the way to Eskashem [M. Yamashita]

human beings and so produces nightmare. The natives told me that they often in their dreams at night saw these evil female spirits, who were a mixture of the beautiful and the dreadful...

"The Wakhans hold that the evil spirits, which they imagine to fill the air, now and again visit the earth and take up their abode in dark ravines, amongst mystical-looking mountains and rocks, or in old trees, and by graves. It is possible that this is why they have lights burning in bowls or lamps in such places, to keep these evil spirits away by the aid of the good spirit, the fire—or at any rate to paralyse their effects...

"The people believe that there are great realms down in the earth, but no human being knows anything with regard to them, except that they are the abode of Shaitan and all his inferior devils. This Shaitan was in the beginning a good spirit, an angel, who lived in heaven. He was very wise and very haughty. One day in his arrogance he spat on the sky ('asman'), and this remained on the sky as a crescent. Then the angel Djabraïl (Gabriel)—in Islam God always speaks to the Prophet through the angel Djabraïl or Gabriel—descended to the earth and formed a man out of earth, and God gave it soul and ordered that all the angels should bow down before this creature (second Sura of the Koran). All the angels obeyed but Shaitan, who held himself too mighty an angel to bow down before man. As a punishment, Shaitan was chained on the sky to the half-moon, which he had himself produced in his arrogance. Later on he was thrown down on the earth and his body covered with hair. He took up his abode inside the earth, but is at the same time omnipresent on earth—nobody sees him or knows him ...

"When there is a solar eclipse or lunar eclipse, the Wakhans kill sheep and goats at their altars and sanctuaries, and the meat is distributed among the poor. When, during winter, the sun can only shine a short while into the narrow mountain valleys, the people say that God ('Khoda') is wrathful on account of the sins of the people—therefore the sun hides behind the mountains, and so, to appease God, they make sacrifices of cattle and light lamps in the sanctuaries.

"Others told us that the sun and moon occasionally themselves sin, and are punished by God by being obscured, as, for instance, after an eclipse; they then have very heavy toil in chasing away the demons who have obtained great power over them during the time of darkness..."

On his way out of Jurm, Wood found and stayed the night at the tomb of Nasir Khusraw, the 11th century mystic and poet:

"Shah Nasir is the patron saint of the Kohistan, and much revered by the inhabitants of the Upper Oxus. For the support of the Ziarat a tract of land was assigned at the time the buildings were erected; and in return for an indulgence which has been confirmed by the subsequent rulers of Badakshan, the Mazar is bound to furnish the wayfaring man with food, water, and a night's lodging. Its inmates complained that wheat will not grow upon their land, though it does of that of their neighbours. The grain, they said, springs up and forms an ear, as in other fields, but no wheat is in it, and the straw alone will not repay them the labour of cutting it down. There must be something in the soil inimical to the growth of this grain; but the inhabitants of the Ziarat have found a better reason, alleging that the saint in compassion to human frailty has kept wheaten bread from them, that their passions might be easier kept under, and their tendency to sin be the less."

Nasir Khusraw was born in Qubadiyan, near Balkh, in AD 1003/4, and was given the fullest possible education in all the branches of knowledge: theology, philosophy and literature—both Islamic as well as those of ancient Greece and Iran—the sciences and mathematics. He worked as a financial clerk in the service of the Seljuk court before undergoing a spiritual experience at about the age of 40, at which he determined to set out on pilgrimage and travel extensively throughout the Islamic world. In Cairo, which was at that time under the rule of the Ismaili Fatimid Caliphs, he decided to convert to Ismailism and to propagate further that version of the Islamic faith. On returning home after seven years, he was declared a

Holy man with bow, Baharak [D. Grossart]

heretic and driven out. After a further period of wandering, he came to settle under the protection of a local prince in Yamgan in Badakhshan, where much of his work came to be written. Aside from a highly-regarded travel narrative, the *Safarnama*, and a set of philosophical works, Khusraw composed a collection of Persian mystical verse which is still considered to be some of the greatest writing in the language. He incorporated many neo-Platonic ideas in his work; like other mystics, he strove to comprehend the unity (*tawhid*) of God, emphasising that it could not be grasped in the transitory physical world; nevertheless, the physical world and its processes were, he maintained, a creation of the World-Soul, an expression of its striving towards understanding and embracing the infinity and unity of God. Unlike many other mystics, he held that the material world was not inherently evil, but if treated properly, could be, as the Book of Common Prayer would put it, "an outward and visible sign of an inward and spiritual grace". Many of these ideas are discernible in this translation of one of his poems.

"In the creator's name, the Pure, the ruler,
He, higher far than intellect or thinking!
He is the First, He is the Last for ever;
No one is prior to Him, none is later.
His essence, an abyss, confuses reason—
Know Him as free from stars and from directions.
How could one see Him with the body's eye?
The soul's eye only sees the Soul of souls!
His nest lies far behind 'There-where-no-place' is—
What can I say? It's always much too lowly!
His attributes, His Essence, are primordial.
To understand that is a mighty journey!
How could one travel there with human feet?
How to arrive there on this earthly steed?
My reason hid its head due to its weakness:
'How could I dare that, don't dare to pronounce it—
I am too small to utter such a word!'
The tongue can not express his Unity—
He is too great, beyond comparison!

I don't say: 'He created four and seven.'
I say: 'He nourishes the intellect.'
Do sun and moon and spheres have any value?
You cannot attribute these things to Him!
Why do you say that He created rubies
And gold and jewels out of clay and water?
You say: 'He brings the flowers forth from dust!'
The vegetative spirit does this work
by planting roses, box-trees, cypresses!
Know: Soul and reason are from God—what's silver?
What's gold? Don't worship forms! What's head and foot?
You also say: 'It is alone from semen
that He made here appear all our forms!'
Don't talk like that! For all these artful acts
come from the influence of stars and natures;
To call the sphere, the elements, the spirit
of vegetation 'god', seems pagan though!
Don't lose your way in thinking how the creatures
were formed! From wheat comes wheat, from barley, barley.
He, who created souls and knows their secret,
He has no company in Being God!
You speak of 'faith' and 'infidelity'—
You don't know the beginning nor the end!
With such an immature weak intellect—
how can you call yourself a Muslim. Say?
For if you have such thoughts concerning God
You are inferior to Christians, Jews!
The erring Parsee does not say such things—
I beg God to forgive such words and thoughts!
Lord of the Universe, All-Knowing, Mighty –
Know Him as One, and one appeared from Him!"

Despite the work he did in Badakhshan—his literary and academic pursuits, and propagation of the Ismaili creed—he would often complain bitterly of his exile in such a distant and remote region:

"Pass by, sweet breeze of Khurasan,
To one imprisoned in the Valley of Yumgan,
Who sits huddled in comfortless tight straits,
Robbed of all wealth, all goods, all hope.
Cruel fate has rudely stolen away by force
All peace from his heart, all rest from his body.
His heart swells fuller with sorrow than a pomegranate bursting with seed,
His body shrinks, more consumed than a shrivelled winter reed.
That beautiful face and that handsome figure
Have now turned to ugliness, misery and ruin
Fallen into weakness, ugliness and ruin.
That face, once bright as spring's anemones,
Crackles now like autumn leaves from exile's miseries.
Even family turn away from him like strangers.
None can help him now, save the mercy of God."

Near the tomb of Nasir Khusraw, Wood took the opportunity to inspect the lapis lazuli mines. By the time of his visit, the mines had been worked for more than 7,000 years, supplying the blue semi-precious stone for even such artefacts as the golden funeral mask of Tutankhamun:

"Where the deposit of lapis-lazuli occurs, the valley of the Kokcha is about 200 yards wide. On both sides the mountains are high and naked. The entrance to the mines is in the face of the mountain, on the right bank of the stream, and about 1,500 feet above its level. The formation is of black and white limestone, unstratified, though plentifully veined with lines... The summit of the mountains is rugged, and their sides destitute of soil or vegetation. The path by which the mines are approached is steep and dangerous, the effect of neglect rather than of natural difficulties. The shaft by which you descend to the gallery is about ten feet square, and is not so perpendicular as to prevent you

The Mask of Tutankhamun, embellished with lapis lazuli from Badakhshan. [Egyptian Museum, Cairo]

walking down. The gallery is eighty paces long, with a gentle descent; but it terminates abruptly in a hole twenty feet in diameter and as many deep. The width and height of the gallery, though irregular, may be estimated at about twelve feet; but at some places where the roof has fallen in its section is so contracted that the visitor is forced to advance upon his hands and knees. Accidents would appear to have been frequent, and one place in the mine is named after some unhappy sufferers who were crushed by the falling roof. No precaution has been taken to support by means of pillars the top of the mine, which formed of detached blocks wedged together, requires only a little more lateral expansion to drop into the cavity. Any further operations can only be carried out at the most imminent risk to the miners. The temperature at the further end of the mine was 36° of Fahrenheit, while in the open air at its entrance it was 29°.

"The method of extracting the lapis-lazuli is sufficiently simple. Under the spot to be quarried a fire is kindled, and its flame, fed by dry furze [gorse], is made to flicker over the surface. When the rock has become sufficiently soft, or, to use the workmen's expression, *nurím*, it is beaten with hammers, and flake after flake knocked off until the stone of which they are in search is discovered. Deep grooves are then picked out round the lapis-lazuli, into which crow-bars are inserted, and the stone and part of its matrix are detached.

"The workmen enumerate three descriptions of lajword [lapis-lazuli]. These are the Neeli, or indigo colour; the Asmani, or light blue; and the Suvsi, or green. Their relative value is in the order in which I have mentioned them. The richest colours are found in the darkest rock, and the nearer the river the greater is said to be the purity of the stone. The search for lajword is only prosecuted during the winter, probably because, labour in the mine being compulsory, the inhabitants are less injured by giving it in a season of comparative idleness than when the fields require their attention. Perhaps, also, during the cold of winter the rock may be more susceptible to the action of heat, and thus be more easily reduced, than when its temperature is higher."

Some way to the north of the lapis mines, at Shignan—as Marco Polo describes—ruby mines are to be found. The remarkable 19th-century American adventurer and soldier of fortune, Colonel Alexander Gardner, before going in the company of a local bai (bey, or petty nobleman) to propitiate a rival chief, made a visit to them:

"On our way we visited the famous ruby mines. To reach them we had to diverge southwards. Before starting we were treated to a sumptuous repast served on wooden trays, on which were spread handsome tablecloths. Everything was served by fair hostesses. We had kababs and pillaos, both sweet spiced and saline, with fresh cheese-curds, washed down by draughts of fine though somewhat acid Kafiristan and Chitral wine. Nor was fine, fat, snow-preserved wild mutton wanting. We had horn spoons and ladles to help ourselves with.

"The presents for the dreaded chief consisted of lion and tiger skins, large red-deer antlers and horns of markhor and ibex, some fine furs, a few bags and bones full of gold dust, some musk-glands, and a few rubies of inferior quality.

"Having taken leave of our hosts and hostesses with outstretched hands, muttering a short prayer after the head mullah, we mounted and started off towards a lonely hamlet where we were to pass the night before going to the mines.

"Here dwelt a solitary fakir of venerable aspect, with long white locks and eyebrows, and evidently of advanced age. He was seated on the only mat in the place, outside his hovel, absorbed in reverie. All his worldly property seemed to consist of some earthen pots of grain placed in a hole dug in the middle of the hut. He was evidently one of those hermits of the mountains who relinquish the world and all its cares. He was a remarkable man—he had visited Turkey, Asia Minor, Arabia, Persia, Turkestan, and Afghanistan; had seen Constantinople, Baghdad, Erzeroum, Mecca, Medina, Ispahan, and Teheran. Moreover, he was known to be the owner of a remarkable ruby, and the old bai was most anxious to become its possessor. He made most urgent entreaties for the gem, but for some time the fakir sat perfectly unmoved. The bai declared that by means of this ruby only could the robber chief, whom he was on his way to propitiate, be induced to spare the lives, property and honour of all the innocent families around. At last the fakir quietly arose, and lifting the plank that covered a hole in the hut, after a little fumbling produced the gem. Having motioned us with a dignified gesture to be seated, he proceeded quietly

The Imperial State Crown. The great stone in the cross at the front—the Black Prince's ruby—(in fact, a spinel ruby) was mined in Badakhshan, and in 1367 passed by way of the King of Castile into the possession of the Prince of Wales. It was worn by Henry V in his helmet at the Battle of Agincourt (1415). © Her Majesty Queen Elizabeth II

to unfold a bit of rag, then with much grace placed the jewel softly in the hands of the bai, bestowed on him his blessing, expressed the hope that the offering might produce the anticipated result, and then relapsed into a silent reverie. The bai offered him a sum of money, but the old man gently declined it, but desired that the allowance of grain, which it appears was made him, should be somewhat augmented, in order that he might be able to relieve way-worn and destitute travellers. This was at once agreed to, when the fakir motioned us to leave his hut, whereupon we departed.

"On examining the gem I found a small Zoroastrian altar cut in high relief on the centre of the oblong face of the stone, and round the altar a double cordon of letters of the same kind of characters that appear on the Scytho-Bactrian coins which are found about Balkh & Bokhara. The stone was very valuable, from 150 to 200 carats in weight—a pure lustrous gem. It was salaamed to by the bai and all his followers. The ruby had been found about the time of Timur by an ancestor of the fakir in a cave near the famous shrine and Kafir city of Esh or Oosh in the Bolor Ranges.

"On the following day we took leave of the holy man and proceeded to the mines. They consisted, somewhat to my surprise, of cave-like burrows about 1000 feet above the river. They were cut in soft, decayed rock, which both above and below alternated with a species of mountain limestone, also in strata. There was a thick, whitish, and in parts yellowish, saline-like crust formed on the sides of the cutting, which extruded from the limestone rock, and which in many places was marked with green, yellow and dirty-white spots, giving evidence of the presence of iron or copper oxides. The upper part and roofs

(Above) *Colonel Alexander Gardner [RSAA]*
(Right) *Wakhan River near Qaleh-ye Panjeh [M. Yamashita]*

of the burrows were utterly neglected and in ruins. After wading diagonally through the slush we emerged. Around were old dismantled forts which once commanded the passage of the river and the entrance to the mines. It was said that there were copper, antimony and lead mines in the vicinity, but that they had not been worked since the days of Timur. In my wanderings I lost no opportunity of inquiring about the various mines which existed in the regions which I visited, but I never found one which seemed likely to repay attention."

Colonel Gardner also described the methods of panning for gold which were practised in the local areas:

"The population generally were herdsmen or farmers, but they added to their income by gold-washing in the rivers and by occasional plundering expeditions. There are three different methods of obtaining gold from the rivers. The first is to wash the river-sand at certain well-known spots, particularly at the inner angles of curves, where the strong current of the main stream causes swift reverse eddies, and allows the gold scales and particles to subside together with quantities of deep purple and black ferruginous sand, in which alone gold is found. This operation is lucrative in the Upper Oxus and several other rivers. The proper season is after the rains, and when the snow-floods have subsided and left the rivers at their lowest. Sometimes as much as four tillahs' weight of gold is collected—about 120 grains. This, when rubbed up with a little mercury, forms a still amalgam. It is then taken home and separated from all impurities. The mercury evaporates through an application of heat, and the

residuum of pure gold is stored in the hollow shank-bones of large birds, such as herons, cranes, etc. The second method, in vogue principally in the neighbourhood of Hazrat Imam, consists in the formation of a sort of gold-trap of fleecy sheepskins, which are laid down in the bed of the river at chosen spots. They are held in place by heavy stones, and care is taken that the natural inclination of the wool faces the stream, so as to keep the entire growth of the wool freely flowing in the water. After two or three day's immersion the fleeces are carefully taken from the river and sun-dried. Without hazarding a suggestion that the fable of the Argonautic expedition of the Golden Fleece may have derived its origin from the immemorial practice just described, it is certain that the possession of these golden fleeces is the cause of severe skirmishes, as armed parties frequently rush upon the men left to watch, and sometimes bear off the prize, leaving its guardians dead on the riverside..."

Beyond Badakhshan lies the Wakhan Corridor, and at the end of this the Great Pamir. Marco Polo followed this route to China in 1272, having recovered from his illness:

"In leaving Badashan you rise 12 days between east and NE, ascending a river that runs through land belonging to a brother of the prince of Badahsan, and containing a good many towns and villages and scattered habitations. The people are Mahometans, and valiant in war. At the end of those 12 days you

Horns of an Ovis Poli, or Marco Polo Sheep. This specimen, in the library of the Royal Society for Asian Affairs, is the fourth largest known; the horns were removed from a dead animal found in the Wakhan in the early 20th century. [RSAA]

come to a province of no great size, extending indeed no more than 3 days journey in any direction, and this is called Vokhan [Wakhan]. The people worship Mahomet, and they have a peculiar language. They are gallant soldiers, and they have a chief whom they call *none*, which is as much as to say 'count', and they are liegemen to the prince of Badashan.

"There are numbers of wild beasts of all sorts in this region. And when you leave this little country, and ride 3 days northeast, always among mountains, you get to such a height that it is said to be the highest place in the world. And when you have got to this height, you find a great lake between two mountains, and out of it a fine river running through a plain clothed with the finest pasture in the world; insomuch that a lean beast there will fatten to your heart's content in 10 days. There are great numbers of all kinds of wild beasts; among others, wild sheep of great size, whose horns are a good six palms in length. From these horns the shepherds make great bowls to eat from, and they use the horns also to enclose folds for their cattle at night. (Messer Marco was told also that the wolves were numerous, and killed many of those wild sheep. Hence quantities of their horns and bones were found, and these were made into great heads by the wayside, in order to guide travellers when snow was on the ground.)

"The plain is called Pamir, and you rise across it for 12 days altogether, finding nothing but a desert without habitations or any green thing, so that travellers are obliged to carry with them whatever they have need of. The region is lofty and cold so that you cannot even see any birds flying. And I must notice also that because of this great cold, fire does not burn so brightly, nor give out so much heat as usual, nor does it cook food so effectually."

The first major settlement to be found in the Wakhan is called Ishkashim (Ishkashm). Wood describes both the houses of the Wakhan, and a case of domestic unhappiness in Ishkashim:

"The houses resemble those in Badakhshan, except that instead of the central fire-place, they have large stoves after the Russian fashion. These occupy an entire side of the house, and throw out so general a warmth, that when once you have fairly domesticated yourself under a Wakhani's humble roof, you are unwilling to quit such comfortable quarters. The smoke is somewhat annoying; but the nearer you lie to the floor, the less of it you inhale. To me a wood-fire is more agreeable than a coal one. I loved to hear its cheerful crackling sound, and to feed it during the long hours that we were compelled to remain indoors was my delight; not that we needed its warmth, but the sight of its long tongues of flame, frisking and roaring under the good wife's enormous pot, induced a contented and happy state of mind, to which a knowledge of the good things it contained might probably no little contribute. It is not uncommon for six families to live together; not in separate apartments as in Badakhshan, but in one, or at most two rooms. As night draws on, the Wakhani pulls down a dry branch of the willow tree out of the many bundles suspended beneath his rafters, and putting one end of the branch to his breast, while the other is held by his wife's foot, takes his knife from his girdle, and with both hands sheaves from off the rod as many lengths as he conjectures will last through the evening. These resinous slips are then deposited above the lintel of the inner door; and they answer all the purposes of an oil lamp or candle.

"By the 1st of March we had reached Ishkashm... and put up in a house, where we had ample opportunity of learning that the matrimonial state is not all sunshine even among Mahomedans; upon whom, in such matters, their Prophet's intended kindness has entailed much misery. Of all the trials which assail a human being in the course from infancy to the grave, I should think a good perfect specimen of a scold of a wife must be the greatest. If a man, whose mind is harassed by contact with the world, have a happy fireside of his own, he soon forgets the rubs of the business day in the comfort in store for him at home. But if he comes into a house where a vixen of a wife galls his very soul with bitter taunts and reproaches, what chance is there for him? Of this calamity, the house in which we were lodged at Ishkashm offered a very striking example. Our host, a young good-looking merry fellow, was tethered to a perfect termagant of a wife. She was a manumitted slave of Afghan extraction. He knew nothing of her temper before marriage, but on being introduced to the father foolishly agreed to take his daughter to wife; and as the poor fellow dolefully expressed himself, 'On that ill-fated day she seized me by the throat, and has held fast ever since.' But, added he (in a half whisper, and by the motion of his hand warning us that his better half was not far distant), 'Never mind, never mind, I am making love to a young woman in the next village, a pretty gentle soul, and when the affair is all settled I will break the matter to my wife. If she heard of my intentions now, my life would not be safe. Did she only bite I could live with her, for teeth can be extracted; but, oh the tongue! The tongue! There never was a husband yet could get rid of that.'"

As with Badakhshan, many of the inhabitants of the Wakhan are Ismaili Shias who revere the Imam Ali, cousin and son-in-law of the Prophet, as the founder of a line of religious leaders represented even today by the Aga Khan. Olufsen describes a major shrine dedicated to Ali which he came across in the area:

"This monument in Wahkan is said to have been erected in memory of the holy Ali having once rested in this place. It is a small mud-built house about six feet high and nine feet square. The entrance to the house is through a small woodendoor, and on each side of this door are the platforms so common in Wakhan, which are used for seats. In the house is a cubical clay altar about three feet high with a base one metre square, chalked all over. On the altar were placed two large rounded black stones of seventeen centimetres diameter; and between these two stones was another like them but smaller, of the size of a hen's egg. Beside the large round stones lay two cow-horns for tooting-horns; round one of these was a copper ring. On a small shelf at the top of the altar was placed a small earthenware bowl which was used as a lamp. On the front of the altar was placed a small lamp in a little triangular niche. It was made out of a hollow stone, and beside it was an iron lamp with a wick ('chirak'). At the foot of the altar, on a shelf, were placed two candlesticks of copper, or rather two bowls which were fastened by some twisted copper branches to stands, the pointed ends of which were fastened to a piece of wood on the shelf. In a hole in the wall, to the left of the entrance, was a white yak-ox tail, which is a still more holy symbol than a dark one. On staffs, which pass from the altar through a hole in the roof, wave red and white banners over the building,

Ancient shrine, Small Pamirs [D. Grossart]

and on the end of these three flagstaffs were the so-called kobba, two of tinned copper and one of glazed clay. The house was surrounded by a shady well-kept orchard, enclosed by a high stone wall. Judging by the good state of repair of the house from the Wakhan point of view, and the care with which the house was cleaned and the orchard kept, and that an old man was appointed to guard the sanctuary—a Sayyid, a descendant of the prophet—this must be considered the very holiest place of the Wakhans...

"The Aksakal of the village told me that at festivals of the new moon, which are celebrated at the house and in the garden, sheep are killed and eaten on the spot, the lamps are lit on the altars, and all present, men and women, stand bowing before the altar, their faces covered with their hands. At each New Year a great festival was celebrated at which a bull was killed. During the festivals they tooted on the cow-horns placed upon the altar.

"The people have a story about the round black stones upon the altars to the effect that when Ali now and again dwells in the house he uses them to play at ball. This is probably a legend to show that the stones are a symbol of the strength of the saint. The horns which are placed on mazars [tomb, sanctuary] and other holy places are a sign of strength."

Olufsen also found another variety of shrine:

"Besides the altar of Hazrat Ali, there is still another sanctuary in Wakhan which is held in special awe by the people. This is the so-called 'mazar' situated about 200 metres west of the cleft through which runs the road from Wakhan to Garm-chashma. Both in the valleys of Pamir and in High Pamir amongst the nomas the name 'mazar' is given to the sepulchral character or the specially adorned tomb of some righteous or holy man. But this sanctuary was called 'mazar,' though nobody knew why it was here; it had no special name; the Wakhans only knew that it was very old, and that no-one was buried under the monument—a statement most likely correct, as the place for a great distance round was solid granite. A Beg from Bokhara, Mirza Abdul Kader... told us that the sanctuary was not a 'mazar' but a 'kadamga'—*footprint*—erected in memory of a holy man having set foot on this place... This one was a stone enclosure on a small rock—the stones were heaped up loosely on each other, and on top of the wall was placed one kiyik [wild sheep] horn beside the other. At one end of the enclosure was a cairn ornamented with horns of the kiyik and with staffs, on the top of which was a kobba of glazed clay. Before entering the enclosure the natives cover their faces with their hands; but they only knew concerning the place that it was good to visit it. Rags, which were hung up, showed that the people appeal here for cures against disease."

The other inhabitants of the Wakhan are the Kyrgyz (Kirghiz) nomads. Unlike the Ismaili Wakhanis, who speak a dialect of Persian, the Kyrgyz are Sunni Muslims, and their language is cognate with Turkish. Wood's first encounter with the Kyrgyz, having left Ishkashm, was coupled with his first ever encounter of a yak, also referred to as a kash-gow:

"Proceeding up the valley of the Oxus, with the mountains of Shakh Durah on our left hand, and those of Chitral on our right, both rising to a vast height, and bearing far below their summits, the snow of ages, we arrived early in the afternoon at the hamlet of Ishtrakh, having before passed Kila Khoja and Pullu, the first inhabited places since we entered Wakhan. We reached the village in the middle of a heavy snow-fall; and its houses built amongst fractured pieces of the neighbouring mountains, must have passed unnoticed, but for a Yak or Kash-gow, as the animal is here called, standing before a door with its bridle in the hand of a Kirghiz boy. There was something so novel in its appearance, that I could not resist the impulse of mounting so strange a steed; but in doing so I met with stout resistance from the little fellow who had it in charge. In the midst of our dispute the boy's mother made her appearance, and very kindly permitted me to try the animal's paces. It stood about three feet and a half high, was very hairy and powerful. Its belly reached within six inches of the ground, which was swept by its bushy tail. The long hair streamed down from its dew-lap and forelegs, giving it, but for the horns, the appearance of a huge Newfoundland dog. It bore a light saddle with horn stirrups; and a cord let through the cartilage of the nose, served for a bridle. The good Kirghiz matron was not a less interesting object than her steed. She was diminutive in stature, but active and strong, and wore some half dozen petticoats under a showy blue striped gown, the whole sitting close to her person, and held there, not by ribbons, but by a stout leather belt about the waist. Her rosy cheeks and Chinese countenance were seen from under a high white starched tiara, while broad bands of the same colour protected the ears, mouth, and chin. Worsted gloves covered the hands, and the feet were equally well taken care of. She chid

her son for not permitting me to mount the Kash-gow; and I quite won the good woman's heart by praising the lad's spirit, and hanging a string of beads about his neck. Strutting up to her steed with the air of an Amazon, she emptied the flour she had obtained at the village into her koorgeens [woven bags], took the bridle out of her son's hand, and vaulted astride into the saddle. The sight appeared to be new not only to us, but to the inhabitants of Wakhan; for the villagers had thronged round to see her depart. They enquired if she would not take the boy up behind her? 'O no,' was her answer, 'he can walk.' As the mother and son left us, a droll looking calf leisurely trod after its dam; and when the party disappeared amid the falling snow-flakes, the rugged half-clad Wakhanis exclaimed, as if taken by surprise, 'None but a Kirghiz boy could thrive under such rough treatment.'

"The yak is to the inhabitants of Tibet and Pamir, what the reindeer is to the Laplander in Northern Europe. Where a man can walk a Kash-gow may be ridden. Like the elephant, he possesses a wonderful knowledge of what will bear his weight. If travellers are at fault, one of these animals is driven before them, and it is said that he avoids the hidden depths and chasms with admirable sagacity. His footing is sure. Should a fall of snow close a mountain pass to man and horse, a score of Yaks driven ahead answer the purpose of pioneers, and make, as my informant expresses it, 'a king's highway.' In this case, however, the snow must have recently fallen; for when once its surface is frozen and its depth considerable, no animal can force its way through it. Other cattle require the provident care of man to subsist them through the winter. The most hardy sheep would fare but badly without its human protection, but the Kash-gow is left entirely to itself. He frequents the mountain slopes and their level summits. Wherever the mercury does not rise above zero, is a climate for the Yak. If the snow on the elevated flats lie too deep for him to crop the herbage, he rolls himself down the slopes and eats his way up again. When arrived at the top, he performs a second somersault, and completes his meal as he displaces another groove of snow in his second assent. The heat of summer sends the animal to what is termed the old ice, that is to the regions of eternal snow; the calf being retained below as a pledge for the mother's returning, in which she never fails. In the summer, the women, like the pastoral inhabitants of the Alps, encamp in the higher valleys, which are interspersed among the snowy

Boy on a yak near Lasht [W. Thesiger]

mountains, and devote their whole time to the dairy. The men remain on the plain, and attend to the agricultural part of the establishment, but occasionally visit the upper stations; and all speak in rapture of these summer wanderings. The Kash-gows are gregarious, and set the wolves, which here abound, at defiance. Their hair is clipped once a year in the spring. The tail is the well-known Chowry [fly whisk] of Hindustan,but in this country, its strong, wiry, and pliant hair is made into ropes, which, for strength, do not yield to those manufactured from hemp. The hair of the body is woven into mats, and also into a strong fabric which makes excellent riding trousers. The milk of the yak is richer than that of the common cow, though the quantity it yields be less. The kourut [type of cheese] made from it is considered to be first rate, even superior to the produce of the Kohistan of Kabul, which has great celebrity in Afghanistan. The Kirghiz never extract the butter.

"The first Yaks we saw were grazing among the snow on the very summit of the rugged pass of Ism Kashm, and at the village of this name, I procured one for Dr Lord, and despatched it to Kunduz in charge of two trusty men. But so cold a climate do these singular animals require, that though winter still reigned in the Kunduz plain, the heat was too great, and the Yak died within a march or two of the town. In fact it began to droop as soon as it had passed Jerm. Some years back, an Afghan nobleman succeeded in bringing two or three of these animals to Kabul, but even the temperature of that city, though situated 6,000 feet above sea-level, is not sufficiently cold to suit their constitution. They declined as the snow left the ground, and died early in the spring."

Having taken his leave of the yak, Wood was received by the Kyrgyz in one of their *kirgahs*, or nomadic tents:

"The arrival of strangers was an important event to the horse. Each kirgah poured forth its male inmates, and all clustered round our little party to hear the news of Kunduz. More rugged weather-beaten faces I had never seen; they had, however, the hue of health. Their small sunken eyes were just visible, peeping from beneath fur-caps, while the folds of a snug woollen comforter concealed their paucity of beard. The clothing of most of them consisted of sheep's skin, with the wool inside; but some wore good coloured cotton chupkuns. Snuff was more in demand with them than tobacco; but to satisfy the

Kirghiz families of Aq Jelqa in felt yurts [R. & S. Michaud]

craving desires of such voracious snuff-takers would have required a larger stock of *Irish Blackguard* than we had brought of charcoal. On presenting my box to the chief of the horde, he quietly emptied half its contents into the palm of his hand, then opening his mouth and holding his head back at two gulps he swallowed the whole. Our boxes were soon emptied, for none of them were contented with a pinch or two for the nose. In this bad habit the Uzbeks likewise indulged, but not to the extent of their relatives the Kirghiz. The latter invariably have bad teeth; many even of their young men are toothless. This they attributed to the coldness of the water they are obliged to drink, but I should imagine the snuff had a good deal to do with it.

"We now asked permission to rest awhile in one of their kirgahs, and were immediately led up to one of the best in the encampment. Its outside covering was formed of coarse dun-coloured felts, held down by two broad white belts about five feet above the ground. To these the dome or roof was secured by diagonal bands, while the felts which formed the walls were strengthened by other bands, which descended in a zig-zag direction between those first

mentioned and the ground. Close to the door lay a bag filled with ice—the water of the family. On drawing aside the felt which screened the entrance, the air of tidiness and comfort that met our eyes was a most agreeable surprise. In the middle of the floor, upon a light iron tripod, stood a huge Russian cauldron, beneath which glowed a cheerful fire, which a ruddy cheeked spruce damsel kept feeding with fuel and occasionally throwing a lump of ice into her cookery. She modestly beckoned us to be seated, and continued her household duties unembarrassed by the presence of strangers...

"The kirgah had a diameter of fourteen feet, a height of eight, and was well lighted by a circular hole above the fire-place. Its frame-work was of the willow-tree, but between it and the felt covering, neat mats, made of reeds, the size of wheat-straw, and knitted over with coloured worsted, were inserted. The sides of the tent, lined with variegated mats of this description, not only looked tasteful, but imparted a snug and warm appearance to the interior. Corresponding to the outside belts were two within of a finer description, and adorned with needle-work. From these were suspended various articles appertaining to the tent and to the field, besides those of ornament and the sampler. Saddles, bridles, rings, thimbles, and beads, all had here their appropriate places. One side of the kirgah had the family's spare clothes and bedding. In another, a home-made carpet hung from the roof, making a recess in which the females dressed, and where the matron kept her culinary stores and kitchen apparatus. The opposite segment was allotted to the young lambs of the flock. A string crossed the tent to which fifty nooses, twenty-five of a side, were attached, to each of which a lamb was fastened. While we were present, they were taken outside to their dams, and after a time again brought back into the kirgah."

The Chinese traveller Hsuen-Tsang (Xuan Zang) left one of the earliest descriptions of the further parts of Wakhan and the Great Pamir:

"On the north-east of the frontier of this country, skirting the mountains and crossing the valleys, advancing along a dangerous and precipitous road, after going 700 *li* or so (250 miles) we come to the valley of Po-mi-lo (Pamir). It stretches 1000 *li* or so (350 miles) east and west, and 100 *li* or so (35 miles) from north to south; in the narrowest part it is not more than 10 *li* (3 miles). It is situated among the snowy mountains; on this account the climate is cold, and the winds blow constantly. The snow falls both in summer and spring-

Kirghiz caravan, Small Pamir [R. & S. Michaud]

time. Night and day the wind rages violently. The soil is impregnated with salt and covered with quantities of gravel and sand. The grain which is sown does not ripen, shrubs and trees are rare; there is but a succession of desert without any inhabitants.

"In the middle of the Pamir valley is a great dragon lake (Nagahrada); from east to west it is 300 *li* or so (100 miles), from north to south 50 *li* (15 miles) It is situated in the midst of the great T'sung ling mountains [Pamirs], and is the central point of Jambudvipa [the world]. The land is very high; the water pure and clear as a mirror; it cannot be fathomed; the colour of the lake is a dark blue; the taste of the water sweet and soft: in the water hide the *kau-ki* fish, dragons, crocodiles, tortoises; floating on its surface are ducks, wild geese, cranes, and so on; large eggs are found concealed in the wild desert wastes, or among the marshy shrubs, or on the sandy islets. To the west of the lake there is a large stream, which, going west, reaches so far as the eastern borders of the kingdom of the kingdom of Tamasthiti, and there joins the river Oxus (Fo-t'su) and flows still to the west. So on this side of the lake all the streams flow westward."

Hsuen-Tsang's dragon lake, 'Nagahrada,' is the modern Zorkul, which Wood reached in February 1838; naming it Lake Victoria (until he discovered that it was already called Zorkul), he declared it to be the true source of the Oxus, discharging —of all the tributaries—the greatest volume of water into the river. Wood's discovery and the maps that he drew up on his expedition were the basis for the 1873 border agreement with the Russians. However, further geographical work and different interpretations of what constituted the source of a river cast doubt on Wood's findings. To the north, the River Bartang, rising in the Little Pamir in present-day Tajikistan, was found to run the furthest distance from the mouth of the Oxus; to the south, in 1894, Lord Curzon found that the highest point of the whole river system was a glacier at a height of 14,700 feet, feeding into another tributary, the Wakhjir; and as late as 1971, the diplomat and explorer Hugh Leach ascertained that Lake Shiva in Badakhshan was the headwater containing the greatest volume of water. Nonetheless, Zorkul ultimately remained the Afghan-Russian border.

Wood did not have the luxury of visiting the lake in summer, and had to rely on a description from his guides as to the nature of the place at that time of year:

"At that season, it is said, the water swarms with aquatic birds, which, as the winter approaches, migrate to warmer regions: many are killed by the cold. The lake is a favourite resort of the Kirghiz, and no sooner is the snow off the ground than its banks are studded with their kirgahs. A spot better adapted to the wants of a pastoral community cannot well be imagined, and the hordes that frequent it seem fully to appreciate its advantages, since they are never weary of expatiating upon them. The grass of Pamir, they tell you, is so rich that a sorry horse is here brought to good condition in less than twenty days; and its nourishing qualities are evidenced in the productiveness of their ewes, which almost invariably bring forth two lambs at a birth. Their flocks and their herds roam over an unlimited extent of swelling grassy hills of the sweetest and richest pasture, while their yaks luxuriate amid the snow at no great distance above their encampment on the plains."

However, Wood only had the opportunity to see the Bam-i-Duniah, the Roof of the World, at the coldest and most inhospitable time of year:

"The aspect of the landscape was wintry in the extreme. Wherever the eye fell one dazzling sheet of snow carpeted the ground, while the sky overhead was everywhere a dark and angry hue. Clouds would have been a relief to the eye; but they were wanting. Not a breath moved along the surface of the lake; not a beast, not even a bird, was visible. The sound of a human voice would have been music to the ear, but no-one at this inhospitable season thinks of invading these gelid domains. Silence reigned around—silence so profound that it oppressed the heart, and, as I contemplated the hoary summits of the everlasting mountains, where human foot had never trod, and where lay piled the snows of ages, my own dear country and all the social blessings it contains passed across my mind with a vividness of recollection that I had never felt before. It is all very well for men in crowded cities to be disgusted with the world and to talk of the delights of solitude. Let them but pass one twenty-four hours on the banks of the Zorkul, and it will do more to make them contented with their lot than a thousand arguments. Man's proper sphere is society; and, let him abuse it as he will, this busy, bustling world is a brave place, in which, thanks to a kind Providence, the happiness enjoyed by the human race far exceeds the misery. So, at least, it has always appeared to me."

Sheep and goats, Buzai Gumbad, Small Pamir [D. Grossart]

BADAKHSHAN AND THE WAKHAN CORRIDOR: TRAVEL INFORMATION

B adakhshan, Afghanistan's most remote and beautiful province, was untouched by the Russian jihad and the lunatic rule of the Taliban, when it provided Ahmed Shah Massoud an impregnable redoubt against his enemies. Its capital, Faisabad (Feyzabad), is the starting point for trips to Lake Shiva and the Blue Mountain, the ancient world's only source of lapis lazuli. It is the jewel in the crown of Afghanistan's tourist attractions.

The Wakhan Corridor, that thin panhandle of territory that leads to the Great and Small Pamirs and pokes out towards China, has always been regarded as one of the most romantic and inaccessible travel destinations in the world. Inaccessible because its position on the Soviet frontier made it a security zone, and could be visited only by the most exalted VIPs. Romantic because it contained the solution to one of the 19th century's most vexed geographical problems: where did the mighty River Oxus rise? Lord Curzon—mobilising all the resources available to a British MP—won the Royal Geographic Society's Gold Medal for his discovery of the highest glacier that feeds the source of the Oxus. It must rank as one of the most spectacularly beautiful areas of the world.

Badakhshan contains the following destinations for a traveller:

1. Faisabad: base camp for all travel in the region.
2. Tomb of Nasir Khusraw.
3. Sar-el-Sang (The Blue Mountain).
4. Lake Shiva.
5. The Wakhan Corridor and Great and Small Pamir.

1. FAISABAD

All travellers in Badakhshan will start their journey in Faisabad, a pleasant mountain town that straddles the gold-bearing Kokcha River, which joins the Oxus at Ai

En route to Baharak [M. Yamashita]

Khanoum. There you can see gold prospectors using sheep fleeces to trap the alluvial gold, just as Gardner noticed (see p. 137).

Faisabad is the commercial centre for Badakhshan but plays a more significant role as a staging post for goods going to Kabul and Peshawar, either via the Anjuman Pass or the Dorah Pass to Pakistan. Furs and lapis are for sale in the bazaar, but the prices to tourists are not significantly cheaper than in the capital. During the 1990s it was the acting capital for the anti-Taliban Northern Alliance and the town's main industry was foreign aid; there are still many NGOs based here.

The Marco Polo hotel near the bazaar is strongly recommended by travellers who have stayed there, although it has no hot water. One room is permanently reserved for BBC correspondents.

Another hotel is the Government Guest House, access to which is controlled by the governor of Badakshan. Go and see him at his office near the main square in the market. The hotel is in two buildings: one (the old guest house) is on an island in the middle of the Kokcha River. It has a certain period charm (sitting on the terrace by the river at night is a fine experience; at this altitude the stars are clear, numerous and do not twinkle), but the accommodation in the new building is much more modern. The new guest house was originally built as a residence for President Rabbani, although he never occupied it. It is at the top of a cliff reached up a long staircase. The view is magnificent, the rooms excellent and the bathrooms have hot water. If you want electric light after dark, you will have to give the staff money to buy petrol for their generator. This is always welcomed because it enables them to watch television, although this can be annoying to the guest.

Cars may be hired from the garages that cluster round the bridge over the Kokcha (see map). If you are planning to visit the Wakhan or Sar-el-Sang, a reliable vehicle and a competent driver are absolutely necessary—probably best arranged in Kabul.

It is also necessary to get a written note from the governor for travel into the Wakhan, which must be presented to the police chief at Ishkashim.

Journey times en route from Faisabad to Ishkashim, the town at the bottom of the Wakhan, are 1.5 hrs to Baharak; 2.5 hrs Kazdeh; 1 hr Zebak; 3 hrs Ishkashim; total 8 hours.

2. TOMB OF NASIR KHUSRAW

Khusraw, an Ismaili holy man, theologian and poet, is burid in the village of Hadrat-i-Sayyid, a two-hour car journey from Jurm. He was exiled to Badakhshan as a heretic and, like Ovid, much of his work laments the solitude of his place of exile, often calling it his prison. He makes frequent references to the fanatics who drove him from his home and reminisces about happier days at with his family in Khurasan. The locals claim that Khusraw introduced Ismaliism to Badakhshan. He died c.1089.

Khusraw's tomb is situated on a hillock and, very curiously, is guarded by Sunnis who discourage visits by Ismailis. They claim Khusraw as a Sufi Sunni holy man and vehemently deny any connection of him with Ismailism. The inscription refers to its renovation in 1697. Nasir Khusraw is often refered to as the Ruby of Badakshan.

3. SAR-EL-SANG (THE BLUE MOUNTAIN)

The lapis lazuli mines at Sar-el-Sang are the oldest continuously worked mines in the world. Until the 20th century, Sar-el-Sang (The Blue Mountain) was the only source in the world. It has been worked for at least 7,000 years—lapis objects have been found in graves of that date. The lapis for Tutankhamun's funeral mask and William Butler Yeats's carving, celebrated in his great poem *Lapis lazuli*, was mined here

To get to Sar-el-Sang, drive to Jurm and then follow the Kokcha River upstream for three hours. From Faisabad it is a one-day journey.

There are more than 20 tunnels, but those producing the best lapis are Number One and Number Four. The Number One shaft has been worked for 7,000 years; as you enter you can see the soot from fires that were used to make the rock friable and the marks made by the iron-age tools that prised the fractured lapis out of the veins. This process was still being used in 1838 when Wood came here (see p. 135). The miners can tell instantly from which shaft a piece of lapis was quarried.

You can spend the night at the tea house at the foot of the valley. To climb to the Number One shaft takes about one hour and is not for those who suffer from vertigo.

The lapis is still transported by donkey and horse to Pakistan, where Peshawar is the main market. It is a three-day journey by horse from the village of Skarzer (see below). I interviewed one of the traders:

"I was a trader for four years in the 1980s when the prices were low because there was no money because of the jihad. I sometimes went to Hong Kong to sell it. I spent a month here negotiating with the miners to buy the stone. I paid 8,500 afs [$105] per kilo depending on the shaft it came from and then hired horses at Skarzer to cross to Pakistan. The horsemen charged me 2,000 afs [$25] for 7 kilos to take it across the Dorah Pass. I had to pay a 17 per cent tax to the Chitral government. I would sell it in Peshawar and made 50 per cent to 100 per cent profit and sometimes more. By taking it to Hong Kong I made another 100 per cent profit. I would send the high quality stone from the Number One shaft by air and the lower quality stone by ship from Karachi. It was a very good business until I was arrested in Karachi for using a Pakistani

River crossing with mule and supplies, Small Pamir [D. Grossart]

passport. You see, they would not let Afghans in so I had to buy a Pakistani passport for 4,000 rupees from a Pakistani official. I spent four days in jail and bought my way out for 18,000 afs [$225].

4. LAKE SHIVA

Visited by Wilfred Thesiger in 1957, this glorious lake is one of the summer grazing grounds of the Kuchi nomads. Its status as one of the sources of the Oxus was first established by British diplomat Hugh Leach. Today a road takes you there in one day, and passes small hamlets along the way. The roofs of the houses are covered with cow dung preserved as winter fuel. There is a chaikhana where the road meets the lake, or you can camp.

The lake itself is an astonishing deep blue colour. A two-day trek around the edge is well worth making.

The road now continues down to Shignan on the Oxus, the location of the balas ruby mines mentioned by Marco Polo (see p. 120), the location of which was rediscovered by the American gem hunter, Gary Bowersox. This is a three-hour journey. From Shignan, one can trek on horses up the Oxus to Ishkashim.

SKARZER TO GARAM CHASHMA IN PAKISTAN, VIA THE DORAH PASS

This three-day trip by horse is the most memorable and exciting journeys that I have made in Afghanistan, although it is physically demanding. You are travelling with the lapis traders, their donkeys loaded with fertilizer bags of the stone, on a trade route that is many thousands of years old. It is necessary to bring your own provisions and American MREs (Meals, Ready-to-Eat); these are easily bought in the Faisal Supermarket in Kabul's Flower Street and are ideal.

Skarzer village is a three-hour drive south from Sar-el-Sang. The road bears sharp right here through a spectacular red sandstone gorge and leads up to the Anjuman Pass and the Panjshir Valley (see p. 222), another outstanding journey that takes you across the watershed between the Indian subcontinent and Central Asia. This is a one-day journey by 4WD, and you can stay at a chaikhana at Lake Anjuman.

But to follow the lapis traders one turns left along the river.

There is only one chaikhana at Skarzer and the horses live in wrecked houses along the main street. The village is dominated by the large house of the local mujahedin commander who has grown rich on the lapis trade. Horses here cost about $20 per day with horsemen who bring them back when one reaches the Pakistani border. Set off early on the first day along the river valley until you reach the first pass. This is, according to the horseman, a low pass, but I found it exhausting and the horses were not fit enough to carry me. Then you descends a steep slope, covered with jagged black rocks down to a flat alluvial valley with a large river that has eroded a 30-foot chasm. The scenery here is spectacular, with great cliffs enclosing the valley. You cross the river by wading and then struggle up the other side. But your sufferings are nearly over—it is only a few miles to the first night's stop. This is a house next to a water mill. You should arrive here in the early afternoon.

The next day's journey is easier and mostly downhill along a river valley with an enormous flood plain that roars like a motorway. This is the sound of the stones grinding along the watercourse. The path is terrifying with a frightful sheer 100-foot drop on your left-hand side. At the bottom of this hill stands a checkpoint. Turn right here, following a river, and you arrive at Jangal, your rest stop for the second night.

Jangal is an awful place, a collection of primitive houses largely made from plastic sheeting. You sleep wedged up against lapis traders, unable to roll over, like slaves on the Atlantic crossing. Fortunately, there is an alternative. A few miles further on from Jangal is a chaikhana, a much better place to spend the night.

The next day's journey involves crossing the Dorah Pass. You pass a turquoise lake and ascend a steep mountainside. The summit is about 4,500m (15,000 feet) and even at the height of summer there are patches of snow, sculpted by the wind into those curious formations known as neves penitents. The rest of the journey is an easy downhill romp to the Pakistani border village of Shai Salim. In 2001, a Pakistani visa was sufficient to cross the border but you now may need a local permit for the border areas. However, it is possible to sneak round the side of the police post at night.

Horseman in the Wakhan [W. Thesiger]

5. THE WAKHAN CORRIDOR AND GREAT AND SMALL PAMIR: A JOURNEY TO THE SOURCE OF THE OXUS

Geographically, the Wakhan is best considered in three parts, the Wakhan Corridor, the Great Pamir and the Small Pamir. The rivers have a multitude of local names but are here referred to as the Oxus, the Pamir and the Wakhan. This journey really begins at Ishkashim. The section below presents: A. The Wakhan Corridor, B. The Great Pamir, and C. The Small Pamir.

A. THE WAKHAN CORRIDOR

The Corridor—well named—is a thin strip of land walled in by huge mountains. Geologically, it has been formed by the upward tectonic pressure that gave rise to the Himalaya and Karakorum ranges, formed in the Tertiary period just two million years ago. This makes the Pamirs a site of special interest to plant scientists; some think that the ancestors of several modern species found as afar away as North America may be found here.[1]

The Corridor is about 280 km (175 miles) long, and at its narrowest is can be just 20 km (12 miles) wide, as it runs between the Tajik and Pakistani borders. The Tajik border is geographically logical, defined by the river that here I shall refer to as the Oxus. The southern side is defined by the Durand Line, a boundary created by Sir Henry Durand in 1891, an artificial border that prevented the Russian and British empires meeting. Afghanistan's ruler at the time, Abdur Rahman, whose foreign policy was controlled by the British, was by no means pleased with the gift and complained that he had "enough problems with his own people and did not wish to be held responsible for the Kyrgyz bandits in the Wakhan and Pamir!"[2] It is said that the Russians were planning to annex the whole area under Leonid Brezhnev; only his death and succession by Mikhail Gorbachev frustrated the plan.

The Corridor can be said to have its mid-point at Qala Panj, where two sources of the Oxus meet. The river goes by a number of names, the most modern being the Amu Darya,[3] but I prefer to use the name by which Alexander and the British knew it, the Oxus.

The people living here call themselves and their language Wakhi,[4] an Indo-European tongue related to the Indo-Iranian group.[5] They are Ismaili Muslims, followers of the Aga Khan. Each village has a *shah* or "king" whose duty it is to accommodate visiting travellers and who levies a tithe for this purpose on his "subjects". He, in turn, is accountable to the Aga Khan. The governor (*woluswai*) of Wakhan is in the village of Khandud and it is courteous for travellers to stop there and pay their respects to him.

Travellers will almost certainly find themselves staying in the guest house of the local shah. It is always difficult to know how to reciprocate their hospitality, but cloth for making clothes (easily bought in Kabul) and pencils and notebooks for the children seem to be appreciated.

The Wakhi have curious burial customs that will be obvious to the traveller: they build houses over the graves, with doors and windows open to the elements. They themselves live in houses made from mudbrick, heated with animal dung or scrub.

Kirghiz Cemetery, Buzai Gumbad, Small Pamir [D. Grossart]

Qala Panj is the major settlement here (see below), and the site of a shrine dedicated to Ali. The main house of the village is the residence of the shah, a Sayed and hereditary leader of the Wakhan. It is possible to stay the night in his comfortable guest room; on one of my visits his hospitality included giving us a new shock absorber for our Land Cruiser.

The Wakhis are transhumance herders and farmers – they both grow crops and herd livestock, which includes Bactrian camels and yaks (further up the valley). They grow barley and various other crops including pulses and opium. The United Nations Environment Programme (UNEP) commented on their "sophisticated system of crop rotation"; even an ordinary traveller can see that these people are very good farmers. While most locals own a few sheep and a cow, larger farmers band together and take their flocks up to summer camps, or *aylaqs*, for four or five months in the summer. They spend the winters in their village, or *geshlaq*.

The long history of Afghanistan is marked by repeated conflicts between sedentary civilisation and the wild nomads of Central Asia. Genghis Khan was only the most brutal of many waves of nomad invaders. But here in the Wakhan a symbiotic relationship exists between the Wakhi and the Kyrgyz. During the winter, the Kyrgyz look after the pregnant yaks and some of the Wakhi's sheep. Payment is made in yak's milk and grain, which the nomadic Kyrgyz cannot cultivate and which they need for bread.

Mountaineering

Many people see the Wakhan as a region for mountaineering. Nowshak (Nurshak) is the most famous and highest peak in Afghanistan at 7,485 metres. In 2003 an Italian expedition ascended successfully; the team of 14 climbers required 128 porters to carry their equipment to base camp—the way is not suitable from horses. Climbing and descending the peak generally takes 7 days. The whole expedition took one month from leaving Kabul to returning. The group's guide—Haji Safit Mir—thinks that a smaller group could do it in two weeks. It was a popular ascent before 1979, though difficult; only four of the Italian team reached the summit in 2003.

View westward, Boroghil, Wakhan Corridor [D. Grossart]

Another fine peak between Qala Panj and Boroghil is called Baba Tangi (6,421m), and outside the Wakhan proper, in the Jurm Valley, stands Dari Sahir (6,428m), also a good challenge.

A journey up the Wakhan corridor to Boroghil via the Wakhan River (southern route)

The end of the first day's journey is Ishkashim, the town that controls the entrance to the Wakhan. You can spend the night here or push on for another two hours to Kazdeh, where you can stay in the guest house of the local shah. The royal guest house is very nice, with a beautiful courtyard and a pool fed by a mountain torrent.

The second night is spent at Qala Panj, a village with a beautiful setting at the Wakhan Corrridor's widest point. The king has a large caravanserai and is always welcoming. A remarkable British doctor, Dr Alex Duncan, and his family have set up a clinic in the village and are planning to build a guest house. Until Dr Alex opened his clinic here, there were no medical facilities at all in the Wakhan and people were dying of septicaemia and appendicitis. His work is heroic and should be supported.

*Young Wakhani shepherd boy,
near Boroghil [D. Grossart]*

Two hours' drive from Qala Panj is the lovely village of Sargaz. An orchard in the middle of the village makes a perfect camping ground but the place's main attraction is its hot spring—and it is really hot. At any rate, make a stop here to bathe and have breakfast.

Four hours' drive from Sargaz is Boroghil, the base camp for trips to the Small Pamir, a high, glacial valley carpeted in grass (see below).

Horses in Boroghil can be hired from Tashi Bey, the local chief. He has built an excellent guest house in what he claims is Tajik style, which seems to mean that it has a window in the ceiling. There is also a spring, though less hot than the one at Sargaz.

From Boroghil there are two passes leading to the Small Pamir. The main one—the Marpej Pass (4,850 m)—leads straight through the cleft to the east of Boroghil. The second—the Gorombez Pass—is slightly longer and has magnificent rocky scenery alternating with green valleys. This adds an extra day to the journey. It is not as steep as the Marpej and has good camping sites. Travel Afghanistan's 2004 expeditions went into the Pamir by the Marpej and came out over the Gorombez. The Gorombez Valley is still Wakhi territory and is used as their summer grazing grounds. One of the herders told me "there are no cows because the yaks eat them.

Bridge, Small Pamir [D. Grossart]

No female horses because they die in the winter." Their sturdy little horses come from Tibet.

The capital of the Kyrgyz country is Buzai Gumbad, ruled by a terrific character called Apandi (sometimes Effendi) Bey.[6] He is extremely rich and told us that he owned 1,500 sheep, 500 yaks, numerous horses and Bactrian camels (a rare sight in Afghanistan). As Ismailis, the women are not veiled and are beautifully dressed.

Haji reproached Apandi Bey for not using his wealth to perform the hajj, a duty incumbent on all Muslims who can afford it. But with disarming honesty he said that his opium habit prevented it. He smoked opium for six days and then slept it off for another six. He claimed to consume 45 to 50 kilos of opium a year, which cost him 120 sheep.

Five-Day Trek to Lake Chaqmartin

Lake Chaqmartin lies between Buzai Gumbud and the Yuli Pass (4,872m), which leads to China; Buzai Gumbud to the lake is approximately 15 km (10 miles). Near

the Yuli Pass is the glacier that Lord Curzon considered to be the icy source of the Oxus, and it takes three days to return to Buzai Gumbad from this glacier.

Journey from Ishkashim to Boroghil (details by Anthony Fitzherbert)

The road from Ishkashim to Qala Panj, though repaired in the mid 1990s, is still subject to damage from floods. Many of the streams in this region that flow into the Oxus have no bridges, and must be carefully navigated, preferably with a member of the party wading ahead of the car.

Alternatively, walk or ride, which allows one to appreciate the scenery and spot wildlife. Marco Polo sheep (*Ovis poli*) are to be found in many of the side valleys of the Wakhan.

Below is the daily record of a 2002 trip that went up the Wakhan River rather than the Pamir River. Numbers represent days of the journey. To visit Syr Kul, it is best to travel up the Pamir River. (Three of the days were spent spotting wildlife rather than travelling.)

1. Ishkashim to Qala Panj. Governor at Ishkashim is Abdul Menan Hashemi; get travel permission. 3.5 hours to Khandud (home of Mohmad Sabir, the king's old shikari, who is an expert on where Marco Polo sheep are to be found). 3 hours more to Qala Panj.

2. Journey to the Great Pamir via Pamir River. 2 hrs by car to Ghaz Khan, where road runs out. Hire horses. 7 hours trekking to campsite at Jangal-i-Gurvash (3,290 m).

3. Jangal-i-Gurvash to Ishkemich Valley (Zaman's camp; *aylaq*, or summer camp). 8.5 hours to Zaman's camp in Ishkemich Valley via plateaus and valleys.

4. Day trip: Ishkemich to Bakhshah's aylaq. At this point the party paused to observe wildlife. It is only half an hour to Bakhashah's aylaq. The party rode up to the junction of the Shikargah and Khoshabad Valleys, where they observed five ibex and, at the bottom of the Shikargah Valley, 28 Marco Polo ewes.

5. Day trip: Bakhshah's aylaq to Shikargah Valley. 4.5 hours to "spying point" below Hawz-i-Chap Lake (4,700 m); observed four mature Marco Polo rams. Returned to aylaq.

6. Ishkemich to Porsan. 7.5 hours riding.

7. Porsan to Yupgaz. At the top of the Yupgaz Valley the party saw fresh tracks of a snow leopard.

8. Yupgaz to Ghaz Khan. 3 hours to Ghaz Khan, where party picked up jeep to drive to Neshkow, 3.5 hours.

9. Ghaz Khan to Boroghil-Sarhad. 1.5 hours.

10. Three-hour climb to Kotal-i-Dalriz Pass, gateway to the Small Pamir.

11. Boroghil-Sarhad to Khandud by car. 6 hours to Qala Panj; 1 hour Qala Panj to Khandud.

12. Khandud to Faisabad. 3 hours to Ishkashim. 7 hours to Faisabad.

B. The Great Pamir

The Great Pamir comprises the main block of mountains that form the western end of the "Pamir Knot". The highest peaks rise above 6,000 metres (20,000 feet), and the region contains high plateaux. Extending about 100 km (62 miles) from east to west and between 20 and 60 km (12–38 miles) in width, the Great Pamir is geographically defined by the Pamir River in the north and the Wakhan River in the south.

Two ethnic groups live here: the Wakhi and Kyrgyz. The latter are Sunni Muslims but there seems to be no animosity between the two groups who trade and occasionally intermarry with each other. The Kyrgyz, being nomads, have a quite different pattern of

Wakhani shepherd boy [D. Grossart]

subsistence. They live in large yurts (called *kirgahs*) built of a wooden framework covered with felt. Inside they are decorated with felt hangings, which they manufacture, and carpets, which are traded or bought from itinerant merchants. The structures are heated by horse-dung stoves ventilated by wonky metal chimneys. In the summer, the top of the dome is open, but in winter (when it gets very cold) it is covered over with plastic. The Kyrgyz are not to be found in the lower Wakhan valley, but in the Great Pamir around Syr Kul, and the Small Pamir around Buzai Gumbad.

These Kyrgyz have a curious history. They are the remains of a much larger community who migrated in 1978 to Gilgit, under the leadership of Rahman Gul Khan, a powerful Kyrgyz chief. There they lived with their flocks until, in 1983, the Turkish government[7] offered them a home in Eastern Anatolia, where they now live around Lake Van, having displaced a Kurdish group.[8] Those who are left in the Great Pamir eke out a poor living compared with their much richer cousins in the Small Pamir. They amount to about 100 families. Much of their business seems to revolve around the Tajik border post on the edge of Syr Kul, and it is probably best not to enquire too closely about what that trade involves.

Most of the Afghan Kyrgyz live in the Small Pamir and are considered very rich. The Kyrgyz people originated long ago on the upper reaches of the Yenisei River in Siberia, then migrated southwards to their present locations between the 9th and 12th centuries, intermarrying with the native communities in their way. Although they speak a Turkic language, in appearance they seem more like Mongols. And though Sunni Muslims, anthropologists report that they maintain certain pre-Islamic customs, which may be Siberian shamanistic. The Pamir Kyrgyz are the only Kyrgyz that retain their character as nomads, as the Soviets settled those living in the USSR. They arrived in Afghanistan as refugees from the chaos and civil war that ensued in the USSR after the 1917 Revolution.

They live in scattered family herding groups and shift their camps according to the seasons and the grazing. They ride stallions which they acquire from the Wakhi.

River crossing at dawn, Khandud, Boroghil Road, Wakhan [D. Grossart]

They eat horsemeat and keep herds of mares but do not appear to drink koumiss, the famous fermented mare's milk.

The Kyrgyz describe themselves as organised into 15 clans, with names like "Falcon", "New Year", "Ram" and "Far Sighted".

In 2002 I spent three days staying with the Great Pamir Kyrgyz in their yurts. They told me that their parents used to make an annual migration to what is now Kyrgyzstan but the Soviets put a stop to that 50 years ago. Their hospitality was striking and they postponed moving their camp to accommodate us. We ate bread and fat-tailed sheep, which was baked rather than boiled as elsewhere in Afghanistan. It seemed to me that it would be best to reciprocate their hospitality with gifts of warm clothes and presents for the children. Their camp was a short distance from the shore of Syr Kul, which drains to the west in a waterfall.

Boroghil and its passes

A difficult road goes from Qala Panj to Boroghil.[9] It should only be attempted in a four-wheel drive car with a very good driver and a mechanic. It has been completely washed away by spring floods in many places. On my journey, we had to pull a Médicins Sans Frontières (MSF) team, foolishly travelling in a Russian Gaz "jeep", out of a ford on several occasions. Our driver had taken a young man, who he

referred to as "the Mad Boy", who spent several long and unpleasant sessions in icy water finding the way for the car through these washes.

As you get towards Boroghil, the village at the end of the road, the valley suddenly and dramatically widens out forming what Fitzherbert accurately describes as a "broad basin". It is a lovely place in summer, bounded on the south side by the huge flood plain of the Wakhan River as it debouches from the narrow pass of the Small Pamir. The village, which contains a hot spring and a room in the shah's house for guests, is the meeting place of three passes. To the south, across the Pakistani border, is Gilgit. To the east is the pass to the Small Pamir, and to the north, to the Great Pamir. This is the base camp for further exploration, where one hires horses and pack animals per day, with guides or horsemen. The flat fields are ideal for camping and the hot spring makes it a pleasant place to spend a few days while haggling over transport. I repaid the villagers' hospitality with a contribution, notionally towards the rebuilding of the bath house. The village headman is called Kachi Beg and his house boasts a telephone with which he can communicate with Khandud. The apparatus is an engineering triumph, with the line recycled from Soviet barbed wire.

Kirghiz man with Caravan camels [R. & S. Michaud]

Taking the passes in order:

To Pakistan: Boroghil Pass, 4,288 m

At present the southerly Boroghil Pass to Pakistan is officially closed, but locals seem to cross without difficulty, and in 2002 I met an English doctor, a veteran of these parts, who was planning to cross into Pakistan with his wife and five-year-old child. He had a Pakistani visa, which should be sufficient. Fitzherbert notes that "This was the pass that haunted the late 19th century imperial Britons as being the one through which they feared the Imperial Russian Cossacks, equipped with cavalry and

artillery, would come to invade India." It was also the pass by which Curzon arrived on his journey to find the true source of the Oxus.[10]

To the Great Pamir: pass name and height unknown

Few Europeans have crossed this pass, which goes northwards over the mountains bringing you out near Syr Kul. This two or three-day journey is recommended only for those with mountain experience, or the masochistic. It requires one night in a Wakhi aylaq and two nights in shepherds' shelters. The summit of the pass itself is a horrific combination of glacier and massive rockfalls that make it very difficult to get horses through. The day after I crossed the pass, a party of Tajik traders (apparently coming from China with goods bought there) crossed and one of them was killed, apparently in a fall on the glacier. My guide also suffered badly from altitude sickness. A much easier way to get to Syr Kul is described below.

To the Small Pamir: Marpej Pass, 4,850 m

A narrow declivity dominates the village a few km to the east. This is the pass eastwards to the Small Pamir and China. Marco Polo would have taken this route (see below for his comments on the Small Pamir itself). It is called the Wagjhir Valley and leads, in an easy three-day ride, to Buzai Gumbad and Syr Kul, the summer headquarters of the Small Pamir Kyrgyz.

C. THE SMALL PAMIR

The Small Pamir is a self-contained ecosystem, a mountain area cut through deeply by the Waghjir River. This river, which originates at the glacier that is Curzon's source, divides the Small Pamir into two distinct halves. To the south lie the Karakoram Mountains and the Pakistani areas of Gilgit and Hunza; the famous Khunjerab Pass on the Karakoram highway into China lies about 50 km west of the Yuli Pass (4,872m), the easternmost extension of this area. The whole area contains peaks rising from 6,500 to 7,000m, with the highest peaks along the Afghan-Chinese border well over 6,500 metres. The pass into China taken by Marco Polo is the Yuli Pass. The Small Pamir is separated from Syr Kul and the Great Pamir by a wilderness of peaks and lakes.

The Small Pamir is home to the majority of the Wakhan's 1,400 Kyrgyz families (UNEP estimate). Their summer base is Buzai Gumbad and their chief is a powerful character named Apandi Bey (the opium smoker). The area between this settlement and Lake Chaqmartin is the loveliest and most fertile in the Wakhan, an area referred to by Marco Polo as a "high place where the traveller finds a plain between the mountains, with a lake from which flows a very fine river. Here is the best pasturage in the world; for a lean beast grows fat in ten days. Wild game of every sort abounds and there are great quantities of wild sheep of huge size." It is this fertility that makes the Kyrgyz of the Small Pamir much richer than their cousins near Syr Kul. The 2002 UNEP survey reported a larger number of Marco Polo sheep here than elsewhere, as well as ibex—both species on the UN's "Red List" of endangered animals. The pasture seems to be fertile enough to support both Kyrgyz flocks and wild Marco Polo sheep.

Travelling in the Small Pamir

This itinerary starts at Qala Panj and assumes that the traveller will be hiring horses and guides at Boroghil. Numbers refer to days along the way.

1. Qala Panj to Boroghil-Sarhad: 6 hours' driving, depending on road conditions.

2. Boroghil-Sarhad to Buzai Gumbad: 3 days' ride. Along the way are a number of camps. The first Kyrgyz camps are at Ak Jilga ("White Mare"), and the others are named as follows: Kotal-i-Dalriz Pass; Baharak; Sang-i-Neveshta ("Inscribed Stone"); Garbin Warm; Aveliz; Kyrchyn; Ak Jilga ("Mountain Camp"); Buzai Gumbad/Wagjhir Valley.

3. From Buzai Gumbad, the Waghjir Valley goes eastwards to the Chinese border at the Yuli Pass, via Birgitikho, which is the Kyrgyz winter quarters. Allow 5 days to get to the Yuli Pass. (Count on eight or nine days on horseback to reach China from Buzai Gumbad.)

4. From Buzai Gumbad the main Wakhan Valley goes to Lake Chaqmartin via a series of campsites named Cheshmeh Arkhar ("Marco Polo Ram's Spring"), Hawz-i-Chaqmartin and Mynarah. The valleys leading off the main route are listed by Fitzherbert as Arghil, Kyzyl Ghoran, Andamin, Tasari Bala, Taysari Pain, Jarmashir and Otobil.

[1] Dr Barrie Juniper of Oxford University, who traced the origin of the European apple to the Ferghana Valley, thinks that the earliest variants of the mulberry may be found here, remaining from the temperate forest that covered these latitudes before the tectonic shifts that created the mountains. I think of it rather like Conan Doyle's *The Lost World*.

[2] Louis Dupree, *Afghanistan*, 1980.

[3] Strictly, a tautology, as Amu means river in Turkic and Darya means river in Dari.

[4] For an excellent account of these people on the other side of the Durand Line, see *The Voice of the Nightingale*, Sabine Felmy, Oxford 1996.

[5] See www.ethnologue.com

[6] Effendi Bey is strictly a tautology: "Mister Mister".

[7] The Kyrgyz speak a Turkic Central Asian dialect and thus have a common ancestor to the modern Turks.

[8] See M.N. Shahrani, *The Kirghiz and Wakhi of Afghanistan*, Univ. of Washington, 2002.

[9] This place is also known as Sarhad, which means "border", or Boroghil-Sarhad.

[10] See his excellent book *The Oxus* (1896), a collection of his three articles that appeared in the *Geographical Journal*, also in 1896. The book has a beautiful map.

THE CARPETS OF AFGHANISTAN
CARPETS, WOVEN GOODS AND THE NOMADIC LIFE

—Richard Parsons

*A*lthough the Turcomans of Afghanistan—the country's leading producers of carpets and rugs—are now a sedentary people, they were originally nomads, herding their flocks of sheep and goats across the rolling steppes of Central Asia. They lived in yurts, those circular domed tents seen from Outer Mongolia to the Caspian Sea. Those wood framed tents, easily dismantled and reassembled, were lined and roofed with felt and skirted with thick reed matting, the whole being bound with woven tent bands. During winter, an open fire burned in the centre of the yurt, the smoke slowly leaving through a chimney hole in the roof. Fuel was dried manure from the flocks, which gave off a pungent smell and soon blackened the felt walls and ceiling. Traditionally, a yurt constructed for a newly-wed couple was white.

A jallar, *or long narrow bag affixed to the wall of the* yurt. This example bears the 'bastani' design. [Parsons]

Not surprisingly, in this largely self-sufficient and ovine-based economy, wool was, and is, used extensively. Besides carpets and rugs, the Turcomans produced countless items made with wool for their daily domestic needs and yurt furnishings, wood and metal being extremely difficult to come by and, not being flexible, difficult to transport. A specially woven carpet, a purdah, would act as a door to the yurt. Having no furniture, the nomads would store their clothes and household possessions in woven and knotted bags of different shapes and sizes, often of magnificent workmanship and design, each of which had a specific purpose. These bags were hung on the inside of the yurt, or placed on the ground and used as cushions.

A koorgeen, or *woven bag, usually used for carrying goods on camels. [Parsons]*

In every family, a minimum of tent bags was necessary for the storing of their possessions. Thus, the wealth and status of the family had a decided bearing on the number of bags owned. Wealth implied a greater number of possessions, while status determined the number of bags which a girl would bring in her dowry.

When a girl approached marriageable age—usually in her early teens—she and the other women in her family would start to weave carpets, bags, and other pieces for her dowry. If a would-be suitor was not considered acceptable, the girl's father would answer that the dowry pieces were not yet completed. This tactful answer saved any loss of face. On the other hand, if the match was considered suitable, a tacit agreement was reached and the weaving of the pieces was accelerated.

THE MAKING OF AFGHAN CARPETS
THE SHEEP

Of the eight or so classified breeds of sheep in Afghanistan, only five contribute their wool to the country's carpet industry. The principal breeds used in making Afghan carpets are the Karaqul from the north and the Ghilzai found predominantly in the south, as well as the Kandahari, the Hazaragi, the Beluchi from Nimroz Province and the strains found around Herat, which include the Arabi and Herati sheep. All are of the fat-tailed variety but because of cross-breeding and migratory movement, as well as not altogether precise geographic boundaries, it is difficult to be absolutely categoric when referring to any specific breed of sheep.

By far the most commonly used wool comes from the Karaqul sheep, indigenous to Uzbekistan as well as northern Afghanistan. This sheep has a dual fleece, which means two types of wool growing simultaneously. The outer fleece has longer fibres than the soft crinkly wool of the inner fleece; both are hardwearing and lustrous and when carefully sorted and blended provide ideal wool for Afghan carpets.

The Karaqul sheep, generally grey or black in colour and recognisable by the kink in its tail lying over the heart-shaped lobes, is a hardy animal, living in regions with extremes of temperature ranging from -30°C up to 48°C in the shade. It is also renowned in the fur trade for the lightly-curled glossy newborn lambskins called variously Karaqul, Broadtail, Astrakhan and Persian Lamb, sold annually at international fur auctions in London and St Petersburg. Some six million Karaqul sheep are raised on the northern slopes of Afghanistan alone.

The Ghilzai, or nomad sheep, is variously coloured. Its fat tail gets very large and its wool tends to be coarse. Much of this wool is bought up by the Hazaras from the nomads who in summer graze their flocks high up in the Hindu Kush and around Beshud in the mountains of the Hazarajat. It is used in commercial Hazara weaving, as well as for warp yarn, which is sold to Turcomans who use it in the production of cheaper quality carpets.

THE WOOL

Shearing, which is done by hand, takes place in the spring, starting about mid-April, and again in the autumn during September, when it may be only partial, depending on the condition of the sheep. The spring clip, with a seven-month growth, provides the better wool and is invariably used in the finer quality of carpet. Wool from the autumn shearing was not, traditionally, used for carpet making. However, with the commercialisation of the Afghan Turcoman carpet, the autumn clip is now increasingly made into carpet yarn.

Turcomans claim that in former times when carpet weaving was primarily for domestic use and the sorting of wool was done with a care that present-day commercialisation does not allow, their carpets never wrinkled or cockled if wetted. Even today many weavers are loath to mix spring wool with wool from the autumn clip. Cockling in Afghan woven goods, as well as a diminished degree of lustre, is caused by bad mixing of wool from different parts of the fleece.

After shearing, the fleeces are twisted and rolled up on themselves. As shearing may take place out in the open grazing regions far from any habitation, the fleeces are transported to the local bazaar by small lorry or by camel caravans.

The fleeces are sorted by colour, and the wool graded by quality; the coarse, rough hairs, known as kemp, are put aside. The wool is then hand-carded, often by the older men and women. The most common method is to place a block of wood embedded with metal spikes on the ground, and to pull the wool through the spikes repeatedly until all the fibres lie in the same direction and *the longer fibres are separated from the shorter ones. Up to one kilo of wool a day can be carded by this method. At this point, the wool is spun, usually by hand—a process that is generally done by both men and women, often by members of the Arabi tribal group, who are principally spinners and not weavers.*

DYEING

A great deal of wool used in the production of Afghan carpets is now treated with synthetic dyestuff of varying quality. Although this makes the manufacturing process somewhat less laborious, it can

Drying the wool after the dyeing process [Parsons]

lead to a poorer result. Otherwise well-made pieces are often ruined by gaudy metallic greens, purples and pinks. Moreover, many of these chemical dyes are unstable, and colours such as blue often oxidise after a short time to give a muddy grey.

However, much of the production is still made using natural dyestuff. The warm mellow red, the predominant colour used by the Turcoman, is obtained from the root of the madder bush, known locally as royan. Yellow comes from the flowers of a wild plant called sparak by the Uzbeks, or zahr-i-choub 'yellow wood' in Persian. Walnut peel, pomegranate peel and wheat straw are other sources of natural dyes. Walnut peel, the section around the shell, gives a dark brown and is often combined with madder to darken the reds. Pomegranate peel and wheat straw give different tones of medium to light brown. Crimson, or kermes, is still occasionally obtained from the dried bodies of certain insects living in oak bark.

The dyeing process is not a little time-consuming. If, as an example, madder is to be used, the root is obtained, cut into one-centimetre lengths, allowed to dry for 40 days, after which the pieces are broken down with a pestle and finally ground into a coarse powder. A careful selection must be made of the raw material; the bark of the root gives a pink-rose dye, while the inner core, depending on its thickness, gives a reddish brown. The thickness of the root determines the shade of red; thus, a section of root the diameter of a cigarette renders a bright pinky red, and a section the diameter of a man's thumb renders a rich mahogany brown.

THE LOOM

Afghan weavers always use a horizontal loom. This is the most basic type of loom and is traditionally and exclusively used by nomad tribes, as it can easily be dismantled and transported. The loom consists of two wooden end beams placed on two side beams to which they are bolted, thus forming a rectangular frame. The end beams are firmly anchored to four stumps hammered into the ground and tightened by a tourniquet lashing or a screw bolt. The frame of the loom is usually of poplar, a cheap and fast growing wood, which is used extensively for building and furniture making.

The warp threads are stretched lengthwise between the end beams in a figure of eight, and are often dampened to increase tensions. To prevent slipping, mud or a flower paste is packed on the warp threads around the two end beams to fix them securely. Weaving only begins when this paste has caked hard.

The vast majority of Turcoman weavers are women and girls, though among the Turcomans, and especially among the Uzbeks, there is an increasing number of boys and youths who are learning this craft. They are usually unmarried, since the responsibilities of marriage force them to abandon this means of livelihood.

When beginning a carpet, the weaver (or weavers) squats on a plank placed immediately under the surface of the warp threads at one end of the loom. As the work progresses, the weaver moves forward sitting now on the pile itself, supported by the plank which is also moved forward. The only instruments used are the heavy metal 'comb' for beating down the wefts, and a knife for cutting the pile yarn after the knot has been tied. A pair of hand shears similar to those used for shearing sheep is used for clipping the pile at the end of the day.

WEAVING

Turcoman carpet designs are woven entirely from memory; graph paper patterns are used only when resuscitating old designs, or weaving totally new and

Weaving on a horizontal loom [Parsons]

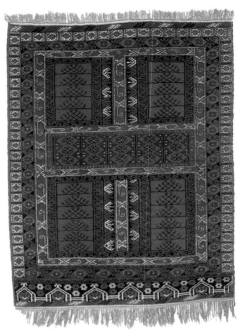

A purdah; *these pieces, recognisable by their cross design dividing them into four different panels, are hung from their upper corners to act as a sort of door into the yurt. [Parsons]*

non-traditional, therefore unfamiliar, designs. Originally, the patterns and designs used would very clearly signify the tribe and clan which wove the carpet; however, with increasing commercial pressures and the breakdown of the tribal system, this is no longer the case.

The width of the carpet being woven determines the number of weavers needed. Weavers only move forward; and the width of their working front will be as far as they can comfortably reach either side, generally about 75 centimetres. An apprentice is placed next to an experienced adult weaver who not only supervises his hard work, but also ensures that the wefts are beaten down to an even tension to avoid a distortion in the design.

A carpet starts and ends in a band of flat weave called the kilim. In some cases, this kilim displays a design; in others, it is made up of lateral bands of colour; sometimes it is embroidered, sometimes plain, dyed or undyed.

A Turcoman rug displaying the fil-pai gul, *or elephant's foot design [Parsons]*

A Baluchi prayer rug from Herat, showing the stylised 'Tree of Life' design. [Parsons]

Many Turcomans are very poor and it is only the wealthier ones who can afford to have in their compounds a room devoted entirely to the housing of a loom, and big enough to hold a loom on which a large, say 300–400 cm carpet can be made. This is why most large carpets are woven in the summer months, when the loom can be assembled for use outside. In the winter, the production of rugs is markedly higher.

A superstition common to most Turcomans in Afghanistan is putting a match to the fringe of a newly-woven piece and burning a small amount of wool. A wish is made that the carpet will be sold as quickly as the burned wool flares up.

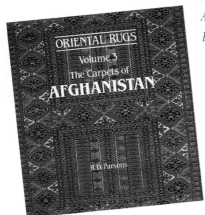

This essay is extracted from *The Carpets of Afghanistan* by the late Richard Parsons. A revised 1999 edition is published by the Antique Collectiors Club, £29.95.

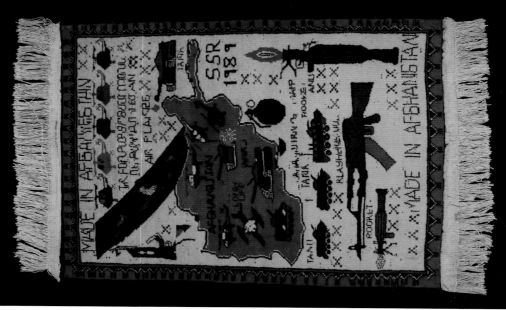

(Above) *A Turcoman Kilim, or flat-woven carpet, from Herat, portraying the Bastani design.* [Parsons]
(Bottom) *A narche jangi, or 'war rug'. These curious items were made in the period after the Soviet invasion, often by Turcomans and Uzbeks in the refugee camps of Pakistan.* [Private collection]

Bagram and the Panjshir Valley

It is almost certain that the first known Western visitors to the Panjshir Valley—Alexander the Great and his followers—were unable to appreciate its beauty without hardship or apprehension. They were travelling this route in pursuit of the rebel Bessus, who had declared himself to be the King of Persia after his murder of the retreating Darius; he had moved his forces back beyond the Hindu Kush to the land of Bactria, and now stood as the last obstacle to Alexander's total conquest of the Achaemenian Empire.

By 329 BC, Alexander's troops had already undergone great privations crossing the mountainous areas between Kandahar, Ghazni and the Kabul River Valley. The historian Curtius describes how the men suffered famine, losing their limbs and eyesight in the freezing snow-bound territory. At length they reached a more fertile area, dominated by the Hindu Kush to the north, where they paused to recuperate and gather supplies. They came across Kapisa, the old capital of the Persian satrapy of Gandhara, and refounded it, settling there over 10,000 native soldiers, camp followers and men no longer fit for active service. Mistakenly believing themselves to have reached the Caucasus Mountains, the new city was named Alexandria-ad-Caucasum (modern-day Bagram, near Charikar). After this, Alexander proceeded northwards towards Bactria by means of the Panjshir Valley and the Khawak Pass. As they went on their way, the native guides pointed out a cave in which, they claimed, the mythical figure Prometheus had been chained to a rock and suffered the constant torture of an eagle tearing out his entrails; "the nesting place of the eagle... as well as the marks of the chains were visible", records Diodorus of Sicily. Despite the astonishment this discovery would have caused amongst the Greek and Macedonian soldiers, they still suffered great shortages. Bessus had ravaged the land beyond the Hindu Kush, and during the 17 days it took them to traverse it, there was little to eat besides silphium (a fennel-like plant) and asafoetida. Curtius further describes their circumstances:

"Alexander had indeed crossed the Caucasus… but the lack of grain had almost reduced his men to starvation. They anointed their bodies with the juice of pressed sesame seeds as a poor substitute for oil, but a single amphora of this substance would now change hands for 240 denarii, an amphora of honey for 390 denarii, and an amphora of wine for 300 denarii, but hardly any wheat was found at all. For the barbarians had pits which they called *siri*, which they hide so skilfully that no-one is able to find them except the person who dug them; in these were all of their crops hidden. In the absence of these supplies, the men lived on herbs and fish from the river. And then, when even those had failed them, they were ordered to slaughter the pack-animals which carried their baggage; on this flesh, until they reach Bactra, were they able to survive."

After the death of Alexander, Alexandria-ad-Caucasum and the surrounding territory eventually reverted to the possession of the Mauryan Empire, ruled by the Indian King Chandragupta and later by Asoka the Great, who converted the area to Buddhism in 260 BC. However, it is believed that the Greek population there was still substantial, and in 184 BC, after the invasion of a Graeco-Bactrian army from the north, the area was placed under Greek rule. Nevertheless, its inhabitants were of

Hazara man fishing [B. Jenks]

particular diversity, originating from Persia, India and Bactria as well as Greece itself. This multi-ethnic realm was at first part of the Graeco-Bactrian Empire, and later stood alone as an Indo-Greek Kingdom (c 125 BC) ruled by King Menander, who became famous to posterity as author of a Buddhist treatise called *Milinda-Panho* or "the Questions of Menander".

Although this kingdom collapsed around 110 BC after being overrun by the Central Asian Sakae tribes, it did not remain unvisited by the Greeks. Perhaps the first record we possess of a short walk in the Hindu Kush is left by a writer named Philostratus, in his biography of Apollonius of Tyana. Apollonius was a Neo-Pythagorean mystic and religious reformer, who, according to Philostratus, walked to India to study under its priests and learned men. Philostratus leaves us a record of a conversation—probably fictional—between Apollonius and a follower, Damis, as they traced back Alexander's route over the Hindu Kush (which they still believed to be the Caucasus):

> "And as they were passing over the summit of the mountain, going on foot, for it was very steep, Apollonius asked of Damis the following question:
>
> 'Tell me,' he said, 'where were we yesterday?'
>
> And he replied: 'On the plain.'
>
> 'And today, O Damis, where are we?'
>
> 'In the Caucasus,' said he, 'if I mistake not.'
>
> 'Then when were you lower down than you are now?' he asked again, and Damis replied: 'That's a question hardly worth asking. For yesterday we were travelling through the valley below, while today we are close up to heaven.'
>
> 'Then you think,' said the other, 'O Damis, that our road yesterday lay low down, whereas our road today lies high up?'
>
> 'Yes, by Zeus,' he replied, 'unless at least I'm mad.'
>
> 'In what respect then,' said Apollonius, 'do you suppose that our roads differ from one another, and what advantage has today's path for you over that of yesterday?'
>
> 'Because,' said Damis, 'yesterday I was walking along where a great many people go, but today, where there are very few.'

'Well,' said the other, 'O Damis, can you not also in a city turn out of the main street and walk where you will find very few people?'

'I did not say that,' replied Damis, 'but that yesterday we were passing through villages and populations, whereas today we are ascending through an untrodden and divine region: for you heard our guide say that the barbarians declare this tract to be the home of the gods.' And with that he glanced up to the summit of the mountain.

But Apollonius recalled his attention to the original question by saying:

'Can you tell me then, O Damis, what understanding of divine mystery you get by walking so near the heavens?'

'None whatever,' he replied.

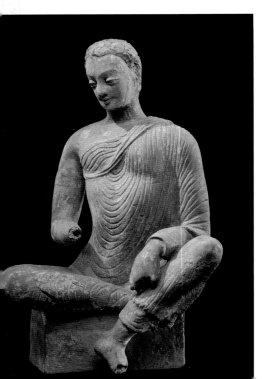

'And yet you ought,' said Apollonius. 'When your feet are placed on a platform so divine and vast as this, you ought at once to utter thoughts of the clearest kind about the heaven and about the sun and moon, which you probably think you could touch from a vantage ground so close to heaven.'

'Whatever,' said he, 'I knew about God's nature yesterday,' I equally know today, and so far no fresh idea has occurred to me concerning him.'

'So then,' replied the other, 'you are, O Damis, still below, and have won

(Top) *Head of a bearded ascetic, Gandhara, E. Afghanistan, 2nd century AD*; (left) *Buddha seated in meditation Gandhara, E. Afghanistan, 2nd century AD [Musée Guimet]*

nothing from being high up, and you are as far from heaven as you were yesterday. And my question which I asked you to begin with was a fair one, although you thought that I asked it in order to make fun of you.'

'The truth is,' replied Damis, 'that I thought I should anyhow go down from the mountain wiser than I came up it, because I had heard, O Apollonius, that Anaxagoras of Clazomenae observed the heavenly bodies from the mountain Mimas in Ionia, and Thales of Miletus from Mycale which was close by his home; and some are said to have used as their observation mount Pangaeus and others Athos. But I have come up a greater height than any of these, and yet shall go down again no wiser than I was before.'

'For neither did they,' replied Apollonius, 'and such stargazings show you indeed a bluer heaven and bigger stars and the sun rising out of the night; but all these phenomena were manifest long ago to shepherds and goatherds, but neither Athos will reveal to those who climb up it, nor Olympus, so much extolled by the poets, in what way God cares for the human race and how he delights to be worshipped by them, nor reveal the nature of virtue and of justice and temperance, unless the soul scan these matters narrowly, and the soul, I should say, if it engages on the task pure and undefiled, will soar much higher than this summit of Caucasus.'"

Carved Ivory plaque with dancing women, Bagram, 2nd century AD [Musée Guimet]

The city of Alexandria-ad-Caucasum, reverting to the name of Kapisa, eventually became one of the leading cities of the great Buddhist Kushan Empire. Although it did not leave behind a great deal of documentary evidence—even the date of its most prominent king, Kanishka, is still a matter of fierce debate—spectacular archaeological finds were made there after excavations which began in 1937.

Painted glass vase showing a Roman gladiator, Bagram, 2nd century AD *[Musée Guimet]*

Objects from all over the ancient world—glass from Syria and Egypt, bronze vessels, bone and ivory carvings from India, Roman sculpture, lacquer bowls from China—bear witness not only to the city's wealth and international commerce, but also to the wide variety of cultural influences that came together to create the distinctive style of Gandharan art, pioneered for use in Mahayana Buddhism.

The Kushan Empire was brought down by invasions of the Central Asian Hephthalties, or White Huns, around AD 465. Eventually, after interventions by the Persian Sassanian Empire, Kapisa, like many of the surrounding areas, evolved into petty Buddhist kingdoms. The Chinese traveller Hsuen-Tsang bore witness to this, visiting Kapisa in AD 630, and hearing various accounts of King Kanishka and the glories of his time:

> "This country is 4000 *li* or so in circuit. On the north it abuts on the Snowy Mountains, and on three sides it borders on the 'black ridge' (the Hindu Kush). The capital of the country is 10 *li* or so in circuit. It produces cereals of all sorts, and many kinds of fruit trees. The *shen* horses are bred here, and there is also the scented root called *yu-kin* (broad-leaved turmeric). Here also are found objects of merchandise from all parts. The climate is cold and windy. The people are cruel and fierce; their language is coarse and rude; their marriage rites a mere inter-mingling of the sexes. Their literature is like that of the Tukhara country, but the customs, common language, and rules of behaviour are somewhat different. For clothing they use hair garments (wool); their garments are trimmed with fur. In commerce they use gold and silver coins, which in appearance and stamp differ from those of other countries. The king is a Kshatriya by caste. His is of a shrewd character, and being brave and determined, he had brought into subjection the neighbouring countries, some

ten of which he rules. He cherishes his people with affection, and reverences the three precious objects of worship. Every year he makes a silver figure of Buddha eighteen feet high, and at the same time he convokes an assembly called the Moksha Mahaparishad when he gives alms to the poor, and relieves the widows and bereaved.

"There are about 100 convents in this country and some 6,000 priests. They mostly study the rules of the Great Vehicle. The stupas and *sangharamas* are of an imposing height, and are built on high level spots, from which they may be seen on every side, shining in their grandeur. There are some ten temples of the Devas, and 1,000 or so of different sects; there are naked ascetics, and others who cover themselves with ashes, and some who make chaplets of bones, which they wear as crowns on their heads.

"To the east of the capital 3 or 4 *li*, at the foot of a mountain in the North, is a great *sangharama* with 300 or so priests in it. They belong to the Little Vehicle [Theravada Buddhism] and adopt its teaching.

"According to tradition, Kanishka Raja of Gandhara in the old days having subdued all the neighbouring provinces and brought into obedience people of distant countries, he governed by his army a wide territory, even to the east of the T'sung-ling Mountains. Then the tribes who occupy the territory to the west of the river, fearing the power of his arms, sent hostages to him. Kanishka-raja having received

Fresco from the niche of the Small Buddha, Bamiyan Valley, 1974 [Y. Crowe]

the hostages, treated them with singular attention, and ordered for them separate establishments for the cold and hot weather; during the cold they resided in India and its different parts, in the summer they came back to Kapisa, in the autumn and spring they remained in the kingdom of Gandhara; and so he founded *sangharamas* for the hostages according to the three seasons. This convent in Kapisa which has just been mentioned is the one they occupied during the summer, and it was built for that purpose. Hence the pictures of these hostages on the walls; their features, and clothing, and ornaments are like the people of Eastern Hia [Xia]. Afterwards, when they were permitted to return to their own country, they were remembered in their old abode, and notwithstanding the intervening mountains and rivers, they were without cessation reverenced with offerings, so that down to the present time the congregation of priests on each rainy season frequent this spot; and on the breaking up of the fast they convene an assembly and pray for the happiness of the hostages—a pious custom still existing.

"To the south of the eastern door of the hall of the Buddha belonging to this *sangharama*, there is a figure of the Great Spirit King (Vaisravana); beneath his right foot they have hollowed the earth for concealing treasures therein. This is the treasury place of the hostages, therefore we find this inscription, 'When the *sangharama* decays let men take of the treasure and repair it.' Not long ago there was a frontier king of a covetous mind; hearing of the quantity of jewels and precious substances concealed in this convent, he drove away the priests and began digging for them. The King of Spirits had on his head the figure of a parrot, which now began to flap its wings and to utter screams. The earth shook and quaked, the king and his army were thrown down prostate on the ground; after a while, arising from the earth, he confessed his fault and returned.

"Above a mountain pass to the north of this convent there are several stone chambers; it was in these the hostages practise religious mediation. In these recesses many and various gems are concealed: on the side there is an inscription that the Yakshas (half-god half-demon creatures) guard and defend these precincts. If any one wishes to enter and rob the treasures, the Yakshas by spiritual transformation appear in different forms, sometimes as lions, sometimes as snakes, and as savage beasts and poisonous reptiles; under various appearances they exhibit their rage. So no-one dares to attempt to take these treasures…"

Kapisa/Bagram dwindled in significance, other settlements such as Kabul being preferred to it, and by the time of the Islamic conquest of the area under Mahmud the Great of Ghazni in AD 988, the city had been virtually abandoned.

A folk story of the history of Bagram up to the time of the first Muslim invasion, quite different to the above account, is still told in Afghanistan; this version was collected by Hackin and Kohzad:

"In the heart of the mountains of Central Asia, two intrepid warriors, united by ties of family, bound by an oath of loyalty, increased their raids on the caravan routes. Having broken out of the existence amongst their pasturing tribe which they found too monotonous, having abandoned their homes and their flocks, they chose this life of adventure which led them far away.

"In a short time, they won a formidable reputation. In order to avoid being pillaged, the caravans were compelled to take long detours, which exhausted both the men as well as the animals. But these two indefatigable warriors, mounted on their magnificent swift horses, possessed an innate sense of the terrain, and took little time to discover the hidden ways that the caravans took to avoid them.

"One day, while they were watching for a caravan on a stony road at the exit of a defile, they came to realise that they were not the only ones of their sort in the area, for they saw a number of unsettled animals charging in all directions, emerging from the road.

"Angry, the two warriors made their way with caution down the defile, but the other robbers had already escaped with the booty, and they had only left behind a single wounded man who called out to them: 'Noble gentlemen, have pity on a poor and wretched man; see, I am wounded. Several armed men attacked the caravan and sacked it. My men fled, the pack animals are scattered, I am on the verge of ruin; for the love of God, help me.' And seeing in their faces a glimmer of kindness, he cried out again, fearing that they would abandon him, 'the kindness of your looks tells me that you are

A typical timber bridge for a side road across a stream near the Salang Pass [B. Woodburn]

not going to leave me to die like an animal on this deserted track.' The two brothers, Parvan, who was the elder, and Marvan, the younger, took up the wounded man, and carried him back to their refuge.

"The man whom they had rescued had the peculiar gift of being able to charm them by telling them stories of many adventures which had taken place in a distant land: 'I was returning from a country of a hundred wonders, and I wish that one day I will be able to lead you there. My caravan was loaded with a variety of rare fruits; had it not been pillaged, I would have been able to let you try them; much more than my words, they would have given you a fore-taste of the excellence of that country, where there is nothing but luxury and opulence. Why do you not gather together a band of men from the land here, and go out to conquer this new world? I will lead you there as a guide.'

"Enticed by the prospect of such a wonderful quest, Parvan and Marvan began to recruit followers: warriors like themselves, hungry for adventure. Helped by their reputation, they soon found themselves at the head of an army of fierce men ready to sacrifice their lives, who swore to accompany the two brothers wherever they went.

Before long, they started their journey towards the west. Neither the gruelling marches, nor the privations of the journey would at all stop them. Every evening when they came to pitch camp, they demanded to hear again the description of the far-off land. In the glimmering light of the flames of the fires they listened attentively, forgetting the troublesome journey over the inhospitable mountain passes. Nothing was in their minds except an immense verdant valley, full of trees laden with fruit, cooling springs, and pleasant shady groves where rest would be a delight. A sweet and melancholy song plunged them into a deep sleep without realising it. Wearied, tired out with fatigue, they allowed themselves to be seized by dreams which carried them into an unknown paradise.

"Who, seeing them in this state, would think that these were the same men who went about strewing terror in their wake, burning and pillaging without mercy?

"It was thus, one morning in autumn, after so many trials which they had courageously withstood, having surmounted difficulties without number, that they finally saw the entrance to the Valley of Salang, the grand fertile plain of the Koh-i-Daman.

"On their faces, scored by the hardship of the journey, appeared expressions of profound astonishment, and it took them several minutes to realise that their dream had been fulfilled. The lushness of the crops, the trees as far as the eye could see excited them no end; they rode about on their horses at full gallop, crying out with exclamations of victory, joy, and covetousness. Snatched up by the crowd, enveloped in clouds of dust, Parvan and Marvan could scarcely extricate themselves, and, judging it impossible to restrain their men, they both went forward with the guide to explore the terrain and to find out what sort of opposition the enemy might field.

"The peaceful inhabitants of the land, for the most part farmers and vine-growers, had mostly left behind their dwellings to take refuge in the mountain. They had been forewarned against the advance of this army, and had fled in haste, carrying out on their animals all that was moveable, and burying all the rest. The closed bazaars, the abandoned houses, all breathed a dull silence when this horde of barbarians descended on the place. They sacked everything, and massacred the few unfortunates who had stayed behind to defend their property. The beating of a drum interrupted them in their work. The sun was at its height, and the frenzy of combat had lasted for several hours. The warriors conferred amongst themselves, and slowly the scattered forces reassembled; obedient to their oath of fidelity, they made their way to the place of muster where their leaders had called them.

"'You have forgotten your duties as warriors: you have been amusing yourselves and enjoying the spoils of victory, when first you should have been ensuring that an enemy close at hand was not going to assail you. We two alone were ensuring your safety, something for which you should be ashamed. The citadel is nearby, the enemy is weak, but they are waiting for us. Your task will be simple; as soon as the resistance is destroyed, then will we be free to enjoy all of the spoils'. Then, at the head of their men, they besieged the citadel. Battle was joined, but the enemy surrendered a short while afterwards. The citadel being occupied, everyone prepared to celebrate the victory.

"Enriched with booty and covered in glory, the guide returned to his own country, not before persuading the elder brother to declare himself king of the land they had just conquered.

"Parvan, in his new position, did not appear satisfied. Every time he walked around the walls of his city, his eye was drawn to another similar fortification not far off, and the thought that a formidable enemy was watching from there did not leave him indifferent. In agreement with his brother, they decided to sweep away the danger. The warriors were again assembled in the middle of the citadel, and again an appeal was made to their courage, and their oath of loyalty. 'As long as we have before us an enemy who looks down at us from the height of his tower, there will never be peace. An enemy so near by, no matter how weak it may be, is always dangerous. If you hope to keep your riches, if you have any regard for your king, ready yourselves for battle with Marvan as your chief; he is the best leader I am able to give you, as we must suppress without delay this danger which threatens us here. But before you leave, you should remember to take care of the population; lay low any resistance, but spare those who are compliant. Once the citadel is in your hands, establish the rule of law to protect the inhabitants.' And, in front of the crowd as they began to disperse, King Parvan took his younger brother in his arms, and recommended him to be prudent, and to fight with courage. 'I am counting on you to accomplish this delicate task: you must surprise the enemy in their sleep; at night, you should cross the river. The preparations have been completed; I gave the orders for them myself. At nightfall, I shall lead you to the place where a set of rafts have been constructed, and together we will find which place would be the best to make the crossing.'

"Parvan watched his brother leave with a great sense of relief. Chosen to be King by his warriors, he doubted that his brother was not jealous. It was in order to avoid any intrigues that Parvan had devised this stratagem of sending him into combat against the fortress of Bagram.

"Marvan crossed the river in silence, and, as day broke, his forces put themselves in order for the assault. 'The citadel of Bagram dominates the river. Before the enemy realises that an attack is in progress, we must be inside.' And so it was done. The cries of surprise were drowned out by the beating of a drum. The adversaries fled. The citadel being in their hands, the town beneath it offered no further resistance.

"The pillage began and the celebrations as well. Drunken with victory, the warriors ranged throughout the town. Feasting began, and continued for several days. Marvan, installed in the opulent palace, received an emissary from his brother Parvan who requested him to take charge of the defence of the newly-captured town, and to give him full authority over it by proclaiming him King of Bagram.

"In this way, affairs were settled, and life started to return to normality. Parvan and Marvan, each one in his own castle, allowed themselves to indulge in a life of idleness and opulence. The warriors shared out the spoils and the dwellings. Little by little, the original inhabitants began to return in order to try and recover their possessions. Everyone seemed to be enjoying the calm, and expressing confidence in their new rulers. Meanwhile, King Parvan, already softened by this sedentary life of luxury, began to feel his trust in his brother ebbing away. 'Is the fidelity I give him properly reciprocated? Or has he become ambitious, and eager to unite the two kingdoms, pushing me aside so that he can become the sole ruler?' In spite of being unsettled, he came to the conclusion that they should maintain their alliance in case of an external danger. To aid this, he decided that a heavy chain should be stretched between

Farmer, Panjshir Valley, 2004 [B. Jenks]

the two citadels across the river. In the event of any threat, the chain would be shaken violently so that one could summon help from the other.

"However, Marvan was too young to get used to the new style of life, which was hardly suited for a warrior of his stamp. The ennui weighed heavy on him, and he began to doubt his brother. His faith in Parvan collapsed, and one morning he went to the chain, and shook it with violence. Parvan, having heard the signal, raised the alarm, and his slaves hurried throughout the town beating the drums. After his warriors had rapidly armed themselves, he led them to relieve his brother. When he arrived, he could not understand why all was quiet; yet, when he found that there was no threat or danger, his rage was indescribable. His brother had played a trick on him, but Parvan was in no mind to forgive, accepting neither explanation nor apology from Marvan's messengers. He returned to his own kingdom, having refused to go to the palace where Marvan had planned to receive him and account for the misunderstanding.

"The quarrel separated the two brothers, and each retired to their own kingdom. All ties were cut between Bagram, and the land ruled by Parvan. But, one day, a real menace approached.

"After a time, a young Muslim general appeared in the land, preaching a Holy War. He gathered round himself fighters from the oppressed people in the area who were weary of living under the dictatorship of strangers. His army became strong, and the general, Abdullah, decided to attack the city of Bagram. During the night, he advanced along the plateau, captured the points of strategic importance, and ordered that an offensive should be made the next day at dawn. He himself went to inspect the areas around the walls, and saw to it that wood was collected to burn out the gates. The tired guards who held the walls raised the alarm during the night; the comings and goings outside seemed suspect to them, and the king was alerted. He left the palace, and passing by the chain which was still linked to Parvan's citadel, he grasped it and shook it with fervour, all the while understanding the futility of his gesture. Reflecting miserably on his fate, he suddenly caught sight of flames which had taken hold of the main gate. This time, he knew the situation was grave: the striking of drums, shouts and cries—his last hopes of survival had vanished. The brave invaders who surrounded the palace were making a great clamour, but one voice rose above all: 'God is great and Mohammed is his messenger.'

"For the first time in his life, Marvan felt his courage abandon him. He gave the order to his men to resist the attackers, but he himself prudently retreated to the safety of his palace. A vicious struggle arose, during which the Muslim general was killed. The fury of his followers was so great that nothing could stop them; the gate was smashed down, and the invaders made a charge towards the palace. But Marvan, seeing his army defeated, profited from the confusion and disorder by disguising himself as a peasant, and escaping by way of a steep path beside the river, deserting the courageous warriors who had chosen him to be king. He made his way into the mountains, not once turning back to take a final look at the smoking ruins of his kingdom."

The Hindu Kush has always been renowned for the mineral riches concealed within its mountains. In early times, the Panjshir Valley based its wealth on silver; an account of the area's silver mines is found in Yaqut al-Hamawi's 12th-century geographical dictionary:

"[Panjshir is] a town in the province of Balkh, close to which is a silver mine. Its population is very mixed, and is always stirred up by fanaticism and discord. Silver is so abundant there, it is said, that even the smallest quantity of vegetables can cost as much as a drachma. The mine is at the top of a mountain which looks over the town and the surrounding area, and the mountain itself, from the sheer amount of excavation which has taken place, resembles a vast cavern; there are also little streams in which are found particles of silver which indicate where the silver is to be found. The inhabitants give themselves over to the search for silver with such ardour that it is not uncommon to see many among them invest more than 300,000 drachmas in their quest. Their efforts are often crowned with success, and they ensure the prosperity of themselves as well as their descendants; other times, they are scarcely able to cover their expenses, and occasionally the coming of torrential floods or other disasters ruin their work, and reduce them to poverty. When two miners happen to pursue different branches of the same vein, custom assigns the rights over the mine to the first person to reach the metal; this causes the miners to surpass themselves in their desperate efforts, and the last person to arrive loses all the fruits of his labour. If they reach it at the same time, custom dictates that they hold it in common. The inhabitants have made so many excavations in the earth over such a period of time, that underground their torches are still able to burn;

On a Hindu Kush trail leading to Lapis and Emerald Mines [G. Bowersox]

but, as soon as they should happen to go out, they stop and retrace their steps, for whoever strays too far may easily meet a sudden death. Moreover, it is scarcely possible to recount the number of people in this place who started the morning rich, and ended up in the evening being compelled to beg for their bread."

In the late 20th century, emeralds were found in the Panjshir Valley at the bottom of craters caused by Soviet bombing; as a result, ad hoc mining for the stones began in earnest. An American expert, Gary Bowersox, who had been invited to inspect the area, describes what he found in his autobiography, *The Gem Hunter*:

"Emerald mining requires expertise. But emerald mining had only been done in the Panjshir Valley for just over a decade. And it didn't look like mining to me. The Afghans were simply digging holes in the ground and looking for green. They worked individually or in small teams, climbing the steep mountain slopes up to the 9,000 to 12,000 foot level. Trails did not exist, so pack animals could not be used. The miners carried the equipment on their backs. Half the people in the valley had been killed during the 1980s; most of those remaining were connected with the industry as miners, or support services. Emeralds meant survival.

"I spent the next days reconnoitring the high rocky slopes of the mountains, examining the conditions at Derik, Darun, Mokoni, and Khenj mines, evaluating current procedures and documenting my findings with photographs. I was astonished at the number of separate mines and disheartened to see the evidence of overuse of dynamite. Many small chips of broken emerald crystals lay scattered everywhere. Their mining methods were destroying their stock-in trade. The mountain looked and sounded like a war zone; they used explosive material scavenged from unexploded bombs and even land mines.

A 36-Carat Emerald crystal with nodule, mined in the Panjshir Valley [G. Bowersox]

"Although post-mining land reclamation is a legal and moral duty in the US, in Afghanistan the concept is far more remote than this region itself. It did not occur to them to fill in the holes or to stabilize areas after they mined them. They figured Mother Nature was large enough to cover a multitude of human sins. There was always another slope, another pass. And these people, scarred as the landscape where they laboured, had no extra energy for such luxuries.

"The working conditions appalled me. The mountainside looked like Swiss cheese, covered with holes of assorted sizes. To see their way in the dark, they used extremely volatile tin can lanterns filled with oil and gasoline and then wicked with cloth—incendiaries with Molotov cocktail potential. One man was boring with an old Chinese road drill, which emitted colourless, odourless clouds of lethal carbon monoxide fumes. The miners obtained most of their explosives by taking apart Soviet bombs, a risky form of recycling. After blasting, men carried out the rubble on a gurney, shook and sorted it for gem rough, and then threw the overburden down the steep mountainside. There was excessive fragmentation of the land and poor recovery of ore—in short, a great waste of the nation's resources. But despite their mistakes, they were making a substantial contribution to the local economy. The emeralds were equal in quality to those of Columbia, the world's largest producer. And there wasn't much other economy to speak of."

Near the mouth of the Panjshir Valley is a peculiar geological phenomenon, which has claimed the attention of travellers for many generations—the singing, or moving sands, known as *Reg-Rowan*. Alexander Burnes visited them in the 19th century:

"As we were now in the vicinity of 'Reg-Rowan,' or the moving sand, we made an excursion to it. It is a phenomenon similar to what is seen at Jubul Nakoos, or the sounding mountain, near Too in the Red Sea. The Emperor Baber thus describes it: 'Between the plains there is a small hill, in which there is a line of sandy ground, reaching from top to bottom. They call it Khwaju Reg-Rowan; they say that in the summer season the sound of drums issues from the sand.'

"The description of Baber, however marvellous it appears, is pretty accurate. Reg Rowan is situated about forty miles north of Kabul, towards Hindu Kush, and near the base of the mountains. Two ridges of hills, detached from the rest, run in and meet each other. At the point of junction, and where the slope of the hills is at an angle of about 45 degrees, and the height nearly 400 feet, a sheet of sand, as pure as that on the sea-shore, is spread from the top to the bottom, to a breadth of about 100 yards. When this sand is set in motion by people sliding down it, a sound is emitted. On the first trial we distinctly heard two loud, hollow sounds, such as would be produced by a large drum. On two subsequent trials we heard nothing, so that perhaps the sand requires to be settled and at rest for some space of time before the effect can be produced. The inhabitants have a belief that the sounds are only heard on Friday; nor then, unless by the special permission of the saint of Reg-Rowan, who is interred close to the spot. The locality of the sand is remarkable, as there is no other in the neighbourhood. Reg-Rowan faces the south, but the Wind of Parvan (Bad-i-Purwan), which blows strongly from the north for the greater part of the year, probably deposits it in an eddy. Such is the violence of this wind, that all the trees in the neighbourhood bend to the south, and the fields, after a few years, require to be re-cleared of the pebbles and stones, which the loss of soil lays bare. The mountains around are, for the most part, composed of granite or mica, but at Reg-Rowan we found sandstone, lime, slate, and quartz. Near the strip of sand there is a strong echo, and the same conformation of surface which occasions this is doubtless connected with the sound of the moving sand."

A folk legend that explains the phenomenon of the Reg-Rowan is recorded by Sirdar Ikbal Ali Shah:

"There is a small hill in Kohistan and a white line of sand is visible in the middle of the green herbage. The sand, curiously enough, is in motion, and they say that at the foot of the hill there is a cave where all the Reg Rowan (Reg-sand; Rowan-running, or in motion) goes down, and weird sounds are heard on dark nights, especially on Thursday nights.

"The legend goes on to say that there was an old man who took up his abode near the cave of Reg Rowan and proclaimed himself as Imam Medhi, who is to come at the end of the world. He soon collected followers, and dressed them as birds and beasts, and advanced towards Kabul. The Amir's troops dispersed his followers and the pretender escaped to the hills of Kohistan. But he did not rest, and men from all parts of the country flocked under his banner, and once again they marched on the capital. The Mullahs and Sufis denounced him as a curse to the peace of the Faithful, and prayed to God that the disturber of the tranquillity might be severely punished; and with this good omen, and backed up by the pious men's spiritual zeal, the Afghan soldiers defeated the hordes of the professed Medhi and killed him near the cave wherefrom he rose.

"It is said that his corpse descended into the cave, and from that time the white streak of sand goes down the pretender's cave to stuff his mouth for speaking blasphemy. The voices heard are his groans for mercy."

Alexander Burnes mentioned the *Bad-i-Purwan*, or Wind of Parvan, which blows from the Hindu Kush towards Bagram, providing relief from the heat throughout the area during the summer months. Another folk story is told to account both for the existence of the wind, and also the great quantity of pottery fragments found around Bagram. This version of the tale was also collected by Hackin and Kohzad:

"In the time of Noah, Bagram was considered to be the richest and most prosperous town in the country. It was renowned not only for the prestige of being the flourishing capital of Kapisa, but was equally well known for its moral degeneracy and the excesses that were committed there.

"The citizens, behind its ill-reputed walls, did not care to think of anything except their own pleasure. A pious and right-thinking man like Noah was evidently not able to live in such an environment of such corruption. But as he was a native of this town, he made a vow to attempt the impossible, by bringing to them the word of God.

"For many years, he sacrificed his time in vain; every day, the ungrateful inhabitants dreamt up new insults to hurl at him, to reproach him for his patience and his love of God. However, seven of his followers, whom he had been able to recruit on a preaching mission, returned with him to Bagram, and began courageously to support him in his task. But often harried by the people, he was the object of base mockery. Bewildered, he prayed that God would come to his aid and intervene to punish the ingrates. Having heard his prayers, God made it known to him that He was going to destroy the world. He ordered Noah to get ready to build an ark with his disciples in order to escape the fate that was reserved for others of the town. 'When your ark is ready, the rains will make their appearance; it is then that you must take refuge—you, your family, and your followers, along with a pair of every sort of animal.'

"But Noah did not reckon on the cunning of the inhabitants of Bagram. Rumours began to spread among them about what he was doing. Having surveyed his preparations, they fathomed out the reason for which he was hurrying to build such a dwelling in wood.

"All of the potters in the city, called together in haste, received an avalanche of commissions. They were called to make great watertight jars, of such a size that an ordinary person would be able to take refuge in them with ease, along with a stock of provisions. A lid of wax would allow the person inside to seal himself in, whilst still leaving holes for him to breathe.

"At last, the rain began to fall with violence. Noah embarked with his disciples, and was not able to rebuke himself for a feeling of justified satisfaction. In his prayers, he thanked the Lord for having chastised these wretches.

Painted truck, Panjshir, 1975 [Y. Crowe]

"The ark began to float and ride upon the waters until Noah took his final look at the cursed town, but doing so, how great was his surprise! Seeing a great number of jars floating on the waves, he turned to his followers. Not able to conceal his anger, he told them to pray.

"And God granted their wishes. A great wind arose, roaring with ferocity. It came from the direction of the plain of Parvan straight towards the plateau of Bagram. As a result, the floating jars began to dance about madly, knock against each other, and break into pieces, sinking quickly in the deep."

Whilst Afghanistan was at peace, the Panjshir Valley attracted many visitors on account of its great beauty. The journalist and writer Rosanne Klass described a coach journey there during the 1960s in *Afghanistan, Land of the High Flags*:

"Although Afghan buses were uncomfortable, they had a compensatory charm all their own. Only the cabs and chassis were imported; the bodies were erected locally on the frames. The side and front panels of the bright blue bodies were painted as elaborately, if not quite so skilfully, as the ceilings at Versailles, with exuberant landscapes, genre views, and scrolled calligraphy in bright primary colours, scalding pink being a favourite. The front window and driver's mirror were often decked with paper flowers and, sometimes, tasteful pin-ups of Indian movie actresses, who incline to palpitating languor. This riotous artistry distracted one in some part from the fact that the seats were hard and fractionally too narrow for an ordinary human bottom, and without much leg room.

"But the impressive thing about the buses—as about all motor vehicles in Afghanistan—was the drivers and their relationship with engines, wheels, transmissions, axels, and the other essentials of the machines they drove. They could keep anything moving no matter what happened, and they did it when necessary with bits of wire, with linseed oil, with spit or, at the last extremity, by sheer will power and nerve.

"As we bumped and swayed onto the road that led north to Panjshir, the driver had a few delicate adjustments to make. Once or twice, without stopping, he leaned out of the window to shout up to the passengers on the roof, who responded to his instructions by redistributing themselves, their goat, and the baggage to eliminate a noticeable list to starboard.

"It was a beautiful day for a trip. The summer sky was, as always, clear blue and cloudless. The sun was brilliant. Along one side of the road the mountains lay rose-brown and grey, criss-crossed with a faint tracery of shepherd's trails beaten hard by the sharp little hoofs of numberless sheep and goats. Furrows on the distant slopes stretched into cracked gullies crossing the road—the channels of springtime torrents which had burst across the road-bed to water the valley a few months before, now lifeless dry beds, bone-dry, baked hard, their pebbles shimmering with stony light in the full glare of the summer sun. On the other side of the road, fields were laid out across the valley as neatly as truck-gardens, each field precisely rimmed with low mud walls and laced with little irrigation ditches to carry the hoarded water, and coloured by late summer ripeness.

"Against the treeless stone-coloured landscape, brilliant little blue-green kingfishers flashed like bits of iridescent enamel as they swung on the telephone wires along the road, with the ever-present big black-and-white magpies stalking about the fields.

"We passed Istalif, its green woods tucked into a ravine; and Charikar, where fine knives are made; and stopped at Gul Bahar, at the mouth of the Panjshir River, in the park where the rivers meet. With kabobs from the bazaar — lamb and young kid, crisp and still smoking—and slabs of fresh bread, and melons, we feasted under the trees. When we set out again, the bus had lost some passengers, including the goat, and picked up a few others. We crossed the rushing waters and started up a tortuous road hewn heroically into the mountain-side, up through the valley of Panjshir, while below us the river tumbled past.

"The landscape changed. Everything cooled and paled—air, light, and colour. On either side, high above, the rocky escarpments were hard yellow-grey in the sunlight; but their lower flanks were covered with trees, and wherever the valley reached out from the river and poked fingers of earth among the roots of the hills, there was green: rich glowing leafy living green, as exciting to find as gold shining in the silt of a miner's pan. The further we went, the richer it grew. As the afternoon waned, the high peaks overhead, rising in majestic order towards the ranges of Badakhshan and the high Pamirs, cut off the sun from the lower gorge. There were shadow and water and verdure and beauty into which the spirit could sink luxuriously, soaking in rich

Gulbahar Bazaar, Panjshir Valley [F. Holt]

green peace. It was a miracle; and the miracle was simply a river which never ran dry.

"You must live in a dry land to know what a garden is. The very word *paradise* comes from the Persian word for 'garden,' and Eden must have been much like the valley of Panjshir: an island of sunlit greenness and coolness and flowing water; that is what Genesis says: that Eden had trees and a river. It is a definition. The men who set down that story knew such landscapes as these, and for them the wilderness beyond Eden must have been like the waterless plains which I had seen stretching to the horizon, a land where there is no substance but what can be wrenched from the earth by endless labour and unrelenting struggle. That was the wilderness they knew, and they must have had a precise understanding of what I could here begin to comprehend: the terror of Adam and Eve, driven from such a world as this green valley out into the sun-blanched rocky earth which they had hardly glimpsed, and never heeded, beyond the leafy edges of their paradise; and forbidden to return."

In 1956, the Panjshir Valley was the site of a famous chance meeting between two English expeditions being made to Nuristan—one led by Eric Newby and Hugh Carless, the other by the great explorer Sir Wilfred Thesiger. Newby recounts the encounter at the end of *A Short Walk in the Hindu Kush*:

"We crossed the river by a bridge, went up through the village of Shahnaiz and downhill towards the lower Panjshir.
'Look,' said Hugh, 'it must be Thesiger.'
Coming towards us out of the great gorge where the river thundered was a small caravan like our own. He named an English explorer, a remarkable throwback to the Victorian era, a fluent speaker of Arabic, a very brave man,

ERRATA

p. 11, for '*Afghanistan, Land of the High Flags*, by Roseanne Klass' read '*Land of the High Flags: A Travel Memoir of Afghanistan*, by Rosanne Klass, by courtesy of the author'

p. 206–208, from 'Although Afghan buses…' to '…forbidden to return', for 'Panjshir' read 'Panjsher'

p. 206, for '1960s' read '1950s'; for '*Afghanistan, Land of the High Flags*' read '*Land of the High Flags: A Travel Memoir of Afghanistan*'; for 'skilfully' read 'skillfully'; for 'colours' read 'colors'; for 'favourite' read 'favorite'

p. 207, for 'grey' read 'gray'; for 'coloured' read 'colored'; for 'colour' read 'color'

p. 208, for 'labour' read 'labor'

p. 725, for 'KLASS, ROSEANNE *Afghanistan: Land of the High Flags*, (New York, 1964)' read 'KLASS, ROSANNE *Land of the High Flags: A Travel Memoir of Afghanistan*, (New York: Random House, 1964)

who has twice crossed the empty quarter and, apart from a few weeks every year, has passed his entire life among primitive peoples.

We had been on the march for a month. We were all rather jaded; the horses were galled because the drivers were careless of them, and their ribs stood out because they had been in places fit only for mules and forded innumerable torrents filled with slippery rocks as big as footballs; the drivers had run out of tobacco and were pining for their wives; there was no more sugar to put in the tea, no more jam, no more cigarettes and I was reading *The Hound of the Baskervilles* for the third time; all of us suffered from persistent dysentery. The ecstatic sensations we had experienced at a higher altitude were beginning to wear off. It was not a particularly gay party.

Thesiger's caravan was abreast of us now, his horses lurching to a standstill on the execrable track. They were deep-loaded with great wooden presses, marked 'British Museum', and black tin trunks (like the ones my solicitors have, marked 'Not Russel-Jones' or 'All Bishop of Chichester').

The party consisted of two villainous-looking tribesmen dressed like royal mourners in long overcoats reaching to the ankles; a shivering Tajik cook, to whom some strange mutation had given bright red hair, unsuitably dressed for Central Asia in crippling pointed brown shoes and natty socks supported by suspenders, but no trousers; the interpreter, a gloomy-looking middle-class Afghan in a coma of fatigue, wearing dark glasses, a double-breasted lounge suit and an American hat with stitching all over it; and Thesiger himself, a great, long-striding crag of a man, with an outcrop for a nose and bushy eyebrows, forty-five years old and as hard as nails, in an old tweed jacket of the sort worn by Eton boys, a pair of thin grey cotton trousers, rope-soled Persian slippers and a woollen cap comforter.

Chaikhana, Panjshir, 1975 [Y. Crowe]

'Turn round,' he said, 'you'll stay the night with us. We're going to kill some chickens.'

We tried to explain that we had to get to Kabul, that we wanted our mail, but our men, who professed to understand no English but were reluctant to pass the gorges at night, had already turned the horses and were making for the collection of miserable hovels that was the nearest village.

Soon we were sitting on a carpet under some mulberry trees, surrounded by the entire population, with all Thesiger's belongings piled up behind us.

'Can't speak a word of the language,' he said cheerfully. 'Know a lot of the Koran by heart but not a word of Persian. Still, it's not really necessary. Here, you,' he shouted at the cook, who had only entered his service the day before and had never seen another Englishman. 'Make some green tea and a lot of chicken and rice—three chickens.'

'No good bothering the interpreter,' he went on, 'the poor fellow's got a sty, that's why we only did seventeen miles today. It's no good doing too much at first, especially as he's not feeling well.'

The chickens were produced. They were very old; in the half-light they looked like pterodactyls.

'Are they expensive?'

'The power of Britain never grows less,' said the headman, lying superbly.

'That means they are expensive,' said the interpreter, rousing himself.

Soon the cook was back, semaphoring desperately.

'Speak up, can't understand a thing. You want sugar? Why don't you say so?' He produced a large bunch of keys, like a housekeeper in some stately home. All that evening he was opening and shutting boxes so that I had tantalising glimpses of the contents of an explorer's luggage—a telescope, a string vest, *The Charterhouse of Parma*, *Du Côté de Chez Swann*, some fish-hooks and the 1/1,000,000 map of Afghanistan—not like mine, a sodden pulp, but neatly dissected, mounted between marbled boards.

'That cook's going to die,' said Thesiger; 'hasn't got a coat and look at his feet. We're nine thousand feet if we're an inch here. How high's the Chamar Pass?' We told him 16,000 feet. 'Get yourself a coat and boots, do you hear?' he shouted in the direction of the camp fire.

After two hours the chickens arrived; they were like elastic, only the rice and gravy were delicious. Famished, we wrestled with the bones in the darkness.

'England's going to pot,' said Thesiger, as Hugh and I lay smoking the interpreter's King Size cigarettes, the first for a fortnight. 'Look at this shirt, I've only had it three years, now it's splitting. Same with tailors; Gull and Croke made me a pair of whipcord trousers to go to the Atlas Mountains. Sixteen guineas—wore a hole in them in a fortnight. Bought half a dozen shotguns to give my headmen, well-known make, twenty guineas apiece, absolute rubbish.'

He began to tell me about his Arabs.

'I give them powders for worms and that sort of thing.' I asked him about surgery. 'I take off fingers and there's a lot of surgery to be done; they're frightened of their own doctors because they're not clean.'

'Do you do it? Cutting off fingers?'

'Hundreds of them,' he said dreamily, for it was very late. 'Lord, yes. Why, the other day I took out an eye. I enjoyed that.'

'Let's turn in,' he said.

The ground was like iron with sharp rocks sticking up out of it. We started to blow up our air-beds. 'God, you must be a couple of pansies,' said Thesiger."

After the Soviet invasion in 1979, the Panjshir Valley saw a great deal of fighting between the Soviet and Afghan communist troops, and the Mujahedin. A Russian conscript soldier, Aleksei Kupriyanov, left an account of a Mujahedin ambush in the area:

"The convoy was lined up on the road at sunrise. Early morning is the best time of day in Afghanistan. The birds are awake and singing; their chirping drowns out the quiet rumbling of engines. There is none of the debilitating daytime heat which is impossible to escape when you're on a march. There came an order to move forward. Twenty minutes later, we went over a small concrete bridge, under which raced a swiftly flowing stream meandering its way down to the valley. An hour later, the convoy turned off the concrete roadway onto a dirt road. The road was lined with villages. Horses hitched to carts appeared, hugging the side of the road. The convoy stopped at one of the villages. All the crews climbed out onto the top of the carriers. We carefully surveyed what was going on in the village; it was the first time I'd seen one at such a close distance. Not far from the road, a very thin Afghan man spread out a small stack of rye onto a flat little square, drove a donkey in from the yard and chased it around in a circle. That's how he threshed rye which had been left over from last year's harvest. His method seemed rather strange to us. Little boys appeared, chasing livestock out to pasture. Unlike the little kids in Kabul, who immediately attack us, asking us for baksheesh, they looked us over warily. Some women had gathered by an artesian well. Their faces were covered with yashmaks [veil]. On the surface, it appeared as if they had assembled to take turns drawing water from the well and had become absorbed in conversation. Instead, they were examining the Russian soldiers sitting on the armoured carriers with curiosity. An unshrouded young Afghan woman came out of the house opposite our APC [armoured personnel carrier] to the yard. She began to call her chickens for feeding. She was standing with her back facing us and didn't see us. When she felt our gazes fixed upon her, she turned around, and glanced above the courtyard wall. When she saw us, and we'd even half-risen so the wall wouldn't block our view, she shrieked, covered her face with her shawl and ran into her house. Several old men sat down near the courtyard wall and looked at us with curiosity. Several minutes passed and one of them approached us and said something. Saburov interpreted for us:

'Russians, there's no need to go further ahead there, beyond the hills, there are a lot of mujahedins.'

'How do you know?' asked Saburov.

'Old men know everything.'

Having spoken with Saburov, the old man screwed up his eyes and looked us over for several minutes. Then he turned around and walked back to where he'd been sitting before.

A large cloud of dust rose up on the dirt road behind the convoy. Soon we could hear the roar of diesel engines. The assistance we'd been promised had arrived: a tank company and an Afghan battalion. Our whole column moved over to the side of the road. A truck came to a stop across from our APC. Two Afghan soldiers were sitting in the back of it. Animated conversations began

Abandoned Soviet Armoured Personnel Carrier, Panjshir Valley, 2004 [B. Jenks]

between the soldiers as the unit commanders were agreeing about our coordinated action. Saburov was our interpreter. The Afghans had their platoon commander, who spoke Russian pretty well. To begin our dialogue, we traded a dozen cans of dry rations; evidently they were just as sick of kidney beans as we were of oatmeal.

An order came over the radio from the battalion commander to reorganize the convoy. Two tanks went ahead, followed by our APC, no. 282, and then Zadorozhny's APC, No. 280. The Afghan battalion went behind the APCs. They were reinforced by several batteries of mortar men, one more APC and then, finally, supply trucks and the main part of our tank company. The convoy had increased to almost twice its original size. It accelerated gradually as it moved out of the village. The road moved closer to the mountains and then rose up into them. In places it was very steep. The convoy's speed waned. This relatively short journey in terms of mileage took a very long time. Only at around 10am did we reach our destination.

The convoy stopped on a hill a mile away from a township, to be more exact, a group of close-knit villages, which were stretched out along the right bank of a river. The river, which rushed out of the Panjshir Ravine in a swift current, became calm at the dam in front of the village. There was the concrete building, a weaving mill on the other side of the river, and next to it stood several houses, among which one ritzy mansion particularly stood out.

Our crew crawled out onto the APC and studied the town very carefully.

'Its weird that no one's walking around the village. It's as if everyone's been killed,' Frolov said. His voice sounded alarmed.

'No one's coming out to meet us. Where the heck are the local authorities? They've perished along with the mujahedins and the battalion commander's scared everyone away with this huge formation,' Bakhtin said in amazement.

'Would it be so, but just you wait, there'll be mujahedins there!' Gogolev answered, not having any faith in the tranquil scene. Several minutes later, the battalion commander gave the 'ok' to move ahead. The deceptive silence had puzzled him as well, and after taking a look at the village through his binoculars, he decided to move to the other side of the river, towards the weaving mill. He consulted with the Afghan battalion commander, and the supply trucks were left behind under the protection of two tanks and two anti-aircraft detachments.

The choppers roared, flew low over the village, and then made a farewell circle over the convoy. Having escorted us all the way to our destination, they wung back towards the base.

Descending slowly from the hill along the road, the tanks headed for the village, and two of our APCs followed them. The Afghan battalion and then the remaining APCs followed us.

The advanced guard of the convoy entered the village slowly along a narrow little street and began nearing a bridge, which was bordered on both sides by high courtyard walls revealing only the tops of trees and the roofs of the houses. Both crews from APC 282 and APC 280 got their submachine-guns in a ready position and scrutinized the roof tops from behind the courtyard walls. Our nerves had been strained to the max. The tanks travelling up front were moving slowly and at times they stopped altogether. Everyone was expecting an ambush.

Silence. Terrifying silence. It would be better to go right into battle than to endure this draining uncertainty. It was quite dark in the APC. Saburov pulled down the front windshield, protecting the driver and the commanding officer from sniper bullets, and drove the vehicle, observing the road through the sights. The APC stopped again and Frolov cracked open the roof hatch and peered outside, telling the half-blind crew about the prevailing situation.

'The Afghans are lagging about two blocks behind. We've gone through the whole village and come out to the river; the tanks have stopped in front of the bridge.'

In several minutes, Frolov continued with his analysis of the situation:

'The lead tank has slowly crawled onto the bridge.'

The thunder from a solitary explosion reached us, and immediately thereafter, we could hear rifle and submachine-gun fire.

'Ambush! To arms! Mujahedins to the left in the gardens!' cried Nikolai, trying to get in touch with the company commander over the radio.

'This is Whirlwind One. Ambush. The bridge has exploded with the lead tank. The road ahead's been cut off; we're engaged in combat. Typhoon, come in.'

But all he heard in reply was loud noise and rolls of thunder, which was totally cutting off commands. Seryogin began to whirl the turret, searching for a target. After evidently discovering something, he opened fire.

Frolov took the earphones, which had become useless, off his head. Worried about grenade launchers, he commanded:

'Everyone except the gunner and the driver, get to the right side of the APC.'

Bakhtin opened the right side hatch, stuck his head out and looked around. He crawled out of the APC feet first. It was then that the machine-guns fell silent; the machine-gun belt had run out. The side hatches of APC-60s, which were part of our regiment's hardware, were situated uncomfortably high. Therefore, one had to first find the ground with his feet and then throw his body out of the hatch. Saburov held out his submachine-gun to me:

'Take it, it's better for close combat.'

After exchanging weapons with the driver, I climbed out at last. Saburov

immediately closed the hatch after me. The APC fired a long round. The noise of large-calibre machine-guns is much louder outside the carrier than inside. My ear-drums started aching in pain. The side hatch of the APC 280 standing several metres in back of us opened. Zadorozhny climbed out first, followed by his whole crew, with the exception, like us, of the gunner and driver. Taking cover from the bullets rustling through the air behind the armour of the APC, both crews fired back with their submachine-guns at the gardens and houses, where the mujahedins had fortified their position. I heard a powerful explosion and turned in the direction of the Afghan soldiers. The Afghans' vehicles were blazing on the road six hundred feet back. The rumble of non-stop machine-gun fire and frequent explosions was reaching us. The Afghans had jumped out to the right side of their vehicles as well. Their officers were trying to get things under control and cut the mujahedins off from the road, but panic had erupted in the battalion.

One man from a mortar crew managed to deploy a mortar and drop several shells into the gardens, but he was cut down immediately by a sniper's bullets. The rest of the mortar men didn't even try to take off the mortar covers. The

(Above) *Derelict Soviet Tank, Panjshir Valley, 2004 [B. Jenks]*
(Right) *Commander Massoud in conference with his officers [M. Yamashita]*

drivers, afraid of taking the ammunition trucks out of the village, left them to the mercy of fate. Several bangs from a grenade launcher rang out, and new fires began to blaze in the convoy.

It was a major, well-planned ambush. Evidently, somehow the mujahedins learned our route and prepared an ambush at the final point of our journey in a very convenient place. Our weapons and equipment, hemmed in by the courtyard walls, couldn't turn around, and the Afghan battalion was fired at as it marched."

The leading Mujahedin commander in the Panjshir Valley—and later, during the time of Taliban rule, leader of the opposing Northern Alliance—was Ahmed Shah Massoud. Massoud was educated as an engineer at Kabul University, but after the 1973 communist-backed coup of Daoud Khan, he joined a party called Jawanan-i-Musulman, or 'Muslim Youth,' which organised an uprising against the new authoritarian government. The group was forced to flee to Pakistan, where they began to organise resistance against the spread of communism in Afghanistan.

During this time, Massoud split from the Jawanan-i-Musulman, opposed to the terrorist methods advocated by one of its other leaders, Gulbuddin Hekmatyar, and instead joined the Jamiat-i-Islami (Islamic Society), newly founded by Burhanuddin Rabbani. After 1979, Massoud returned to the Panjshir Valley, where he began to fight against the Soviets. At one time near the beginning, his fighting force was reduced to just ten men; however, after his capture of Dara-i-Khanj in 1981, where emeralds had been discovered, he came into possession of the financial resources necessary to fund the resistance against the invaders.

Massoud was generally acknowledged to be a brilliant military tactician, scoring many victories against the communist armies. He came to be regarded as a hero by many Afghans, as much for his extraordinary magnetic character as his abilities on the battlefield. His personality was much remarked upon; the journalist Sandy Gall, on meeting him, said that he possessed "an aura, a mystique that seemed to set him apart". Gary Bowersox, on first being introduced to Massoud, recalled: "He seemed to draw power from somewhere else: from the earth beneath his feet and the mountains beyond. I felt an energy I just can't describe—but I knew that before me stood an extraordinary man. It wasn't anything he did or any way he looked. It was whom he *was* that left the impression."

Massoud was assassinated in the Panjshir Valley by two suicide-bombers masquerading as journalists on 9 September 2001. The last night of his life, spent with the Northern Alliance ambassador to India, Massoud Khalili, is recorded by Jean-Marie Pontaut and Marc Epstein in *Ils ont assassiné Massoud*:

> "The discussion had been going on for an hour, when suddenly Massoud turned towards Khalili.
>
> 'Tell me, as you live in India, have you yet visited any Hindu temples?'
>
> The Ambassador was puzzled. 'Of course,' he replied, 'in the North, South, East, West: they're all over the country.'
>
> 'What are they like? And why did you visit them?'
>
> Embarrassed, Khalili began a long speech about these religious places. He explained that India counted mosques amongst them also, as well as Buddhist

temples. Massoud encouraged him to continue. He went on to say that it was enshrined in the Indian constitution that the state was secular, but that spirituality permeated every aspect of daily life.

'We Afghans think that we are good Muslims because we observe a fast once a year during the month of Ramadan. But in India, certain wise Hindus fast for periods of two years! And in it, there are others who, out of veneration for the Creator, have not spoken a word for many years! If men believe in God, what does it matter if they go to a mosque, a temple, a synagogue, or a church? When your faith is strong, the rest is only a matter of colour: it is like the different hues that can be seen in a single tapestry.'

The commander was fascinated: 'Tell me again what you've just said.'

Khalili was pleased; he loved to captivate his audience. He noted in particular how much his friend had changed. He wondered whether the media plaudits Massoud had won during his journey in Europe, and the welcome he received at the European Parliament in Strasbourg in April, had broadened his horizons. Khalili found him more interesting than others, and particularly foreigners.

It was 5pm when their discussion came to an end. The chief of the Northern Alliance called together several of his officers for a staff meeting. That evening, after dinner and another period of reflection, the two friends found themselves in the commander's house. Stretched out on a mattress, Khalili began to leaf through various books of poetry.

'Read,' murmured Massoud, 'read me a poem.'

And thus, for more than four hours, Khalili went through the *Divan* of Hafiz [14th century], his monumental collection of texts. Of this, the Commander possessed a full edition, bound in white, with notes and explanations at the bottom of the page. Although tired, Khalili did not protest, wrapped up in his enjoyment of the evening.

Like many Tajiks and Persians, Massoud appreciated the *ghazals* of the poet. The ghazal—literally, a 'gazelle'—is similar to a ballad. The art of the ghazal, explains Cheryl Benard in her novel *Moghul Buffet*, consists of portraying the moment when the gazelle, pursued by the hunter, realises that her death is imminent: 'The hunter, although paralysed by the beauty of the gazelle, realises that this dream-like stupor will not last, and will come to an end as he kills the animal. The ghazal sings of that second of eternity when the eyes meet of the hunter and the prey. Petrified with fright, the gazelle is not able to flee; overcome with its grace, the hunter is not able to shoot. They each lose themselves in the sight of the other, but both knowing that the moment is not destined to last: when it comes to an end, it is inescapable that the grace will be finished, and turned into carrion. All the energy of the ghazal hangs on the idea that this fatal moment is, in every respect, an analogy of love.'

A number of those who read Hafiz look in his writing for signs—*faals*—about their future. They open his work at random, and the first verse they see is taken as a prediction.

That night, remembers Khalili, he chose a page in this fashion, and translated it from Old Persian into Tajik:

O, you two, cherish this night,

Cherish the words that you exchange,

Cherish the time you pass together,

For many nights will pass on,

And many days will pass on,

And many months will pass on,

And many years will pass on,

When you will be unable to see each other...

A silence. Massoud stood up, and stared at Khalili. 'Read it again,' he said. Khalili did so, three times. Massoud asked him 'do you remember that poem by Jami? You read it about three years ago; it was about a candle.' Khalili began to recite:

Like the candle, I died, suffocated by my own tears.

Like a candle, I have become silent.

And like a bow in the hair of my lover,

I am a wanderer balanced on the shoulders of time,

Remembering you so many days and nights

That I forget my own soul.

The Commander closed his eyes, and bit his lip. 'God, how beautiful.' It was 4am when the friends finally went their separate ways.

Khalili said nothing at the time, but he was proud: 'That night, I was able to tear him away from his hellish life, the life of a solider and a warrior, to lead him into the garden of paradise and the muses. He was happy; that was enough for me.'"

THE PANJSHIR VALLEY: TRAVEL INFORMATION

This is one of the most beautiful valleys in Afghanistan. Its closeness to Kabul made a popular destination in the good old days of tourism. It was the scene of some of the fiercest fighting during the jihad of the 1980s; the great Ahmed Shah Massoud defeated the Russians 13 times here and so comprehensively that they stopped trying to defeat him. Much of the television footage shown in the West of the jihad was shot here. That the Panjshir is now once again a beautiful and well-cultivated valley is a tribute to the Afghan's astonishing resilience.

The valley's principal attraction for visitors is its extraordinary natural beauty. There are very few sights to see, but a trek up to the Anjuman Pass, camping in

CHAIKHANA IN CHARIKAR

mulberry orchards on the way, makes it an unforgettable trip. The Panjshir is famous for its fruit, principally grapes and mulberries. Mulberries are harvested in July and August and grapes in September. These are the best months to visit. There are only tea houses (*chaikhanas*) at Bazarak, Khenj, Safit Chir and Dasht-i-Rewat, and a guest house at Astana, so camping is probably a better option.

To reach the Panjshir, drive northwards out of Kabul, through

Chaikhana in Charikar [F. Holt]

Charikar, until you come to the village of Jebal Seraj. Here the road to the Panjshir branches right (the one straight on goes to the Salang Pass).

The road narrows as you drive along and enter the Panjshir proper. The administrative centre is at Rokha, with a police checkpoint, though no special permission is required to enter the valley. Most of the major Tajik leaders of the jihad came from this village and those further up.

The first sight of interest is the tomb of Ahmed Shah Massoud, "Lion of the Panjshir", who was assassinated at his headquarters in Khawja Bahauddin by two of Osama bin Laden's suicide bombers on 9 September 2001. It is on the top of a hill that dominates his home village. When I first visited the grave a few months after his death, it was just a simple barrow of earth measuring the length of his body, with a green flag at the head showing it to be the grave of a martyr. Since then a more elaborate dome has been erected over it and the grave covered in marble. There are plans to rebuild it on a more magnificent scale.

It is a moving place and a visitor's book is kept nearby. In it, one visitor wrote in 2002 Churchill's magnificent epitaph on Orde Wingate, equally applicable to Massoud: "He was a man of genius, who might well have become a man of destiny."

The view from the hill is magnificent, the steep mountainsides contrasting with the patchwork of corn fields and fruit orchards.

After passing through Massoud's village of Jangalak, the next stop is at Astana where there is an excellent guest house kept by Massoud's logistics chief, Jon Mohammed. It was built for visiting dignitaries and the chiefs of the Northern Alliance. The enormous dining room was in fact the cabinet room. Opposite is Massoud's helicopter base. The plain by the river, dotted with mulberry tress is gorgeous and an excellent picnic or camp site.

Further up stream, at Bazarak, is an old Russian command post and 4 kilometres beyond that is the shrine of Panji Piran, a local holy man. According to some sources, he was one of the five men whose exploits gave rise to the name Panjshir, which means Five Lions. Previously it was known as Banj Hir or Kushkim.

Mausoleum of Ahmed Shah Massoud, 2004 [B. Jenks]

According to this tale, Mahmud of Ghazni was building a dam at Ghazni. His workers were slow and idle. Frustrated, Mahmud forced five strong men from the valley to come to Ghazni to do the work. They far exceeded his expectations and built the dam in one day. Impressed, Mahmud said that they were not five men, but five lions. Hence the name. Massoud, of course, earned the honorific "Lion of the Panjshir" and his colleague, Ismael Khan, is known as the "Lion of Herat".

Further up stream, at the village of Marz, is a large marble-faced house belonging to Marshal Fahim, the commander who took over from Massoud. Upstream from here is the village of Khenj, with a chaikhana, but the place is notable for its proximity to the emerald mines . They are not being worked at the moment because primitive mining techniques have exhausted what can be easily extracted by burrowing with stone tools and explosives, and have turned the area into a very dangerous Swiss cheese. Explosives are extracted from unexploded bombs, a highly dangerous procedure done at home that often wipes out whole rows of houses. And the high explosives damage more emeralds than are recovered. The mines are a four-hour climb up the beautiful valley that runs into the Panjshir opposite the village of Khenj. A further set of mines exists at Buzmal, near the village of Dasht-i-Rewat.

Two hours' drive from Dasht-i-Rewat finds a junction of two rivers, where the Parian, flowing down from the Anjuman Pass, meets the Panjshir. Rising northwards is the Khawak Pass, a site of enormous historical interest because here, in the middle of winter and in appalling conditions, Alexander marched his troops to surprise Bessus. It takes about six hours to climb to the top and in the summer the place is full of Kuchi nomads. The view from the top is spectacular. Alexander had been taught—by Aristotle, no less—that from the summit of the Hindu Kush one could see the Ocean, the sea that was believed to encircle the earth. But by the time Alexander had got here, he had probably realized that Aristotle was wrong.

A fairly bleak chaikhana stands at the foot of the pass. From here you can either head up the Parian and the trekking areas around Mir Samir (see below), or follow the Panjshir up to the Anjuman Pass. This 14,700-foot pass is truly spectacular and provides the best vantage point that I have found to see the Hindu Kush, with jagged ranges of mountains stretching to the horizon and beyond. Descending the Anjuman Pass, the road takes you to Skarzer (see p. 159).

TREKKING ROUND MIR SAMIR

Mir Samir is the mountain that Eric Newby and Hugh Carless tried to climb in 1957. Their adventures are recounted in *A Short Walk in the Hindu Kush*, a brilliant book that has a claim to being the greatest travel book in English and must be read by anyone coming to this area. The peak has still never been climbed.

Carless and Newby's exploits have left a curious folk memory in the area, told to me by Haji Safit Mir, a native of Dasht-i-Rewat. "When I was five, two Englishmen came to climb Mir Samir. All the children and men ran out of their houses to see them when they arrived. Then we heard that they had climbed up and fell off, but were saved because they had parachutes. They left an ice axe there, which a German lady got a few years later. She also parachuted down."

Mir Samir is near the border of the Panjshir and Nuristan, and the Chamar Pass leads into Nuristan at 4,570 m (15,000 feet). The mountain itself is in the Chamar Valley, below the pass.

To trek round Mir Samir, hire horses at Chamar village. It takes one day to reach the glacier used as a base camp by Newby and Carless. Four days of trekking round the base of the mountain make a genuinely enjoyable short walk in the Hindu Kush.

THE GEOLOGY OF AFGHANISTAN

—Catherine McMullen

*A*fghanistan's landscapes tell a tale of sea and wind and rain and snow…and plate tectonics. When the dinosaurs still walked the earth, more than 65 million years ago, the land that is now Afghanistan's interior was a low swampy coast along the northwest edge of the Tethys Ocean. A huge continent to the south stared to break up and one chunk, the Indian subcontinent, moved to the north and west. It collided with that swampy coast of Asia first, and so began the most complex and powerful mountain-building process that we can study.

The Tethys Ocean narrowed as the continental plate with the Indian land mass began to dive, or subduct, under the larger and more stable Asia. Volcanic islands emerged in the Tethys and, together with shards of the giant southern continent moving ahead of India, they crashed against Asia and were sheered into elongated blocks that now populate the mountainous area we call the Hindu Kush. The sheering and deposition and erosion have continued for millions of years; the rocks and mountains of Afghanistan tell the story of this process and the story has not yet been fully transcribed—after so many years of instability in this part of the world, the geology remains uninterpreted, undocumented. The big picture is part of the story of the Himalayas and the great tectonic tale of continental collision between India and Asia. The details of this huge tale are still unexamined in Afghanistan.

There are two major faults cutting through the Hindu Kush. The first, the Chaman Fault, forms the edge of the Indian plate. It emerges from the Arabian Sea and passes to the west of Karachi to Quetta and Chaman. Then it curves to the northeast from Kandahar to Kabul. The Hari Rod (Rud) Fault, further north, marks the boundary of the Asian plate. It crosses northern Iran and slices east through Herat, up the Hari Rod valley, and then forms the valleys of Bamiyan and Ghorband. The two faults meet near Jabal Saraj and head up through the Panjshir and Andjoman (Anjuman) valleys, through Badakhshan, to curl into the Pamir Knot. The area between the two faults is filled with those blocks that were once islands in the Tethys Ocean, squeezed and distorted by the pressures of continental collision. From west to east, these blocks include the Lut Block in Iran, the Afghan Block east of the Helmand River and the Kabul Block that includes the Shomali Plain, as well as the Kohistan and Ladakh blocks in Jammu and Kashmir. The pressure on these blocks and the fractures that weave through them are responsible for the preponderance of major and deadly earthquakes that continuously shake eastern Iran, Afghanistan, Tajikistan, and Pakistan.

The high mountains block water-laden southern winds from reaching Central Asia. The rain and snow of the Hindu Kush flow through a thousand valleys and ravines—down to the Indus, down to the Amu Darya and down into the sand. The headwaters of the Kabul River lie in the Paghman Range to the west of the city. Over the last decade, lack of rain and snow has had its inevitable effect. The Kabul River is now dry for most of its length, until it reaches Sarubi and meets the surging waters from the Panjshir. If the Lataband Pass east of the city continues to uplift faster than the feeble waters of the river can erode its bed to maintain its slope, the Kabul River may no longer reach the Indus and then the sea.

Most of the water flowing through the Amu Darya—the Oxus River of history and legend – is captured in Badakhshan. It once gained even more from the Hindu Kush; the Maimana, the Qaysar, the Shirin Tagab and many more long rivers used to flow into the Amu, as the Kunduz River still does. But the extensive irrigation channels braiding over the northern plain slowed, then absorbed, the waters. Finally, the shifting sands moved in and built dunes that move back and forth like sentries, only infiltrated when the inland waters reach fullest flood.

Further to the south, the Helmand River and the Farah Rod drain the immense tracts of southwest Afghanistan, feeding the Sistan basin – a vast and legendary inland water body that formerly straddled Afghanistan's boundary with Iran. Scientists have found that the ecologically diverse lakes of the Sistan basin, valuable overwintering sites for migrating waterfowl, fluctuate in size between wet spells and droughts. The current drought affecting the region of the Iranian plateau, which seems to have had only one year of respite—in 2002—is producing tragic desiccation in this unique ecosystem. The 200-km north-south natural depression has been occupied by human populations since 3000 BC, and their irrigated, agricultural societies have left potentially rich archaeological sites.

The region's dynamic tectonics produce geothermal springs and chemical deposits. Near its headwaters in the west of the Bamiyan Valley along the Hari Rod fault, the Band-i-Amir River is so saturated by carbonates that the chemicals precipitate along small obstructions, building lips *that grow and grow. The travertine barriers gleam like abalone 10 metres high, enclosing intensely cyan lakes that sit like stepped jewels along the bottom of a barren canyon. Geothermal activity is also responsible for the oddly shaped ridge that identifies the Darya Ajdahar, or Valley of the Dragon, southwest of Bamiyan. A 100-metre-long fissure along the spine of the ridge, left by Hazrat Ali's deadly thrust with his mighty sword Zulfiqar, and a number of mineral-rich springs have come to represent through legend the doomed dragon's oozing blood and repentant tears; these phenomena demonstrate the continuing geological forces of heat and pressure that reach the surface along the Hari Rod fault.*

And so we have the rocks and we have the water. But the most striking features about Afghanistan's landscapes may be those left by glaciation—by solid rivers of ice that can grow to be 1,000 metres thick. Like tongues of steel, they scoured the valleys; ripped the sandstones; ground the sands to silt and clay; captured boulders, cobbles, pebbles, and grains; and pushed the soils and rocks and hills into distorted patterns throughout most of Afghanistan's precipitous valleys. In the Panjshir, for example, remnants of end moraines mark the front of the last glacier as it stopped and then retreated up the valley. Lateral moraines run up the sides of the valleys like sinuous shelves, and reworked deposits fall out of side valleys as alluvial fans. All these features are obscured to varying degrees by a silt drape left by the lakes, the cold, milky, blue lakes that form everywhere around melting ice. The Panjshir ridge, where Ahmad Shah Massoud's burial shrine gleams, is a remnant of moraines and glacial lakes. It may have started as a terminal moraine that then served as the upper shoreline for a lake blocked by a plug in the slender pass at the bottom of the valley—likely an ice plug. When the pass cleared, the water drained suddenly and a silt veil covered the up-valley ridge as a giant ripple mark.

In the Bamiyan Valley, the south facing cliffs that once housed the famous Buddhas are unconsolidated siltstone-like beds of glacial lacustrine (lake-formed) deposits. The characteristic rubble-supporting silt is only lightly cemented and throughout Afghanistan these deposits have been colonized by people looking for shelter from searing summer heat and blasting winter cold. Caves and tunnels designed for human habitation honeycomb many glacial lacustrine beds in the mountains of central and eastern Afghanistan.

While numerous valleys in the Hindu Kush once contained lakes, only a few of these blue gems remain, such as Caqmaqtin (Chaqmartin) and Zorkul in the Wakhan Corridor. The remarkable blue results from sunlight reflected by particles—glacial silt—of a specific size suspended in the water. The word for the silt that blows in the wind and settles into every crevice and shelf is khaki —and that's its colour. This khaki is also the major component of Afghan soils, which are so rich, people just add water to grow lush fields of wheat, barley, cotton, flax, sesame, squash, potatoes, tomatoes, eggplants, peppers, melons and orchards of fruit and nuts.

A skirt of plains, or Dashts, extends from the mountains. These are flat, compacted silt deposits forming a drab khaki veneer on top of the Turan platform to the north and the Iranian plateau to the west. Golden sand dunes roll over the plains, migrating back and forth before the dominant winds of different seasons. These Dashts have local names with varying pronunciations and meanings. From southwest to northeast some of these names are Dasht-i-Margho (Desert of Death), Dasht-i-Baxil, Dasht-i-Khuspas, Dasht-i-Babus, Dasht-i-Hamdamab, Dasht-i-Layli (Plain of the Lilies), Dasht-i-Sortepa, Dasht-i-Abadan Mir Alem and Dasht-i-Sermahi.

Afghanistan's landscapes have one odd characteristic: the difficulty in distinguishing between natural features and those built by humans. A rock face will become a rock wall, an overhang shades a dug cave, a crevice becomes a staircase, a stream starts to braid, then one loose end bends into an irrigation channel. If you find your eyes resting on a feature that makes no sense, like a perfectly round hill sitting atop a perfectly flat plain, it is likely a remnant of human endeavour. Villages, towns and cities grew and thrived and then died out. Sometimes they passed away gradually, but sometimes settlements would be abandoned in a generation, or a week. When Genghis Khan swept through in the 13th century, many settlements were left in rubble. What was once a citadel, then rubble, after 500 years is now a mound sitting forlornly out on an endless plain. On the road from Charikar to Bamiyan, the iron in the rocks to the south have left them red as blood in the setting sun, then the walls and crenellations begin to form the ruins of Shahr-i-Zohak, the Red City of an evil legendary king. If the sun is not right, it appears as just another wall of rock. Often, a rounded exposure will allow a glimpse into the ground or a slope, or sometimes a row of these small craters will appear at semi-regular intervals—these are landmine craters and they mark where some being trod and probably died, or lost limbs.

Afghanistan's irrigation is not all above the ground. In the dry south and west, where open irrigation channels would lose much of their water to evaporation, the people have built karez, or underground water channels. These tunnels reach from the alluvial fans that edge mountain *ranges out into the dry-lands, sometimes for hundreds of kilometres. These tunnels have a diameter of about 1.5 metres and they slope gradually so several centimetres of water flow gently through sections maintained by communities along the way. Every 200 metres or so, a vertical shaft descends from the surface for water to be removed and for small workers to enter. Once in the tunnel, the worker clears any debris that may have collected in that section. The task is usually performed by a boy from the family responsible through countless generations for building and maintaining the karez. At the far end of the tunnel, the water usually emerges into a pool that forms the centre of an oasis with a steady water supply far, far from the mountains where the water first accumulated. These irrigation tunnels can be very old. The technology is sophisticated and the efforts are made by communities that must plan the tunnels in three dimensions, perform backbreaking excavations to precise specifications and commit many years of vigilance to maintain the system.*

The irrigations skills of the country support amazing gardens hidden within the walls of family compounds in every province. In most villages, households maintain small orchards of fruit and nut trees as well as gardens for vegetables and flowers. Tenderly cared for roses are found at every location that could possible grow them. Unfortunately, outside of family-owned properties, deforestation has ravaged the gentle slopes of hills, the defiles of canyons and the floodplains of the rivers. The loss of trees leads to further erosion, and future research may show that Afghanistan was not always such a desert. With natural forests covering mountains and plains, their cycling of water through the ground and air would have maintained a far moister climate. History tells us that the Panjshir Valley was heavily forested until around AD 1000. The mining and refining of silver consumed all the green forests and today the mountainsides are blighted by scree slopes that continually pour rocks and debris, like festering sores on the mountainsides. The years of war and drought have not helped the landscapes to heal. Populations hiding in valley heads and escaping over mountain passes burn what they can find for heat and for cooking. What they might leave to regenerate will probably be eaten by their sheep and wicked goats that can forage 2 metres up into trees. Those trees that can be found, such as mountain ash, often have a tropical look to them with a high canopy and no lower branches. This is the result of goats, not nature.

People can divert streams, fell trees, wall cities, nurture gardens and excavate tunnels. Ultimately, the landscapes of Afghanistan are controlled by forces of nature: by earthquakes, by flood and by drought. With continental collision wrapping mountains around each other and major faults anastomosing (joining) like blood capillaries underfoot, it is no wonder that scientists believe 5,000 earthquakes occur every year in Afghanistan. Five hundred of these are significant enough to register on global seismic detection networks.

Along the southeastern side of the Chaman fault, along the Sulaiman Mountain Range, the mountain ridges seem to pour like molasses down to the Indus Valley. Geologists suspect there is an obstruction beneath this range—something that will not dive under the Asian plate. So the rocks stretch and slide around the obstruction and the earth shakes and groans, producing quakes that literally bury societies. In 1935, death came to 30,000 people when an earthquake devastated Quetta. Further north along the Chaman fault, 2,000 people were killed around Zarahrr Sharan in Logar province on 9 June 1956. The confluence of the Chaman and Hari Rod faults has been quiet lately, but there is a history of anti-social behaviour: Jabal Saraj and nearby Gulbahar were completely destroyed by an earthquake on 18 October 1874. Most recently, the worst hit areas are farther north where the two faults seem to break into many shard-like transform faults within Tokhar and Badakhshan provinces. In 1998, two earthquakes hit these regions, each killing at least 4,000 people. These earthquakes can trigger landslides—the evidence can be seen in countless valleys—which contribute to the death toll when human settlements are in the way.

Finally, the landscapes of Afghanistan display the signs of flood and drought. Narrow defiles are prone to flash flooding, especially during the weeks when ice is breaking up in downstream reaches. The surpluses of water drain away and Afghanistan is left with the ongoing drought. Although the good rains of 2002 and bountiful harvests seemed to mark the end of a five-year drought, 2003 and 2004 harvests have been disappointing due to lack of rain and the World Food Programme is starting to organise relief efforts for the winters ahead.

Catherine McMullen is an earth system scientist and writer. After writing a book on Solid-Earth Science for the US National Academy for Sciences, she advised the Canadian Foreign Affairs Department on science and environment policy and CIDA on climate change impacts in developing countries. She served as a specialist on the effects of ozone depletion for Friends of the Earth Canada and on climate change vulnerability and adaptation for Greenpeace International.

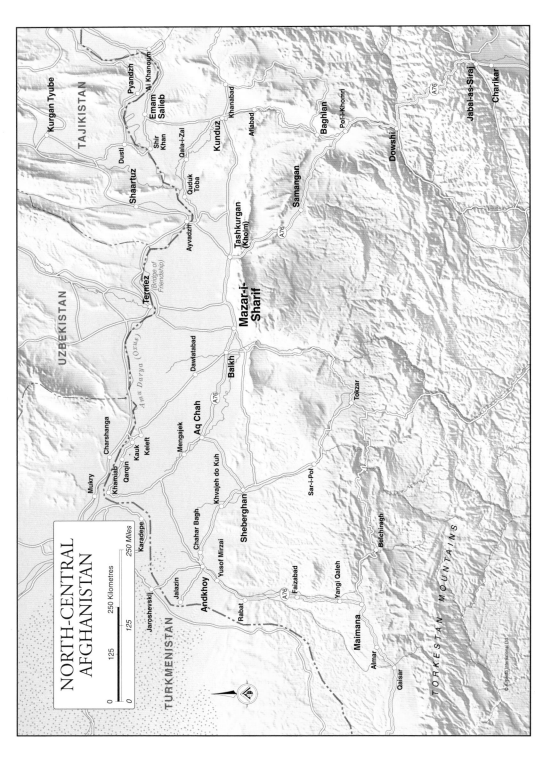

NORTH-CENTRAL AFGHANISTAN

0   125   250 Kilometres

0   125   250 Miles

TURKMENISTAN

UZBEKISTAN

TAJIKISTAN

Kurgan Tyube

Pyandzh

'Ai Khanoum

Emam Salieb

Shir Khan

Dustl

Qala-i-Zal

Kunduz

Khanabad

Aliabad

Baghlan

Pol-i-Khomri

Jabal-as-Siraj

Charikar

Shaartuz

Quduk Toba

Ayvadzh

Dowshi

Tashkurgan (Kholm)

Samangan

A76

A76

Termez (Bridge of Friendship)

Amu Darya (Oxus)

Dawlatabad

Mazar-i-Sharif

Mukry

Charshanga

Kauk

Keleft

Mengajek

Balkh

Khamiab

Qarqin

Aq Chah

Khvajeh do Kuh

A76

Tokzar

Karadepe

Chahar Bagh.

Sheberghan

Sar-i-Pol

Jaroshevskij

Jalazin

Yusof Mirzai

Belchiragh

Andkhoy

Rabat

Faizabad

A76

Yangi Qaleh

Maimana

Almar

Qaisar

TORKESTAN MOUNTAINS

© Upfront International Ltd.

Uzbek Woman's boots, Andkhoy, NW Afghanistan, c. 1965 [Pavia]

BALKH: CITY OF THE HIGH-LIFTED BANNERS

O f all the great cities of Central Asia, few can compete with Balkh for importance in history or prominence in legend. Although the small town now based on its site has been eclipsed by the nearby settlement of Mazar-i-Sharif, and gives little hint as to its previous significance, to the Islamic geographers Balkh (classical Bactra) was *maadar-i-shahrha*—"the Mother of Cities"; to the Zoroastrians, the beautiful land of "the high-lifted banners", one of Ahura Mazda's first creations; and, overall, a major junction on the trade route between the West, China and India: a cradle of religion, meeting point of cultures and a capital of empire.

One of the earliest stories to reach us about Balkh is the myth of its siege and capture by Ninus, King of the Assyrians, along with an army of over two million men. Although the tale is of uncertain historicity—the Greek sources date the beginning of Ninus' reign to 2189 BC, whereas other evidence states that Ninus, properly known as Tukulti-Ninurta, ruled around 1200 BC—the story is not without interest. Not only does it record the early reputation the area possessed for wealth; it also bears witness to one of the first great strong women of history, Semiramis, whose tactical genius both brought the siege to a successful conclusion and also won the heart of King Ninus. The main account we possess of the siege is from the Greek Historian Diodorus of Sicily, who, amongst other things, points to Semiramis as the inventor of Persian national dress—a costume that, particularly with respect to the use of trousers, the Greeks found unsettlingly androgynous, if not downright effeminate:

> "After completing the foundation of the city which bore his name, Ninus turned his attention to the planned campaign against the Bactrians. Bearing in mind their great numbers and courage in battle, and that the country possessed many strong-points which could not be attacked by an enemy, he enlisted a great body of troops from all of the nations he ruled. In his previous attempt

to conquer Bactria he had done poorly, but this time he was eager to march against it with an absolutely overwhelming force. Thus, when the army had been assembled together from every side, it numbered, as Ctesias records in his history, one million seven hundred thousand foot soldiers, two hundred and ten thousand cavalry, and slightly under ten thousand six hundred scythe-bearing chariots. These huge numbers may, at first sight, seem improbable, but anyone who considers the great size of Asia and the huge number of people that inhabit it, will agree that the size of Ninus' army is not at all incredible...

"The country which he was invading was difficult to enter, and could only be approached through narrow passes; as a result, he was compelled to divide up his enormous forces before leading them onwards. The land of Bactria had many great cities, but the most famous, in which the royal palace was situated, was called Bactra; in size, and in the strength it drew from its acropolis, it exceeded all the other cities by far. Oxyartes, the King of the country, had conscripted all the inhabitants of military age into a force which numbered around four hundred thousand men. Taking this force and encountering the enemy at the passes, he allowed a part of Ninus' army to make its way into the country; when he thought that a sufficient number of the enemy had spread itself out on the plain, he readied his own men for battle. After a fierce struggle, the Bactrians put the Assyrians to flight, pursuing them as far as the mountains overlooking the battlefield, and killing at least one hundred thousand of them. However, after this, when the whole Assyrian force had managed to enter the country, the Bactrians were overwhelmed by their sheer numbers, and each man withdrew to his own city, intending to defend their own against the attackers. As a result, Ninus was easily able to subdue all of the smaller cities, but remained unable to overcome Bactra itself, as it was well-defended, and extremely strong.

"After a time, the siege began to drag on. One of Ninus' officers, Onnes, who still felt a great passion for his wife Semiramis, summoned her from home to come to him. Being not only intelligent and daring, but also excellent in every other respect, she seized the opportunity to display her native ability. First, as she was about to set out on a long journey, she devised a garment that made it impossible for anyone to distinguish whether the wearer of it was a man or a woman. This was well adapted to her needs, allowing her to travel in the heat, protect her complexion, and, since it allowed for the ease of movement that a young person would require, enabled her to do as she wished. (In fact, it was so pleasing that in later times the Medes, who became dominant in Asia, adopted Semiramis' garment as their national dress, as did the Persians after them.) When Semiramis arrived in Bactria, she surveyed the progress of the siege. She observed that the attacks were always made on the plains and other weak positions, but that no-one ever moved against the acropolis because of its strength; moreover, the soldiers defending the acropolis would always leave their posts there and assist those guarding the walls below whenever they came under pressure. Therefore, she took a group of soldiers who had a knowledge of rock-climbing, made her way with them up a certain hazardous ravine, captured a part of the acropolis, and gave a signal to those who were besieging the wall down on the plain. Those within the city, struck with terror at the sudden seizure of the height, decided that there was no hope of saving the situation, and consequently they abandoned their defence of the walls.

"When the city had been taken in this fashion, King Ninus, marvelling at the woman's ability, at first honoured her with magnificent gifts; later on, he became infatuated with her because of her great beauty. He tried to persuade

Gold from the Kushan grave hoard of Tillya-Tepe,
found near Balkh (see p. 655) [V. Sarianidi]

her husband to yield her to him of his own accord, promising to give him in exchange his own daughter, Sosane, as a new wife. When he reacted unfavourably to this offer, Ninus threatened to put out his eyes unless he immediately acceded to his commands. But Onnes, partly out of fear of the Kings' threats, and partly out of love for his wife, fell into a certain kind of madness or frenzy, and hanged himself. In this way, Semiramis came to be the Queen.

"Ninus captured the treasures in Bactra, which consisted of a great amount of gold and silver, and when he had settled the affairs there, he disbanded his forces."

Despite the eminent position accorded by Diodorus to Balkh in the history of warfare, we should perhaps venerate it more for its role in the development of religion. It was at the court of the legendary King Goshtasp in the city of Balkh that the preacher and prophet Zardusht (known to the West as Zoroaster) began his

The Walls of Balkh [B. Woodburn]

ministry, laying the foundations for the faith of Zoroastrianism—the official religion of pre-Islamic Persia, still practised by some adherents even today, notably the Parsees of India. Little is known for certain of Zardusht's life. It is believed that he was born in the Iranian city of Rey, and that he travelled extensively before reaching Balkh. Nonetheless, even his dates are completely unclear. Greek and Latin writers say that the lived "5,000 years before the fall of Troy" or around 6000 BC, whilst other sources place him as late as the establishment of the Achaemenian Empire in the 6th century BC. Despite this wide margin of possibilities, the majority of academic opinion currently holds that he was active around the middle of the first millennium BC. The poet Firdousi portrayed the appearance of Zardusht at Goshtasp's court in the Iranian national epic, the *Shahnameh*:

> "Time passed over these events. Out of the earth a tree appeared. It sprang up in the hall of Goshtasp and grew till it reached the dome; a tree with many roots and multitudinous branches. Its leaves consisted of pieces of good counsel and its fruit was wisdom: how shall one who consumed fruits of this kind ever die? Of happy augury was this phenomenon named Zardosht (Zoroaster). He it was who slew Ahriman the maleficent [the devil]. He said to the king of the world:

> "I am a messenger and I am a guide to God.' Producing a brazier of blazing fire he said further, 'I have brought this out of Paradise and the Creator of the world has bidden you to accept this religion, saying, Gaze on this heaven and earth which I have brought into being without earth or water. Observe how I fashioned it and see whether any other has achieved its like. Surely it is I who am Lord of the world; there is none besides. Since you know that I composed it, it is your duty to acclaim me Creator of the world. Accept the goodly faith from me that addresses you; learn from me the Way and Practice. Observe what I say and do accordingly. Choose wisdom, hold worldly things in contempt. Learn the way of the religion of goodness, for without religion kingship is without worth.'

> "When the good king heard of the good religion, he received it and the practice of it at his hands. So also did his gallant brother, the fortunate Zarir (he that could bring down a raging elephant), and the old king his father who had retired to Balkh when the world turned bitter in his heart. Then too the great nobles of every clime as well as the sages and skilled physicians received it. All

came to the king's court, bound on the girdle and entered the faith. There then appeared the divine glory, evil disappeared from the hearts of the wicked, tombs were covered by the radiance of God and seed was cleansed of all defilement.

"The noble Goshtasp, after having ascended the throne, despatched troops to every clime and sent priests about the world to establish domed fire-temples according to the ritual. He first laid the foundation of the temple of the bright fire of Mehr. Zardosht planted a noble cypress before the temple gate, placing an inscription on the tree to proclaim that Goshtasp had adopted the good religion. He thus made the noble cypress his memorial, and thus does wisdom spread right conduct abroad in the land.

"Years in number passed over these events and the slender cypress increased steadily in growth. So greatly did it expand that no lasso could encompass it, and it put out many branches aloft. At last the king built a goodly dome about it, forty ells in height and forty in diameter, yet in its foundation neither water nor earth were used. To it he added a great hall of pure gold, the interior being silver and the floor of amber. On the outside he caused to be painted a picture of Jamshid [legendary first king of Persia], worshipper of moon and sun. He commanded also that Faridun [successor of Jamshid] with his bull headed mace should also be represented, and all the highest were similarly portrayed. Think who else could have executed such a masterpiece!"

Zoroastrianism preaches the existence of two contrary and coeval powers: Ahura Mazda and Angra Mainyu. Ahura Mazda is the "Wise Lord": Creator of Wisdom, Light and Truth, Maker of the Righteous Order and the Lord of Life. Angra Mainyu is the destructive spirit, or, more properly, "Demon of the Lie"; corrupter of the world, responsible for all illusions, deceptions and discord. The religion holds that creation, being a product of Ahura Mazda, was, at the beginning, essentially good. Despite its corruption by Angra Mainyu, the ethical actions of human beings have the power to redeem it and bring it back to the original blessed state. The world is a battle-ground between the two great Powers over a period of 12,000 years; the appearance of Zardusht marks the beginning of the last 3,000 years of this time, at the end of which, with the help of humans doing good acts, Ahura Mazda will overcome Angra Mainyu.

Malang, or Wandering Dervish, Mazar-i-Sharif [R. & S. Michaud]

From Ahura Mazda, certain powers emanate which have the capacity to awaken their counterparts in man. These powers, or *Amesha Spentas*, are said to be both "God" and also "of God"; they include Good Mind, Righteous Order, Divine Piety, Excellence and Immortality. Likewise, from Angra Mainyu come malignant *Daevas*: Evil Mind, False Appearance, Cowardice, Hypocrisy, Misery and Extinction.

It can thus be seen that Zardusht introduced many innovations into the sphere of religion. Beforehand, it was generally thought that the world was corrupt by nature. It was folly for mankind to believe that it could bring about any real change. Man's best chance of contentment was to acknowledge himself a hollow player in the face of the great cosmic cycle of ages. Ethical judgements, dualities and human will were meaningless in the face of the essence of the world, the "ultimate Being of beings". The way of ascent was to abstain from all activity and purge oneself of any hope of renovation.

To Zardusht more than anyone, the great monotheistic faiths owe their belief in the paramount importance of human will, free choice and ethical actions. From Zardusht, they obtain the concept that the universe is not an endless unchanging cycle, but a lineal progression from perfection, to fall, to restoration. Angels and devils in the later religions are derived from the *Amesha Spentas* and the *Daevas*, as well as notions of rewards in Heaven and torments in an impermanent hell.

The oldest scriptures of Zoroastrianism are contained in the *Avesta*. One section of this, called *Yasna*, contains the *Gathas*, or inspired hymns of Zardusht; these are written in a more archaic dialect than the rest of the Avesta, and are generally reckoned to the work of Zardusht himself. In the following hymn, *Yasna 31*, addressed both to the *Amesha Spentas* as well as the adherents of the faith, Zardusht meditates on the nature of Ahura Mazda; the necessity of following God's moral precepts and the rewards for doing so; and the punishments that will come upon those who fail to act ethically, or with regard to the truth:

1. [To the *Amesha Spentas*] Having in mind your doctrines, we utter forth words heard not by those who through the doctrines of the Evil One destroy the beings of Righteousness, but words which are most excellent for those who devote their heart unto Ahura Mazda.

2. [To the followers] Since, then, owing to these false doctrines, the better path for the soul is not clear, I am come unto you all as a judge—as Ahura Mazda knows—between the two ways, that we may live according to the law of righteousness.

3. [To Ahura Mazda] What joy will you give through Your Spirit and Your Fire, the united pair—and, as you promise through Righteousness—Thy decree for the wise-in-heart; this, may you speak unto us, that we may know it, with the word of your mouth, O Mazda, in order that I may convert all men living.

4. [To the followers] If Righteousness be strong, and Truth and Good Thinking appear, and also Reward and Piety, then through the Best Mind I will implore for myself the mighty Power by whose force we may overcome Satan.

5. [To Ahura Mazda] Tell me this, that I may discern and know it through Your Good Mind and lay it to heart, what you through Righteousness will give me as the better lot, in which my reward shall consist. Tell me even those things, Ahura Mazda, which shall or shall not be.

6. [To the followers] The very best reward shall be for the knowing man, who can tell me the real teaching concerning the truth of His completeness and Immortality: as the reward, the Kingdom of Mazda, which by his Good Mind he increases for Him.

7. Mazda who in the beginning conceived the thought to fill His heavenly realms with light—He by His wisdom founder of Righteousness (the Law), by which to keep up His Best Mind in His people; [To Ahura Mazda] may you increase these blessed realms with Your spirit, Ahura Mazda, who are even until now and forever more unchanging.

8. Therefore in the beginning, O Mazda, I conceived you to be worthy of worship when I first beheld you in a vision, as the father of the Good Mind, the very founder of the Law of Righteousness, the Lord amidst the deeds of life.

11. Since you, O Mazda, in the beginning for us formed our beings, our consciences, and our intelligence through Your Own Mind, since you made life clothed with a body, since you gave us the works and words whereby one may freely express his belief.

12. So lifts up his voice alike the false prophet and the true, the foolish and the wise, according to his heart and mind; but Piety unceasingly with Thy Spirit inquires wherever faults may be.

13. What open faults or secret ones, O Mazda, she inquires into in her search, or when on the other hand for a slight sin one seeks out for himself the greatest absolution—all these in Your eye, O All-seeing One, guardian with Righteousness, you behold.

14. Therefore I ask you, O Ahura, what is coming and is to come; what claims in the accounts above shall be made upon the righteous, and what upon the wicked, and how these will stand when the entries are balanced.

15. I ask You about this: what wrath awaits him who advanced the power for the wicked of evil deeds, O Ahura; he who cannot find his livelihood without harm to the flocks and men of the righteous husbandman.

16. About this also I enquire: how, and when, and by what deeds, he, who in wisdom devotes himself to advancing the power of the house, the district and the land through righteousness, shall become even as you, O Ahura.

17. Which of the two—that which the righteous man or the wicked man believes—is the greater? Let the enlightened to the enlightened speak, nor let the unenlightened deceive; be Thou to us, O Ahura Mazda, the revealer of Thy Good Mind.

18. Let no one of you hearken unto the words and commandments of the wicked, for the wicked man will bring house, village, district and land into distress and death. Therefore smite all such with the weapon!

19. Let each give ear to Zardusht, an enlightened healer of the world, who has conceived what is Right, O Ahura, who will have power at will over the words of his tongue—so that they will be verified through Your red Fire, O Mazda, in when Your good will fall upon both sides.

20. Whosoever comes over to the righteous, for him hereafter will be spared the long duration of misery and darkness, the evil food and woeful words—such is that life to which, O ye wicked, your conscience through your own deeds will lead you.

21. May Ahura Mazda then, out of His rich store grant unity with Weal and Immortality, with his Righteousness and Power—the full enjoyment of the Good Mind, to him who is faithful to Him in word and deed.

22. Clear are these things to the wise as to one confident in mind; it is he that in word and deed promotes Righteousness with the Good Power; it is he, O Mazda, that will be to Thee a most profitable servant.

Still in the age of legend, the banks of the River Oxus to the north of Balkh form the setting for a famous episodes from Firdousi's *Shahnameh*: the single combat between the great hero, Rustam (Rustum), and his long-lost son, Sohrab. Rustam was the son of Zal, king of the southern land of Seistan. From the moment of his birth, his exceptional strength and stature were immediately apparent. Firdousi writes of him:

The Faravahar, *or symbol of the Zoroastrian faith, from a relief at Persepolis, Iran (4th century* BC*) [A. Cassidy]*

> "Ten foster-mothers gave Rustum the milk which provides men with strength and then, when after being weaned from milk he came to eating substantial food, they gave him an abundance of bread and flesh. Five men's portions were his provision and it was a wearisome task to prepare it for him. He grew to the height of eight men so that his stature was that of a noble cypress; so high did he grow that it was as though he might become a shining star at which all the world would gaze."

In Rustam's time, the Oxus formed the boundary between Iran and its rival kingdom, Turan; against the latter, Rustam often fought in defence of Iran. On one occasion, he was hunting near this frontier when his horse, Ruksh, was stolen. Whilst pursuing its thieves, he was informed that it had been recovered by the servants of the king of Semenjan, a nearby city. Making his way there, he presented himself at the king's court, where the king's daughter, Tamineh, moved by stories of Rustam's prowess, fell in love with him. Although the King of Semenjan was a vassal of Afrasiab, King of Turan, and hence an enemy of Iran, Rustam and Tamineh were married, and a child was conceived. Rustam was called away before the child could be born, for what he thought would only be a short time; before parting, he gave his wife a stone of onyx, asking her, if the child was a son, to bind the gem on his arm, and if a daughter, in her hair. The child turned out to be a son, whom Tamineh named Sohrab. However, she feared, if Rustam were to learn he had a son, that he would send for him and leave her bereft; therefore, she sent word to him that the child was a daughter. As a result, he never returned to his wife, and never came to know his child.

Sohrab grew into a warrior as formidable as Rustam. Eventually, when he was told of his parentage, he determined to find his father. Taking an army from the king of Turan, he marched southwards, making war against Iran. He hoped, if he could force the Iranians into great difficulties, that Rustam would appear; if he did so, Sohrab intended to challenge him to a single combat, disclose his identity to him, and thus reunited, fight to secure for themselves the thrones of both Iran and Turan.

The army of Sohrab scored many successes against the Iranian forces under Iran's weak king, Kai Kaoos. Fearful that he would ultimately be defeated, he summoned Rustam, who appeared only tardily, having spent eight days feasting before responding to the call. The pair quarrelled, and Rustam would have been put to death had not Kai Kaoos been in such danger. Eventually, Rustam went reluctantly to join the Iranian camp by the Oxus. There, Sohrab called on the Iranians to put forward a champion to engage in single combat. Rustam accepted the challenge, but, still piqued at his treatment by Kai Kaoos, went out to fight under a false identity, and in disguise. A fierce and prolonged struggle ensued between the two, at the end of which—only after Sohrab had been mortally wounded—did they realise, after the onyx stone was displayed, that they were father and son.

The tale is not only told in Firdousi's *Shahnameh*. The poet Matthew Arnold, finding the story of great appeal, drew from a version that had appeared in India to write an English adaptation in blank verse called *Sohrab and Rustum*. The following excerpt describes the moment of recognition, to the death of Sohrab on the banks of the Oxus:

> He spoke; but Rustum gazed, and gazed, and stood
> Speechless; and then he utter'd one sharp cry:
> O boy—thy father!—and his voice choked there.
> And then a dark cloud pass'd before his eyes,
> And his head swam, and he sank down to earth.
> But Sohrab crawl'd to where he lay, and cast
> His arms about his neck, and kiss'd his lips,
> And with fond faltering fingers stroked his cheeks,
> Trying to call him back to life; and life
> Came back to Rustum, and he oped his eyes,
> And they stood wide with horror; and he seized
> In both his hands the dust which lay around,
> And threw it on his head, and smirch'd his hair—
> His hair, and face, and beard, and glittering arms;
> And strong convulsive groanings shook his breast,
> And his sobs choked him; and he clutch'd his sword,
> To draw it, and for ever let life out.
> But Sohrab saw his thoughts, and held his hands
> And with a soothing voice he spake, and said:

"Father, forbear! for I but meet to-day
The doom which at my birth was written down
In Heaven, and thou art Heaven's unconscious hand.
Surely my heart cried out that it was thou,
When first I saw thee; and thy heart spoke too,
I know it! but fate trod those promptings down
Under its iron heel; fate, fate engaged
The strife, and hurl'd me on my father's spear.
But let us speak no more of this! I find
My father; let me feel that I have found!
Come, sit beside me on this sand, and take
My head betwixt thy hands, and kiss my cheeks,
And wash them with thy tears, and say: My son!
Quick! quick! for number'd are my sands of life
And swift; for like the lightning to this field
I came, and like the wind I go away—
Sudden, and swift, and like a passing wind.
But it was writ in Heaven that this should be."

So said he, and his voice released the heart
Of Rustum, and his tears broke forth; he cast
His arms round his son's neck, and wept aloud,
And kiss'd him. And awe fell on both the hosts,
When they saw Rustum's grief; and Ruksh, the horse,
With his head bowing to the ground and mane
Sweeping the dust, came near, and in mute woe
First to the one then to the other moved
His head, as if enquiring what their grief
Might mean; and from his dark, compassionate eyes,
The big warm tears roll'd down, and caked the sand.
But Rustum chid him with stern voice, and said:

"Ruksh, now thou grievest; but, O Ruksh, thy feet
Should first have rotted on their nimble joints,
Or ere they brought thy master to this field!"

But Sohrab look'd upon the horse and said:

Young Horseman, Kunduz,
1975 [Y. Crowe]

"Is this, then, Ruksh? How often, in past days
My mother told me of thee, thou brave steed,
My terrible father's terrible horse! and said,
That I should one day find thy lord and thee.
Come, let me lay my hand upon thy mane!
O Ruksh, thou art more fortunate than I;
For thou has gone where I shall never go,
And snuff'd the breezes of my father's home.
And thou hast trod the sands of Seistan
And seen the River of Helmund, and the Lake
Of Zirrah; and the aged Zal himself
Has often stroked thy neck, and given thee food,
Corn in a golden platter soak'd with wine,
And said; O Ruksh! bear Rustum well!—but I
Have never known my grandsire's furrow'd face,
Nor seen his lofty house in Seistan,
Nor slaked my thirst at the clear Helmund stream;
But lodged among my father's foes, and seen
Afrasiab's cities only, Samarcand,
Bokhara, and lone Khiva in the waste,
And the black Toorkmun tents; and only drunk
The desert rivers, Moorghab and Tejend,
Kohik, and where the Kalmuks feed their sheep,
The northern Sir; and this great Oxus stream,
The yellow Oxus, by whose brink I die."

    Then, with a heavy groan, Rustum bewail'd:
"Oh, that its waves were flowing over me!
Oh, that I saw its grains of yellow silt
Roll, tumbling in the current o'er my head!"

    But, with a grave mild voice, Sohrab replied:
"Desire not that, my father! thou must live.
For some are born to do great deeds, and live,
As some are born to be obscured, and die.
Do thou the deeds I die too young to do,
And reap a second glory in thine age;

Kala Fath, on the Helmand: Citadel and Fort. By T.H. Holdich, c. 1885 [RGS]

Thou art my father, and thy gain is mine.
But come! thou seest this great host of men
Which follow me; I pray thee, slay not these!
Let me entreat for them; what have they done?
They follow'd me, my hope, my fame, my star.
Let them all cross the Oxus back in peace.
But me thou must bear hence, not send with them,
But carry me with thee to Seistan,
And place me on a bed, and mourn for me,
Thou, and the snow-hair'd Zal, and all thy friends.
And thou must lay me in that lovely earth,
And heap a stately mound above my bones,
And plant a far-seen pillar over all.
That so the passing horseman on the waste
May see my tomb a great way off, and cry:
Sohrab! the mighty Rustum's son, lies there,
Whom his great father did in ignorance kill!
And I be not forgotten in my grave."
    And, with a mournful voice, Rustum replied:
"Fear not! as thou hast said, Sohrab, my son,
So shall it be; for I will burn my tents,
And quit the host, and bear thee hence with me,
And carry thee away to Seistan,
And place thee on a bed, and mourn for thee,
With the snow-headed Zal, and all my friends.
And I will lay thee in the lovely earth,
And heap a stately mound above thy bones,
And plant a far-seen pillar over all,
And men shall not forget thee in thy grave.
And I will spare thy host; yea, let them go!
Let them all cross the Oxus back in peace!
What should I do with slaying any more?
For would that all whom I have ever slain
Might be once more alive; my bitterest foes
And they who were call'd champions in their time,

And through whose death I won that fame I have—
And I were nothing but a common man,
A poor, mean soldier, and without renown,
So thou mightest live too, my son, my son!
Or rather would that I, even I myself,
Might now be lying on this bloody sand,
Near death, and by an ignorant stroke of thine,
Not thou of mine! and I might die, not thou;
And I, not thou, be borne to Seistan;
And Zal might weep above my grave, not thine;
And say: O son, I weep thee not too sore,
For willingly, I know, thou met'st thine end!
But now in blood and battles was my youth,
And full of blood and battles is my age,
And I shall never end this life of blood."
    Then, at the point of death, Sohrab replied:
"A life of blood indeed, thou dreadful man!
But thou shalt yet have peace; only not now,
Not yet! but thou shalt have it on that day,
When thou shalt sail in a high-masted ship,
Thou and the other peers of Kai Khosroo,
Returning home over the salt blue sea,
From laying thy dear master in his grave."
    And Rustum gazed in Sohrab's face, and said:
"Soon be that day, my son, and deep that sea!
Till then, if fate so wills, let me endure."
    He spoke; and Sohrab smiled on him, and took
The spear, and drew it from his side, and eased
His wound's imperious anguish; but the blood
Came welling from the open gash, and life
Flow'd with the stream; all down his cold white side
The crimson torrent ran, dim now and soil'd,
Like the soil'd tissue of white violets
Left, freshly gather'd, on their native bank,
By children whom their nurses call with haste

Indoors from the sun's eye; his head droop'd low,
His limbs grew slack; motionless, white, he lay—
White, with eyes closed; only when heavy gasps,
Deep heavy gasps quivering through all his frame,
Convulsed him back to life, he open'd them,
And fix'd them feebly on his father's face;
Till now all strength was ebb'd, and from his limbs
Unwillingly the spirit fled away,
Regretting the warm mansion which it left,
And youth, and bloom, and this delightful world.
    So, on the bloody sand, Sohrab lay dead;
And the great Rustum drew his horseman's cloak
Down o'er his face, and sate by his dead son.
As those black granite pillars, once high-rear'd
By Jemshid in Persepolis, to bear
His house, now 'mid their broken flights of steps
Lie prone, enormous, down the mountain side—
So in the sand lay Rustum by his son.

It may be said that Balkh passes from the age of legend to that of history in the 6th century BC, with the rise of the Achaemenian Empire under the Persian King Cyrus. The city and surrounding territory formed one of his satrapies and, according to Herodotus, paid an annual tribute of 360 gold talents to his successor, Darius the Great. Herodotus also informs us that a Bactrian military contingent accompanied the later king Xerxes in his invasion of Greece in 480 BC; he notes that they wore caps and were armed with cane bows and short spears. At around this time, Balkh is thought to have become a centre of worship for Anahita, the Persian goddess of water and tutelary deity of the Oxus. The Greek geographer Strabo claims that the population of the city in this period still possessed many nomadic traits; he also passes on the report of one of his sources, Onesicritus, that those who had become helpless through sickness or old age were customarily thrown alive as prey to dogs known as "undertakers" kept specifically for that purpose. "While the land outside the walls of the metropolis of the Bactrians looks clean," he adds, "most of the land inside is full of human bones." Otherwise, it seems, the area was not wholly unpleasant. The historian Quintus Curtius writes:

> "The land of the Bactrians is of a diverse and varied nature. In some places, a great multitude of trees and vines give a plentiful harvest of rich fruits, and the fertile soil is irrigated by a large network of springs. Those areas which are milder are cultivated for grain; the rest is set aside for fodder. Beyond this, sterile sands cover a great part of the same territory; a region of terrible dryness, which supports neither man nor beast. Indeed, when the winds blow in from the Pontic Sea, they sweep together whatever sand lies on the plain; when it is all heaped together, it assumes the appearance from far off of a number of great hills, and every trace of the earlier road disappears beneath them. Therefore, those who travel across them make their way like sailors, observing the constellations at night, and plotting the course of their journey by them; and the shade at night is just as bright as daylight. Thus, during daytime the area is impassable because they can find no traces to follow, and the shining of the stars is obscured. Moreover, if the wind which rises from the sea comes down on them, it buries them in the sand. But, where the land is more pleasant, it supports a great population of men and horses."

It was this pleasant land which Alexander the Great reached in 329 BC, having crossed the Hindu Kush in pursuit of the rebel Persian Bessus and final control of the whole of Asia. Bessus had taken refuge in Balkh, where he had hoped to make a stand against Alexander's forces. However, terrified by the speed with which they had managed to traverse the Panjshir Valley and Khawak Pass, a great part of his army deserted, and Bessus himself fled with a small contingent across the Oxus. This allowed Alexander and his men a short respite between the difficulties of crossing the mountains and the hardships they were to face as they continued their chase of Bessus across the desert regions:

> "After entrusting the territory of the Bactrians to Artabazus, he left there the packs and baggage there with a garrison, whilst he himself advanced with a light-armed column into the Sogdian desert, leading his army by night. The scarcity of water… stirs up thirst through despair of finding any, before it does so by desire of drinking. For 400 stadia, not the slightest trace of water is to be found. The heat of the summer sun makes the sands hot; when they begin to

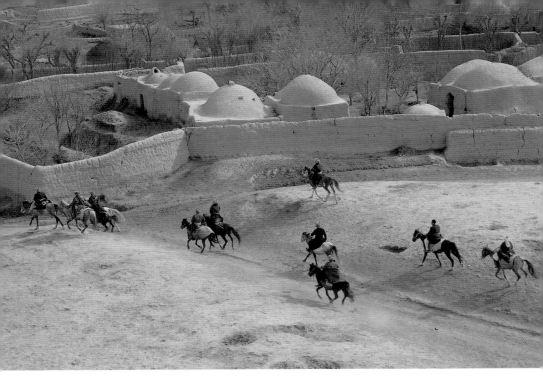

Turcoman village on the steppe North of Balkh [R. & S. Michaud]

glow, everything is burned, as if by a continuous fire. Moreover, a mist, caused by the excessive heat of the earth, obscured the light, and the plain took on the appearance of an enormous and deep sea. The journey at night seemed tolerable, as the bodies of the men were refreshed by the dew and cool of the morning. But, with the onset of day the heat returns, and dryness absorbs every drop of natural moisture; one's mouth and inner body is parched. As a result, their spirits and then their bodies began to fail, and they became reluctant to stand still or go forward. A few, who had been advised by those who knew the region, had furnished themselves with supplies of water; this kept off their thirst for a while, but as the heat rose, their desire for liquid again was kindled. Whatever wine and oil they had was greedily consumed, and such pleasure did they take in drinking, that they did not worry about a future lack of supplies. Then, heavy with their over-consumption, they were neither able to carry their weapons nor fight, and those who had no water seemed more fortunate, since those who had were compelled to vomit up what they had taken without moderation.

"The king was anxious at these troubles; however, his friends begged him to remember that it was his strength of character alone that would prove the remedy for the deficiencies of the army. At this point, two of them who had gone forward to choose a place to pitch camp returned bearing skins full of water; they intended to rush it to their sons, who were in the same column, and scarcely able to endure the thirst. When they met Alexander, one of them opened a skin and filled a cup which he was carrying, offering it to the king. He inquired for whom the water was intended; when they replied that it was for their sons, he returned the cup full, as it had been given to him, saying 'I cannot bear to drink alone, nor can I divine such a small amount amongst everyone; hurry and give to your children what you have brought by your own efforts.'

"At length, Alexander reached the river Oxus at around sunset. However, a great part of the army had been unable to keep up with him; he therefore ordered fires to be lit on a high hill to indicate to those who were following with difficulty that they were not far from the camp. Those who were at the front of the column, having strengthened themselves with food and water, filled

Raft made of inflated skins, Kunar River, Nuristan [R. & S. Michaud]

skins, containers, and whatever else they could find that would hold water, and went to aid the stragglers. But those who had imbibed earlier with little moderation, died through choking fits; a greater number were lost in this way than perished in any battle. Alexander himself, still clad in his breastplate, refusing to take any food or drink, stood on the way by which the army was coming, not going to refresh himself until the whole column had gone past. Later, he spent a sleepless night with a greatly troubled mind. Nor was he in better spirits on the next day as he had no boats, and was not able to raise a bridge over the river, as the land all around was bare and lacking particularly in timber. He therefore adopted the only solution that necessity allowed him: he distributed as many skins as possible, stuffed with straw; lying on these, they swam across the river, with those who had crossed first remaining on guard until the rest had crossed. In this way, he brought his whole army across the river in five days."

Having crossed the Oxus, Alexander made an extraordinary discovery: a community of Greeks who, for over a century and a half, had been in exile in the depths of Asia. His response to this find was equally astonishing:

"While Alexander and his forces were pursuing Bessus, they arrived at a small town; it was inhabited by the Branchidae. They, at one time, had lived at Miletus, but left at the order of Xerxes as he was retreating from his invasion of Greece; to please him, they had desecrated the temple known as the Didymeon, and he had settled them in this distant spot. They had not yet departed from their ancestral Greek customs, but were already bilingual, degenerating little by little from their original tongue under external influence. They greeted Alexander with great joy, surrendering to him both their city, as well as themselves. Alexander called together a meeting of the Milesians who were serving with him; they bore a long-standing hatred for the race of the Branchidae. The King said that he would allow the Milesian contingent, who had been betrayed by these people in Xerxes' time, to do as they saw fit to the Branchidae—whether they would prefer to remember their common ancestry, or else the betrayal. However, since they could not agree amongst themselves, he eventually decreed that he would do as he himself saw fit.

"The next day, having met the Branchidae, he ordered them to go with him, and when they had reached the city, he himself entered the gate with a light-armed company. The phalanx was ordered to surround the walls, and, when a signal was given, to plunder the city—a hideout for traitors—and to slaughter them to the last man. The inhabitants were unarmed, and everywhere there was butchery; neither their common language, nor prayers, nor olive branches held out to the attackers were able to prevent the cruelty. At length, so that the walls could be pulled down, their foundations were undermined, so that no even the slightest trace of the city would remain. Moreover, their woods and their sacred groves were not only cut down, but also utterly uprooted, so that, nothing but a vast and sterile desert wilderness would be left behind.

"If this revenge had been brought against the original authors of the betrayal, it would have been just, and not at all cruel; now, however, people who had never even seen Miletus, were now being compelled to pay for the sins of their forebears."

In this final part of the pursuit, the only real bloodshed was amongst the Branchidae; Bessus was betrayed by his companions, sentenced to death by Alexander in Balkh in the winter of 329–28 BC (his greatest offence being the murder of his own king, Darius), and sent to Ecbatana for execution in the presence of an assembly of Medes and Persians. Alexander was afterwards compelled to mount a further campaign in the Transoxiana region, founding cities and suppressing dissent, before turning his attention south towards India. One notable event which took place whilst he was still in the area was his marriage to a local princess, Roxanne (Roxane). Different accounts are given by different historians; this version is also drawn from Quintus Curtius:

Turcoman wedding, 1973
[R. & S. Michaud]

"Alexander came to the region governed by Oxyartes, a noble satrap, who submitted himself to the power and good faith of the king. Alexander allowed him to continue in government, asking from him only that two of the satrap's three sons should serve him as soldiers. Oxyartes delivered to him also the last son who was with him, and prepared a banquet of oriental magnificence, at which he entertained the king. While this was being enjoyed with great friendliness, he ordered thirty noble virgins to be brought in. Amongst these was his own daughter, Roxanne, who possessed a beauty and dignity of bearing that was uncommon amongst barbarians. Although she went forward amongst an elect group, the eyes of all were on her, particularly those of the king, who was now not so much a master of his desires thanks to the constant indulgence of fortune (against whom no man is sufficiently on his guard.) Once, Alexander had looked on Darius' wife and daughters—who alone could compare with Roxanne in beauty—with no other feeling than that of a parent. Now, he was so transported with love for this girl—of ignoble stock in comparison with the royal blood—that he said it was necessary for the Persians and Macedonians to be joined together in wedlock, so that his empire may be made more stable. He added that by this way alone could the shame of the conquered and the pride of the victors both be banished. Achilles also, from whom he traced his descent, married a captive; so that the conquered did not think that wrong was being done to them, he desired to be joined with her in lawful wedlock.

"The father was elated with joy at the king's unexpected announcement, and Alexander, in the height of his ardour, called for a piece of bread to be brought, according to his own country's customs—this was amongst the Macedonians a most sacred pledge of those contracting marriage—which was divided using a sword and tasted by each. I suppose that those who established this Macedonian custom wished to show, by means of an everyday and common food, that those joining together their wealth should be content with their lot. In this way, the King of Asia and Europe took in matrimony a woman who had been brought in as a party entertainment, intending to raise from a captive one who would rule over victors."

After Alexander's death in Babylon in 323 BC, his empire began to break up into its constituent parts. Following around 15 years of confusion and struggle, the eastern territories from Syria to India fell to one of his generals, Seleucus. Under him and his successors, known as the Seleucids, Bactria was governed as a province by a series of unknown satraps or deputies. However, as time went on, the area became progressively more autonomous; by around 250 BC, it appears to have evolved into an independent entity ruled by a king named Diodotus.

It is difficult to know what to say about this new Greek kingdom standing alone in the middle of Asia. Scarcely any literary evidence has been preserved, and most of the historical data we possess about it is derived from archaeological finds and the remarkably fine coins minted by it over its relatively brief existence. The dates and even names of its kings are still putative, and the whole nature of the enterprise is the subject of continual academic debate. One of the pioneering scholars of Graeco-Bactrian studies, W.W. Tarn, argued that the kingdom was the best realisation of Alexander's dream: a place where foreigners and Greeks lived together in an equal brotherhood, learning and practising the Hellenistic arts of civilisation as imported from the Mediterranean. Other more recent experts hold that this view is too rose-tinted. Not only did the Greek settlers there live in a climate of political and civil instability, at conflict amongst themselves as well as with the Seleucid Empire; they also lived under the constant threat of invasion from the barbarian nomads. They cared little for teaching the arts of civilisation to the Bactrians, preferring instead to stress their foreignness in order to prevent themselves from embracing, like the Branchidae, native customs. Indeed, their whole concern was to preserve their Greek way of life in the midst of this distant and hostile region. The rediscovery in

1964 of a Greek city near the modern village of Ai Khanoum (perhaps the settlement of Alexandria Oxiana) at the junction of the Oxus and River Kokcha appears to support this latter hypothesis: enormous pains had been taken to recreate, hundreds of miles from Greece, the typical Greek *polis*. The only theatre east of Babylon, cut into the mountainside by the side of the main street, a gymnasium, wrestling-ground and library all served to affirm the identity of the inhabitants. A shrine, or heroön, dedicated to one Kineas, reputed founder of the city, engraved with maxims brought by the philosopher Klearchos from the Oracle of Apollo at Delphi— "As a child, be wise; as a youth, be self-controlled; as an adult, be just; as an elder, be wise; as one dying, be without pain"—tied this far-flung outpost firmly to the heart of the Greek religious world. Olive oil was imported from the west, wine was made in the city itself and Ionic and Corinthian column capitals were carved from local stone as a substitute for marble. Native citizens seem to have lived apart from the Greeks, and, in 200 BC, further lines of defence were built against the danger of attack from the indigenous wandering tribes.

It appears that this peculiar kingdom flourished for some time, even extending its influence south of the Hindu Kush, where its generals ruled over petty Indo-Greek states until around AD 10. However, the Greek Kingdom in Bactria itself was overwhelmed after 150 BC by successive invasions of the Sakae and Yueh-Chih— Central Asian tribes, probably displaced by the unification of China. Of these, the latter seem to have taken control of Bactra, eventually making it a leading city of the Buddhist Kushan Empire.

In 130 BC, a Chinese diplomat named Chang-Kien (Zhang Qian) travelled through the region of Bactria, exploring the prospects in the area for trade and diplomatic alliances. His brief notice of Balkh throws some light on this period of Greek collapse, whilst also stressing the continuing prominence of the city as a major commercial hub:

> "Ta-hia (Bactria) is more than 2000 *li* (600 miles) to the southwest of Yüan, on the south bank of the K'ui-shui (Oxus). The people have fixed abodes and live in walled cities and regular houses like the people of Yüan. They have no great king or chief, but everywhere the cities and towns have their own petty chiefs.

(Left) La Genie aux Fleurs, *E. Afghanistan, 3rd–4th centuries* AD; (top) *Head of a Barbarian, E. Afghanistan, Kushan Period. [Musée Guimet]*

While the people are shrewd traders, their soldiers are weak and afraid to fight, so that, when the Yueh-Chih migrated westward, they made war on the Ta-hia, who became subject to them. The population of Ta-hia may amount to more than a million. Their capital is called Lan-shï (Balkh), and it has markets for the sale of all sorts of merchandise. To the southeast of it is the country Shön-tu (India). Chang K'ien says in his report to the Emperor: 'When I was in Ta-hia, I saw a stick of bamboo of Kiung (Kiung-chou in Ssï-ch'uan), and some cloth of Shu (Ssï-ch'uan). When I asked the inhabitants how they had obtained possession of these, they replied: 'The inhabitants of our country by them in Shön-tu.' Shön-tu may be several thousand *li* to the southeast of Ta-hia…"

Bearded man and sheep, Kunduz, 1975 [Y. Crowe]

Throughout its time under the Kushan Empire and its successor, the Hephthalites or White Huns, Balkh continued prosperous thanks to its position on the trade routes. It is referred to briefly around AD 545 in a work named *Topographia Christiana* by Cosmas Monachus, who claims that "among the Bactrians… there is an infinite number of churches with bishops, and a vast multitude of Christian people, and they have many martyrs and recluses leading a monastic life." The Chinese traveller, Hsuen-Tsang, who visited Balkh around AD 630 on the eve of the Islamic invasion, leaves us a description of the city with particular reference to its opulent Buddhist monuments:

"This country is about 800 *li* (250 miles) from east to west, and 400 *li* (125 miles) from north to south; on the north it borders on the Oxus. The capital is about 20 *li* (6 miles) in circuit. It is called generally the little Rajagriah. This city, though strongly fortified, is thinly populated. The products of the soil are extremely varied, and the flowers, both on the land and water, would be difficult to enumerate. There are about 100 convents and 3,000 monks, who all study the religious teaching of the little vehicle.

"Outside the city, towards the southwest, there is a convent called Navasangharama, which was built by a former king of this country. The Masters (of Buddhism), who dwell to the north of the great Snowy Mountains, and are authors of Sastras, occupy this convent only, and continue their estimable labours in it. There is a figure of Buddha here, which is lustrous with noted gems, and the hall in which it stands is also adorned with precious substances of rare value. This is the reason why it has often been robbed by chieftains of neighbouring countries, covetous of gain.

"This convent also contains a statue of Pishamen (Vaisravana) Deva, by whose spiritual influence, in unexpected ways, there is protection afforded to the precincts of the convent. Lately the son of the Khan Yeh-hu, belonging to the Turks, becoming rebellious, Yeh-hu Khan broke up his camping ground, and marched at the head of his horde to make a foray against this convent, desiring to obtain the jewels and precious things with which it was enriched. Having encamped his army in the open ground, not far from the convent, in the night he had a dream. He saw Vaisravana Deva, who addressed him thus: 'What power do you possess that you dare to overthrow this convent?' and then hurling his lance, he transfixed him with it. The Khan, affrighted, awoke, and his heart penetrated with sorrow, he told his dream to his followers, and then, to atone somewhat for his fault, he hastened to the convent to ask permission to confess his crime to the priests; but before he received an answer he died.

"Within the convent, in the southern hall of Buddha, there is the washing-basin which Buddha used. It contains about ten pints, and is of various colours, which dazzle the eyes. It is difficult to name the gold and stone of which it is made. Again, there is a tooth of Buddha about an inch long, and about eight or nine tenths of an inch in breadth. Its colour is yellowish white; it is pure and shining. Again, there is the sweeping brush of Buddha, made of the 'Ka-she' (kasa). It is about two feet long and about seven inches round. Its handle is ornamented with various gems. These three relics are presented with offerings on each of the six fast-days by the assembly of lay and cleric believers. Those who have the greatest faith in worship see the objects emitting a radiance of glory."

The first attempt by the Arab Muslims to conquer Balkh is thought to have been made in the reign of the third Caliph, Othman, around AD 653 (AH 32). During this time, the famous Buddhist monastery of Nowbahar is believed to have been destroyed, but little progress was made against the city itself on account of its strenuous opposition; further attacks led to it being largely ruined. An Arab garrison was built a short distance away at Baruqan, but after 725 Balkh was lavishly rebuilt and returned to its former prosperity. Towards the end of the 9th century AD it formed a part of the Samanid Empire, ruled from its capital Bokhara; under their control and that of their successors, the Ghaznavids and the Seljuks, Balkh became a major centre for the study of the arts and sciences.

One of the more remarkable characters to have been produced by the city in the Samanid period was Rabia Qozdari (or Balkhi), the first poetess known to have written verse in Persian. According to somewhat uncertain sources, she was the daughter of Kab, son of Harita, an Arab who acted principally as governor of Balkh. A 19th century Iranian poet, Hidayat, describes her as "The Jewel of the Arabs… With her beauty, grace, merits, perfection and knowledge, she was unique at her time, the pearl of her epoch…" Tradition relates that she was a mystic, and that she engendered in herself a platonic love for one of her brother's slaves, Bektash, in order that she might better understand the love of God. The poet Jami writes "The Sheik Abu Sa'id ibn Abi'Khayr said that Ka'b's daughter was in love with a slave; but according to great mystics this word cannot be applied to a creature of this earthly world; it applies to another world. One day, this slave, meeting the girl all suddenly, seized her sleeve. She cried: 'Is it not enough for you that I, being with God and inflamed with love for Him, have projected that love into you? And you ask me to love you with profane love!'" Legend relates that Rabia's brother, unjustly believing her to be guilty of adultery with this slave, stabbed her to death; using her blood, she wrote on the wall her final verses.

Portrait of a Turcoman woman, 1979, N. Afghanistan [R. & S. Michaud]

Few of her poems, which are primarily love lyrics, survive. Of the two translations below, one is an example of a *molamma*, or poem made up of alternating Arabic and Persian couplets:

> You make me patient in love with your ruses; what
> Excuse will you make when you appear in front of God?
> Even if I rebelled against my faith, I would not dare
> to rebel against my love for you.
> I do not want the delights of paradise without you,
> but with you even hell would suit me.
> Because sugar without you tastes like poison and
> with you poison is sweet like honey.
> Do not trust a beautiful face: in a few days, even if
> it were as beautiful as the planet Saturn, it will be
> covered with the first down.
> In any case what the sage says is by no means untrue:
> 'He who becomes too proud one day will fall
> the lower the higher he is.'

> [Arabic] *I noticed one of the birds that cried.*
> *It roused my sorrow and my memories.*

> [Persian] *When the night had passed, the bird perched in a branch*
> *continued to lament and wail bitterly.*

> [Arabic] *I asked it: 'Why do you wail and weep*
> *in the dead of the night when the stars shine?'*

> [Persian] *'I bewail my departed friend.'*
> *'Why wail if you are with a friend who helps you?*
> *I do not say anything, though I shed my wails and my blood,*
> *You who do not shed anything, why do you speak?'*

Balkh's prosperity lasted until the arrival of the Mongols in 1220. Some of the city's estimated population of 200,000 flew westwards before their arrival (including the 12-year-old Jalal-al-din Rumi, who was to become one of the greatest of the Persian mystical poets); many others were slaughtered in the utter destruction of the city by Genghis Khan. One of the first descriptions of its ruins comes from Marco Polo:

The walls of Balkh [B. Woodburn]

"Balkh is a noble city and great, though it was much greater in former days. But the Tartars and other nations have greatly ravaged and destroyed it. There were formerly many fine palaces and buildings of marble, and the ruins of them still remain. The people of the city tell that it was here that Alexander took to wife the daughter of Darius."

In 1333 the Arab traveller Ibn Battuta also visited the wasted city, giving some impression of its past glory as well as further details of Genghis Khan's depredations

"Next we crossed the river Jaihun (Oxus) into the land of Khurasan, and marched for a day and a half after leaving Tirmidh and crossing the river through uninhabited desert and sands to the city of Balkh. It is completely dilapidated and uninhabited, but anyone seeing it would think it to be inhabited because of the solidity of its construction (for it was a vast and important city), and its mosques and colleges preserve their outward appearance even now, with the inscriptions on their buildings incised with lapis-blue paints...

"The accursed Genghis devastated this city and pulled down about a third of its mosque because of a treasure which he was told lay under one of its

columns. It is one of the finest and most spacious mosques in the world; the mosque of Ribat al-Fath in the Maghrib resembles it in the size of its columns, but the mosque of Balkh is more beautiful than it in all other respects.

"I was told by a certain historian that the mosque at Balkh was built by a woman whose husband was governor of Balkh for the Abbasid Caliphs, and was called Da'ud bin Ali. It happened that the Caliph on one occasion, in a fit of anger against the people of Balkh for some rebellious act on their part, sent an agent to the to exact a crushing indemnity from them. On his arrival in Balkh, the women and the children of the city came to this woman who had built the mosque (i.e. the wife of the governor) and complained of the situation and the suffering which they had to endure because of this indemnity. Thereupon she sent to the Amir who had come to levy this tax on them a garment of her own, embroidered with jewels and of a value greater than the indemnity that he had been ordered to collect, with a message to him saying 'Take this robe to the Caliph, for I give it to him as alms on behalf of the people of Balkh, in view of their poverty.' So he went off with it to the Caliph, laid the robe before him, and related the story to him. The Caliph was covered with shame and exclaiming 'Shall the woman be more generous than we?' commanded him to annul the indemnity extracted from the inhabitants of Balkh, and to return there to restore the woman's robe to her. He also remitted one year's taxes to the people of Balkh. When the Amir returned to Balkh, he went to the woman's dwelling, related to her what the Caliph had said, and gave the robe back to her. Then she said to him, 'Did the Caliph's eye light upon this robe?' He said 'Yes.' She said 'I shall not wear a robe upon which there has lighted the eye of any man other than those within the forbidden degrees of relationship to me.' She ordered the robe to be sold and built with its price the mosque, the hospice, and a convent for Sufi devotees opposite it, [which] is still in habitable condition today. After the buildings were completed there remained of the price of the robe as much as one-third, and the story goes that she ordered it to be buried under one of the columns of the mosque, that it might be available and come to light if it should be needed. This tradition was related to Genghis, who gave orders in consequence to pull down the columns in the mosque. After about a third had been pulled down without finding anything, he left the rest as they were."

The area around Balkh, in the north of present-day Afghanistan, is known as Afghan Turkestan. It is now predominantly inhabited by the Uzbeks, a Turkic people who are reputed to be descendants of the followers of Uzbek Khan, a 14th century chief of the Golden Horde. They passed over into the area mainly during the 15th century, as the Timurids attempted to revive the fortunes of Balkh, and still make up one of Afghanistan's most significant minority populations. In the early 19th century, the English explorer Sir Alexander Burnes travelled extensively around Balkh and recorded some of his impressions of these people:

> "Men here sell their wives, if they get tired of them. This is by no means uncommon: but the man is obliged to make the first offer of her to her family, naming the price, which if they do not give, he is at liberty to sell her to anyone else. On the death of a man his wives all become the property of his next brother; who may marry them or sell them, giving the pre-option, as before, to their own families.

> "Jandad, a Kabuli Attari, to whom I spoke of the custom of selling wives, which I did not entirely credit, said 'I'll tell you what happened to myself. I was one day returning from Khanabad; and, being overtaken by darkness, halted for the night at Turnab, three kos short of this. After feeding my horse and going to the house for shelter, I found three men busily engaged; and, inquiring the subject of their conversation, was told that one of them was selling his wife to the other, but that they had not agreed about terms. Meantime, Khusa Berdi Ming, Bashi and chief of the village, came in, and

Portrait of a Turcoman woman, 1973, N. Afghanistan [R. & S. Michaud]

whispered to me that, if I could go halves with him, he would purchase the woman, as he had seen her, and found her very beautiful. I agreed, upon which we purchased her for seventy rupees, thirty-five each, and she went home with me for that night. Next morning Khusa Berdi came, and said that partnership in a woman was a bad thing, and asked me how I intended to manage. I said she should stay with me one month, and then go to him next. To that he would be no means agree; because, if sons or daughters were born, there would be disputes to know to whom they belonged. 'In short', said he, 'either do you give me five rupees profit on my share, and take her altogether, or I will give you the same profit on your share and she shall be altogether mine.' To this latter alternative I consented; and she is now living with him, as every one well knows.

"A man who has a daughter marriageable must give intimation of it to the Mir, who sends his chief eunuch to inspect her: if handsome, he takes her; if not, he gives permission that she should marry another.

"A child is circumcised at the age of seven or ten years. This is a time of greatest festivity among the Uzbeks; and on such occasions considerable expense in incurred, and feasts given which last fifteen or twenty days. The eating is truly enormous; but, indeed, to our ideas, it is always so: two Uzbeks not unfrequently devouring an entire sheep, with a proportional quantity of rice, bread, ghee, etc, between them; and afterwards cramming in water-melons, musk-melons, or other fruit: but these they say go for nothing, being only water. On the occasions to which I have referred horse-racing is a favourite amusement, and the horses for the purpose are generally trained for a fortnight or three weeks preceding; and they require this, for a race here is not a matter of one or two mile heats, but a regular continued run for twenty or twenty five kos (forty or fifty miles) across the country, sometimes wading through morasses and swimming rivers, but more frequently crossing their magnificent extended plains; one of which, as level as our best race-courses and

Buzkashi being played near the Bala Hissar
at Kabul, 1972 [B. Woodburn]

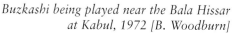

with a beautiful green turf covering, not unfrequently extends the entire distance to be run. The scene set on these occasions is highly animated, as not only the racers, generally about twenty in number, set off, but the whole of the sporting assembly, perhaps 100, or even 500 in number, accompany them, at least for the first three or four miles. A judge has been sent on in advance; and the competitors seldom return till the next day. The prizes are certainly worth some exertion; and in one case, when the donor was a man of good substance, they were as follows: the first, and most classical, was a young maiden, generally a Hazara or Chitrali, both prized for their personal attractiveness; the second, fifty sheep; the third, a boy; the fourth, a horse; the fifth, a camel; the sixth, a cow; and the seventh, a water-melon, the winner of which becomes an object of ridicule and banter for the rest of the meeting.

"Another and more amusing kind of race is the following: One man places a goat on the horse before him, and sets off at full gallop; fifteen or twenty others immediately start off after him, and whichever of these can seize the goat, and get safe off with it beyond the reach of the rest, retains it for his prize.

The rapidity with which the goat sometimes changes masters is very laughable; but the poor animal is occasionally torn to pieces in the scuffle."

The Hungarian traveller, Ármin Vámbéry, who travelled in the area during the 1860s, made a collection of some Uzbek sayings:

"If you cling to two boats, you are sure to drown."

"Shame is worse than death."

"Tears from the heart can start a blind man weeping."

"It is bad for a horse to be thin, and a soldier to be in a foreign land."

"The young man *may* die, but the old man *must*."

"If you are frightened for the sparrows, don't sow millet."

"I'm talking to you, my daughter, although my sister-in-law should hear."

"A donkey without a load feels like tasting a rest."

"Thick smoke only rises from a thick log."

"Better a living mouse than a dead lion."

"Whom God has beaten the Prophet will poke with his stick."

"Animals lick, men address each other."

"Animals are held by their horns, men by their words."

"An open mouth does not hunger for long."

"God would lead even the prophet Elijah astray."

"Do not rejoice for the new-fallen snow, for bitter cold follows it. Do not rejoice over the priest's visit, he wants something from you."

"If drinking doesn't satisfy you, licking never will."

"If the hand could give all that the tongue promises, there would be no beggars and all men would be princes."

"Two mullahs are worth one man; one mullah is worth a woman."

"If you look for blood you'll find the vein."

"Travelling is good, however long the journey."

"A virgin is beautiful, however ugly she is."

In 1933, Robert Byron visited Balkh as part of his quest to reach the River Oxus, then out of bounds to foreign travellers on account of the mutual distrust between the USSR and British India:

"After Akcha (Aq Chah), the colour of the landscape changed from lead to aluminium, pallid and deathly, as if the sun had been sucking away its gaiety for thousands and thousands of years; for this was now the plain of Balkh, and Balkh they say is the oldest city in the world. The clumps of green trees, the fountain-shaped tufts of coarse cutting grass, stood out almost black against this mortal tint. Sometimes we saw a field of barley; it was ripe, and Turcomans, naked down to the waist, were reaping it with sickles. But it was not brown or gold, telling of Ceres, of plenty. It seemed to have turned prematurely white, like the hair of a madman—to have lost its nourishment. And from these acred cerements, first on the north and then on the south of the road, rose the worn grey-white shapes of a bygone architecture, mounds, furrowed and bleached by the rain and sun, wearier than any human works I ever saw: a twisted pyramid, a tapering platform, a clump of battlements, a crouching beast, all familiars of the Bactrian Greeks, and of Marco Polo after them. They ought to have vanished. But the very impact of the sun, calling out the obstinacy of their ashen clay, has conserved some inextinguishable spark of form, a spark such as

Desolation within the walls of Balkh [B. Woodburn]

a Roman earthwork or a grass-grown barrow has not, which still flickers on against a world brighter than itself, tired as only a suicide frustrated can be tired.

"Yet by degrees the country became greener, pasture covered the adamant earth, trees multiplied, and suddenly a line of bony dilapidated walls jumped out of the ground and occupied the horizon. Passing inside them, we found ourselves amid a vast metropolis of ruins stretching away to the north; while on the south of the road, the shining greens of mulberries, poplars, and stately isolated planes were balm to eyes bruised by the monstrous antiquity of the preceding landscape. We stood in Balkh herself, the Mother of Cities.

Citadel of Balkh from the air, 1967 [Y. Crowe]

"Our guard, surveying the ruins, which were mostly left in this state by Genghis Khan, remarked: 'It was a beautiful place till the Bolsheviks destroyed it eight years ago.'"

BALKH AND THE ROAD TO OXIANA: TRAVEL INFORMATION

PUL-I-KUMRI VIA THE SALANG TUNNEL

The town of Pul-i-Kumri is often used as an overnight stop on a journey from Kabul to the northern cities and Afghan Turkestan, but I would recommend Baghlan instead, 22 kilometres beyond towards Kunduz (see below, p. 292). The road is good, and takes you across the Hindu Kush[1] through the Salang Tunnel (renovated in 2004), which at 3,363 m (11,030 feet) is claimed by Afghans to be the highest road tunnel in the world. It was built by the Russians in 1965 and proved an extremely convenient route for Soviet tanks in 1979. Its construction suggests that the Russophobes like Lord Curzon were right and a Russian invasion of the country had been long planned. Until this tunnel was built, northern Afghanistan was effectively isolated from the south during the winter when the other passes froze.

During the civil war that followed the Soviet retreat in 1989, the Salang Tunnel became a strategic prize for almost every faction and the tunnel was repeatedly mined, re-mined and blocked by explosions at its northern end. When I first travelled through the Salang in 2002, small side tunnels were still mined, but the main tunnel is reputed to be safe no. Like the Anjuman Pass, the Salang marks the watershed between Central Asia and the Indian subcontinent, between the Oxus and the Indus River systems.

This dividing line becomes obvious when one has descended from the mountains. The traveller is now in Central Asia proper. Almost everything is different from the dry, dusty India plain that forms southern Afghanistan, with its Pashto speakers. Now one is in Tajik country;[2] the lingua franca is Dari; the countryside is formed of the soft, sensuous hills formed round rocky outcrops made from loess, the fertile dust blown in over millennia from Central Asia. Rice, hemp and wheat grow easily, and the finest *buzkashi* horses bred here. In the spring, the hills in the north are a startling green colour and carpet-patterned with red tulips and asphodels.

There are two villages where one can stop, either for the night or simply to explore the new world that you have entered. One is Malkhan, with a chaikhana, the other Khinjan, with an old *Klub* (club). Both are lovely places, shaded by mulberry trees and with a view of the tremendous mountains that one has just crossed. At Khinjan, the road divides and its eastward branch leads up the Anderab Valley to the Khawak Pass, which leads over the Hindu Kush into the Panjshir. This pass is of great historical interest. It was used by Massoud during the civil war to transport Russian-supplied arms from his stronghold in northern Afghanistan (his headquarters was, until 2000, at Taloqan) into the Panjshir Valley, his home and redoubt throughout the Soviet and Taliban wars. 2,300 years previously, Alexander used it during one of his most astonishing military achievements, leading (literally by personal example) his army across in the middle of winter and descending on Bessus like the wolf on the fold. Bessus had smugly and stupidly assumed that such a march was impossible in winter. He had underestimated Alexander—as Darius had done—and his troops were massacred; Alexander ordered Bessus's ears and nose to be cut off, the traditional Persian punishment for treason. By now Alexander saw himself as the rightful King of Asia, and was determined to play the role, to the dismay of many of his Macedonian companions.[3]

The Anderab River has good trout fishing.

Further north, one comes to the town of Doshi, where the road forks again. Westwards lies Bamiyan and the Ajar Valley along the Surkhab River, a valley made beautiful by its opium poppy crops.

PUL-I-KUMRI

Find a number of hotels and chaikhanas here. Most prominent is the Zadran Hotel. It is clean and comfortable, with a fine bathroom, but the management claim (no doubt mendaciously) that the police prevent them from hiring the $20 rooms to foreigners but have to put them in identical but "safer" rooms at $30. The hotel has a huge marble-floored dining room with a shelf along two sides on which Afghan men are stacked neatly, wrapped in brown patous or white sheets, to sleep. It serves good boiled dumplings (*mantu*).

Mahmad Niyaz, 'the man with the rose', Tashkurgan [R. & S. Michaud]

Market—fish stall, Kunduz, 1975 [Y. Crowe]

The only attraction I have been able to find in Pul-i-Kumri is a hot spring, something that is always welcome in Afghanistan. This spring is just beyond the bridge over the Anderab, on the left, as one leaves the town. A little rill of hot water runs from the rocks down into the river and five showers are supplied from it. The cost is 20 afs. The spring has attributed to it curative properties that, if true, would knock the BVM at Lourdes off her pedestal. It is called Cheshmi Shifar, or Healthy Spring, and the custodian said, "When somebody is going to wash their body, they will not become ill, you know."

A nice chaikhana with its own garden and flat lawn stands on the river bank—an ideal campsite; also a shop operating out of a blue sea container.

The road out of Pul-i-Kumri passes through exceptionally fertile countryside, much of it growing cotton, which was once a big export industry centred on Kunduz. Just south of Pul-i-Kumri is a major junction where the road splits. The right fork goes to Kunduz, Taloqan and Ai Khanoum, the left to Mazar-i-Sharif, the capital of Afghan Turkestan.

FROM PUL-I-KUMRI TO MAZAR-I-SHARIF AND BALKH SAMANGAN (295 KM)

Keep straight on at the roundabout in Pul-i-Kumri for Samangan, another lovely little town with few cars, most transport by droshky and the streets lined with plane trees. One feels in touch with Kipling's India.

The sight to be seen here is the complex of Buddhist caves known as Takht-i-Rustam (Rustam's Throne). Afghanistan has a number of places with the same name, Rustam being the main character in the Persian national epic, the *Shahnameh* (Book of Kings), and he makes a famous appearance in English literature in Matthew Arnold's *Sohrab and Rustum*. The opening description of the "Chorasmian wastes" (an Anglicisation of the ancient kingdom of Kwarezm) is surely one of the reasons why the Oxus has always seemed such a romantic travel destination to British travellers.

The poem is worth reading. It articulates one of the basic folktales studied by structural anthropologists, in this case an inversion of the Oedipus myth: Rustam volunteers as his army's champion and is killed in single combat by a man who turns out to be his father.

The Rustam aetiology has been grafted onto a much earlier Buddhist shrine. Now that Bamiyan has been destroyed, this is undoubtedly the most important Buddhist site in Afghanistan, the one most evocative of the Kushan Buddhist period.

Entrance to the site is $5, payable to the guardian, who can produce a letter of accreditation from the Ministry of Culture. The sign at the entrance is a classic: "Takht-i-Rustam is one of historical places in Afghanistan and according to some quotations the construction of it began early of Christmas and lasted in the last half of the fourth century. The wedding party of Takhmina with Rustam was in this place."

The shrine is a stupa—the earliest burial mounds that contained relics of the Buddha (and other treasures). Originating in India and later spreading to Sri Lanka, these domed structures became more elaborate over time, eventually evolving into pagodas. A stupa forms the centrepiece of a Buddhist religious complex; the one here is particularly interesting for being carved entirely out of the rock. What must have been a jagged peak has been levelled, a gigantic inverted pudding basin carved as the stupa by means of an excavated trench 30 feet deep and a square shrine carved on the summit containing a small room that would have held the reliquary. It is a similar construction to the famous rock-hewn underground churches at Lalibela in Ethiopia, though this resemblance is presumably entirely coincidental.

The carved building at the top, known as "Rustam's throne", gives its name to the entire complex. On the top is a hole—technically known as a *harmika*—which would have held the pole of a large umbrella, or *chatra*. But post-Buddhist legend explains it as a bowl from which Rustam would drink wine, which is not only obviously un-Islamic but also extremely inconvenient. A wooden bridge takes you across the chasm excavated to form the stupa and allows the visitor to see how precisely and carefully the work has been executed. You can enter into the harmika and see the small chamber that would have contained a relic of the Buddha. Dupree points out that this open display is unusual, and certainly in Sri Lanka the relics are buried in the very centre of the dome, which is usually constructed of earth and plaster. Elsewhere in Afghanistan the practice of burying relics has led to most of the stupas being excavated and robbed.

Descending the outcrop, one comes to a wide passageway that conducted pilgrims to the base of the stupa. They would then have processed clockwise around the dome, and doing so allows the modern visitor to marvel at how such an amazing piece of work could have been produced by the simple tools available in the 4th century AD. Around the base are ledges and a large cave in which pilgrims and holy men stayed or lived.

Dupree dates this structure to the 4th and 5th centuries AD and its destruction to the Hephthalites.

Below the stupa is a series of five caves hollowed out of the rock, where the monks lived. This is similar to the great complex at Bamiyan, though the limestone here is very much harder than the flood-laid composite from which Bamiyan was carved.

Taking the caves in order, as shown in the plan:

Cave 1 is self-contained, about 9 m (30 feet) wide. The dome reaches 12 m (40 feet) high and is carved with a beautiful lotus flower, now sadly obscured by soot from fires kindled in the cave. Legend attributes this to be the room of Rustam's mother.

Cave 2 is a long thin corridor off of which the monks' living quarters are carved. The corridor has an arched roof and is lit by light filtering in through openings that act as windows, giving the same contemplative feel as a Benedictine monastic cloister.

Cave 3 has a barrel-vaulted antechamber with niches, also badly obscured by soot. This corridor leads into a beautiful square room leading upwards into a domed roof by means of ornamental squinches. An attempt has been made here to clean off the soot and gives a better idea of the original effect. The four large niches on each wall would have held images of the Buddha, but most interesting is that over each niche is a simple but classically perfect Doric column—another example of the Buddhist-Greek cultural fusion initiated by Alexander, which gave rise to the glorious Gandharan school of art.

Cave 4 is a bathroom judging from the square pool in the centre of the entrance chamber, and the large room off the corridor seems to have benches along the sides, making it appear very much like a *hammam* (bath house).

Cave 5 is, apparently, regarded by experts as a toilet block, of interest only to the most obsessive sightseer, and is probably something on which the muse of travel writing should draw a veil.

As you drive along the road, notice the beehive domed houses. This architectural feature was noted by Alexander's troops when they were fighting Bessus after they had crossed the Hindu Kush via the Khawak Pass, east of here.

At km 33 is the shrine of Hazrat Sultan.

MAZAR-I-SHARIF
HOTELS

Mazar Hotel, built on a monumental scale, is a relic of the good old days of tourism. It has 40 rooms, varying in price from $30 to $43 for rooms described by the manager as "very beautiful, with showers". It has large and attractive sitting and dining rooms with air conditioning, and the gardens have a swimming pool. I believe this is the hotel described by Byron as "equipped with every comfort known to the great hotels of the West", and looks as if it had been designed by Albert Speer, with great square pillars dominating a symmetrical three-sided quadrangle.

Farhat Hotel has 30 rooms varying in price from $30 to $50 and most have bathrooms. There is no restaurant but food is brought in from the bazaar. There is air conditioning in the public rooms and an internet connection.

Kefayat Hotel is the Ritz of Mazar, and a building of surpassing vulgarity. Its reflective blue glass windows mean that it can be seen from a very great distance. It has a large well-kept garden with concrete edged flowerbeds, a fibreglass deer, a yurt, a souvenir shop and a swimming pool. The rooms are luxurious, and not just by Afghan standards. The one I was shown contained two double beds, a fridge, air conditioning, TV and an ensuite bathroom with a Western bath and toilet. This cost $100 per night. It only has ten rooms but ample public rooms and a restaurant serving lunch and dinner for $5 per meal. No internet. Curiously, the hotel belongs to a 93-year-old religious teacher (*maulawi*).

Barat Hotel is situated next door to the shrine of Ali. It has 40 bedrooms and 16 shower rooms costing from $30 to $50 per night, varying on the quality of the room. All rooms are air conditioned. The manager is Ghulam Haidar.

THE SHRINE OF ALI

As you walk in through the side entrance you will notice a large pillar punctured with holes that serves as a dovecote. It is said, and devoutly believed, that doves of any other colour, "like red or black", go white within 40 days. "You see," said Haji. "There are no brown doves."

The Shrine of Hazrat Ali at Mazar-i-Sharif [B. Woodburn]

The mosque is impressive though not equal to the Friday Mosque in Herat. The quality of the tiling is definitely inferior, though it has the same polychrome dazzle in the bright sunlight. The tiles are individual squares that have been hand painted, rather than the mosaic patterning which is used at Herat, a technique of Timurid provenance. To the north of the main entrance is a pool, which is home to ducks (of no sacred significance, apparently) and used as a swimming pool by small boys.

There are separate women's and men's entrances and the entire mosque is given over to women on Wednesdays.

The shrine has a curious history. Ali, the Prophet's son-on-law, is reputed to be buried here after his assassination in AD 661. One other site vies with Mazar-i-Sharif for the honour, nearer to the actual place of death in Kufa, Iraq. The Mazari's story, excellently re-told by Dupree, is that "Ali's companions placed his body on the back of a white she-camel which wandered until she fell, exhausted on this spot, where the body was buried."

Pilgrims at the Shrine of Hazrat Ali at Mazar-i-Sharif, 1972 [B. Woodburn]

All knowledge of the final resting place was lost until the beginning of the 12th century, when its existence was revealed to a mullah in a dream. The great Seljuk Sultan, Sanjar, ordered a shrine built here in 1136.

Genghis Khan destroyed this building, having heard that there was great treasure buried underneath its pillars, and again the grave lay unmarked until a second revelation occurred during the reign of the Timurid sultan, Husayn Bayqara. He ordered an elaborate shrine constructed in 1481. None of the 15th-century decoration remains. What you see today is a modern restoration.

SHOPPING

Karakul was always the staple product of this area. This very tightly wound sheep's coat is rather disgustingly produced. Ten days before the ewe is due to give birth, she is disembowelled and the unborn lamb skinned. It used to be popular for the collars of Western men's coats but is hardly ever seen on them now. It is still used for Astrakhan hats, the type that President Karzai wears. (Tom Ford, the chief designer of Gucci, has described Karzai as the best dressed head of state in the world.) Mazar is also the manufacturing centre of the beautiful striped silk chapans, also modelled by Karzai.

Two turbaned men with sheep, Kunduz, 1975 [Y. Crowe]

Carpets and kilims have traditionally been major trade items for the entire Central Asian region including the former Soviet Union. Mazar is famous for these —cheaper here than in Kabul, though not by much. Many carpet shops are to be found east of the shrine. They also sell fine embroidery, including Arabian Nights embroidered leather slippers from Turkmenistan. It is an excellent place to go shopping. There are also shops selling antiquities, some of which may even be more than two years old.

BALKH (KM 435)
THE MOUND OF THE OLD CITY

As you drive into Balkh, you will be struck by the enormous mudbrick wall that long predates Alexander's arrival here. It was already a large well-fortified capital city of the Aryans, and later the home of the king-prophet Zoroaster (Zardusht), better known in the West by his German name Zarathustra. He worshipped the sun and was a monotheist before the Jews[4] (though his dates are uncertain). The magnificent C-major opening of Richard Strauss's *Also Sprach Zarathustra* represents the sun rising; it is worth getting up early to watch the sunrise over the Oxus plain while listening to this music. Many of the religious ideas in Christianity and Islam (including Heaven and Hell) originate with Zoroaster. He is known to us through the Zoroastrian holy book the *Avesta* and is as elusive and fascinating a character as that other early sun-worshipping monotheist, Akhenaten of Egypt.

Balkh (then called Bactra) was Alexander's headquarters for his three-year campaign in Soghdia (the region north of the Oxus), the longest period he spent in one place during his life, Macedonia excluded. It was here that he married Roxanne, "the most beautiful woman in Asia", daughter of the local Persian satrap Oxyartes, in a ceremony that historians are prepared to admit was as much of a love-match as politically expedient. Already, Alexander's policy of bringing together Greeks and Persians in a new commonwealth was in full swing. Bactra became the site of one of Alexander's foundations and the resulting city was the capital of Bactria, a significant Greek kingdom.

The Shrine of Khawja Abu Nasr Parsa at Balkh, 1972 [B. Woodburn]

Archaeologists have been searching here for remains of this Greek city since the 1920s, but with no success. This has caused the head of the French archaeological delegation to lament that Bactria was a mirage, hinted at by coins and written records but with nothing left in the ground.[5] Then came the discovery of Ai Khanoum (see below, p.295), which went a long way towards giving substance to the mirage. Yet nothing turned up at Balkh.

But in 2002, what can reasonably be called a major archaeological discovery occurred here by accident. A local treasure hunter, digging at the bottom of the wall outside the city, stumbled upon an underground chamber with column heads that were definitely Hellenistic. It could be that this is the first site anywhere in the world to be linked directly to Alexander's life. Excavations began again under the Délégation Archéologique Française en Afghanistan (DAFA), led by Roland Besenval and Prof. Paul Bernard, the distinguished excavator of Ai Khanoum. Much more work needs to be done, but it is possible to hope that the very paving stones on which Alexander walked have been discovered.

THE SHRINE OF KHAWJA PARSA

The main sight of Balkh is the late-Timurid (late 15th century) shrine of Khawja Parsa, built by Sultan Husayn Bayqara. The building should be understood and examined by comparing it with other Timurid monuments in Herat, particularly the tomb of Gawhar Shad. The turquoise pumpkin dome with its fluted tiling is very similar. However, unique in all Afghan Timurid architecture are the twin corkscrew pillars. Much of the tiling, unfortunately, is the product of modern restoration, made (I would guess) at the tile factory in the Herat Friday Mosque. Note the geometric patterns of coloured tile alternating with buff bricks, identical to the decoration in the mihrab at Gazargah, in which Byron detected Chinese influence. To enter the shrine, which is at the edge of a park and usually locked, you need to locate the guardian, Baba Hakim.

This shrine is dedicated to the saint Khawja Parsa (d. 1460), a theologian who taught at the madrassah on the other side of the park. No one in the West has ever been moved to erect such a magnificent memorial to a mere academic.

Just outside the back entrance of the shrine is a collection of graves and a gorgeous garden. The most modern tomb commemorates Abdul Ahat, a *maulawi* who died in 1992 at the age of 105, and the most celebrated one is of Rabia Balkhi, the famous poet-princess of Balkh. The grave is hideously restored with machine-made yellow lavatory wall tiles on a concrete plinth. However, experts are sceptical that this is in fact her grave, but if Hazrat Ali is buried in Mazar, why should Rabia not be here? The inscription records that she was martyred by her brother and tradition claims that this was because she wanted to marry a Turkish slave. Dying, she wrote the following

Interior of dome, Shrine of Khawja Abu Nasr Parsa, Balkh, 1975 [Y. Crowe]

poem in her blood on the wall of the dungeon in which she was incarcerated, addressed to her brother:

I pray God you fall in love

With someone as cold and indifferent as you

Then may you understand

The pain of love, the suffering and torture of separation

And may you appreciate my devotion.

On the other side of the park stand the remains of the madrassah of Sayyid Subhan Quli Khan—an arched gateway of a building destroyed by Genghis Khan, who had been told that treasure was buried in the foundations. He didn't find any. Whether his massacre of the inhabitants of Balkh was in revenge for this, history does not relate. Again, notice the Chinese geometric pattern in the walls.

THE MOSQUE OF HAJI PIARDEH

This is slightly difficult to find. When Bruce Chatwin was looking for it he asked a passer-by who said "I don't know. It must have been destroyed by Genghis." Go down the road from the shrine of Khawja Parsa, across the main road and down another path. The mosque is visible a few hundred metres down this lane; notice the tin roof erected over it to prevent further erosion. Turn right to get to the building past fields devoted to the cultivation of marijuana and cotton.

Masjid-i-No Gumbad (the Mosque of the Nine Domes), Balkh, 1971 [Y. Crowe]

Haji Piardeh was a holy man who made nine pilgrimages to Mecca. It is the earliest Islamic building in Afghanistan and one of the earliest mosques in the world, of a type known as *No Gumbad* or Nine Domes, the structure still obvious from the three rows of three pillars. Nancy Dupree's description is excellent:

> Built during the early years of the 9th century when the first local Islamic dynasties were asserting their independence from the harsh rule of Arabic governors, it coupled outside influences with local ingenuity. As such it

(Above left) *Tile mosaic spandrel lotus, Khawja Abu Nasr Parsa, Balkh, 1975 [Y. Crowe]*
(Bottom left) *Ruins of the 17th century Madrassah of Sayyid Subhan Quli Khan at Balkh [B. Woodburn]*

Haji Piardeh, Detail,
Balkh, 1975 [Y. Crowe]

continued a tradition…[found] throughout Afghan history, from the Achaemenid, Greco-Bactrian and Kushano-Sasanian periods. Few datable examples of mosque architecture exist anywhere in the world from this early period. Only a handful featuring an architectural plan with nine domes are scattered over the former Arab empire, from Balkh to Cairo to Toledo in Spain, dating from the 9th to the 12th centuries AD.

The building, though crumbled, is still a stunning and fascinating example of Islamic architecture. Small pieces of carving poke through the mud. Only the tops of the pillars are visible, the mudbrick roof now forming a thick layer of earth that obscures the bottom of the pillars. The site has never been excavated. Pillars and arches are inscribed with beautiful patterns, some resembling Indian paisley designs, and others include palmettes, circular leaves, pomegranates and lotus blossoms.

To visit Mazar-i-Sharif from here requires returning to Pul-i-Kumri and taking the east fork in the road mentioned earlier.

TASHKURGAN (FORMERLY KHULM) (KM 361)

The approach to this town is breathtaking. One has been travelling through tortured rock formations for hours until one comes up against a wall of peaks that is punctured only by an opening about 40 metres wide, cut over millions of years by a small river, where the walls of rock rise up a thousand feet in height. Suddenly the enormous pancake-flat plain of Afghan Turkestan—the country of Oxiana—

Part of the Bazaar at Tashkurghan, 1972 [B. Woodburn]

comes into view. From here the land runs flat down to the River Oxus, a short journey by road to the river itself. To go is a cheap triumph over Robert Byron, who was here on 3 June 1935, the closest he got to seeing the Oxus itself, but did not attain the object of his quest.

It was not for want of trying. At Mazar-i-Sharif he and Christopher Sykes wrote their grotesque letter to the governor of Afghan Turkestan, Mohammed Gul, requesting permission to see the Oxus:

Your Excellency

Knowing from personal experience that Your Excellency's day is already too short for the public welfare, it is with signal reluctance that… we venture to lay before Your Excellency a trifling personal request.

In undertaking the journey from England to Afghan Turkestan, the tedium and exertions of which have been thrice repaid by the spectacle of Your Excellency's wise and beneficent administration, it was our capital object to behold the waters of the Amu Darya, famed in history and romance as the river Oxus and the theme of a celebrated English poem from the sacred pen of Matthew Arnold. We now find ourselves, after seven month's anticipation, within forty miles of its banks.

Understanding… that an extraordinary permission is necessary to visit the River, we request this permission for ourselves, confident that Your Excellency will not be deluded into imputing a political motive to what is but the natural curiosity of an educated man.

The fact that others, in their lesser wisdom, may be victims of this delusion, reminds us that Afghanistan and Russia are not the only countries in the world to be separated by a river. We dare observe that an Afghan traveller, sojourning in France or Germany, would encounter no regulations to prevent his enjoying the beauties of the Rhine.

There are indeed some countries where the Light of Progress has yet to pierce the night of medieval barbarism and where the foreign visitor must expect to be obstructed by ill-conceived suspicions[6]. *But we consoled ourselves, during our stay in Persia, by the consideration that we should soon be in Afghanistan, and thus should escape from a parcel of vain and hysterical women to an erect and manly people, immune from ridiculous alarms, and happy to accord that liberty to strangers which they justly demand for themselves.*

Were we right? And on returning to our country shall we say that we were right? The answer lies with Your Excellency. Certainly we will tell of the hotel in Mazar-i-Sharif equipped with every comfort known to the great capitals of the West; of a city in the course of reconstruction on lines that London itself might envy; of bazaars stuffed with all the amenities of civilisation. But are we then to add that though Your Excellency's capital holds everything to delight the visitor, nevertheless, the chief attraction of the district is denied him? that in short, he who comes to Mazar-i-Sharif will be treated as spy, a Bolshevik, a disturber of the peace, if he asks to tread the shores where Rustam fought? We believe that Your Excellency, jealous of your country's good name, would deprecate such sentiments. We believe also that when you have read this letter, they will not be necessary."

But to no effect. Byron admitted that Mohammed Gul was "not simply being disagreeable. High policy is involved."

This town was home to the last surviving traditional Central Asian bazaar in the world, but it was destroyed in an appalling ideologically-inspired piece of "modernisation" and sheer vandalism,[7] a loss over which one can only weep. It has left Tashkurgan a dull place for the visitor; the only attraction is a palace built by Abdur Rahman, the 19th-century creator of modern Afghanistan who forcibly converted the Kafirs to Islam and mended all the clocks in Kabul.[8] He was appointed governor of this town at the age of nine and cherished a fondness for it throughout his reign. You can climb up onto the roof for a splendid view of the Turkestan plain and—even more impressive—the pink mountain ranges through which one has just travelled.

The palace is somewhat decayed but is a good example of 19th-century British Indian colonial architecture, from which it was presumably copied. An arched portico facing the north side of the palace resembles Delhi's Connaught Circle. Until King Zahir Shah's deposition in 1973, it was used as a state guest house.

I was warmly welcomed by the guardian, who had not previously received any tourists. He can show the visitor a small museum consisting of pots and coins found by local farmers when ploughing their fields. They look to my inexpert eye Islamic,

Interior of the Tashkurgan Bazaar, now destroyed [R. & S. Michaud]

not Hellenistic, though there are a couple of finely thrown pots resembling ones I have picked up at Ai Khanoum.

There was a 5,000-volume library, assembled by a bibliophile whose photograph hangs in the room that was formerly the library. The Taliban took all the books and burned them, a pastime of which they were fond. A delightfully eclectic, though tiny collection is taking its place, mostly from an old American library in Kabul, including a high school textbook on the US Constitution and a gardening book entitled *Plants in Peace and War*.

PUL-I-KUMRI TO KUNDUZ

This is one of my favourite parts of Afghanistan. It is still comparatively unspoiled by modernity and sometimes I get the feeling I am in touch with remnants of Kipling's India. There are few cars and transport in the towns is by horse drawn tongas or carts. Westerners are comparatively unknown here (or were in the few years after the fall of the Taliban) and Europeans should expect to be stared at as exotic beasts. In the spring, the countryside is stunning, the loess hills bright green like psychedelic sand-dunes. These are common features from here to northern Iran, but come as a shock to travellers who have not seen them before. Byron's response to them reminds us that he was a painter as well as an writer:

"Suddenly, as a ship leaves an estuary, we came out on to the steppe: a dazzling open sea of green. I never saw that colour before. In other greens, of emerald, jade or malachite, the harsh deep green of the Bengal jungle, the sad cool green of Ireland, the salad green of English summer beeches, some element of blue and yellow predominates over the others. This was the pure essence of green, indissoluble, the colour of life itself."[9]

BAGHLAN (22 KM FROM PUL-I-KUMRI)

This is a lovely little town, infinitely preferable as a place to stay than Pul-i-Kumri. The main street is lined with citrus trees and on the left a large flat lawn, resembling a cricket pitch but with cows grazing on it. On the right is an arched arcade of shops. Traffic consists of droshkies and bullock carts.

A delightful hotel in Baghlan is the Sugar Klub. "Klubs" were the hotels where tourists stayed in the good old days and most have fallen into disrepair, but this one is being restored by a German team who are restarting the sugar factory. You get a feel of what made Afghanistan such a special tourist destination in the 1960s. A suite and dining room here were kept for the king and queen. It has a big garden at the back and 23 large rooms, three bathrooms with Western baths and a big dining hall. Prices are likely to be about $50 per night.

74 kilometres from Pul-i-Kumri on the road to Mazar-i-Sharif, at a place called Sayat, is the most beautiful rest stop that I have found in Afghanistan. You sit on a rug underneath a mulberry tree next to a flour mill, a small rill running past. Buy a Kunduz melon and admire the scenery and the huge pink mountains. You can go into the mill and watch it working. It is of a design that has not changed for centuries, and mills of this exact type are found right across Asia and beyond. The millstones turn at about 150 rpm and throw out flour hot from the friction. I have seen identical mills in Morocco. The miller takes 5 per cent of the flour that he mills for the local farmers and pays a rent of $3,500 a year. The mill produces 3.5 tonnes of flour each 24 hours, worth $350.

KUNDUZ

Dusty Kunduz has not yet been despoiled by asphalt. Entering the town at dusk is like entering a cloud of fog. Still, it is definitely exotic— women on tongas bouncing over the potholes, looking like ghosts (the burqas are white here rather than Kabul-blue). In the morning, though,

Old rider, child and beggar, Kunduz, 1975 [Y. Crowe]

the dust has settled, the shopkeepers are damping down the streets with buckets of water. The bazaar is wonderful and probably the cheapest place in Afghanistan to buy a *chapan* (silk robe).

The town is dominated by the defunct Spinzar Cotton Mill. Somewhere in this complex of buildings there is (or was) a museum of Greek antiquities collected by the founder of the Spinzar ("golden cotton") company, possibly still including pieces from Ai Khanoum, of which he can be said to be the discoverer (see below). But I have never found it.

Kunduz also has a fine hammam (bath house), probably the best I have seen in Afghanistan, and very necessary to remove the dust.

TALOQAN

This small town was Massoud's headquarters until a Taliban offensive in November 2000 forced him to move to Khawja Bahuddin, near Ai Khanoum (see below). It is utterly unspoiled, the main street beautiful with enormous *chinar* (plane) trees and its bazaar full of fruit. Marco Polo said that the melons from here are "the best in the world" and I would agree. They are best in the late summer. People have tried to grow them elsewhere—including Hawaii—but they do not taste the same. It must be something to do with the soil and climate. But you have not really experienced a melon until you have eaten one from here.

Marco Polo also writes about the salt mines: "the mountains to the south of it [Taloqan] are very large and are made of salt. Men come from all the country round, for thirty days journey, to fetch this salt, which is the best in the world. It is so hard that it cannot be fetched except with a stout iron pick." This is what I wrote in my diary at the time:

> "You can find the salt market in the bazaar in an old caravanserai, behind the row of shop fronts. Men were unloading horses of large oblong blocks of salt, that looked like white granite. The sides were marked with what I took to be the marks of drills where it had been worked, in a herringbone pattern. Machines milled it into powder—surprisingly modern, brightly painted machines.

'Is it harder than normal?'

'Yes, it's the hardest in Afghanistan.'

'And is it good quality?'

'Yes' he said proudly, 'Much better than Pakistani salt.'

'How?'

'It is very clean.'

I had seen rock salt in the bazaar in Peshawar. It was a dirty brown colour and presumably had to be refined before using. This salt could be milled as it came from the ground.

I asked where it came from and they drew a sketch map, showing the road to take just to the south of the town.

'It will only take you half an hour.'

This proved to be a gross underestimate, as usual.

High Street, Taloqan [D. Grossart]

You can visit the mines quite easily. They are, as Marco Polo says, a few miles to the south of the town. You can drive part of the way and then walk for half an hour up the valley and then one comes to the workings. I went down into one of them.

"Looking up I could see the natural opening, a crevasse, where the mine had started. Below, the working widened making a sort of partial dome above us, whiter than the surrounding rocks and textured with the marks of tools. It looked like the work in progress of a monumental sculpture, perhaps the nose of a president on Mount Rushmore.

It was cooler down here. The floor, the area that was being worked, was on two levels and a man sat on each, one ten feet above the other. With great ill manners I asked if I could have some water and he offered me a plastic pot covered in sacking.

The only tools they had were: two picks; a crowbar and an iron wedge. He worked by using a pickaxe to cut a block out of the floor perhaps five feet long and nine inches wide and deep. This gave the blocks the characteristic herringbone texture.

This left the block attached below. He then used the wedges to drive holes underneath and, when he had made enough, used the crowbar to break the whole block free.

Then he used the pick to score a groove with a series of chips across the top and used the crowbar to lever the block up, inserted a wedge exactly underneath the groove, and tapped the top. It broke into exactly the same shape I had seen in the market.

I got pleasure from seeing the task so expertly done. He had been doing this, he told me, for 23 years. In a day he could produce about twelve donkey loads. A donkey boy had told me earlier that each donkey carried eighty kilos. So he was producing one tonne a day and earned from this about four dollars. He was making about twelve hundred dollars a year. He paid a tax to the government of about 10 cents a day.

He had been working this mine for a year, and he thought that there was another three years work in it. It was an old working that he had re-opened and was now his as long as he paid the tax to the government.

Below there was the old working, a series of steps leading down into it carved out of the salt. The salt here was brown and showed why the mine had been abandoned. The rock salt I had seen in Pakistan was of this colour and the contrast showed why Taloqan salt was such good quality.

I looked up again. His new working had enlarged the hole and the worked salt curved up, creating an overhang of perhaps 20 feet of rock salt above us.

'Aren't you afraid of a collapse?' I asked.

'No, the salt is very hard. Even the rain doesn't affect it.'

'Where will you mine next?'

He pointed to the other side of the hole, which was presumably part of the original natural crevasse. The surface was like snow, a clean white unlike the mined rock salt which was grey. It was formed of knobbly round protrusions and the surface was of fine crystals that came off as I brushed it.

Two donkeys entered down the steep path and the blocks tied on to them with blue nylon cord. We left and I was delighted, feeling I had discovered something; that Marco Polo had actually been here."

There has been scholarly debate, sparked off by Frances Wood's excellent book *Did Marco Polo go to China?*, whether Marco Polo actually went all the way to China. I am certain, though, that he (or whoever wrote the section dealing with the journey from Taloqan to the Chinese pass at the Wakhan) did in fact come here. It is the quality of detail that is so convincing; the location, the stout iron picks, the description of the salt, in particular the hardness. None of this could have been imagined by a storyteller sitting in a Genoese prison or remembered second-hand. It is a writer's love of detail.

From Taloqan, a road leads southeast towards Faisabad (see p. 152), joining the Kokcha River at Pul-i-Begum. From there, the road follows the river valley to Faisabad. This arduous drive can take 12 uncomfortable hours. At many places the road has been washed away and you are driving along the river-bed. But you may well want to spend longer in the Oxus valley, visiting little towns and villages like Aliabad and Khanabad. You can hire horses in Kunduz to do this and follow the flood-plain of the Oxus, keeping yourself happily occupied for weeks.

AI KHANOUM

The other major sight in the middle-Oxus valley is the Greek city of Ai Khanoum, about a day's journey by car from Taloqan. It is the only Greek city to have been excavated in Central Asia and is almost certainly Alexandria-Oxiana, one of Alexander's foundations. The evidence for this is that the *heroön* (hero-shrine) is dedicated to Kineas, a Thessalian name, and we know that Alexander discharged his Thessalian cavalry here.

It has always been claimed that the site was discovered by King Zahir Shah during a hunting party in 1961. This is true, and he then sent a mission from the Délégation Archéologique Française en Afghanistan (DAFA) to assess the site. The head of the mission immediately recognised that it was Hellenistic and of great importance. But, in fact, the founder of the Spinzar Cotton Mill already knew of its existence and had pieces in his private museum from here.[10] The site has been badly looted, mostly during the Taliban war. Many valuable antiquities appeared in the 1990s on the markets, whether in Peshawar or in the West, with an Ai Khanoum

Dish from Ai Khanoum, Kabul Museum, Kabul, 1971 [Y. Crowe]

provenance, though Paul Bernard doubts whether many such cases are genuine. His excavations—very revealing about the Bactrian kingdom—have turned up few objects which could be described as treasure, except the Plate of Kybele, which, happily survived the Taliban by being hidden in the vault of Kabul's central bank.

Much of Ai Khanoum remains untouched and the French plan to continue excavations here. The top of the acropolis has been left untouched and there is a mound a mile or so upstream with Kushan pottery on it, which may well cover an earlier settlement. It commands the best crossing point of the Oxus for miles around and would be my bet for the site of Alexander's original foundation.

A map from the four-volume excavation report marks neatly the Temple, Gymnasion, Palace, Theatre, House no. 1 and others, though it is difficult to relate these to the moonscape you see *in situ*. The site is a flat plain at the junction of two rivers, the Oxus and the Kokcha. The Oxus is enormous and as you look upstream it seems like an inland sea. Ai Khanoum was superbly defensible: the land on the opposite side of the Oxus rises straight up in a cliff face nearly 500 feet high, the rocks stratified upwards towards the right, a fortress wall far different from the rounded loess hills of elsewhere. At the other side of the plain is the acropolis, perhaps 200 feet high, defending the city from the warlike Central Asian nomads who finally burned the city in 148 BC.

When visiting the site, I have always stayed at the guest house of Mamoor Hassan, the local commander. It is also worth visiting Khawja Bahuddin, Massoud's final headquarters, where he was murdered on 9 September 2001. The column bases from the palaestra of Ai Khanoum have been used to decorate the traffic islands, and the chaikhana has its roof supported with two Corinthian column heads, mounted upside down.

[1] The traditional etymology of Hindu Kush—*Killer of Indians*—was first given by ibn Battuta and may not be accurate. Nonetheless, it has always formed an almost impassable barrier between Central Asia and the subcontinent.

[2] The villages of Pashto speakers in the north were generally planted here by Abdur Rahman in the late 19th century in a Stalinist-like attempt to remake his country as more of an ethnic unity.

[3] See above, p. 34, and Robin Lane Fox.

[4] During their early period, the Jews were monolatrous; that is, they accepted the existence of other gods but refused to worship them. Hence the lawyer's wording of "Thou shalt have no other gods but me" in the Ten Commandments.

[5] See the essay by Foucher, *Le mirage de Bactria*, c. 1920.

[6] A snide reference to Iran and the Shah's competition with the Amanullah of Afghanistan to Westernise his country faster, one of the comic themes of the book. It brought both regimes to a bad end, but to Amanullah's first. He was murdered, among other reasons, because his wife appeared in a dress that revealed her shoulders. He is buried on the golf course in Jalalabad, another Western feature he had introduced to Afghanistan. The son of Marjoribanks (as Byron refers to the Shah) survived till 1979.

[7] It was the socialist revolutionary Bakunin (a friend of Wagner's) who opined, "The urge for destruction is also a creative urge", inspiring countless acts of Year Zero cultural vandalism, the apogee of which was the Cultural Revolution (1966–76) in China.

[8] From Abdur Rahman's memoirs, published in 1900.

[9] Byron, *The Road to Oxiana,* Folio Society edition, p. 225

[10] See Paul Bernard, *Comptes Rendues des Académies des Inscriptions* (2001), for the full story.

Holding History in Your Hands: Graeco-Bactrian Coins

—Professor Frank L. Holt

*I*n his legend of lost Atlantis, Plato tells us that a great civilization once sank out of sight beyond the Pillars of Hercules (modern Gibraltar). We may never know what truth lies beyond this mythic image, but something equally dramatic did occur at the other end of the ancient world where an entire Greek kingdom disappeared into the sands of Central Asia. Bactria (modern Afghanistan) flourished as "the land of a thousand cities" for 200 years following the conquests of Alexander the Great. Eclectic palaces and temples rose along the banks of the Oxus River (modern Amu Darya); trade routes pulsed with precious cargo at the hub of the emerging Silk Road; powerful Greek kings grew richer still by raiding India. Bactria quickly became the celebrated "Jewel of all Ariana"—and then, just as suddenly, disintegrated. History faded into fable.

The reliable accounts of Bactria written by the Greeks fell out of use and were forgotten. Only the strangest tales survived in "believe it or not" fashion: gold-digging ants grew as big as dogs in Bactria; rivers of honey oozed on the Bactrian frontier; dragon-like griffins prowled the skies. For Propertius and other Roman writers, Bactria seemed no more than a synonym for the mystical ends of the earth. By the time of the Renaissance, the names of but two Bactrian kings could be found in the works of Boccaccio and Chaucer. Were such monarchs any more real than the monsters who threatened them? Who could be sure? But in 1738, the existence of one of those kings— Eucratides the Great—was dramatically affirmed by the discovery of an ancient silver coin bearing his name and portrait. Through numismatics, the modern world came face to face with a vanished Bactrian of flesh and blood. Gradually, the reigns of other Greek kings came to light as enthusiastic experts and amateurs collected thousands of coins in Afghanistan, often at great peril. Today, more than 40 lost kings and queens have been ransomed by their own money in one of the most exciting adventures of our time.

Coinage may seem an unheroic witness to the lost worlds of antiquity. After all, we hate to think that a dime or nickel instead of a library or computer database might someday serve as the

Portrait of a Turcoman woman, N. Afghanistan [R. & S. Michaud]

chief repository of all our records. But ancient coins were worthy of this burden. They acted as carefully designed disks of information technology capable of transmitting important data at great speeds over incredible distances. As they circulated in a world with no better means of mass communication, coins were deliberately fashioned to disseminate the latest news and propaganda.

Fortunately for us, this technology was also very durable. Thus, experts can now hack into these ancient files for all sorts of clues about the lives of the lost Bactrians. Who were they? Who ruled them and for how long? How were they related? What did they look like? Which gods did they worship? What regalia did they wear? What weapons did they use? What languages did they speak? Some of the Bactrian currency was actually bilingual, with Greek on one side and an early Indian script on the other!

Fig. 1

The first Greek rulers of independent Bactria, when the realm broke away from the empire of Alexander's successors in the third century BC, bore the name Diodotus (fig. 1). This father-son duo identified themselves with Zeus, whose dynamic image—hurling a thunderbolt—

Fig. 2

they emblazoned on their gold and silver coins. Their money shows how the elder Diodotus groomed his son for power, giving the young man a royal title and mint so that someday Diodotus II could more easily step into his father's place (fig. 2). The son did succeed his father, but the short-lived dynasty suffered calamity at the hands of another ambitious Greek named Euthydemus, who seized power and founded a royal house of his own. King Euthydemus chose to portray Hercules on his money (fig. 3), as did his son Demetrius (fig. 4). With almost photographic realism, Euthydemus is shown growing old on his coinage during a patently long reign. Demetrius followed in dramatic fashion, sporting

Fig. 3

Fig. 4

*for the first time on Bactrian coinage a military cloak
and special headgear. In this case, the king wears an
elephant scalp, tusks and all, symbolizing his ambitions
in India.*

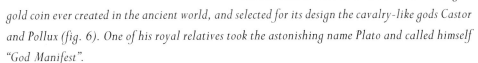

Fig. 5

*Close royal associates of Demetrius depicted themselves
in many interesting ways. A King Agathocles (fig. 5) issued a
special series of coins celebrating his predecessors on the Bactrian throne, each one given a divine
epithet such as "Saviour" or "God". He also portrayed on some square silver coins the remarkable
images of the Indian deities Vashudeva-Krishna and Samkarshana. King Antimachus wore a
distinctive Macedonian cap, the kausia, and
chose Poseidon as his protective deity. The
sea-god may seem out of place in land-
locked Bactria, but Poseidon also promoted
skilled horsemanship—for which the region
has always been renowned. Helmeted and
heroic, Eucratides the Great minted the largest
gold coin ever created in the ancient world, and selected for its design the cavalry-like gods Castor
and Pollux (fig. 6). One of his royal relatives took the astonishing name Plato and called himself
"God Manifest".*

Fig. 6

*At about this time in Bactria's history, the quarrelsome yet grandiose Greek kings faced a
threat none of them could turn back. Nomadic invaders swept down into the Oxus valley and
displaced many of the Greeks, who abandoned their cities and streamed over the Hindu Kush
Mountains towards new realms in India. This intensified a process already underway by which the
Greek and Indian civilizations amalgamated in the area of modern Pakistan. Indo-Greek kings
such as Menander converted to Buddhism, yet continued to issue coins depicting traditional Greek
deities. With few exceptions, these hybrid rulers also faded from sight, and their remarkable story
disappeared except for the ancient coins that still come to hand in this Atlantis of the East.*

Frank Holt is Professor of ancient history at the University of Houston,
and author of *Thundering Zeus*, on the history and numismatics
of the ancient Graeco-Bactrian kingdoms of Afghanistan.
Coins reproduced by courtesy of Spink of London.

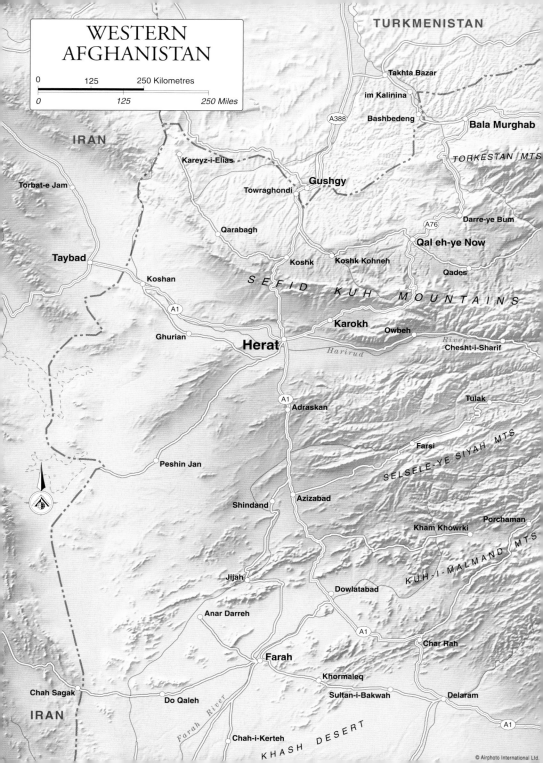

HERAT: THE PEARL OF KHURASAN

The city of Herat lies in the west of modern-day Afghanistan, in the fertile valley of the Hari Rud River. It owes its existence to the cultivation made possible by a benign climate and the ready supply of water, and also to its location: in early days, it was both a natural halting place on the journey between the western and eastern halves of the Persian Empire, and a point of convergence for routes between Balkh, Bamiyan, Khiva, Bokhara, and, by way of Kandahar and the Bolan Pass, northwestern India. As a result, it has always been one of Central Asia's leading centres of trade.

Kuchis (Nomads) crossing the Hari Rud by moonlight [F. Holt]

The age of the city is not at all clear. It is mentioned as 'Haraewa' in the *Avesta*, from which is derived the classical 'Aria' or 'Ariana' and the modern 'Herat'. Scholars generally argue that this name is cognate with the word 'Aryan', and assert—although not with universal acceptance—that the Aryan tribes who are thought to have sojourned there around 1500 BC left behind this echo of their presence in the names of the city and the river. At any rate, Ariana is known for certain in the 6th century BC as a satrapy of the Achaemenid Empire—an area already irrigated with underground water canals, and paying, according to Herodotus, 390 talents annually to the treasury of Darius the Great.

Like all cities in Afghanistan, Herat possesses a plethora of legends to account for its foundation. The one most often quoted is contained in a simple Persian quatrain, attributing its establishment and subsequent development to the mythical

Iranian kings Lohrasp, Gushtasp, Bahman, and finally Alexander the Great. Other less well known accounts link different characters from eastern antiquity to the appearance of the city—for instance, Ardashir-i-Babakan, founder of the Sassanian Empire, or Zohhak, an early ruler of Iran—and give more elaborate detail, needless

to say without any basis in fact, about the process of construction. For example, Sayf ibn Muhammad Harawi, a Herati historian writing around AD 1300, says that the city was built by colonists who had left Kandahar in the time of King Bahman, seeking to build a larger settlement elsewhere:

"The reigning King, Bahman, did not want to finance a new city out of public funds, and was only willing to allow it to be built if the colonists were ready to pay for it themselves. They agreed. The local governor, Arghaghoush, assembled a group of architects and craftsmen, asking them to determine how many men would be required for the project. They decided that 16,000 workers would be required to be present

City Gate, Herat, 2004 [B. Jenks]

every day: 4,000 at each corner of the city, supervised by 400 experienced masters. They then employed astrologers to judge what moment would be most auspicious for the building work to start. As the chosen hour approached, the workers made themselves ready, taking up the bricks in their hands; it was necessary that work start on all four corners at the same time. However, at that moment, a beggar was baking some bread, a piece of which was stolen by an urchin. The beggar, being foolish, made an uproar, shouting out and calling for the boy to be stopped. This disturbance upset the governor, who feared that it was a bad omen. Seeking the astrologers' advice, however, his fears were dispelled: the citizens of Herat were to be hospitable people; it was becoming that they should be generous, and hence, the incident was not at all inauspicious. Their reassurances led to the resumption of the work. The 16,000 men toiled for eight years to build the foundations. They then waited four years for these to dry. Another eight years was consumed in the construction of the walls. A wall encompassing Herat and Kandahar was also erected. At the four corners of the walls were four towers, on top of which strong defences were placed, as the reigning king was afraid. They then constructed a very deep moat. Four gates were also built, each being given a name: Firouz, Sara, Khosh, and Kandahar. All of these were truly unique."

Harawi also preserves a different tradition, this time associating the foundation of Herat not with an Iranian, but with the mother of Alexander the Great. The story is without value as history, but nevertheless possesses interest for its sheer peculiarity:

"Another account is that Alexander asked his mother's permission to travel to Kandahar and then on to the area of Herat, where he wanted to build a great new walled city. Apart from Kandahar, there was not any other amenity in the vicinity, and that city itself was constantly harassed by the Turks, who carried off slaves and other goods as plunder. For this reason, his mother asked him to spend no more than a year there. At length, Alexander reached Kandahar, where he started to draw up his plans for Herat, and then proceeded to the area of the new city itself. The local population reacted, it is said, by pleading with him to desist from his plan to build a city there. Alexander was angered at this, and decided to lengthen his stay there to two years. Having heard this, his mother wrote to him, ordering him to return to Kandahar, but Alexander refused, saying that his reputation would be damaged by acquiescing in such a way to the local inhabitants. His mother replied, asking him to send her samples of soil from each corner of the new city's site. When she received these, she saw that the soil was of diverse sorts: some was soft, some was hard; parts of it were white, and others black. Concluding that there must be some sort of secret hidden in this soil, she took some and hid it beneath a number of carpets, on which she then invited various noblemen of Rum [the West broadly speaking] to assemble and be seated. She informed them of Alexander's desire to build the city of Herat, and asked them their opinion as to whether this should be permitted to proceed. One group advised against it, saying that on account of its distance and its location, it would be subject to plots and disturbances. Another group, by contrast, disagreed, saying that the king would be able without difficulty to dispel whatever plots may happen to arise. The nobles adjourned for the evening, but when they reassembled the next day, and sat down on the carpets, they all suddenly came to an agreement, saying that the work should go ahead. As a result, Alexander's mother wrote a letter to him, stating that the soil had shown that the natives of the area would behave in a changeable and unpredictable fashion. Alexander read the letter with interest, but went on to complete the building work, sparing no expense. However, the very day on which the city was finished, he put to death 1,700 of the local people, flogging some and hanging others from the towers of the city, choosing instead that the place should be populated with tribes from the cities of Khurasan and Iraq."

More reliable information about Alexander's activities in the vicinity of Herat is given by the earlier Greek and Roman historians. Alexander first entered the area of modern-day Afghanistan by way of the city in 330 BC; it is recorded that at around this time, Alexander first adopted Persian dress and customs in order to convince the subject peoples of Asia that he was their legitimate ruler. Diodorus of Sicily writes:

"... First, he installed ushers of Asiatic race in his court, and then he ordered the most distinguished persons to act as his guards; among these was Darius' brother Oxathres. Then he put on the Persian diadem and dressed himself in the white robe and the Persian sash and everything else except the trousers and the long-sleeved Median cloak. He distributed to his companions cloaks with purple borders and dressed the horses in Persian harness. In addition to all this, he added concubines to his retinue in the manner of Darius, in number not less than the days of the year, and outstanding in beauty, selected from all the women of Asia. Each night these paraded about the couch of the king so that he might select the one with whom he would lie that night. Alexander, as a matter of fact, employed these customs rather sparingly, and kept for the most part to his accustomed routine, not wishing to offend the Macedonians. Many, it is true, did reproach him for these things, but he silenced them with gifts."

Alexander embarked on his course through the eastern satrapies of the Persian Empire intending to overtake Bessus and defeat him. Bessus, originally one of the officers of the Achaemenid King Darius, had turned against his master on the retreat from Alexander's forces, murdering him as he fled in an oxcart. Declaring himself to be Artaxerxes V, the new king of the Persian Empire, he withdrew by way of Ariana, hoping to make a concerted stand against the invaders in his native territory of Bactria.

When Alexander had reached Aria in the course of this pursuit, the local ruler, Satibarzanes, tendered his submission to the conqueror, who accordingly confirmed him in his position. Having settled matters peacefully in this fashion, Alexander installed a small garrison of Macedonian soldiers in the city and proceeded on his way. However, a time after his departure, Satibarzanes rebelled, slaughtering the garrison in its entirety. News of this reached Alexander when he was some distance from the city. In response, he selected a detachment under the commanders Erigyius and Caranus, and ordered it to go back and crush the uprising, so that he himself with the majority of the army could continue after Bessus. The detachment marched at speed back towards Aria, taking Satibazarnes somewhat by surprise. Battle was joined between Alexander's forces and the Arian natives, but the result was determined by a remarkable single combat, an account of which is narrated by the historian Quintus Curtius:

> "The traitor Satibarzanes commanded the barbarians. When he saw that the battle was coming to a stalemate, and that the forces were equal on both sides, he rode to the front ranks, took off his helmet, ordered the men to stop throwing their weapons, and issued a challenge to anyone who wished to fight a single combat. He added that he would go into the struggle bare-headed. Erigyius could not put up with the arrogance of the barbarian leader. Although he was of advanced years, he was no inferior to the young men in courage or bodily strength. Therefore coming forward, he removed his helmet, and displaying his white hair, declared: 'The day has come when, either by a victory or an honourable death, Alexander shall have a proof of what sort of soldiers and friends he possesses.' Speaking no further, he drove his horse against the enemy.
>
> "You would believe at this point that the order had been given for both sides to stop fighting. Straightaway, the two front lines drew back to leave a free

space; all those watching were intent not only on the fate of their leaders, but their own as well—the future of the men and their generals were inextricably bound together. The barbarian was the first to throw his spear, but Erigyius avoided it with a slight movement of the head. Then, spurring on his horse, he thrust his lance into the middle of the barbarian's throat, so that it stuck out through the back of his neck. The barbarian, although thrown down from his horse, still continued to fight back. But Erigyius, pulling the lance from the wound, directed it for a second time at his face. Satibarzanes, seizing it with his hands, aided the enemy's blow, so that he would perish more quickly. Then, the barbarians, having lost their leader—whom they had followed more through necessity than their own free will—not forgetful of the good qualities of Alexander, surrendered to Erigyius."

There is little further mention of Herat in the historical record until the AD 652 Muslim conquest led by the Governor of Basra, Abdullah bin Amir. In AD 822, as the power of the Caliphate over the area declined, the city came under the control of a local Islamic dynasty known as the Tahirids. From this time, the historian Khwandamir gives an account of the conflict in the city between the Muslim population and the Zoroastrians, who, it seems, were then still numerous. This version of Khwandamir's story is given by the French scholar d'Herbelot:

> "Khwandamir... relates that during the reign of Abdallah, Prince of the Tahirid Dynasty, there was, close by Herat, a temple of the Magi, or fire-worshippers—a magnificent edifice, for whose preservation these Idolaters would pay every year an enormous sum in tribute to the Muslims. Not far from this great temple stood a small and insignificant mosque.

Rooftops of Herat [R. & S. Michaud]

"The grandeur of this Temple, or 'House of Fire' as the Persians called it, would attract great crowds of Magi, or 'Gerbers' as they are known, who would make their way there from every region. One day, an Imam, who was conducting a service at the Mosque, transported with zeal for his religion, declared with much fury in his sermon that no-one should be surprised Islam was every day in decline at Herat, since the temple of the Idolaters was so close to that of the faithful, and since there were no Muslims who had the zeal or the initiative to do anything about this situation.

"The congregation, stirred up by this speech, did not fail on the next night to mount an arson attack on the Temple, which was entirely burnt to the

ground, along with the small neighbouring Mosque. The latter, however, was rebuilt in a finer style than it had been previously.

"The Fire-worshippers, after this event, went to Prince Abdallah to complain against the violence of the Muslims. The Prince called for further information on the matter, and summoned 4,000 of Herat's inhabitants to appear before him as witnesses, so that he could learn from their statements precisely how the fire was caused. However, every one of the 4,000 testified that they had never before seen a Fire Temple in that place; only the neighbouring mosque. Against this evidence, so apparently authentic and solemn, although false, the Magi were unable to win their case, and since that time the temple has never been rebuilt."

At the beginning of the 9th century AD, Herat was incorporated into the Samanid Empire, governed from the city of Bokhara north of the Oxus. Despite this, history relates that one of the dynasty's most famous rulers, Nasr ibn Ahmad, on visiting Herat found it so pleasant that he was loath to return home. The story is recorded by Nizami, a poet and physician of the 12th century:

"They relate thus, that Nasr ibn Ahmad, who was the most brilliant jewel of the Samanid galaxy, whereof the fortunes reached their zenith during the days of his rule, was most plenteously equipped with every means of enjoyment and material of splendour—well-filled treasuries, a far-flung army and loyal servants. In winter he used to reside at his capital, Bokhara, while in summer he used to go to Samarqand or some other of the cities of Khurasan. Now one year it was the turn of Herat. He spent the spring season at Badghis, where are the most charming pasture-grounds of Khurasan and Iraq, for there are nearly a thousand water-courses abounding in water and pasture, any one of which would suffice for an army.

"When their beasts had well enjoyed their spring feed, and had regained their strength and condition, and were fit for warfare or to take the field, Nasr ibn Ahmad turned his face towards Herat, but halted outside the city at Margh-i-Sapid and there pitched his camp. It was the season of spring; cool breezes from the north were stirring, and the fruit was ripening in the districts of Malin and Karukh—such fruit as can be obtained in few places, and nowhere so cheaply. There the army rested. The climate was charming, the breeze cool, food plentiful, fruit abundant, and the air filled with fragrant scents, so that the soldiers enjoyed their life to the full during the spring and summer.

"When Mihrgan (the autumn equinox) arrived, and the juice of the grape came into season, and the basil, rocket, and fever-few were in bloom, they did full justice to the delights of youth, and took tribute of their juvenile prime. Mihrgan was protracted, for the cold did not wax severe, and the grapes ripened with exceptional sweetness. For in the district of Herat one hundred and twenty different varieties of the grape occur, each sweeter and more delicious than the other; and amongst them are in particular two kinds which are not to be found in any other region of the inhabited world, one called Parniyan, and the other Kalanjari, thin-skinned, small-stoned, and luscious, so that you would say they contained no earthly elements. A cluster of Kalanjari grapes sometimes attains a weight of five maunds, and each individual grape fire dirhams' weight, they are black as pitch and sweet as sugar, and one can eat many by the reason of the lusciousness that is in them. And besides these there were all sorts of other delicious fruits.

"So the Amir Nasr ibn Ahmad saw Mihrgan and its fruit, and was mightily pleased therewith. Then the narcissus began to bloom, and the raisins were plucked and stoned in Malin, and hung up on the lines, and packed in store-rooms; and the Amir with his army moved into the two groups of hamlets called Ghura and Darwaz. There he saw mansions of which each one was like highest paradise, having before it a garden or pleasure ground with a northern aspect. There they wintered, while the Mandarin oranges began to arrive from Sistan and the sweet oranges from Mazandaran; and so they passed the winter in the most agreeable manner.

"When the second spring came, the Amir sent the horses to Badghis and moved his camp to Malin, to a spot between two streams. And when summer came and the fruits again ripened, Amir Nasr ibn Ahmad said, 'Where shall we go for the summer? For there is no pleasanter place of residence than this. Let us wait until Mihrgan.' And when Mihrgan came, he said, 'Let us enjoy Mihrgan at Herat and then go': and so from season to season he continued to procrastinate, until four years had passed in this way. For it was then the heyday of the Samanian prosperity, and the land was flourishing, the kingdom unmenaced by foes, the army loyal, fortune favourable, and heaven auspicious;

A market by the Citadel in Herat, in the autumn of 1972 [B. Woodburn]

yet withal the Amir's attendants grew weary, and desire for home arose within them, while they beheld the king quiescent, the air of Herat in his head and the love of Herat in his heart; and in the course of conversation he would compare, nay, prefer Herat to the Garden of Eden, and would exalt its charms above those of a Chinese temple.

"So they perceived that he intended to remain there for that summer also. Then the captains of the army and nobles of the kingdom went to Master Abu Abdillah Rudagi, then whom there was none more honoured of the king's intimates, and none whose words found so ready an acceptance. And they said to him, 'We will present you with five thousand dinars if you will contrive some artifice whereby the king may be induced to depart hence, for our hearts are craving for our wives and children, and our souls are live to leave us for longing after Bokhara.' Rudagi agreed; and, since he had felt the Amir's pulse and understood his temperament, he perceived that prose would not affect him, and so had recourse to verse. He therefore composed a qasida; and, when the Amir had taken his morning cup, came in and sat down in his place; and, when the musicians ceased, he took up the harp, and, playing the 'Lover's air,' began this elegy:

> 'The Juyi Muliyan we call to mind,
> We long for those dear friends long left behind…'

Then he strikes a lower key, and sings:

> 'The sands of Oxus, toilsome though they be,
> Beneath my feet were soft as silk to me.
> Glad at the friends' return, the Oxus deep
> Up to our girths in laughing waves shall leap.
> Long live Bokhara! Be thou of good cheer!
> Joyous towards thee hasteth our Amir!
> The Moon's the Prince, Bokhara is the sky;
> O Sky, the Moon shall light thee by and by!

Bokhara is the mead, the Cypress he;
Receive at last, O Mead, the cypress tree!'

"When Rudagi reached this verse, the Amir was so much affected that he descended from his throne, all unbooted bestrode the horse which was on sentry duty, and set off for Bokhara so precipitately that they carried his leggings and riding-boots after him for two parsangs, as far as Buruna, and only then did he put them on; nor did he draw rein anywhere until he reached Bokhara, and Rudagi received from the army the double of the five thousand dinars."

The Arab traveller Ibn Hawqal leaves behind a 10th century account of the city, bearing witness both to its early prosperity and lingering religious diversity:

"The city of Herat has a castle with ditches. This castle is situated in the centre of the town, and is fortified with very strong walls. Kehendiz, with its mosque, belongs to this city. The governor's palace is situated in the suburb called Khurasan Abad.

"Herat extends about half a farsang (parsang) on the road of Busheng or Pusheng. There are four gates; one on the road to Balkh, another, on the Nishapur road, called Zeyadi; another, which they call Derwazeh Khushk. All the gates are made from wood, except that on the road to Balkh, which is of iron, and situated in the middle of the city. In all Khurasan and Maweralnahr there is not any place which has a finer or more capacious mosque than Herat. Next to it we may rank the Mosque of Balkh; and after it the mosque of Seistan.

"At the distance of two farsangs from Herat there is a mountain, between which and the city there is not any garden, orchard, nor water, except the river of the city and a bridge. In all the other directions there are gardens and orchards. This mountain, of which we have spoken, produces not either grass or wood, or anything except stones, which serve for mill-stones. Here is a place inhabited called Siccah, with a temple or church of Christians."

Herat passed into the hands of the Ghaznavid Empire at the end of the 10th century, and then into the control of the Seljuk Turks under Torghul Beg in 1038. Despite these changes in government, the city continued to flourish throughout the whole period. The Arab geographer Yaqut al-Hamawi wrote that, at this time, Herat was pre-eminent for "its grandeur and prosperity, the fertility of its soil, its

Herat, from the air in 1972. The Friday Mosque is in the left centre with the minarets at the Musalla complex in the distant left. [B. Woodburn]

large population, the beauty of its gardens, the abundance of water, and most of all for the great number of scholars and famous men which it had produced." The foremost member of this crowd of famous men is, without any doubt, the religious scholar and ascetic Abu-Isma'il 'Abdullah Ansari.

Ansari was born in Herat in 1006, where, aside from various short periods of study in Nishapur, he spent virtually all of his life. He was renowned for his learning and erudition, but nevertheless spent long periods under suspicion from both the Ghaznavid and Seljuk rulers. As an adherent of the Hanbalite legal school of Islam,

which advocated a strongly literal understanding of the Koran, he ran into frequent conflict with the state, which promoted the Asharite school and a more metaphorical reading of the Muslim Holy Book. He was briefly exiled on account of his beliefs in 1066, but after a change of heart on the part of the authorities he was recalled, and in 1070 given the title of 'Shaykh al-Islam' by the Abbasid Caliph in Baghdad. Ansari spent much of his time teaching, writing treatises in defence of the Hanbalite school, and also pursuing his own studies and contemplations of mysticism. He believed that by meditation on the words of the Koran and the Hadiths (traditions of the Prophet), one could come to an inner knowledge of the essence of faith, the unity of the divine, and a personal experience of God Himself. Nevertheless, he still held, unlike some others, that a strict adherence to the external laws and customs of the religion complemented rather than hindered this process. He also stressed the danger of pride; self-abasement itself could lead to vanity, leading ascetics easily astray from the inner knowledge of God.

Ansari is perhaps best known today for his *Munajat*, or "Intimate Conversations"—a compilation of mystical utterances from all of his other works put together by his students. The following extracts are from the translation made by W.M. Thackston:

In the agony suffered for You,
the wounded find the scent of balm:
The memory of You consoles the souls of lovers.
Thousands in every corner, seeking a glimpse of You,
cry out like Moses, 'Lord, show me Yourself!'
I see thousands of lovers lost in a desert of grief,
wandering aimlessly and saying hopefully,

'O God! O God!'
I see breasts scorched by the burning separation from You;

I see eyes weeping in love's agony.
Dancing down the lane of blame and censure,
Your lovers cry out, 'Poverty is the source of my pride!'
Ansari has quaffed the wine of longing:
Like Majnun he wanders drunk and perplexed through the world.

O God, You are merciful in Your might,
You are glorious in Your beauty.
You are not needful of space,
You require not time.
No-one resembles you;
You resemble no-one.
It is evident that you are in the soul—
Nay, rather the soul lives by something which you are.

O God, when You brand a heart with your love,
You scatter its heap of being to the winds of non-existence.

O God, whosoever comes to know You
And raises the banner of Your love
Will cast off all that is other than You.
What use has he of his soul who has known You?
What use has he of offspring and family?
When You drive one mad,
You give him both this world and the next:
What use has the madman for this world or the next?

O God, when I look upon you,
I see myself a king among kings,
A crown on my head.
When I look upon myself,
I see myself among the humble,
Dust on my head.

O God, outwardly I am dishevelled
and inwardly I am in ruins.
My breast is aflame
and my eyes atear.
At times I burn in the fire of my breast

Inside the shrine of Gazargah, by Robert Byron, 1933 [Conway Library]

and at times I drown in my tears.

O God, from Your victim flows no blood.
From one burned by You rises no smoke.
He who is killed by You is happy to be killed.
He who is burned by You is glad to be burned.

O God, would that Abdullah had turned to dust
that his name could be effaced from the register of existence!

Ansari died in 1089—killed, so legend relates, by unruly boys pelting him with stones whilst he was at prayer. He was interred at the burial-ground of Gazargah, which since that time has been a leading site for pilgrimage. The English traveller Arthur Conolly left this account of it after an excursion there in the 1830s:

"…We made a party, with our host's brother and the Aukhoondzadeh, to visit the shrine of Khojeh Abdollah Ansari, a Sunni Saint and philanthropist of great celebrity, who lies buried in a garden on the hills which are to the north of the city. The morning was lovely, and my companions, having plenty of pipes to keep them in spirits, exerted themselves to be witty, and we rode in the greatest possible harmony to the village of Gazar Gah. Here we picketed our horses under a fine tree, and proceeded to the gate of the garden, on either side if which was a small mosque, kept by attendant servants of the shrine, who desired us to enter and say a mass, and to leave as much money as we were anxious should be given in charity. We deposited our slippers here, and then passed into a walled garden, the trees of which shaded several tombs of white marble built over the dust of the descendants of Timour-leng (Tamerlane). At the end of the garden, under a low spreading tree, was the grave of the saint, covered by a large stuccoed mound, of conical shape, and headed by a pillar of white marble, on which were sculpted choice Arabic sentences. The shape of the pillar was very elegant; but, unfortunately, when the [Persians] came to Herat they cracked it, in their desire to dishonour a saint of a sect opposed to their own. All our party were Shias, so that, if they did not consider the act a very meritorious one, they in now way found fault with it, and, as they entertained no great idea of the sanctity of the place, I was enabled to indulge my curiosity without constraint. About the tomb were many rags, left there by the votaries who had bad husbands, or who were childless, etc, and several rams' horns, which, I could not learn why, are brought to all holy places. Near the head of the tomb was a withered tree, stuck full of nails, which had been driven in by persons afflicted with toothache—a certain cure...

"The shrine is very well endowed, a Motwullee and 30 attendants being retained to perform the duties of reading the Koran and keeping the garden in order; and they, and numberless cats, lounge about and sleep, and profit by the visitors. Khojeh Abdullah Ansari extended his philanthropy to the brute species, and was very fond of cats, of which I should think not fewer than 100 are kept in honour of his memory; not that the shrine is put to much expense, for the townspeople continually make picnic parties, to enjoy the prospect from these hills, and what they do not eat they leave for the cats and beggars.

A pilgrim at the shrine of Ansari, Gazargah [B. Woodburn]

"Timour-leng's descendants constructed summer palaces on this hill, made other gardens and basins of water; but these only remain as evidences of a grandeur which has passed away. We wandered among the ruins and over the hill, enjoying varied prospects of the beautiful valley below us, and then sat down to dine under a shady tree. Our host had munificently kebaubed a sheep, and our cloth was besides spread with bread and cheese, curds, grapes, and pistachio-nuts; our beverage was clear and sparkling water from the rill, and the repast was seasoned with the best humour and Persian wit. While we feasted and were surrounded by cats, who watched and fought for the morsels thrown to them, and two or three old beggars shared with them the fragments of our repast. The glow of an autumn sun, which had bathed the whole valley in a flood of light, was fading into the grey of evening when we mounted our horses to return home: the moon rose almost as soon as the sun had set; by its light we visited other gardens on our way to the city, which we reached when its inhabitants were at rest, and retired to our couches in that pleasant state of weariness which closes a day happily spent."

The travel writer Bruce Chatwin also visited the shrine in 1970, recording his impressions in a notebook:

"Set in a garden. Single white roses, beds of purple petunias, vegetable plots behind neat box hedges, cypresses and pomegranate trees.

"The Iwan… Diamond lozenges blue and white. The two side-panels key-fret (time of the Chinese embassies) pale turquoise and dark blue. Olive green and ochre centre. Central Iwan the domed heavens, blue stars in an orange sky. Zoroastrian survival. Tomb of Ansari with green painted palings. Decorated Kufic balustrade in buttery white marble. Small pistachio trees. Red and green prayer flags. Soldiers praying.

'Old man lying in the shade. Women walking in wavering blue. White turbans and white marble tomb slabs. The knotted pine's craggy branches with cones. The tree peppered with nails of the faithful. Abrasion of devotion. Wild wind whistling through the pines and briar roses. Lattices and blue carpets spread on the stone tile. Horned sheep on a tomb—the Ram of the Faith. Octagonal guest house cream with green shutters. A huge and sinister hornet flexing its repulsive body on a white marble rose decorating an inscription."

The inscription by Ansari's tomb reads:

"In order that the cup-bearer of the divine knowledge may give your heart the liquor of wakefulness, come to the assembly of Khaja Abdullah Ansari.

"The tombstone of his sepulchre is a beautiful cypress which, by its excessive beauty, has so moved the angles that they exclaim and cry like turtle-doves."

The greatest catastrophe to befall Herat was, beyond question, the Mongol invasion of the 13th century. The city was besieged

Detail of the tilework at the entrance to the shrine of Ansari at Gazargah, 1972 [B. Woodburn]

twice; first, in 1219 by Tolui Khan, the son of Genghis, and for a second time in 1222 by Eljigidäï Noyan, another of the Mongol commanders. Herat had become, not long before, a possession of the growing empire of the Khwarazm Shahs under Sultan Jalal-ud-Din Muhammad, and was now administered by his governor, Malik Shams-ud-Din Muhammad Jurjani. The historian Khwandamir narrates the fierce resistance to the siege led by Jurjani, and the affair's relatively amicable conclusion:

"[Tolui encamped in the Mashartu meadow outside the city], and sent an envoy named Zambur to the leaders of the city with a message that the king, cadi, khatib, and famous men must come out to greet him so that they might bask in the sun of imperial favour, secure from untoward events. When Malik Shams-ud-Din Muhammad Jurjani, Sultan Jalal-ud-din Muhammad's governor in Herat at that time, heard Zambur's message, he killed him in a fit of rage, saying, 'May the day never dawn that I submit to infidels.'

"When the news of Zambur's murder spread in Tolui's camp, the Mongols swarmed out enraged and, at Tolui Khan's command, surrounded the city, killing everyone they encountered. Malik Shams-ud-Din Muhammad had readied himself for battle, and for seven days great valour was displayed on both sides, as many from both the Muslim and infidel camps went to heaven and hell, among them seventeen hundred Mongols. On the eighth day Malik Shams-ud-Din Muhammad and a large group were out fighting when an arrow hit him and killed him. The Heratis divided into two groups. Those who supported Sultan Jalal-ud-Din and the adherents of Malik Muhammad Jurjani said, 'We will not stop fighting so long as there is a breath of life left in us.' The cadis, ulema, nobles, and grandees of the city, however, were inclined to make peace. Since Tolui Khan liked the sweet waters, pleasant air, pleasure parks, and gardens of the region, he did not want Herat to suffer the same devastation as other places, and so on the very day that a truce was proposed by the Heratis, he and two hundred horsemen rode up to the moat at the Firuzabad Gate. He himself said, 'People, know that I am Tolui Khan, son of Genghis Khan. If you want your life spared, cease fighting and come forth in obedience. Render to our representatives half of what you used to give in annual taxes to the Khwarazm Shah's agents, and you will receive imperial favour.' And he swore a solemn oath that if they stopped resisting and opened the gates, they would be dealt with justly and equitably.

"When the people of the city heard these words from the mouth of Tolui Khan, they ceased fighting and sent out to Tolui Khan Amir Izzuddin Muqaddam Haravi, the chief of the weavers guild, with a hundred weavers, each carrying nine suits of expensive clothing. Then the nobles and grandees came out of the

[R. & S. Michaud]

city to receive imperial favour. Tolui Khan killed 12,000 men of Herat who were followers of Sultan Jalal-ud-Din, but he did not bother any of the rest of the population. Tolui stationed Malik Abubakr as governor and Mangtai as *shahna* and then set out for Taloqan, where his father was encamped."

However, this peace was not to last; as the historian goes on to declare, "the pen of fate had inscribed the destruction of Herat". A short while after Tolui left the city, news came that Genghis had suffered a serious reverse in his offensive against the forces of the Khwarazm Shahs. As a result, it was rumoured that the Mongols were on the verge of retreat. The people rose up, killed the new governor, and rescinded their allegiance to the invaders—a situation not dissimilar to that faced by Alexander in the same place one and a half thousand years previously. When the news reached Genghis—who was certainly not intending to cease his campaign—he became furious and scolded Tolui, saying "If you had killed the people of Herat, this revolt would never have happened." As a result, Genghis gave orders for the second siege of the city, which Khwandamir describes, along with its aftermath:

"Genghis Khan dispatched Eljigidäi Noyan and 80,000 warriors to Herat and charged them to take the city and not to leave a thing alive. Eljigidäi sped across the distances and camped on the banks of the Herat River, where he kept his men for a month in order to make preparations to take the citadel. Assistance was requested by Genghis Khan's order from some other forces of Khurasan… and 50,000 additional men joined Eljigidäi's forces…

"After a month Eljigidäi apportioned the gates of Herat and stationed 30,000 men all around the city, saying, 'Anyone who deviates from the line of duty will be executed, and anyone who displays valour will be extremely well rewarded.' Then he attacked from all four sides at once, and the Heratis, trusting in God, began their defence. For six months and 17 days battle and bloodshed continued. In the year AH 619 [AD 1222] Eljigidäi kept up battle continuously for several days, and in every assault nearly 5,000 of his men were killed or wounded. However, so many stones were hurled that holes were made in the outer walls, and the towers were nearly toppled by tunnels bored beneath sawhorses. One day fifty yards of the wall fell in on the sawhorses, and 400 renowned warriors of the Tartar army were crushed to death. Three days after this event, the Heratis were driven to desperation by lack of supplies, and divisions began to appear among the ranks. On a Friday morning during the month of Jumada II 619 [July–August 1222], Eljigidäi took Herat by force from the Khakbarsar Tower (which is now known as Khakistar) and unleashed a general massacre in which men, women, old, and young were killed. For seven days and nights the Mongols did nothing but kill, plunder, burn and dig up. More than 1,600,000 Heratis were martyred.

"Then Eljigidäi went to the province of Harirud, and when he reached the town of Obey, he sent 2,000 Mongols back to Herat to dispatch anyone who might have crept out of hiding. Those 2,000 wretched infidels returned to

Herat, gathered together nearly 3,000 people, and then killed them. Aside from sixteen people, one of whom was Mawlana Sharaf-ud-Din, the khatib of the village of Jighartan, who had hidden in a hole in the dome of the Friday mosque, not a soul was left alive in Herat. In the history of Herat it has been related that when the city was vacated by the Mongols, one of those sixteen who had survived came out of the mosque, went to the market and sat down on the counter of a sweet shop, looking all around but seeing no-one. Then he stroked his beard and said, 'Thank God for a moment of peace and quiet.'

"Later another twenty-four people from the surrounding areas joined the sixteen survivors, and for fifteen years there was no-one but these forty people in the entire city and surrounding countryside. They all lived next to the Friday mosque... feeding themselves for a long time on dried meat belonging to the slain. They searched through the pantries of houses and horse stables, picking up every grain of wheat and barley they saw. When they had gathered a few maunds of grain, they managed to plough a small patch of earth and plant it so that the next year each one would have a handful of wheat and barley at harvest time. These forty people made Mawlana Sharaf-ud-Din their leader and with difficulty kept themselves alive until such time as Ögödäï Qa'an, Genghis Khan's son, decided to rebuild Herat..."

Despite the scale of the devastation, the city still recovered. Aided by its natural advantages—the fertility of the ground, the ready supply of water and its position on

The entrance to the shrine of Khwaja Abdulla Ansari at Gazargah, 1972, much as Bruce Chatwin would have seen it. [B. Woodburn]

the trade routes—Herat was able, in a short while, to regain its former eminence. Under the capable government of the Kurt dynasty, which had come to rule Herat by the middle of the 14th century, the walls of the city were rebuilt, commerce was encouraged and protected, and Herat re-acquired to a great degree the luxury and wealth which Yaqut al-Hamawi had praised a century before.

However, the city was again to suffer. In 1381, the Emperor Timur (Tamerlane), having seized power in the regions beyond the River Oxus, moved southwards with the intention of capturing Persia. Ghiyas-ud-Din, the Kurt's leader then in charge of Herat, at first attempted to resist the impetus of this new invader, but seeing at

length that he would be unable to do so, instead decided to surrender. Nevertheless, Timur did not desist from sacking the city: the treasuries were emptied, the city walls were pulled down and the gates carried away and installed in the town of Kesh, Timur's birthplace. Yet, within a few years he came to realise the strategic importance of Herat, and consequently his son, Miran Shah, was sent with orders to restore it.

In 1396, Timur appointed his fourth son, Shah Rukh, to the governorship of Khurasan. It was a decision that was to mark the beginning of an extended period of cultural and artistic endeavour—indeed, a renaissance—throughout the whole Timurid Empire. In 1404, Shah Rukh acceded to his father's throne. Setting up his brilliant son, Ulugh Beg—one of the foremost astronomers of his time—as his viceroy in Samarkand, he moved the capital of the empire to Herat. There, along

with his formidable wife Gawhar Shad, he presided over a flowering of the arts, architecture, painting, learning and literature, that was—despite a period of instability in the middle of the 1400s—to last for the next 100 years.

Much of the architectural heritage from this time in Herat has been lost. However, the Emperor Babur, who visited the city in 1506, left behind a list of the mosques, palaces, gardens and other buildings he was able to compass during his stay there. The bare recital of these names is enough to evoke an idea of the grandeur and opulence of the city in this era:

"In the course of these twenty days I saw perhaps everything worthy of notice except the Khanekh (convent) of Sultan

The Walls of Herat; some of the Timurid tilework which once covered them is still visible, 2004 [B. Jenks]

Huseyn Mirza. I saw the Gazer-Gah, the garden of Ali-Shir Beg, the paper mills, the Takht Astaneh (royal residence), the bridge of Kah, the Kadastan (race-course), the Nazar-gah Gardens, the Niamat-abad (Pleasure-place), the Khiaban (public pleasure walks), the Khatirat of Sultan Ahmad Mirza, the Safar Palace, the Nawai Palace, the Barkir Palace, the Palace of Haji Beg, the Palaces of Sheikh Bahaudin Umar, and Sheikh Zain-udin; the honoured Mausoleum and tomb of Jami, the Nimazgah-i Mukhtar (place of prayer), the Fishpond, the Saq-i-Suliman, the Imam Fakir, the Avenue Garden, Mirza's colleges and tomb, and congregational mosque, the Raven Garden, the New Garden, the Aksarai, or White palace, built by Sultan Abusaid Mirza, near the Irak gate, Puran and Sufeh-i-Sirandazar (the Warrior's seat), Chirgh Alanik and Mir Wahid, the Bridge of Malan, Khwajeh's porch, the White Garden, the Tarab-Khana (Pleasure House), the Bagh-i-Jahanara, the Kioshk and Makavi Khaneh (Mansion of Enjoyment); the Sosni-Khana (Lily Palace), the Doazdeh Burj (Twelve Towers), the great reservoir on the north of the Jahanara, the four edifices on its four sides, the five gates of the town walls, the King's Gate, the Irak Gate, the Firuzabad Gate, the Khush Gate, and the Kipchak Gate, the King's Bazaar, the Charsu, or great public market, the college of the Sheikh-ul-Islam, the Grand mosque of the Kings, the Bagh-i-Shahar (City Garden), the College of the Badia-i-zaman Mirza on the banks of the River Anjil, Ali Shir Beg's dwelling-house, which they call Unsia (Palace of Ease), his tomb and great mosque, his college and convent, his baths and hospital, all these I saw in the short space I had to spare."

One of the most magnificent monuments to be constructed at this time was the Musalla, or religious college, commissioned by Gawhar Shad. After the Timurid period, this fell prey first to neglect, and then was finally destroyed in the Pandjeh crisis of 1885, with only a number of minarets still left standing. However, descriptions of it still remain from western visitors. The British Army officer, C.E. Yate, who was responsible for carrying out the order of the Amir of Afghanistan to demolish it, spoke of it thus:

"... a huge massive building of burnt brick, almost entirely faced at one time with tiles and mosaic work, all the various patterns of which are beautifully fitted together in minute pieces set in gypsum plaster. Musalla means, I believe, a place of prayer; and doubtless, on this account, the walls were covered with the numerous texts in tile-work that now ornament them. The main building consists of a lofty dome some 75 feet in diameter, with a smaller dome behind it, and any number of rooms and buildings around it. The entrance to this dome is through a lofty archway on the east, some 80 feet in height, the face of which is entirely covered in tile-work and huge inscriptions in gilt; while above the archway is a lot of curious little rooms and passages, the use of which I cannot tell. To the east of this arch is a large courtyard some 80 yards square, surrounded with corridors and rooms several stories in height—all covered with tile-work. The main entrance of all is on the eastern side of this court, through another huge archway, also some 80 feet in height; but though the inside of the arch is all lined with tiles, or rather mosaic-work in regular patterns, the outside is bare, and looks as if it had never been finished. Four minarets, some 120 feet in height, form the four corners of the building: a good deal of the tile-work has been worn off by the weather—especially towards the north, the side of the prevailing winds; but when new, they must have been marvellously handsome. It is hoped that they may be preserved from the general demolition..."

The ribbed dome of the Mausoleum of Queen Gawhar Shad at Herat, in 1972. The drum is partly restored but the dome still has some of its original tiling. [B. Woodburn]

An anonymous member of Yate's party in Herat published a more evocative description in *Blackwood's Edinburgh Magazine* of August 1885:

> "The face and interior of the Musalla (except the wings), as well as the exterior of the minarets… are all covered with enamel-work, illustrating the delicate beauty of an art which is lost. Shades of blue and green, from azure and emerald to the deep tones of indigo and of a lustrous peacock green (I don't know how else to describe it), varied with yellows from lemon to russet, including all the tints of dying and dead leaves in autumn, are blended in the devices of this *faïence*. It is not the coarse tile-work such as is common in India (though in general effect it resembles Multan pottery, which is very effective in its way), but all the delicate tracery of the design is carefully graven into the clay before the enamel is burnt on… This *faïence*, I think, constitutes the chief beauty of the Musalla. Yet the gigantic size of the whole hill, and the halo of history surrounding the slender stems of those broken minarets, were very impressive on that still May evening. And surrounding it, of course, were ever the same saintly-looking poppies, like deceiving angels, with delicate creamy-white complexions, beguiling the senses even as they stood, and making the air heavy, faint, and oppressive."

A story of one of Gawhar Shad's visits to the Musalla with her ladies-in-waiting,

The Musalla Minarets at Herat, from the air in 1972 [B. Woodburn]

here narrated by Mohun Lal, demonstrates her thoroughly enlightened attitude towards scholars:

> "It is alleged, one day, Gawhar Shad, accompanied by 200 beautiful ladies, came into the college, and ordered all the students to go out; she passed all the day in the place, and had the pleasure of seeing every room.
>
> "One of the students, being sleepy, was not aware of her coming, and therefore he remained in the college. He awoke, and peeped fearfully through the holes of the window. He cast his eyes on a ruby-lipped lady, one of the companions of Gawhar Shad. She caught the sight of the scholar, and fell in love with him. She left her associates, and entered the room of the student, who gained the pleasure of her society.
>
> "She was a delicate virgin, and after leaving the student, she joined her party, who suspected her by the irregularity of her dress and manners.
>
> "Gawhar Shad, on the information of this, was very much vexed, and to wipe away the reproach, she married all her associates to the students of the

Minarets at the site of the Musalla, 1972 [B. Woodburn]

college, who were first ordered to avoid the friendship of the women. She gave them clothes, fine beds, and good salaries to live upon; she made rules for the collegians to meet their wives after seven days, on the condition not to forget their studies. She did all this to arrest the adultery."

In 1438, the year after the completion of the Musalla, the poet Mahmud Arifi composed the *Halnama*, or 'Book of Ecstacy' (also known as 'The Ball and Polo Stick). Like Ansari's *munajat*, the work meditates on the total and self-annihilating love which the mystic bears for the infinity and unity of God. Arifi uses as the central image a polo mallet ceaselessly striking a ball, hitting it in all directions without any regard, to portray the relationship between the mystic devotee and the divine. The poet envisages the ball addressing the polo mallet with such a speech:

"Oh my beloved, I will sacrifice my head for your love.
Since I stand tall in your presence, why should I not lose my head at your feet?
Every moment you are with me, you save me from the dust
You have carried me on this path; I shall fall onto the dust of your feet.
Even if you leave me, you will soon hurry back to me.
I am at your feet, not wishing to leave you; listen to my words—they are
                                                                not idle.
Even if you strike me a thousand times, I shall still be at your feet.
I shall always look up to you; you will always find me at your feet.
Your thoughts will never leave my head, and I will always fly on your wings.
I ceaselessly proclaim your excellence, so how can I escape you?
Although you are elusive, I intend to catch you and kiss your feet.
Even if you harm me, and break my head a hundred times,
I shall not turn away from you—I have no weapon except my head.
I may be as beautiful as the moon, but in your presence I am no more than
                                                        the soil beneath your feet.
As long as I can remember, I have been under your spell:
It was you who made me, and spread my fame…"

After the death of Shah Rukh, and the short reign of his son Ulugh Beg as the Emperor in Herat (1447–49), a period of internecine strife overtook the Timurids. This disorder only came to an end 20 years later with the accession of Sultan Husayn Bayqara (1468–1506) to the imperial throne. Sultan Husayn is generally

Watercolour of the Musalla, Herat, 1933, by Robert Byron [Byron Estate]

acknowledged to have been one of the greatest princes of the dynasty; he was not only himself a capable writer and poet, but also an enlightened and discerning patron. With the help of his Vizier, Mir Ali Shir Nawai (who is recognised as a pioneering author in Turkish) he surrounded himself with luminaries such as Bihzad, the miniaturist, Mirkhwond, the historian, and Jami, one of the greatest Sufi mystic poets produced by Herat, and indeed, the whole Islamic world.

Jami, however, is also known as a writer of prose. In the *Lawa'ih*, he describes—with distinct echoes of Plato—the path that mystics must take in their meditation on the divine:

> "God has not made man with two hearts within him. The Incomparable Majesty who has conferred the boon of existence upon you has placed within you but one heart, to the end that with a single heart you may love him alone, and may turn your back on all besides, devoting yourself to Him alone, and refraining from dividing your heart into a hundred portions, each portion devoted to a different object...

> "Distraction or disunion consists in dividing the heart by attaching it to diverse objects. Union, or collectedness, consists in forsaking all else and being wholly engrossed in the contemplation of the One Unique Being. Those who fancy that collectedness results from the collecting of worldly goods remain in perpetual distraction, whilst those who are convinced that amassing wealth is the cause of distraction renounce all worldly goods...

> "The 'Truth', most glorious and most exalted, is omnipresent. He knows the outer and inner state of all men in every condition. Oh, what a loss will be yours if you turn your eyes from His face to fix them on other objects, and forsake the way that is pleasing to Him to follow other roads...

> "Everything other than the 'Truth'... is subject to decay and annihilation. Its substance is a mental figment with no objective existence, and its form is merely an imaginary entity.

> "Yesterday, this universe neither existed nor appeared to exist, while today it appears to exist, but has no real existence: it is a mere semblance, and tomorrow, nothing thereof will be seen. What does it profit you to allow yourself to be guided by vain passions and desires? Why do you place reliance on these transitory objects that glitter with false lustre? Turn your heart away

from all of them, and firmly attach it to God. Break loose from all these, and cleave closely to Him. It is only he who always has been and always will continue to be. The countenance of His eternity is never scarred by the thorn of contingency.

"The Absolute beauty is the Divine Majesty endued with the attributes of power and bounty. Every beauty and perfection manifested in the theatre of the various grades of beings is a ray of His perfect beauty reflected therein. It is from these rays that exalted souls have received their impress of beauty and their quality of perfection. Whosoever is wise derives his wisdom from the Divine wisdom. Wherever intelligence is found it is the fruit of the divine intelligence. In a word, all are attributes of Deity which have descended from the zenith of the Universal and Absolute to the nadir of the particular and relative. They have descended to the end that you may direct your course from the part towards the Whole, and from the relative deduce the Absolute, and not imagine the part to be distinct from the Whole, nor be so engrossed with what is merely relative as to cut thyself off from the Absolute...

"Man, in regard to his corporeal nature, stands at the lowest point of degradation; nevertheless, in regard to his spiritual nature, he is at the summit of nobility. He takes the impress of everything to which he directs his attention, and assumes the colour of everything to which he approaches. Hence, philosophers say that when the reasonable soul adorns itself with exact and faithful impressions of realities, and appropriates to itself the true character of such realities, it becomes such as if it were itself altogether essential Being. In like

Caravanserai, Herat, 2004 [B. Jenks]

manner, the vulgar, by the force of their conjunction with these material forms and extreme preoccupation with these corporeal bonds, come to be such that they cannot distinguish themselves from these forms or perceive any difference between the two... Therefore, it behoves you to strive and hide your *self* from yourself, and occupy yourself with Very Being, and concern yourself with the 'Truth'. For the various grades of created things are theatres of His revealed beauty, and all things that exist are mirrors of his perfections.

"And in this course you must persevere until He mingles Himself with your soul, and your own individual existence passes out of your sight. Then, if you regard yourself, it is He whom you are regarding; if you speak of yourself, it is He of whom you are speaking. The relative has become the Absolute, and 'I am the Truth' is equivalent to 'He is the Truth.'"

Towards the end of his life, Sultan Huseyn wrote an apologia for his reign, elucidating and surveying his achievements:

"...During the time of some there has been endless tyranny and innumerable acts of aggression against the poor, miserable peasantry on the part of the self-willed, highly positioned princes and mighty ministers of state. In my time, however, the poor have been delivered of these sorrows and the unlucky peasantry freed of these bonds.

"In the time of some, tyrannical ministers and wrong-thinking potentates wrecked the pious foundations and, spending the proceeds on debauchery and entertainment, have indulged in ungodliness and sacrilege. However, the overseers appointed to the foundations have repaired all the damage and gladdened the people of merit. Because in former times the foundations were in ruins, students were aggrieved and teachers deprived; but now, thank God, there are in the capital nearly one hundred educational institutions where religious learning and certain knowledge are to be found. From the farthest reaches of Anatolia to the borders of China, capable students from all the lands of Islam, hearing of the limitless opportunity for study, choose the hardship of exile from their homes and turn their faces to this imperial city. Of God's favour all expenses are met by the income of the foundations, and they pass their days in freedom from want. Near the above mentioned places of study is a *khanaqah*, in every corner of which those in need are tended to and those deserving receive a portion of good things.

A craftsman in the tile workshop at the Friday Mosque, Herat [B. Woodburn]

"If, in former days, travelling merchants, other strangers and wayfarers had insurmountable difficulty going from their homes to their destinations because of brigands and highway robbers, now swift retribution has rid the realm of the chaff of that God-forsaken group's existence and dispatched them to hellfire. At every stage there are lofty caravanserais for travellers and towering fortresses to provide safety for wayfarers where they may find protection from the cold and shade from the heat. Aside from protection, they can obtain whatever they need therein, and at every turn are stationed troops and police to prevent crime and prohibit robbery.

"If, during the time of some, mosques were allowed to go to wrack and ruin, and the congregations were held captive by brutes, in my time the amount spent on mosques would be beyond the reckoning of accountants, and the congregations can scarcely fit inside, every spot therein being as resplendent as the sanctuary at the glorious Ka'ba.

"If, in the days of some, the precepts of divine legislation and the people of Islam have been subjugated to heretical hordes, during these days the arm of the Prophet's law and precepts has become so strong that the enforcers of public morals can almost snatch the lute and harp from Venus, the Singer of the Third Heaven, and dash them to the ground."

Sultan Huseyn's last claim here was, perhaps, not entirely accurate. Shortly after Huseyn's death in 1506, the Emperor Babur visited Herat, which was by then on the verge of capture by the approaching Uzbeks. Not only did he find Huseyn's sons and successors sunk in decadence, entirely incapable of leading a defence of the city; he himself was sucked into their sin:

"A few days after Muzaffar Mirza had settled down in the White-Garden, he invited me to his quarters; Khadija Begim was also there, and with me went Jahangir Mirza. When we had eaten a meal in the Begim's presence, Muzaffar Mirza took me to where there was a wine-party, in the Tarab-khana (Joy-house) built by Babur-Mirza, a sweet little abode, a smallish two-storeyed-house in the middle of a smallish garden. Great pains have been taken with its upper storey; this has a recess in each of its four corners, the space between each two recesses being like a balcony; in between these recesses and balconies is one large room on all sides of which are pictures which, although Babur-Mirza built the house, were commanded by Abu-sa'id Mirza, and depict his own wars and encounters.

"Two divans had been set on the north balcony, facing each other, and with their sides turned towards the north. On one Muzaffar Mirza and I sat, on the other Masud Mirza and Jahangir Mirza. We, being guests, Muzaffar Mirza gave me place above himself. The social cups were filled, the cup-bearers ordered to carry them to the guests; the guests drank down the mere wine as if it were water-of-life; when it mounted to their heads, the party waxed warm.

"They thought to make me also drink and to draw me into their own circle. Though up till then I had not committed the sin of wine-drinking and known the cheering sensation of comfortable drunkenness, I was inclined to drink wine and my heart was drawn to cross that stream...

"Amongst the musicians present at this party were Hafiz Haji, Jalal-ud-din Mahmud the flautist, and Ghulam shadi's younger brother, Ghulam *bacha*, the Jews'–harpist. Hafiz Haji sang well, as Herati people sing, quietly, delicately, and in tune. With Jahangir Mirza was a Samarkandi singer, Mir Jan, whose

Decaying latticework,
Gazargah, 2004 [B. Jenks]

singing was always loud, harsh, and out of tune. The Mirza, having had enough, ordered him to sing; he did so loudly, harshly, and without taste...

"After the Evening Prayer we left the Tarab-khana for a new house in Muzaffar Mirza's winter-quarters. There Yusuf-i-ali danced in the drunken time, and being, as he was, a master in music, danced well. The party waxed very warm there. Muzaffar Mirza gave me a sword belt, a lambskin surtout, and a grey tipuchaq horse. Janak recited in Turki. Two slaves of the Mirza's, known as Big-moon and Little-moon, did offensive, drunken tricks in the drunken time. The party was warm till night when those assembled scattered; I, however, stayed the night in that house."

Herat was captured by the Uzbeks in 1507, bringing to an end this brilliant period in its history. According to Khwandamir, "So many lustrous pearls, emeralds, Badakhshan rubies and other gems and gold vessels were obtained that not a decimal of a tenth could be contained in the imagination of any emperor." Only three years later, the city fell into the hands of the Persians, who held it with only occasional interruptions until the establishment of the Afghan Empire in the 18th century. Their policy of attempting to divert trade to other regional centres in Khurasan, whilst being only partially successful, still caused a general decline in the state of the city; something which Afghan rule from then did little to reverse. Charles Masson, who stayed there for some time during the 1830s, wrote in a memorandum to the British government that '...the residence of the sons of Timur no longer retains its ancient splendour…' He went on to add, with great foresight, that '…the ancient palaces of its kings still exist, but in decay, so destructive has been the hand of time upon them, that another century may witness their entire demolition.'

At the time when Masson made these comments, Herat and the surrounding territory existed as a virtually autonomous fiefdom outside Afghanistan; it had earlier been seized by one of the deposed Afghan kings, Shah Mahmud, and was administered on his behalf by his vizier, Yar Mahommed. In 1837, the Persians, with Russian aid and encouragement, thinking that Herat was in no fit state to defend itself, entered the country and encircled the city. However, after a siege lasting into 1838, they were eventually compelled to retreat. One cause of their defeat was the presence of a British army officer, Lt Eldred Pottinger, who had offered his services to the vizier. G.A. Henty, the renowned writer of boy's own adventure stories, drawing from historical sources, describes how Pottinger's actions almost single-handedly saved the city from capture on one of the most difficult days of the siege:

"Upon the 24th of June, Herat went through the most terrible experience of the siege. At daybreak a heavy fire opened from the Persian batteries on all four sides of the city. It ceased suddenly after a time. Pottinger, who was at breakfast, exclaimed to Angus, as he leapt up from his seat: 'They are going to assault; the batteries have done their work. Quick, to the wall!'

"Warning the soldiers they came upon as they ran, they made their way to the wall. Just as they arrived there another gun was fired, and at the signal the batteries on all sides again broke into life. A storm of rockets carried dismay into the town, the mortars dropped their shells into it, and, most conclusive of all, a rattle of musketry broke out, growing every moment in power. Against five points was the assault directed. That on the gate of Kandahar was repulsed, and the enemy chased back to their trenches. That upon the south-west angle was but a feint, and was never pushed home against the western gate. The Russian regiment under Sampson, and a strong force under a Persian officer, pressed up to the breach; but the Persian was killed and Sampson carried off wounded, and the troops fled after suffering immense loss. The attack on the north-western face was similarly repulsed, but the fifth contest was desperate. The storming party gained the *fausse braye*. The Afghans defending it fought desperately, and all fell at their post. The storming party rushed up the slope. The officers and leading men were mown down by a heavy musketry fire, but after a fierce struggle the upper *fausse braye* was carried, and some of the assailants gained the head of the breach.

"But now the Afghan reserves were brought up, and the Persians on the breach were driven back. Again and again, the Persians, fighting this time with desperate courage, struggled to effect a lodgement, only to be repulsed, and fell back in confusion on their comrades behind. For a long time the issue was doubtful; a desperate hand-to-hand conflict ranged, the assailants and defenders swayed up and down the breach, which was covered with corpses and slippery with blood.

"Yar Mahomed arrived almost at the same time as Pottinger and Angus, for these, before coming here, had seen that all was going well at the other points attacked.

"They had observed, as they came along, men leaving the breach by twos and threes under the pretence of assisting wounded comrades, and Pottinger saw to his dismay that the men were losing heart. As they came to the breach they found other soldiers coming up. The wuzeer [vizier], was sitting down close by. Pottinger ran up to him. 'You must encourage your men, wuzeer; go forward and join them, or all will be lost.'

"The Afghan scarcely seemed to hear what he said. 'You must come,' Pottinger repeated loudly; 'there is no time to be lost.' Then he turned to Angus: 'Do what you can,' he said. 'I must rouse the wuzeer; evidently his nerves have suddenly given way.'

"Glad at last to be free to join in the struggle, Angus drew his sword and ran down, thrusting back those who were mounting, and pushed his way forward to the front, shouting in Pushtoo: 'Fight, men! Fight for your faith, your wives, and your children! Everything is going well elsewhere. Are you alone going to fail?'

"The bearded Afghans, astonished at seeing this young Englishman rushing forward in advance of them, followed him, and again the Persians were beaten back. But although the Afghans in front had been animated by the lad's example, those behind were still dropping off. The wuzeer, aroused by the vigorous exhortations of Pottinger, had risen up and neared the breach. The

Persians were renewing their attack, and the wuzeer called upon his men to fight. The fugitives paused irresolute. The wuzeer's heart failed him again, and he turned back, his action still further discouraging the men. Pottinger, in the most vehement language, exhorted him to set an example. Again, he turned, and advanced, but again shrank back. Pottinger now, instead of entreating, reviled and threatened him, called him opprobrious names, and at last, seizing him by his arm, dragged him forward to the breach. This astounding treatment maddened the Afghan. He shouted to the soldiers to fight, and as they continued to fall back, seized a large staff, and, rushing like a madman upon the soldiers, drove them forward again with a shower of heavy blows, while Pottinger, sword in hand, seconded him. Cooped up as they were, and seeing no other outlet of escape, many of them leapt wildly down over the parapet, rushed down the slope, and fell upon the Persian stormers. Believing that great reinforcements must have arrived, these were seized by a panic, abandoned their position, and fled."

Herat is notable, perhaps more than any other city in Afghanistan, for its sheer resilience, and its ability to regenerate itself after even the most major of cataclysms. Just as it was able rapidly to re-establish itself after the devastation wrought by Genghis Khan and Timur in the 13th and 14th centuries, within the last ten years it showed itself capable of surviving and maintaining its culture in the face of the philistine repression of the Taliban. The

Wedding dress shop, Herat, 2004 [B. Jenks]

Sunday Times correspondent Christina Lamb in her recent book, *The Sewing Circles of Herat*, describes an interview shortly after the fall of the Taliban in 2001 with

Ahmed Said Haghighi, the president of the Literary Circle of Herat, and a lecturer at the university, Professor Rahiyab. Together, they described the subterfuge they employed to ensure that women in the city continued to receive an education, and that the literary culture of the city was preserved as well as possible:

> "Three times a week for the previous five years, young women, faces and bodies disguised by their Taliban-enforced uniforms of washed-out blue burqas and flat shoes, would knock at the yellow wrought-iron door. In their handbags, concealed under scissors, cottons, sequins and pieces of material, were notebooks and pens. Had the authorities investigated they would have discovered that the dressmaking students never made any clothes. The house belonged to Mohammed Nasir Rahiyab, a forty-seven year old literature professor from Herat University, and, once inside, the women would pull odd their burqas, sit on cushions around a blackboard and listen to him teach forbidden subjects such as literary criticism, aesthetics and Persian poetry as well as be introduced to foreign classics by Shakespeare, James Joyce and Nabokov.

> "Mr Haghighi banged on the door and it was opened by a small boy who showed us into a long and windowless room with cushions on the floor, a board at one end, an oil painting of a man at a desk, and some glass wall-cases containing a few books including a Persian-English dictionary, some volumes of Persian poetry, and a book in English on Poisoning. Professor Rahiyab came and sat down with us beneath his own portrait, and a flask of green tea and a dish of pistachios were brought even though it was Ramadan. 'I don't go to the mosque,' he explained with a shrug. He was a shy soft-spoken man who only became passionate when talking about his beloved Russian writers and he showed me his bust of Pushkin, which he used to keep hidden, only taking it out for classes.

> "While lessons were underway his children would be sent to play in the alleyway outside. If a Talib or any stranger approached, one of the children would slip in to warn him and he would then escape into his study with his books while his place running the class was quickly taken by his wife holding up a half-finished garment which they always kept ready.

> "Only once were they almost exposed when the Professor's daughter was ill in bed and his son had to run to buy bread so there was no one to raise the

alarm when a black turbaned Talib rapped at the door. 'Suddenly he was in the courtyard outside. I just got out of the room in time and my wife ran in and the girls hid their books under the cushions. I realised that I had not cleaned the board or hidden Pushkin. I sat in the other room, drinking tea, my hand shaking so much my cup was rattling. Fortunately the Taliban were such ignorant people they did not know what they were seeing.'

"In a society where even teaching one's own daughter to read was a crime… I asked the professor why he had taken such a risk.

"If the authorities had known that we were not only teaching women but teaching them high levels of literature we would have been killed,' he replied. 'But a lot of fighters sacrificed their lives over the years for the freedom of this city. Shouldn't a person of letters make that sacrifice too?

"We were poor in everyday life,' he added. Why should we be poor in culture too? If we had not done what we did to keep up the literary spirit of our city, the depth of our tragedy would have been even greater…

"A society needs poets and storytellers to reflect its pain—and joy,' said Professor Rahiyab as we got up to leave. 'A society without literature is a society that is not rich and does not have a strong core. If there wasn't so much illiteracy and lack of culture in Afghanistan then terrorism would never have found its cradle here."

'The only masonry bridge between Kabul and Herat', near Charikar. [F. Holt]

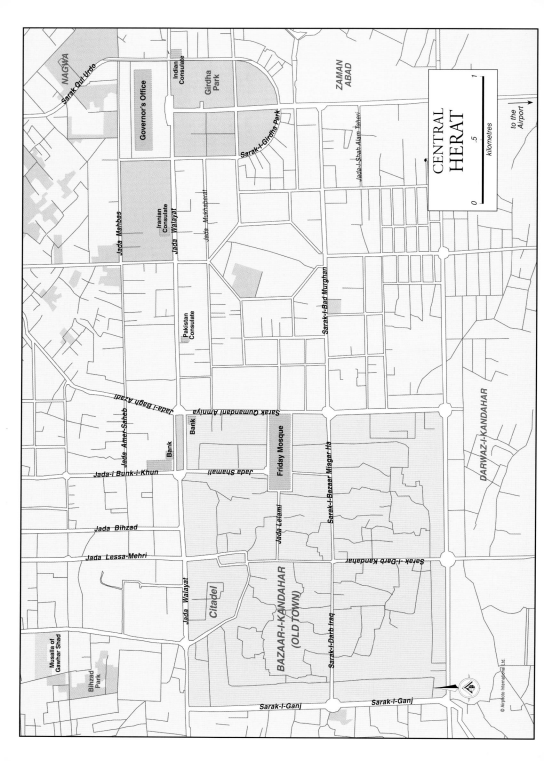

CENTRAL
HERAT

kilometres

0   .5   1

to the
Airport

NAGWA

Sarak Qut Urdo

Governor's Office

Indian Consulate

Girdha Park

ZAMAN ABAD

Sarak-I-Girdha Park

Jada-i Shah Alam Taheri

Iranian Consulate

Jada-Mahbas

Jada Walayat

Jada-Mukhaberat

Pakistan Consulate

Sarak-i-Bad Murghan

Jada-i Bagh Azadi

Jada-Amer-Saheb

Bank

Bank

Sarak Qumandani Amniya

Friday Mosque

Jada-i Bunk-i-Khun

Jada Shamali

DARWAZ-I-KANDAHAR

Jada Bihzad

Jada Lessa-Mehri

Jada Lelami

Sarak-I-Bazaar Misgar-Ha

Sarak-i-Darb Kandahar

Jada Walayat

Citadel

BAZAAR-I-KANDAHAR
(OLD TOWN)

Sarak-i-Darb Iraq

Musalla of
Gawhar Shad

Bihzad Park

Sarak-I-Ganj

Sarak-I-Ganj

© AirPhoto International Ltd.

Herat Area Guide

Accommodation

1. Green Place Guest House

Tel: 224219, (mobile) 0704 05095; address: Jardeh Mahbas, street no. 2

This guest house is easily found because the proprietors have helpfully stenciled signs pointing to the place on concrete walls all around Herat. It is a modern building with a nice garden and a slightly surprising topiary hedge. It is in fact a family house, occupied by the same family who now run it as a guesthouse, and this gives it a particularly good atmosphere for tourists. The son of the house speaks excellent English.

There are 7 bedrooms and the whole house can sleep 25 people. All the rooms have at least two beds. A new building contains single rooms, and a swimming pool is being built.

There are three bathrooms, two with Western-style baths. Bed and breakfast costs US$20 per person per night, which means at least $40 per room. There is a slow internet connection. Heating is supplied in the winter and air conditioning has been promised for the summers. A satellite TV provides the usual 600 channels of rubbish.

Lunch and dinner may be had and the menu varies in price from $1 for a sandwich through $6 for "Chlow Muscle" (?) to $8 for Lamb Chops.

The entire place is very clean and well decorated and I strongly recommend it.

2. Marco Polo Hotel

Tel: 221944, 221947, (mobile) 0704 03340; address: Badmurghan Street email: heratmarcopolo@yahoo.com; website: www.heratmarcopolo.com

This is the place for journalists and people in Herat on business. It is a newly-built hotel with laundry, air conditioning and free internet. It has 30 rooms and two large dining rooms. The manager is Mr Aref Ehsan.

SIGHTS IN AND AROUND HERAT

1. Citadel and museum
2. Old Town and bazaar
3. Chahrsuq and water tanks
4. Friday Mosque and tile factory
5. Minarets and Mausoleum of Gawhar Shad
6. Shazar Dahar: tombs of the two princes
7. Pul-i-Malan
8. The northern hills, Bagh Milat and Takhti Safar
9. Gazargah: a Sufi shrine
10. Ziaratgah: a one-day picnic
11. Karokh
12. Kohsan
13. Obey and Chishti Sharif
14. Minaret of Jam

1. CITADEL AND MUSEUM

Although the present citadel structure dates from 1305, settlement here is very ancient. It long precedes the arrival of Alexander, whose fortress is said to lie underneath the mound. The tiling on the side of the fortress is attributed to Shah Rukh. The museum—long closed to the public—is said to contain fascinating Greek and Timurid pieces, and there are plans for it to be reopened. Enter the citadel itself to walk around the battlements and towers, which afford magnificent views of the city and surrounding hills.

2. OLD TOWN AND BAZAAR

The fun way of getting around the Old Town, and perhaps out to Gazargah, is to use one of the horse drawn taxis that queue at the beginning of the road leading to the bazaar and citadel. They are decorated with bells and red pompoms. The covered bazaar has gone, but arched mudbrick tunnels lead off the main streets to more houses, surprising squares, turns, then more houses round an unexpected courtyard. Be prepared to get lost.

Fortified village in ruins, near Herat [R. & S. Michaud]

The bazaar caters to all needs: silk turbans, aluminium cooking pans, firewood, the motor trade, lorry motors charging car batteries, Wellington boots, bikes, plastic shoes, brushes for sweeping floors, bright piles of oranges, popcorn.

You should spend at least half a day here, alone or in small groups. It is not a place that you can appreciate as part of a big crowd.

SHOPPING

On the north side of the Friday Mosque are the shops that sell handicrafts and antiquities, some of which may be genuine. The stock of most shops has not changed since 1979. Herat's speciality is hand-blown blue glass, with bubbles in, very rustic but attractive.

3. CHAHRSUQ AND WATER TANKS

As one of the biggest cities in central Asia, Herat needed a reliable water supply. Reservoirs supplied this need, and a number of these still dot the town. The most famous is Chahrsuq, near the Friday Mosque, but it is by no means the only one. Such water tanks (reservoirs) follow the same basic design: a roofed pool with steps leading down to different levels, to allow access to the water during different seasons. They are said to derive from the 15th century, during the rule of Sultan Bayqara.

(This page) *Goods on sale in the Herat Bazaar [B. Jenks]*; (right) *The Friday Mosque (Masjid-i-Jami). The present mosque was laid out on the site of an earlier mosque in the 13th century during the rule of the Ghorids. [B. Woodburn]*

Another water tank exists at Baq Marad, a mosque of hideous Soviet-style concrete construction. The pool was emptied following the death by downing of two children, and it is partly filled by rubbish. It was fed from the river rather than a spring. The beautiful lapis-blue inscription on the street attributes the water tank to Bayqara.

4. FRIDAY MOSQUE AND TILE FACTORY

This is one of the major sights of Afghanistan and although I have visited many times, it never fails to give me a thrill. The western end faces out over a garden and you should take your orientation from this, looking west. Pilgrims, covered with patous (long thin brown blanket) sleep in the niches, awaiting the next time for prayer. The mosque has a number of interesting elements to note.

COURTYARD AND MIHRAB

Enter the main courtyard along the long arched passageway on the right of the main entrance from the gardens. The passageway is dark and cool and entering the huge, brightly tiled courtyard, hot from the Central Asian sun, is an unforgettable experience of sudden space, light and colour.

PRE-TIMURID MOSQUE

On the left-hand side, looking from the garden, stands a courtyard that contains the remains of a Ghorid arch (12th century, the same period as the minaret of Jam), which later was covered by a Timurid arch. The top of the Timurid construction has been partially removed so you can see behind it the Ghorid arch. Notice the much more geometrical tiling decoration, a contrast to the swirling mosaics of Timurid design. The geometric turquoise lettering forms quotations from the Koran; an inscription says it is 650 years old and built by Ali Shah.

TILE FACTORY

The photographs and text of Robert Byron show that when he visited, the Friday Mosque was plain and unadorned, with little tilework remaining. The stunning decoration you see today has all been produced since 1943 from the tile factory situated within the mosque itself. It claims to be the oldest tile factory in the world and probably dates back to the original Ghorid construction in 1200. When I first visited in 1993, as the owner of an English tile manufactory, it was to help re-start this workshop. I arranged for a shipment of chemical colours from a supplier in Stoke on Trent, to mix in the glaze—these colours exactly matched the ancient ones. This assistance predated UNESCO's involvement by several months.

5. MINARETS AND MAUSOLEUM OF GAWHAR SHAD

The five minarets are all that survive of the madrasa (theological college; also *musalla*) of Gawhar Shad, the famous Timurid queen. Until the jihad of the 1980s, another minaret stood as well, though today only a stump can be seen to the southwest of Gawhar Shad's mausoleum. Their chief glory was the tilework, and remains of blue and turquoise tiles can still be seen on them. When Byron visited in 1933 a great deal more could be seen and he commented, "If the mosaic on the rest of the Musalla surpassed or even equalled what survives today, there was never such a mosque before or since". Byron rightly laments the destruction with dynamite of the musalla by British soldiers in 1885, in order to clear a sight line for their guns, the better to kill the Russian hordes, who never arrived.

Courtyard of the Friday Mosque, Herat [B. Jenks]

MAUSOLEUM OF GAWHAR SHAD

The interior of the mausoleum is stunning—a set of interlocking niches painted in slightly faded colours. There are three graves: of Gawhar Shad, Huseyn Bayqara and a child. Leaning against the walls of the mausoleum interior are beautiful panels of carved marble, presumably screens from the Musalla destroyed by the British. The curator told me that they had been dug up from between the minarets, during the 1990s (possibly as part of de-mining operations).

Getting inside is not usually a problem; a variety of people have access to the key that opens the padlock. If this fails, the key is easily obtained from the cultural office at the Friday Mosque, although baksheesh may be needed.

6. SHAZAR DAHAR: TOMBS OF THE TWO PRINCES

These two mosques, which house the tombs of two 9th-century princes, from where one can see to the south the citadel, and to the north the minarets of Gawhar Shad across the jumble of mudbrick houses. Perhaps come here by droshky. The mosques themselves have some of the most stunning internal decoration I have seen in Afghanistan.

Looking northwards, towards the minarets, is the tomb of Qasim. The portico has sculpted and patterned decoration that I have never seen elsewhere in such profusion. The background is lapis-blue. On each side of the entrance is one column, carved with palmette decoration. The inscription over the door gives the date of Qasim's death as 190 AH (811 AD). The interior is breathtaking, largely because of the painting on the domes and squinches as well as the panelled tilework at ground level. The pir, who is the guardian, speaks good English. As you walk from Qasim's to Abdullah's tomb, notice the pigeon house.

THE TOMB OF ABDULLAH

Inside this mosque is the best Timurid tilework I have ever seen, though dulled with age. An aid project could easily remedy this. The outstanding interior evoked distant memories of Hagia Sophia in Istanbul.

7. PUL-I-MALAN

Some miles to the west of Herat is the Pul-i-Malan, a bridge of 15 arches praised by Babur, who visited in 1506. The wooded area that runs along the side of the river is a fine place for a picnic. The most famous legend about this bridge's construction is given by Nancy Dupree: "The bridge is attributed to Bibi Nur and her sister Bibi Hur who devoted much time, effort and money in collecting egg shells to mix with the clay from which the bridge was built. This made it stronger than steel and Heratis delight in recounting the fate of countless modern bridges washed away by floods while the Pul-i-Malan remains."

8. THE NORTHERN HILLS, BAGH MILAT AND TAKHTI SAFAR

These hills, to the north of the city, are where Heratis gather to watch the sun set behind the mountains that close the southern plain of the Hari Rud valley. Herat's golden sunsets have been celebrated for many years and a number of gardens and pleasure spots here were built by various rulers to command the best view. Bagh Milat and Takhti Safar refer to two well-known viewing sites in the hills. Ismael Khan, the great mujehad, has continued this tradition and is often to be found in this area as the sun goes down. All visitors should try to do this too, from one of the several spots built recently or over the centuries.

Along the way to Takhti Safar, notice the collection of cannons. One was fired each midday, but Herat seems to have a much larger collection. Going down the row of guns, north to south, the first two are dated 1802 and show the initials and seal of George III; further down are two Vickers 1915 cannon, made in La Spezia; a British artillery piece of 1938; a Russian-manufactured gun with Cyrillic inscription and the last is of Persian manufacture.

Another popular place to watch the sunset is Ghar Darwishan, where the king used to come in the evening. It is more famous now for a mosque, up a short, steep hill, built in front of a cave and thus likely to be the site of a pre-Islamic shrine. The inscription says that it was built during the reign of Shah Rukh and Gawhar Shad for the Sufis to worship in. The cave has a low bench of bricks around it and a domed brick roof extends the cave forward. When I visited there were many men gathered to watch the sunset, and blue specks of women climbing up to the picnic spots. A significant number do not wear burqas but black robes, with just oval faces showing where they clasp the robe round their necks.

Further down the hill is a round building that contains a diorama display of the war based on a Russian design, I suspect the one at Stalingrad. The plain you look across was a main battlefront between the Russians and Ismael Khan's troops and a guide who was a mujahedin (as mine was) will describe the "security strips", long straight roads that the Russians bulldozed and mined through the town in an attempt to secure their hold on the place. Mines were a big problem but now seem to have been cleared by dedicated NGOs and the UN.

Here, too, is the Bagh-i-Milat Hotel, a modest building built on the site of one of the Herati king's sunset-watching spots. Ismael Khan often uses it in the late afternoons to hold meetings.

9. GAZARGAH

A highlight of Herat is the Sufi shrine of Gazargah, a complex of buildings east of the city where Abdullah Ansari, the Sufi poet, is buried. Ansari lived between 1006 and 1089. The buildings were started under Shah Rukh.

A detail of the restored tile work in the Friday Mosque, Herat, 1972 [B. Woodburn]

Remove your shoes at the portico. There is a hallway with a domed and painted roof. On the left-hand side is a mosque; on the right-hand side is a staircase that leads to a room containing a hair of the Prophet Mohammed. It is housed in a circular cupboard that is covered in green cloth, often surrounded by women in blue burqas.

The floor of the hallway is made up of beautiful worn white marble paving stones of various sizes and heights, hundreds of years old. They have been stupidly removed inside the shrine and replaced by light brown machine cut oblongs of stone from Iran, presumably as part of Ismael Khan's programme of urban beautification.

The tiling of blue interlocking lozenges in the hall is magnificent and ancient. Notice also the lovely plaques carved with lines of Persian poetry and Koranic verses. In the courtyard are fine examples of the tilework known as *haft rangi*, or "seven colours", for which Timurid Herat was famous.

Threshing, near Herat [F. Holt]

Another important site of Gazargah is the Golden House (Khana Zarnegar). It is perfectly possible to get in here: the culture office at the Friday Mosque has the key, so go and see them first. Bring a powerful torch because there is no lighting and the decorations, gold leaf against a lapis lazuli background, are well worth seeing. The Golden House normally opens once a week, when it is used by Sufi dervishes.

Inside is a room about 40 sq ft, with a dome supported by squinches. These are decorated with gold leaf on a lapis lazuli background. The bottom row of the dome is a series of pointed arches and above a plain brick dome. On one wall is a white cloth painted with green Sufi sayings of Ansari.

10. ZIARATGAH: A ONE-DAY PICNIC

This is a day in an entirely traditional Afghan village, culminating in a walk across several miles of flat grassy steppe to a spring with the grave of a holy man.

Make the journey to Ziaratgah by car. On the way you will notice the pigeon towers, which provide the dung to fertilise fruit, especially grapes, for which the Herat area used to be famous. Such towers and pigeon houses have over the years evolved a beautiful style, noteworthy for the geometric patterns of brickwork around the holes through which the pigeons enter.

The village of Ziaratgah itself is an example of the continuation of traditional Afghan rural life, though houses and mosques wrecked by the Russians are still visible. It is a village of mudbrick houses and fields surrounded by cob walls. The doors of the houses are irregular in shape, sometimes curved, and set deep in the mudbrick walls, suggesting troglodyte dwellings.

The name Ziaratgah means "Place of the Shrine" and is noteworthy for a superb plain brick mosque from the Timurid period (c. 1370–1507)—the power of its design heightened by its lack of decoration. Outside flows a rill from an attractive spring-fed reservoir, with an iwan-vaulted roof, steps leading down to allow children to fill water containers and a building for the required Islamic ablutions.

The mosque itself is one of the most important Timurid buildings in Afghanistan and certainly my favourite. Over the entrance is Koranic lettering in blue and white ceramic, probably original.

The stunning courtyard of the mosque alone justifies the journey out here. Its austere beauty and buff brickwork are the antithesis of the baroquerie of the Friday Mosque in Herat. In the centre of the courtyard is a square pool in which, surprisingly, goldfish swim. I heard the plops as they swam away from me and the towers shimmered in the spreading concentric rings. In the *qibla* are beautiful blue and white hexagonal tiling, made by a simple and perhaps Chinese-influenced aesthetic and technique of blue cobalt applied to a white clay and then covered with a soft transparent glaze. The triangular painted decorations interlock perfectly with the tessellation of the hexagons. Some appear to have been painted over and some smashed—perhaps in another spasm of iconoclasm. Much more elaborate polychrome tiling appears about 15 feet below the summit of the minarets

Stand on the far right-hand side of the courtyard and see the straw domes over the one-story buildings fronting the mosque and the mauve mountain peaks behind them. Then go and say hello to the children in the school on the right as you go in. Boys sit outside with their reading primers, near dozens of tiny plastic shoes, blue, pink, turquoise, black. Pens and notebooks, easily bought in Herat, are always welcome.

Behind the mosque, and belonging to the headmaster of the village school, Sayyid Gul, is an orchard. This is the place to have a picnic, perhaps to the accompaniment of the village musicians.

Further on in the village is a mosque named Chahel Satun, destroyed by the Russians. Its name means "forty arches", though only four stand now. The ground is comprised of broken bricks and glazed pottery.

Then one can walk, ride or drive across a huge grass plain ringed on the horizon with mountains. You are heading for the spring and picnic area of Mullah Nasband and an orchard of fruit trees. This is a special place with red sandstone cliffs towering over the grove of trees. Find the rather beautiful house covering a spring-fed pool, as clear as a vodka martini. The water is not hot, but warm enough to bathe in.

11. KAROKH: A SUFI SHRINE AND A COLD SPRING

This village, though badly damaged during the anti-Russian jihad, is in the most magnificent setting and represents a perfect example of an old-fashioned Afghan country village, with winding mudbrick streets and women in burqas. Do not photograph the women, though without their splash of colour a photo is merely dull. Now that the refugees are returning the village is being reconstructed.

There are two sights here: the cave with a cold spring and the Sufi shrine.

To find the cave with the spring, on the other side of the Hari Rud River, is not easy. It is not marked and the driver must keep a lookout for the narrow, red-clay track that leads sharply up from the river bed and gives access to the cave and pine trees above. This popular summer picnic spot for Heratis is probably best visited with a hired local guide, to avoid wasting time looking for it.

You walk up a small hillside and look up at the cave, which is fronted by a clump of pine trees with unnaturally tall trunks pushing into the sunlight, reminding one of giraffes. The site is striking with the cliff jutting out 30 feet above your head and making a cool shaded area. Its use by man must be very ancient and I would guess that neolithic humans lived here. Concrete steps have been built up the slope, a necessary precaution since the natural clay is very slippery when wet.

The spring drips from a section of the ceiling in one corner of the overhang, where the roof is made of tiny stalactites green with algae. The water is gathered into a brick tank and is very cold but tastes excellent. You can sit on the edge of the tank and hear the slow, random dripping of water from the roof into the pool.

Near the pool is an Islamic shrine, a small building with Koranic verses engraved in Persian and Arabic, its corners decorated with curved horns. Behind this shrine is a long cave, my guide assured me, almost certainly a pre-Islamic holy place, which has been sealed up with a wall. If true, it would be worth a proper examination. Modern handprints from the local red clay on the white plaster of the shrine put the idea of Lascaux into a European visitor's head.

The shrine of Hazrat-i-Karokh is worth a visit. It is entered through an arched doorway with a vaulted ceiling, rather like Gazargah (see above) but in need of cleaning. This leads into a lovely grove of pine trees through which you can see the mosque and shrine. The upper story of the lodge contains a room where pilgrims (or perhaps mere travellers) may stay "as long as they like". The keeper told me that many pilgrims still come here "from Turkestan".

The mosque itself is of unusual design, its chief feature being a wooden portico with a row of carved pillars about 20 feet high supporting the roof. The brick-paved floor makes it a beautiful arcade. Inside, the mosque is long and narrow and architecturally undistinguished. Its only points of interest are some carved marble Koranic verses. Notable also is the painted decoration of flowers and geometric patterns in the *mihrab*.

The shrine of Hazrat-i-Karokh stands outside, a raised brick platform with beautifully carved Koranic marble inscriptions, one of which dates the shrine to 1220 AH (1841). Pillars stand at each corner, surmounted with animal horns. For a small fee, the keeper will open the gate and show the lovely white marble tomb of the saint, its top a mosaic terrace of carved stones. There are some smaller graves and a cypress tree.

A nearby grove of trees makes this a lovely place for a picnic.

12. KOHSAN: ANOTHER TOMB OF GAWHAR SHAD

I think there is no truth whatsoever in the local's story that Gawhar Shad is in fact buried here rather than in the magnificent tomb amidst the minarets in Herat. The long journey to get here is recommend only for the most obsessive student of Timurid architecture.

The mausoleum stands in the middle of the village, another elegant buff brick design. Only a small patch of tiling remains on the roof. Wind certainly played a part, though locals blame the *shuravi* (Russians) and say that a series of explosions blew the tiling off.

By climbing up onto the roof through a staircase you can reach the inside of the dome. As with other Timurid domes, there are at least two domes (some authorities claim three, but I could only see two here), each steeper than the one below, resting on top of each other. The mausoleum in Herat is similarly constructed. On the roof you can see the surviving tiling, which looks to me very old. The mullah told me that the dome had once been covered with beautiful blue and green tiling.

The internal decoration of the mausoleum is mundane. The walls of the room containing the tombs are covered with unglazed hexagonal tiles, and the main room contains some well-executed fresco paintings of trees, in blue.

On the way back there is a fine bridge, probably from the same period as the Pul-i-Malan. Pontoons of huge stones support five pointed arches—really rather beautiful.

13. OBEY AND CHISHTI SHARIF

Obey is famous for its hot springs, popular with Heratis, and is definitely worth a visit. A fairly ambitious hotel is being constructed here.

The road to Obey is beautiful, especially in the spring, across the flat flood plain of the Hari Rud River, edged with folded loess hills. Villages along the way are composed of mudbrick houses with beehive roofs, a style typical of this area.

You can stop at the tea house (*chaikhana*) at Marwa (60 km from Herat), the walls of which are decorated with abstract circular patterns divided into four differently coloured quadrants—hippy influence perhaps. At 87 km, you enter Obey district at the village of Shahr-i-Nur (New City), about two hours from Herat. Turn left up into the hills as you leave the village, just past the graveyard, to get onto the road to the springs. In the spring, the hills are green and the jagged mountains still snow-covered.

The setting of the hotel and hot springs is stunning, in a canyon between tortured volcanic mountains. A further spring lies about 4 km upstream, reputedly hotter than the ones here, and accessible only by foot.

Obey Springs Hotel: this hotel will have 18 bedrooms, 16 with ensuite bathrooms with hot water. Downstairs is a large restaurant and a room where travellers can spend the night on mattresses on the floor, as in a chaikhana. The top floor has a stunning view of the mountains. The manager, Abdul Baqi, has only vague marketing plans, but some Americans have already stayed here.

HOT SPRINGS

The springs take two forms: the six "modern" baths, and behind them a much older building in which one can swim, which I think is far preferable. Therefore bring swimming things as well as shampoo and towels, which the management do not provide. Or you can dry yourself Afghan-style with your headcloth.

The six modern baths are full-size enamel ones, of which only four were working when I visited. The one at the right end is larger and better than the others. The baths are filled by uncorking a pipe stoppered with a plug of wood and car tyre. The water temperature is perfect and the water slightly sulphurous, no doubt healthy but not at all unpleasant.

But behind this is a much older and more beautiful building, an octagonal domed room with a pool about 20 feet across. Light can be let in by going onto the roof (on the same level as the saint's grave) and removing the stone plug at the apogee of the dome, which lets in a shaft of light visible in the steam. The building has four large and four small arches supporting the roof. The pool is about five feet deep and completely clear with a slight aquamarine tinge. I recommend this strongly rather than the baths. The room is usually locked but the key is easily found, and to open the padlock requires banging with a stone.

I suspect this site is ancient. The steps to the modern baths are made from blocks of beautiful cream-white marble, and I found another block embedded in a bank. Locals say this marble is from a building of long ago.

THE SAINT'S GRAVE

Just above the baths, easily reached, is the tomb of the pir, or holy man. It has four pillars at each corner, with concave tops in which stones sit, rather like a pestle and mortar. The inscriptions are in Kufic—the oldest Islamic Arabic script, angular in appearance—and no one could read them to me. They are rather beautiful and have, unforgiveably, been painted green. As a shrine it is visited by childless women; tied onto the tree that grows over the saints grave are little stones wrapped in cloth, symbolising a baby in a cradle. Above the shrine is the cave in which the holy man lived.

A further drive of several hours due east brings one to Chishti Sharif, site of some curious Ghorid (12th century) ruins.

14. MINARET OF JAM

The road to Chishti Sharif continues on eastwards to the Minaret of Jam, one of Afghanistan's most extraordinary and mysterious structures. It is in a place so isolated that it was not re-discovered until 1943, when—it is said—a pilot spotted it from the air. The minaret was first studied in 1957, and shortly thereafter Freya Stark visited and wrote her famous book, *The Minaret of Jam*. Today it is a UNESCO World Heritage site.

The minaret stands 65 m (213 feet) high and leans off the vertical. Only the Qutb Minar in Delhi is higher. Its provenance has always been a mystery although its inscriptions date it to the Ghorid period (the name of Ghiyasuddin, 1157–1202, is set into the structure), making it the only large-scale building to have survived from that important period.

Scholars debated the purpose of the minaret and some argued that it was part of the Ghorid capital of Firuzkoh. Sceptics pointed to the absence of any other buildings. But in 2002 and 2003 illegal digging uncovered a great deal of archaeological remains, which seem to suggest that the Firuzkoh advocates were right. Rory Stewart's *The Places in Between* is the only published account to describe the present situation there.

OTHER PLACES

Southeast of Herat is a place called Pirosokha, or Pira Sar, in Gozara district, with a spring, a valley and trees 1,000 years old. Along the way are many historical monuments.

The journey to Mazar-i-Sharif from Herat via Maimana takes two days and is safe.

Minaret of Jam, 1971 [Y. Crowe]

ART OF THE BOOK IN TIMURID HERAT

—Dr Ebadollah Bahari

*A*fghanistan is part of the earliest civilisation extending from the Mediterranean in the west to India in the east and China in the north. There is ample evidence of artistic activity in the region from as early as 18,000 BC. Within Afghanistan itself, objects have been excavated to show this, such as the "Sculptured Head" from Aq Kopruk.

Most of the western part of present-day Afghanistan fell within greater Khurasan, which includes parts of eastern Iran and Mavaraunnahr (Transoxiana). This area has been an important centre of civilisation and development down to modern times, and by virtue of its geographical situation, it was a link between the three major civilisations of Iran, India and China.

In the Islamic era, Khurasan was still a centre of art and culture. The Ghaznavid rulers of the 10th to 12th centuries made their capital at Ghazni, and the Ghorid and other local rulers reigned in Afghanistan. But during the Timurid rule, particularly when Timur's son, Shah Rukh, made Herat his capital, the area prospered and flourished in every respect.

Timur (Tamerlane), the founder of the Timurid dynasty, who conquered most of the old Sassanian Empire, India and Central Asia, had a high regard for men of learning, artists and artisans. He encouraged many such men in the conquered lands and despatched them to his capital, Samarkand, where he had elegant buildings erected. After Timur's death in 1405, Shah Rukh, who inherited most of the Iranian lands, set up his capital in Herat, which during 100 years of Timurid rule became the greatest centre of cultural activity, including arts, literature and architecture.

Shah Rukh was particularly interested in history and humanities and had fine illustrated books produced for him. His Iranian wife, Gawhar Shad, also established fine buildings such as the famous Gawhar Shad mosque in Mashhad, with exquisite tile-work and dedicatory inscriptions by Baysunghur, and the famous Mausoleum and Madrassah in Herat (fig.1, see overleaf). However, Shah Rukh's sons—including Baysunghur—were the major patrons of the fine arts in Herat, Fars and Samarkand. Baysunghur, who was appointed to the governorship of Herat by his father, established an important atelier for the production of finely illustrated books and other outstanding works of art for buildings and a variety of projects. He gathered the best artists and calligraphers in his atelier, called Kitabkhana, which employed some 200 artists, including 40 master calligraphers. A report by the head of the Kitabkhana , Ja'far Tabrizi, datable to about 1433, is indicative of the atelier's activities: book production, designs for decorating tents, saddles, buildings etc. The illustrated books produced by this atelier rank among the finest ever produced, and include the famous Shahnameh, known as Baysunghur Shahnameh, completed in 1430.

The artists responsible for these books—originally sent to Samarkand by Timur—included the famous Abdulhay, Mir Khalil and Pir Ahmad. Baysunghur further attracted other master artists to his atelier in Herat; the books produced here now have pride of place in various libraries and museums in Iran, Turkey, Europe and America. Master architects, musicians, and literary men were also attracted to Herat.

Later in the century under the long and stable rule of Sultan Husayn Bayqara, arts and culture flourished further and Herat became a renowned centre of excellence. Many famous artists, literati, builders and musicians flocked to the city. The Sultan and his able Vizier, Amir Ali Shir, generously patronised these men. The celebrated poet, Sufi and writer Abdul Rahman Jami lived there as well, and his presence was a magnet for other literary men.

Thus in the last quarter of the 15th century many able painters were active in producing superb illustrated books, including Kamal al-Din Bihzad, the greatest master of Persian painting. His efforts elevated book illustration to its zenith.

Surpassing all predecessors, Bihzad remains the unmatched master of Persian painting. The conjunction of high culture, supreme aesthetics, great literary personalities, Sufis and sympathetic rulers made Herat the mecca of artists and cultured men of the Islamic lands. In this atmosphere, Bihzad flourished as both a superbly talented painter and a master of spiritual learning. He went beyond the visual appeal of painting to the deeper meaning of reflecting the text that he was illustrating, and thus had a particular mastery in depicting spiritual or Sufi narratives. Bihzad —supreme in his design, colouring and fineness of brushwork—gave a dynamic and naturalistic touch to his paintings, which are unique in Islamic painting.

The importance of the cultured assembly in Herat of that time is emphasised by the surviving documents, which show the powerful Ottoman Sultan lavishing generous donations and presents on the celebrated poet Jami, pleading him to attend his court where he will be revered and

welcomed. Jami politely declines. Similarly, the Ottoman Sultan, who has heard the fame of Bihzad, sends a portrait by his chief Venetian artist, Gentile Bellini, to Sultan Husayn Mirza of Herat; he has the same superbly copied by Bihzad and sends it back to the Ottoman Sultan.

Many contemporary and later historians have written glowing reports of life and the cultural events of the period. For example, the poet and writer Wasifi, in his readable book Badayi al-Waqayi (Wonderful Events), gives an example of the spirit of the cultural gatherings in this period:

"It is reputed that the said Master (Bihzad) brought an illustrated page to the paradise-like cosmically adorned reception of the Great Amir, Mir Ali Shir... It depicted a finely planted garden containing a great variety of trees, on whose branches were perched many kinds of fine, colourful birds, streams, flowing in every direction, and brilliant flowers blooming; it also showed a fine portrait of the Mir standing, leaning on his staff, with trays full of gold set before him as is customary in present-giving ceremonies. Observing the illustration on that delicate page, the gardens of [Mir Ali Shir's] mind were adorned with flowers of delight and happiness, and from the nightingale of his conscience cries of 'well done, well done' [Ahsan, Ahsan] were uttered on the branches of joy and appreciation... Then he turned to those present at the reception and said, 'How would the dear guests describe the praiseworthy illustration?' Mawlana Fasih al-Din, who was a teacher of the Mir, and one of the renowned of Khurasan, responded: 'After seeing these fine blooms, I was tempted to pick some and fix them on my turban'. Mawlana Sahib Dara who was a friend and companion of the Mir said: 'I felt the same inclination, but was afraid that if I do so, the birds might fly off the branches.' Mawlana Burhan, who had a great reputation for humour in Khurasan and was constantly cracking jokes to

(Above) Fig. 1: Tilework at Gazargah, Herat [E. Knobloch]
(Right) Fig. 2: 'The Dance of the Sufi Dervishes', attributed to Bihzad, c. 1490
[Metropolitan Museum of Art]

his Excellency the Mir, said: 'I withhold my hand and my tongue lest [in the picture] his Excellency the Mir be offended and grimace.' His Excellency the Mir then said: 'The dear ones spoke well, and if it hadn't been for the cheek of Mawlana Burhan, I would have showered all this gold on their heads.' After that he presented Master Bihzad with a horse and saddle and a suitable robe, and gave all the others present some fine garments too."

Another event during the usual gatherings of writers and poets with Mir Ali Shir, who was a poet himself, is reported: When the Mir, sitting on the floor, stretched his leg, he inadvertently hit the backside of a poet sitting nearby. The Mir then said: "What has this city come to that you cannot stretch your leg without hitting the backside of a poet?"; to which one of those present retorted, "You will do the same again when you gather your leg again."

Other historians have written about the fine palaces and gardens resounding to the sound of music and entertainments. One of these, Babur, the founder of the Mughal dynasty in India, who was related to the Timurid rulers, in his book, Baburnama, gives a fascinating account of the splendour of the court and palaces and gardens in Herat when he visited the city in 1505–6.

An illustration of the Suma (Dance) of the Sufis (fig.2) demonstrates an event in Herat around 1490. In this vivid and dynamic illustration one can confidently say that the white-bearded man at top-centre is the Sufi sage and poet Jami, the other man leaning on his staff to his right is Mir Ali Shir and the young man holding a book on the left is none other than the painter Bihzad himself, who has immortalised the gathering in this fine illustration.

Further illustrations listed below give a broader appreciation of painting of the period:

Fig.3, from a book of deprived lovers, Layla and Majnun of Nizami, shows a scene of battle between a tribe sympathetic to the dejected lover Majnun with Layla's tribe, who oppose their daughter Layla's wedding to Majnun. Despite the small number of camel-mounted warriors shown in this confined space, one can feel the intensity of the battle. Majnun is seen gazing at this scene from beyond the hill at top-right of the illustration.

Fig. 4–5, a double-page frontispiece to the Hasht Bihisht by Amir Khusrow Dehlavi produced in 1496, attributed to Bihzad, shows a royal hunt in action. Hunting was a princely pastime and here the artist has depicted the riotous scene of the hunt in its different stages.

Fig. 3: 'The Battle of the Clans' by Bihzad,
from Khamsah of Nizami, c. 1490 [British Library]

(Above & right) *Fig. 4&5: 'A Royal Hunting Scene', attributed to Bihzad, from a* Hasht

Bihisht *of Amir Khosrow Dihlavi, 1496. [Topkapi Palace Museum Library, Istanbul]*

*Fig. 6: The Construction of the Palace of Khwarnaq' by Bihzad,
from* Khamsah *of Nizami, 1494 [British Library]*

Fig.6, The construction of the Palace of Khawarnaq, *is a masterpiece of design, skilfully showing all those involved in the construction in an expressive and dynamic manner.*

Sultan Husayn Mirza died in 1506, and the following year Herat was captured by the Uzbeks, who were then driven out by the Safavid Shah Ismail in 1510. The Safavid rulers of Iran had a high regard for the Timurids and attached great importance to Herat, which was treated second only to their capital of Tabriz. The heir to the throne of Shah Ismail, Tahmasp Mirza (later Shah Tahmasp) and later his brother, Sam Mirza, were appointed to the governorship of Herat. Thus the Safavid not only respected the artists and scholars gathered at Herat, but in fact retained the Kitabkhana, appointed Bihzad as its head and encouraged other artists under their domain to join the renowned atelier. This assured continuity in the arts; some of the best illustrated manuscripts up to 1528, including the first part of the world-famous Shahnameh *of Shah Tahmasp, were produced in Herat. However, due to constant threats to the city from the Uzbek Shaybanid rulers of Samarkand and Bokhara, the Kitabkhana was transferred to Tabriz in 1528. Herat nevertheless continued to be an important artistic centre well into the 17th century, after which —due to many historical and political reasons—it fell into decline.*

For further reading, see Timur and the Princely Vision *by T.W. Lentz and G.D. Lowry, Los Angeles County Museum of Art (1989), and* Bihzad—Master of Persian Painting *by E. Bahari, IB Tauris, London (1996).*

Dr Ebadollah Bahari is the author of *Bihzad: Master of Persian Painting*, a fully illustrated work on the art of the period, available from I.B. Tauris, $95.00.

A horseman at Band-i-Amir near Bamiyan, 1972 [B. Woodburn]

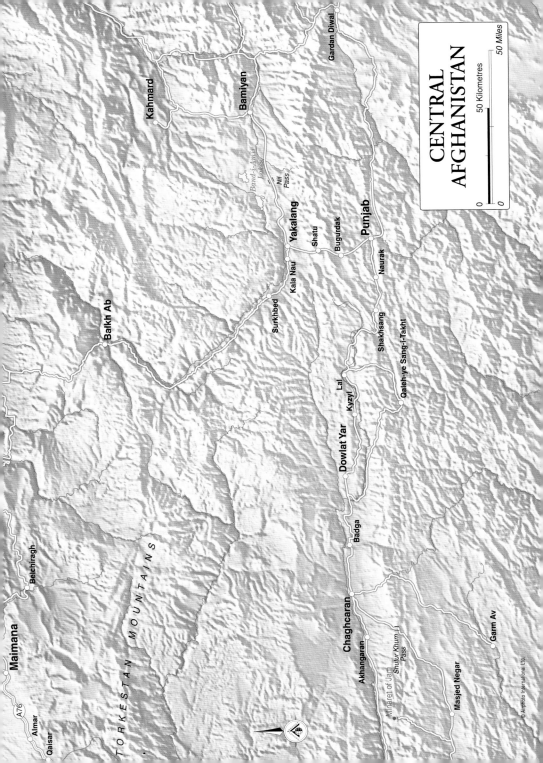

BAMIYAN AND THE HAZARAJAT

Like many places in Afghanistan, the early days of Bamiyan have left little trace in written history. Some scholars argue that it first appears in the classical writers under the guise of Alexandria-ad-Caucasum, a foundation established by Alexander and the Macedonians in their trek across Asia; yet this assertion is by no means universally accepted. Beside a few mentions of its name in Chinese records, nothing specific is known for certain before the 5th century AD.

This lack of texts, however, does not leave us wholly in the dark. Bamiyan lies in a fertile valley beneath the Koh-i-Baba mountain range. Its geographical location, combined with its possession of abundant pasturage, a supply of fresh water and shelter from the wind, would have made it an ideal resting place for caravans plying the trade route between the Kushan capital of Kapisa and the great cities of Balkh and Tashkurghan to the north. Occupying a position between several great empires, it would have seen travellers of many nationalities, and goods from many lands. From China, silk; from Badakhshan, rubies and lapis lazuli; from India, spices and chrysotile; from Iran, silverwork; from the Roman Empire, finished goods—gold, cut gems, glass vessels, amber, frankincense, asbestos cloth, amphorae and statuary.

To the trade route, Bamiyan owed not only its early prosperity but also its religion. Buddhism was greatly popularised south of the Hindu Kush by the conversion of the great Mauryan King Asoka in 260 BC, and it would have been about this time that Buddhist ideas began to reach Bamiyan, carried there as much by merchants as by missionaries. However, the colossal sculptures of Buddha for which the valley was celebrated would not be created for at least another 500 years. Around 130 AD, Kanishka, who ruled the Kushan Empire which held sway over the area of present-day Afghanistan and beyond, called a synod of Buddhist elders to meet in Kashmir. A result of this conference was the deepening presence of the new doctrine of Mahayana Buddhism, or the 'Greater Vehicle'. One of its central tenets was an emphasis on the divine nature of Buddha's own person. The need for adherents to contemplate his humanity encouraged not only the veneration of relics and pilgrimages, but also a demand for representational imagery. An upsurge in patronage supported this nascent artistic impulse, which reached an apogee with the construction of the Bamiyan sculptures.

An early account of the community at Bamiyan is given by the Chinese traveller Hsuen-Tsang, in AD 630. By the time of his visit, control over the Afghan territories had changed hands several times. The Kushan Empire disintegrated after an invasion by Shapur I of Iran in AD 241, which extended Sassanian rule towards the Indus River. This was overturned in the 5th century by incoming waves of a Turco-Mongolian horde, the White Huns or Hephthalties. After a time, they themselves were brought back under control by the Sassanians, and continued to live as vassals of the Persian Empire. Despite these upheavals, Hsuen-Tsang found Theravada Buddhism (Hinayana, Little Vehicle) flourishing at Bamiyan; the settlement's strong geographic position deterred attackers from making any concerted assault against it, and it continued to exist as an autonomous entity:

"This Kingdom is about 2,000 *li* (600 miles) from East to West, and 300 *li* (90 miles) from North to South. It is situated in the midst of the Snowy Mountains. The people inhabit towns either in the mountains or the valleys, according to circumstances. The capital leans on a steep hill, bordering on a valley 6 or 7 *li* in length. On the North it is backed by high precipices. The country produces spring-wheat and a few flowers or fruits. It is suitable for cattle, and affords pasture for many sheep and horses. The climate is wintry, and the manners of the people hard and uncultivated. The clothes are chiefly made of skin and wool, which are the most suitable for the country. The literature, customary rules, and money used are the same as those in the Tukhâra country. Their language is a little different, but in point of personal appearance they closely resemble each other. These people are remarkable, among all their neighbours, for a love of religion; from the highest form of worship to the three jewels (Buddhism), down to the worship of different spirits, there is not the least absence of earnestness and the utmost devotion of heart. The merchants conjecture in coming and going whether the gods and spirits afford propitious omens; if the indications are calamitous, they offer up their prayers. There are ten convents and about 1,000 priests. They belong to the Little Vehicle, and the school of Lôkôttaravâdins (one of the Little Vehicle schools).

(Following pages) *Cliff, fortified farms and ploughed fields, Bamiyan, 1974 [Y. Crowe]*

"To the North-east of the royal city there is a mountain, on the declivity of which is placed a stone figure of Buddha, erect, in height 140 or 150 feet. Its golden hues sparkle on every side, and its precious ornaments dazzle the eyes by their brightness.

"To the East of this spot there is a convent, which was built by a former king of the country. To the east of the convent there is a standing figure of Sâkya Buddha, made of metallic stone, in height 100 feet. It has been cast in different parts and joined together, and thus placed in a completed form as it stands.

"The King of this country, every time he assembles the great congregation of the Wu-che (a meeting of the priests every five years), having sacrificed all his possessions, from his wife and children down to his country's treasures, he gives in addition his own body; then his ministers and the lower order of officers prevail on the priests to barter back these possessions; and in these matters most of their time is taken up."

In 642, the recently converted Muslim Arabs made their conquest of Sassanian Iran, along with Balkh, Merv and Herat. Nevertheless, like many before them, the Arabs were unwilling to attempt an attack on the Buddhist kingdom. An early 8th century Korean monk and pilgrim, Hui-ch'ao (Hye Ch'o), confirms that Bamiyan was continuing as before, but with Great Vehicle Buddhism now becoming prominent:

"Then, from the kingdom of Sie-yu after passing Ki-pin (Kapisa), we travelled toward the north for seven days, and reached the kingdom of Fan-yin (Bamiyan). The king is an Iranian. He is not a vassal of any other kingdom; his foot soldiers and cavalry are strong and numerous; the other kingdoms dare not come to attack them. For clothing, the people wear shirts of cotton, cloaks of fur, and cloaks of felt. The country produces sheep, horses, and cotton; it abounds in grapes. This country is built in the snow and is very cold; many of the dwellings are built on the mountains. The king, chiefs, and the people are very devoted to the three jewels (Buddhism); monasteries and priests are in abundance; they practice the Great and the Little vehicle. In this kingdom, as in Sie-yu and other kingdoms, they clip their beards and cut their hair. Their habits are very similar to those of Ki-pin though there are many differences. The language of the country differs from that of other kingdoms."

Bamiyan Valley in Winter [R. & S. Michaud]

By the time of Hui-ch'ao's arrival, the cliffs around the great Buddhas would have presented a very different appearance to that of the present day. Caves had been hollowed out from the soft stone over the whole height of the rock face to accommodate the monks, and allow them to participate in the pious practice of circumambulating the figures. The Buddhas themselves were coloured red, blue and gold; their niches were covered in frescoes depicting scenes from the Buddha's life, and even the side of the cliff was decorated, as Nancy Dupree says, "with realistic representations of wooden structures such as jutting roof beams and carved doorways and windows, each painted in rich polychromatic hues".

On the road from Bamiyan to the lakes at Band-i-Amir [B. Woodburn]

One of the first Western travellers to reach Bamiyan, and indeed, one of the first travellers at all to leave a description of the caves, was Sir Alexander Burnes, writing in 1834:

> "Bamiyan is celebrated for its colossal idols and innumerable excavations, which are to be seen in all parts of the valley, for about eight miles, and still form the residence of the greater part of the population. They are called "Soomuch" by the people. A detached hill in the middle of the valley is quite honeycombed by them, and brings to mind our recollection of the Troglodytes of Alexander's historians ... The hills at Bamiyan are formed of indurated clay and pebbles, which renders their excavation a matter of little difficulty; but the great extent to which it has been carried excites attention. Caves are dug on both sides of the valley, but the greater number lie on the northern face, where we found the great idols: altogether they form an immense city. Labourers are

frequently hired to dig in them; and their trouble is rewarded by rings, relics, coins, &c. They generally bear Cufic inscriptions, and are of a later date than the age of Mahommed. These excavated caves, or houses, have no pretensions to architectural ornament, being no more than squared holes in the hill. Some of them are finished in the shape of a dome, and have a carved frieze below the point from which the cupola springs. The inhabitants tell many remarkable tales about the caves of Bamiyan; one in particular—that a mother had lost her child among them, and recovered it after a lapse of twelve years! The tale need not be believed; but it will convey an idea of the extent of the works. There are excavations on all sides of the idols; and below the larger one, half a regiment might find quarters."

100 years later, Robert Byron examined the site, commenting on the apparent mix of cultural influences from East and West in the sculpture and painting. His judgement was far from sympathetic:

"That Buddha is 174 feet high, and the smaller 115; they stand a quarter of a mile apart. The larger bears traces of a plaster veneer, which was painted red, presumably as a groundwork for the gilt. Neither has any artistic value. But one could bear that; it is their negation of sense, the lack of pride in their monstrous flaccid bulk, that sickens. Even their material is unbeautiful, for the cliff is made, not of stone, but of compressed gravel. A lot of monastic navvies were given picks and told to copy some frightful semi-Hellenistic image from India or China. The result has not even the dignity of labour.

"The canopies of the niches which contain the two figures are plastered

Detail, pleats in the vestment of the Small Buddha, Bamiyan Valley, 1974 [Y. Crowe]

and painted. In the smaller hangs a triumph scene, red, yellow, and blue, in which Hackin, Herzfeld, and others have distinguished a Sasanian influence; but the clue to this idea comes from Masson, who saw a Pahlevi inscription here a hundred years ago. The paintings round the larger head are better preserved, and can be examined at close quarters by standing on the head itself. On either side of the niche, below the curve of the vault, hang five medallions about ten feet in diameter which contain Bodhisattvas. These figures are surrounded by horse-shoe auras of white, yellow, and blue, and their hair is tinged with red. Between each medallion grows a lotus; at least we supposed it to be that, though in other surroundings it might be taken for an ecclesiastical gas-bracket upholding three glass globes. The next zone above is occupied by a pavement in squares out of Pompeian curtains furnished with a border of peacocks' feathers. On top of this come two more rows of Bodhisattvas, seated against auras and thrones alternately, the thrones being decked with jewelled carpets. Between these stand large cups on stems, resembling Saxon fonts and sprouting cherubs. The topmost zone overhead is missing. The colours are the ordinary fresco colours, slate-grey, gamboges, a rusty chocolate-red, a dull grape-tint, and a bright harebell blue.

"The subjects suggest that Persian, Indian, Chinese, and Hellenistic ideas all met at Bamiyan in the 5th and 6th centuries. It is interesting to have a record of this meeting. But the fruit of it is not pleasant. The only exception is the lower row of Bodhisattvas, which Hackin says are older than the rest. They achieve that air of repose, graceful but empty, which is the best one can expect of Buddhist iconography."

In contrast, Peter Levi took a more contemplative view of the two great statues:

"In the morning, the Buddhas are in shadow and you see a whole parade of almost nude brown hills faintly dusted with green and deeply picked out into shadows. The Buddhas are not naturalistic; they are more like the seagull-eyed image of the virgin of which Robert Lowell speaks, *non est species, neque decor* (neither beautiful, nor charming). The faces have been cut away and the restored pieces have a coldness, the feet a solid stance. No statue which has had its face removed can express justice or law or illumination or mercy, but there is a disturbing presence about these two giants that does express something. I do not know if it is 'expressionless, expresses God' or not."

Large Buddha, Bamiyan Valley, 1974 [Y. Crowe]

The head of the Large Buddha at Bamiyan, in 1972. The upper part of the face was destroyed in the 17th century. In the arch cut out of the cliff above it are remains of paintings from the late 5th–7th centuries. [B. Woodburn]

Bamiyan was to continue as a Buddhist kingdom until 970. At this time, the Samanid Empire ruled much of the Afghan territory from the city of Bokhara, north of the River Oxus. On account of Bokhara's distance from its outlying provinces, the day-to-day administration of these areas was generally delegated to Turkish slave-officers, who acted as governors and military commanders. One of these, Alptigin, governor of Nishapur, after falling into conflict with the Samanid ruler Mansur I, decided to take advantage of his relative power and independence by marching an army south to capture for himself the small town of Ghazni. His route took him towards Bamiyan, where the local king attempted to arrest his progress. Alptigin therefore decided to force a battle by planning an ambush. Selecting a detachment of 500 soldiers, he ordered his deputy Subuktigin to advance with 100 of them, whilst he himself hid with the rest of the party in a narrow gorge. The troops of Bamiyan, seeing the small number of attackers, thought that they were nothing more than a raiding party, and went out heedlessly in force to see them off. As they went on the offensive, they suddenly found themselves surrounded by Alptigin's men, and were cut down. The king of Bamiyan was captured, and Bamiyan itself became a fief of Alptigin and his successors, the Ghaznavid dynasty, continuing in their control until it fell to the rival Ghorid Empire in the mid-12th century.

The Arab historian, Yaqut al-Hamawi, writing around 1200, left a brief description of Bamiyan under Ghorid control in his geographical dictionary:

> "Bamiyan is the name of a town and large district between Balkh and Ghazni in the mountains; it has a citadel. The town is small, but it is the capital of an extensive area. A 10-day march separates it from Balkh, and an eight-day march from Ghazni. One may see there a building of an extraordinary height; it is supported by giant pillars and covered in paintings representing all the birds created by God. In the interior, there are two immense idols carved out of the rocks and rising from the base to the top of the mountainside. One is called the 'Red Idol' and the other the 'White Idol'. No statues equal to these may be seen anywhere in the world."

Bamiyan continued to prosper under the Ghorid Shansabani dynasty until 1215, when it was taken by the ruler of Khwarazm and given as a possession to his son, Jalal-ud-Din. His reign was to be short. In 1220, Genghis Khan crossed the Oxus with his Mongol warriors, utterly destroying Balkh, Merv and Nishapur. Seeing that he intended next to attack Bamiyan, Jalal-ud-Din mustered a force of 70,000 men, with which he prepared to make a stand outside Ghazni. Genghis therefore sent 30,000 Mongols ahead to meet Jalal-ud-Din's troops, whilst he himself went with the main body of his army to surround Bamiyan. Jalal-ud-Din managed to overcome his opponents, but this advantage was squandered by violent disagreements between his commanders, which caused his forces to disintegrate. In the meantime, Genghis was enraged at the death of his grandson at the siege of Bamiyan, which was now becoming protracted. When the city finally capitulated, he completely razed the citadel as an act of revenge, massacring the inhabitants and destroying its irrigation systems. He proceeded southwards, pursuing Jalal-ud-Din across the Indus and annihilating all opposition. Bamiyan, now desolate, its agriculture and trade in ruins, was unable to regain its former prominence, and dwindled to being no more than a small and sparsely populated settlement.

The extensive ruins of the citadel still stand above the valley. Named Shahr-i-Gholghola—The City of Noise, or Screaming—from the screams of the inhabitants caught in the massacre, folk stories are still told of its fall to Genghis. The following version of the legend was prepared by Nancy Dupree, combining tales collected from residents of the area with verses made on the story by Charles Masson:

> "During its days of glory, Shahr-i-Gholghola was the central city of a kingdom ruled by the Khwarazmian ruler Jalal-ud-Din Manguberti. Standing on its sugar loaf hill, and towering above the whole valley, the citadel contained within its well-defended walls a succession of buildings which formed the king's palace.
>
> "Jalal-ud-Din, though still a young man, was already a widower and his friends and advisors were insistent that he should remarry. The king had several daughters but none to compare with Lala Khatun, a dazzling beauty who exercised considerable influence over her father, for he trusted her and had the fullest confidence in her judgement. She reigned as a despot in the palace and this was the cause of jealousy in many quarters. Plots were laid against her but she kept close watch in those whom she suspected, demanding their expulsion from the palace. Many had thus been sent to distance and lonely posts, and she was cordially hated for her cruelty.
>
> "One day when her father told her of his plans to remarry, she recognised the hand of her enemies. Having no intention of allowing the presence of a strange woman in the palace, she called on her father to abandon the idea. But when, after weeks of quarrelling, she learned that envoys had been sent to the Court of Ghazni to ask for the hand of the princess, she realised that she had lost.

The ruins of the citadel of Shahr-i-Gholghola ('City of Srcreaming' or 'Lamentation') which was the heart of the Islamic city of Bamiyan. It was totally destroyed by Genghis Khan in 1221. [B. Woodburn]

"Pining now to leave the palace, she despatched a messenger to her father, the king: 'Lord, Lala Khatun, the Light of the Eyes, sends me to thee with the following request: East of the palace, on the high ground, there is a shady garden. When evening falls, a cool air breathes among its trees, the fragrance of its flowers causes lovers to swoon, the light of the moon waits on those who listen to the song of the nightingale. This garden in which thou lovest to walk in a summer night, and which thou hast laid with so much pride and care, Lala Khatun asks thee to give to her, that she may build in it an abode where she will live in peace, far from the intrigues of the harem which would impair her delicate health.

"Hoping that the estrangement would be forgotten and anxious that good understanding should again prevail between them, the king at once agreed to give up his wonderful garden.

"'Send to me all those who are builders by trade', she wrote to her father, 'for I wish my castle to be an image of myself, and I beg you to leave to me the

entire care of its construction'. Jalal-ud-Din not only accepted these conditions, but also informed Lala Khatun she could spend as much as she liked and choose within the palace whatever pleased her fancy for the decoration of her new abode.

"Accordingly, in a short time there arose in the midst of the fairy garden a very large building with four corner towers and ramparts of such giddy heights as to excite the wonder of wayfarers. When the roof was nearing completion, she made an inspection of the most beautiful carpets, ordered all of the most valuable hanging to be removed, as well as many lovely caskets full of useless ornaments. The king was none too happy to find one half of his possessions thus carried away to Kalah-i-Dokhtar, Castle of the Daughter, as the new palace was called, but to conceal his dismay he decided to feast the people on the day when his daughter was to move.

"The great day came at last; the people were excited, preparations were made everywhere. Coffers bursting with silken garments filled Lala Khatun's room; veils of gauze as light as diaphanous clouds lay here and there. Suddenly, the ladies-in-waiting were startled by the sound of groans coming from the

A fortified farm in Bamiyan [B. Woodburn]

inner room, and the old nurse, on entering, found the princess sobbing. "Look at my legs: I can no longer move them." The king rushed to his daughter's side. Pressing her palsied ankles between his hands, he called for all the most learned physicians to assemble. In great numbers they examined her, yet in spite of all their treatments, in spite of all the magic spells, there was no sign of improvement. Time passed, and people began to talk of other matters.

"One day, Lala Khatun, unable to bear the tedium, asked to go to her own castle, and was accordingly carried to the uppermost story of one of the lofty towers. Here she lay gazing at her father's palace from whence she was banished forever. She saw no one other than her old nurse, terminating the visits of her father, and an oppressive silence fell over the whole kingdom.

"Winter passed; spring was at hand.

"One of the early days of that spring, a holy man with seven disciples stopped to rest in a hamlet near Bamiyan. Cold and weary after walking 200 miles across the mountains from Herat, he sent his disciples to the cave-dwellers to ask for fuel. The undisguised mistrust with which they were met and the meagreness of their offerings so enraged the old man that he sent the disciples to the hills for cakes of ice which he set on fire. The whole valley was soon informed of the miracle accomplished by the holy man who they called Mir Ali Yakhsuz, the Ice-Burning Saint, and sick people were brought to him from every corner of the realm that he might heal them.

"Jalal-ud-Din too went out to visit the saint. Having reached the camp, the king was asked to take the seat of honour. At a sign from the master, a disciple brought to the king a bowl of deer's milk, and on being served this precious offering realised that his daughter would be healed. Even so, before he had time to submit his request, a messenger announced the sudden and complete recovery of Lala Khatun. In token of his gratitude, the king gave the saint one of his daughters in marriage…

"The king's heart was at peace once more. His daughter was healed, he was no longer tortured by anxiety, and there was nothing in the way of his marriage. His suit, having met with a favourable reception at the Court of Ghazni, he could now make preparations for his journey there. Thus hopeful of the future, the king set out with a large retinue of high officials.

"This sudden departure took Lala Khatun by surprise. All hope of recovering her former power was dispelled, and she shut herself up once more, the better to feed her resentment and meditate on revenge.

"Then, one day rumours reached Kalah-i-Dokhtar that the warriors of Genghis Khan were invading the country, leaving naught but death and ruin in their wake. Shahr-i-Zohak, a military outpost only 10 miles down the valley, was soon besieged by the Mongols. Lala Khatun became frantic with joy, for here she saw her chance for revenge. One the roof of one of her towers she danced, spinning around in a cloud of gossamer veils, and dragging into the mad whirl the old nurse who followed her like a shadow. Shahr-i-Zohak was captured and, no further resistance being possible, the menace now fell directly upon Shahr-i-Gholghola. The barbarians surged up the valley and encamped in the valley of Kakrak for the evening.

> Now beams the moon resplendent queen of night!
>   Full on the earth its golden radiance pours;
> On Bamiyan's vale it sheds a holy light,
>   Where in its arch, the idol darkly lours,
> And the temple grots—mysterious sight!
>   Fit shrines and fanes of supernatural powers!
> Nor less benignly its rich lustre falls,
>   On proud Gholghola's stately towers and walls
>
> Now from the Tartar squadrons on the plain,
>   The captains with the banners in advance,
> Loud drums and trumpets bellow forth amain,
>   Amid the clang of buckler and of lance:
> The chieftain eyes them, of their bearing vain,
>   And bids his heralds to the walls advance,
> And there, a parley sounded, boldly flings
>   His proud defiance to the Tajik King.
>
> Swift with exalting cries and wild despair
>   On the proud fortress rush the maddened host,
> That lengthened ladders to its walls they bear,
>   And press contending for the dangerous post;
> Gholghola's bands an equal fervour share,

And oft its battlements are won and lost—
Whole crowds unpitied fall! When shines the day,
The tartar sword for once hath missed its prey.

The Tartar chief informs his serried host:
  'Tomorrow morn we lead our bands away.'
Such was the chief's resolve; and in his tent
  He musing sat, and mighty projects planned—
When told, a female from the fortress sent
  Disguised, attends with letter in her hand.
Received—he reads the missive, speaks content,
  Thus: 'Tell your lady, I salute her hand.'
Then rising shouts, 'Our Tartar Gods are just,
And Gholghola yet shall yield to woman's lust!'

"The letter was of course from Lala Khatun, and it ended thus: 'On the tableland, you can see four watermills fed by a mysterious underground canal which also supplies the city with water. As the spring yields but little water it is not easy to discover this canal. You will have to go upstream as far as the spring and throw into it a quantity of chopped straw; then, keeping your eye on the motes, you will follow them downstream until they start whirling as though caught in some eddy. This is the spot where you will find the underground canal begins. If you block it up with felt matting, the whole city will be deprived of water and it must perforce surrender.'

"Genghis followed her advice, and was soon able to penetrate the citadel.

Now gallant warriors, raise a mighty shout—
  'The welcome signal to our friends without'.
The bands without return a deafening yell,
  And forward rush with loud promiscuous din.
On every side they scale the walls pell mell,
  And join their conquering friends already in.
On every side the reeling Tajiks fell,
  To spare a Tajik dog is deemed a sin—
'Spare none!' The chieftain cries 'Spare none, kill, slay!
The night for slaughter and the morn for prey!'

And comes the morn at length: amidst the dead

And dying, takes the Tartar chief his stand—
'Gholghola's glory has for ever fled,
And we are now the masters of the land!
Enough of blood, since none remains to shed—
The city's treasure lies at your command:
But heed—a woman's lust hath brought this shame
On Gholghola and the Tajik fame!'

"Meanwhile at Lala Khatun's castle, Lala Khatun had summoned her old nurse and ordered her to dress her as a bride. The old woman massaged her, anointed her with perfumes; combed and oiled her hair, and tied in her forelock her most costly jewel; a necklace of golden bells encircled her slender throat; numberless rings adorned her henna-tinted fingers; a veil of gold covered with flowers was draped about her head. Thus apparelled, she awaited the visit of the warrior.

"Days passed. There were no visitors to her chamber. Then, on the seventh day, a band of soldiers broke down her door, and told Lala Khatun and her nurse to travel with their captain. Senseless, unable to stand on her feet, Lala Khatun was dragged out, her nurse behind her, and hoisted onto a saddle. A dozen horsemen surrounded the two women and they rode off at a quick pace. Lala Khatun was soon faint: they laid her on a carpet on the ground. Genghis, who halted suddenly and inquired into the cause for the delay, looked down at her, his face a hard mask.

"The warriors were summoned. Genghis told them the tale, sparing not particulars of her treachery, ending thus: 'That girl deserves no mercy; she must be punished for having abominably betrayed a father who was too good to her.' The two women, huddled together in their distress, fell under a hail of stones where they lay until they passed away without a word of lamentation.

"The news of the siege of Shahr-i-Gholghola reached Jalal-ud-Din during the festivities of his wedding with the beautiful Ghaznavid princess. Quickly raising an army, he marched North, but on reaching the narrow valley of Ghorband, he heard of his daughter's betrayal, and of the complete devastation which had been done. He fell to earth, as though struck by a thunderbolt."

Masson visited the ruins of Shahr-i-Gholghola around 1830:

Shahr-i-Gholghola [F. Holt]

"The evidences of Gholghola are many and considerable, proving that it must have been an extensive city. The most remarkable are the remains of the citadel, on an isolated eminence in the centre of the valley, its base washed by the river of Bamiyan. They are picturesque in appearance, although bare and desolate, as well from the form and disposition of the walls and towers, as from the aspect of the eminence on which they stand, whose earthy sides are furrowed by the channels silently worn in them by rains. Many of the apartments have their walls pretty entire, with their niches well preserved; they are, of course, filled, more or less, with rubbish and debris.

Some few are distinguished by slight architectural decorations, as to their plaster mouldings, but all of them must have been confined and inconvenient dwellings, being necessarily, as to extent, affected by the scanty area comprised within the limits of the fortress. Excavations have been sometimes made by the inhabitants of the vicinity, and arrow-heads, with masses of mutilated and effaced manuscripts, are said to have been found. The latter are plausibly supposed to have been archives, and are written, it is asserted, in Persian characters. Chance also frequently elicits coins, but so far as I could learn, they are invariably Cufic, which, if true, would fix a period for the origin of the place. On the eastern front the walls of the outer line of defence are in tolerable repair, and are carried much nearer the base of the eminence than on the other sides. They are tastefully constructed, and have loop-holes, as if for matchlocks, though they may have been intended for the discharge of arrows; still we are not certain whether the ruins extant are those of Genghis Khan, or of some more recent edifice, which, adverting to native traditions, may have succeeded it. The walls of the citadel, and of all the enclosed buildings, have been formed of unburnt bricks. The adjacent castle, called Killa Dokhtar, the castle of Alladad Khan, is built of superior kiln-burnt bricks.

Besides these primary objects, there are very many dilapidated mosques and tombs, as might be expected, on the site of a decayed Mahomedan city, and the broken undulating ground South of the river of Bamiyan, to the foot of the hills confining the valley, is strewed with mounds, and the remains of walls and buildings; and these, say the present inhabitants, occupy the 'assal' or veritable site of the city of Gholghola. The traveller surveying from the height of Gholghola, the vast and mysterious idols, and the multitude of caves around him, will scarcely fail to be absorbed in deep reflection and wonder, while their contemplation will call forth various and interesting associations in his mind. The desolate spot itself has a peculiar solemnity, not merely from its lonely and startling evidences of past grandeur, but because of mystery and awe. The very winds, as they whistle through its devoted pinnacles and towers, impart tones so shrill and lugubrious as to impress with emotions of surprise the most indifferent being. So surprising is their effect that often while strolling near it the mournful melody irresistibly riveting my attention, would compel me involuntarily to direct my sight to the eminence and its ruined fanes, and frequently would I sit for a long time together expecting the occasional repetition of the singular cadence. The natives may be excused, who consider these mournful and unearthly sounds as the music of departed souls and of invisible agents; and we may suspect that their prevalence has gained for the locality the appellation of Gholghola, slightly expressive of the peculiarity."

A few miles to the west of Bamiyan lies the Darya Ajdahar—Valley of the Dragon. This small valley is blocked by a large and curious barrage of rock, coloured by deposits from mineral-rich springs in the middle of the formation. Hsuen-Tsang, when travelling to Bamiyan, spoke of a large recumbent Buddha in the vicinity of the settlement, and a certain French archaeologist, Foucher, claimed that he was in fact referring to this feature. Nonetheless, the local people possess a more elaborate legend on the matter, casting Ali, the son-in-law of the Prophet, as its hero. In the following story, recounted by Mir Ali, a Tajik living near Bamiyan, the Darya Ajdahar is also called the "Red Valley":

"Bamiyan, a small but prosperous locality, was, along with all of the neighbouring valleys, living in terror. A great evil had fallen on the population in the form of a voracious dragon that had made its home in the base of the little Red valley.

Threshing with oxen in the Ghorband Valley, on the way to Bamiyan [B. Woodburn]

Every day on waking it roamed through the area, spitting flames and destroying everything in its path. Behind it was left a trail of nauseating odour which caused the crops to perish. For fear of being taken unawares by the monster, the farmers remained in their dwellings in hiding. The monster cared little about the destruction it was causing; each day it sought new prey, and had as its preference young girls with tender flesh.

"Seeing his kingdom on the verge of ruin, having already sacrificed his best warriors by sending them in combat against the monster, the king was compelled to negotiate with the dragon in order to reach an agreement. The dragon was pitiless in his demands; it promised, nevertheless, no longer to trouble the area with its daily visits and to remain in its own narrow valley on the condition that its appetite was satisfied. With no other option, the King agreed to the conditions imposed by the dragon, and undertook to deliver the dragon daily a girl still living, two camels, and six hundred pounds of meat.

"Once this accord was reached, a custom was established that each one of the King's subjects had to furnish, in his turn, the provisions for the dragon. Officers were employed and a census was organised, which every day determined the person who was to fulfil the duty. There were many tears, and many heart-wrenching scenes, but everyone acted according the decree of the king. For

fear of the dragon resuming its devastation of the valley, no one dared to evade their duty, and, every day at dawn, the new victims could be seen being led to the lair of the dragon.

"A relative peace was established, and with confidence to a certain extent restored, the farmers began again to work in the fields. However, one day, the job of providing for the dragon fell to a poor widow who possessed only a beautiful daughter and a little livestock. Like everyone else, she had to submit herself to the cruelty of fate. While it was still night she began the journey, leading her child by the hand, and ahead of her driving her camel and two sheep. All the time as she made her way down the track towards the Red Valley, she prayed that God would come to her aid.

"Dawn had scarcely broken when the two women reached their destination. Seating themselves on a rock, they began to wait for the monster to rise. The mother could not at all resign herself to sacrificing her daughter to the hunger of the dragon. In her misery, she failed to see a young man sleeping just a few feet away from them. In the features of this young man, one could recognise the legendary hero, Ali.

"Woken by the women's wretched lamentations, he rose up, and going over to them, asked why they were weeping. When the mother had explained the reason for her despair, Ali told her to return to her village. Announcing his intention of killing the dragon, he promised her that he would take charge of

her daughter's safety. The mother departed, without any real hope of seeing her daughter again, but was nevertheless consoled by the reassuring words of this young man with a face almost other-worldly and radiant.

"Ali approached the girl, and sitting by her said, 'I shall rest myself while waiting for the monster to appear; do not fear as I do so, but watch carefully the approaches to the valley, and the moment you see any sign of life, no matter how slight, wake me.' He laid his head on her knees, and fell asleep.

"The faint light of dawn began to fill the valley; the sun began to throw its first rays on this peculiar scene, when Ali, disturbed by a tickling sensation on his cheek, awoke. It was the tears of his companion which fell on his face like a light and refreshing rain. Ali understood the reason for her sudden agitation, for he had just perceived in the light of dawn, the silhouette of the monster, which was stealing lazily towards them. Immediately he got to his feet, and warned his companion to take refuge in a cave not far from where they were.

"The monster was advancing peacefully towards the place where every morning he was accustomed to find his provisions; suddenly, he found himself in the presence of the young hero who straightaway began to strike him with his sword. Still heavy with sleep, it could not at first grasp what was happening. However, when it understood the situation, it became furious.

"To escape the fierce jet of flames which shot from the nostrils of the monster Ali would jump either side of the dragon, now to the left, now to the right, over its body covered in scales and trembling with anger. In vain did he strike it with his sword: the blade slid harmlessly across its thick skin without making the slightest impression.

"However, finding itself unable to finish off the intrepid adversary, the dragon attempted a ruse. Using its powerful breath, it inhaled, and sucked towards it the assailant; now at its mercy, the dragon began to wind itself around him like a serpent. This done, the monster readied itself to swallow him. Its eager jaws opened, and began to water in anticipation. Sure of its power over the hero, it made to tear off his head, but by some phenomenon it came to be out of reach. Every time it tried, although it held him firmly in its grasp, Ali's head seemed always to be beyond the range of its jaws. Infuriated, the dragon released the hero, and flung him with full force against

A roadside stop beside the Ghorband River, on the road from Kabul to Bamiyan [B. Woodburn]

the side of the valley. Yet, instead of being dashed to pieces against the solid rock, the dragon to its great surprise saw the young man get up, and, brandishing his sword, rush back to resume the fight. The dragon responded by scorching the earth about him with a sheet of poisonous flames.

"'The hero will surely be overcome,' gasped the terrified girl as she watched the struggle; she entreated God to protect the life of this youthful hero who fought with such ardour and courage to save her from a hideous death. But at the moment when she thought all was lost, she saw with astonishment a miracle. Ali, just before the venomous flames were about to reach him, took his sword, and traced around himself a circle on the ground; when the flames had crossed over the boundary he had marked out, they crashed against his feet in the form of red tulips.

"The monster began to cry out and rage so that the whole valley shook; nevertheless, Ali allowed it to approach him. When, at last, it was within striking distance, he seized the moment, and laid the monster low with an almighty kick.

"The attack was aimed at its mouth; the force of the blow reduced its brain to a pulp, and it expired in a final burst of rage, spitting out its teeth in front of Ali. Sword in hand, Ali went forward to the body of the dying animal; he wished to take to his master a souvenir of the exploit. Cutting in half the corpse of the beast, he cut away a thin band of skin from its head to its tail. At the same moment, he saw in the valley a camel; seizing it, he tried to load it with the precious evidence of his conquest, but it collapsed under the unexpected weight of the burden. Instead, Ali took back the skin, and wound it round his waist like a belt. Then, he whistled, and his faithful companion, the horse Doldol, mysteriously appeared, which he mounted and rode towards the cave where he had told the girl to hide; but he found she was no longer there. But he could not linger; a new adventure called him to the valley of Chaidan, where another dragon was raging and oppressing the people.

"As for the girl, miraculously saved from death, she had started to run back towards Bamiyan to recount the extraordinary feat of her protector. Yet, everyone she met without exception was horrified at her appearance—no-one believed her story, and after she returned terror began to spread amongst the people; all demanded an immediate punishment for her disobedience to the king.

"A gathering crowd demanded she be sent to the royal palace; perfectly calm, she allowed herself to be led there, all the while telling her mother to trust in God. The mob continued to grow following the procession going down into the valley, when, to its consternation, it saw a great black cloud from the direction of the red valley spreading rapidly across the sky, preventing them from going any further. Soon, a sickening odour began to fill the air. The people, taken aback, sought to muster in the darkness, and, scattered about in confusion like a herd of cattle lost in the night, they began to wait. Suddenly, rumours started to spread amongst them, and they came to understand the signs of their deliverance.

"After only three days, when the sky had cleared, and a fresh breeze swept away the vile stench, the first journey out into the depths of the valley was accomplished. At the head of the party went the king; behind him, on a camel richly adorned and laden with offerings, went the girl who had been the only witness to this exploit of Ali.

"To pay homage to the hero, the saviour of the people of Bamiyan, a great festival was ordained, and everyone piously rejoiced at the spot where the petrified corpse of the dragon lay across the Red Valley."

Several other sites of geological interest in the region of Bamiyan, including the Band-i-Amir, have similar legends attached to them. An almost identical formation is located 88 miles south of Bamiyan; this is said to be a child of the dragon slain by Ali in the Darya Ajdahar, which itself met the same fate as its parent. Charles Masson also left an account of this site:

"The Azdha [Ajdahar] of Bisut is indeed a natural curiosity, which the creative imagination of the Hazaras supposes to be the petrified remains of a dragon, slain by their champion Hazrat Ali. Nor are they singular in their belief, for all the classes of Mahomedans in these countries coincide with them, and revere the object as an eminent proof of the intrepidity of the son-in-law of Mahomed, and as a standing evidence of the truth of their faith. It is, geologically speaking, of volcanic formation, and a long projected mass of rock about 170 yards in length; the main body is in form the half of a cylinder, of a white honey-combed friable stone; on its summit is an inferior projection, through the centre of which is a fissure of about two feet in depth and five or six inches in breadth, from which exhales a strong sulphurous odour; and a portion of the rock having been set on fire, it proved to contain sulphur. This part of the rock is assumed to have been the mane of the monster. In the superior part of the projection, which is supposed to represent the head of the dragon, there are numerous small springs on the eastern face, which trickle down in small lucid currents, having a remarkable effect from rippling over a surface of variously coloured red, yellow, and white rock, and exhibiting a waxy appearance. The water of these springs is tepid, and of a mixed, saline, and sulphurous flavour. They are supposed to exude from the Azdha's brains. On the back of what is called the head are a number of small cones, from the apices of which tepid springs bubble forth. These cones are of the same description of white friable porous stone, but singular from being as it were scaled over, and this character prevails over the greater portion of the Azdha. On one side of the head large cavities have been made, the powdery white earth there found being carried away by visitors, extraordinary efficacy in various diseases being imputed to it. The vivid red rock which is found about the head is imagined to be tinged with the blood of the dragon. Beneath the numerous springs on the Eastern face occur large quantities of an acrid crystalline substance resembling sal-ammoniac, and I was told it occurs in some of the neighbouring hills in vast quantities; lead is also one of the products of the hills near this place. I afterwards found that an analogous mass of rock, but of a much more imposing size, occurs in the vicinity of Bamiyan, and is alike supposed to represent a petrified dragon.

"Near the North-western extremity of the dragon of Bisut, on high ground, is a small building, a ziarat. Here are shown impressions on a mass of black rock, said to denote the spot where Hazrat Ali stood when with his arrows he destroyed the sleeping dragon, the impressions being those of the hoofs of his famed charger Daldal. At the entrance is also a stone, with some other impressions, and over the door is an inscription, on black stone, in Persian, informing us that the building was erected some 150 years since. In various parts of Afghanistan are found impressions on rock, certainly resembling the cavity which would be formed by the hoof of an animal, rather than anything else. Most of such impressions have ziarats erected over them, but I have seen them in spots where they have not hitherto been so consecrated, and where they occur, beyond doubt, in the solid rock of the hill."

Rock formation on the Ajdahar of Bisut. According to folk lore,
this feature is the petrified horn of the dragon slain by the Hazrat Ali. [B. Jenks]

The mountainous areas in the centre of Afghanistan around Bamiyan—known as the Hazarajat—are predominantly inhabited by the Hazara people. The debate over their origin has not been finally resolved. Some ethnographers have argued that they are autochthonous, descended from the original population of the area. However, the predominant opinion is that their ancestors were military settlers who colonised the territory in waves after the time of Genghis Khan. Their physical characteristics are Mongoloid—high cheekbones, square faces, small eyes and thin beards—and their language, Hazaragi, although being a dialect of Persian, contains a significant amount of Mongolian vocabulary. The name "Hazara", which in Persian means "thousand", stands as an equivalent of the Mongol term "Ming", denoting a unit from the Mongol army.

The Hazaras are adherents of Shia Islam, which they most likely adopted in the early 17th century during a period of Safavid Persian domination. As a result of this, they have suffered much discrimination at the hands of other Afghans, who are predominantly Sunni Muslims. Burnes commented on their condition in 1834:

> "The Hazaras are a race of good disposition; but are oppressed by all the neighbouring nations, whom they serve as hewers of wood and drawers of water.

Many of them are sold into slavery; and there is little doubt that they barter their children for cloth and necessaries to the Uzbeks. All the drudgery and work in Kabul is done by Hazaras, some of whom are slaves and some free: in winter there are not less than 10,000 who reside in the city, and gain a livelihood by clearing the roofs of snow and acting as porters. They make good servants, but in their native hills their simplicity is great: A Sayyid (descendant of the Prophet), who has been much among them, tells me that, if he bared his head, they did the same."

Whilst Burnes was commenting on the Hazaras in Kabul, Charles Wood was making his way towards the Oxus; on his journey, he found them suffering depredations in their own heartlands:

"Every day we encountered parties of half-famished Hazara, abandoning their inclement mountains for the less rigorous winter of the plains. Some of the groups presented sad objects of compassion; their torn garments ill protecting them from the cold. To see the aged of both sexes, ill-clothed and scantily fed, toiling on through the snow, and exposed to all the asperities of the season, might almost induce one to tax Providence as partial in the distribution of its gifts. But to the honour of these poor people, though hard pressed by misfortune, and lacking even the common necessaries of life, they viewed their lot with another eye and in a better spirit. Though not cheerful, they were resigned, and if the destitute condition of his children did sometimes cloud a father's brow, could it be wondered at? For, can any trial of a parent's fortitude be more severe than to hear his offspring call upon him in vain for bread. The early fall of snow this year, had, they told us, destroyed the crops, and as they had been unable to pay the usual tribute to the Amir of Kabul, Dost Mohamed, their sheep had been seized. Without the means of passing the long dreary winter now closing in upon them, they were compelled to emigrate to the plains where the wealthy would employ them in keeping the roofs of their houses free from snow, clearing the footpaths, bringing firewood, and in the other drudgery of the household. This is a misfortune that often overtakes the Hazara, and yet so improvident are they, that they never think of providing against it."

Wood also left an account of his reception as a guest in a Hazara dwelling:

"We passed the night at Gulgatui, under the roof of an Hazara family. The house was of stone, low, flat-roofed, and contained a considerable number of apartments, in one of which the females slept, and in another the men of the family and ourselves. The fire-place in the kitchen or sitting-room was merely a hole scooped in the earthen floor, while the smoke found a vent through two apertures in the roof. On top of the house was piled, in bundles, the winter's store of fuel. On the whole, an Hazara house, with a cheerful fire on its hearth, is a snug berth enough, could custom but reconcile one to its smoky atmosphere. The head of the family was a hale, hearty old man, who had been married 30 years, the last 20 of which he had lived in this house. The whole stock on his farm consisted of two cows, as many calves, and a few sheep. For the little spot of ground which he occupied, he paid to the ruler of Kabul a portion of the village tax of 60 rupees. He told us that in this bleak region the men, for seven months out of the twelve, have little other employment than to bring fuel from the hills. We retired early to rest; and when they imagined us to be sleeping, the whole family cautiously entered the room in which we

Hazara women and a baby, in the Ghorband Valley [B. Woodburn]

were lying, and which adjoined the kitchen, lit the candle, and minutely examined such articles as had been left upon the table. A plated candlestick, in particular, astonished them; and after handling it over and over, a young woman, casting a furtive glance at Doctor Lord and myself, deposited the treasure in a corner of the room. Having finished their survey, a large basin of water was brought in, from the half-frozen stream before the door. This and a few mouthfuls of coarse barley bread formed the frugal supper of the family. The fire was now extinguished, and all retired to rest. Next morning, when we were prepared to start, the fair thief enquired if we missed nothing; and we, wishing to discover the motive that led her to secrete the candlestick, pretended a total ignorance of the scene we had witnessed the preceding night. The secreted treasure was now produced; but whether the laughing culprit had hidden it for better security, or merely to frighten us with the loss of so costly an article, we could not well determine. To these simple-minded people it must have appeared of immense value. At all events it was evident that no dishonest motive had prompted the conduct of the Hazara maiden; and we left the house well pleased with our reception."

The Hazaras enjoyed a semi-autonomous status, governed by their own tribal leaders, until the end of the 19th century. At this time, the Amir, Abdur Rahman, embarked on a policy to establish strong centralised government in Afghanistan. His position—along with a sudden rumour that he was seriously ill—caused the Shaykh Ali tribe to revolt briefly in 1888; three years later, a more general uprising followed under Muhammad Husayn, a Hazara commander who had previously been loyal to the government in Kabul. The movement was crushed after an anti-Shia jihad was declared by the Amir, during which many of the tribesmen fled, either eastwards towards Quetta in Baluchistan, or else westwards to Mashhad in Iran. The Amir commented on the matter: "The Hazaras had raided and plundered the neighbouring subjects for about 300 years past, and none of the Kings had had the power to make them absolutely peaceful. They considered themselves rather too strong to be defeated, and were very proud of their power." Throughout the following century, attempts were made to discriminate against the Hazaras by means of dispersion, the settlement of other tribes in their native areas and the dismemberment of the Hazarajat into different administrative entities in order to foment internal disputes. Pressure was also put on them to speak Pashto rather than Hazaragi, and to accept Sunni rather than Shia doctrines. In spite of this, Hazara culture, music and poetry has continued to flourish, and, according to Sayed Askar Mousavi, an eminent scholar in the field, has been used in recent years to raise political consciousness amongst them.

Hazara folk poetry is generally divided into two categories: that which is sung with musical accompaniment, and that which is not. Unaccompanied poetry includes the Daido or Bolbi—love lyrics, recited using both yodelling and the ordinary voice, sung at weddings, festivals and by shepherds in the field. It also includes the Makhta—laments sung by women at times of mourning, a genre thought to have been evolved during the uprising of 1890. Accompanied poetry is primarily composed of love lyrics, distinguished by their various verse forms. When musical accompaniment is provided, instruments include the *dambura* and *ghichak* —plucked and bowed two-stringed instruments; the *nay*—flute—and *dayerah*— tambourine. Dr Mousavi has collected and translated various examples of these lyrics, of which three examples are given below. The first was composed by the Shahrestani poet Abu Sahl:

Last night I went to her side, it was not morning then,
But the middle of the night.
One little kiss I took: the moon-browed one slept.
At once the old mother-in-law awoke
And with damned ill-luck made a racket like no sheep's dropping,
But a good half brick.
Her dog yapped ready to bite me,
And I kicked it just as if it were thrown backwards like a light cap.
My cap on one side and my boots on the other, I escaped,
You know this making off, which always means running from it.
Oh, my new moon! Abu Sahl fell in love with you,
Do you remember the time you lived in Garmew?
I said to her, 'My dearest, here is your long-time lover!'
She said, 'Woe! My head was under the quilt.'

It's a full moon tonight, but my moon has not come,
I waited for him until dawn, without sleeping,
I waited for him until dawn,
The dawn has arrived, but my lover has not.

Come, sit by me and tell me first the news from home,
Then tell me of my sweet-talking nightingale,
Everything my loved one has told you,
Come and tell me it all word by word.

I would give my life for your tall slender body,
I put my head at your feet,
You look at me, but with no compassion,

But how have I wronged you?

My love, your body is slender, your face tender,
My love, with a mole on your fine face,
If I do not see you twice or thrice a day,
Every passing moment feels like a year to me.

My love, do not make any noise, I am in the middle of cooking
Kiss me discretely, so that my husband may not see

The light of my life climbs up and down the valley
I cannot bear to see him go under the heat of the mid-day sun.

The old man could be my grandfather,
The young man, the light of my life.

An improvised band plays at a teahouse, near Band-i-Amir, 1972 [B. Woodburn]

Bamiyan: Travel Information

Bamiyan stands at 2,500 m (8,204 feet) above sea level and is best visited when the weather is warm. From Bamiyan, the road from Kabul continues westwards to the Minaret of Jam (in Ghor province) and Herat. In the old days, this was a main tourist route (the trip to Herat today can take up to nine days). A road also runs northwards to Afghan Turkestan and is the alternative to the Salang for crossing the Hindu Kush.

Getting there from Kabul

Two routes lead to Bamiyan from Kabul: each route takes its name from the pass it crosses, the Shibar or the Hajigak. Both take 8 hours or so, depending on the speed of the driver.

Most tourists arrive by private car hired in Kabul, which costs about US$50. Buses cost about $5 (250 afs); the Bamiyan bus station is next door to the Zohaq and Hammam hotels.

1. Via the Shibar Pass and Charikar (northern route, 148 miles)

Charikar is two hours from Kabul. The Shah Darweish Hotel, owned by Haji Khalil, serves lunch and dinner (cost between 45 and 100 afs). Accommodation from 100 afs per person, in rooms that sleep up to four people. There are six bedrooms with at least one iron bedstead per room and Afghan mattresses. Disgusting bathroom. Petrol station in town.

The town is famous for metalworking: knives and horseshoes. Flower Hill (Gul Gundi) is a short journey to the west. It is popular for picnics from May to July.

Hazara territory starts at Chardi Ghorband, from where buses go to Kabul—a three-hour journey—for 80 afs; also a shared taxi for 100 afs. There is no hotel but one can stay at Ghorband restaurant, which has sleeping platforms on a balcony that would be perfect in high summer. A wonderful bazaar reflects this area's role as the fruit basket of Afghanistan, selling walnuts, apricots, mulberries, pomegranates, melons and apples.

Recently constructed University of Bamiyan [B. Jenks]

FONDUKISTAN SCULPTURES

This route passes the site of Fondukistan, the name given to a Buddhist monastic complex excavated by the French in the 1930s. It produced some of the most beautiful sculpture to be discovered in Afghanistan and can be regarded as the very latest flowering of the Gandharan style, made all the more sensuous and beautiful by Indian influences. The Fondukistan sculptures were exhibited in the Kabul museum and until 2004 were thought to have been destroyed. Happily, they turn out to have been safe in the basement of the central bank along with the Scythian gold.

2. Via the Hajigak Pass (southern route, 110 miles)

This is my favourite route to Bamiyan. The entrance into the Bamiyan valley is spectacular. It is suggested that you leave the car at the beginning of the final approach and walk through a defile and past magenta cliffs and the Wagnerian castle of Shahr-i-Zohak (see below). To do this, you should stop the car at the hot springs 6 kilometres from Shahr-i-Zohak, and then resume driving once through. On tours, ask your guide to arrange for horses to meet the party here. The springs are a dull orange colour, caused probably by iron oxide "fixed" by bacteria. They are also slightly gaseous and bubble like a cooking pot.

SIGHTS IN BAMIYAN

Bamiyan has a number of things to see, amongst which the Dragon Valley and the lakes of Band-i-Amir must be counted as wonders of the world.

1. Giant Buddhas
2. Shahr-i-Gholghola
3. Bazaar
4. Foladi and Kakrak Valleys
5. Dragon Valley
6. Shahr-i-Zohak
7. Band-i-Amir and the lakes
8. Ajar National Park (old royal hunting grounds)

ACCOMMODATION AND BATHING

The main Bamiyan Hotel (ATO-owned) is next to the governor's office on the town's main hill. It is managed by Mr Najaf Ali; bookings can be made via the ATO in Kabul (tel. 23 00 33 8; 0702 76152). I have always just turned up and found a warm welcome. Rooms are $30 per night ($3 for breakfast and dinner); $50 for yurts. Horses cost between $20 and $40 per day.

Inside the fortified walls of Qala Bolola Village, near Bamiyan [F. Holt]

The existing hotel has ten rooms, of which three are single. Six yurts on the hotel grounds have bathrooms with Western lavatories en suite. There is hot water in all buildings, including the yurts. A neighbouring building should provide another 6 rooms. Laundry can be done by one of the boys at the hotel for a few dollars.

Another hotel, the Zohaq Hotel, is in the New Bazaar and the manager is Mohammed Saddiq.

This more modest establishment has 10 rooms, each with two beds. There are two bathrooms, with shower and hot water, and two toilets. $20 per room (=$10 per person; breakfast 50 afs extra). The restaurant serves lunch and dinner (60 afs per meal).

Trips can be arranged in the hotel's 1994 Landcruiser for $60 a day, with a guide/interpreter for an extra $20.

In 2004 the Bamiyan Heights Hotel opened on the west side of the plateau and commands the best view in Bamiyan of the niches that once contained the Buddhas. The building is attractive, with a large central sitting area and was the mujahedin governor's private house. It is run by Shir Hussein, the Fonz of Bamiyan, a philoprogentive international man of mystery with a New York accent. He has a Thuraya satellite phone so you can book in advance; the number is 00 88 216 211 97621. He hopes to offer heli-skiing in the winter.

Ten rooms of varying sizes have 30 beds in all. The charge is $30 per bed, regardless of how many people are in the room (a strange but common practice in Afghan hotels). The charge includes breakfast. Lunch and dinner from $5. There are plans to erect yurts in the garden.

There are two bathrooms, one for women and one for men. The women's bathroom contains a Western toilet and bath. Hot water is available from a gas-fired boiler and there is satellite TV. The generator operates between 5pm and midnight.

Hammam Ali Dad, a 10-year-old "bathhouse" made up of individual baths, is one of the better ones I have seen in Afghanistan. Women are welcome but tend not to use it. Shampoos and razors are sold. The proprietor is Ghulam Mohammed.

SIGHTS

1. GIANT BUDDHAS

The principal reason to visit Bamiyan in the old days, the two enormous Buddhas cut out of the cliffs, no longer exists. The niches stand like empty sarcophagi looking out over the valley. The surrounding cliffs are riddled with caves that themselves contained more carvings and frescos. In the dim morning or evening light from plateau across the valley, it is easy to imagine faces in the folds of rocks and this may well have inspired the Buddhist monks to carve statues there.

It is still possible to visit the caves and ascend to head-level of the large Buddha, which affords a magnificent view across the valley. The cost is 160 afs, payable at the office by the site entrance.

Of the two giant images, more

Empty Buddha niche, Bamiyan, 2004 [B. Jenks]

remains of the smaller Buddha and one can still see the rock scraped into folds and dotted with holes to take the plaster.

The destruction wreaked by the Taliban (see below) may be partly compensated by the discoveries of two archaeological campaigns in 2003 and 2004. One, undertaken by Japan's National Research Institute of Cultural Properties, used Ground Penetrating Radar (GPR), a new technology for archaeologists, which shows remains up to six metres below the earth's surface.

Large Buddha 'new hall' ceiling detail, Bamiyan Valley, 1976 [Y. Crowe]

In 2003, the Institute undertook two projects. One, funded by UNESCO, was to preserve what remains of the caves and their frescoes. The second was a GPR survey of the valley in order to identify and preserve underground antiquities.

Their main target was to try to locate the 1,000 foot (300m) Buddha whose existence was recorded by Hsuen-Tsang in the 7th century. He wrote: "To the east of the city 12 or 13 *li* there is a palace in which there is a figure of the Buddha lying in a sleeping position, as when he attained nirvana. The figure is in length about 1,000 feet or so." I suspect that the report of this colossal reclining Buddha actually refers to the stone outcrop in the Dragon Valley (see below). And a Buddha carving 1,000 feet long is surely unfeasible. However, Professor Yamaouchi thinks that it may exist. His team did find evidence of buildings underground, which probably correspond to a palace complex referred to by the Chinese traveller. "We found traces in two places and we have a reflection of the monuments underground. Just a trace." In August 2003 they found fragments of Buddhist manuscripts in Sanskrit and the Gilgit script, which date from the 7th century AD. The texts themselves simply relate to contracts of land and marriage.

The second mission was undertaken by a French-Afghan team led by Professor Tarzi from Strasbourg University. They discovered six Buddhist heads below the stupa near

Frescoes, Cave C, Large Buddha, Bamiyan Valley, 1974 [Y. Crowe]

the smaller Buddha, which are now stored in a sealed room in the compound by the large Buddha. They were described as "magnificent wrecks" by a London art dealer who saw the photos.

DESTRUCTION OF THE BUDDHAS

Cave, two rows of carved arches, Bamiyan Valley, 1974 [Y. Crowe]

The following account was given to me by Mohammedi, who had been imprisoned by the Taliban as a mujahedin and then forced at gunpoint to plant explosives in the statues. He now works at the Bamiyan Hotel; here is his first-hand story.

> "The Taliban were standing at the top of the cliff with their rifles. Most were Pakistanis and Arabs and bin Laden's people and a few Afghans. There was a piece of wood on the top and with that they slowly pulled us up and down.
>
> "They lowered us down, and at the bottom of the Buddhas were holes where doves were. First they told us to clean the dove holes and then they gave us mines with a timer and we put them in the holes. Because I'm a military man I knew what they were, and they were made in Britain, America and Pakistan—but mainly Pakistan. There were Pakistanis with radios below giving comments to tell us to put them there or there.
>
> "After we finished this process they took us opposite the Buddhas, near the ATO hotel, and the interpreters (who were from Kandahar) said, 'Look, now we are going to blow up the Buddhas.'
>
> "I asked a mullah who was there, and the mullah said: bin Laden, Mutaqi [Taliban Minister of Culture], the Minister of Defence and some other communists [by which he meant villains]. I knew bin Laden because I had seen his photograph but I didn't know Mullah Omar. But all of them were here. Four aeroplanes came to the airport. And about 300 or 400 Taliban were here with Datsuns.

Ruined tower in Shahr-i-Gholghola [B. Jenks]

"The explosions all went off together, all at once, and the Taliban shouted 'Allahu Akbar! [God is Great!]' The whole of the valley shook. They were all laughing and happy, like they were at a wedding or it was the end of Ramadan."

2. SHAHR-I-GHOLGHOLA

Shahr-i-Gholghola—the City of Screaming—is the hill that looks like a Swiss cheese at the eastern end of the valley. It was destroyed by Genghis Khan and the screams of its inhabitants as they were butchered gave the place its name. From the top there is a magnificent view of the hills and the cliffs in which the Buddhas were carved.

In Afghanistan, the Mongol invasions are still remembered, almost as if they were recent history. The ATO's chief guide, Haji Safit Mir, recounted for me the story of Gholghola and the Mongols' arrival in Bamiyan.

"In 1221, when Genghis Khan crossed the Amu Darya, Jalaludin was governor of Afghanistan with his capital at Gor, near Jam. Ghenghis destroyed Balkh and came down the Shikari valley and sent his grandson, who was 14 or 15 years old, to take Bamiyan, but he was killed by the people of Bamiyan. Genghis besieged Gholghola in revenge for the death of his grandson and told his troops to kill everything, people, animals and children. Yet he could not take the castle.

"But down in the valley, there was a large house called Qal-i-Duqtar, where Jalaludin's daughter lived. She sent a message to Genghis by shooting an arrow and stated two things: first, if I show you the way to take the citadel you will not destroy my fortress, and second, you must marry me. He said he would. [Haji pointed to the south.] She said, go there, and there is an underground canal that brings water and if you stop the water you will be able to occupy this area. They shut off the water and took this citadel.

"But to the princess Genghis said, 'You killed your father and maybe if you meet another young man you will kill me.' So they put her inside a rug and wrapped her in a sack and then the horsemen pulled her like a buzkashi game. But he didn't destroy her house. It is called Gholghola because many people were noising, you know."

3. BAZAAR

The old bazaar in Bamiyan ran along the road immediately below the large Buddha. It was destroyed by the Taliban as part of their persecution of the Hazaras. Professor Yamaouchi said that it is possible to find leather Bactrian manuscripts in Greek in the new bazaar. He recommends the following tests to see if they are genuine: 1. Do they smell of clay and earth? 2. Are they very light? 3. Are they very dry? 4. If a manuscript has oil on it, it has been forged.

Restaurant menu, Bamiyan, 1974 [Y. Crowe]

SHOPPING IN BAMIYAN

In the new bazaar, just below the plateau where the Bamiyan Hotel is located, you can find mink coats, flintlock muskets, an unattractive Buddha for $20,000. Your purchases need only be fettered by taste, not price—what about a mink bedcover? The shopkeeper produced a Persian seal. "It is Bacterian," he said. Whether genuine is another matter.

4. FOLADI AND KAKRAK VALLEYS

A short distance away from the main valley are two other valleys worth visiting that contain caves with carvings. In 2003 archaeologists surveyed here; it is possible they will discover more Buddhist remains in the future.

5. DRAGON VALLEY

About five km (three miles) to the east of the Buddhas is an astounding rock formation, one of the most remarkable natural sights I have ever seen. It is a long tongue of lava cracked open by an earthquake, with mineral water pouring out from springs at the north end, deep springs that emit subterranean bubbling and groaning. It makes an extraordinary impression. Nancy Dupree wrote: "In escorting visitors to the Bamiyan dragon, I have found their initial scoffing quickly turns into genuine sympathy for this dragon who has lain here groaning, bleeding and crying through the centuries."

The dragon's body is a long peninsula of solidified lava about 300 m long, flat on the top where it is broken by a crack running the entire length of the body. This is where Hazrat Ali's sword bisected the beast.

The fissure down the back is obviously the product of an earthquake and at its widest gapes open about 1 m (three feet). At the tail end it seems about 2 m deep

(six feet) but then deepens rapidly and in the middle could be hundreds of feet deep. It is easy to believe that it goes through the crust and magma right to the centre of the earth. The sheer rock formations along the crest suggests that the dragon itself must have looked similar to those dinosaurs who, for obscure evolutionary reasons, had plates along their backs.

(Top) *Crack in the Ajdahar of Bisut, which, according to folk lore, is a scar left behind from a sword-blow of the Hazrat Ali. [B. Jenks]*
(Bottom) *Within Shahr-i-Zohak [B. Woodburn]*

As you walk down the spine, your footsteps ring hollow on the rock. The northern tip of the peninsula does indeed look like the head of a creature and the fissure is only inches wide here, like a skull split open by a Mongol scimitar. The waters from the springs at the north end, which correspond to the dragon's eyes, have given rise to soft waves of white calcium, over which the water still flows silently, forming patterns like those left by a retreating tide on a tropical beach. These are the dragon's tears; its ears are formed of plugs of lava eroded into cones 5m (15 feet) high. The surrounding countryside is of soft loess hills, green in the spring, making the dragon all the more astonishing.

By pressing your ear to the rock, you can hear the trapped dragon's moans as it chafes at its captivity. Locals say that the sounds used to be much louder; presumably the underground springs are drying out.

Half-way along the dragon's back is the key to the scientific puzzle. The sides of the fissure at its widest point are ribbed and smoothly finished with shiny calcium, giving them the appearance of mother of pearl. Aeons ago, a much stronger flow of water issued from here and eroded this patch flat. At one end was a wide channel, perhaps 1 m (three feet) wide where the water had poured out and the spongy tufa below has been eroded into a series of pools. A shrine here must be originally pre-Islamic.

Shahr-i-Zohak, Bamiyan Valley, 1976 [Y. Crowe]

6. SHAHR-I-ZOHAK

This immensely impressive fortress, with its crenellations and towers against the skyline, announces that you have arrived in the Bamiyan Valley. Dated to the Ghorid period, it was destroyed by Genghis Khan in 1221, although buildings stood here long before; archeological work dates a preceding castle to the 6th century AD. The fort on the top stands 150 m (500 feet) above the fields.

You need a guide from the local police station to take you up because the pathways are slippery and dangerous. However, soldiers regularly walk up to the gun emplacement at the top, which has a magnificent view up the Hajigak Valley and the Koh-i-Baba mountain range. This view dramatizes Bamiyan's strategic position, a knot at the heart of the Silk Road, the meeting place of the two passes from Kabul, the route northwards across the Hindu Kush and the westerly road towards Herat.

7. BAND-I-AMIR AND THE LAKES

Band-i-Amir is about two hours' drive from Bamiyan. You can stop at Qharqana where there is a chaikhana. The landscape is undulating and featureless, but in the

spring and summer bright green like a sea, through which fleets of nomads move.

Beyond this stop is a Pushtun graveyard, called Kabre Afghan by the Hazaras (who refer to Pushtuns simply as "Afghans"). Hazaras have attacked and broken up the graveyard in revenge for their persecution by the Taliban.

You first catch sight of the main lake of Band-i-Amir as the road breasts the top of a hill. It is a good idea to leave the car just after this and follow the path that leads down from the road and walk around the edge of the lake. Send the car ahead and meet it at the village.

The lakes are astonishingly beautiful and their water is a deep blue-black, an extraordinary colour tinted by the mineral salts from springs that feed them. The lakes are themselves the craters of volcanoes, with 20-foot walls made of pumice stone.

BAND-I-AMIR HOTEL

Mohammed Hussein Azimi has owned this 10-room hotel for over 40 years. There is no phone but the ATO in Bamiyan can get a message to him, and he can hire horses ahead of time. The chaikhana does dinner for 100 afs and breakfast for 50.

THINGS TO DO

1. See the shrine after visiting the lakes.

2. Make a one-day excursion round the 5 lakes.

3. Hire a rowboat or motorboat to see the waterfall.

1. Visiting the The Shrine:

The shrine is the tomb of Aus-ud-Din, dated in Arabic AH 1213 (AD 1835), and an inscription over the door reads AH 1222 (AD 1844) and records the construction of the building itself.

(Left) *Two forest lakes, Band-i-Amir,1976 [Y. Crowe]*
(Above) *Beside a solidified "waterfall" at Band-i-Amir [B. Woodburn]*

You will be immediately surprised by over 100 locked padlocks, all of Chinese manufacture. These are put there as tokens of vows, for example (said the guardian) "I will marry that person". Inside is the tomb of a holy man with two beautifully carved stones, one wedge-shaped and the other a broken circle. It seems semi-pagan; placed on top are money, a piece of emery paper, a Koran wrapped in a brightly coloured Pakistani scarf, a staff with cloths attached. In the mudbrick tomb is set a beautiful basalt carving in Arabic. The round stone with the inscription reminds me of a Buddhist wheel of life and there is probably an influence in this area where Islam displaced Buddhism.

The waters of the very cold main lake, called Band-i-Zulfiqar and closest to shrine, are said to be a cure for madness. "They bring some ladies or some man which they are mad, you know? And they tie with a rope two, four, five people they will hold him, one part of the rope, the other part of the rope they will take that person and throw them into the lake and immediately take them out—because they will die, you know—and when they go into the room they will take their clothes and give it to the people and he or she will other new clothes and they will become well." Haji explained that madness was caused by a djinn. "Where does the djinn go?" I asked. "Into the lake," he said, laughing. "I do not think they can swim.'"

The lake itself is a curiosity. Nobody knows the source of the spring that gives rise to it,

(Top) Basalt carving at the tomb of Aus-ud-Din, c. 13th century; (right) Padlocks on the door of the Shrine of Aus-ud-Din, Band-i-Amir, 2004 [B. Jenks]

though it must be subterranean. Neither has its depth ever been measured. They tried once, but ran out of rope. In a perfectly ordered world it would be warm.

2. Hire a horse and walk round the lakes, which takes about five or six hours. Horses can be hired at an expensive $10 an hour.

3. Take a boat to the waterfall that feeds the main lake, Band-i-Haibar. It should cost 300 afs in a rowboat and 1,000 in a motorboat. Bring a can of petrol to get the motorboat working.

A Note on Afghan Expressions of Time

"Yek minute" (lit. one minute) means a wait of several hours is in store.

To a man going up hill: May you live forever.

To a man going down hill: May you never be tired.

Typical Afghan lack of connection with reality I thought.

8. AJAR NATIONAL PARK (OLD ROYAL HUNTING GROUNDS)

The Ajar Valley—still the personal property of King Zahir Shah and his family— is one of Afghanistan's most beautiful, remarkable places; it makes the somewhat difficult journey from Kabul well worthwhile. The almost completely enclosed valley reminds British travellers of Xanadu, not least because it is watered by a large river that rises from a cave at its far end. Rich wildlife still survives here. The scenic Surkhab Valley, which leads to Ajar, contains an interesting and sometimes belligerent mixture of Sunni, Shiite and Ismaili villages. Occasionally there are fisticuffs along sectarian lines.

GETTING THERE

There are two ways to travel to Ajar from Kabul. One crosses the Hindu Kush via the Salang Tunnel, the other goes via Bamiyan. Both require a good four wheel drive vehicle with an expert driver. Be careful; in spring 2004 the Bamiyan-Surkhab road involved crossing a bridge near the end of its life. The driver had to remove planks from behind the car and place them in front. The steel required to rebuild the bridge was ready at one end, but no one seemed to know when it would be built.

The bridge notwithstanding, the Bamiyan route is preferable. Travellers can break the journey at one of Bamiyan's hotels rather than the chaikhana at Tala-i-Barfak (Barfak). Plan to spend a few days at Bamiyan and visit Band-i-Amir before pushing on to Ajar. The Bamiyan-Ajar journey took over ten hours in 2004.

Beside the Surkhab River, north-east of Bamiyan, 1972 [B. Woodburn]

However, the longer route takes the traveller through the Salang Tunnel and along the Surkhab Valley from Doshi to Doab-i-Mikh Zarin (Doab). This is astonishingly picturesque, particularly in the spring when the opium poppies paint the valley mauve, red and white. The road to the Salang Pass goes via Charikar and is in good repair until the north side of the tunnel. Beyond, though, it has not been repaired and in May 2004 the sides of the roads were still mined. Take care. The Salang Tunnel, built by the Soviets in 1965, provided an excellent route for their tanks in 1979. It seems that, as Lord Curzon and the 19th-century Russophobes always feared, the invasion of Afghanistan had been a long-cherished plan. Follow the road northwards until you get to Doshi. From this town the road leads northwards to Pul-i-Kumri along the Larkab Valley, and another road leads up the Khinjan Valley.

Ploughing, with ox and wooden ploughshare, in the Ghorband Valley [B. Woodburn]

North of Doab was the main pass across the Hindu Kush before the Salang Tunnel existed; this pass has seen most of the invaders of Afghanistan from Alexander the Great onwards, including Josiah Harlan, the 19th-century American "Prince of Ghor" whose story is told in Ben Macintyre's excellent book, *Josiah the Great*.

Our main concern here is the road to Doab via Barfak. The poor road makes this a prolonged and sometimes unpleasant journey, only redeemed by the glorious countryside. Barfak (the name means "not much snow") makes a convenient overnight stop. There is a chaikhana with rooms that can be hired in the back yard. You can also stay with the charming local headman (*nayamandeh*), Sayid Ahmad Ranjibar, if he is at home. It is courteous to make a present to him—fabric for a new shalwar kameez is always welcome, and pencils and books for the children.

Between Doab and Barfak are a number of valleys. Wadu (just before you arrive in Barfak district) is Ismaeli and houses are decorated with pictures of the Aga Khan and Hazrat Ali. The entrance to this is found behind a small bazaar and chinar tree. The ethnic patchwork of this area is obvious in the neighbouring Tormush ("black mouse") Valley, which is Sunni yet contains a shrine where a relative of the Eighth Imam is buried, still tended by a small community of five Shiite families.

The little town of Doab (full name Doab-i-Mikh Zarin, "two waters of the golden nail") marks the start of the Kahmard Valley, which leads to Ajar. Here begins the characteristic scenery of high pink walls, and a fertile flood plain. You should buy any provisions and fruit you need at the bazaar and eat at the chaikhana. They are the last in the valley. You drive across a ford in the river and towards the high cliff walls of the valley. The dirt road, built for Zahir Shah, improves somewhat although it is difficult after much rain. This part of the valley, being fed by the

underground river in Ajar, is very fertile, intensely cultivates and has been unaffected by the drought that started in 1997.

Before reaching Ajar, you will see a dramatic cut in the rock face which is the narrow entrance to the Darreh Modar ("valley of the mother"). Inside it is honeycombed with man made caves. The valley itself contains old orchards of apricots and almonds.

Then one arrives in the Ajar Valley (*ajar* means "rock" in Arabic). Apart from its extraordinary natural beauty, Ajar drew the king because of its profusion of wildlife. In his time, the valley and surrounding mountains were maintained as a wildlife reserve,[1] full of game including urial wild sheep (*Ovis orientalis*), ibex (*Capra ibex sibericus*), a population of Bactrian deer (*Cervus elephus bactrianus*), introduced from the Oxus Valley, and a herd of wild yaks, introduced from the Pamirs. The valley is also on a north-south migration route for birds. Partridge can be bought from locals coming down from the mountains, who shoot them with antique shotguns.

Some of this wildlife has been killed by the Taliban, who sacked Ajar in 1998 —certainly the yaks and deer. However, local reports suggest that the indigenous wildlife remains. Mir Abdul, the king's shikari (a title meaning "great hunter"), recounted that in the spring of 2004 he saw a snow leopard (*Uncia uncia*) killing an ibex. He kept the head and had it stuffed as proof[2]—the leopard took a side of the ibex and buried it.

The valley itself is 1,830 m (6,000 feet) and the mountains rise to 4,270 m (14,000 feet). Follow the river up between a narrow defile to discover a huge lake, which was formed in 1956 by an earthquake that dislodged the huge boulders. The river downstream was dry for three days and then some of the rocks were dynamited to let the water through. You can see the remains of a pathway that was reached up a ladder, higher than the path you use today which consists of stepping stones along the left-hand wall. The cliffs rise sheer up, well over 300 m (1,000 feet) high. At the end lies a sacred cave called Chiltan from which the river rises. It is said that

Ajar Valley, 2004 [B. Jenks]

centuries earlier, 40 holy men entered, and are still there, asleep or praying until Judgement Day.

The cave is decorated with tiny scraps of fabric, each placed there to mark a request. Locals say that the water originates at Band-i-Amir and flows underground until it rises here. Certainly the colour of the water matches the deep blue of those lakes. By turning left here and continuing up, one reaches a juniper forest. Haji Safit Mir, the ATO's head guide, in the 1960s followed this route all the way to Band-i-Amir, a seven-day journey through a desolate landscape. He had been commissioned to survey the area to see if a trekking route for tourists could be established here.

In 2003, Jonathan Ledgard of *The Economist* interviewed Mir Abdul. This is his story.

Mir Abdul is the head of the village of Ajar and has 24 living children by five wives. He is a short man with a snow-white beard and watery grey eyes. "I have served the king all my life and I continue to serve him to the best of my ability and with dignity". He started to work for the king aged 17. Hunting came easily to him:

Boy in the Ghorband Valley, 1972, with a British smoothbore musket dating from 1856. It was loaded with metal scraps for hunting birds. [B. Woodburn]

"It was like pulling a plant out of the ground." The orchards in the valley were planted by his grandfather and father.

In 1999, the Taliban raided the valley, destroyed the king's house, chopped down many of the trees and shot the yaks and deer with kalashnikovs. "We were beaten and killed. We had no home, no animals, no seed." Since then, two NGOs have rebuilt the houses so he no longer lives in a tent. New Zealand troops have built desks for the school.

His happiest memories were of hunting, especially trailing snow leopards, working out where they had been and in what numbers. He had killed three of them and three steppe eagles with a rifle the king had given him. The last leopard measured nine feet from nose to tail. "The king was first in hunting. He was strong. He was brave. He took risks. We had the best times together."

Mir Abdul's son, Sultan Aziz, also worked as a hunter. "Because we had no dogs in Ajar, I was trained as a boy to take the place of a dog. I ran after the birds shot down by the princes. On one occasion I dived into the river and pulled out two wild ducks brought down by the crown prince. The prince liked me for doing this and promised to bring me to Kabul and pay for my schooling there." But before this happened, Zahir Shah had been deposed.

The king, too, remembered the valley for Jonathan. "There were four or five of us. We climbed with Mir Abdul to the top. We lit campfires at night on which we cooked our food. Everyone told a story, whether true or invented. The social distance between us just disappeared. We were just friends sitting together. Afghans. Equals. You know, those were the happiest moments of my life."

[1] See Jonathan Ledgard's piece in the Atlantic Monthly April 2004—available on the internet at www.theatlantic.com—which contains an interview with the King.

[2] However, Anthony Fitzherbert—probably the leading foreign expert on Afghan flora and fauna—remains sceptical of this story. He thinks it may have been a common leopard.

CERAMICS OF AFGHANISTAN

—Dr Yolande Crowe

A *small number of sites have been scientifically excavated yielding sufficient information to provide an outline of Afghan ceramic history, notwithstanding a gap in the early centuries of the Christian era, partially filled by the excavations in old Kandahar. Ceramic production in Afghanistan followed, it seems, the traditions of neighbouring Central Asian lands, the Iranian plateau and the Indus valley. In prehistoric times the site of Mundigak, crossroad of trade routes, about 20 km from Kandahar, spread across an area of about 20 hectares. All seven excavated levels have yielded earthen wares, some goblets and beakers with geometric or animal decoration in black or brown on a lighter ground. They echo the early ceramics of Quetta and Kulli in Pakistan as well as those of Susa in the 3rd millennium BC Later less attractive pieces are decorated in black on a red slip recalling similar schemes of the 2nd millennium in the Ferghana valley in Uzbekistan. Some terracotta figurines represent animals such as the Indian buffalo well known from the site of Harappa in Pakistan. The site was abandoned after the 1st millennium BC.*

Just south of the upper Oxus valley, the Graeco-Bactrian site of Ai Khanoum (late 4th century until c. 145 BC) has produced numerous shards that have been gathered into three main groups: the first relates to Persian wares of the Achaemenian period, with white and red slip decoration, and some new Greek shapes of fish dishes and craters. The second group indicates closer relations with the Greek world of Asia minor, with a dark grey body and a black slip for small and large ewers, dishes and bowls. The latter often have an incised inner circle surrounded with four stamped palmettes. In the third group new large dishes with a black or white slip have been found as well as ewers with handles decorated with a female head.

Sgraffito and green dish, Kabul Museum, 1976 [Y. Crowe]

The use of glazes appears with the Islamic period, when from roughly the 10th century slip-painting and sgraffito techniques begin to enhance dishes, bowls and pourers. Comparisons with Central Asian and Persian examples suggest simplified patterns for slip-painted wares, although a few fragments with calligraphic decoration show some sophistication. Furthermore, fairly dense patterns on shards from dishes and bowls are also painted in the same dark almost black manganese slip as well as in a russet slip. The motifs range from complex squares and "S" shapes to pseudo-Kufic lines. Sgraffito examples display simple incised bands along plain areas with slight copper-green splashes. Other wares have only champlevé denser palmettes and pseudo-Kufic broad inner bands on bowls without any splashing. Monochrome green wares are fairly common. As to the few lustre bowls found in the Ghazni excavations, they appear to have been imported presumably from Persia. Other excavated sites, such as the immense Ghorid palace in Lashkari Bazaar, the walls of ancient Balkh and sites in the Bamiyan valley, have also yielded shards mostly belonging to the period prior to the Mongol conquest (13th century). A bowl recovered from Ghazni and surface finds in southwest Afghanistan indicate a possible local production of later blue and white ceramics before the area was abandoned at the end of the 15th century. In the 1970s excavations of old Kandahar a series of late Safavid blue and white dishes and bowls was recovered from several pits.

(Top) *Sgraffito and green dish, from Ghazni;* (bottom) *Slip-painted bowl with pseudo-calligraphy, 12th century, Kabul Museum, 1976 [Y. Crowe]*

As in neighbouring lands from the 12th century, monuments were soon enhanced by glazed brick decoration. The most famous of such ornamentation in turquoise stands high on the minaret of Jam, which was erected in 1193–94. Square tiles about 20cm x 20cm (7 x 7 inches) are said to have come from baths in Ghazni; they display relief representations of birds, quadrupeds with a leafy tail and even a horse with its rider. A square frame of pearls surrounds each of them. The glazes are usually green or amber.

During the rule of the Timurids in the 15th century, a series of monuments was erected in Herat, one of its capitals, such as the tomb and musalla of Gawhar Shad, the forceful wife of Shah Rukh, son of Timur (Tamerlane). The outer walls of the tomb are covered in bannai technique,

where plain brick is patterned in with blue, turquoise and black glazed bricks. What is now left of three minarets shows intricate tile-mosaic work, like colourful lace applied to their shafts. Further examples of complex tile designs of the 15th century enhance the shrine of Sufi Ansari nearby at Gazargah. Noteworthy are the two great panels of the main iwan in front of the tomb, itself in the open air. A few parts of the Friday Mosque in Herat still carry Timurid panels including fragments over an earlier lateral doorway. Another shrine near Balkh, dedicated to Khwaja Abu Nasr Parsa, is dated 1460–61. The intricate architecture of the grand façade has recovered its colour by several restorations, which have renewed the floral motifs amongst which the lotus is set impressively within its spandrels.

(Top) *12th century Ghaznavid tile [Y. Crowe]*
(Left) *Minaret of the Herat Musalla [E. Knobloch]*

Repairs of outdoors tile work is a constant requirement owing to sharp temperature contrasts between winter and summer as well as torrential rains, whenever they happen. These restorations have been undertaken at irregular intervals over the years by local and foreign teams on the great mosque of Herat, the shrine of Balkh and the later shrine of Mazar-i-Sharif. Although very colourful with its blue tile work, this last shrine does not possess the quality of tile design seen on earlier monuments.

In the village of Istalif near Kabul the folk production of potters used to create attractive, if haphazard, turquoise glazed wares which attracted visitors before the recent wars. These included four-legged beasts and farm animals, figurines and common bowls and dishes. Nowadays only a couple of potters still work in the village, without great success. Too much wood is required for the firing of kilns at a time when scarce fuel is required for more essential needs.

Mention should also be made of all the utilitarian unglazed wares that used to be produced in most important villages. These ranged from kilns for baking bread to the yearly supply of ewers, which allow for fresh water in hot weather as their porous walls maintained cool water within. In the past any visitor to a chaikhana may have recalled the numerous teapots on the shop shelf for black or green tea according to the season. In the 19th century these pots were provided by the Russian porcelain factory set up in Moscow by Gardner. Later the market was taken up by the Japanese. Today, sadly, the foreign porcelain has been replaced by metal pots made abroad and usually coloured blue.

Yolande Crowe's Book, *Persia and China: Safavid Blue and White Ceramics in the Victoria and Albert Museum 1501-1738*, is published by Thames and Hudson, £60.00.

The Walls of Ghazni [E. Knobloch]

GHAZNI AND MAHMUD THE GREAT

The early and rapid expansion of the Islamic Empire, not long after its appearance in the 7th century AD, brought as many troubles as it did advantages for its rulers, the caliphs. One of their main difficulties, as the territory of Islam reached from Spain in the west to Central Asia in the east, was the maintenance throughout these far-flung areas of their authority. By the middle of the 9th century, the Abbasid Caliphs in Baghdad found themselves compelled to delegate substantial powers to governors in the more distant regions, allowing them to raise revenue and maintain armies. Although the caliphs hoped to ensure the obedience of these governors by means of a network of intelligence, they found this to be impossible. Over a period of time, the influence of the governors increased substantially, so that although they owed nominal allegiance to Baghdad, in reality they became virtually independent, and free to found their own ruling dynasties.

One such case was the Samanid dynasty, which came to prominence in Transoxiana towards the end of the 9th century. The capital of the empire was established at Bokhara, and at its height it ruled over much of Afghanistan, as well as lands as far away as the Aral Sea, the Ferghana Valley, the borders of India and Iraq. However, this new entity suffered from the same problems as did the Abbasid Caliphate itself. It was, in truth, only a loose association of provinces, whose leaders, whilst promising allegiance to the centre, carried on their affairs as normal; only the areas close to the capital came under any great control. Moreover, like the Abbasid Caliphs, the Samanids came to rely on Turkish slave-troops—known as *mamluks*—to reinforce their authority over various territories. In 961, one of these mamluks—Alptigin, governor of Nishapur—came into conflict with the Samanid ruler in Bokhara, Amir Mansur I. Deciding to revolt, he first marched to Balkh with 7,000 Turkish soldiers, where he defeated a force of 12,000 men sent by Mansur I to quash the rebellion. After this success, he proceeded south, and captured the city of Ghazni; although he took it in the name of the Amir, it was to be the home and capital of a new and separate empire.

GHAZNI FROM THE SOUTH WEST.

Published by Smith, Elder & C.º 65 Cornhill, London, 1867.

M & N. Hanhart, lit!

Capt.ⁿ P. S Lumsden, del!

View of Ghazni, 1857 [RSAA]

It is generally thought that the city which he had captured was of some little antiquity. Many have argued that Ghazni was mentioned by Ptolemy under the name of "Gazaca"; it has also been suggested, notably by the scholar Sir Alexander Cunningham, that it was also spoken of as "Gazos" by two late Greek poets, Dionysius (c. AD 300), and Nonnos of Panopolis (c. AD 500). Both emphasise its strength and impregnability; Nonnos, in his great epic, the 48-book *Dionysiaca*,' writes of it as:

> "…fortified Gazos, with a rampart of linen built with blocks of plaited threads, impregnable, well made with well-spun foundations, a steadfast fortress of Ares: no enemy hand has ever broken with bronze that line of linen-clad towers…"

However, the first extensive description of the city is handed down by the Chinese traveller Hsuen-Tsang. Visiting the city around AD 644, he reported that it was the joint capital of a Buddhist kingdom called Tsu-ku-cha—an area thought to correspond to Arachosia. He calls Ghazni "Ho-si-na", and names the other capital as "Ho-sa-la", a settlement that still remains to be identified:

> "This country is about 7,000 *li* (2,500 miles) in circuit, and the capital, which is called Ho-si-na (Ghazni), is about 30 *li* (10 miles) round. There is another capital, Ho-sa-la, which is also about 30 *li* round. Both of them are naturally strong and also fortified. Mountains and valleys succeed each other, with plains intervening, fit for cultivation. The land is sown and reaped in due season. Winter wheat is grown in great abundance; shrubs and trees grow in rich variety, and there are flowers and fruits in abundance. The soil is favourable for turmeric and for asafœtida…
>
> "The climate is cold; there are frequent hail and snow storms. The people are naturally light-hearted and impulsive; they are crafty and deceitful. They love learning and the arts, and show considerable skill in magical sentences, but they have no good aim in view.
>
> "They daily repeat several myriads of words; their writing and language differ from those of other countries. They are very specious in vain talk, but there is little body or truth in what they say. Although they worship many spirits, they also greatly reverence the three precious ones (are Buddhists).

There are several hundred *sangharamas*, with 1,000 or so priests. They all study the Great Vehicle. The reigning sovereign is sincere and honest in his faith, and is the successor of a long line of kings. He applies himself assiduously to religious work and is well-instructed and fond of learning. There are some ten stupas built by King Asoka, and several tens of Deva temples, in which sectaries of various denominations dwell together.

"The Tirthaka sect is very numerous here; they worship principally the Deva Kshuna. This Deva spirit formerly came from Mount Aruna in Kapisa, and took up his abode here in the southern districts of this kingdom, in the Mount Sunagir. He is severe or good, causing misfortune or exercising violence. Those who invoke him with faith obtain their wishes; those who despise him reap misfortune. Therefore people both far off and near show for him deep reverence; high and low alike are filled with religious awe of him. The princes, nobles, and people of this as well as of foreign countries assemble every year at a season of rejoicing which is not fixed, and offer gold and silver and precious objects of rare value, with sheep, and horses, and domestic animals; all which they present in simple and confiding trust, so that though the earth is covered with silver and gold, and the sheep and horses fill the valleys, yet no-one would dare to covet them: they consider them as things set apart for sacred purposes. The Tirthakas, by subduing their minds and mortifying their flesh, get from the spirits of heaven sacred formulae. By the use of these they are frequently able to control diseases and recover the sick."

It is not entirely clear when Ghazni ceased to be a Buddhist city. It is thought to have been attacked by Islamic forces in 662–63 and 747, but not to have come under their full control until 870, when the warrior Yakub bin Lais mounted a campaign against Arachosia and Kabul. It is believed that the city was captured by him around this time, and then passed to his brother, Amr bin Lais, who caused it to be fortified. Ghazni fell to the Samanids in 934, and remained wholly under their sovereignty until its capture, as stated, by Alptigin in 961.

Alptigin ruled the city as a nominal vassal of the Samanids, but in practice was fully independent; however, he died only two years after obtaining this position. Likewise, his son and successor Ishaq, after working hard to overcome challenges to his authority by the family of the ousted governor of Ghazni, Abu Bakr Lawik, was unable to enjoy the fruits of his labour; he died after a reign of three years in 966. A short period of some instability followed, but by 977, Subuktigin, a former mamluk of Alptigin, had managed to obtain the throne.

Subuktigin was noted by contemporaries for his military prowess. Before 977, he had mounted a successful campaign against the king of Kabul, who had formed an alliance with Abu Ali, son of Abu Bakr Lawik. It was this ability as a soldier, combined with his marriage of Alptigin's daughter, which brought him to power in Ghazni. However, the historian Ferishta, who had a penchant for recording somewhat apocryphal tales, gave the following as the ultimate cause of Subuktigin's rise to prominence:

> "The author of the *Jama-ul-Hikayat* relates that 'Subuktigin was at first a private horseman in the service of Alptigin, and being of a vigorous and active disposition, used to hunt every day in the forest. It happened on a time, as he was engaged in the amusement of the chase, he saw a doe grazing along with her fawn. On which, spurring his horse, he seized the fawn, and binding its legs proceeded on his return home. Having ridden but a short distance, he looked back, and beheld the doe following him, exhibiting every demonstration of affliction. The soul of Subuktigin melting with pity, he unbound the fawn and restored it to liberty: the happy mother turned her face to the wilderness, often turning round to gaze on Subuktigin. He is said to have seen during that night, in a dream, the Prophet of God (on whom be peace) who said to him 'That generosity which you have this day shown to a distressed animal has been appreciated by God, and the kingdom of Ghazni is assigned to you in this world as your reward: let not thy power, however, undermine thy virtue, but thus continue the exercise of benevolence towards mankind.'"

Under Subuktigin, the influence of Ghazni increased. In 986, he mounted another campaign against Kabul; within two years he had driven out the final king of the Hindu Shahi dynasty, and annexed Kabul to his own dominions. Six years later, the Samanid ruler, Nuh II, who presided over an empire that by this time was waning in significance, appealed for help to Subuktigin to put down a rebellion in Khurasan. He responded by sending an army under his eldest son, Mahmud, which succeeded in this endeavour. As a result, Nuh II appointed Subuktigin governor of the region—a position exercised on his behalf by Mahmud. Hence, when the ruler of Ghazni died in 997, he bequeathed to his son an emergent kingdom that stretched from Khurasan in the west, to the banks of the Oxus, to Peshawar in the east.

It was under Mahmud that the new dynasty of Ghazni achieved its greatest power and magnificence. Having come to the throne, he disassociated himself from the collapsing Samanid Empire, and instead applied to the caliph in Baghdad for formal recognition of his sovereignty. The Abbasid Caliph, Al-Kadir Billah, responded by sending him a robe of honour, and bestowing on him the title of *Yamin-ad-Daulah*, or "The Right Arm of the State". From this title, the Ghaznavid dynasty also came to be known as the Yamini.

Mahmud was supported by a number of Turkish troops initially in excess of 10,000. In order to ensure their loyalty, he saw to it that they received a regular salary from the public treasury, and were also given the opportunity to go on as many campaigns as possible; four-fifths of booty taken on any expedition fell to the ordinary soldiers, and constant warfare guaranteed for them rich rewards. In his time, he made 17 expeditions into India, and as a result built up not only a huge amount of wealth, but also an empire that reached from the Caspian Sea all the way to Delhi.

The 13th century Persian historian Juzjani, in his work on the Islamic dynasties of Asia, records one of Mahmud's most famous exploits—the raid on the Temple of Somnath—and also portrays the splendour of his reign:

> "When Sultan Mahmud ascended the throne of sovereignty, his illustrious deeds became manifest unto mankind within the pale of Islam, when he converted so many thousands of idol-temples into mosques, and captured so many of the cities of Hindustan, and overthrew and subdued its Kings. Jaipal, who was the greatest of the Kings of Hind, he made captive, and kept him a prisoner at Manyazid, in Khurasan, and commanded that he might be ransomed for the sum of eighty thousand dirhams. He led an army into Nahrwalah of Gujarat, and brought away Manat, the idol, from Somnath, and had it broken into four parts, one of which was cast before the entrance of the great mosque at Ghazni, the second before the gateway of the Sultan's palace, and the third and fourth were sent to Mecca and Medina respectively.

"Concerning this victorious expedition the poet Unsuri composed a Kasidah, or poem, two couplets of which are here inserted:

When the potent sovereign made the expedition to Somnath,
He made the working of miracles his occupation.
He staked the Chess of dominion with a thousand kings:
Each king he check-mated, in a separate game.

"Out of the different occasions in which the Sultan's greatness showed itself pre-eminent, one occurred during this expedition. When he retired from Somnath, and desired to lead back the army of Islam by way of the desert, to Sindh and Mansurah, out of Gujarat, he directed that guides should be procured. A Hindu presented himself, and offered to act as guide, and that sovereign, with the army of Islam, proceeded on his way. After the army had marched all night and next day, and the time had come round for the troops to halt, although search was made for water, none was anywhere to be found. The Sultan directed that the Hindu guide should be brought before him, and inquiries made from him. This was done, when the Hindu guide replied to the Sultan, saying: 'I have devoted my life for the idol Somnath, and I have led you and your army into this desert, in any part of which water is not to be found, in order that you may all perish.' The Sultan commanded that the Hindu should be despatched to hell, and that the troops should halt and take up their quarters for the night. He then waited until night had set in, after which he left the camp, and proceeded some distance from it, aside. Then, kneeling down, and with his forehead to the ground, he prayed devoutly and fervently unto the Most High for deliverance. After a watch of the night had passed, a mysterious light appeared in the horizon, and the Sultan gave orders for the troops to be put in motion, and to follow him in the direction of the light. When the day broke, the Almighty God had conducted the army of Islam to a place where there was water, and all the Musalmans were delivered safely out of this impending danger.

"The Almighty had endowed that ruler with great power of performing many miraculous and wonderful acts, such as He has not bestowed since upon any other sovereign, nor such vast military resources, so large a number of troops, and unbounded wealth. Sultan Mahmud possessed 2,500 elephants; and his court was guarded by 4,000 Turkish slave troops, who, on days of public audience, were stationed on the right and left of the throne—2,000 of them with caps ornamented with four feathers, bearing golden maces, on the right hand, and the other two thousand with caps adorned with two feathers, bearing silver maces, on the left.

"This monarch, by his manliness, his bravery and intrepidity, his wisdom and foresight, and his prudent counsels and wise measures, considerably extended the Muhamadan conquests in the east, and greatly increased the dominion of Islam in that quarter. The whole of Ajam, Khurasan and Khwarazm, Tabaristan, Iraq, the territory of Nimroz, Fars, the mountain district of Ghor, Tukharistan, all came under the control of his officers. The Maliks, or rulers, of Turkistan paid him obedience and acknowledged his superiority. He threw a bridge over the Jihun (Oxus), and marched his forces into Turan, and Kadr Khan had an interview with him, as had the Khans of the Turks likewise; and the Khakans of Turkistan came and presented themselves before him, and tendered him their allegiance."

In order to ensure the support of the Abbasid Caliph, Mahmud enforced a strict policy of Sunni orthodoxy throughout his dominions. Although the following story told by Ferishta is almost certainly untrue, it nevertheless records his reputation for piety:

"A petitioner one day complained, that owing to his having a handsome wife, the king's nephew had conceived a passion for her, and came to his house every night with armed attendants, and beat him and turned him into the street, till

he had gratified his adulterous passion; that he had frequently complained to who ought to have done him justice, but that the rank of the adulterer had hitherto protected him.

"The king, on hearing this, shed tears of indignation, and reproved the poor man for not making his complaint sooner. The man replied he often attempted, but could not gain admittance. He was then commanded to return to his house, and to give the king notice the first time his nephew was guilty of the like violence, charging those who were present, on pain of death, to let nothing of the subject transpire, at the same time ordering the poor man to be admitted at any hour. Accordingly the man returned to his house.

"On the third night, the king's nephew as usual came, and having whipped the husband severely, turned him into the street. The poor man hastened to the king, but the captain of the guards refused him admittance, saying that his majesty was in the seraglio. The man immediately vociferated loudly, so that the porter, fearing the court might be disturbed, and the noise reach the king, was under the necessity of conducting him to the officers of the bed-chamber, who immediately acquainted Mahmud.

"The king instantly arose, and wrapping himself in a loose cloak, followed the man to his house. He found his nephew and the man's wife sleeping together in one bed, with a candle standing on the carpet near them. Mahmud, extinguishing the candle, drew his sword, and severed his nephew's head from his body. Then commanding the man to bring a light, he called for water, and having taken a deep draught, he told him he might now go and sleep with safety, if he could trust his own wife.

"The poor man fell at the king's feet in gratitude, but begged him to say why he put out the candle, and afterwards called so eagerly for water to drink? The king replied, he put out the candle that pity might not arrest his hand in the execution of his duty, for that he tenderly loved the youth; and moreover, said, he had made a vow to God, when he first heard the complaint, that he would neither eat nor drink till he had brought the criminal to justice, which was the cause of his intense thirst. Let it not be concealed from my learned readers, that although we have many well authenticated stories of the inflexible justice of some virtuous monarchs, we have no other instance of this nature. God only knows the hearts of His people."

Remains of an 11th century Ghaznavid Palace near Lashkar-i-Bazaar, 1971 [Y. Crowe]

'Firdousi encounters the Court Poets of Ghazni' attributed to Bihzad, from Shah
Tahmasp's Shah-nameh, c. 1525 [Collection of Prince Sadruddin Aga Khan, Geneva]

Mahmud was as much renowned for being a patron of the arts as he was for being a warrior. He attracted many Persian poets to his court, the most prominent being Firdousi, writer of the greatest Iranian national epic, the *Shahnameh*, or 'Book of Kings.' Very little is known of Firdousi's life, except for a story of the enmity which one of Mahmud's viziers, Ahmad Mymundi, bore towards him. When Mahmud commissioned Firdousi to work on the *Shahnameh*, he commanded the vizier to pay him a gold dinar for every line that he composed. A 19th-century translator of the epic, James Atkinson, completes the story:

> "The Minister, in compliance with the injunctions of Mahmud, offered to pay the sums as the work went on; but Firdousi preferred waiting till he had completed his engagement, and receiving the whole at one, as he had long indulged the hope of being able to do something of importance for the benefit of his native city.

> "It appears that Firdousi was of an independent spirit, and not of that pliant disposition which was necessary to satisfy the expectations and demands of the proud Vizier, who, offended at his unbending manners, did everything in his power to ruin his interest with the king. Several passages in his poems were extracted and invidiously commented upon, as containing sentiments contrary to the principles of true faith. It was alleged that they proved him to be an impious philosopher, a schismatic, and a follower of Ali. But in spite of all that artifice and malignity could frame, the Poet rose in the esteem of the public. Admiration followed him in the progress of the work, and presents were showered on him from every quarter. The Poems were at length completed. The composition of 60,000 couplets appears to have cost him the labour of thirty years. The Sultan was fully sensible of the value and excellence of that splendid monument of genius and talents, and proud of being the patron of a work which promised to perpetuate his name, he ordered an elephant-load of gold to be given to the author. But the malignity of the Minister was unappeased, and he was still bent upon the degradation and ruin of the Poet. Instead of the elephant-load of gold, he sent to him 60,000 silver dirhums! Firdousi was in the public bath at the time, and when he found that the bags contained only silver, he was so enraged at the insult offered to him, that on the spot he gave 20,000 to the keeper of the bath, 20,000 to the seller of

refreshments, and 20,000 to the slave who brought them. 'The Sultan shall know,' he said, 'that I did not bestow the labour of thirty years on a work, to be rewarded with dirhums!' When this circumstance came to the knowledge of the King he was exceedingly exasperated at the disgraceful conduct of the Minister, who had, however, artifice and ingenuity enough to exculpate himself, and to cast all the blame upon the Poet. Firdousi was charged with disrespectful and insulting behaviour to his sovereign; and Mahmud, thus stimulated to resentment, and not questioning the veracity of the Minister, passed an order that the next morning he should be trampled to death under the feet of an elephant. The unfortunate Poet, panic-struck and in the greatest consternation, heard of the will of the Sultan. He immediately hurried to the presence, and falling at the feet of the King, begged for mercy, at the same time pronouncing an elegant eulogy on the glories of his reign, and the innate generosity of his heart. The King, touched by his agitation, and respecting the brilliancy of his talents, at length condescended to revoke the order.

"But the wound was deep and not to be endured. He went home and wrote a Satire against Mahmud, with all the bitterness of reproach which insulted merit could devise, and instantly fled from the court. He passed some time at Mazinduran (Mazanderan, N Iran) and afterwards took refuge at Baghdad, where he was in high favour with the Caliph Al-Kadir Billah, in whose praise he added a thousand couplets to the *Shahnameh*, and for which he received a robe of honour and 60,000 dinars...

"Mahmud at length became acquainted with the falsehood and treachery of the Vizier, whose cruel persecution of the unoffending Poet had involved the character and reputation of his Court in disgrace. His indignation was extreme, and the Minister was banished forever from his presence. Anxious to make all the reparation in his power for the injustice he had been guilty of, he immediately dispatched to Baghdad a present of 60,000 dinars, and a robe of state, with many apologies for what had happened. But Firdousi did not live to be gratified by this consoling acknowledgement. He had returned to his friends at Tus, where he died before the present from the King arrived. His family however scrupulously devoted it to the benevolent purposes which the Poet had originally intended, viz. the erection of public buildings, and the general improvement of his native city."

The Persian scholar E.G. Browne provides us with an excerpt of the satire:

"They said 'This bard of over-fluent song
Hath loved the Prophet and Ali for long.'
Yea, when I sing my love for them, I could
Protect from harm a thousand like Mahmud.
But can we hope for any noble thing
From a slave's son, e'en were his sire a king?
For had this king aught of nobility,
High-throned in honour should I seated be.
But since his sires were not of gentle birth,
He hates to hear me praising names of worth."

Mahmud died in 1030. Ferishta supplies us with more doubtful stories of Mahmud's behaviour towards the end of his life:

"It is a well established fact that two days before his death, he commanded all the gold and caskets of precious stones in his possession to be placed before him: when he beheld them he wept with regret, ordering them to be carried back to the treasury, without exhibiting his generosity at that time to anybody, for which he was accused of avarice. On the following day, he ordered a review of his army, his elephants, camels, horses, and chariots, with which having feasted his eyes for some time from his travelling throne, he again burst into tears, and retired in grief to his palace.

"Abul Hassan Ali, the son of Hassan Mymundi, relates, that the king one day asked Abu Tahir Samani, what quantity of valuable jewels the Samanid dynasty had accumulated when it became extinct? He replied, that in the reign of Amir Nuh Samani the treasury

Bazaar Merchant, Ghazni, 1967 [Y. Crowe]

contained seven ruttuls weight of precious stones. Mahmud flung himself prostrate on the floor, and cried out 'thanks to thee, all-powerful being, who hast enabled me to collect more than 100 ruttuls.'

"It is also said that in the latter end of his reign Mahmud, on hearing that a citizen of Nishapur possessed immense wealth, he commanded him to be called into his presence, and reproached him for being an idolater and an apostate from

Pilgrims at the Mausoleum of Sultan Mahmud (998–1030), who chose this site in a favourite garden near Ghazni. The triangular tombstone is carved from Afghan marble. [B. Woodburn]

the faith. The citizen replied 'O king, I am no idolater nor apostate, but I am possessed of wealth; take it, therefore, but do me not a double injustice, by robbing me of my money, and my good name.' The King, having confiscated his whole property, gave him a certificate under the royal seal, of the purity of his religious tenets. According to the *Tubket Naasiry* it appears that Mahmud was sceptical on certain religious points, and questioned the orthodoxy of the opinions of the learned, especially on the use of penances. He even professed

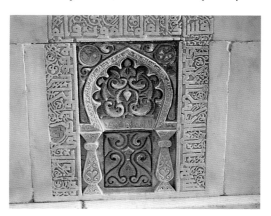

his doubt of a future state, and did not hesitate to say he questioned whether he really was the son of Subuktigin. He dreamed, however, one night that he saw the Prophet standing before him, who addressed him thus: 'O son of Amir Nasir Subuktigin, may God give thee honour in both worlds, as he has conferred it on man by his precepts!' So that the three points of his scepticism were removed by this short sentence…"

Mahmud's tomb detail, Ghazni, 1974 [Y. Crowe]

Mahmud was buried in a mausoleum erected in a garden just outside the city, known originally as Bagh-i-Firuzi—"The Garden of Victory"—but now named Rauza (tomb with an attached mosque and garden). The mausoleum, tradition holds, was fitted with the sandalwood doors looted from the Hindu temple of Somnath. The large entranceway into the garden stands as one of the last remaining monuments—along with the palatial ruins at Lashkar-i-Bazar and the "Towers of Victory"—of the great period of Ghaznavid architectural patronage. Robert Byron visited the site in 1933, and described the Sultan's marble tomb within:

> "Three old men were chanting from large Korans, while our guides leant over a wooden railing to take off the black pall, shaking the rose-petals that covered

it into a heap at one end. There emerged an inverted stone cradle with triangular ends, five feet long and twenty inches high, and mounted on a broad plinth. The stone is marble, white and translucent. On the side facing Mecca runs a Kufic inscription in two lines beginning 'a gracious reception from God for the noble Prince and Lord Nizam-ad-Din Abulkasim Mahmud ibn Subuktigin.' On the other side,

Mahmud's tomb, detail, marble calligraphy, Ghazni, 1975 [Y. Crowe]

a small trefoil panel says: 'He died... in the evening of Thursday when seven nights remained of the month of Rabiat II in the year 421.' That was February 18th, 1030.

> "The virtue of the Tomb as a work of art lies in the depth and fullness of the carving, in the glow of the marble where age has caressed it, and above all in the main inscription. Kufic lettering has a functional beauty; regarded as pure design, its extraordinary emphasis seems in itself a form of oratory, a transposition of speech from the audible to the visible. I have enjoyed many examples of it in the last ten months. But none can compare with these tall

rhythmic ciphers, involved with dancing foliage, which mourn the loss of Mahmud, the conqueror of India, Persia, and Oxiana, nine centuries after his death, in the capital where he ruled."

After a struggle between Mahmud's sons, he was eventually succeeded by his eldest offspring, Masud I. With his accession, the Ghaznavid dynasty, like its predecessors, started to go into decline; the governors of outlying provinces— particularly in India—embarked on various revolts, and the Seljuk Turks began to press down from the north across the Oxus. Nevertheless, the Empire displayed a late period of strength at the beginning of the 12th century under its final rulers, Masud III and Bahram Shah, and Ghazni itself continued to be a centre of rich artistic patronage.

One of the most notable poets to be maintained by the later Ghaznavid court was the Sufi mystic Sana'i, who flourished during the reign of Bahram Shah. Little is known of his life, but his mausoleum is still to be seen in a garden on the outskirts of the city. Nonetheless, he left behind a significant body of verse, most famous of which is the *Hadiqatu'l-Haqiqat*, or "The Garden of Truth". Like other mystics, he struggles with the question of the infinity of God, trying and failing to pin it down in terms of human reason and perception; in the end, he concludes that God's infinity and unity is beyond expression in these terms, and implies that the only way to articulate it is in paradox, absurdity or an acceptance of not knowing—as the English mystic George Herbert put it, "they that know the rest know more than I". Here are Sana'i's words:

> "When he shows His Nature to His creation, into what mirror shall He enter? The burden of proclaiming the Unity not everyone bears; the desire of proclaiming the Unity not everyone tastes. In every dwelling is God adored; but the Adored cannot be circumscribed by any dwelling. The earthly man, accompanied by unbelief and anthropomorphism, wanders from the road; on the road of truth thou must abandon thy passions; rise, and forsake this vile sensual nature; when thou hast come forth from Abode and Life, then, through God, thou wilt see God.

"How shall this sluggish body worship Him, or how can Life and Soul know Him? A ruby of the mine is but a pebble there; the soul's wisdom talks but folly there. Speechlessness is praise—enough of thy speech; babbling will be but sorrow and harm to thee: have done!

"His Nature, to one who knows Him, and is truly learned, is above 'How' and 'What' and 'It is not' and 'Why.' His creative power is manifest, the justice of his wisdom; His wrath is secret, the artifice of His majesty. A form of water and earth (the human being) is dazzled by His love, the eye and the heart are blinded by His Nature. Reason, in her uncleanness, wishing to see him, says, like Moses, 'show me'; when the messenger comes forth from that Glory, she says in its ear, 'I turn repentant unto thee.' Discover, then, the nature of His Being through thy understanding! Recite his thousand and one pure names. It is not fitting that His Nature should be covered by our knowledge; whatever thou hast heard, that is not He. 'Point' and 'line' and 'surface' in relation to His Nature are as if one should talk of His 'substance' and 'distance' and 'six surfaces'; the Author of those three is beyond place; the Creator of these three is not contained in time. No philosopher knows of imperfection in Him, while He knows the secrets of the invisible world; he is acquainted with the recesses of the mind, and the secrets of which as yet there has been formed no sketch upon thy heart...

"Reason is made up of confusion and conjecture, both limping over the earth's face. Conjecture and cogitation are no good guides; wherever conjecture and cogitation are, He is not. Conjecture and cogitation are of His creation; man and reason are His newly-ripening plants. Since any affirmation about his nature is beyond man's province, it is like a statement about his mother by a blind man; the blind man knows he has a mother, but what she is like he cannot imagine; his imagination is without any conception of what things are like, of ugliness and beauty, of inside and outside.

"In a world of double aspect such as this, it would be wrong that thou shouldest be He, and He thou. If thou assert Him not, it is not well; if thou assert Him, it is thyself thou assertest, not He. If thou know not that He is, thou art without religion, and if thou assert Him thou art of those who liken Him. Since He is beyond 'where' and 'when', how can He become a corner of thy thought? When the wayfarers travel towards Him, they vainly exclaim, 'Behold! Behold!'

"If thou wilt, take hope, or if thou wilt, then fear; the All-wise has created nothing in vain. He knows all that has been done or will be done; thou knowest not, yet know that he will assuage thy pain. In the knowledge of Him is naught better than submission, that so thou mayest learn His wisdom and His clemency. Of His wisdom He has given resources to His creatures, the greater to him who has the greater need; to all He has given fitting resources, for acquiring profit and warding off injury. What has gone, what comes, and what exists in the world, in such wise it was necessary; bring not folly into thy conversation; look thou with acceptance on His decrees."

Sana'i stresses again and again the necessity not to commit the sin of idolatry by placing one's reliance on anything in the transitory world. In the following extract, he describes how the prophets had, by lives of dispossession and humility in the material world, obtained not only true contentment in the midst of their physical lives, but also a glimpse of the Divinity:

"Dost thou desire thy collar of lace to be washed, then first give thy coat to the fuller. Strip off thy coat, for on the road to the King's gate there are many to tear it. At the first step that Adam took, the wolf of affliction tore his coat: when Cain became athirst to oppress, did not Abel give up his coat and die? Was it not when the prophet Idris (Enoch) threw off his coat that he saw the door of Paradise open to him? When the Friend of God (Abraham) remorselessly tore their garments from star and moon and sun, his night became bright as day, and the fire of Nimrod became a garden and a rose-bower. Look at Solomon, who in his justice gave the coat of his hope to the fuller; jinn and men, birds and ants and locusts, in the depth of the waters of the Red Sea, on the tips of the branches, all raised their face to him, and all became subservient to his command; when the lustre of his nature had been burnt in the fire of his soul, the heavens laid his body on the back of the wind.

"When the venerable Moses, reared in sorrow, turned his face in grief and pain towards Midian, in bodily labour he tore off the coat from his anguished heart. For ten years he served Shu'aib (Jethro), till the door of the invisible was opened to his soul. His hand became bright as his piercing eye; he became the crown on the head of the men of Sinai.

"When the Spirit (Jesus), drawing breath from the spiritual ocean, had received the grace of the Lord, he sent his coat to the cleanser of hearts at the first stage of his journey. He gave brightness to his soul, He gave him kingship, even in childhood. By the Eternal Power, through encouragement in secret and grace made manifest, he lost the self; the leprous body became dark again through him as the shadow on earth, the blind eye became bright as the steps on the throne. Whoso like him seeks neither name nor reputation, can produce ten kinds of food from one jar. A stone with him became as fragrant as musk; the dead rose to living action and spoke. By his grace life broke forth in the dead earth of the heart; by his power he animated the heart of the mire.

"When predestined fate had closed the shops, and the hand of God's decree lay in the hollow of non-existence (the *fitrat*, or time between Jesus and Mohammed), the world was full of evil passions, the market full of ruffians. Then He sent a vicegerent (Mohammed) into this world to abolish oppression; when he appeared from mid-heaven, fervid in soul and pure in body, wore no coat on the religious path; then what could he give to the fullers of the land? When he passed from this mortal state to eternal life he became the ornament and glory of this perishable world."

In another part of the work, Sana'i rehearses the view, generally held by Sufis, that the Koran (Qu'ran) can be understood at two levels: the outer level of meaning, to the letter, known as *zahir*; and an inner spiritual level—clear only to a few initiates—known as *batin*:

"Glorious it is, though concealing its glory; and a guide, though under the veil of coquetry. Its discourse is bright and strong; its argument clear and apt; its words are a casket for the pearl of life; its precepts a tower over the water-wheel of faith; to the Knowers it is love's garden, to the soul the highest heaven.

"O thou to whom, by reason of thy heedlessness and sin, in reading the Qu'ran there comes upon thy tongue no sweetness from its words, into thy heart no yearning from their comprehension; by its exceeding majesty and authority the Qu'ran, with argument and proof, is in its inner meaning the light of the high road of Islam, in its outward significance the guardian of the tenets of the multitude; life's sweetness to the wise, to the heedless but a recitation on the tongue—phrases upon their tongue whose sweetness they cannot taste, while careless of their spirit and design.

A view of Ghazni, 1841. Note the minarets, which at this time still bore see their upper portions, now collapsed. (Bellew)

"There is an eye which sees the spirit of the Qu'ran, and an eye which sees the letter: for this the bodily eye, for that the eye of the soul; the body, through the ear, carries away the melody of its words; the soul, by its perceptive power, feeds on the delights of its spirit. For strangers the curtains of majesty are drawn together in darkness before its loveliness; the curtain and the chamberlain know not aught of the king; he knows who is possessed of sight, but how can the curtain know aught of him?

"The revolutions of the azure vault have brought no weakening of its power, no dimming of its lustre; its syntax, form and pronunciation, prevail from earth to Pleiades.

"Now hast thou in thy daily provision tasted the nut's first husk; the first skin is rough and harsh, the second is like the serpent's slough, the third is silk, pale and fine, and fourth is the succulent cool kernel; the fifth degree is thy abode, where the prophets' law becomes thy threshold. Seeing then that thou mayest delight thy soul with the fifth, why halt at the first? Thou hast seen of the Qu'ran but its veil; thou hast seen its letters, which do but hide it. It does not reveal its countenance to the unworthy; him, only the letters confront. If it had seen thee to be worthy, it would have rent this subtle veil and shown its face to thee, and there thy soul might have found rest; for it heals the wounded heart, and cures the disappointed soul; the body tastes the flavour of the dregs that it may live; the soul knows the taste of the oil.

"What can sense see, but that the outward form is good? What there is within, wisdom knows. Thou recitest the form of its suras, and its true nature thou knowest not; but know, that to him who truly read the Qu'ran, the feast it gives comes not short of the guest-house of Paradise. It has made the letter its veil, because it is to be concealed from alien eyes; material existence knows naught of its inmost soul; know its body is one thing, its soul a thing apart— from its outward form thou seest but so much as do the common men from the appearance of a king."

Other relics of the latter part of the Ghaznavid dynasty are the two minarets— or "Towers of Victory"—which still stand outside the city. Their purpose is unknown, and they do not stand in their original form—the upper cylindrical sections of the minarets collapsed in an earthquake in 1902. Robert Byron describes them as he saw them in 1933:

"The difference between [the towers] is in breadth, the diameter of the larger, excluding the stone base, being about twenty-four feet, and that of the smaller about twenty-two. Both are built of a rich toffee brick tinged with red, and are adorned with carved terra-cotta of the same colour. In each case, each of the eight recesses between the star-points is divided into eight ornamental zones of varying depths. Between the third and fourth, fifth and sixth, and sixth and seventh zones, the brickwork is interrupted by wooden joists.

"Apart from zigzag patterns in which the bricks are set, the ornament of the smaller tower is confined to the sixteen panels of bold Kufic lettering at the top, which describe Mahmud as 'the august Sultan, King of Mussulmans, help

of the poor, Abulkasim Mahmud—may God illuminate his constancy—son of Subuktigin Gazi... Commander of the Faithful.' The larger tower is richer, its bricks are closer set, and all eight zones are filled with elaborate ornament, sometimes bordered with lesser inscriptions. Another sixteen panels round the top proclaim the titles of Masud; their Kufic is taller and more graceful, standing out from a maze of pattern like soldiers from a crowd. Generally, when it is a question of comparing two buildings of similar design but different dates, the simplicity of the older is preferable. Here that is not so. The fineness of the larger's brickwork and the elaboration of its ornament have a functional propriety. They weight the tower to the earth, giving it that air of strength and cohesion which it needed to support the shaft above. An old photograph in the Legation at Kabul, taken about 1870, shows the detail of this shaft. The first

Detail of inscription, Minaret of Bahram Shah, Ghazni, 1967 [Y. Crowe]

twenty-five feet were plain and were probably hidden, when the tower was first built, by a wooden balcony. Thereafter it was divided into ornamental ribs, alternately curved and flat. These were surmounted by eight pairs of elongated niches and by a belt of carving which looks as if it contained a Kufic inscription."

The Ghaznavid dynasty began to collapse in the middle of the 12th century. To the west of Ghazni lay the mountainous area of Ghor, inhabited by the Shansabani, who had been pagan until the Ghaznavids had conquered and forcibly converted them in the early period

A back street in Ghazni, 1972 [B. Woodburn]

of their empire. However, by the time of Bahram's reign, the territory had been taken over by the Seljuk Turks, as a result of which serious conflicts began to arise between Ghor and Ghazni. The latter city was briefly captured in 1148 by the ruling Ghorid prince, Saif-ud-Din, who held it until Bahram was able to oust him and put him to a shameful death by torture. One of his brothers, Ala-ud-Din, determined to avenge him, led an army against Ghazni and put Bahram to flight; having entered the city, he gave it over to looting, massacre and destruction. This ruination of what was universally acknowledged to be one of the finest and most beautiful cities of Central Asia won Ala-ud-Din the title of *Jahan Suz*, or "World Burner". The Ghaznavid monarchs retreated to Lahore, where they met their final defeat at the hands of the Ghorids in 1192. As for Ghazni itself, after further devastation by the armies of Genghis Khan, it failed to regain its former prominence. A small population remained there for the sake of trade, but the city's past glory was never to return; as an 18th-century traveller, George Forster, said:

"But, ah! what humiliating sorrow did I feel, how quickly did every spark of the pride incident to humanity subside, on beholding the fallen state of Ghazni! In vain did I look for its 'gorgeous palaces and cloud-capped towers.' They had been long levelled with the dust, and save some scattered masses of misshapen ruins, not a monument is to be seen of Ghazni's former grandeur."

The settlement, however, did not cease to be of strategic importance. In 1504, it was captured by Babur, who referred to it in his memoirs:

"Ghazni has little cultivated land. Its torrent, a four or five-mill stream, makes the town habitable and fertilizes four or five village; three or four others are cultivated from underground water courses (karaiz). Ghazni grapes are better than those of Kabul; its melons are more abundant; its apples are very good, and are carried into Hindustan. Agriculture is very laborious in Ghazni because, whatever the quality of the soil, it must be newly top-dressed every year; it gives a better return, however, than Kabul. Ghazni grows madder; the entire crop goes to Hindustan and yields excellent profit to the growers. In the open country of Ghazni dwell Hazara and Afghans (Pushtuns). Compared with Kabul, it is always a cheap place. Its people hold to the Hanafi school of Islam, and are good orthodox Musalmans, many people keep a three months' fast, and their wives and children live modestly secluded..."

"The year I took Kabul and Ghazni… people told me there was a tomb in a village there, which moved when a benediction on the Prophet was pronounced over it. We went to see it. In the end I discovered that the movement was a trick, presumably of the servants at the tomb, who had put a sort of platform above it which moved when pushed, so that, to those on it, the tomb seemed to move, just as the shore does to those on a passing boat. I ordered the scaffold to be destroyed and a dome built over the tomb; also I forbad the servants, with threats, ever to bring about the movement again.

"In books it is written that there is in Ghazni a spring such that, if dirt and foul matter be thrown into it, a tempest gets up instantly, with a blizzard of rain and wind. It has been said also in one of the histories that Sabuktigin, when besieged by the Rai of Hind, ordered dirt and foulness to be thrown into the spring, and by this aroused, in an instant, a tempest with blizzard of rain and snow, and, by this device, drove off his foe. Though we made many enquiries, no intimation of the spring's existence was given us."

Like Babur, later travellers also noted the karaiz (karez, qanat), or underground canals, examples of which—though often in ruins—can be seen in many parts of Afghanistan. H.W. Bellew, who briefly passed through the city in 1857, left a fuller description of them:

"The Karaiz is a subterranean aqueduct, connecting several wells, and conducting their united waters in one stream to the surface of the earth at a lower level. The object of this arrangement is to obviate the loss by evaporation, which, were the stream to flow for any distance over the open surface, would be so great that it would be mostly dissipated before it reached the fields it was to supply with water. The Karaiz is thus constructed: On the slope of some neighbouring hill, or on other rising ground, where it is supposed there are underground springs, a large shaft or well is sunk till it opens on one of these springs. If a sufficiency of water is indicated, the construction of a Karaiz for its conveyance to the desired spot is determined on, and the work is commenced on the site where it is intended that the water shall issue on the surface. At this spot a shaft of three or four feet in depth is sunk; and at regular intervals of twenty, thirty, or more paces from this, in the direction of the hill or other

Outside Ghanzi, Tomb of Ulugh Beg Miranshah (d. 1501), a descendant of Timur. The design of this monument prefigures that of the Taj Mahal. [Y. Crowe]

side, where, by the sinking of the first shaft, it has been previously ascertained that water will be obtained, a series of similar shafts or wells is sunk, and they are all connected together by tunnels bored from the bottom of one shaft to the base of the one next above it, and so on, up to the first shaft sunk over the spring from which the water is to be drawn away. The depth of the shafts gradually increases with their distance from the one near the spot at which the stream is to issue on the surface, and in proportion to the slope of the ground and the number of the shafts. The length of the Karaiz depends on the supply of water to be obtained, and the distance of the springs from the site selected for habitation or cultivation. From the shaft sunk near the land to be irrigated the water is conducted into the fields through a tunnel which, commencing at the base of the shaft, opens on the surface by a small aperture at about twenty or thirty feet distance, and from this point the water flows onwards in a narrow and shallow stream along a superficial trench that winds through the fields. The position of the shafts is marked by circular heaps of earth excavated from them and collected on the surface around their openings, which are usually closed over by a roofing of beams and matting, covered with earth. These coverings are removed at intervals of a couple of years or more, according to circumstances, for the purpose of clearing out the shafts and tunnels (which are mere excavations of the soil, without the aid of bricks and mortar), which become coated with a more or less thick deposit of earthy matter from the streams

flowing through them... Some Karaizha (plural of Karaiz) afford a constant stream of water for ages, whilst some, on the other hand, become exhausted ere they have yielded a return commensurate with the cost of their construction. The oldest Karaiz in Afghanistan is at Ghazni, and is said to have been constructed by the Sultan Mahmud Ghaznavi, whose

A horse-buggy near Ghazni in 1972, when animals still provided the commonest means of transport. [B. Woodburn]

name it bears. This Karaiz, which is said to be upwards of twenty miles in length, has for this long period of time watered the garden in which lies the tomb of its constructor, with the fields in the vicinity."

Bellew also experienced the bad weather for which, according to Babur, Ghazni was renowned:

"At Ghazni our party halted a day, in order to rest the animals. On the day after our arrival, a tremendous dust-storm, followed by thunder and rain, passed over our camp. The sky had been lowering and cloudy all day, and a high south-west wind was blowing with increasing force, till in the afternoon, somewhat suddenly, the atmosphere became darkened, and a loud sound of rushing air indicated the near approach of a heavy storm. During this short interval the air felt as if rarefied, and insufficient for respiration, and both men and animals appeared disturbed and excited by instinctive efforts to escape the approaching tempest. At the first sign of the coming storm, most of our escort hastily struck their tents, and piling them over their bedding, seated themselves on the heap, and with turban-enveloped heads and faces quietly awaited the (to them) well-known dust storm. During all this bustle and haste, which only occupied a few minutes, the horses neighed and pawed the earth with impatience, and, sniffing the now close at hand storm, snorted and screamed with fear. In a moment more it was upon us. The tents still left standing were blown down, whilst many of the horses, kicking themselves loose from their head and heel ropes, went rushing wildly through camp, biting and kicking each other in vicious passion, and, adding still greater confusion to that already produced by the tumult of the elements. During all this a gloomy darkness overwhelmed the whole camp, and a fierce wind, carrying clouds of fine dust and sand along with it, impelled them with such force as to be quite blinding to the eyes and painful to the exposed portions of the body, whilst withal an indescribable confusion and Babel of voices prevailed. Men shouting at each other, horses screaming and fighting, shreds of tent-cloth or portions of horse-clothing blowing about in every direction, and above all, the howling of the storm, formed an indescribable scene of disorder and discomfort, which lasted for some ten minutes or more, and then gradually subsided, being followed by a temporary lull and a clearing of the atmosphere, after which a cold wind ushered in the rain that closed the storm, and laid the dust raised by it. During this interval, and before the rain reached us, the whole camp was as busy as a colony of ants; one-half of them were occupied in re-pitching their tents, whilst the rest were engaged in capturing and picketing the loose horses; and this done, each individual set to work to rid himself of the dust with which he had become begrimed. The sensations produced by the dust-storm, while they last, are very trying and disagreeable. I noticed a peculiar oppression on the chest and sense of suffocation, as if the air inspired were not of sufficient quantity or density to fill the lungs. After these sensations had continued for a minute or two, a feeling of heat about the head, and a dryness of the air-passages, succeeded. These were, perhaps, simply owing to the quantities of fine dust with which the nostrils, mouth, and eyes were filled. But besides this, there was, I believe, some peculiar meteoric change in the atmosphere, which also had a share in producing these symptoms. The succeeding rain had a most delightful effect, and at once revived the feelings of faintness, and dispelled the uncomfortable symptoms above described."

The buildings in Ghazni, as in most Afghan towns, have no windows at ground level on the street side; light comes from internal courtyards. [B. Woodburn]

Charles Masson visited the city a few years before the First Afghan War (1839–42) and gives a general picture of its situation at that time:

"About an hour and a half before sunset we started for Ghazni. Castles and small villages chequered either side of the road. It was daylight when we distinguished in the distance the walls and castle of the once famed capital of Mahmud, but it was night before we reached it, having crossed near it the river, over which is an ancient and ruinous bridge. We skirted the walls on the southern face, and halted in front of the Kabul gate.

"The kafila (caravan) had here to pay duties, which were collected in a courteous manner by a Hindu farmer of the revenue. No person is allowed to enter the town unless he deposits his weapons with the guards at the gates. The bazaar is neither very large nor well supplied, and the town itself probably does not contain above one thousand houses. It is built on the projecting spur from a small mass of rounded hills, and the citadel, or residence of Amir Mahommed Khan, is perched on the higher portion of the spur. Its appearance is sufficiently picturesque, and it enjoys an extensive view over the country to the South, but there are no objects to render the landscape interesting. We look in vain over the city for any traces of the splendour which once marked the capital of the great Sultan Mahmud, and almost question the possibility that we are wandering about its representative. There are traditions that the ancient city was destroyed by a fall of snow overwhelming it at an unusually late

Spices in the Ghazni Bazaar, 1967 [Y. Crowe]

period of the season, or nine and a half days after No Roz, but its destruction may be equally imputed to the desolating armies of Hulaku and other Barbarian conquerors. The low hills, which close upon and command the city on the side of the Kabul gate, are covered with old Mahomeddan cemeteries, and under them, about a mile distant from the town, is the village of Rozah; contiguous to which is the sepulchre and shrine of the mighty Mahmud. This has been suffered to dwindle away into ruin, and broken figures of marble lions, with other fragments, alone attest the former beauty of its courts and fountains. In the present gates, fragments, which have escaped the avidity of the pious collections of relics, are said to be portions of the celebrated Sandalwood gates of Samnath, and the interior of the apartment covering the tomb of the once-powerful monarch is decorated with flags and suspended ostrich eggs. The tomb itself is enveloped in carpets and palls of silk. There are numerous gardens belonging to Rozah, and the houses of the village have an antique appearance. Between this village and the town are two brick columns, which are the most ancient vestiges of the place, and may be held undoubted testimonies to the ancient capital. They are usually ascribed to Sultan Mahmud, but I am not aware on what authority. They are, however, due to the period when Kufic characters were in use, for the bricks of which they are constructed are so disposed as to represent Kufic inscriptions and sentences. They are hollow, and may be ascended by flights of steps, which are, in truth, somewhat out of order, but may be surmounted. Ghazni is surrounded by walls, formed of mixed masonry and brick-work, carried along the scarp the entire length of the spur of hill on which it stands. The walls are strengthened with numerous bastions, and a trench surrounds the whole. The citadel is built on an eminence overlooking the town, and owes its present appearance to Amir Mohamed Khan, who since its capture by Dost Mohamed Khan has made it his residence.

I saw but two gates, one leading towards Nani, the other towards Kabul, but conclude there are also gates on the opposite side. Ghazni commands a most extensive plain, which is but indifferently furnished with villages and castles, although not absolutely without them, and the river of Nawar runs beneath the town walls on the northern side. The town is seated in the midst of a rich grain-country, and in the adjacent plains of Nawar it has immense fields of pasture... The country being more elevated than Kabul, the temperature of the atmosphere is generally lower, and the winters are more severe. The apples and prunes of Ghazni are much famed, and exceed in goodness those of Kabul."

The wall of the Citadel at Ghazni. Considered impregnable by the Afghans, it was taken by the British during the First Afghan War, when an engineer officer blew in the only gate that had not been bricked up. [B. Woodburn]

Ghazni played a major part in the First Afghan War. It was a stronghold of the forces of the ruler of Kabul, Dost Mohammed, but fell on 23 July 1839 to an advancing British column, which blew out one of its gates with gunpowder and took the city by storm. The day before this lightning raid, the British, encamped outside the walls with the ex-King Shah Shuja, whom they were attempting to return to power, came under a fierce attack. The historian Sir John Kaye describes the event:

"On that 22nd of July was made known to us, with fearful demonstrativeness, the character of those fanatic soldiers of Islam, who have since become so terribly familiar to us under the name of *Ghazis*. Incited by the priesthood, they flock to the green banner, eager to win Paradise by the destruction of their infidel foes, or to forestall the predestined bliss by dying the martyr's death in the attempt. A party of these fearless followers of the Prophet had assembled in the neighbourhood of Ghazni, and now they were about to pour down upon the Shah's camp, and to rid the country of a King who had outraged Mohammedanism by returning to his people borne aloft on the shoulders of infidels. A gallant charge of the Shah's horse, led by Peter Nicolson, who took no undistinguished part in the after-events of the war, checked the onslaught of these desperate fanatics; and Outram, with a party of foot, followed them to the heights where the cavalry had driven them, and captured their holy standard. Some fifty prisoners were taken. It is painful to relate what followed. Conducted into the presence of Shah Shuja, they gloried in their high calling, and openly reviled their King. One of them, more audacious than the rest, stabbed one of the royal attendants. Upon this, orders were issued for the massacre of the whole.

"The Shah ordered them to be beheaded, and they were hacked to death, with wanton barbarity, by the knives of his executioners. Coolly and deliberately the slaughter of these unhappy men proceeded, till the whole lay mangled and mutilated upon the blood-stained ground... It is enough simply to recite the circumstances of a deed so terrible as this. It was an unhappy and an ominous commencement. The Shah had marched all the way from Ludhiana without encountering an enemy. And now the first men taken in arms against him were cruelly butchered in cold blood by the 'humane' monarch. The act, impolitic as it was unrighteous, brought its own sure retribution. That 'martyrdom' was never forgotten. The day of reckoning came at last; and when our unholy policy sunk unburied in blood and ashes, the shrill cry of the Ghazi sounded in its funeral wail."

After, as Kaye puts it, the "day of reckoning", or the 1842 massacre of the 16,000 British troops and camp followers on the retreat from Kabul, a British army of retribution visited Ghazni in the same year. One of its orders, received directly from the new Governor-General of India, Lord Ellenborough, was to recover the "Gates of Somnath" from the Mausoleum of Mahmud. The gates were almost certainly not those taken from the Indian shrine over 800 years previously, but Ellenborough was insistent; he hoped to use it as a political gesture to win approval from the Hindus—an act which eventually backfired, being treated with derision by the Indians. The British officer charged with carrying out the order, Major Rawlinson, made a note of the incident in his journal:

"We moved our camp this morning [8 September] from the west to the east of Rozah, preparatory to fairly setting out on the march to Kabul; and during the day the measure was put into effect of removing the gates of Mahmud's tomb. The work was performed by Europeans, and all possible delicacy was observed in not desecrating the shrine further than was absolutely necessary. The guardians of the tomb, when they perceived our object, retired to one corner of the court and wept bitterly; and when the removal was effected, they again prostrated themselves before the shrine and uttered loud lamentations. Their only remark was: 'you are lords of the country, and you can of course work your will on us; but why this sacrilege? Of what value can these old timbers be to you; while to us they are as the breath of our nostrils?' The reply was: 'The gates are the property of India—taken from it by one conqueror, they are restored to it by another. We leave the shrine undesecrated, and merely take our own.'"

THE SANDAL WOOD GATES OF SOMNAUTH.

Translation of the Kufic Inscription.

"In the name of the merciful and compassionate God. there is mercy from the habitation of God for the most illustrious Ameer and Surdar, (whose Ancestors were Kings) The right hand of the State, the defender of the Faith and the father of Casim, Mahmood son of Subuktugeen. may the merciful God be with him. and if God have pardoned, There is mercy for him

GHAZNI: TRAVEL INFORMATION

This town (which at present is off-limits to travellers on account of security concerns) is one of the main historical sights of Afghanistan, especially famous for the Towers of Victory, or minarets, visited by Robert Byron in the 1930s. Its apogee was under the dynasty that took its name from the place, the Ghaznavids. Nancy Dupree writes: "The Ghaznavids took Islam to India and returned with fabulous riches taken from both prince and temple god. Contemporary visitors and residents alike write with wonder of the ornateness of its buildings, the great libraries, the sumptuousness of its court ceremonies and the wealth of precious objects owned by its citizens. This glorious city was also razed in 1151 by the Ghorid, Alauddin. Again it flourished, only to be permanently devastated, this time by Ghenghiz Khan in 1221."

There are two minarets, which are capped with corrugated iron. Originally they were very much taller and almost certainly served as the model for the Minaret of Jam in Bakakhshan. The more ornate one was built by Masud III (1099–1114), the other by Bahram Shah, whose reign (1118–1152) was terminated by Alauddin's victory. Just south of Masud's tower are the remains of his palace, excavated by the Italians. Masud's tomb, beautifully carved out of marble, survives and is to be found just outside the town, on the road to Kabul.

The other highlight of Ghazni is the Buddhist sanctuary at Tepe Sardar, excavated by the Italians in the 1970s. It is not known how much remains of this, and how much has been looted, as has happened at the other great Buddhist site in the south, Hadda.

Ghazni was famous for its poets, the most celebrated being Sana'i. He is buried near the river to the east of the city. As at Gazargah, the site has many other graves and the carving on their marble gives a good idea of the splendour of Ghaznavid art.

Islamic Architecture in Afghanistan

—Edgar Knobloch

General

*T*he origins of Islamic architecture in the Middle East have to be sought in the earlier periods, in Iran, in India as well as in Byzantium. The Buddhist stupa, the vihara (monastery), the Iranian fire-temple, the Byzantine basilica, all have left their marks. Thus, for example, the main features of Islamic architecture, the arch and the dome, originated in Sassanian Iran; the rectangular courtyard surrounded by cells, which is the main feature of the religious college, can be traced back to the vihara; the drum on which rests the dome of a mosque is a vestige of the stupa (domed structure to house relics) etc.

The only important contribution of Islam was the mosque, originally a simple courtyard with a qibla wall and the mihrab niche. It later became covered with a roof of reed matting resting on rows of wooden columns. Later still these rows, mainly under the influence of Iran, became arcades of solid brick arches supporting low cupolas; a domed prayer-hall was added, flanked by one or more minarets. The entrance became a monumental portal framed with a high portal-screen and everything was profusely decorated with monochrome and, later, polychrome ornament and calligraphy.

The urban design is closely connected with secular and military architecture. In the centre of a typical town was the citadel built on a strategically convenient place. Within its precinct were the palace, the prison and the garrison quarters. The main/Friday mosque was either within or nearby. Around the citadel were the merchants' and artisans' quarters with the bazaars, the workshops and the houses of the wealthier inhabitants. The shahristan, as this part of the town was called, was surrounded by walls equipped with bastions and towers; it was entered by several fortified gates. Outside, in the rabads (suburbs), were the houses of the poor, the open markets for cattle and horses, the gardens, the orchards and the cemeteries. The rabads were sometimes protected by a second line of walls.

The bazaar was sometimes situated in a large street covered with reed matting. In later periods arcaded brick buildings were constructed for it. A particular feature was the chahar-su ("four rivers"), a vaulted domed structure built over the crossroads of two streets. Another type of secular building was the caravanserai, built on a convenient spot on a caravan route, often like a fortress, with bastions, protective towers, etc. It had a large courtyard to accommodate animals with one or two-storey buildings around it, with lodgings, kitchens and a prayer-hall.

The bridge was another important type of building, a solid structure of stone or fired bricks. The best surviving example is the Pul-i-Malan Bridge in Herat.

The shrine, or mausoleum, was built in a place where a particular saint was venerated. It was, generally, a cube-shaped structure covered with a dome and entered through a monumental portal. Often it was surrounded by a courtyard entered by another portal. Other types of religious architecture, apart from the mosque already mentioned, were the stupa, the khaniga, and the minaret. The general layout consisted of a rectangular courtyard surrounded by one or two-storey buildings housing small living cells, lecture rooms, and kitchens. It had a large entrance portal on one side and often a domed prayer hall opposite. The khaniga was a kind of monastery for meditation. The minarets were towers of various shapes and heights, circular, conical or star-shaped. They were either free-standing or connected with a mosque. Their purpose was to make the site of the mosque visible from afar. Some of the towers in Afghanistan, however, seem to have no apparent connection with a mosque—Ghazni and Jam—and were probably intended as a kind of victory tower.

A word should be said about a particular feature of Iranian architecture, the iwan, which in Islamic times can be found in mosques, stupas, as well as mausolea and caravanserais. It first appeared in early Sassanian architecture in the form of an open audience-hall, which gradually evolved into a monumental entrance, a function similar to that of a portal of a cathedral. In a stupa it often served as an auditorium, while in caravanserai it was used as a kind of common room. A spectacular monumentality was achieved with the system of four iwans, one in the middle of each side of the rectangle, all facing inside, while the entrance iwan was backed by another facing outside. In the 14th–15th centuries it became a deep ornamental recess, the monumental effect of which was enhanced by a high portal screen / pishtaq, as well as by two flanking minarets. Some constructions were made even more impressive by their colossal dimensions.

The building material, from the earliest times, was mostly sun-baked bricks. On more important buildings and also where more solidity was required, such as on bridges, outer layers of ramparts, covered bazaars and, also in some areas, on underground water canals, baked bricks of fired clay were used. Stone was rare, although not unknown. Wood was a common material for the supporting columns in early mosques. In mountain areas small wooden mosques can still be found, with porches richly decorated with ornamental carving. In secular buildings wood was used much more frequently. The most famous wooden structure to survive until recently, was the bazaar in Tashkurgan.

The barrel vault, the earliest example of which, found in southern Iran, dates from the Elamite period—around 1500 BC—was still used in the iwan. The dome, an early Iranian element, posed certain problems when its circular form had to be positioned on the square base of a cube-shaped structure. The corners had to be somehow decoratively covered, and the solution was found in the squinch. The earliest squinches appeared in the Firuzabad palace in southern Iran in the third century AD. In principle, the squinch was an arch built across each corner of the square which provided a zone of transition by reducing the square to an octagon. Sometimes small arches were added further to bridge the corners, thus producing a 16-sided figure coming close to the circle of the dome. The squinches came in many shapes and forms, the most sophisticated of which was the mukarnas or stalactite vault. It consisted of clusters and tiers of cells arranged in "rows of super-imposed out-curving panels, generally miniature quarter-domes, the apexes apparently leaning on empty space". Its planning was a baffling task and although it might have had a structural function in the early stages, it became purely decorative later.

The dome or cupola was itself known in early Sassanian and Byzantine times. It was, originally, single; in the 12th century a double dome appeared, making the whole structure higher and more monumental. To enhance its effect still further, it was later raised on a drum. A triple dome appeared in the late 15th century but only one specimen is known: the Mausoleum of Gawhar Shad in Herat. Pyramid roofing, sometimes encountered in Iran, seems to have been unknown in Afghanistan.

A particular feature of Iranian and Afghan agriculture are underground water canals, called qanat or karez. They carry water for many miles from the mountains to the oases in the plains and are still indispensable for the economy of these countries.

The surfaces of Islamic buildings were profusely decorated, especially the entrance, the iwan and the portal screen. The purely architectural elements in this decoration were niches and recesses, lintels, colonettes with capitals and bases, etc. However, the most prominent elements, *typical for Islamic architecture, were the ornament and calligraphy. Whereas in its structural elements Islamic architecture was extremely conservative, in decoration it shows astonishing liveliness and inventiveness. The material was usually brick and stucco, which had already been used in pre-Islamic times. Small bricks were laid in various geometrical configurations, variations in brickwork could emphasise architectural lines, etc. Stucco was used to fill gaps between bricks and stucco panels complemented brick ornaments. Another material was terracotta, pieces of hard pottery laid in ornamental forms that later developed into mosaic faience. In the early period this decoration was strictly monochrome. The arrival of glaze, sometime in the 11th century, brought with it the use of colour. Glaze was made of cobalt, sulphur, arsenic and various metal oxides. At first, small glazed bricks were used for inscriptions and epigraphic friezes to decorate the mihrab niche and the entrance gate, but from the 14th century onwards the use of colour became virtually universal. The first colours were white, turquoise and blue. The 15th century buildings,*

Mosque of Khwaja Abu Parsa (The Green Mosque) Balkh [E. Knobloch]

such as the Green Mosque in Balkh, the shrine of Gazargah and the mausoleum of Gawhar Shad in Heart, mark the peak of this technique, after which a decadence set in. Technically, various methods were used: carved stucco, incised terracotta, flat panels composed of glazed, polychrome small bricks—the so-called banai technique to be found, for example, in the shrine of Gazargah—as well as some rare cases of wall painting, such as the frescoes found in the palace of Lashkar-i-Bazaar. Wall painting became more frequent only from the 17th century onwards—parts of Gazargah and Takht-i-Pul.

There was a wide range of ornamental motifs that basically fall into two categories, geometrical and floral / vegetal. Exceptionally, some Chinese motifs—clouds, dragons—could be found as well as landscapes in wall paintings. Geometrical ornament consisted at first of simple forms and patterns, combinations of squares, circles or triangles, while later more sophisticated forms appeared such as the knot/girikh, which sometimes reached an astonishing degree of complexity. Floral and vegetal motifs were at first used only as a background for inscriptions and only at a later stage did they form independent panels and patterns. Some abstract design may be found in the form of medallions, which often incorporated inscriptional elements.

In the absence of figural motifs, which were frowned upon in Islam, calligraphy became, next to the geometrical ornament, the most important element of decoration. Here again various techniques or styles were used. The angular, geometrical Kufic script (after Kufa in Iraq) was well suited for monumental patterns and large, long surfaces. The early, austere Kufic developed into more decorative floral, foliated and plaited varieties. An angular version developed in Herat became known as Herati Kufic. The cursive scripts first used in manuscripts made their appearance in architecture, too. Their main types were the naskhi and the thuluth.

SITES AND MONUMENTS

The oldest surviving example of monumental Islamic architecture in Afghanistan is the mosque Noh Gumbad (Nine Domes) near the town of Balkh, dating from the 9th or early 10th century. Its nine domes rest on massive columns joined by low, pointed arches and decorated with stylised floral motifs in incised stucco, which are divided into geometrical fields

(Top) *Tilework at Gazergah, Herat;* (left) *Detail of floral motifs, No-i-Gumbad, Balkh [E. Knobloch]*

separated by meanders or straight or circular bands, as well as with some geometrical ornaments of circles, octagons and four-leaf figures. The Noh Gumbad mosque belongs to the transitional period of medieval architecture when pre-Islamic traditions began to mix with emerging new features, foreshadowing a new architectural style that later dominated the country in the 10th–12th centuries.

Nearby, south of the town, the remnants of the late 14th century walls can be seen, but the circular site of the citadel and the rectangle of ancient ramparts belong to the early centuries of our era.

The Shrine of Khoja Abu Nasr, called the Green Mosque, also near Balkh, is a late 15th or possibly 16th century building with a large iwan flanked by two truncated minarets and, behind it, an octagonal building with a ribbed dome on a high drum. The portal screen (pishtaq) is flanked by two 'corkscrew' pillars with vase-shaped bottoms and, behind them, remains of truncated minarets. A band of mukarnas can be seen between the dome and the drum. Kufic inscriptions decorate the drum, the minarets and the pishtaq. Floral ornaments in mosaic faience adorn the pillars. All decoration is in glazed tiles, mostly black, blue and white. Inside, the dome is carried by a triple band of mukarnas and is painted with repetitive floral motifs.

In the south of the country, the ruins of the city of Bost (Lashkargah) and of the palaces of Lashkar-i-Bazaar date from the end of the 10th and the beginning of the 11th century. The group consists of three palaces with courtyards, gardens and auxiliary structures inside a walled enclosure. The main palace had a vast forecourt with a mosque, an entrance iwan, two lateral iwans and a main iwan with a throne room. There was also a small private courtyard with apartments. The decoration was of carved stucco and terracotta. Epigraphic bands and geometrical ornaments date probably from the 12th century. Wall paintings were also found with remnants of more than 40 figures out of perhaps 60, clad in ceremonial robes and carrying insignia of rank. They were moved to the Museum of Kabul; it is not known if they have survived. An elegant arch stands at the foot of the citadel of Bost, probably built in the 11th century with a somewhat later decoration. In 1978 it began to show some cracks and to secure it a supporting structure was built inside.

From the same period date the monuments in Ghazni, the tomb of Sultan Mahmud and two isolated towers. The tomb is a marble-faced sarcophagus decorated with superb calligraphy in

Kufic and naskhi. The ornamental decoration shows some Indian influence. The towers were originally much higher but the top circular parts no longer exist. The towers are star-shaped with intricate decoration in monochrome small bricks and carved terracotta. Panels of geometrical and floral motifs alternate with Kufic inscriptions and are arranged horizontally in eight ornamental zones. Each tower stands on a stone base and the decorative panels are laid out in stages narrowing to the top. The larger tower, of Masud III, is slightly older (between 1099 and 1114), the smaller one, of Bahramshah, can be dated to the middle of the 12th century. Nearby are the ruins of a palace, recently discovered, also attributed to Masud III (around 1111). The lay-out is

Detail, Ghazni Minaret [E. Knobloch]

similar to that of the Lashkar-i-Bazaar. The decoration consisted of ornamental panels in carved marble, stucco and terracotta. The inscriptions were in Kufic and naskhi, in gold and yellow on a blue and red background. The most spectacular items found were 510 epigraphic panels in Kufic script painted blue on a red background and forming a 250-m-long eulogy in Persian of the Ghaznavid dynasty.

The 16th century Mausoleum of Sultan Abdul Razzak is a plain brick structure with semi-circular corner towers and four iwans with high pishtaq walls. There is no decoration.

In the desolate mountainous region of Ghor in the centre of the country stands an isolated monument from the 12th century, the Minaret of Jam. With its 65-m height, it is the second tallest in the Islamic world. It consists of an octagonal base and three cylindrical stages decorated with geometrical patterns in fired bricks, glazed tiles and stucco, separated by bands of Kufic inscriptions.

In the valley of Bamiyan the fortress of Shahr-i-Zohak was originally a pre-Islamic castle built probably in the 6th or 7th century and rebuilt in the 11th or 12th. The old city of Bamiyan, the ruins of which are known as the Shahr-i-Gholghola (City of Murmurs), was built in the 11th century and destroyed, like Shahr-i-Zohak, by the Mongols of Genghis Khan. The patterns of the bazaars, the mosques, the palaces and the caravanserais are still discernible among the debris of clay walls.

In the west of the country and most exposed to Iranian influence is the city of Herat where some of the most outstanding monuments in Afghanistan can be found. The citadel (Arg, Bala Hissar) is an imposing building constructed in the 9th or 10th century on an artificial mound on the site of an earlier fortress. Its ramparts and round towers were rebuilt several times. A 15th century bastion linking the citadel to the city fortifications created a single defence complex. A decorative frieze of glazed bricks with a pseudo-Kufic inscription and some geometrical ornament can be seen at the bottom of one tower. Originally, an inscriptional frieze carrying a panegyric to Shah Rukh ran around the whole complex, but nothing remains of it.

The Friday Mosque now presents a picture of a 14th–15th century building, but it bears the marks of many reconstructions that point to earlier origins, some of them going back to the beginning of the Islamic era. It is, basically, a traditional Iranian four-iwan mosque. Each courtyard iwan has its counterpart on the outside. Inside the arcaded wings enclosing the courtyard are halls of columns concealed inside the façade niches. Each outer iwan is flanked by

two minarets. The oldest surviving part of the building is a 12th century portal incorporated in the eastern façade and decorated in monochrome geometrical and floral ornament in carved stucco and terracotta. The main parts of the building, heavily restored, are decorated in 15th–16th century tilework, mostly in black, dark blue and white, both ornamental and inscriptional.

North of the citadel, a vast site where a number of tall minarets still

Courtyard of Friday Mosque, Herat [E. Knobloch]

Restored tilework, Friday Mosque, Herat [E. Knobloch]

stand is the former Musalla, or what may be called a "university district". The main building, still standing in 1885, was blown up by the British when the city was preparing its defences against an expected Russian attack. Only six minarets and a mausoleum now remain from the whole complex. One of the minarets was decorated with panels of mosaic faience in deep blue, azure and purple with white moulding separating the panels and calligraphy. It was hit by a shell in 1984 or 1985 and only a stump of it now remains. Another minaret has galleries decorated with mukarnas and brick ornaments alternating with tilework on the tower itself. The four minarets of the original stupa have geometrical ornaments in mosaic faience, turquoise, blue and white. The white mosaic somehow survived while the turquoise fell off.

The mausoleum ascribed to Queen Gawhar Shad is a squat square structure with a ribbed dome on a high drum. Only remnants of the original decoration remain on the outside; on the drum a band of rectangular medallions can be seen with floral ornament and inscription in white and

Dome of the Mausoleum of Gawhar Shad, Herat [E. Knobloch]

blue. On the dome there are geometrical ornaments in turquoise, blue and white on the ribs; at the bottom is a band of rosettes and stylised lettering. The interior and the inside of the dome are among the most impressive achievements of Islamic architecture. Intersecting pointed arches divide the space into various polygons and mukarnas-decorated half- and quarter-domes with ornaments painted in blue, gold, ochre and white.

North of the city lies one of the most complex and interesting sites in the Islamic world, the Shrine of Khoja Abdullah Ansari, better known as the Gazargah (Bleaching Ground). Although its origins go back perhaps to the twelfth century, the present state is the result of two building periods in the fifteenth century. There is a vast open forecourt separated by a high iwan from the inner court, at the eastern end of which is the tomb of the saint. Above it is a monumental iwan with an enormous pishtaq. On both sides of the courtyard are arcaded wings, each with an iwan in the centre. The buildings are of bricks and the decoration is either in mosaic faience, in the banai technique (glazed bricks laid in decorative patterns) or in the inset technique (a series of plaques made up of mosaic faience or majolica tiles). In a room of the north wing is the famous cenotaph of black stone, called Haft qalam (seven pens), bearing "the most intricate and delicate carvings". The most imposing part of the shrine is the eastern iwan. Its pishtaq is completely covered with glazed tiles made into complex geometrical figures, a Kufic inscription (in fact a naskhi executed in banai technique), a thuluth inscription on the iwan and, on the arch, a kaleidoscopic design of small squares, rhomboids and triangles centred around a hexagon. A great variety of ornamental motifs and inscriptions can be found on the other buildings of the shrine as well. The tomb of the Khoja is hidden behind a latticework in front of the iwan. Six black cenotaphs are set on a platform in front of the southern iwan, decorated in white marble inlaid with black. The southern wing is on the whole in a poor state of preservation. Other buildings in the complex are a twelve-sided kiosk called Namakdan (Salt Cellar), an underground cistern and a domed pavilion, Zarnigar Khana, with a remarkable decoration of gold and blue paintings on its dome.

The Shrine of Hazrat Ali in the city of Mazar-i-Sharif in the north is the last monumental building of any significance, built in the late fifteenth century, just before decadence set in. It has been rebuilt and restored several times. An important place of pilgrimage, it shows strong Indian influence in its architecture. The tile decoration, mostly turquoise and blue, is of mediocre quality. The painted floral ornament in the inner chamber dates from the 19th century.

East of Balkh, the mosque Takh-i-Pul has three domed halls with well-preserved painted decoration on the inside, the style of which is a mixture of Indian and Islamic tradition.

The Shrine of Mazar-i-Sharif [E. Knobloch]

The town of in the northeast used to be famous for its wooden bazaar, but this was apparently destroyed in the recent war. The citadel, south of the town, stands on the site of the old city, the name of which was Khulm. It is in ruins, as is the citadel of Kunduz nearby.

Edgar Knobloch is the author of *Monuments of Central Asia: A Guide to the Archaeology, Art and Architecture of Turkestan*, available from I.B. Tauris, £15.99, and *The Archaeology and Architecture of Afghanistan*, available from Tempus Publishing, £17.99.

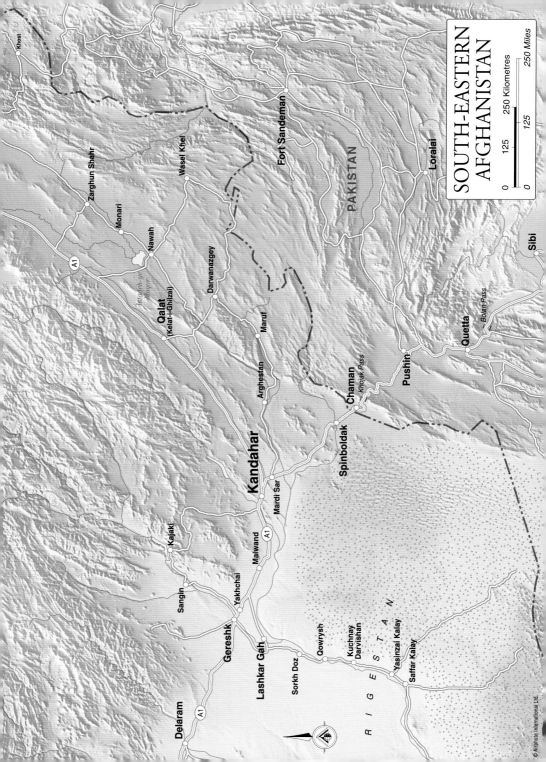

SOUTH-EASTERN
AFGHANISTAN

0   125   250 Kilometres
0   125   250 Miles

Khost

Zarghun Shahr

Monari

Nawah

Wasel Khel

Fort Sandeman

PAKISTAN

Loralai

Sibi

A1

Qalat
(Kelat-i-Ghilzai)

Istalif-ye
Rigor

Darwanazgey

Maruf

Arghestan

Quetta

Bolan Pass

Khojak Pass

Pushin

Chaman

Kandahar

Spinboldak

Mardi-Sar

Kajaki

Maiwand

A1

Sangin

Yakhchai

Gereshk

Lashkar Gâh

Sorkh Doz

Qowrysh

Kuchnay
Darvishan

Yasinzai Kalay

Saffar Kalay

R   I   G   E   S   T   A   N

Delaram

A1

© Arjhode International Ltd.

KANDAHAR AND THE PUSHTUNS

The city of Kandahar is thought to have come into existence by around 1000 BC. It stands at a confluence of routes from India, Seistan, Kapisa and Herat, and as a result is likely to have gained its early importance as a centre of international trade. It is first heard of as *Haraiwati* in inscriptions of Darius, who, in the early 5th century BC, consolidated Persian rule over the area and designated it as a satrapy of the Achaemenid Empire. By this time, Kandahar had become the pre-eminent settlement in the Southern Afghan territory, eclipsing its more ancient rivals such as Mundigak. The city next features in the campaigns of Alexander the Great, who captured it in 329 BC during his pursuit of the rebel Bessus, and refounded it as Alexandria Arachosia. Although many believe that the present name "Kandahar" is a variant of "Iskander"—the name by which Alexander is known in Central Asia— it is now rather thought to be a corruption of the Indian "Gandhara". Even though the name of the city may not bear witness to Alexander's conquest, he is still remembered there in folk myth. One of the popular tales relating to him was collected by Sirdar Ikbal Ali Shah in 1928:

> "They say that the Rigestan desert which lies to the South of Kandahar, was once a land where grew immense gardens of pomegranates and figs, and there were many prosperous towns. But during the time of Alexander the Great a beast was born in one of the cities of Rigestan, and whosoever caught his gaze was instantly killed. The beast roamed about devastating the towns and laying waste all that came in his way, till the whole part of that country became a desert.
>
> "Alexander was very anxious to have the beast killed, but none dared look at the animal, whose gaze was fatal. The king consulted his ministers, but no one could suggest a plan nor volunteered to go and face the beast of the desert. Aristotle at last stepped out and said he would undertake to combat the evil-eyed monster.
>
> "He caused a mirror of about six feet to be fastened to a carriage. Sitting in this carriage he propelled it himself and placed the big mirror in front. When

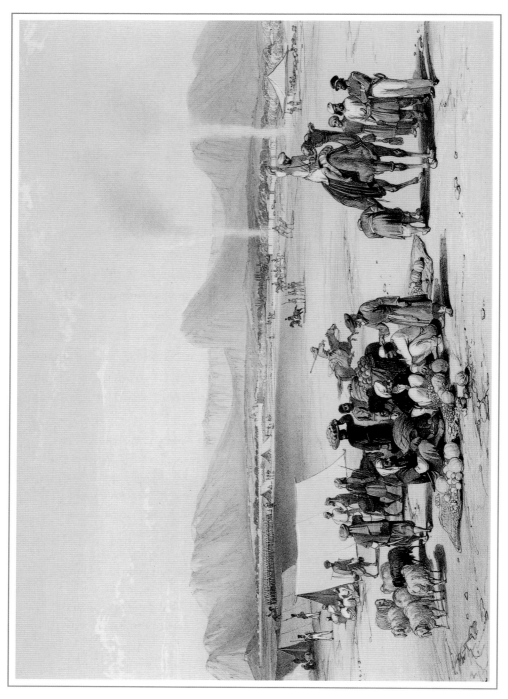

The City of Kandahar, 1841 [Bodleian]

the beast smelt the scent of a human being he advanced towards the carriage, but Aristotle placed the glass in front of the monster, and as soon as he saw his reflection in the mirror he gave a loud growl and was dead, having seen his evil eye in it. The King honoured the Minister and asked him how it was, and how did the monster actually come into being.

"'My master', he replied, 'the people of that region were very unclean, and this monster was born of filth and a product of uncleanliness, so he purged the earth of such people, and as his sight was death to man, I thought that if he could see himself in a mirror his end would also be complete.'"

After the death of Alexander, control over the eastern part of his empire eventually passed to one of his generals, Seleucus. In order to assert his authority throughout Asia, he spent several years on military campaigns between Babylon in the west, and Alexandria-Eschate on the Jaxartes River in the far northeast. In 303 BC, he passed through southern Afghanistan, crossed the Indus, and made to attack the Mauryan kingdom, at that time ruled by Chandragupta. However, on account of Chandragupta's overwhelming strength and potential threats to Seleucus' power in other areas of Asia, the two leaders decided to avoid a battle by means of a treaty: the Indian ruler gave 500 war-elephants and a large quantity of gold to Seleucus and accepted one of his daughters in marriage; in return, Seleucus ceded Arachosia to him, along with parts of the territory on the far side of the Hindu Kush. As a result, Kandahar now came under the control of the Mauryan Empire.

Chandragupta reigned until 298 BC. His throne passed to his son Bindusura, and then, in 273 BC, to his grandson Asoka. Asoka was reputed, at the beginning of his kingship, to have been a particularly brutal character. Various sources of uncertain reliability claim that on his accession he murdered several of his brothers to consolidate his hold on the monarchy; nevertheless, it is known that he operated an expansionist policy, spending much of his time fighting to extend the sphere of Mauryan rule. However, after a time, he underwent an extraordinary Damascene conversion. In 261 BC, having finished a campaign against Kalinga (roughly equivalent to modern-day Orissa), he became unsettled at the extreme suffering caused by his warlike behaviour, and as a result, under the influence of the sage Moggaliputta,

Buddhist statue, Gandhara, Afghanistan,
3rd century AD *[Musée Guimet]*

embraced the teachings of Buddhism. His change of heart was sudden and complete. Histories record that he worked to ensure free medical treatment for his population; that he built highways, placing trees, wells and inns at intervals along them; that he outlawed the slaughter of animals on certain holy days, and prohibited their consumption in the royal kitchen; and that he went on pilgrimages to places associated with the life of Buddha, building 84,000 stupas, or shrines, in the process. As a result of his actions, Buddhism was raised from its status as a local Indian creed to become a major world religion.

Kandahar bears witness to Asoka's conversion. Throughout the Mauryan Empire, stone inscriptions were erected—known as the "Rock Edicts" or "Pillars of Morality"—in order to proselytise and spread the new belief. In 1958 and 1964, two of these edicts were discovered in Old Kandahar, the former, a bilingual text in Greek and Aramaic, the latter solely in Greek. Although fragmentary, they stand not only as important documents in the history of Asoka himself and the spread of Buddhism; they also demonstrate a lingering Greek and Persian presence on the borders of India long after the passing of the Achaemenid and Macedonian empires.

The two texts refer to King Asoka under the title of Piodasses—"the one of amiable appearance". The latter inscription in Greek alone is the longer of the two,

and is distinct from all other Rock Edicts in that it was carved on a chiselled marble
block, ostensibly prepared for incorporation in a building:

> "...piety and self-mastery in all the schools of thought; and he who is master
> of his tongue is most master of himself. And let them neither praise themselves
> nor disparage their neighbours in any matter whatsoever, for that is vain. In
> acting in accordance with this principle they exalt themselves and win their
> neighbours; transgressing in these things they misdemean themselves and
> antagonise their neighbours. Those who praise themselves and denigrate their
> neighbours are self-seekers, wishing to shine in comparison with the others but
> in fact hurting themselves. It behoves to respect one another and to accept
> one another's lessons. In all actions it behoves to be understanding, sharing
> with one another all that one comprehends. And to those who strive thus let
> there be no hesitation to say these things in order that they may persist in piety
> in everything.

> "In the eighth year of the reign of Piodasses, he conquered Kalinga.
> A hundred and fifty thousand persons were captured and deported, and a
> hundred thousand others were killed, and almost as many died otherwise.
> Thereafter, pity and compassion seized him and he suffered grievously. In the
> same manner wherewith he ordered abstention from living things, he has
> displayed zeal and effort to promote piety. And at the same time the King has
> viewed this with displeasure: of the Brahmins and Sramins and others practising
> piety who live there—and these must be mindful of the interests of the king
> and must revere and respect their teacher, their father and their mother, and
> love and faithfully cherish their friends and companions, and must use their
> slaves and dependents as gently as possible—if, of those engaged there, and has
> died or been deported and the rest have regarded this lightly, the king has taken
> it with exceeding bad grace. And that amongst other people there are..."

The bilingual text, dated to 258 BC, is inscribed on a large boulder. Thirteen and
a half lines of Greek remain, along with eight lines of an incomplete Aramaic text.
A translation of the Greek reads:

> "Ten years having passed, King Piodasses revealed piety to men. Thenceforth
> he made men more pious and made all things prosper throughout the entire
> land. The king abstained from eating living creatures, and following his
> example other men did likewise, and all who were hunters or fishermen have

ceased their work. Those lacking self-control have, as far as possible, overcome their weakness and, unlike before, have become obedient to their father, mother, and elders. By doing these things, they will live more profitably in the future."

The south of Afghanistan and the North-West Frontier Province of Pakistan are the abode of the Pushtuns (or "Pathans" in the Anglicised form of the word). The origin of this generally nomadic people is uncertain. The ancient Indian Vedic texts speak of the "Paktua", who may have inhabited the northwestern areas of India, and Herodotus makes reference to an ethnic group of the same name, which he describes as the "most warlike of the Indian tribes". From this evidence, and that of their language, Pashto, a member of the Indo-Iranian language group, many conclude that they are indigenous inhabitants of the territory. Others believe that they descend from the Sakae, who were driven south ahead of the migration of the Yueh-chih from Central Asia around 130 BC, or else that they spring from an intermarriage of the Sakae and the original Paktua tribes.

The Pushtuns themselves, however, will tell a different story: that they look for their origins not to the north, but to the far west, as a lost tribe of the people of Israel. H. W. Bellew, who was attached to a British mission to Kandahar in 1857, prepared a condensed version of the legend from several manuscripts dating back to the 16th century which he found in the city:

"All Afghan histories first refer to Saul (Sarul), of the tribe of Benjamin (Ibnyamin), as the great ancestor of their people. Saul, on becoming king, was entitled 'Malik Twalut' (which is said to denote 'Prince of Stature'—a signification borne out by the literal meaning of the words). His history, as recorded in the books of the Afghans, is in the main much the same as that brought down to us in the Bible. They have accounts of his going in search of his father's missing asses, his enmity to David, his dealings with the witch 'Salih' at 'Andor' and so on. Saul is said to have had two sons, named 'Barakiah,' or Barachiah, and 'Iramia,' or Jeremiah. They were both born in the same hour, of different mothers, who were, however, both of the tribe of 'Lawi,' or Levi. These sons were born after the death of their father, who, together with ten other sons, was killed fighting against the Philistines. During their infancy, these sons lived under the protection of David, who succeeded Saul on the throne. Subsequently, each of them rose to exalted positions under the government of David. Barakiah officiated as prime minister, and Iramia as commander-in-chief of the army. The former had a son named Assaf, and the latter one named Afghana. These, after the deaths of their respective fathers, filled the same important positions under the government of 'Sulaiman,' or Solomon, David's successor, that their fathers did during the reign of David. Assaf is said to have had 18 sons, and Afghana, 40. Afghana, under Sulaiman, superintended the building of 'Bait-ul-mukadas', or Temple of Jerusalem, which David had commenced. At the time of the death of Sulaiman, the families of Assaf and Afghana were amongst the chiefest of the Israelitish families, and multiplied exceedingly after the death of Assaf and Afghana. At the time that Bait-ul-mukadas was captured by 'Bukhtu-n-nasr,' or Nebuchadnezzar, the tribe of Afghana adhered to the religion of their forefathers, and on account of the obstinacy with which they resisted the idolatrous faith of their conquerors, were, after the slaughter and persecution to death of many thousands of the Bani Israil (Children of Israel), banished from 'Sham' or Palestine, by order of Bukhtu-n-nasr.

"After this they took refuge in the Kohistan-i-Ghor and the Koh-i-Faroza. In these localities they were called by their neighbours 'Afghan, or 'Aoghan,' and Bani Israil. In the mountains of Ghor and Faroza the Bani Israil increased very greatly; and after a protracted period of warfare with the original heathen inhabitants of the hills in which they had taken refuge, they at length succeeded in subduing them and becoming masters of the country, and establishing themselves in the mountain fastnesses. Some centuries later, their numbers having greatly increased, and the country becoming too small for them, this colony of Afghans extended their borders by force of arms to the Kohistan-i-Kabul, Kandahar, and Ghazni.

"During all this time, and, indeed, until the appearance of Mohammed as the Prophet of God, this people were, according to all accounts, readers of the Pentateuch, or 'Tauret Khwan,' and in all their actions were guided by the ordinances of the Mosaic law. But in the ninth year after the announcement by Mohammed of his mission as the Prophet of God, and more than 1,500 years after the time of Sulaiman, the Afghans for the first time heard of the advent of the new Prophet through a fellow Israelite (one named Khalid bin Walid);

Cap.ⁿ P.S. Lumsden, del.^t

A F R Ī D Ī S

M & N. Hanhart, lith.

Published by Smith, Elder & C.º 65, Cornhill, London 1862.

Afridi Tribesmen, 1857 [RSAA]

and, in a very few years, being convinced of the truth of his new doctrines, adopted his religion, as will be mentioned presently.

"This Khalid bin Walid was an Israelite who had settled in Arabia after the dismemberment of the Jewish nation. He was one of the earliest of Mohammed's disciples, and, on his own conversion, sent word to the Afghans of the advent of the 'last Prophet of the times,' and exhorted them to accept his doctrine.

"On the receipt of Khalid bin Walid's message by the Afghans, they deputed to him, then at Medina, one Kais—a man who was remarkable among them for his piety and learning, and belonged to one of the best Afghan families. He was accompanied on this mission by some six or eight of the chief men and elders of the Afghan people. All of these, soon after their arrival at Medina, embraced the new faith on Khalid's exposition of its doctrines, and subsequently, under his guidance, vigorously aided the Prophet in diffusing his doctrine by slaying all who rejected or opposed its progress. It is reported of Kais and his companions that, in the height of their religious zeal, they slew upwards of 70 unbelieving Koreshites in one day. As a reward for this meritorious service they were presented before the Prophet, who treated them with kindness and distinction, and inquired their respective names. But on finding that they were all of Hebrew origin, the Prophet, as a mark of his favour, changed them for Arabic names, and promised them that the title of 'Malik,' or king, which had been bestowed by God on their great ancestor 'Sarul,' should never depart from them, but that they should be called 'Malik' till the last day. (At the present day, it may here be mentioned, the head of every Afghan house, or tribal subdivision, is styled 'Malik.') And for the name 'Kais,' the Prophet substituted 'Abdur Rashid' or Servant of the Wise; and afterwards, when Kais was about to depart for his own country, the Prophet conferred on him the title of 'Pihtan' or 'Pahtan'—a term which in the Syrian language signifies a 'rudder'; and at the same time, with much kindness, and smiling, the Prophet drew a simile between his now altered position as the pilot of his countrymen in the new faith, and that part of the ship which steers it in the way it should go."

The two major tribal divisions of the Pushtuns are the Durranis (formerly called the Abdalis), who live primarily in the south of the country between Herat and Kandahar, and the Ghilzai, who live between Kandahar and Ghazni. Other smaller tribes that inhabit the mountainous areas in the southeast of Afghanistan and the

North-West Frontier Province of Pakistan include the Mohmands, the Khattaks, the Wazirs and the Afridis.

Many of the Pushtuns still live a nomadic existence. Mountstuart Elphinstone wrote a description of the Durranis' pastoral life, which had continued unchanged for many generations:

> "In spring, when grass is plenty in all places, and the season for lambing renders it inconvenient to drive the flocks far from home, the shepherds break up their camps and disperse over the country, pitching by twos and threes, wherever they meet with an agreeable spot. Many such spots are found in the beginning of spring, even in the worst parts of the Durrani country, and the neighbourhood of the high hills especially affords many delightful retreats in sequestered valleys, or in green meadows on the borders of running streams.

Portrait of a Pushtun boy [R. & S. Michaud]

> "The delight with which the Durranis dwell on the description of the happy days spent in these situations, and the regrets which are excited by the remembrance of them, when in distant countries, can only be believed by those who have seen them; while the enthusiasm with which they speak of the varieties of scenery trough which they pass, and of the beauties and pleasures of spring, is such as one can scarce hear from so unpolished a people without surprise.

> "Though these camps are so small, and situated in such retired situations, we must not suppose that their inhabitants live in solitude. Many other camps are within reach, and the people belonging to the often meet to hunt, by chance or by appointment. Sheep-shearing feasts and ordinary entertainments also bring men of different camps together; and they are besides often amused by the arrival of an itinerant tradesman, a wandering ballad-singer, or a traveller who avails himself of their known hospitality.

Veil of a Pushtun nomad, c. 1960 [Pavia]

"This sort of life is perhaps seen in most perfection in the summer of Toba, which belongs to the Achakzais [a Durrani sub-tribe]. The extensive district is diversified and well wooded. The grass is excellent and abundant, and is mixed with a profusion of flowers; and the climate is so mild as scarcely to render shelter necessary either by night or day. This agreeable country is covered in summer with camps of Durranis and Tarins, who all live on the most friendly terms, visiting at each others camps, and making frequent hunting parties together. They often invite each other to dinner at their camps, where the strangers repair in their best clothes, and are received with more ceremony and attention than is usual in the more familiar intercourse of immediate neighbours. On these occasions, companies of twelve or 15 assemble to dine in the open air, pass the evening with part of the night in games, dancing, and songs, and separate without any of the debauchery and consequent brawls which so often disturb the merriment of common people in other countries. Their fare at that period is luxurious to their taste: lamb is in season, and koroot, maust (a soft sort of curd, which is slightly acid), curds, cream, cheese, butter, and everything that is produced from milk, are in abundance. Thus they pass the summer; at last, winter approaches, snow begins to fall on the tops of the hills, and the shepherds disperse to their distant countries, to Urghessaun, to Pisheen, to Rabaut, and to the borders of the desert."

A Pushtun wedding, c. 1920 [Holmes]

Other Pushtuns live in more settled communities, making a living by means of agriculture and farming. Elphinstone also spoke of the Durrani villages found in the vicinity of Kandahar:

"It is a common form of the Durrani villages, to have four streets leading into a square in the centre. There is sometimes a pond, and always some trees in this space, and it is here that the young men assemble in the evenings to pursue their sports, while the old men look on, and talk over the exploits of their youth, or their present cares and occupations.

"The houses are constructed of brick, burnt or unburnt, and cemented with mud, mixed with chopped straw. The roofs are sometimes terraces laid on beams, but far more frequently are composed of three of four low domes of brick joining to one another. An opening is left in the centre of one of the domes, and over it is a chimney made of tiles, to keep out the rain. This sort of roof is recommended by its requiring no wood for rafters, a great consideration in a country where timber is so scarce. Most dwelling houses have but one room, about 20 feet long and twelve broad.

Portrait of a Pushtun man [R. & S. Michaud]

"There are two or three outhouses adjoining to the dwelling house, built exactly in the same manner, and designed for the sheep and cattle; for the hay, straw, grain, firewood, and implements of husbandry. Most houses have a little courtyard in front of the door, where the family often sit when the weather is hot. The room is spread with Gulleems (a kind of red carpet) over which are some felts for sitting on. The villages are generally surrounded with orchards, containing all the fruit trees of Europe, and round them are scattered a few mulberry trees, poplars, planes, or other trees, of which the commonest are one called marandye, and another tree, with broad leaves, called purra."

The Pushtuns, and particularly those who live in the mountainous areas towards the east, place a premium on their personal liberty and independence, and as a point of honour are ready to fight fiercely to protect them. This point is strikingly illustrated by the following description of the Jaji tribe. As the British mission to Kandahar proceeded through the Paktia province in 1857, the tribe, fearing an attack from the military detachment accompanying the mission, occupied a nearby hilltop and performed a war dance in order to intimidate them. Bellew made a record of the incident:

"Their war dance was a most exciting performance, and, as far as I could make out from watching the proceedings of a crowd occupying an eminence some 300 yards off, was conducted somewhat in this fashion. Some dozen or 15 men of their number, after divesting themselves of their rifles, shields, etc, uncovered their heads, and tied the 'paggri,' or turban, round the waist. Each man then unsheathed his 'charah' and took his place with his fellows, the whole together forming a circle. They then commenced chanting a song, flourishing their knives overhead, and stamping on the ground to its notes, and then each gradually revolving, the whole body moving round together and maintaining the circle in which they first stood up. Whilst this was going on, two of the party stepped into the centre of the ring and went through a mimic fight, or a series of jumps, pirouettes, and other movements of a like nature, which appeared to be regulated in their rapidity by the measure of the music, for towards the close of the performance the singing ceased, and the whole party appeared twirling and twisting about in a confused mass, amidst the flashing of their drawn knives, their movements being timed to the rapid roll of their drums. It was wonderful that they did not wound each other in these intricate and rapid evolutions with unsheathed knives. On the conclusion of the dance, the whole party set up a shrill and prolonged yell, that reverberated over the hills, and was caught up by those on the neighbouring heights, and thus prolonged for some minutes.

"Whilst all this was going on upon the heights around our camp, several parties of armed Jajis ranged in columns, three or four abreast and eight or nine deep, followed each other in succession round and round the skirts of our camp, all the time chanting an impressive and passionate war-song in a very

A Pushtun tribesman, R.M Grindlay, 1809 [RSAA]

An Eusofzye.

peculiar sonorous tone that seemed to be affected by the acoustic influences of the locality, which, as already mentioned, was a deep basin enclosed for the most part by bare and rocky eminences and hills. This effect was most marked in the chorus 'Woh-ho, Ah-hah,' the slowly-repeated syllables of which were echoed back in a continuous and confused reverberation of rumbling noise. At the conclusion of the war-song, they all leapt simultaneously into the air, and, on again alighting on terra firma, the whole party together took a leap or skip forwards, at the same time yelling and screaming like fiends. The excited appearance of these men, and the wild antics they performed, are hardly credible. They were mostly dressed in loose shirts and trousers of cotton, dyed blue; over one shoulder was supported a 'jezail' (rifle), with its long forked rest; whilst from the other depended, against the back, a large circular shield of camel's or buffalo's hide: around the waist were suspended by leather straps three or four powder flasks of uncured sheep-skin, together with a host of other paraphernalia belonging to the jezail, such as tinder-box, flint and steel, hammer, pick, etc. Those not armed with the rifle carried a 'charah', the sheath of which was stuck in the folds of the waistband, whilst the blade itself was flourished about in the air overhead with grotesque antics and grimaces. Added to these, the tangled meshes of their long loose hair were jerked about in a wild manner by their movements, and contributed greatly to the fierceness of their features and actions."

The Pushtuns have throughout their history been governed by an unwritten honour code, known as the "Pushtunwali". Elphinstone described its principle tenets:

"The general law of the kingdom is that of Mahomet, which is adopted in civil actions in the ooloses (courts) also; but their particular code, and the only one applied to their internal administration of criminal justice, is the Pushtunwali, or usage of the Afghans; a system of customary law founded on principles such as one would suppose to have prevailed before the institution of civil government.

"The opinion that it is every man's right and duty to do himself justice, and to revenge his own injuries, is by no means eradicated from among the Afghans; and the right of the society even to restrain the reasonable passions of individuals, and to take the redress of wrongs, and the punishment of crimes, into its own hands, is still very imperfectly understood; or if it is understood, is seldom present to the thoughts of the people. This practice must have had its origin at a time when the government afforded no protection to individuals, and in such circumstances, it must be allowed to be beneficial, and even necessary; but it has taken root in the habits of the Afghan nations, and although in most parts of their country, justice might now be obtained by other means; and though private revenge is everywhere preached against by the mullahs, and forbidden by the government, yet it is still lawful, and even honourable, in the eyes of the people to seek that mode of redress. The injured party is considered to be entitled to strict retaliation on the aggressor: an eye for an eye, a tooth for a tooth, and so on. If the offender be out of his power, he may wreak his vengeance on a relation, and in some cases, on any man of the tribe. If no opportunity of exercising this right occurs, he may defer his revenge for years; but it is disgraceful to neglect or abandon it entirely, and it is incumbent on his relations, and sometimes on his tribe, to assist him in retaliation.

"Retaliation thus exercised, of course leads to new disputes; the quarrel becomes inveterate, and in serious cases, it is often transmitted from father to son for several generations."

Nevertheless, the necessity of protecting one's *ghayrat*, or personal honour, by means of revenge is not the only element of Pushtunwali. Equally prominent in the code is the obligation on all tribesmen to provide hospitality—*milmastia*. It is the custom of the Pushtuns to receive guests, even if they happen to be enemies against whom a vendetta is being waged, and to do everything possible to protect them whilst under the power of the host.

It seems that Kandahar maintained its prosperity under the Kushan Empire in the first few centuries AD, with archaeological finds indicating that it continued both to benefit from its position on the trade route and also to adhere to the Buddhist religion. However, at the end of the Sassanian period, around 700 AD, it appears to have gone into a sharp decline, standing virtually abandoned until the rise of the Ghaznavids. The city was taken under their control, and began to recover its former importance. The 12th century Arab scholar al-Idrisi bears witness to this with a somewhat enigmatic entry in one of his geographical works:

"The town of Kandahar is of a large size and has a big population. They are a people distinguished from others by their beards. They let their beards grow until the major portion of it reaches down to their knees and even beyond. It is wide and very hairy. They have round faces. It is proverbial to talk of their huge and long beards. They dress in the Turkish fashion. They have in their country wheat, rice, grains, goats and cows. They eat dead goats, and certainly do not eat cows, as we have mentioned before."

Following this spell of prosperity, Kandahar was not to know any prolonged period of stable government for many centuries. Genghis Khan sacked the city in his sweep across the south of Afghanistan, after which it came under the power of the Kurt Maliks, a local dynasty that also held Herat. In 1383, it was captured by Timur, and eventually passed to the Arghuns, a family descended from the Mongol Il-Khanids of Persia. Although still being nominally under the control of the Timurid princes then ruling in Herat, the Arghuns were constantly in rebellion against them. However, this state of affairs came to an end in 1507; Herat fell to Uzbek invaders from the north, and Babur, founder of the Moghul Empire, seized Kandahar briefly for the first time. After Babur's failed attempts to recapture possessions north of the Oxus, he turned his attention towards India, and having made several putative expeditions there he retook Kandahar to protect his southern flank in 1522.

With the establishment of the Moghul Empire, Babur (Baber) ordered a monument to be erected in Kandahar to commemorate his second conquest of the city. An early site—probably dedicated to the Kushan royal house—was chosen in the hills to the city's western side, and converted to commemorate the Moghul victory. Named the *Chihlzina*, or Forty Steps, Bellew explored it whilst with the British Mission:

"Half way up the north-east face of the hill… and situated between two guard

Chihlzina, from the base of the hill, J.C. French, 1932 [RSAA]

*Chihlzina; the headless stone lion and the Moghul inscription
of the 16th century can clearly be seen. J.C. French, 1932. [RSAA]*

towers on adjacent portions of the rock, is a flight of forty steps, that leads to a recess in the rock. At the top of the steps, and on each side of the entrance to the recess, is the figure of a crouched leopard, nearly life-size. The whole, viz. steps, recess, and leopards, is carved out of the solid limestone, and is said to have occupied 70 men for nine years before the work was completed. The chamber in the rock is bow-shaped and dome-roofed. The height is about 12 feet in the centre, the width from side to side is about eight feet, whilst the depth from the entrance inwards equals the height. The sides of the interior are covered with Persian inscriptions, carved in relief out of the rock; the work is beautifully executed, and is said to have kept the artist hard at work for four years. The writing is to the effect that on the 13th of the month Shawal, AH 928 Baber Badshah conquered Kandahar, and appointed his sons Akbar and

> Humayun successively as its rulers. A long list of the virtues and noble qualities of these princes then follows, together with an enumeration of the principal cities of Baber's Empire, extending from Kabul to the sea-coast of Bengal, and including the names of many of the chief cities now existing between these limits."

Despite the sentiments of this monument, Kandahar was still not to experience any long-lasting settled rule. The newly resurgent Persian Empire began to show interest in possessing Kandahar, and when Babur's eldest son and heir Humayun was driven into exile at the court of the Persian Shah Tahmasp, the opportunity afforded by his presence was not missed. Tahmasp promised Humayun help to recover the Moghul throne from his scheming younger brothers, on condition that he surrendered Kandahar to him after his victory. Accordingly, Humayun set out with a large Persian army and took the city in 1545. However, he failed to honour the agreement with Tahmasp, and eventually the Persians snatched the city on Humayun's death in 1556. After this, control over the city oscillated frequently between the Moghuls and Persians, falling more permanently into the hands of the latter in 1649, where it was to remain until the Pushtun uprisings of the 18th century and the foundation of the kingdom of Afghanistan.

The situation of Kandahar was not the only long-term problem facing the rulers of the Moghul Empire. In order to ensure the security and economic prosperity of the empire, it was necessary to keep open the road link between Peshawar and Kabul, so as to maintain trade and communication links with further parts of Central Asia. These mountainous areas around the present-day North West Frontier Province were in the possession of the Pushtun hill-tribes, none of which were at all amenable to foreign domination, and which generally posed a threat to any traffic making its way through the passes. Nevertheless, emperors such as Akbar, Jahangir and Shahjahan managed to pacify the Pushtuns with bribes, titles, occasional official employment, or else the occasional punitive raid. However, when Aurangzeb claimed the Moghul throne in 1657, he reversed the conciliatory policy of his predecessors and decided to launch a campaign to bring the Pushtuns fully under his power. In 1667 there was a rising of the Yusufzai tribe in response to the new stance of the empire, but this was put down with overwhelming force. Five years later, the Afridi tribe proclaimed a jihad against the Moghuls, which led to the destruction of a 20,000-strong Moghul army near the Khyber Pass and the capture of a huge amount of treasure. Fortunes continued to be mixed for Aurangzeb until 1675, when he decided to revert to the earlier position, a move that carried with it far greater success. A new governor, Amir Khan, was put in charge of Kabul, and managed to ensure quiet amongst the Pushtuns by the payment of subsidies and the encouragement of inter-tribal feuding to prevent them from turning their energy against the Moghuls in organised revolts.

Pushtun Merchant, Tashkurgan
[R. & S. Michaud]

An outstanding figure from this time is the Pushtun warrior-poet Khushal Khan Khattak, chief of the Khattaks, a tribe of the Khyber Pass area. Born in the reign of Jahangir, he came of age in the reign of Shahjahan, who recognised his abilities and entrusted him with various diplomatic and imperial duties. However, Aurangzeb decided to imprison him as part of his fight against the Pushtuns, a move that backfired when he escaped, and, fired with hatred against Aurangzeb, assumed leadership of the rebellion against the Moghuls. After Aurangzeb's abandonment of his belligerent policy against the Pushtuns, Khushal railed against his own people for their acquiescence to foreign influences and bribery, and spoke as contemptuously of them in his verse as he did of Aurangzeb himself. Nonetheless, his poetry is not solely concerned with the situation of the Pushtuns, but ranges widely over all areas of human experience, from war to philosophy, religion, love and the beauties of nature. A small selection of his poems, translated by C. Biddulph, is given here:

Infatuated have the Pushtuns become for ranks and titles,
May God preserve me ever from such desires!
Whose is knowledge and counsel, if not the warriors?
Plain is all to them as the Koran read in the schools.
There is none of them who knows aught of plans or schemes,
Well am I informed of the tempers of them all.
Great is the weakness of the Pushtuns, as thou seest;
By the titles of the Moghuls they are led away.
No thought is theirs of honour, fame or pride;
All their talk is of either rank or gold.
Far preferable to me is the Khattak buckler over my loins,
Than the golden badge of service hanging round my neck.
The nights in the Emperor's prison are ever in my mind,
When all night long I called to God in vain.
When the Pushtuns drew their swords on the Moghuls,
Every Pushtun led a Moghul bound beside his horse.
No thought have they for honour now, Khushal;
Of what stock can these Pushtuns then have been sprung?

If but once her face shows from forth her veil,
Lost will be forever all claim of radiance to the Sun.
The tulips will borrow colours from her face,
Shamed will be the Hyacinth at the sight of her tresses.
Why do people lay charges against fortune?
It is she that with her eyes the world hath desolated,
Is it with the effects of wine her eyes are thus flushed,
Or has someone out of sleep awoke her too early?
The blood of hearts she quaffs in place of wine,
Again for relish with it she takes broken hearts.
The special fate of those slaughtered by my fair one
Is that without question straight to paradise they go.
My heart is as a compass, fixed its bearing,
It points ever to the altar of thy eyebrows.
Be not gladdened with her promises, Khushal:
From the bubble what constancy does one expect?

Jesus never in his life made a fool a wise man,
Though by miracles he made many blind ones seeing.
He whom God at his birth has not with wisdom gifted,
Who can have the power to make such foolish wise?
What though the fool learns lessons, what will be his state?
As though the dye upon his hair restored to age his youth!

No great deed will ever be wrought by the Pushtuns;
Heaven has ordered that petty should be their undertakings.
However much I try to straighten them, they straighten not;
Crooked is the vision of the evil-natured.
No regard have the Yusufzaies for Pushtun honour;
Get you gone from amongst these disgraced Pushtuns, Khushal.
Go to Bunnoo, and there collect your followers,
And spread fire and clouds of smoke right up to Khushab;
Or in retirement in your house give yourself up to devotion;
Or go to Mecca—these three things I can advise you.
In war and violence there is no profit, Khushal;
The fire burns up alike the grain and chaff.

After the end of the 16th century, on account of increasing feuds between the Abdali (later Durrani) and Ghilzai Pushtuns, the former were forcibly relocated to the southern and western parts of Afghanistan by the Persian overlords in order to preserve the peace. Kandahar, therefore, was left to the Ghilzais under Persian government. Safavid rule over the city was not oppressive early on, but became more so with the progress of time. In 1704, an increasingly weak Persian court, fearing that the Ghilzais were conspiring against them with the Moghuls, sent a ruthless Georgian prince named Gurgin Khan to act as governor of Kandahar. His depredations eventually lead to his murder and an uprising headed by the Ghilzai leader, Mir Wais. Mir Wais died in 1715; his second son, Husayn Sultan, assumed control of the city, whilst his elder brother Mahmud raised an army and marched on Persia, taking for himself the Safavid throne in 1722. However, a Turkish adventurer, Nadir Kuli Beg, managed to rally the Persians, drive back the Ghilzais and claim for himself the Persian crown, being acclaimed as Nadir Shah in 1736.

City of Kandahar, 1857 [RSAA]

Having fought groups of Abdali tribesmen around Herat, he realised their effectiveness as soldiers and decided to employ a number of them as a mercenary army. With this force, he marched on Kandahar in 1737, destroyed the old city and built a new settlement to the southeast named Nadirabad. Lands taken from the Abdalis in the 1600s were restored to them, and they replaced the Ghilzais as the leading power in the area. However, on Nadir Shah's assassination in 1747, the Abdali army contingent broke away from the Persians, captured a treasure convoy that included the Koh-i-Noor diamond, and returned to Nadirabad. Here, in a tribal council, they resolved to declare independence, and chose the leader of the Abdali mercenary contingent, Ahmad Shah, as their first king. The Abdalis were renamed the "Durranis" in recognition of one of the king's new titles—"Dur-i-Durran", or "Pearl of Pearls'—and the king himself ordered Nadirabad to be abandoned, and Kandahar to be refounded as the capital of the Empire.

Charles Masson visited the new city about 50 years after the death of Ahmad Shah:

> "The city of Kandahar is surrounded by mud walls, which have a circumference of three miles. There are, I believe, seventeen towers on each face, besides the angular ones; and a trench was carried round, under the direction of the late Sirdar (governor) Shir Dil Khan. Its situation is convenient, as it is on no side commanded; and it has five gates, one of which opening upon the id-gah [mosque], and leading onto the citadel, is generally closed up. The citadel occupies the north-west quarter of the city, and is said to have been built by Shahzada Kamran [an earlier crown prince], who formerly held the government of the city and country. The present city was projected by Ahmed Shah, the founder of the Durrani monarchy, and on that account in all public documents is styled Ahmed Shahi [of Ahmad Shah]. It superseded another city, designed by Nadir Shah, whose ruins are to be seen a little to the South-east, as that replaced the more ancient city, taken by the conqueror from the Ghilzais, and then dismantled by him. Its ruins are about two miles distant from the present city, seated at the foot, and on the acclivity of a hill, and are still considerable.

> "At the point where the roads from the principal gates intersect each other is a covered building, called the Chahar Su, whose lower apartments are

occupied by traders, and the upper ones called the Naubat Khana, from the Naubat [ceremonial drum-beating] being daily performed there. The principal bazaars are wide and spacious, and had originally avenues of trees, and canals, leading along either side of them, but they are not now well preserved. No city can be better supplied with water, which is brought by large canals from the Arghassan river, and then distributed by so many minor ones, that there is perhaps no house which has not one of them passing through its yard. There are also many wells, and the water is considered preferable to that of the canals as a beverage.

"Of the area included within the city walls so much is spread over with ruinous and deserted houses, extensive courts, gardens, and ranges of stabling, that it is probable that there are not above 5,000 inhabited houses, by which estimate the population would be from twenty-five to thirty-thousand souls. Notwithstanding the city is acknowledged to be the takht, or metropolis of the Durranis, the public mosques, and other buildings, are by no means handsome, arising principally, perhaps, from a deficiency of materials; and this evil has been detrimental to the substantial erection of the city generally, the houses being almost universally built of unburnt bricks, and covered with domes, there being no fuel to burn bricks, and no timber to make flat roofs.

"Ahmed Shah was consistently interred in the city of his creation, and his tomb is one of its most interesting objects. It stands in an enclosure surrounded with apartments, and lines of mulberry trees. Of octagonal form, it is surmounted with a cupola, and is farther embellished with minarets. In the central chamber of the interior is the king's tomb, of white marble, covered with rich carpets. The ceiling is gorgeously gilded, and painted with lapis lazuli, and at the top is suspended a brazen or gilded globe, supposed by popular belief to have been closed by the sovereign before his death, and to contain his soul.

"The residences of the sirdars, while large and sufficiently commodious, display no architectural taste or beauty; the balconies of their balla khanas, or upper rooms, are, indeed, curiously carved in wood, and constitute their chief ornamental appendages. The arg, or citadel, being constructed of kiln-burnt bricks, appears to advantage from the exterior, and the entrance is somewhat imposing. Within, the palaces of the former kings, with their painted chambers, are desolate, or occupied by the menials of the present rulers, who seem studiously to avoid residing in them.

"The bazaars are well supplied with good and cheap provisions, and with a great abundance of excellent fruits. Kabul is famed for the quantity, Kandahar for the quality of its fruits; yet I found them so reasonable that a maund, or several English pounds of grapes, was purchased for a pais; and figs, plums, apricots, peaches, pears, melons, and almonds, were nearly as cheap. The pomegranates of Kandahar are, perhaps, unsurpassed, and justly enjoy a great repute in these countries. Meat, while very good, is not perhaps so cheap as at Kabul, but roghan, so generally used, and bread, are cheaper, as are curds and eggs; of the latter ten or twelve being sold for one pais. It is a great blessing to these countries that subsistence is so cheap, and that the poorer classes are, consequently, little affected by the struggles for political ascendancy amongst the chiefs."

Fruit merchant, Kandahar [R. & S. Michaud]

Ahmad Shah Durrani not only re-founded the city of Kandahar and established the Afghan empire, but also won renown as a poet. According to Major H.G. Raverty, who translated a number of his poems in 1860, the majority of his work was produced during a period of relative peace between 1752 and 1756, after the Afghan conquest of Kashmir. Throughout this period, Ahmad Shah would preside at regular Majlis-i-ulema, or Assemblies of the Learned, in which he himself, as a *molawi* or Doctor of Divinty, would participate fully. Discussion would begin with matters of theology and law, and then conclude with questions of science and poetry. His poetry, written in Pashto, is tinged with Sufi mysticism, particularly placing an emphasis on seeking the eternity of God behind the transitory world, and repeatedly using the imagery of intense human love to depict one's love for God:

Alas, Alas, for sweet life, that passeth away!
  That, like unto a stream, floweth past and is gone.
Wherefore, then, is the heart not aware of its departure,
  When life, alas, passeth so swiftly away?
Why, O my heart, hast thou become thus from grief,
  When existence, like the breeze, bloweth for ever away?
Though thou may'st erect mansions, in all symmetry and grace,
  Filled with regret, alas, Thou must leave them all behind.
Sorrow, sorrow, and for ever sorrow, O my heart!
  That loving friends from each other are severed so soon.
Those dear ones are like unto spring's fragile flowers,
  That in autumn's heats, alas, wither and fade away.
This separation is as hell, and absence the heated stones of hell,
  That fall, alas, upon the poor devoted lover's head.
It behoveth us here to renounce the world, for it is inconstant:
  Alas, it possesseth neither good nor advantage to carry away.
Had meeting never taken place, we had not known separation:
  Alas, it is from meeting that the very heart's blood floweth.
If friendship be thy aim, with bereavement make friends;
  For, alas, it cometh upon thee from thine own hands' deeds.
Friendship is like the rose; but its produce is the thorn:
  The thorn becometh sharp, and alas, pierceth to the quick.
Why grievest thou, Ahmad Shah, for it is a period of joy?
  The drum of meeting soundeth: alas, union's hour is near.

O heart-ravisher! There will be none other in the world like unto thee:
  Draw aside thy veil, or thy lover will of grief and sorrow expire!
With thy breast consumed by passion, I ever follow in search of thee;
  But thy abode is neither in earth nor in the heavens to be found.
I will wander throughout the world, as a Santon or Dervish;
  Or I will saturate my garments with the flood of my tears.
O fragrant zephyr of the morn! News of her bring thou to me!
  Make thou my heart to smile the garden of flowers within!

When thus I weep and bewail, my object, in doing so, is this,
  That my heart may be a nightingale in the rose-bower of thy face.
The heart, at the depredations of thy beauty, lamenteth,
  Like as the nightingale's heart bewaileth when autumn arriveth.
In this world, the heart will not from spoliation be exempt;
  Thou consumest hearts—a wondrous fire in thy nose-jewel is.
The world's censures and reproaches he taketh not to heart:
  The lover standeth in the plain, and raiseth his voice on high.
With all her tyranny and injustice, I would not abandon love,
  Were I, Ahmad Shah, with the powers of endurance prepared.

With the onset of the 19th century, although Kabul had assumed the role of capital city, more travellers began to visit Kandahar. One of them, General Ferrier, a French soldier of fortune, described a particular hazard of the journey there—the pestilential wind, or *simoom*:

"At three o'clock in the afternoon we were again in the saddle and continued our way along a deep valley; but in about two hours the horses absolutely refused to advance further against the burning hot wind. This terrible hot blast, which inflicts upon animals the same tortures as on the human race… blows by sudden squalls, the approach of which is indicated by a certain perturbed state of the atmosphere. It is filed with masses of livid opaque vapour, which conceal the horizon, and not infrequently objects that are at no great distance from the traveller: the light of the sun comes through it tinted red, and causes visible alarm to the animals, who drive their noses into the sand, or turn their backs to the squall until it has passed, and men are almost suffocated by it; perspiration is suddenly arrested, an impalpable sand fills up every pore—eyes, nose, ears and mouth; the pulse beats violently, and the sufferer falls down suddenly, as if struck by apoplexy. Decomposition always rapidly follows death under these awful circumstances, and at the slightest touch the corpse becomes dismembered—everything attending the prevalence of this death-charged blast is singular, exceptional, startling. In the vast southern steppes of Central Asia it rarely blows in squalls, it is only in the deserts of Seistan that it exhibits that characteristic; but here it blows about three days in moderate force, in which one suffers much, though death rarely ensues. There is no protection against it, except a house hermetically closed on the side from which it comes."

A Document newly known to exhibit otherwise Lost Vessel — 1041 (B.N.J. 1.)

A legend is still told to explain the cause of the great heat around Kandahar, here again related by Sirdar Ikbal Ali Shah:

> "There is a mazar, or grave, it is said, of Sheikh Fareed or Baba Fareed in the district of Safid Koh. He was a renowned Sufi. During his younger days as a poor man he roamed about the streets of Kandahar begging bread. None gave him any, and people were all busy with their games and sports. Fareed wanted no alms, for he could at any time produce great quantities of foodstuffs if he desired, but he had heard that people round about were not very charitable and he came to ascertain the truth for himself. As no one took any notice of the poor Fakir, he jumped into the river, caught a fish, and held it up to the sun. The sun descended from his height and roasted the fish. The people were all scorched to death. The water boiled in their vessels and the earth became red hot. Fareed left the town and henceforth the heat of the sun is great over those parts during summer."

When General Ferrier reached Kandahar in 1845, the city was under the control of the half-brothers of Dost Mohammed, who was now ruling from Kabul after the defeat of the British in the First Afghan War. Kandahar was still unsettled, partly on account of the conflict's aftermath, but also because of the brothers' rapacious government. On arriving there, Ferrier was arrested on suspicion of being a British spy, and led before one of the governors, Kohendil Khan. Their subsequent conversation casts much light on the causes for the brothers' unpopularity throughout the city:

> "The conversation then turned on a variety of subjects; the Sirdar took much interest in the details that I gave him respecting the different countries of Europe, and their respective riches and power. He had heard much of France, and talked a long time about it, making me specially repeat all that concerned her commerce, manufacturers, and modern inventions worked by steam. The Asiatics believe everything; they imagine that in an hour they can be made to understand arts and sciences of the most complicated character, and which it has required ages to bring to their present perfection. He was also quite surprised that I could not make easy to him the political economy of the nations of the West, nor enable him clearly to understand by what means the population had been brought under obedience to the laws without coercion by physical force.

"'I have confiscated, bastinadoed, tortured, and cut heads off,' said the wise and merciful Kohendil Khan, 'but I have never yet been able to bring my savage Afghans to obey my decrees; and yet there is not a Sirdar in my principality, not excepting even my brothers, my sons, or my nephews, who would not seize with joy a chance of wrenching the sovereign power from my grasp, if they thought it at all probable they should succeed in the attempt. Here might is right; why is it otherwise in Europe?'

"'It is,' I answered, 'because with us the governments act for the benefit of the people, without regard to their personal interest. All the acts of a government are subordinate to the law, while yours are regulated only by your good pleasure.'

"'But', he replied, 'what is the use of power if it is not to enable one to get rich? What is a government without absolute power? What is a king who cannot, when he pleases, bastinado one of his subjects and cut off his head? It is turning the world upside down, the most terrible thing that can be seen; it must be permanent anarchy—I know it; I can judge by my Afghans. They are like other men, but they respect me because they fear me: and it is by constant oppression that I succeed in inspiring this fear. If God had not inspired men with terror, by pointing out the torments with which they would be punished, would they obey the dictates of his Holy Book the Koran? I think despotism, therefore, appears the best form of government for doing good; nevertheless, if you can teach me a better, I will hasten to put it in practice.'

"'The system,' I said, 'was shown you by the English when they were in your country: do as they did; regulate everything according to justice and equity, encourage commerce and agriculture, carry out works of public utility, make your roads safe from robbers, repress the tyranny of subordinate agents, let the people know what they owe to the state, and be exempt from extortion when they have paid for it; fear not then that your country will be rich and prosperous, the population will increase instead of emigrating, and venerate the prince who shall first teach them the value of order, justice, and abundance, and their gratitude to him will be the best security for the endurance of his power.' Kohendil Khan listened, but it was plain that he thought me a short-sighted Utopian visionary, devoid of any real idea of the science of good government."

The British were, in fact, to take control of Kandahar during the Second Afghan War. However, their government there was far less happy than Ferrier might have expected. A column of troops, led by General Donald Stewart, took the city in January 1879; command of the garrison left behind there was later passed on to General George Burrows, a less experienced officer. As time went on, and the country began to slide into anarchy despite British efforts to install a new administration in Kabul, news came that Ayub Khan, a son of the ousted ruler of Afghanistan, Sher Ali, was collecting a rebel force. This new army mustered in Herat, and proceeded to attack the British garrison in Kandahar, meeting General Burrows' force outside the city at Maiwand on 27th July 1880. The engagement was a disaster for the army of occupation, with 1,000 out of the original detachment of 2,500 British and Indian troops being killed on that day. The British retreated back into the city, and, finding themselves surrounded by the men of Ayub Khan, expelled the native population of Kandahar in its entirety, the better to withstand the siege. The Government of India, realising that help needed immediately to be sent to the beleaguered garrison, ordered Sir Fredrick Roberts (Later Lord Roberts of Kandahar) who was then in Kabul, to select 10,000 men, and lead them to the city to save the situation. This forced march from Kabul to Kandahar was later to be hailed as a great military achievement; the distance between the two cities—313 miles—was covered by the column in 22 days, and Roberts, on his arrival at the end of August 1880, was able to disperse the rebel army. Howard Hensman, a correspondent for the *London Daily News* embedded with the British forces, described the march in a despatch sent on 23rd August from Kelat-i-Ghilzai (Qalat), some 70 miles outside Kandahar:

> "Today is the fifteenth from Kabul, and the eighth from Ghazni, and so far Sir F. Robert's march has been most successful. We have come through an enemy's country without any show of opposition being made, and the merit of the march is therefore its unequalled rapidity. From Ghazni we have covered 136 miles in eight days, giving an average of 17 miles per day, continuous marching; while, taking Beni Hissar as our starting point, we have done 236 miles in 15 days, or on an average 15.7 miles per day. For a regiment alone to

KILATI GHILZAI.

Capn F S Lumsden. del. t

M & N Hanhart, lith.

Published by Smith, Elder & C° 65 Cornhill, London, 1862.

Citadel of Qalat (Kelat-i-Ghilzai), which lay on the route of General Roberts' 1880 march from Kabul to Kandahar [RSAA]

do this would not be extraordinary, but for a force numbering 18,000 souls, with between 8,000 and 9,000 baggage animals, to cover this distance without a day's halt, is a feat in marching which is perhaps unrivalled... Only those who have shared in the march can form an idea of the discomfort and hardship involved; and I, as a non-combatant, with no one but myself to take care of, have had many opportunities of seeing how splendidly the men have behaved, and how officers have not spared themselves in carrying out the orders of the General directing the movement. The regiments forming the fighting line have, after marching for eight hours, often through sandy soil or over rough ground, to furnish on arrival at camp parties for all kinds of duty; one party for wood, another for *bhoosa* and green forage, a third for guards, while sentry-go and picquet duty at night have allowed what is technically known as 'three nights in bed.' Then the rear-guard work has been terribly heavy: regiments on this duty reach camp sometimes as late as nine o'clock, having been under arms since four o'clock in the early morning. The next day's march begins at 4 AM, and the men have had to turn themselves out at *reveillé* (2.45 AM), load up their baggage animals, and fall in as if they had enjoyed a long night's rest. The nights have luckily been deliciously cool, and the early mornings even bitterly cold: but two hours after sunrise the heat makes itself felt, and from eight o'clock until four the sun beats down upon the open treeless country with great fierceness. Marching, one does not feel it so much, but in the trying pauses when cast loads have to be replaced on broken-down mules, and when waiting in camp for the tents to come up, the heat punishes the men fearfully. Blistered hands and faces were common enough during the first days of the march, and although these have come to be little regarded, there remain that bodily exhaustion and lassitude resulting from long exposure in the sun and a short allowance of sleep at night. The extremes of temperature may be appreciated when I state that the thermometer at 4am registers 45° Fahrenheit in the open, and at 4 PM 105° in a double-fly tent. For the last two marches we have turned out at 1 AM and marched at 2.30, in order to get the main body into camp early in the day, and as we have had a bright moon to light up the road, the marching has been excellent. The rear-guard gets in by about three o'clock in the afternoon, and the troops have ample time to prepare their food before 'turning in' at half-past seven.

"It is well for us that food has been plentiful along the route, for without liberal rations no men could stand the constant call upon their powers; and we have been lucky also in getting plenty of green forage for our animals. The villages… we have found all fairly well peopled; the villagers had sown their crops of Indian-corn, which we have been able to purchase for transport requirements. We expected to find a howling desert, whereas we have found a strip of cultivation, narrow enough, but still sufficient for our needs. We could not possibly have maintained our rate of rapid marching if this had not been so, for continuous work will break down the best mule ever bred if the animal be not properly fed.

"I have already alluded to our followers as being the greatest drag upon us, and the *kahars* have undoubtedly had a struggle to keep up. They are such fatalists that they believe it is part of their *kismut* to wander off the road into obscure *nullahs*, there to fall asleep, and take the risk of being cut up by Afghans… Wonderful to say, men straggle into camp long after midnight, unharmed and perfectly self-satisfied. They have enjoyed their sleep in obscure ravines, and have then resumed their march as if in a friendly country. Some of them tell strange stories of having been stripped by Afghans and then allowed to escape; but these are Mohammedans who have claimed fellowship in religion with the tribesmen. Our actual loss in dead and missing since we left Kabul is, I believe, as follows: Died—Europeans, one; sepoys, four; *kahars*, five; follwers, five; missing—forty-three. Of the men who have died, one private of the 72nd and one sepoy of the 23rd Pioneers committed suicide; three sepoys died from obstruction of the bowels caused by eating unripe Indian-corn, and then drinking large quantities of water."

H.W. Bellew, a far more sympathetic observer of Kandahar and the Pushtuns, reached the city in the company of the British mission at the same time as the outbreak of the Indian Mutiny. Despite the dangers hanging over the mission from the weak position of the British government in India, Bellew portrays a period of relative tranquillity in the city before its involvement in the Second Afghan War (1878–80):

"Towards sunset yesterday evening (31 July 1857), a discharge of artillery warned the Kandaharis of the commencement of the 'Id-i-Kurban.' This is a religious festival observed by Mohammedans in commemoration of the sacrifice by Abraham of his son Ishmael, as they have it. The festival lasts three days, during which business is suspended, and all shops are closed, excepting only those of hucksters and grocers, and a few others of the same sort. During this season the people of all grades give themselves up to pleasure and amusements of various kinds. They dress themselves in their best clothes, pay visits to their friends and relatives, and, with presents of fruit, clothes, or trinkets, efface previous misunderstandings or quarrels, and cement a new friendship. Those devoutly inclined, after the morning prayers at the mosque, visit their favourite 'ziarat,' or holy shrine, and spend a few hours in religious exercises. Some visit the tombs of their departed relatives and friends, and strew the graves with flowers; and the rich employ a priest to recite a certain number of prayers or read a chapter or two of the Koran for the benefit of the departed souls.

"On the first day of the festival the head of every family, if he can afford it, kills a lamb, and divides its flesh amongst the members of the family, a portion being also reserved for their priest. Generally the animal intended for the sacrifice has been prepared for the occasion by careful feeding for some weeks previous to the festival. This is always the case with the rich or well to do, who sometimes, instead of a lamb, kill a camel, ox, or buffalo, on this occasion. Those who do not kill their sacrifice on the first day can do so on the second or third, but not later than this.

"In the afternoon of each day of the festival a fair was held on the plain to the north of the city. Almost the whole population turned out to amuse themselves, chatting, smoking, eating sweetmeats and fruits, and drinking sherbets freely. There were none of those amusements or shows that characterise a fair in the home country, and the crowds of holiday folks were remarkable for their quiet and orderly demeanour. The women and children found amusement round the different little parties of musicians to whose obscene songs they listened with delight, every now and then testifying their approbation by bursts of merriment and applause. The men wandered about from one part of the crowd to another; here dividing a dish of parched lentils, raisins and almonds, with some friend who stood as host; there, over a bowl of sherbet and a chilim, discussing the politics of the day; now quail-fighting, by and by cracking eggs with the first passer-by. By way of parenthesis, I must here note that quail-fighting is a very popular amusement of the Afghans. Almost every man has his one or more birds, and they frequently gamble on the averred powers of their respective favourites. In the early summer quail visit the cornfields and vineyards in vast numbers; they are usually caught in a large net thrown over the standing corn at one end of the field, and they are driven towards this by the noise produced by a rope being drawn over the corn from the other end, a man on each side of the field holding an end of it. Sometimes they are caught in horsehair nooses fastened to lumps of clay; and these are scattered about the borders of the field where the birds are accustomed to run from one to the other. When a quail has been beaten in a fight, and runs from its rival, his owner at once catches him up and screams in his ears; this is supposed to frighten the remembrance of his defeat out of his memory.

"The custom of cracking eggs ('tukhm-jangi') is the characteristic amusement of this festival. The eggs are boiled hard and their shells are dyed red. Immense numbers are prepared for this occasion. The people go about wagering the strength of their eggs against those in the hands of any passer-by. The point is settled by each party's alternately tapping the other's egg on its small end by a sharp stroke with the small end of his own, the object of each being to crack his adversary's egg first. In either case, the owner of the egg that chances to break loses the wager and forfeits his broken egg to his successful rival. In this manner one individual sometimes collects several scores of eggs, which he shares with his family and friends for consumption during the fair.

"Towards evening, a party of horsemen appeared on the ground and displayed their skill at 'neza-bazi' before crowds of admiring spectators. This is a manly exercise requiring skill in the handling of the lance, beside good equitation, and taxes the powers of the horse as much as those of the rider. It consists in riding full speed, with the lance at the point, at a wooden peg driven into the ground, and picking it out, at the moment of passing, in its point, which is for this purpose formed of a sharp-pointed iron spike. The Afghans are very fond of this exercise, and from frequent practice generally excel in the use of the lance. An ordinary skilful man at this exercise will with ease, whilst riding by at full speed, pick off on the point of his lance a lime or apple held at arm's length in the open palm without touching the hand itself.

"With such amusements as these, the greater part of the time at the fair was passed."

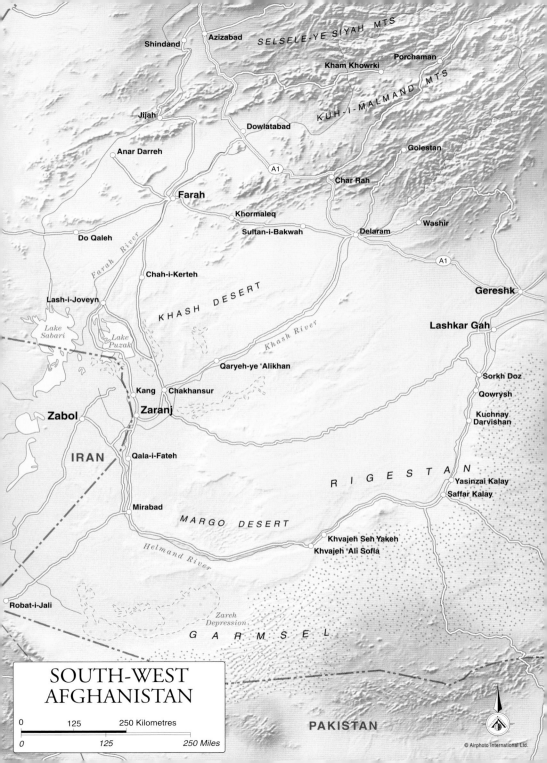

SELSELE-YE SIYAH MTS

Shindand
Azizabad
Kham Khowrki
Porchaman

KUH-I-MALMAND MTS

Jijah
Dowlatabad
Golestan

Anar Darreh

A1

Char Rah

Farah

Khormaleq
Washir
Do Qaleh
Sultan-i-Bakwah
Delaram

A1

Gereshk

Chah-i-Kerteh

KHASH DESERT

Lash-i-Joveyn

Lashkar Gah

Lake
Sabari

Khash River

Lake
Puzak

Sorkh Doz

Qaryeh-ye 'Alikhan

Qowrysh

Kang
Chakhansur
Kuchnay
Darvishan

Zabol

Zaranj

IRAN

Qala-i-Fateh

R I G E S T A N

Yasinzai Kalay

Saffar Kalay

Mirabad

MARGO DESERT

Khvajeh Seh Yakeh
Khvajeh 'Ali Sofla

Helmand River

Robat-i-Jali

Zareh
Depression

G A R M S E L

SOUTH-WEST AFGHANISTAN

0   125   250 Kilometres

0   125   250 Miles

PAKISTAN

© Airphoto International Ltd.

Kandahar: Travel Information

Kandahar—capital of the Pushtun parts of Afghanistan—is the country's second-largest city. It was the capital under the eighteenth-century Durrani dynasty, from which the current royal family claim descent. At present, concerns about security render the city off limits to western travellers; yet when the situation becomes sufficiently stable, there will be much matter of interest to the visitor. Kandahar as a settlement long precedes the Durranis. Excavations in the 1970s uncovered Achaemenid remains and an inscription that—although the subject of academic dispute—almost certainly refers to the site as Alexandria.[1] It seems that the conqueror refounded a Persian city as an Alexandria, and the name Kandahar probably derives from Alexander's name, Iskander. This makes it unique in Afghanistan as a site that can be definitely identified as one of Alexander's.

Kandahar is also the setting of two of Asoka's Rock Edicts (c. 3rd century BC), unearthed in the Zor Shah or Old City. A copy of one and the original of the other can be seen in the Kabul Museum—in the hall as one enters the building. One is in Aramaic and Greek, the other just in Greek. The longer one records the conversion of Asoka (or Piodasses, in Greek) to Buddhism after an exceptionally bloody career: "In the eight year of his reign, Piodasses conquered the Kalinga. A hundred and fifty thousand persons were captured and deported and almost as many died otherwise. Thereafter pity and compassion seized him and he suffered grievously. In the same manner wherewith he ordered abstention from all living things and he has displayed zeal and an attempt to promote piety."

The main sight of Kandahar is the tomb of Ahmed Shah Durrani, the "Father of Afghanistan". Although externally simply decorated, the inside is strikingly colour-ful. The inscription underneath the squinches is in hyperbolic praise of Ahmed Shah: "In his time, from the awe of his glory and greatness, the lioness nourished the stag with her milk. From all sides in the ear of his enemies there arrived a thousand reproofs from the dagger of his tongue."

Kandahar is also home to a shrine containing the cloak of Mohammed. This was acquired, along with a hair of his beard, by Ahmed Shah from the Amir of Bokhara in 1768. It is clad in green marble. The cloak has been exhibited three times in the last century: in 1929 by Amanullah, in 1935 to banish a plague of cholera and in 1996 when the Taliban leader Mullah Omar proclaimed himself Amir-ul-Momineem, or Commander of the Faithful. The hair of the prophet is in a mosque by the bazaar.

The bazaars of Kandahar are famous for their fruit and handicrafts.

[1] See P M Fraser, "The Son of Aristonax at Kandahar", in *Afghan Studies* 1979.

Pushtun embroidered napkin, c. 1920 [Pavia]

ART AND HISTORY OF THE GANDHARA
REGION AND THE KUSHANS

—Jonathan Tucker

THE KUSHANS

*D*uring the first century AD, a group of nomadic warriors known as the Kushans conquered the ancient region of Gandhara, situated in the Peshawar Valley of modern day northwest Pakistan. Most of the information we have on the Kushans comes from Chinese annals —especially those of the Han dynasty historian Sima Qian (c. 145–90 BC) and from the study of coins. Sima Qian describes how a nomadic tribe called the Yuezhi (Yueh-chih) originally occupied an area in China's Gansu province, between the Tianshan (Heavenly) Mountains and Dunhuang. A once powerful nation, they were attacked and defeated by another nomadic tribe, the Xiongnu (Hsiung-nu). The Xiongnu leader Maodun is said to have killed the king of the Yuezhi and made his skull into a drinking vessel. After their defeat they were led westwards by the son of the slain king and conquered the kingdom of Daxia (Bactria), setting up their capital on the north bank of the River Oxus on the borders of what we now call Afghanistan and Uzbekistan. The Yuezhi appear to have begun their migration in about 165 BC and arrived in Bactria in about 140 BC, thus migrating over a distance of more than 4,000 km within a single generation. They steadily extended their rule across Bactria and the Kabul region and, during the first century AD, into the Gandhara kingdom and the Punjab. Much of this was accomplished during the reign of Kujula Kadphises (r. c AD 30–80), ending Parthian rule in the area, unifying the entire region and establishing the foundations for the Kushan Empire. Kujula issued coins that imitated the styles of the Scythians and Parthians who preceded him. Fascinatingly, some of these coins include depictions of the Roman Emperor Augustus (r. 31 BC–AD 14), with modifications made to the design for his own use.

By the early part of the second century AD the great Kushan King Kanishka I (r. c. 100–126 or 120–146 AD) ruled an empire that extended from the Gangetic Plain of northern India to Sogdiana. Kushan rule brought prosperity and security and led to an increase in trade throughout the region. Kanishka was the greatest of all the Kushan rulers, his empire encompassing parts of

Central Asia, Bactria (modern Afghanistan), Northwest India (modern Pakistan) and Northern India as far east as Bihar. Contemporary sources indicate that Kashmir was also part of his empire.

Another, closely related portrait sculpture of Kanishka from Surkh Khotal, Afghanistan was in the Kabul museum's collections and was regarded as one of the world's great works of art. It survived the Russian occupation, civil war and looting; only to be destroyed in March 2001 by a Taliban official wielding a sledgehammer. Both images depict Kanishka in the guise of a warrior but he was also a man of great intellect with eclectic views on religion. His coins include depictions of almost the entire pantheon of Persian, Greek and Indian deities but it is the appearance of the Buddha image for the first time that has created such excitement among historians. A celebrated gold coin of Kanishka's reign in the British Museum is generally regarded as containing the first firmly dated depiction of the Buddha in human form. Kanishka may not have been a Buddhist himself but there is no doubt that he was a patron of the Buddhist faith. The construction of an immense stupa (a domed structure for relics), now destroyed, at his capital Kanishkapura or Purushapura (modern Peshawar), was accompanied by a surge in the activities of sculptors of Buddhist art.

The last of the great Kushan rulers was Vasudeva I (c. 164–200 AD or 184–220 AD). During Vasudeva's reign the Kushan Empire—with its capital at Mathura on the banks of the Yamuna River in modern Uttar Pradesh, northern India had attained its apogee. Vasudeva's patronage of the Mathura style of art has endowed us with exquisite creations, most notably in the mottled red sandstone sculpture of the period. These sculptures reflect a time of great splendour and opulence (fig 3.).

Fig.1 Red sandstone portrait statue of King Kanishka I, Kushan period, Mathura, ca. AD 100–146, H. 185 cm; inscribed Great King, the King of Kings, the Son of God, Kanishka. From Mat, Uttar Pradesh, India. [Archeological Museum, Mathura. Jonathan Tucker]

Fig. 2 Grey schist frieze with depiction of a Kushan prince or king making offerings to the Bodhisattva Maitreya (the Buddha of the future). Kushan period, Gandhara, 2nd or 3rd century AD, W. 84 cm, H. 61 cm. [Private collection]. An interesting feature is the 'Phrygian' cap worn by the obeisant servant—a conical wool or felt headdress that originated in Phrygia in Asia Minor.

The Kushan Empire entered a period of slow decline after Vasudeva's death. The Sassanian King Ardashir I (r. c. 224–40 AD) began a campaign to absorb the area into his empire, a campaign completed by his son Shapur I. From about 230 until 360 AD, the Sassanians ruled this eastern province of their empire through their own princes, governing as Kushan kings. During the rule of the Kushano-Sassanian kings, a small remnant of the Kushan Empire survived in Kashmir and in the Punjab but came under increasing pressure from local tribes and, subsequently, from the Gupta Empire of northern India. The appearance of various groups of Huns, from the mid-fourth century onwards, brought about the final demise of the Kushans and also led to the decline of Sassanian power in the region. The first of these groups was the Kidarites, who began by seizing Balkh from the Kushano-Sassanians and then invaded Gandhara. At around the same time, the Hephthalites or Chionites (also known as the White Huns) moved into Bactria from northwest China. Their empire was enlarged throughout the fifth century, until it threatened the Gupta rulers of the Punjab region. The Hephthalites were essentially nomadic and, as a consequence, did not produce sculptural art. They did produce coins and carved gems, however, and it is within this medium that we discover that they, like their predecessors, were influenced by both Persian and Greco-Roman art.

Techniques such as cameo and intaglio carving are clear examples of the importation of Western technology via the Silk Road at this time.

A peculiar aspect of Hephthalite custom was a belief that an artificially deformed head was a symbol of high social status. This disfigurement was achieved by binding the head during infancy. As a result, many Hephthalite coins include extraordinary depictions of their kings with dome-shaped skulls. Hephthalite rule lasted until about 560 AD, when an alliance was formed between the Sassanian King Khusrau I (r. c. 531–79) and the Western Turks of northern China. They succeeded in gaining control of the Kabul region and of Gandhara, and ruled the area until the coming of Islam in the late seventh and early eighth centuries.

Fig. 3. Red sandstone Bacchanalian Relief depicting the story of the 'Intoxicated Courtesan' and Vasantasena. Kushan period, Mathura; late 2nd century, H. 97 cm, W. 76 cm [National Museum, New Delhi. Jonathan Tucker]

GANDHARA AND MATHURA ART

By the time of Kanishka I, the Kushan Empire had two capital cities: Mathura (in modern Uttar Pradesh, Northern India) and Peshawar (ancient Purushapura, in what is now Northwest Pakistan). Two broad schools of art have been identified: a more Hellenised form in the northwest and a more 'Indianized' style around Mathura. These styles were far from distinct, however, and numerous common elements have been identified.

THE MATHURA SCHOOL OF ART

Mathura is located on the right bank of the Yamuna, a tributary of the Ganges River some 150 km south of Delhi in Uttar Pradesh. It sits at the junction of India's trade routes and by the first century AD was a thriving religious and commercial centre. Described by Ptolemy as a 'City of Gods', early Indian texts state that the inhabitants lived by trade rather than by agriculture. Hinduism, Buddhism and Jainism all coexisted peacefully, along with the worship of nature-spirits, and traders and acolytes brought religious and cultural influences to the city. Mathura's heyday lasted from the first century AD until the Sassanian incursions of the mid-third century. Despite a partial revival under the Gupta rulers of the fourth to the seventh century, the city never regained its former glory and eventually lost its position as a commercial and religious centre. Mathura sculpture is typically produced from mottled red sandstone quarried locally (fig. 3). Popular motifs include sensual young women, nature and water spirits (yakshis and nagas), architectural elements, flora and fauna and bacchanalian scenes. Mathura sculpture is often fleshy and full figured, and its protagonists (both religious and secular) are dressed in diaphanous clothing with multiple folds. While its form is essentially Indian, the influences of Greece and Rome, assimilated via the Silk Road, are also present.

THE GANDHARA SCHOOL OF ART

'In the entrance-hall stood the larger figures of the Greco-Buddhist sculptures done, savants know how long since, by forgotten workmen whose hands were feeling, and not unskilfully, for the mysteriously transmitted Grecian touch.' (Rudyard Kipling, Kim. Kipling describes the Gandhara sculpture of the Lahore Museum, 'The Wonder House', at which his father, Lockwood, was curator.)

The long-destroyed stupa of Kanishka, built at Kanishkapura, near Peshawar in today's Northwest Pakistan, measured almost 100 metres across and was admired by many early travellers, including the Chinese monk Xuanzang during the seventh century. Peshawar (Purushapura) was the seat of the Kushan Empire, at least during its early period. Other centres were at Taxila, the later capital, the Swat Valley and Hadda and Begram (Bagram) in modern Afghanistan. All of these cities sat astride the ancient routes linking China, Central Asia and the Western world, and were part of a region that modern writers have called 'the crossroads of Asia'. The art of Gandhara — almost exclusively Buddhist in nature — draws its influences from Greek, Roman, Persian and local Indian styles. Grey or blue schist seems to have been the preferred medium; stucco and terracotta were used in areas where stone was unobtainable, and gold and bronze also used, though much more sparingly. The fully developed Gandhara style was extant by the end of the first century AD. It is generally accepted that stucco and terracotta images are somewhat later than schist sculpture, perhaps because of the depletion of supplies of stone. Early stucco and terracottas have been found, at Taxila for example, but the majority have been attributed to the third to fifth centuries, compared to the first to third for stone.

An extensive repertoire of classical motifs is found in the art of Gandhara. Mythological figures such as Eros (Cupid) and wingless Puttis (young boys) with garlands of flowers; figures of Herakles (sometimes transmuted to become the Buddhist deity Vajrapani) and Atlas, centaurs and sea monsters, Corinthian columns and capitals with acanthus leaves and floral scrolls (rinceaux). The British Museum even has a schist frieze that tells the story of the Trojan horse!

Images of the Buddha in Gandhara art are devoid of ornament and are formally posed, adhering closely to the designs of Kanishka-era coins. Standing Buddha images typically have a high usnisha (a raised chignon, indicative of princely origins and superior wisdom), eyes half-closed in meditation and a heavy monastic robe with multiple pleats. Despite the simplicity of style of these Buddha images, Greco-Roman elements are still to be found and, indeed, it has been suggested that they derive from the figure of the Western philosopher or statesman known as Togatus, found in the classical world.

Gandhara Buddha images were created in vast numbers. Free-standing (or sitting) images, usually in stone, were produced, as were figures placed in niches against a wall, in common with many stucco or terracotta examples. Very few examples of the latter survive in situ; the Jaulian monastery at Taxila being a rare example. At Jaulian there are tiers of niches containing stucco figures of Buddhas, Bodhisattvas and devotees in acts of worship or meditation.

Perhaps the most famous examples of the Gandhara ideal were the colossal Buddhas, 55 and 38 metres in height, hewn out of the rock at Bamiyan, to the west of the Afghan capital of Kabul. For the 1,500 years that they survived they ranked among the greatest artistic creations of the earth but in March 2001, in one of the most colossal acts of stupidity of recent history, they were blown up by the country's Taliban rulers. A network of caves adorned with exquisite wall paintings surrounded the Buddhas. Many of the paintings were executed in a style referred to by art historians as 'Indo-Sassanian' but they, like the Buddhas, did not survive the vandalism of the Taliban era.

Images of the Bodhisattva (those destined for Buddhahood), in the guise of a Kushan prince, are among the most elegant of all Gandhara sculptures. Typically, these images wear a turban-

diadem that holds in place an elaborate coiffure. The hair is sometimes in the form of a topknot or cockade, sometimes secured by a line of pearls encircling the head. Unrestrained by the austerities associated with the Buddha, Bodhisattva images are adorned with an abundance of jewellery: heavy earrings (often in the form of lions), basubands for the arms and as many as four necklaces, all in a style which evokes the classical world. The robes, too, follow Greco-Roman models and the upper torso is generally bare and muscular. Such Bodhisattva images can be as much as two metres in height but even much smaller images can be magnificent and imposing (fig.4).

Fig. 4. A grey schist figure of a Bodhisattva Kushan period, Gandhara, 2nd or 3rd century AD, H: 110 cm. Probably from the vicinity of Takht-i-Bahi near Sahri Bahlol, Northwest Pakistan [Private Collection]

Sculpture from this middle period of the Gandhara School is not always monumental in style—scenes from the Buddha's previous incarnations, known as the Jataka stories, are frequently rendered in the most delicate and sensitive manner (fig. 5). In the example shown in fig. 5, Queen Maya, wife of King Suddhodana of Kapilavastu, conceives Prince Siddharta, the future Buddha, while dreaming of a white elephant that enters her right side. In this relief she stands holding the branch of a sala tree as the child emerges from her side, a pose that evokes the theme of fertility and is often seen in depictions of yakshis (nature spirits). Supported by her sister Mahaprajapati, Queen Maya is attended by her servants, one of whom holds a palm branch. Similarities between this frieze and the 'intoxicated courtesan' relief from the New Delhi museum (fig. 3) provide clear evidence that the Mathura and Gandhara schools of Kushan sculpture were far from distinct.

The technique of working in stucco, a cheap and readily available substitute for the grey schist stone favoured by the sculptors of Gandhara, attained its apogee around the third century at Hadda, near Jalalabad. Hadda's numerous monasteries (viharas) were still active at the time of a visit by the Chinese pilgrim Fa Xian in around 400 AD, but the city was ruined and desolate when Xuanzang passed through in 630, wrecked by Hephthalite invaders. Sculpting

with stucco, a plaster made from calcium oxide or calcium sulphate, seems to have been invented in or near the Roman port of Alexandria in Egypt. It is extremely easy to work, with large figures built up around a core of wood or stone. This enables the sculptor to infuse his creations with a

Fig. 5. A grey schist frieze depicting the birth of the Buddha. Kushan period, Gandhara, 2nd or 3rd century AD, H. 24 cm, W. 24 cm [Spink and Son Ltd]

greater degree of naturalism and spontaneity. Hadda stuccos still retain the classical elements seen at Taxila and Begram but the city's artists have adapted them to produce a unique style that reveals the full flowering of Gandhara art.

LATER BUDDHIST ART OF GANDHARA

During the seventh and eighth centuries, before the coming of Islam, the Buddhist art of Gandhara entered its final phase. The paintings and sculptures discovered in 1937 by the French at the monastery of Fondukistan, on the Ghorband River to the northwest of Kabul, continue the Indo-Sassanian style that we first saw in the wall paintings of Bamiyan. Figures in similar style were found at Tepe Sardar (near Ghazni), and at Kakrak. The technique of painting unfired clay, sometimes mixed with horse hair and chopped straw and modelled around a wooden framework, is seen for the first time and replaced the old media of schist, limestone stucco and terracotta. It became the method of choice among the artists of the Silk Road, occurring in Kashmir, in China and parts of Central Asia, and embodied a refined and somewhat feminine style. The sculptural counterparts of the Fondukistan paintings are equally flamboyant and sensual and may have their roots in the art of the Gupta dynasty of northern India.

The sudden appearance of the marble figures of the Hindu Shahi dynasty, just before the advent of Islam, was a surprising development in the art of the region. The most important finds were at Khair Khaneh 15 km north of Kabul. The sun god Surya and Vishnu were popular subjects for the Shahi artists and their styles are linked to those of Kashmir. Other sites such as Tagao and Gardez have also yielded sculptures of Hindu deities, including Siva and Durga, although a number of Buddhist images have also been found. When Xuanzang visited the kingdom of Kapisa, north of Kabul, in 630, he recorded that there were 100 monasteries and about 6,000 monks in the city, but that there were also ten Hindu temples. Very little is known about the Hindu Shahi (after the Persian title, 'Shah' or 'King'). It appears that they emerged as a result of a palace coup among the Turki Shahi at some point before the ninth century and established their capital at Udabhandapura (modern Hund) in Pakistan, to the northwest of Taxila. Although the Hindu Shahi dynasty was established only around the ninth cenury, Hindu sculpture was already being produced in the area and has all been labelled 'Hindu Shahi' as a matter of convenience. It seems likely that the Western Turks and the Turki Shahi were one and the same tribe or, at least, were part of the same confederation, but information about both groups, and particularly the latter, is scarce and contradictory. The Turki Shahi are not even referred to by name until the eleventh century, when they are given mention in Al-Biruni's work 'The History of India' (Ta'rikh al-Hind).

The coming of Islam to Central Asia and Afghanistan during the late seventh to eighth century brought monotheism and iconoclasm to the region. Within a hundred years of its arrival the activities of artists and monks, Buddhist and Hindu alike, had come to an end and creativity became the exclusive domain of the new religion.

RECOMMENDED READING

Czuma, S. J. Kushan Sculpture: Images from Early India. Cleveland: Cleveland Museum of Art, 1985.

Errington, E. and Cribb, J. (eds.). The Crossroads of Asia. Exhibition Catalogue, Cambridge: Ancient India and Iran Trust, 1992.

Hallade, H. The Gandhara Style and the Evolution of Buddhist Art. London: Thames and Hudson, 1968.

Kurita, Isao, Gandharan Art I: The Buddha's Life Story, 2 vols. Tokyo: Nigensha publishing, 2003.

Rosenfield, J. M. The Dynastic Arts of the Kushans. Berkeley: University of California Press, 1967.

Zwalf, W. A Catalogue of the Gandhara Sculpture in the British Museum. London: British Museum Press, 1996.

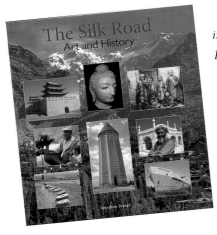

Jonathan Tucker's acclaimed book *The Silk Road: Art and History* (published by Philip Wilson Ltd.) is a detailed, lavishly illustrated account of the ancient trade routes between Europe and Asia.

NURISTAN: THE COUNTRY OF LIGHT

It is said that Alexander the Great came across many wonders in the course of his travels. He found the rock to which Prometheus had been chained and tortured by the angry god Zeus, and a herd of cattle branded with a club, marking the furthest extent of the wandering of Hercules. However, in 327 BC, he made his most remarkable and peculiar discovery. As he crossed the Hindu Kush on his way towards India, he ordered the main body of his forces to proceed directly through the Khyber Pass, whilst he himself with a detachment of infantry and elite cavalry went northeast through the Kunar Valley. Here, he encountered a distinct people, Greek in spirit, and further evidence of the past presence of a god. The historian Arrian narrates the tale:

> "Alexander continued his advance into the country between the river Kophen (Kabul) and the Indus; here, it is said that there was a city called Nysa, which, it is claimed, was founded by Dionysus after he had conquered the Indians. When Alexander approached this city, its inhabitants sent out one of their leaders, named Acuphis, and with him thirty respected elders, to beg him to leave the city to the god. History relates that they came to Alexander's tent, and found him sitting down, covered in dirt from the journey, and still wearing his armour, helmet, and even clutching his sword. Amazed at the sight, they fell to the ground and for a long time remained silent. But when Alexander raised them up and told them to be of good cheer, Acuphis began to address him:
>
> "Your Majesty, the citizens of Nysa beg you to allow them to remain free and independent, out of reverence for Dionysus. It was he who founded this city with some of his soldiers—who were also his bacchants—unfit for active service, when he had subdued the Indians and was returning to the Greek Sea. He did this so it would stand as a memorial to posterity of his wanderings and his victory. In the same way, you yourself have founded an Alexandria on Mount Caucasus, and another Alexandria in Egypt; you have already founded many cities, and you will in time establish many more, all of which will go to prove that your achievements are greater than those of Dionysus. Dionysus

A young Pashaie in Kurgal Village, 1956 [W. Thesiger]

called the city Nysa, and the country Nysean, after Nyse, his nurse. He also called the nearby mountain Meros because, as the story says, he grew sewn-up in the thigh (Gk: *meros*) of Zeus, rather than in his mother's womb. Since that time, our city has retained its liberty, and we ourselves have remained independent, living in a well-ordered civic fashion. Moreover, the proof that this city is a foundation of Dionysus is still to be seen: ivy grows no-where else in India, except here.'

"Alexander was greatly interested to hear all of this; he wanted to believe the tales about the wanderings of Dionysus, and he wanted it to be the case that Nysa was established by Dionysus, so that he would be in a position to exceed his achievements. He also thought that the Macedonians, out of their eagerness to rival Dionysus, would gladly go further with the campaign. And thus, he granted freedom and independence to the citizens of Nysa. He furthermore enquired about their laws, and when he learnt that the best men were in charge of the government, he voiced his approval.

"Alexander then became very eager to see the place where the Nyseans proudly displayed certain relics of Dionysus. It is said that he went to Mount Meros with the Companion Cavalry and the infantry division, and saw it covered in ivy and laurel, and all sorts of groves. The Macedonians rejoiced to see the ivy, as they had not seen any for a long time (for no ivy grows in the

country of the Indians, not even where there are vines); eagerly, they wove garlands from it, crowned themselves, and sang hymns to Dionysus, calling on the god by his many names. After this, Alexander made a sacrifice to the god and ate a feast with his Companions. Some historians have even claimed, if such a story can be believed, that many eminent Macedonians in his company, after crowning themselves with ivy and performing the rites of the god, were possessed by him, raised the Dionysiac shout, and went running through the groves in a Bacchic frenzy."

Silver wine goblet from Nuristan [Pitt-Rivers Museum]

Since Alexander's time, the inhabitants of the area, perhaps on account of its extreme isolation, have been markedly different to the wider population around them. They are often Western in appearance—Elphinstone described one of them as having the complexion of "an Irish haymaker"—and, until the end of the 19th century,

Typical carved wooden Nuristani houses at Burg-i-Matral, 1964 [W. Thesiger]

were wine-drinking pagans rather than Muslims. As a result of their refusal to embrace Islam, they became known as "Kafirs", or unbelievers, and their territory as "Kafiristan". One of Elphinstone's companions, Mullah Najeeb, went on an expedition there sometime before 1815 in order to gather information about them; Elphinstone later related his general account of their mode of living:

> "The houses of the Kafirs are often of wood, and they have generally cellars where they keep their cheese, clarified butter, wine and vinegar. In every house there is a wooden bench fixed to the wall with a low back to it. There are also stools shaped like drums, but smaller in the middle than at the ends, and tables of the same sort, but larger. The Kafirs, partly from their dress and partly from habit, cannot sit like other Asiatics, and if forced to sit down on the ground, stretch out their legs like Europeans. They have also beds made of wood and thongs of neat's leather: the stools are made of wicker work.
>
> "Their food is chiefly cheese, butter, and milk, with bread or a sort of suet pudding. They also eat flesh (which they like half raw); and the fruits the have, walnuts, grapes, almonds, and a sort of indifferent apricot that grows wild. They wash their hands before eating, and generally begin by some kind of grace. They all, of both sexes, drink wine to great excess: they have three kinds, red, white and dark coloured, beside a sort of the consistency of a jelly, and very strong. They drink wine, both pure and diluted, out of large silver

cups, which are the most precious of their possessions. They drink during their meals, and are elevated, but not made quarrelsome, by this indulgence. They are exceedingly hospitable: the people of a village come out to meet a stranger, take his baggage from those who are carrying it, and conduct him with many welcomes into their village. When there, he must visit every person of note, and at each house he is pressed to eat and drink. The Kafirs have a great deal of idle time; they hunt a little, but not so much as the Afghans; their favourite

amusement is dancing. Their dances are generally rapid, and they use many gesticulations, raising their shoulders, shaking their heads, and flourishing their battle axes. All sexes and ages dance. They sometimes form a circle of men and women alternately, who move round the musicians for some time with joined hands, then all spring forward and mix together in a dance.

"They dance with great vehemence, and beat the ground with much force. Their only instruments are a tabor and pipe, but the dancers often accompany them with the voice. Their music is generally quick, but varied and wild.

"Their religion does not resemble any other with which I am acquainted. They believe in one god, whom the Kafirs of Kamdesh call Imra; but they also worship numerous idols, which they say represent great men of former days, who intercede with God in favour of those worshippers.

"These idols are of stone or wood, and always represent men or women, sometimes mounted and sometimes on foot. Mullah Najeeb had an opportunity of learning the arts which obtain an entrance to the Kafir pantheon. In the public apartment of the village of Kamdesh, was a high wooden pillar on which sat a figure, with a spear in one hand and a staff in the other. This idol represented the father of one of the great men of the village, who had erected

(Above) *Nuristani Grave figure, Brumboret Valley, Nuristan. Although many of these figures have been destroyed, some are still to be seen in the Kabul Museum, and the Pitt-Rivers Museum, Oxford.* [W. Thesiger]

it himself in his lifetime, having purchased the privilege by giving several feasts to the whole village; nor was this the only instance of man deified for such reasons, and worshipped as much as any other of the gods. The Kafirs appear indeed to attach the utmost importance to the virtues of liberality and hospitality. It is they which procure the easiest admission to their paradise, which they call Burry Le Boola, and the opposite vices are the most certain guides to Burry Duggur Boola, or hell."

Their distinct nature and way of life has prompted much speculation over their origins. Many have argued that they are indeed, as Arrian's story suggests, the descendants of Greeks who settled there in some early period of history, or else the Greek colonists who established themselves there after the time of Alexander. The explorer Sir Thomas Holdich, quoting one of their hymns to the war god Gish, went so far as to find in it echoes of the ancient Greek religion:

"O thou who from Gir-Nysa's lofty heights was born
Who from its sevenfold portals didst emerge,
On Katan Chirak thou hast set thine eyes,
Towards the depths of Sum Bughal dost go,
In sum Baral assembled you have been.
Sanji from the heights you see; Sanji you consult?
The council sits. O mad one, whither goest thou?
Say, Sanji, why dost thou go forth?"

On which Holdich commented:

"Gir-Nysa means the mountain of Nysa, Gir being a common prefix denoting a peak or hill. Katan Chirak is explained to be an ancient town in the Minjan valley of Badakhshan, now in ruins; but it was the first large place that the Kafirs captured, and is apparently held to be symbolical of victory. Sum Bughal is a deep ravine leading down to the plain of Sum Baral, where armies are assembled for war. Sanji appears to be the oracle consulted before war is undertaken. The chief interest of this verse (for I believe it is only one verse of many, but it was all that our friends were entitled to repeat) is the obvious reference in the first line to the mountain of Bacchus, the Meros from which he was born, on the slopes of which stood ancient Nysa. It is, indeed, a Bacchic hymn (slightly incoherent, perhaps, as is natural), and only wants the accessories of vine-leaves and ivy to make it entirely classical."

A different opinion is proffered by the Jesuit Benedict Göes, who, in 1602, was making a journey towards India. He presumably was not aware of Arrian's account, and rather predictably jumped to a conclusion which, to him, seemed obvious:

> "Further on, whilst on their way to another small town, they fell in with a certain pilgrim and devotee, from whom they learned that at a distance of thirty days' journey there was a city called Capperstam (Kafiristan), into which no Mohammedan was allowed to enter, and if one did get in he was punished with death. There was no hindrance offered to the entrance of heathen merchants into the cities of those people, only they were not allowed to enter the temples. He related also that the inhabitants of that country never visited their temples except dressed in black; and that their country was extremely productive, abounding especially in grapes. He offered our brother Benedict a cup of the produce, and he found it to be wine like our own; and as such a thing is quite unusual among the Mohammedans of those regions, a suspicion arose that perhaps the country was inhabited by Christians."

The hypothesis that the Kafirs were of Greek origin has, however, little hard evidence to support it. Whilst similarities have been observed between Kafir sacrifices and those of the Ancient Greeks, no literature, coins or inscriptions have yet appeared to substantiate the claim; the ancient city of Nysa still remains undiscovered. The various

Puchal in the Ramgul Valley; a Nuristani villager sits on a chair backed with ibex horns. The general use of chairs in Nuristan—unusual for this part of Asia—led many early explorers to believe that the Nuristanis possessed a racial affinity with the Greeks and Europeans. [W. Thesiger]

tribes in the area speak not a derivative of Greek, but various languages of the Dardic group (some of which are mutually unintelligible), belonging to the Indo-European family of languages. If there are various parallels between the Kafirs and the Ancient Greeks—e.g. the use of chairs and tables, the drinking of wine from silver goblets, adornment with ivy—it is more likely that these are vestigial remnants of Greek influence south of the Hindu Kush from after the time of Alexander. It is now generally thought that the Kafirs are composed of a number of Aryan tribes who originally inhabited both the Hindu Kush and the lowland areas to the west as far as Kandahar. From around the 10th century AD, the area under Islamic rule began to grow strongly, and Muslims came into confrontation with those who still adhered to pagan practises. These Aryan tribes, refusing to convert to the new faith, were forced into a slow retreat, eventually taking refuge in the mountain strongholds around the Kunar Valley and Chitral, where, until recently, they remained in their pristine state.

The Kafirs were divided into two principal groups—the Siah Posh, or Black-robed Kafirs, and the Safed Posh, or White-robed Kafirs. These groups were further divided into tribes, the Katirs, Madugul, Kashtan, Kam and Gordesh belonging to the former, and the Presuns, Wai and the Ashkund to the latter. The tribes differed not only in their locations, but also in their dress, languages and customs. Religious beliefs also varied from tribe to tribe. The religion practised by the Kafirs appears not to have been a derivative of the ancient Greek Pantheon or Dionysus worship, but rather a version of early Hinduism with later foreign accretions. The creator god Imra was universally accepted, along with Moni, his prophet, and Gish, the popular war god. Different tribes and settlements would also have their own favoured local deities. Kafirs also appear to have believed in a heavenly abode of the gods, called *Urdesh*, and an underworld, called *Yurdesh*, in which place is located the various rewards or punishments for the virtuous or the sinners.

In 1890, a British agent, George Scott Robertson, made a prolonged stay with the Kafirs, and subsequently wrote *The Kafirs of the Hindu Kush*—the last and fullest account of them before their conversion to Islam. Amongst other things, he collected stories relating to the god Imra:

> "Once Imra took the sun and the moon from the heavens and the world became buried in darkness. Everybody died except one man, who prayed to God for a little light. Moved by pity, Imra gave the man a bit of the sun and a bit of the moon, which he fastened on each side of him, and then, mounting his horse, rode away. Wherever he went there was just sufficient light for him to guide his horse. After a time he reached Presungul [a village sacred to Imra] when Imra appeared in front of him. 'Hullo,' said the man, 'who are you?' 'I am Imra,' was the reply. The horseman was speechless with awe and astonishment. 'Let us perform the ceremony of friendship,' suggested Imra, but the man pointed out that he had not a goat [the ceremony of friendship required the sacrifice of a goat]. 'Never mind that,' replied Imra, 'I will soon fetch one.' Saying which he stepped over to the mountains by the Zidig Pass, and returned with a fine goat. 'But,' objected the man, 'where is the knife to sacrifice it with?' He had no sooner uttered these words than the goat began to dig up the ground vigorously with its forefeet, shaking its body all the time as a wet dog does. At the bottom of the shallow hole made by the goat a knife was revealed. Imra seized it, and he and the man went through the ceremony of swearing brotherhood. When it was over Imra said, 'Now what are you going to give me?' 'I have nothing,' replied the man; 'what can I give?' 'You have your horse,' persisted Imra, 'give me that.' 'But I shall have nothing to go about on,' protested the man; 'no, I cannot give you my horse.' Thereupon Imra summoned an angel, who quietly stole the man's horse and led it away. As it was being carried off the horse cried out, 'I have a sword in my ear; pull it out and kill all your enemies.' Imra drew the sword out of the horse's ear, and used it against his enemies. He subsequently replaced the sun and moon in the sky, and light was restored to the earth."

As has been mentioned, the Kafir gods were worshipped with sacrifices. Mullah Najeeb, during his expedition, witnessed the sacrifice of a goat:

> "There is a stone set upright about four feet high, and in breadth about that of a stout man. This is the Imrtan, or holy stone, and behind it to the north is a

wall. This is all the temple. The Stone represents God. They say 'this stands for him, but we know not his shape'. To the south of the Imrtan burns a fire of Kanchur, a species of pine which is thrown on green, purposely to give a great deal of smoke. A person whose proper name is Muleek, and his title Ota, stands before the fire, and behind him the worshippers in a row. First, water is brought him, with which he washes his hands, and taking some in his right hand, throws it three times through the smoke or flame on the Imrtan, saying every time 'Sooch,' that is, pure; then he throws a handful of water on the sacrifice, usually a goat or a cow, and says 'sooch', Then, taking some water, and repeating some words which mean 'do thou accept the sacrifice,' he pours it into the left ear of the sacrifice, which stands on his right. If the animal now turns his head to heaven, it is reckoned a sign of acceptance, and gives great satisfaction; afterwards in the right ear, and a third time on the forehead, and a fourth on its back. Each time 'sooch' is once said. Next throwing in some fuel, he takes a handful of dry wheat flour and throws it into the fire on the stone; and this flour they reckon a part of God; and again he throws both hands full of ghee into the fire; and also, this is a portion of God. They do not in either of these ceremonies say 'sooch', but now the priest says with a loud voice 'He!' and after him three times the worshippers say 'He umuch!' that is 'accept!' This they accompany each time with a gesture. They put their palms expanded on the outside of their knees, and as they raise them in an extended position, say 'He umuch!' The priest now kills the goat with a knife, and receiving in both hands the blood, allows a little to drop into the fire, and throws the remainder through the fire on the Imrtan (or idol, in case of an idol), and again three 'He umuch' The head is now twisted off (to the left) and thrown into the fire, but no 'He umuch'. Wine is then brought in a bowl, and the priest dropping a little into the fire, throws the rest through it (the ghee too was thrown out of a bowl), and three 'He umuch'. The priest now prays god 'Ward off the fever from us! Increase our Stores! kill the Mussulmans! after death admit us to Burelebola! (or paradise!)' and three 'He umuch' are said. The priest now springs forward and places before himself a pshur, or person possessed by a spirit, who after stretching forward his head into the smoke, and shaking in it, turns up his eyes to heaven, and prays as before; the priest and worshippers three times say loudly 'He umuch!' Next each man puts the fingers of each hand together to his mouth and kisses them, next to his eyes, and lastly to his head; then all retire, and sit or lie down in one place. They now put the blood of the victim, with a little water, on the fire, and after it has simmered a little, put in the flesh, which is soon taken out half raw and eaten. But if the victim be a cow, it is divided, and each man carries his own home. The priest gets a double share in both cases. During the meal they sip some wine, mixed with a deal of water, and furnished by the person who gives the victim."

The Pshurs, who might be thought of as mediums for spirits and the departed, did not confine their activities to sacrifice ceremonies, but were liable to become possessed at any time. According to Robertson, the reputation of the Pshurs varied according to the tribe and location; Pshurs in the Bashgul Valley, predominantly occupied by the Siah Posh Kafirs, were generally distrusted and despised, whereas those in the Presungul Valley were held in great esteem. Robertson himself had an opportunity to draw his own conclusions after spending an evening with one of them, named Shahru, and his friend, Utah:

"In the evening Shahru the Pshur came for a long talk over the events of the day. He even endeavoured to explain his own position towards the gods during sacrifices, but our limited means of intercommunication left the subject still obscure. He told me he had attended four sacrifices that day, and four times had he become possessed, speaking with tongues. The obvious result was that he was very tired. Tobacco had a good effect for a time. We discussed the looting and destruction of a house which was going on two hundred yards or so in front of us, in a philosophical spirit, much in the same quiet way in which we referred to an earthquake which had startled us during the day, for it now took a great deal to turn my curiosity into keen inquisitiveness. Under the combined influences of warmth, tobacco, and friendliness, Shahru revived gently, and on Utah coming in, the three of us, with my Pathan servant, Mir Alam, sat round the fire, and discussed everything in the world, from the general inferiority of the Presungulis in comparison with all other Kafir tribes, to the family connections of her Majesty the Queen-Empress. I invited my guests to take some brandy, or rather I should say they led up to the subject in so marked a manner that I could not do otherwise than send for the spirit. They only drank a very little, greatly diluted with water, but even in this condition they were astounded at its fire and potency. We were continuing the conversation quietly when Shahru suddenly jumped to his feet, powerful tremors shaking his body.

He sprang to the door, where he turned and faced us. His face was pallid, his lips uttered indistinct words, while he held his down-stretched writhing hands tightly clasped together. He kept raising himself on his toes, and then lowering his heels to the ground. If other assurances had been necessary, a glance at Utah's face told me that no farce was being enacted. Utah, serious and priestly, had risen to his feet. Mir Alam had done the same, while I sat and looked on. Shahru presently recovered himself with many strokings of the beard and long-drawn sighs. Utah made him sit down by his side, and gave direction in low but authoritative tones for more wood to be quickly placed upon the fire, which had burned somewhat low. Then the explanation came. Shahru had seen a female spirit, a vetr, just over my door. As was customary on such occasions, whatever the spirit wished to say she spoke through him. It appears that she had come all the way from London, and, after merely asking, 'is the Frank [European] here?' at once disappeared. Her face, Shahru said, was like the moon, especially in its shining qualities. Utah requested me to send at once for some very pure article of food to eat. I produced the remains of a box of sweets which were considered to fulfil the stated requirements. We each solemnly took a morsel of toffee, and munched it silently and thoughtfully. I had summoned up my most sympathetic look, and was rewarded for my trouble. Utah begged me on no account to go to sleep before midnight, adding that he himself, after what had happened, would be afraid to sleep at all that night. He said that on one occasion, near Utzun, he saw Shahru seized by a spirit and whirled away some distance before being thrown down to the ground with such violence that all his clothes were torn into ribbons. He now doubted the wisdom of leaving me at all during the night, and proposed that he and his brothers, Utah, Ding, and Aramallik, should sit with me by turns. If there had been a certainty of further 'manifestations' their company would have been most welcome. Shahru was not humbugging. He remained tired and silent until we made a move, my friends to their homes, and I to keep a vigil, if I would be ruled by priestly advice."

Mullah Najeeb, whilst on his travels, saw the great carved wooden idols erected to commemorate the most eminent men and women of the Kafir tribes. However, Robertson had the opportunity to attend the funeral ceremonies at which these were put up, and to witness the dancing that accompanied the rites:

"When I arrived the first day, escorted by one or two young braves, friends of mine, the performance was in full swing. In the centre of the dancing place, close by the rough altar, was the effigy of a man. It was carried on the back of a slave, above whose head and shoulders it towered a couple of feet. The long straight legs were covered at the ends—there were no feet—by tufted dancing boots. A Badakhshan silk robe was thrown over the shoulders, and the head was bound round with a silk turban, into which eight paint-brush-shaped contrivances of peacock's feathers were thrust. The odd-shaped face, huge and solemn, the white stone eyes set close together, and the bobbing up and down of the big image as the slave bearing it shifted from one foot to the other in time to the music, and every now and then gave it a sudden bunch up, made a curious picture. In the present case it seemed a wonder that one man should be able to sustain so heavy a burden. He always looked tired, and was frequently changed, but nevertheless, the wood from which the image was cut must have been extremely light for one man to be able to uphold it. During intervals of the dance the image was propped up against the altar, and left in charge of the women. Of these during the dance, about two dozen, including little girls, the seniors wearing horned headdresses, circled slowly round the figure, keeping time by a slow bending of the knees, and moving the feet only a few inches at a time. They incessantly moved one hand, palm upwards and breast high, slightly backwards and forwards, towards the bobbing effigy. The action of the hands is intended to symbolise the words 'as this dead person is, so shall I become.' All the women and little girls were shockingly dirty and unkempt, their garments being much torn. The women wore the large serpentine earrings, and two or three had on silver blinkers also. Outside the women was a dense

An Old Nuristani tomb, Kunar Valley [F. Holt]

throng of men, all dancing round from left to right. The women of the inner circle were of the family of the deceased, while their male relations in the dancing crowd were distinguished from the others by wearing bright-coloured clothes and all the bravery they possessed, and by each carrying a dancing axe. They wore gorgeous sham kinbob chappans, or long robes and white cloth turbans.

"The music was supplied by professionals, kindly assisted at times by amateurs. It consisted of three tiny drums and two or three of the ordinary wretched-toned reed pipes. The drums did not exceed four inches in the diameter of the heads, and were contracted in the middle like hourglasses. The performer beats with a small stick, while he keeps up the tension of the drumhead by pulling at certain leather thongs with his left hand, by which the tightness of the stretched hide surfaces could be regulated. I was told that these little drums are costly, being each of them worth a cow, because, out of many, not more than one or two turn out a credit to the maker. The 'time' allowed great latitude to the dances, who indulged their individual fancy, either walking slowly round and round the dancing circle, taking several steps of not more than six inches in length to the bar, or two skips on each foot alternately; or sometimes prancing, stamping, or rushing forward. It was a question of pace.

"A favourite movement seemed to be to march round more or less steadily, merely raising the knees slightly, and the suddenly to rush violently at the orchestra with the head bent, as in the act of butting. Nearly all the dancers were in pairs, with arms over one another's shoulders. Characteristically, if a man wanted to scratch his nose, he was just as likely to use his encircling arm as the free one, without the slightest thought of the discomfort he was causing his partner by twisting the latter's face round. The splendidly dressed relations danced singly. Often in the mob, especially when near the musicians, the leading pairs would face round to those behind them, hammering their feet with great force on the ground, and bending over to watch the effect. Round and round they went, round and round, smiling, very happy, fully conscious of the excellence of their own performances, and never tiring. Aged men, with that touch of nature which makes us all akin, danced with an added grace, from the consciousness that they were showing their juniors how the thing should be properly done. With wooden step they doubled up their knees, gyrated, performed the back-step, side-kick, all the figures of the highest style. These men never smiled, while they were frequently out of time. Axes were twirled by some, jerked with both hands by others, or were merely bobbed up and down on the shoulder. Every time the band stopped the head-drummer sounded a few last taps to show his finished touch and his reluctance to stop. The intervals in the dancing were filled up by extemporary addresses to the wooden image by an individual specially appointed for that duty. He extolled the liberality of the deceased, his bravery, and his good deeds, as well as the virtues of his ancestors. As the orators on these occasions are always members of the dead man's family, they probably say all that is to be said on the subject, and never err of the side of false modesty His style was curiously like that of certain uneducated itinerant speakers one sometimes hears in England. Breathless staccato sentences, with pauses, all the speech broken up into passages of nearly equal length, while the pauses show a constant tendency to grow longer and longer. I could hardly understand a single word uttered until my companions made it clear to me; but it was obvious that the orator thought little of repeating himself over and over again.

"While the orator declaimed, the dancers refreshed themselves with wine ladled from a tub with wooden cups. The same not particularly generous fluid was also circulated among the spectators constantly. Sometimes the musicians would stop altogether, and the dancing would recommence to the chanting of men's voices. The singers crowded round a central figure, a lame friend of mine, who was the highest musical authority in the tribe. In leading the choir he vibrated violently from head to foot with the rapture of his song or hymn, but his notes were inaudible in the accompaniment of his fellows. Poor fellow! I hope he did not know this, for, like all really fine singers, and some others also, he liked to be heard. The men's voices intoned a perfect church chant. Shut your eyes, and you would believe a full-voiced choir was sounding a Gregorian prayer; open them, and it was something quite different."

Kafiristan, throughout its history, was famous for the production of wine. An early mention of it was made by the Emperor Babur, who, being a connoisseur, spoke with authority on the various varieties of grapes grown there, particularly around the area of Lamghan:

"The valley grows grapes also, all trained on trees. Two sorts of grapes are grown, the *arah-tashi* and the *suhan-tashi*; the first are yellowish, the second, full red—of fine colour. The first make the more cheering wine, but it must be said that neither wine equals its reputation for cheer."

Holdich also tried the Kafir wine, 400 years later than Babur; his reaction was much the same:

"Through the kindness of the Sipah Salar, the Amir's Commander-in-Chief, I have had the opportunity of tasting the best brand of this classical liquor, and I agree with Baber—it is not of a high class. It reminded me of badly corked and muddy Chablis, which it resembled much in appearance."

H.W. Bellew learnt much concerning the production of Kafir wines whilst staying in Kandahar in 1857:

"September 1st—The Sirdar (governor) paid us a visit this afternoon. He said he had received no later news from Kabul or Herat than what we knew already; and assured us that there was no doubt about the latter place having been abandoned by the Persians and fallen into the hands of Sultan Jan. He then changed the topic of conversation, and broached the subject of wines and spirits, their varieties and qualities. He appeared to have a fair acquaintance with many of those commonly consumed by Englishmen, although, with ludicrous dissimulation, he pretended profound ignorance of their distinctive qualities, and professed extreme aversion to all such noxious drinks. In the eagerness of conversation, however, he quite forgot his pretence and profession, and launched out in praise of a delicious red wine produced at Kabul, the flavour of which was superior to that of brandy, champagne, or beer, with each of which he now seemed to be well acquainted, as well by name as by quality. This red wine, it appears, was first introduced into Kabul from Kafiristan by the border tribes in communication with the Kafirs, from whom they obtained it by barter, in leathern bottles of goat-skin. It is now largely produced in the Kabul district, especially in its northern parts, by the nobility, most of whom have their own wine-presses. The Sirdar described the method of making this wine as very simple. The juice of the grapes is squeezed into a large earthen vessel, or masonry reservoir, by treading under foot. From this the expressed juice flows through a small hole into a large earthen jar with a narrow opening

Munjanis near the top of the Munjan Pass, 1965 [W. Thesiger]

at the top. When nearly full, the mouth of the jar is closed and the liquor allowed to stand for 40 days. At the expiration of this time an empty flagon of fine porous clay is floated on the surface of the wine, which it gradually absorbs till full, when it sinks. The flagon is then taken out, its mouth closed air-tight with luting of dough, and placed aside in a cool place to ripen. If kept for three years it is said to acquire great body and flavour. The Sirdar, after this description, was on the point of ordering a bottle to be brought for our inspection, but remembering himself in time, attempted to throw off suspicion by promising to make inquiries whether anyone in the city could make or procure some for us. He, however, forgot his promise, and we did not remind him of it."

Despite the Kafirs' reputation as a "harmless, affectionate, and kind-hearted people" in the words of Elphinstone, their tribes were often at war with each other. Moreover, the long-term threat they felt from the surrounding Islamic population led to perpetual feuds between them. Kafirs came to honour greatly those of their number who had managed to kill any Muslims, and it became impossible for Kafirs to gain any respect from their people without doing so. Although Mullah Najeeb was well received by the Kafirs in spite of his different faith, he saw the signs of their wars against the Muslims:

"They sometimes go openly to attack their enemies, but their commonest more is by surprisals and ambushes, and they expose themselves to the same misfortunes by neglecting to keep watch by night. They often undertake remote and difficult expeditions, for which they are well suited, being naturally light and active: when pursued, they unbend their bow, and using it as a leaping pole, make surprising bounds from rock to rock. Mullah Najeeb saw the men of Kamdesh march out against another tribe. The rich wore their best clothes, and some put on black fillets ornamented with cowry shells, one for every Mussulman whom the wearer had killed. They sung a war-song as they marched away, in which were the words 'chera hi chera hi Mahrach', and he learned that when they had succeeded in coming on an enemy unprepared, they set up a loud whistle, and sing a song, of which the chorus is 'Ushro oo ushro': on such occasions they put every soul to death. But their chief glory is to slay the Mussulmans: a young Kafir is deprived of various privileges till he has performed this exploit, and numerous distinctions are contrived to stimulate him to repeat it as often as may be in his power. In the solemn dances on the festival of Numminaut, each man wears a sort of turban in which is stuck a long feather for every Mussulman he has killed: the number of bells he wears round his waist on that occasion is regulated by the same criterion, and it is not allowed to a Kafir who has not killed his man to flourish his axe above his head in the dance. Those who have slain Mussulmans are visited and congratulated by their acquaintances and have afterwards a right to wear a little red woollen cap (or rather a kind of cockade) tied on the head; and those who have killed may erect a high pole before their doors, in which are holes to receive a pin for every Mussulman the owner has killed, and a ring for every one he has wounded. With such encouragement to kill them, it is not likely that the Kafirs would often make Mussulmans prisoners: such cases have happened when the Kafirs were defending their own village; and they then made a feast with great triumph, and put the unfortunate prisoner to death in much form; or perhaps sacrificed him to their idols.

"They, however, sometimes have peace or truce with the Mussulmans. Their way of striking a league is as strange as their mode of war. They kill a goat and dress the heart, bite off half, and give the rest to the Mussulman; the parties then gently bite each about the region of the heart, and the treaty is concluded."

In September 1864, a Pushtun convert to Christianity, Fazl Huq, set off with a companion called Nahrulla on a missionary journey to Kafiristan, all the time keeping a journal using lime juice as invisible ink. The journal was summarised in the *Church Missionary Intelligencer*, and records, amongst other things, a massacre of Muslims by the Kafirs:

"A fearful initiation into their work now lay before them, exhibiting to them Kafir ferocity in its worst features. The next march was to Nikera, on the tops of the mountains. They here found twenty-eight armed Mussulmans, who had been invited by the Kafirs over from Mungoo. It was many years since a number of Kafirs had been slain in their village, and they thought the fact forgiven or forgotten, and believed themselves to be quite safe when they came armed, and in such numbers, to accept the Kafirs' hospitality. Their hosts feasted them bountifully, and, after removing all suspicion from their minds, had persuaded them to leave their arms in the huts assigned to them. It was at this time that our travellers arrived, and had much conversation with these Mungoo men, two of whom were Mullahs, and six students from Koonur, when suddenly their friend Ghara called out to them in Hindustani to come away. 'What for?' they asked. 'Because they were going to dance.' 'Then we, too, will stop and see it.' 'But there will be a scene (*tamasha*), and you must come away'. All this was in Hindustani, which none but they understood. They withdrew quietly, and sat down on a rock above. The Kafirs brought a drum and pipes, and began to sing and dance, throwing their hands and feet about, the women looking on. Then suddenly, without one moment's warning, each Kafir knife was unsheathed, and seen poised high above his head, and, with a loud whistle, four or five Kafirs rushed on each Mohammedan, stabbing him in every part. The whole was over in a moment, and all had sunk down dead, covered with many wounds. They then beheaded them, and threw them all down into the rivulet below. Our travellers were speechless with horror, when Ghara again told them not to fear, for not one hair of them should be touched. They pointed to the dead bodies below, and gasped out that they, too, one short quarter of an hour before, had been the Kafirs' guests. He told them the reason of such dreadful vengeance. The blood feud was still unremoved, and the Kafirs had never forgotten their own brethren murdered long before. He told them, however, never to leave him. Three days after, the Kafirs sent to Mungoo to tell them to send men for the property of the slain: for Kafirs never plunder, they only kill the Mussulman. Some people went from Malel, and brought back their muskets and daggers (which the Kafirs so much valued, but could not take) and also their heads or hands."

This behaviour of the Kafirs understandably caused great resentment and fear amongst the Muslims who lived in proximity to them. From the 10th century and the time of the Ghaznavid Empire onwards, there were several attempts to conquer the area of Kafiristan and bring it under Islamic rule. One of the most famous was made by the Emperor Timur (Tamerlane), who attacked the Kafirs in 1398 before going on to invade India. Despite the positive gloss put on the expedition by his biographer, Sharaf al-Din Ali Yazdi, it was far from being a success:

"Whilst Timur was encamped at Enderabe, the inhabitants came to cast themselves at his feet, to complain of the insults and trouble they received from the idolaters of Ketuer, and from the Siah Poshes: they represented to him that there were a great number of Muslims, from whom the infidels exacted every year excessive sums of money, under the name of tribute and carriage; which if they failed to pay punctually, they killed their men, and made their women and children slaves.

"The emperor, touched with their complaints, and excited by zeal for the religion of which he was protector and defender, marched immediately against these tyrants: he chose three soldiers out of every 10 ... and marched with so much diligence, that he made two days journey in one. He soon arrived at Perjan in Badakhshan, whence he sent Mirza Rousten, accompanied by Burhan Aglen, and other Emirs, with 10,000 men towards the left, to seek the Siah Poshes; and following his road, he arrived at Caouc (at the foot of Mount Ketuer), where he found a demolished citadel, which he caused to be rebuilt. Many emirs and soldiers left some of their horses at Caouc, and ascended on foot to the mountain of Ketuer, where though the sun was in Gemini, the snow lay in so great abundance, that the feet of most part of the horses, which the lords would have carried up, failed them; yet some of them were spurred on so much during the night and the frost, that they were constrained to get up: but day being come, and the snow turned to ice, they kept these horses under felts till evening, when they continued to ascend the mountain, so that at length they arrived at the top, and then sent for the rest of the horses. And as the infidels dwelt in narrow passages and precipices, and there was no road to get to them, besides what was covered with snow, some of the emirs and soldiers descended by cords, while others lying on the snow, slid down to the bottom. They made a sort of raft for Timur, to which they fastened rings, that they might tie cords to it of 150 cubits in length: he sat upon it, while many person let him down from the top to the bottom of the mountain, as far as the cords would reach. Others dug with pickaxes in the snow a place where he might stand firm. They who were on the top having gently descended, they let down Timur in the machine. The place also was marked out where he should stay next; and so on till the fifth time, when he arrived at the foot of the mountain. Then this monarch took a staff in his hand to rest on, and walked on foot a great way. ... They also let down some of the Emperor's horses, girding them about the belly and neck, with great precaution; but most of them through the fault of the guides fell headlong down, so that there remained but two fit for service.

"The infidels of this country are strong men, and are as large as the giants of the people of Aad (certain Arabs in the time of Nimrod). They go about naked; their kings are named Oda and Odachouch; they have a particular language, which is neither Persian, nor Turkish, nor Indian, and know no other than this: and if it was not for the inhabitants of the neighbouring places, who are found there by chance, and having learnt their language, serve for interpreters, no one would be able to understand them.

"These infidels were in a citadel, at the foot of whose walls passes a great river; and on the other side of this river there was a high mountain. As they learnt of the approach of Timur twenty-four hours before his arrival, they abandoned this post, crossed the river, and carried their effects to the top of this mountain, imagining it inaccessible, especially with the entrenchments they had made there.

"When the army after long fatigues arrived at the citadel, they found nothing there by some sheep the enemy had left, which they made themselves masters of: then having set fire to the houses, they immediately crossed the river. The Emperor ordered them to ascend the mountain by many narrow passes; which our soldiers did, and at the same time returned thanks to God.

"The enemy defended themselves rigorously, notwithstanding the great slaughter of their men. The fight lasted three days with unheard of obstinacy: but at length these unfortunate men finding themselves no longer able to make resistance, begged quarter with tears in their eyes. Timur sent to them Ac Sultan Rechi, with orders to tell them that if they would come to him with submission and obedience, abandon their errors, and take up a resolution to acknowledge but one God, and embrace the Mohammedan religion with sincerity, he would not only give them their lives and effects, but also leave them to enjoy their principality as before. They had no sooner learnt this from an interpreter, than the fourth day they came to cast themselves at the feet of the emperor, conducted by Ac Sultan Rechi: they abjured their idolatry, and embraced the Mohammedan religion, promising to submit entirely to the emperor, and obey all his commands. Timur, according to his wonted generosity, gave them clothes, and sent them away, after having encouraged them by the most affectionate speeches.

"Night being come, these wretches, whose hearts were more black than their garments, fell upon the regiment of Chamelic, and put all the soldiers of it to the sword, except a few, who, though wounded and lame, escaped their hands.

"As soon as this treason was discovered, our men slew near 150 of them. All the army got upon the mountain, and following the precept of Mohammed, who orders the women to be spared, they put to the sword all the old and young men of these infidels, and carried away their women and children. At length, they built towers on the top of the mountain and the end of the bridge, with the heads of these traitors, who had never bowed their head to adore the true God. Timur ordered to be engraved upon marble the history of this action, which happened in the month of Ramadan in the year of the Hijra 800 (June 1398 AD); and he added the particular epoch which this people used, that their posterity might have some knowledge of the famous valour of the ever-victorious Timur. This pillar so inscribed gave the greater pleasure to Timur, in that these people had never been conquered by any prince in the world, not even Alexander the Great."

Kafiristan remained as an autonomous and virtually independent entity until 1895. At this time, the British government in India and Abdur Rahman—the Amir of Afghanistan—signed the Durand Agreement, by which the British agreed not to advance beyond a newly-demarcated boundary line, beyond which lay nearly all of the Kafir territory. Abdur Rahman at this point decided to make a final attempt to bring Kafiristan under central control from Kabul. Not only did he wish to end the perpetual fighting between the Muslims and the Kafirs; he also feared that the Russians, who had for the whole of the 19th century been advancing south into Central Asia, would try and snatch the area for themselves if it were left unoccupied by his forces. He began the process by diplomatic means, making approaches to Kafir chiefs, but in the end he decided to launch a full-scale invasion. An English doctor, Lillias Hamilton, who was working in Kabul at the time, gave a full account of the action in a letter to *The Times*:

"The plan of action was as follows: Ghulam Hyder Khan, the Commander-in-chief of Jalalabad, with all the troops under his command, marched from Asmar towards the country of the Kafirs known as Sufed Posh from their white clothes. In one decisive battle he conquered Kamdesh and the neighbouring villages, losing only about 70 men killed and wounded, whilst the Kafirs left from 400 to 500 on the field. All the rest were taken alive. These were at once sent to Jalalabad, and from there to Lozman, where they will remain with their wives and families till the winter is over. Those on the Badakhshan side of Kafiristan surrendered without striking a blow. Thus none were left but the tribe called Siah Posh (black dress) Kafirs. These engaged in a fierce fight with the Amir's troops at a place called Sheshpoos. They were all armed with good firearms and commenced the battle in the open. The Afghans under Captain Mahomed Ali Khan, consisting of several battalions of well-trained men beside Ghazis from Panjshir, Anderab, and Lozman, made considerable havoc among the undisciplined Kafirs, who were forced to retire to their fortified villages, whence they continued to

A Nuristani boy with armed with a bow [W. Thesiger]

fire on the Afghans through holes in the walls. The tables were now turned, the Kafirs lost but few men, the Afghans many. So, contrary to the express orders of the Amir, who wished everyone to be taken alive, the captain was obliged to make use of the heavy guns. In this way many of the houses were destroyed, and the Kafirs were obliged to fly for protection from one village to another, until finally they were completely routed. The Afghan soldiers then rushed into one of the villages to capture all the remainder alive, but some 400 or 500 of them set fire to their own buildings and perished in the flames rather than fall into the hands of the enemy. Wakil, the chief, was, however, captured alive, and is expected to arrive in Kabul in a few days. He is an old man, and the roads being covered with snow he can only travel by very easy stages. The

prisoners captured at Kooloom have all been sent to Charikar, where the Amir has given orders that they are to be supplied, as are those at Lozman, with good houses, warm clothing, one resai, or quilt, between each two persons, and food. When the cold season is over they too will be brought to Kabul. In the meantime, they are enjoying luxuries hitherto unknown, for they are very poor people indeed, and in winter hardly leave the shelter of their houses, where they shut themselves up and keep themselves warm with large fires made of the wood with which their mountains are covered."

Dr Hamilton had close links with the court of the Amir, and was eager to defend his actions. She gives a full and detailed picture of events as seen from the seat of power in Kabul:

"So long ago as the Summer of 1894 the Amir used to tell me stories about these people. He never spoke of them except in terms of the greatest kindness and pity for their ignorance, declaring that the priests alone were responsible for their having fallen away from Mahomedanism, which he believes had at one time been their religion. At the same time he explained at that the name Kafir (unbeliever) had been given to them unjustly, as even now there is no difference between their religion and that of orthodox Mahomedanism. I have myself seen large numbers of these people entertained as guests by the Amir. In fact, I shall never forget in the early spring of 1894 seeing some hundreds of them dance almost naked, with knives either in one or both hands, round a huge bonfire that had been made in a field near the khirgah (Turkestan felt-covered tent) in which the Amir was at that time spending a few days outside the city of Kabul. It was a wild, weird scene! There was no moon, though the hour was about 10pm, so that nothing but the flames of the fire showed up their not

(Top) *Flat-roofed houses, Pech valley, Nuristan, 1971;*
(right) *Rice planting near Chagaserai, Kunar valley, 1971 [Y. Crowe]*

ungraceful forms and rather Jewish cast of countenance as they threw themselves with an ever-increasing rapidity into the excitement of the dance, to the measure of which some 12 or 20 musicians beat a not unpleasing humdrum sort of air. As the more fatigued fell out of the ranks they were not replaced until the last man had given in, when he received both praise and reward from the Amir himself. Then another batch began, and so on. All seemed in the best of good humour, and no wonder, for they had been well fed and had received both clothes and money with which to return to their own country. This, the Amir explained, was his policy, that they might go home and tell others of the kindness and generosity with which they had been treated. To the more intelligent of these visitors the Mahomedan religion was explained, and they were themselves surprised to find how little theirs differed from it. Many of them embraced Islamism without hesitation and undertook to explain the mistakes they had been making to their fellow countrymen. Others, of course, refused, and returned to their country enriched by the Amir's bounty, but imbued with no desire to acknowledge either his supremacy or his religion. Many of them now say they were persuaded by the English in Chitral and the neighbouring towns not to forsake their religion, but to abide both by it and their independence. If there be any truth in this 'the English' were no doubt

most excellently intentioned missionaries, who were anxious not to lose sight of their new converts, which they knew they must do if the country were taken over by the Amir Abdur Rahman, in whose eyes the British Missionary is but the pioneer of the British soldier.

"Beside these newly-converted Kafiristan Mahomedans, the Amir has sent messengers throughout the country to proclaim that, Kafiristan having now been given under his rule and being included in his dominions, the people have become his subjects and must acknowledge his authority. This policy of clemency was continued for two years and with a considerable measure of success. By degrees the people in the more accessible parts gave in, and only the most obdurate retired within their mountainous fastnesses there to await the consequences of their refusal to submit.

"I happened to be with the Amir last Friday when Captain Mahomed Ali Khan, who had been placed in charge of the troops that had been drawn from Panjshir, Anderab, and Lozman, was presented before him. This Captain had brought a roughly coloured map and three boys with him. These boys were the sons and nephew of Wakil, the greatest of their chiefs. The Amir could not have been more charming to any one than he was to these boys, giving them tea and biscuits of which he himself was eating at the time, and allowing them to sit close beside him whilst his own officials and the man who had conquered their nation remained standing. Finding themselves at home, these boys, whose clothes were conspicuous by their absence and whose hair hung in tangled, irregularly-cut masses down their backs, became quite familiar and ventured to poke fun at anyone and everyone. I myself became the butt of some of their jokes, which another Kafir boy, who has been some years in the Amir's service, and is brother of Melik, the favourite page boy who died about three years ago, translated, to the immense amusement of the Amir, who was delighted. Before sending them away, clothes were ordered to be at once made for these little half-naked urchins, and, if the government tailors had their hands too full to start at once, the work was to be put out in the bazaar. Food and warm quarters were also to be provided at government expense.

"In the map brought by Captain Mahomed Ali Khan one place was marked Kali Timur—the Fort of Timur—and he explained that on a stone there he had found the following words engraved: 'The Amir Timur of the Mogul Dynasty conquered this country so far, but was unable to proceed any further.' The Amir's officer then went on to say that on that same stone he has engraved the following words from the Koran: 'The true faith in one God has overcome the infidels or believers in many gods.' Also the following inscription: 'In the year 1313, during the reign of the wise King, Amir Abdurrahman Khan, the whole of Kafiristan was conquered and incorporated into the Kingdom of Afghanistan.' He pointed out to the Amir a place called Kooloom, which was considerably further into the heart of this mountainous province than Kali Timur. This place which, if properly pronounced, ought to be Kooloohoom, which means 'all together,' is an almost impregnable natural fortress surrounded by high mountains and approachable only by one narrow pass. Here, for centuries, the Kafirs have assembled when any foreigner has attacked them. This place it would have been almost impossible to have taken, but when all the rest of the country had given in, those who had collected in this last stronghold, hearing of the kindness with which all those who had surrendered had been treated, also laid down their arms and consented to acknowledge the authority of the Amir."

After the annexation of Kafiristan and the conversion of its people to Islam, Abdur Rahman renamed it "Nuristan", meaning "The Country of Light".

In 1934, Georg Morgenstierne, a Norwegian professor of languages, visited Nuristan and collected from the tribesmen a number of short songs, which commemorated the recent invasion and upheaval. Three of them are quoted below:

Alas, what awful news has reached us!
The Amir has taken away the twelve Kate clans to Kabul
O Skelik, your precious bones have been scattered.

I will not give up my Kafir lock, my own lock!
O Koli, son of my maternal uncle Gumaro, son of Barmuk!
O Koli, with the silken, golden Kafir lock!

Go, O princess, let us go up!
Our children have been lost—what shall we do?
Did our marriage customs exist for this, I wonder?

(Above) *Wooden carved tomb at Chagaserai, 1971;*
(right) *Towards Nuristan, rivers and fields, 1971 [Y. Crowe]*

NURISTAN: TRAVEL INFORMATION

Nuristan is, at the time of writing, a risky destination to visit. There are insurgents loyal to Gulbuddin Hekmatyar based in the area and across the border. When the security situation improves, Nuristan will once again take its place as one of the most remote and beautiful places in the world to visit. It is an extremely mountainous area with wooded, steep-sided valleys and travel is really only possible by foot, something apparent from Tamerlane's account of his campaign here. He and his horses had to be lowered by rope down a cliff face. Eric Newby, recounting this story, comments that "across the centuries one gets the impression that he wished he hadn't come".

The inhabitants of Nuristan seem to be ethnically different from other Afghans. Many have red hair and blue eyes and are probably descended from a wave of Indo-European migration from Central Asia. This question is being investigated with genetic testing.

There are two ways of entering the country, from Jalalabad and from the Panjshir Valley. From Jalalabad, one drives to Kamdesh, through Kunar province and the villages of Ashadabad, Asmar and Barikot. The road crosses the Alingar River on a bridge at Barikot, which may sometimes be washed away. The road forks and to the right hand turns towards Chitral in Pakistan. This road, after Chitral, goes to Garam Chashma and the Dorah Pass back into Afghanistan; the route is described on p. 000, where one is following the ancient trade route from the lapis mines at the Blue Mountain. Kamdesh is the capital of Nuristan and the base camp for any trek in the area.

Nuristan consists of a number of valleys that can be classified by their languages. Although all belong to the Indo-Iranian subgroup, each valley has its own mutually unintelligible language. Linguists classify them under their own heading of Nuristani.[1] The most recent classification of this subgroup gives six Nuristani languages: Ashkun, Kamviri, Kati, Prasuni, Tregami and Waigali.

As for the geography of Nuristan, the best description is still Eric Newby's: "Nuristan is drained by three main rivers. The one farthest east is the Bashgul river; in the centre is the Pech and on the west, next to the Panjshir, is the Alingra whose upper waters are called the Ramgul; the Bashgul and the Pech discharge into the Kunar and the Alingar into the Kabul river just above Jalalabad."

To enter Nuristan from the Panjshir (as Eric Newby did), one follows the trail past Mir Samir and across the Chamar Pass.

One of the most recent western travellers to enter Nuristan was Jonny Bealby; an account of his visit can be read in *For a Pagan Song: In the Footsteps of the Man Who Would Be King*, published by Arrow.

---

[1] See www.ethnologue.com for the most recent classification.

THE CUISINE OF AFGHANISTAN

—Helen Saberi

A *fghanistan has been a melting pot for a large number of cultures and traditions over the centuries. Situated on the crossroads of the ancient Silk Road linking East and West, its position has played a vital role in the exchange of food, plants, skills and knowledge. These different influences can be detected in the rich variety and diversity of Afghan food, the flavours and the regional specialities. It is all the more interesting because the cuisine often mirrors the tastes and flavours of its neighbours. All pervading and unifying are the unforgettable aromas of the herbs and spices—saffron, cardamom, coriander and cumin, which are used to add flavour and fragrance to dishes, with results that are neither too hot and spicy, nor too bland.*

Bread is the staple food, usually made of wheat flour in the form of either nan, which is leavened and baked in a tandoor (oven), or chapati, usually cooked over a tawa (concave griddle). Bread is very often eaten on its own with tea but is important as a scoop for food or as an accompaniment to dishes such as soup.

Although bread is the staple, rice is of great importance. Long grain rice is used for the many types of pilau (e.g. qabili—with carrots and raisins; norinj—with orange peel, almonds and pistachios; zamarud—with spinach; yahkoot—with tomatoes; reshta—with fine noodles. It is also used for chalau, the plain white rice dish usually served with a qorma or burani (vegetables such as aubergine, fried and served with a yoghurt sauce, flavoured with garlic and mint). Short grain rice is used for the basic sticky rice dish called bata which, like chalau, is served with a qorma or vegetables. Ketcheree quroot is a sticky rice served with a qorma or meatballs and accompanied by a minty yoghurt sauce made from reconstituted quroot. Quroot is strained yoghurt (chaka) which is dried and formed into pebble like balls. Mastawa is a hearty winter rice dish using dried lamb, chickpeas and yoghurt. There are also many types of shola, both savoury and sweet, including shola-i-Ghorbandi; shola-i-zard (the dish often prepared for a sort of thanksgiving called Nazr); shola-i-shireen and many other sweet rice dishes often flavoured with cardamom and rosewater, such as daygcha.

Noodles and pasta dishes also play an important part in Afghan cuisine. Aush is the name given to a wide variety of noodle soups. There is also ashak, a pasta stuffed with gandana (a member of the leek family) and served with reconstituted quroot and a minced meat sauce; and mantu, a sort of dumpling filled with chopped meat and onions. Savoury fried pastries are also very popular, particularly as snack foods such as boulanee (pastry stuffed with gandana or with mashed potato and spring onion); sambosa; and pakora. These snack foods are part of the numerous foods available from street vendors, called tabang wala. Other street foods include shour nakhod (chickpeas with a mint sauce) and haleem (a wheat and meat dish).

Lamb is the favourite meat although goat, beef, water buffalo and camel are also eaten, as are poultry and game. Lamb, apart from being used for qorma, is also used for making the many different types of kebab. These include chapli kebab, the fiery hot speciality of Jalalabad chapli means 'sandal' and so-called because of its sandal-like shape. Other kebabs include tikka or sikh kebab, shami or lola kebab, kofta, karayi, chopan and Shinwari. Dumba, the fat from the tail of the fat-tailed sheep, is often cooked with kebabs to keep them succulent and moist or boiled with lamb to make the dish known as dopiasa.

Fish does not play a large part in the Afghan diet, although in the winter months some sea fish (not shell fish) are imported from Pakistan. This fish is usually fried and traditionally served with jalebi, a fried sweetmeat. River fish such as trout and sheer mahi are also popular when available, as is mahi laqa, a large catfish found in the Kunduz River.

Dairy products loom large in the Afghan diet, especially in the high mountainous regions where fresh meat and vegetables and fruit are often scarce. Yoghurt (mast) is used extensively in cooking. It is often strained to make a creamier substance called chaka, which in turn is often dried and formed into balls to make quroot. Cheese (panir) is also made. In the springtime a traditional dish called kishmish panir, white cheese served with red raisins, is popular. Qymaq is another milk product (a kind of thick cream), similar to the kaymak of the Middle East. It is sometimes eaten with nan for breakfast, but is better known for its use in the special Afghan tea called qymaq chai (see below).

Desserts, sweets, cakes, biscuits and pastries are considered to be luxuries. Many resemble those of Iran, the Middle East and India, such as the milk-based firni and sweet rice puddings.

'Preparation for a Feast' attributed to Bihzad, 1490 [Metroplitan Museum of Art]

Halva is also popular, as are pastries such as baklava and the pastry shaped like elephant ears called goash-i-feel.

Abrayshum kebab (abrayshum means silk) is an unusual Afghan sweet, made with egg in such a way that the egg forms threads which are then rolled up like a kebab and sprinkled with syrup and ground pistachio nuts. The egg threads are supposed to resemble silken threads, hence the name.

For the Afghan New Year (Nauroz), a pre-Islamic festival marking the first day of spring, a traditional dried fruit and nut compote consisting of seven fruits and nuts, called haft mewa, is prepared.

At the end of every meal fresh fruits in season are served. In summer this includes melons and grapes, of which there are numerous varieties and for which Afghanistan is famous. Grapes are made into both red and green raisins. Nuts (pistachios, almonds, walnuts, pine nuts) are often nibbled as snacks but are also used extensively in cooking, mainly as garnishes.

Tea, both black and green, usually served without milk but often flavoured with cardamom, is consumed copiously all over Afghanistan. Noql (sugared almonds) are often served with tea as an accompaniment. Chaikhana (tea houses) are an important institution. They not only furnish tea from a constantly boiling samovar, but very often provide accommodation and meals for travellers (such as the traditional 'tea pot' soup, i.e. soup literally made in a teapot).

Qymaq chai is served for special occasions. It is made from green tea in such a way that, with the addition of bicarbonate of soda and the process of aeration, the tea becomes red. Milk is added, producing a purply pink tea which is then topped with qymaq.

Helen Saberi is the author of *Noshe Djan: Afghan Food and Cookery*,
published by Prospect Books, £12.00

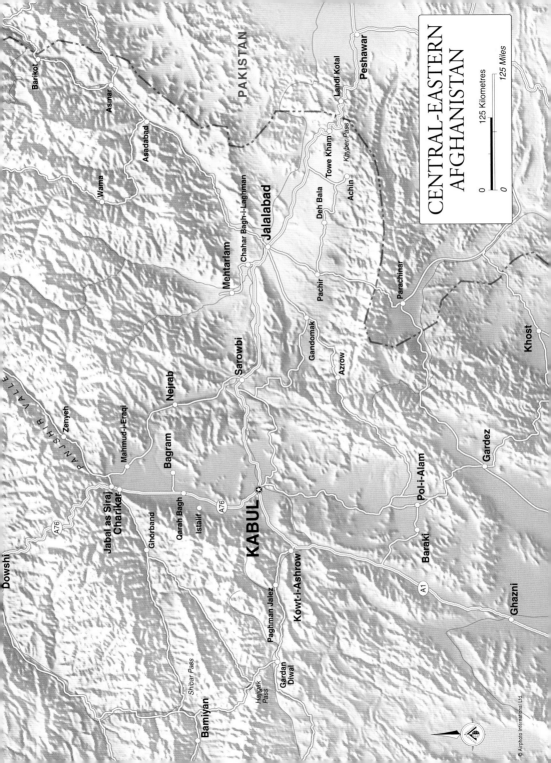

CENTRAL-EASTERN
AFGHANISTAN

125 Kilometres
125 Miles

0
0

PAKISTAN

Barikot

Asmar

Asadabad

Wama

Peshawar

Landi Kotal

Towe Kham

Khyber Pass

Deh Bala

Achin

Chahar Bagh-i-Laghman

Jalalabad

Mehtarlam

Pachir

Parachinar

Gandomak

Azrow

Khost

Sarowbi

Nejrab

PANJSHIR VALLE

Zenyeh

Mahmud-i-Eraqi

Bagram

Gardez

KABUL

Pol-i-Alam

Jabal as Siraj

Charikar

A76

Ghorband

Qarah Bagh

Istalif

A76

Baraki

Dowshi

A76

Kowt-i-Ashrow

Paghman Jalez

A1

Ghazni

Shibar Pass

Gardan
Diwal

Hajigak
Pass

Bamiyan

© Airphoto International Ltd.

KABUL: LIGHT GARDEN OF THE ANGEL KING

F ew writers would disagree with Sir Alexander Burnes' observation that "the ancient history of Kabul... is unsatisfactory"; little, if anything, is known for sure about its foundation or the events of its earliest times. It is generally thought that the city is first mentioned by the Greek geographer Strabo under the name of Ortospana, as being a settlement located on a junction between various roads towards Bactra and India. However, it seems unlikely that it derived any great benefit at that time from its situation. The main trading route from the north down

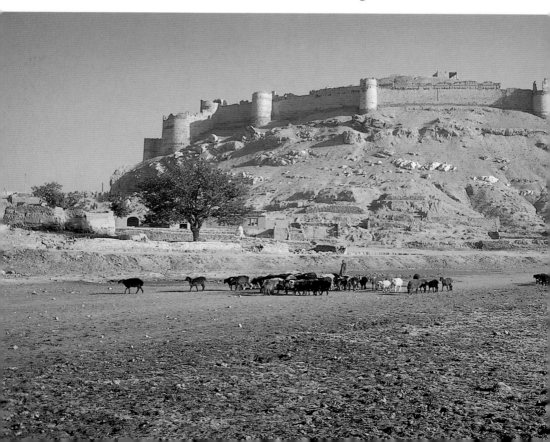

to India bypassed Kabul, running directly from the more important capital of Kapisa (modern-day Bagram) to Jalalabad and the Khyber Pass; hence, Kabul tended to receive little attention in the historical record. The paucity of written material is matched by the lack of firm archaeological data. The oldest site in Kabul—the Bala Hissar, or City Castle—still awaits proper excavation, and although various finds of pre-Kushan pottery have been unearthed in the vicinity, little can be said for sure until the mound on which it sits is subjected to a thorough examination.

Nevertheless, legend supplies what history lacks. Various myths have been chronicled relating to the foundation of Kabul. Burnes himself heard from its inhabitants that the place was founded by the two sons of Noah: Cakool and Habool (a different story from the Bible, in which Noah has three sons). When these two brothers quarrelled over what name their city was to receive, they "at length agreed to form it by taking a syllable from each name, hence Ka-bul". On another occasion, he was told that the "the remains of the tomb of Cabool, or Cain, the son of Adam" was to be seen in the city; he also encountered a popular belief that "the devil fell [in Kabul] when cast out of heaven".

Another story is often repeated in the Kharabat quarter of the city, which has traditionally been populated by musicians and dancers. This version was recorded in the 1930s by Hackin and Kohzad:

"A king of the East, known for his extreme prudishness, harboured a great resentment towards one of his tribes, and began to deliberate on a plan to expel them from his capital.

"In the midst of one of his journeys through his kingdom, he took the opportunity to inspect a

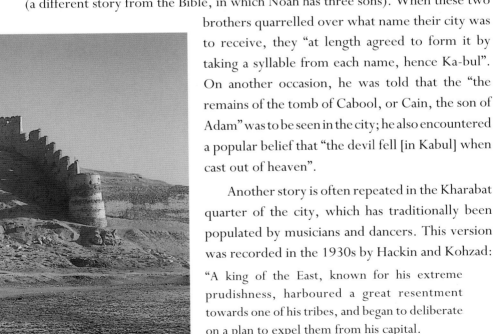

The Bala Hissar (High Fort) at Kabul, in 1972. For many centuries, this fortress contained the seat of the local rulers. [B. Woodburn]

certain marshy area, and decided that it would be the perfect place to deposit the members of this tribe in disgrace. When he returned home, he made this intention known to them.

"All of the tribe, composed for the most part of musicians and dancers, chased out of their lands and properties which were confiscated in their entirety, were made to seek refuge on this swampy island under the surveillance of armed men in the pay of the king.

"No inhabitants in the immediate area; an unhealthy climate; a marsh infested with mosquitoes; such a sight did this land of exile present to them. Courageously, they took it on themselves to build huts out of reeds. From the nearby mountain, they brought down rocks and fresh earth to fill in certain parts of the marsh, and build a solid path to where the earth was firm. They lived by hunting, the game round about being abundant. Little by little, they succeeded in making their island habitable, which visibly began to grow. Soon, they started to dig trenches to bring in water, in order to recover the land beside the swamp; this soon became fertile, and favourable for cultivation.

"In just a few years, the hard-working exiles succeeded in transforming their wretched village into a strong and prosperous town.

"In the meanwhile, their king died. One day, his successor found himself in difficulty with one of the tribes which occupied the region of Wardak. He found it necessary to hurry to the place as quickly as possible in order to punish those who refused to observe the laws of the land. The shortest way there would lead him by the marsh of Kabul. Either they had to cross it on small boats, which they did not possess, or else make their way around it at the cost of the fatigue of his men and a considerable loss of time. Consulting with his generals, the king pointed out the grand foundation on the other side, and suggested that they go there to collect information.

"His emissaries were received with suspicion; however, they quickly came to an agreement with the population, who promised their help on the condition they would be suitably reimbursed. Having had much experience of filling up certain parts of the marsh, they suggested the construction of a route by means of large pieces of rock, which would link them to the other bank. The emissaries approved of this idea. Immediately everyone started to work on the project, the population aided by the soldiers; and soon, a pathway had been improvised going right across the quagmire. The king generously compensated the people for their help, and furthermore bought a great deal of straw, which he spread over the bridge to prevent the horses from harming themselves on the sharp rocks.

"On the return from his punitive expedition, the king halted for several days beside the marsh to go hunting. Warmly congratulating the people of the Kharabat tribe for the great works they had accomplished, he pledged to help them improve their settlement and promised to buy a certain portion of land, which they were in a position to recover from the swamp.

"At length, the marsh diminished little by little, the cultivable land increased in size, and the town became fully developed, stretching on firm ground right to the edge of the mountains."

This story is also used to account for the name of Kabul, derived in this instance from the combination of the Persian *ka* (straw) and *pul* (bridge).

After AD 565, with the fall of Hephthalite rule in Afghanistan, Kabul began to grow in prominence. It became the capital of a petty kingdom ruled over by the Turki Shahi, a Buddhist dynasty descended from the rulers of the Kushan Empire. According to popular legend, it was at this time that the unfinished city walls, traces of which can still be seen today, were begun:

"The king of Kabul, Ratbil Shah, was heartily detested by his people: he had the reputation of being the most oppressive ruler of his age. One day, he came up with the idea of building a wall to encircle his capital; although he kept it with an iron grip, he wished to ensure its safety against invaders.

"The day when he wanted the construction to begin, he was obliged to press gang a large proportion of the city's population into working on the project without pay. No one dared to try and escape the laborious toil, as a strict watch was kept over the people, which would deal with them mercilessly. The lazy were the first to be eliminated; the feeble-bodied followed them down the same route. To punish those who were not able to work at a sufficient rate, the king had instituted this penalty: 'Anyone not able to perform their duty will be immured alive in the fortifications: their example will put muscles on those who are inclined to idleness.'

"And so, everyone worked under this threat without let-up. The cries of the unfortunate did not cease up until their deaths; the workers did not even stop to think about what was happening, seized as they were with fear. They worked at speed, and without respite.

"The wall was three-quarters finished when an important event interrupted the work. Amongst the hundreds of labourers, there was one young man who was about to get married. Terrified like all the others, not daring to seek a holiday, he was bitterly rebuked by his fiancée. She scorned him for his weakness, and point-blank refused to get married under such conditions. At the same time, stung with remorse, she conceived a most audacious plan.

"The next day, a young woman was seen climbing the Sher Darwaza; with a resolute air, she explained on arriving that she was replacing her brother who had suddenly fallen ill. Courageously, she worked away at her task without complaint. Meanwhile, her fiancé, terrified, was hidden at home, biting his nails and trying not to think of the peril in which he found himself. Regretting that he had made this deal with her, he dreaded to think of the situation she was now in, and held himself responsible for it; he was haunted by terrible sights

of the poor wretches who had been immured, and began as if he were already in their place, groaning and perishing for want of air.

"The days passed by; nothing happened to snap him out of his torpor. His valiant fiancée, still dedicated to the task which she had brought upon herself, would always complete the duties allotted to her. Then, one day at the building site it was announced that the king

View of Kabul, 1954 [W. Thesiger]

was about to make a visit. With rage in their hearts, the workers continued to toil feverishly. On appearing in the midst of his entourage, he made a minute inspection of what had been accomplished, considering it to be 'his own work', and not even caring to cast the slightest glance at the labourers. As he was doing so, his attention was arrested by a peculiar sight: a young woman who, at his approach, promptly threw on a veil to disguise her face. Calling her over, he demanded an explanation: 'Why do you veil yourself when I come near? I saw you just a moment ago uncovered, working with the men.'

"'These are not men', she replied.

"'What do you mean?' shouted the king angrily.

"'No,' she went on, 'because if they were men, they would never have put up with being treated like slaves. If they were men, they would have started to think of revolt. But I, who am only a poor little woman, I will not submit myself to the cruelty of your laws.' Matching her words with deeds, she grabbed a stone and hurled it at him. It struck him violently in the stomach, and he fell to the ground from the force of the blow.

Section of the walls of the Bala Hissar, 2004 [D. Grossart]

"A murmur of revolt went round the crowd. At that moment, a detachment of labourers flung themselves at the followers of the king, who were staring in astonishment at his body lying on the ground: they were too shocked to mount a defence, and were massacred where they stood by the delirious mob.

"News of this event was immediately known throughout the city, spreading rapidly through the streets and bazaars: the oppressor was dead, overthrown by his own people.

"In procession, the people made their way down the mountain, abandoning the walls which were never completed. All prepared to celebrate not just their liberation, but also the marriage of the young heroine who, through her courage and energy, had succeeded in sparking the revolt."

Despite his tyranny, the ruler of Kabul was justified in his fear of invasion. In AD 652, the Muslim governor of Basra, Abdullah ibn Amir, sent out an expedition under the general Abdul Rahman to capture further territory in the east. This army, after taking Zaranj and destroying a golden idol in the mountains of Ghor, advanced towards Kabul and captured its king. However, the occupation was brief and the force retreated on condition of an annual payment of tribute money. This was only sporadically forthcoming. As a result, the Arabs endeavoured to capture the city again in AD 698, but failed disastrously, having to pay a ransom for the release of their army. Further attempts were made in the following years by the Muslims to take Kabul under their control, but aside from the brief adherence of the king of Kabul to Islam for a short time after AD 815, little progress was made.

The city was eventually captured in AD 870 by a Muslim warrior named Yakub bin Lais, who founded the Saffarid Empire which ruled cities such as Herat, Kerman and Shiraz. However, his occupation of Kabul was brief. A short while before the city fell to the Saffarids, the Turki Shahi dynasty was ousted by the Hindu Shahi, which retook Kabul in 879. Although Islam at this time began to take a hold amongst the people, a combination of Buddhist and Hindu worship still predominated. An enduring monument to this era in Kabul's history is still to be seen in the area's many stupas (or topes)—reliquary mounds, which were raised for use in Buddhist devotion. The traveller William Moorcroft wrote of seeing a number of these around 1820:

"Here, at Bala Beg, we found a burj (stupa), but we were much disappointed by its appearance. It differed considerably from the structure we had before seen, and, though evidently ancient, was much less substantially built, its exterior being formed for the most part of small irregular pieces of slate piled together without cement. We did not pause long to examine this, as nine others were in sight, one of which, more to the westward, appeared to be larger than the rest. We therefore proceeded to it, and found that is was situated on a stony eminence at the base of the hills, on the opposite side of which lies the main source of the Kabul river, and nearly in a line with the garden of Chahar Bagh. It was of the same style and form as the others, but was larger, and more entire. It rose from a square platform, about 76 ft on each side, ornamented with pilasters, with simple bases but rather curious capitals: were it a tomb, it might be imagined that the centre of the latter represented rudely a skull, supported by two bones placed upright, and side by side, or by a bolster or half-cylinder, with its lower part divided into two. On each side of this were two large pointed leaves; and the whole supported two slabs, of which the lower was smaller than the upper one. A singular feature on this decoration was its being composed of small pieces of thin slate, cleverly joined together. A flight of steps had formerly led up the southern side of the platform, but nothing remained of them except a projecting pile of ruins. On the centre of the platform stood the building called by the people a burj. The lower half rose by perpendicular sides, and was surrounded by a cornice, whilst its centre was marked by a semicircular moulding, and the space between the moulding and the cornice was ornamented by a band of superficial niches, like false windows in miniature, arched at the top, and separated by small pilasters. The upper half of the building was smaller in diameter than the lower, and of a conical outline, but much of the top had fallen down. Intermixed with the brown slate of which it was chiefly constructed were pieces of quartz, or of some white stone, which at a distance gave to the exterior the effect of being chequered, or of a chess board. This, although the largest edifice on the spot, was smaller than the tope of Manikyala [in the Punjab], although evidently of the same character. Many of the smaller topes seemed to have been simply cylindrical towers surmounted by a dome. The greater part of them were in a very ruinous condition."

Examples of Buddhist remains in the vicinity of Kabul and Jalalabad,
from Ariana Antiqua, *1841 by H.H. Wilson. [Private Collection]*

The Arab scholar Ibn Hawqal made a brief reference to Kabul under Buddhist control in one of his geographical works, written around AD 977. In it, we see one of the first references to the pleasant climate of the city, which was to benefit it so much in later years:

> "Kabul is a town with a very strong castle, accessible only by one road: this is in the hands of the Mussulmans; but the town belongs to the infidel Indians. They say that a king is not properly qualified to govern, until he has been inaugurated at Kabul, however distant he may have been from it. Kabul is also, like Ghazni, a pass into Hindustan. The fruits of a warm climate, which abound at Balkh, are brought to Kabul, except dates, which do not grow at Balkh, where snow falls. Kabul is situated in a warm climate, but does not produce date trees."

Ten years after Ibn Hawqal's account is reputed to have been written, Kabul was lost for the final time to its Buddhist rulers. The Turkish general Subuktigin, founder of the Ghaznavid Empire, conquered the city and annexed it to his dominions.

Although the city had, by this time, been facing the threat of invasion for many years, it was nevertheless highly prosperous. Around 70 years after its fall, in the mid-11th century, the poet Asadi Tusi in his *Garshaspnameh*—an epic on the legendary King Garshasp, grandfather of Rustam—included a portrayal of the city's opulent Subahar Buddhist Monastery:

> "He saw, when he came to the Temple of Subahar, an edifice that seemed like the spring in its beauty. The pavement was of onyx; the walls, of marble; the gates of sculpted gold; the floor, of native silver; the stars were everywhere depicted; crenellations were ranged around the *iwan*; the sun, in the middle of the sign of Leo, was picked out in brilliant rubies and freshwater pearls; and in the vestibule, seated on a throne of gems, a golden idol as beautiful as the moon. Sometimes, this idol would raise its arms and open its hands, raising a cry; straightaway, its hands would fill with water, and it would rinse its face and its body. Anyone who drank a draught of this water would see in his dreams everything he desired. A sterile fruit tree, sprinkled with some of this water, would bear new fruit. And in front of this idol a host of girls would stand and

wait, their cheeks the colour of roses, devastating in their beauty; each was dressed in a veil of painted silk, a brocaded tunic bound up with a sash. All of them fanned the idol with peacock feathers whilst chanting praises to it. But these women, in their desire for paradise, would give way to the vile desires of men in return for money, some of which they would pay in tribute to the idol—such as happens nowadays in India.

"In this temple, Garshasp saw sixty shamans surrounding an old man who was carrying a candle. Garshasp asked him 'Who are these girls? What are they doing in front of the idol? And who is the idol?' 'It is our God,' he replied, 'and these girls keep the flies away from him.' Garshasp responded 'Why do you call this powerless idol a god, which doesn't talk, can't see, doesn't understand words, and cannot tell good and evil apart? It is only right to call the God of the universe that Being which knows and looks over all things, good and evil: by His command, the world appeared; it is he who at the beginning created all things that exist except Himself; time itself is at his behest; he frees from every need whomsoever he pleases. Such is the all-powerful God who truly exists— not like this one here, which hasn't any power even against a mosquito! How can this thing, which can't even stand up to a fly, keep others around it safe from evil?'"

The geographer Al-Idrisi gave a further and more extensive notice of Kabul after its fall to the Ghaznavids. Again, an emphasis is placed on its benign climate:

"Kabul is one of the towns of India, neighbouring on Turkharistan. It is a town of magnificent size and beautiful structure. On its mountains fine-quality aloes wood, coconut, and the black myrobalan of Kabul, called after it, are grown. Then the saffron bulb grows in its mountains, and it is also cultivated in its swamps. It is reaped here in large quantities, and exported to neighbouring countries. It is one of the choicest and most pleasant towns as far as the climate is concerned. It has a fortress which is distinguished for its entrenchment, and which has only one way to climb it. There is a large population of Muslims living in it. It has a suburb where Jewish infidels live.

"The indigo cultivated throughout the villages of the land of Kabul has no match in its abundance or in excellence in any of the surrounding countries. It is carried from here to every region of the world, and is known by its name.

"Again, from Kabul fine cloth made of cotton is also supplied. It is carried to China, and is exported into Khurasan. It is also carried there to Sind and its dependencies, and is used in great quantities there.

"In the mountains of Kabul there are iron mines. They are well known and very profitable. Their iron is extremely sharp and beautiful, when turned into swords."

Like all other cities in Afghanistan, Kabul suffered grievously at the hands of Genghis Khan. He attacked and pillaged the city around 1221, taking revenge for the resistance shown to his army by its chiefs. The scale of the devastation can be understood from a brief comment made by the traveller Ibn Battuta, who passed through Kabul in 1325: "This was in former times a great city, and on its site there is now a village inhabited by a tribe of Persians…" However, at length, it began to regain its former prominence. In 1398, it was captured by the Emperor Timur, who married a daughter of the governor, and later, in 1504, Kabul fell to Babur (sometimes spelt Baber). It would not be an overstatement to say that this date marked the beginning of one of the great love affairs of Asia—between the Emperor Babur and the city of Kabul. Being an avid gardener, Babur relates in his memoirs —the *Baburnama*—the profusion and excellence of the horticultural life to be found in and around the district:

"In the country of Kabul, there are hot and cold districts close to one another. In one day, a man may go out of the town of Kabul to where snow never falls, or he may go, in two sidereal hours, to where it never thaws, unless when the heats are such that it cannot possibly lie.

"Fruits of hot and cold climates are to be had in the district near the town. Amongst those of the cold climate, there are had in the town the grape, pomegranate, apricot, apple, quince, pear, peach, plum, jujube, almond, and walnut. I had cuttings of the *alu-balu* (a kind of plum) brought there and planted; they grew and have done well. Of fruits of the hot climate people bring into the town: from the Lamghanat, the orange, citron, and sugar cane; this last I had had brought and planted there; from Nijrau, they bring the *jil-ghuza* (pine seeds), and from the hill-tracts, much honey. Bee hives are in use; it is only from towards Ghazni that no honey comes.

"The rhubarb of the Kabul district is good, its quinces and plums very good, so too its *badrang* (a citron-like fruit); it grows an excellent grape, known as the water-grape. Kabul wines are heady, those of the Khwaja Khawand Sa'id hill-skirt being famous for their strength; at this time however I can only repeat the praise of others about them:

'*The flavour of the wine a drinker knows;*

What chance have sober men to know it?'

"Kabul is not fertile in grain; a four or five-fold return is reckoned good there; nor are its melons first-rate, but they are not altogether bad when grown from Khurasan seed.

"It has a very pleasant climate; if the world has another so pleasant, it is not known. Even in the heats, one cannot sleep at night without a fur-coat. Although the snow in most places lies deep in winter, the cold is not excessive; whereas in Samarkand and Tabriz, both, like Kabul, noted for their pleasant climate, the cold is extreme."

He also spoke with approbation of its commerce:

"Kabul is an excellent trading centre; if merchants went to Khiva or Rum (Istanbul), they might make no higher profit. Down to Kabul every year they come, 7, 8, or 10,000 horses, and up to it from Hindustan, come every year caravans of 10, 15, or 20,000 heads-of-houses, bringing slaves, white cloth, sugar-candy, refined and common sugars, and aromatic roots. Many a trader is not content with a profit of 300 or 400 percent. In Kabul can be had the products of Khurasan, Rum, Iraq, and China, while it is Hindustan's own market."

Babur would make frequent journeys to enjoy the pleasure gardens in the vicinity of Kabul, particularly those near the village of Istalif, 35 miles (56 km) to the north of the city. The following entry in the *Baburnama* records a journey he made from Istalif to Kabul in 1519:

"*August 12*—This day we dismounted at Istalif; a confection was eaten on that day.

August 13—On Saturday there was a wine-party at Istalif.

The village of Istalif, north of Kabul, was a favoured picnic spot of the Emperor Babur. 1972. [B. Woodburn]

August 14—Riding at dawn From Istalif, we crossed the space between it and the Sinjid valley. Near Khwaja Sih-yaran a great snake was killed as thick, it may be, as the fore-arm, and as long as the span of the arms. From its inside came out a slender snake, that seemed to have been just swallowed, every part of it being whole; it may have been a little shorter than the larger one. From inside this slenderer snake came out a little mouse; it too was whole, broken nowhere.

On reaching Khwaja Sih-yaran there was a wine-party. Today orders were written and despatched by Kich-kina, the night watch, to the Begs (lords) North of the Hindu Kush. Giving them a rendezvous and saying 'An army is being got to horse, take thought, and come to the rendezvous fixed.'

August 15—We rode out at dawn and ate a confection. At the infall of the Parvan water many fish were taken in the local way of casting a fish-drug into the water. Mir Shah Beg set food and water before us; we then rode on to Gulbahar.

At a wine-party held after the Evening Prayer, Darwish-i-Muhammad was present. Though a young man and a soldier, he had not yet committed the sin of wine, but was in obedience. Qutluq Khwaja Kukuldash had long before abandoned soldiering to become a darwish; moreover he was very old, his beard was quite white; nevertheless he took his share of wine at these parties. I said to Darwish-i-Muhammad, 'Qutluq Khwaja's beard shames you! He, a darwish and an old man, always drinks wine; you, a soldier, a young man, your beard quite black, never drink! What does it mean?' My custom being not to press wine on a non-drinker, with so much said, it all passed off as a joke; he was not pressed to drink.

August 17—Riding on Wednesday from Gul-i-bahar, we dismounted in Abun village, ate food, remounted, went to a summer-house in the orchards, and there dismounted. There was a wine-party after the midday prayer.

August 18—Riding on next day, we made the circuit of Khwaja Khawand Sa'id's tomb, went to China-fort, and there got on a raft. Just where the Panjshir water comes in, the raft struck the naze of a hill and began to sink. Rauh-dam, Tingri-quli and Mir Muhammad the raftsman were thrown into the water by the shock; Rauh-dam and Tingri-quli were got on the raft again; a china cup, a spoon and a tambour went into the water. Lower down, the raft struck again opposite the Sang-i-barida (the cut-stone), either on a branch in mid-stream or on a stake stuck in as a stop-water. Right over on his back went Shah Beg's Shah Hasan, clutching at Mirza Quli Kukuldash and making him fall too. Darwish-i-Muhammad was also thrown into the water. Mirza Quli went over in his own fashion! Just when he fell, he was cutting a melon which he had in his hand; as he went over, he stuck the knife into the mat of the raft. He swam on and got out of the water without coming on the raft again. Leaving it that night, we slept at raftsmen's houses. Darwish-i-Muhammad presented me with a seven-coloured cup exactly like the one lost in the water.

August 19—On Friday we rode away from the river's bank and dismounted below Aindiki on the skirt of Koh-i-Bacha where, with our own hands, we gathered plenty of toothpicks (thorns from bushes). Passing on, food was eaten at the houses of the Khwaja Khizr people. We rode on and at the Midday prayer dismounted in a village of Qutluq Khwaja's fief in Lamghan where he made ready a hasty meal; after partaking of this, we mounted and went to Kabul."

The practice of making excursions to pleasure gardens was restricted neither to the emperor, nor just to his time. Alexander Burnes recalls a similar journey from Kabul to Istalif he made just over 300 years later:

"We set out from Kabul in the morning, and halted at Kareez-i-Meer, about fifteen miles from which we could see, in the hazy distance, a vast vista of gardens extending for some thirty or forty miles in length, and half as broad, terminated by Hindu Kush itself, white with snow. Next day we reached Shukurdura, where there is a royal garden, but which is now in a state of decay. Our next march was to Kahdura, and thence to Istalif, the next great point of attraction. No written description can do justice to this lovely and delightful country. Throughout the whole of our route we had been lingering amidst beautiful orchards, the banks of which were clustered over with wild flowers and plants, many of them common to Europe, and which were also in profuse abundance along the margins of the innumerable brooks which intersect the valleys.

"The roads were shaded by noble and lofty walnut trees, which excluded the sun's rays, never powerless in this climate. Every hill with a southern aspect had a vineyard on it, and the raisins were spread out on the ground, and imparted a purple tinge to the hills. There were very few songsters however to enliven the scene, most of the feathered tribe having flown to a warmer climate. The coldness of the air, which had driven them away, was to us bracing and delightful, and only served to increase our enjoyment. I must not, however, speak in detail of this charming country, nor do the far-famed gardens of Istalif require any aid from me to establish their supremacy. We pitched our camp on one side of the valley, and directly opposite to us, at a distance of about a thousand yards, rose the town of Istalif in the form of a pyramid, terrace on terrace, the whole crowned with a shrine embosomed among wide-spreading plane-trees. Between us lay a deep and narrow valley, at the bottom of which was a clear, rapid, and musically-sounding brook, on both sides of which the valley was covered with the richest orchards and vineyards. Looking down this stream, the dell gradually opens out, and presents to they eye a vast plain, rich in trees and verdure, and dotted over with innumerable turreted forts: beyond all this, rocky mountains are seen with the fresh snow of yesterday on them; and over these again tower the eternal snow—clad summits of Hindu Kush. The scene was sublimely grand as it was beautiful and enchanting. The yellow autumnal leaves rustled in the breeze, and the crystal waters rushed in their rapid course over craggy rocks with a noise which reached the summit of the valley. Thessalian Tempe could never have more delighted the eyes of an Ionian, than did Istalif please Bœotian Britons. The people illuminated their town in the evening, in honour of their visitors. It had a pretty effect, but the beauties of art could not in our opinion compete with those of nature. Not so with our escort; they declared that Istalif had at all times been the abode of pleasure, and that, without wine, not only would the illumination lose its value, but nature herself would be worth nothing. We accordingly sent a few bottles of wine, to which they did the amplest justice, although the 'Moohtussib', a chief constable of Kabul, was of the party. On the following day I taxed him with this departure from the rules of his sect. He bore my bantering with great equanimity, and replied with mock heroic dignity, 'Who, my lord, suspects me,—me, the Moohtussib—of indulging in wine? My duty is to reform the morals of others.'"

Although he was the founder of the Moghul Dynasty of India, Babur had little affection for the country, and commanded that on his death he be brought back

to his beloved Kabul for burial. Burnes, on his first visit to the city, made haste to see the emperor's tomb:

"I lost no time in making excursions near Kabul, and chose the earliest opportunity to visit the tomb of the Emperor Baber, which is about a mile from the city, and situated in the sweetest spot of the neighbourhood. The grave is marked by two erect slabs of white marble; and, as is common in the East, the different letters of a part of the inscription

The tombstone of Babur, with the headstone erected by the Moghul Emperor Jahangir in the 17th century. [B. Woodburn]

The tomb of Babur, 1972 [B. Woodburn]

indicate the number of the year of the Hegira in which the Emperor died. The device in the present instance seems to me happy: 'When in heaven, Roozvan asked the date of his death. I told him that heaven is the eternal abode of Baber Badshah.' He died in the year 1530. Near the Emperor, many of his wives and children have been interred; and the garden, which is small, has been once surrounded by a wall of marble. A running and clear stream yet waters the fragrant flowers of this cemetery, which is the great holiday resort of the people of Kabul. In front of the grave, there is a small but exquisite mosque of marble; and an inscription upon it sets forth that it was built in the year 1610, by order of the Emperor Shah Jehan, after defeating Mahommed Nuzur Khan in Balkh, and Badakhshan, 'that poor Mahommedans might here offer up their prayers.' It is pleasing to see the tomb of so great a man as Baber honoured by his posterity.

"There is a noble prospect from the hill which overlooks Baber's tomb, and a summer house has been erected upon it by Shah Zeman (third King of Afghanistan), from which it may be admired. If my reader can imagine a plain, about 20 miles in circumference, laid out with gardens and fields in pleasing irregularity, intersected by three rivulets, which wind through it by a serpentine

course, and wash innumerable little forts and villages, he will have before him
one of the meadows of Kabul. To the north lie the hills of Pughman, covered
half way down with snow, and separated from the eye by a sheet of richest
verdure. On the other side, the mountains, which are bleak and rocky, mark
the hunting preserves of the kings; and the gardens of this city, so celebrated
for fruit, lie beneath, the water being conducted to them with great ingenuity.
I do not wonder at the hearts of the people being captivated by the landscape,
and of Baber's admiration; for, in his own words, 'its verdure and flowers
render Kabul, in spring, a heaven.'"

Above the entrance to the mosque in the cemetery, Peter Levi recorded this
inscription:

"Only this mosque of beauty, this temple of nobility, constructed for the prayer
of saints and the epiphany of cherubs, was fit to stand in so venerable a sanctuary
as this highway of archangels, this theatre of Heaven, the light garden of the
God-forgiven angel king whose rest is in the garden of Heaven, Zahiruddin
Muhammad Baber the Conqueror…"

On the death in 1773 of Ahmad Shah Durrani, the first King of the Afghan
Empire, the capital was moved from Kandahar to Kabul. With this change, and the
onset of British dominance in India in the 19th century, the volume of Western
visitors to the city began to increase. Charles Masson described the fashion in which
the travellers were received by the people of Kabul, and the co-existence of
religions therein:

"There are few places where a stranger so soon feels himself at home, and
becomes familiar with all classes, as at Kabul. There can be none where all
classes so much respect his claims to civility, and so much exert themselves to
promote his satisfaction and amusement. He must not be unhappy. To avow
himself so, would be, he is told, a reproach on the hospitality of his hosts and
entertainers. I had not been a month in Kabul before I had become acquainted
with I know not how many people; had become a visitor at their houses, a
member of their social parties. No holiday occurred that did not bring me a
summons to attend some family circle, in some one of the many gardens of the
city. The stranger guest will not fail to be astonished at the attentions paid to
him on such occasions. It seems as if the entertainment had been expressly

designed for him, and that the company had no other object than to contribute to his gratification. The most rigid mind must admire such politeness, and the feelings which prompt its exhibition.

"I was accustomed to stroll freely about the city and its immediate neighbourhood, and was never interrupted, or noticed offensively, but on one day, when a cap I wore, rather than myself, elicited some ill-feeling. I had, by chance, left my house with a Persian cap on my head, in lieu of the usual lunghi (turban). I have seen many changes in Kabul, and do not know what may yet come to pass there, but I cannot forget that the sight of a Persian cap would, in 1832, have brought insult upon the wearer.

"It is a matter of agreeable surprise to any one acquainted with the Mahomedans of India, Persia, and Turkey, and with their religious prejudices and antipathies, to find that the people of Kabul are entirely free from them. In most countries, few Mahomedans will eat with a Christian; to salute him, even in error, is deemed unfortunate, and he is looked upon as unclean. Here none of these difficulties exist. The Christian is respectfully called a 'kitabi,' or 'one of the book.' The dissolute Vizier Fateh Khan, when, occasionally, an Armenian Christian presented himself, desiring to become a convert to Islam, was wont to inquire what he had found deficient in his own religion that he wished to change it? And would remark, that persons who possessed a book, and would adopt a new faith, were scoundrels, actuated by love of gain, or other interested motive…

"Living with the Armenians of the city, I witnessed every day the terms of equality on which they dwelt amongst their Mahomedan neighbours. The Armenian followed the Mahomedan corpse to its place of burial; the Mahomedan showed the same mark of respect to the deceased of the Armenian community. They mutually attended each others' weddings, and participated in the little matters which spring up in society. The Armenian presented gifts on Id Noh Roz, or the Mahomedan New Year's Day; he received them on his own Christmas day. If it happened that a Mahomedan had married an Armenian female who was lost to the Church of the Cross, I found that the Armenians had retaliated, and brought Mahomedan females into their families, and inducted them into their faith. An Armenian, in conversation with the present head of the Wais family said, that some person had called him a Kafir or infidel. The reply was, 'he that calls you a Kafir is a Kafir himself.'"

A Kebab Shop in Kabul, manned by a Hazara proprietor, 1841.
This is possibly the first ever pictorial representation of a kebab shop. [Bodleian]

Although much of the goodwill shown by the people of Kabul towards foreigners and the British in particular was needlessly squandered in the First and Second Afghan Wars, a certain rapprochement took place towards the end of the century under the new king, Amir Abdur Rahman. At this time, a British doctor, John Gray, was sent as part of a political mission to Kabul. His memoirs, *At the Court of the Amir*, provide us with a vivid and well-observed account of Afghan life. Here he gives a panoramic description of the various goods and tradesmen in the shops and bazaars around Kabul:

"Some parts of the bazaars are reserved for the sale or manufacture of particular articles. There is, for instance, the shoe bazaar. This is in the street leading from the wooden bridge south. The Afghan shoes are of heavy make, are sewn with strips of leather, and have the pointed toe turned upwards. Some are elaborately embroidered with gold. The women's shoes or slippers are generally green in colour, and are made with a high heel. They are almost sandals, having an upper only at the toe. They are awkward things to walk in, I have noticed, for they drop at the heel at every step. The native shoes are those most on show, but one can buy English boots of all kinds, from the elaborate patent leather of Northampton to the three-and-sixpenny army boot. There are also long Russian boots made of beautifully soft leather: these are the fashion among the highest class; and a cheaper Turkoman boot of similar shape with a high heel that cavalry soldiers who can afford luxury invest it. A shopkeeper is, however, none too ready to show you his best goods. He does not exhibit them in the shop, for the Government officials have a way of buying anything that takes their fancy at their own price.

"I noticed in the boot bazaar that in the three-foot space under the floor of the shop the poorer men, the cobblers, did their business. There was just room to sit, and there the cobbler sat stitching, with his nose on a level with the knees of the passers by. A customer with a shoe to mend squats down beside him and gives his orders. Cobblers who can't afford to rent even such a 'shop' as this, sit by the road-side in the shade of a wall or a tree and carry on their business.

"There is a copper bazaar. Though copper is found in Afghanistan, most of that used comes from India. This bazaar is in the street running east though the middle of the city. Here, there is shop after shop of men hammering out copper into the different shaped utensils: the long necked vase for the chillim, or hubble-bubble pipe: bowls and pots for cooking kettles: water vases with long neck and handle and tapering curved spout. The shapes are all those made by their fathers and forefathers; there is no new design invented. The pots used for cooking are tinned over inside and out. Supposing the tin has worn off your cooking pots, you send to the bazaar for one of these men. It is interesting to watch how he sets to work.

"He brings a pair of hand-bellows with him and a stick of tin. Settling himself on the ground in the garden he digs a shallow hole six or seven inches across. This is to be his furnace. From it he leads a little trench about six inches long, which he covers over with clay, placing his finger in the trench as he moulds each piece of clay over it. Thus he has a pipe leading to his furnace. The nozzle of his bellows is fitted to the distal end of the pipe. He begs a little lighted charcoal from the cook with which to start his 'furnace,' piles it over with black charcoal, blows his bellows, and soon has what fire he wants. A small boy with him having cleaned the pots with mud and sand, he places the first one, supported on three stones, over his furnace. When it is at the proper heat he rubs it round with a rag smeared with wood ashes, touches it with the stick of tin, then rubs it round again with his wood ashes, and the pot is tinned. If you are watching him he may make it extra superfine with another touch of tin and another rub with the wood ashes, and so he goes on till he has finished them all.

"Describing the way that the 'furnace' is made reminds me that I have seen men prepare an impromptu tobacco pipe the same way. The principle is exactly the same, only instead of blowing air through the pipe they suck the smoke from the tobacco which they have lit with a match. To lie on your face on the ground in order to get a smoke seems rather excessive, but if a man has tobacco, a match, and cannot get a pipe, this is one way out of the difficulty. I have also seen a soldier use his bayonet for a pipe. He filled the cylindrical part that fits on the muzzle of the rifle with tobacco, and having put a lighted match on the top, he fitted his hands round the lower end and sucked the smoke between them. Most Afghans are inveterate smokers. The tobacco they smoke is not the American tobacco that we have. It grows in Kabul, Kandahar, Herat, and many parts of Afghanistan, but the best comes from Persia. The leaf is paler, apparently uncured and is not pressed, nor cut, but simply broken up. I have smoked it, but it is very hot in a short pipe. It smokes best in the chillim.

The Amir himself when he smokes, which is not often, generally has a Turkish cigarette. The eldest Prince, Habibullah, smokes cigars from India. Prince Usuf, the Amir's uncle, one of the younger sons of Amir Dost Mohammed, smokes American birdseye tobacco. He is a courtly old gentleman, dresses exceedingly well, and is of the bluest of the blue blood, and it strikes one as very incongruous to see him puffing away at a short clay pipe; he never smokes anything else.

"In the tea-drinking shops you see a large samovar, about three feet high, in one corner, where water is kept boiling hot by the glowing charcoal in the centre pipe. Men drop in and seat themselves, cross-legged, for a chat and a cup of tea. The shops will hold some three or four. The Afghans like their tea very hot, weak, very sweet, and flavoured with cardamoms, which are put unpowdered into the teapot. They pay a pice, that is a little less than a farthing, for a cup of tea. If a man has some tea with him, and he often has, he can always send to one of these shops for a teapot and hot water. He pays a price for it. There is also a preparation they call 'kaimagh-chai,' but this is comparatively expensive, and is drunk only at festivals or times of rejoicing. It is a mixture of tea, sugar, cream, soda, and cardamoms. It is thick, curdy, pink, and very sweet—not at all bad to taste, but very rich. The teapots, cups, and saucers in use are generally from Russia. Some of the richer men have them from China or Japan.

"Besides the tea-drinking shops there are the eating-houses. These have no marble-topped tables or velvet coloured chairs. The shop is the same as any other shop, except that it looks rather dirtier, probably from the amount of fat or oil used in the cooking. The customer carries his lunch away with him, or stands outside to eat it. The space inside the shop is taken up by the cook and the cooking pots. They sell kabobs—little cubes of meat skewered on a long stick and grilled over charcoal. A stick of kabobs, with some bread, is uncommonly good if you are hungry; you tear the meat off with your fingers. They have also meat, finely minced and mixed with fat, which they squeeze in their hand round a thin stick and cook over charcoal. It looks rather like sausage; I don't know what it is called. They use any kind of meat for this—mutton—or, failing that, the flesh of the camel or horse that age or infirmity has rendered unfit for further service. There are many kinds of pilau too. Rice, boiled skilfully till every grain is soft without being soppy, is piled over the meat, stewed to such tenderness that you can easily tear a piece off with the fingers. There are chicken pilau, mutton pilau, sweet pilau with raisins in it, and so on. Kourma is another dish—meat stewed in small pieces and eaten with stewed fruit.

"For his pudding the Afghan goes to another shop, the confectioner's. Here, there are sweets of many kinds: sugared almonds, 'cocoa-nut ice,' sweets made in the shape of rings, sticks, animals, or men; gingerbread, soft puddings made of Indian corn, much sweetened. In the summer different kinds of iced sherbet, lemon, orange, or rose are sold in the street.

"In the bread shop, the baker squatting on the floor kneads out the dough into large flat cakes and claps it in his oven. The oven is a large clay jar about three feet across and three feet deep in diameter. This is buried beneath the shop, the mouth being level with the floor, and is packed round with earth. It is heated by making a fire inside. When the heat is sufficient, and the fire has burnt out, the baker puts his hand in the mouth and flaps the flat doughy cake against the wall of the oven, where it sticks. When baked, it generally brings away some grains of charcoal or grit with it. You pay two pice (a little less than a halfpenny) for a cake of bread a foot and a-half long, a foot wide, and an inch thick. The Afghans are very particular about eating their bread hot, and don't care to eat it cold unless they are on a journey. One of their proverbs is, 'Hot bread and cold water are the bounteous gifts of God.'"

Kabul was later to become internationally renowned for a sight other than its bazaars. The wife of an American official resident in Kabul in the late 1960s, Kathleen Trautman, describes, in *Spies Behind the Pillars*, her first encounter with a hippie:

"I was getting into our car when he approached me from behind and tapped me on the shoulder. He was young, with curly golden hair that fell in ringlets to his shoulders, and his eyes were aesthetic-looking, an almost transparent blue. He looked rather like the picture of Jesus Christ that had hung on the wall of my Methodist Sunday School classroom in Wichita. He was barefoot and dressed in rags.

'Are you rich, lady?' he asked me.

I didn't know how to answer his question. I hadn't been in church in years, but the parable of Jesus disguised as a stranger crossed my mind and I felt uncomfortable.

'Why do you ask?' I finally replied.

He looked at me with amusement. 'I'm asking for a handout, lady.'

There are few beggars in Kabul, because Afghans take care of their own. Only once had I ever given money to a beggar, and that was with Abdul, when we had gone to the bazaars to shop. A woman had stuck her head in our car window and said her child was sick and she needed money for medicine. I gave her some coins, but she hurled them on the ground, furious, and burst into angry talk. Abdul explained that I had not given her enough money to buy the necessary medicine. When I explained to him that the coins were all the change I had, he reminded me of the Oriental adage which says that once you give to a beggar he is your responsibility for life. As we drove away I saw the woman pick up the scattered coins from the dust. Interestingly enough, if Abdul was with me when someone asked for money, he often reached into his own pocket and dropped a coin in the outstretched hand, contradicting his own philosophy.

The young man with the golden hair standing by our car was not an Afghan, but an American from the large colony of Western hippies living in Kabul. They were very much in evidence on the streets, but this was the first time I had ever been approached by one for money.

'No, I'm not rich and I guess I'm sorry that I'm not,' I answered frankly. 'Do you need money very badly?'

He looked at me and laughed. 'Right now, yes. Tomorrow, I don't know. My parents financed my trip here and my dad would pay my way back home, I guess, if I asked him.'

He didn't seem angry that I had deflected his request, and he gave me a warm smile as he continued on down the street. I stood there wishing I had asked him where home was and how long he'd been gone and who his parents were and if they wondered how he was.

Counsellor officers at the various embassies were full of pitiful stories—of letters received from anxious parents, sometimes with a photo enclosed, asking for any information about a missing son or daughter.

It had been a revelation to me that hippies were not an American invention and that, indeed, much of the youth of the world was in revolt. Those in Kabul came from everywhere – nations with socialized governments, like Sweden; nations with dictators, like Spain; democratic countries, like the USA and England. They didn't seem to have any common background in nationality, religion, or economics; just their age, but perhaps that was enough. One thing that all these young people shared, whether Russian, Chinese, or Western, was the fact that they wanted nothing to do with our generation.

The hippie colony in Kabul was a worry to everyone concerned. The Afghan government was exasperated with them, and rightfully. In a nation of little resources, where everyone works extremely hard to care for his own, the authorities were suddenly swamped by the sons and daughters of richer nations around the world. The kids came to extol the beauty and poetry of poverty and to enjoy the simple life. Many of them had discovered Kabul on their way to an international gathering of hippies in Kathmandu, Nepal, in 1966, liked it, and had simply returned when the hippie festival was over. One of Kabul's draws was that hashish could be purchased for less than ten cents a day.

Many got to begging on the streets and found that the Afghans, although poor themselves, were warmly hospitable and often would take them into their homes as a gesture of friendship. But some of the kids stayed on as parasites, living off the good-heartedness of their hosts. While some of the boys begged, some of the girls had turned to prostitution to earn money. The Afghan tourist officials were in a dilemma as to what to do with them.

After the first bloom of the simple life had worn off and the winter and cold of poverty had set in, the bearded boys and long-haired girls would flood the embassies of the very establishments they had scorned and run away from. Many were sick and suffering from malnutrition or racked with dysentery or diseases more serious, and begging for funds to fly back home."

A little while before this inundation, the American travel writer Lowell Thomas visited Kabul. Faced with the prospect of an audience with the king, Amanullah Khan, whilst knowing little of Afghan history, he sought advice from a venerable Sufi mystic resident in the city. Seated together in the gardens by the mausoleum of Babur, Thomas heard from him an account of Afghanistan's past:

"My informant was Mirza Shahabuddin Khan, a learned Kizilbash related to the royal family of Khiva. We sat under a deodar on thick Kerman rugs while a young slave from Kafiristan stood behind us with a cow-tail whisk to keep the midges away. As if by magic a brass tray appeared with little cups of Persian sherbet and packets of American cigarettes, containing pictures of 'movie' stars. Fortunately we could dispense with an interpreter, since Shahabuddin spoke French.

"'Soon,' he was saying, 'you will be received by his Majesty. And what do you know of our hopes and difficulties—and the King's dangers? You come and you go so quickly; there is no time for understanding in your country. Yet I am told that you write.'

"'True, Mirza Sahib, I write, and therefore I ask questions. I would hear the truth from your lips.'

"'We might hold converse for years in this garden. But would it be the truth? Who knows but that history is lies? We in the East have the ancient philosophy of those who lived here in the Cradle of Mankind uncounted ages ago. Under many names and forms it has always been the creed of the One God. That is more than your tales in lesson-books. But you want names and forms; that is what the West always wants. I will tell you what I know of them.

"'Tradition has it that Zoroaster, the prophet of your modern Parsis, lived in Balkh, in Afghan Turkestan. More than two and a half centuries later—and what is time but a breath of Allah?—soldiers of the great Alexander ravished the women of this valley and left a seal of beauty behind them in the blue eyes that some of us have to this day. Who can tell what else is between and behind these eyes?'

"Mirza Shahabuddin stopped and was lost in thought. He was a Sufi and no doubt versed in mystical tenets. 'The beautiful Roxana, wife of Alexander,' he continued, 'came from the North of my country. Her form was slender as yonder cypress, and her two eyes made the Pleiades weep with envy. But she was a pagan, of course, and indeed for long centuries after the Prophet Isa [Jesus], whose name be blessed, the land was under the rule of idolatrous or Buddhist kings. But after Mohammed, our holy prophet, to whom be dominion, power, and glory, had rested from his earthly labours, some Arabs in the caliphate of Moawiya came to these mountains. For another two centuries the land was divided between the followers of the Prophet of Islam, the Buddha, and the black cults of ancient faiths. But finally Yakub the Ghazi conquered Ghazni and Kabul and made the idolaters bend the knee of humility and place the forehead of subjection upon the carpet of true religion.'

"'When was it that you were all converted to Islam?'

"Mirza Shahabuddin spread his hands with a nescient gesture. 'A thousand or two thousand years ago. Your Western dates are nothing to me,' he replied.

"While he motioned to his slave-boy to put another cigarette into his long amber holder and light it for him, I made a note. Later I found it was AD 870 that Yakub conquered Afghanistan. Sultan Mahmud ascended the throne of Ghazni AD 997.

"Mirza Shahabuddin puffed and thought. 'Whenever it was, there came a time when we were all warriors of the One God, and it was then that our glorious days arrived. Under Mahmud, a slave like the one behind us—but uglier, for he was pocked—our soldiers conquered all Hindustan from here to the navel of the world in the Himalaya and to the Gujarat peninsula. Then came Timur and Baber, Akbar, Jahangir, and Shah Jahan, whose names are stars in the sky of story. It was in the reign of Jahangir that the park at Nimlah was laid out by Nur Jahan, his empress. Nur Jahan was an Afghan girl. If you want to see what our girls are like, look at the miniatures of her.'

"'Mirza Sahib,' I laughed, 'I should prefer to look on flesh and blood. But since I may not, tell me about her.'

"'She was a foundling who rose to be queen. She was born on the caravan route between Kabul and Peshawar and abandoned by her parents; for a girl baby was of no value to them in their quest for fortune at Akbar's court. But a rich merchant found her and carried her to Lahore. Fifteen years later she made her mark there by attracting the notice of the young Prince Jahangir. After many adventures she married him and became empress of Afghanistan and India. She is the only queen of Islam whose signature is on documents of state. During her reign the English came.'

"There was an interlude here while the slave-boy brought a Kabuli muskmelon such as Baber wrote of regretfully from the plains of India.

"'There is a woman behind every trouble,' I prompted my Kizilbash historian.

"'It was a servant of Nur Jahan who gave the British their foothold,' he said. 'She was a favourite maid of the empress. As she was going up-stairs one night, her skirts took fire from an oil-cresset. Being badly burned and near death, she was permitted to have the services of a British doctor who happened to be at the court. He prescribed philtres of such marvellous power that she was cured. As a reward, instead of asking for a bag of gold or a flagon of attar of roses, he stipulated that his country should be granted certain trading privileges on the Hugli River. Thus it was that you came to Kabul.'

"'But I am an American.'

"'There is no difference,' said Mirza Shahabuddin. 'You would fill our country with machines and smoke, make slaves equal to their masters, and destroy true religion. Not you, my friend, but the destiny behind you.

"'After the Great Moghuls passed their zenith with Aurangzeb, the story of my country is written in the blood of murdered kings. One after another they died of knife, poison, or bullet. But always in our hills we have demanded that we should rule ourselves.

"'Seventy-five years ago the British sent an embassy here. We murdered them all, carried the ambassadors head through the street, and hung his body in the bazaar. Of the army that was with him—a thousand white men, four thousand Indians, and ten thousand camp-followers—one single and solitary man reached Peshawar alive. Later, Great Britain sent us another ambassador, and him we also killed, along with his three British officers and seventy-five men of his escort. Of course Great Britain made war with us, but she accomplished nothing—just wasted men and money. Finally, about fifty springs ago, as nearly as I can remember, Abdur Rahman, a grandson of the great Amir Dost Mohammed, came down from Turkestan and took the Emirate. Between Russia, Persia, and Great Britain, our ruler guided his footsteps sternly by the Light of Divine Providence.

Well can I remember him, a very king among men, a pillar of the faith and a sun of wisdom.

Truck picture, Kabul, 1971 [Y. Crowe]

"'Next came his son, Habibullah Khan, who mounted the throne in peace, for the first time in our history—so auspicious was the rule of his father. Habibullah went down to India about twenty years ago and met Lord Curzon and Lord Kitchener. Of the latter he often spoke with admiration. At this great man's hands he received initiation into your Masonic mysteries. The degrees, which take months for the initiate to pass, as do our Sufi ceremonies, were conferred on our Amir by royal dispensation in the course of a single night. He was a friend of the English, but no Englishman came to Kabul except by his invitation. During the World War he stood foot to foot and knee to knee with Great Britain. Outwardly he did many things to please the missions from Germany and Turkey that came to us during the fighting. But a trusted messenger had meanwhile gone to Delhi to clasp the viceroy's hand in secret amity.

"'These things happened in my lifetime,' concluded the Kizilbash, simply.

"'But what of today?' I asked. 'For tomorrow I may meet his Majesty.'

"'Today, ah, if you ask an Afghan about today, he will talk about the scenery. And why not? Look at the stars, my friends. In their light, so calm and clear and cold, of what import are our petty plots and counterplots? Better it is to turn our thoughts to prayer and to the Most High, the Giver of Light.'

"With that Mirza Shahabuddin Khan, the Kizilbash, rose and went to the fountain, kicked the slippers off his feet, rinsed hands and feet and mouth, and, with the suppleness born of long practice and devotion, performed the two-bow prayer with his face toward Mecca. As the mountains rising above Kabul to the west threw the long shadows of twilight across the valley, we left the garden together."

KABUL: TRAVEL INFORMATION

POSTCARDS

You will probably want to send lots of postcards to emphasise the bragging rights you have obtained in coming here. The best selection in town is at the Shah M Book Store and they will also stamp them and post them. If you want to post them yourself—and as an experience it is quite fun—go to the central post office near the Ministry of Communications, near Pushtunistan Square. Use this one rather than the sub post offices which are said to be less reliable. But my experience of the Afghan postal system in sending letters abroad has been good. The woman there will stick the stamps on and frank them in front of you, expertly gumming the stamps on a water-soaked sponge and a stringendo rhythmic bang bang bang as she stamps them.

10 TOP GUEST HOUSES

This is a sector that is developing rapidly. The huge influx of aid workers, election monitors and journalists combined with the sublime awfulness of the Intercontinental in 2002 created a market opportunity for comfortable accommodation with good food. The following information specifies whether a guest house has a generator: the erratic nature of the Kabul electricity supply makes this a requirement for guests using computers.

1. GANDAMACK LODGE

This gap in the market was first spotted and exploited by Peter Jouvenal, the legendary cameraman who "liberated" Kabul with John Simpson, and his Gandamack Lodge (named after a bloody British defeat in the First Afghan War from which the Rugby fag-roaster Flashman VC effected a particularly cowardly escape and from which he took the name of his country seat[1]). Flashman's face, with fine period mutton-chop whiskers, decorates the hotel's china and writing paper. It is probably the best guest house in Kabul and oozes class.

Peter found the house because bin Laden's wife-number-four lived here and he was searching for incriminating papers. The restaurant's cooks—about to be trained by a one-star Michelin chef – serve European food; the menu proclaims the place to be a "rice-free zone", and to anyone who has spent long periods of time in the country eating nothing but rice and tough mutton, this is very welcome. Peter once spent a month in the interior on assignment during the jihad and ate nothing but rice. Hence the policy, once memorably denounced by a lefty American guest as "neo-colonial".

Peter Jouvenal is the manager. Email gandamacklodge@yahoo.com The hotel has 21 rooms including four doubles. Five rooms have ensuite bathrooms and the other rooms share five bathrooms. Rooms cost from $55 to $130 including full English breakfast and unlimited internet access in each room. Lunch $10, dinner $15. Laundry and two generators. Pub called Navy and Cricket Club for guests and members. It is in Passport Lane near the Indian Embassy.

2. KABUL LODGE

Running the Gandamack a close second is the Kabul Lodge, run by staff from the Gandamack. The Manager is Haidar Jailani, owner of three guest houses in Kabul.. There are 14 rooms in main lodge and 16 in the other two lodges. Ten rooms in the main lodge have ensuite bathrooms. Rooms cost from $40 to $120. Lunch is about $6 and dinner $15. A laundry service is offered. The hotel has its own generator and internet access; television and fridge in every room. The food is excellent and makes it worth a visit just for dinner. It also has a swimming pool that, in 2005, will probably be the only filtered one in Kabul (the rest have to be drained and refilled every couple of days). Tel. 0792 82643 and 0702 82643;

website: www.kabullodge.com and email: kabullodge25@yahoo.ca

3. SERENA HOTEL

The Serena, on Faruj Gah Street, will certainly challenge the Intercontinental as Kabul's leading hotel. It is more centrally positioned, and has been built with help from the Aga Khan Development Network.

4. KABUL INN

Rather nice vine trellising in the garden and bright hangings on the wall. This inn has 29 double rooms, which can be charged as single-occupancy. All but three rooms have bathrooms ensuite. Single room is $58 per night; double $78, including breakfast. Ten per cent government tax should be added to these figures. Suites with sitting room and bath are $90 per night. Restaurant serves English and Italian food—steak, tuna sandwich and beef shashlik and Kabuli pillau as a nod to Afghan cuisine. Generator ensures continuous power. Internet broadband access in a business centre with 6 computers.

5. PARK PLACE

A modern building with two-storey green marble-faced buildings round a very green central quad. It is a proper hotel rather than a guest house with a certain impersonality, which the best guest houses lack. Park Place has 70 rooms: single $55, double $85, includes breakfast and laundry. Lunch not served. Dinner $6; internet connection $7 per day; business centre $3 per hour. All rooms have bathroom ensuite. Three suites at $100 per night with kitchen for long-term guests. The attractive quad has well-kept grass and trees.

6. DAS DEUTSCHER HOF

Teutonic and depressing interior design with sentimental pictures, including one of a snow covered and gemutlich Deutsche Hof in Tabarz, Germany. Nice German bar with imported German beer. Definitely a place to get drunk in, teutonically, sentimentally, depressively. On Thursday nights in the summer there are "eat as much as you can" barbecues in the garden. 9 double rooms 70-90 Euros. Lunch and dinner for 10–15 Euros. Business centre where computers can be plugged in.

address: Kalah Fatullah, Street 3, House 60
website: www.deutscher-hof-kabul.de
mobile tel. 0702 322582/0793 322583

7. ASSA GUEST HOUSES

Assa has two guest houses under the same management. Number 1 is off Flower Street; number 2 nearby. Number 1 has a swimming pool, internet access in all rooms and prices are $50 for a single and $80 for a double.

mobile tel. 0702 74364

satellite tel. 88 216 211 31509

email: assa_kabul@hotmail.com

8. MUSTAFA HOTEL

Turned into a legend by Christina Lamb, Wais Faizi—the Fonz of Kabul—presides over a hotel with over 100 rooms. Prices vary from $10 to $100 a night. The Fonz can fix practically anything, from a drink to prescription drugs to heli-skiing in Bamiyan. Every Thursday evening there is a barbecue on the roof terrace. For the extraordinary ambience of its bar, see separate section.

mobile tel. 0702 76021

email: Mustafa_hotel@hotmail.com

Website: www.mustafahotel.com

Shah M, *the Bookseller of Kabul,*
with Peter Lowes, 2004 [B. Jenks]

9. THE INTERCONTINENTAL

In 2002 this was definitely the worst hotel in the world. After a number of disagreements with the manager over what he viewed as a decadent colonialist desire for cold water to wash in, I told him I was going to write an article about him called 'The Worst Hotel in the World.' I did, even if it was only in the *Literary Review*, and have not been able to visit since. In those days the lifts didn't work and I had to get to my room through the kitchen. I didn't mind there being no hot water but I felt that no cold water at $65 a night was too much. When I wanted to use the swimming pool, I was told I couldn't because two guests had recently drowned in it. It had an excellent bookshop (owned by Mr Shah, the famous Bookseller of Kabul), which sold Tajik vodka that gave one a particularly nasty form of hangover, like a new and even more unpleasant version of consciousness. Journalists stayed there because it was expensive and this, they felt, punished their employers for their discomfort.

But people tell me that the hotel has now been revamped for $10 million, the management completely changed and is perfectly acceptable, though expensive.

It has 200 rooms from $80 to $130, high-speed internet cafe, internet with high-speed centre in the basement, air conditioning and swimming pool. The Friday Brunch is very popular and the Talk of the Town cafe is probably Kabul's best.

Satellite tel. (873) 761 469690

10. The Afghan Garden

This is unique, a designer hotel in Kabul. The interior designer of this fabulous building is the owner of Nomad (see Shopping) and his rugs on the walls give a feeling of Liberty's in Kabul. The proprietor is a remarkable young woman, Nadene Ghouri.

address: Shahshdarak, next to Danish Demining Group
mobile tel. 07930 4635, 0702 96878
email: nadeneghouri@hotmail.com

The Afghan Garden also has a second branch, with 19 rooms, all with ensuite bathrooms with Western toilets. Price per room is $70 per day, including breakfast and dinner, with reductions on long-term stays. Its only disadvantage is that there is no lunch or dinner on Fridays.

tel. 0700 25446
email: nadeneghouri@hotmail.com

RESTAURANTS AND BARS

Restaurants and bars are opening rapidly in Kabul to cater for the enormous contingent of European expatriates, and this snapshot will date quickly. For up-to-the-minute information, see www.kabulguide.net, the online version of the excellent Bradt guide to Kabul. The following listing was compiled from information supplied by *Kabul Scene* magazine's reviewers.

1. The Mustafa is the drinking parlour preferred by Kabul's more macho elements. They swagger round with crewcuts and khaki waistcoats and drink straight from the bottle. Like Freemasons and Catholics, they have subtle methods of signalling to you their status, which verbally usually hinges on having "spent a bit of time in Hereford"; Hereford is the HQ of the SAS (Special Air Service). The Mustafa late on a Thursday night is not for the faint-hearted. On my last visit an excess of tequila combined with the appearance of battery-operated dancing, chanting, Kalashnikov-waving Osama bin Laden dolls on the bartop made me wonder whether I had lost my reason.

2. L'Atmosphere is the first French restaurant in town and boasts a swimming pool. Closed on Sundays. Reports of the food were not good in its early days (2004). It is in Qala-i-Fatullah, Street 4; tel. 079 300 264/070 026 56

email: latmospherekabul@yahoo.fr

3. Jaisalmer Tandoor Kitchen and Lounge is a genuine Indian restaurant run by enterprising Goanese. The music is often loud and Indian and dancing is encouraged, which might not appeal to everyone. Qala-i-Fatullah, House 4, Street 1

tel. 079 20 0570; email: jaisalmer_afg@yahoo.com

4. The Flower Street Cafe has a good reputation for fresh sandwiches and brunch on Friday and Saturday and is open between 8am and 7pm. It is not, though, in Flower Street, but in Qala-i-Fatullah, Street 7, House 57.

tel. 0702 93124/079 356319
email: flowerstreetcatering@hotmail.com

5. The Feelings Club, originally a bar, became a restaurant too in 2004. It specialises in pizzas, which the chefs used to make for ISAF (International Security Assistance Force) and the UN, both reputedly homes of the best pizzas in Kabul. Wazir Akbar Khan Street 13; tel. 0702 37687

6. The Mediterraneo Club advertises itself as a "European restaurant, a cozy pub-bar, espresso café, leafy courtyard dining, pool table and big-screen TV". It is slightly difficult to find so give your driver these directions: "Take the road to the former British embassy, turn left opposite the new mosque and then take the third on the right. The Club is at the end of the road." tel. 079 44 77 33

7. The Elbow Room has something of a cult following, perhaps as Kabul's newest and most Westernised bar and restaurant. "SoHo has come to Kabul" marvelled one diner (or perhaps Soho). It serves excellent strong cocktails. Address: at the end of the lane between the UNDP and the Chinese embassy on the Ministry of Foreign Affairs Road, Shah-i-Nao; tel. 079 352 538/ 070254 432

email: elbowroom_kabul@hotmail.com

8. The Sufi restaurant is in Bagh-i-Bala, once one of Kabul's most popular gardens. The address says it is in the "cellar of the Cinema Aryub". It certainly works hard to present the best side of Afghan food and culture, with art nights, traditional Afghan music, poem-evenings and *mantu* (dumpling) evenings.

9. B's Place deserves a special commendation as the first Westernised restaurant to open in Kabul, in 2002. It is still a lovely place, with a large garden lit by paraffin lamps, where one can eat.

10. Anaar, behind Unica Guesthouse, serves unbelievably hot food, to the point that a patron complained that it contravened the Geneva convention, citing napalm coated chips—perhaps the elusive al-Qaeda WMD. My party was soon coughing and sneezing like survivors of a WW1 gas attack. Bring your own wine and a bottle opener. My companions had a higher pain threshold than me but our Afghan companion concluded: "It is better to go somewhere else". The ambience is nice with paraffin lamps strung up along a washing line. A delightful period touch is given by a VW Beetle in the garden. Address: House no 6, Street no 4, Kolola Pushta.

mobile tel. 0702 843151, 07956 7291

email: anaarkabul@yahoo.com

11. Everest Guest House. Restaurant famous for pizza, with all the ingredients brought in from Iran and with free delivery. Kabul's answer to Domino's Pizza.

12. Lai Thai Restaurant. This is run by an absolutely remarkable woman, Lalita Thongngamkam, who specialises in setting up restaurants in the world's more difficult places, and has opened restaurants in Kosovo and East Timor. The food is very good, too, and great attention has been paid to getting the detail right, including furniture specially made in Pakistan.

13. The Kabul Lodge has, on a good night, the best European food in Kabul and is definitely worth a visit even if you are not staying there.

INTERNATIONAL STORES (PX STORES)

A number of PX stores, selling essential imported goods like wine and Marmite have opened. The first, and still the best known, is Supreme Food and Wine, Airport Road, Khojarawash; tel. 079 320914;

email: bdodge@supremefoodservice.com.

DRY CLEANING

A dry cleaners has recently opened near Chicken Street.

TAXIS

Driving in Kabul is a contact sport. And unless you speak Dari, getting a taxi in Kabul can be traumatic. The drivers are unlikely to know where your destination is, although they will nod vehemently when you tell them the address. Once you are irrevocably inside, the driver must stop a series of pedestrians until he finds one that speaks English and can interpret. One way round this is to ask your hotel to write down the address of the place where you want to go. Prices are negotiable; experienced Kabul hands tell me that one shouldn't pay more than a dollar for a journey within the city limits.

My experience is that if you have a number of errands to run, or sights to see, it is better to hire a car with a "fixer" from one of the reputable firms who supply this service to NGOs and journalists.

SIGHTS IN KABUL

One of the best pieces of travel advice I have ever received was "get out of the capital as soon as you can". Kabul has a few sights, but the dust and pall of war damage that hang over the place encourage one to get out to the Wakhan or Taloqan. But you will probably have a few days in Kabul and there are some things worth seeing. Pity the NGO workers who never leave the place.

TELEVISION MOUNTAIN

A popular place to go for an overall view of the city of Kabul, and to realise just how enormous the place is. Houses carpet the plain and creep up the sides of the mountains that ring the city. It is one way of orientating yourself in Kabul.

THE ROYAL MAUSOLEUM

This square domed building, situated atop a hill known as Teppe Maranjan (Teppe Nadir Shah) in the east of the city, has suffered—its metal dome is punctured with shell holes and most of the marble facing has been blasted off. The design, with monumental square black marble pillars, has a curious resemblance to Albert Speer's designs, and given that the Germans were very active in Kabul in the 1930s —establishing a radio station, trying to draw Nadir Shah into an alliance to threaten British India—this resemblance may not be coincidental. In fact, in 1928 Speer was offered a job by King Amanullah to be Kabul city planner and professor of architecture.

The square black marble plinth in the centre of the domed hall is purely decorative. Tombs of the Royal Family are in a catacomb underneath the building and the custodian can unlock the door to let you in. The central grave is that of Nadir Shah, assassinated in 1933; on the left sits the tomb of Zahir Shah's queen who, sadly, died in Rome before returning to her native country. On the right is Nadir

Shah's queen, mother of the present Zahir Shah. The rest of the tombs belong to other family members.

OMAR MUSEUM

At the bottom of Teppe Maranjan is a branch of the Omar Museum. Omar, the first de-mining operation in Afghanistan, have gathered an amazing collection of guns, tanks, aircraft and biplanes that looked to my inexpert eye to be relics of World War II but were probably Soviet state-of-the-art weaponry during the jihad. The battered collection of rockets includes an alleged Scud missile. Omar also have a smaller and more gruesome museum in Wazir Akbar Khan displaying mines. Notice the passenger jet that has been decorated with happy de-miners and the slogan "Destruction of One Landmine shuts the Door of Poverty, Disability and Bigging". An admirable sentiment.

FOOTBALL STADIUM

This infamous site for public executions by the Taliban saw hanging as a favoured option, but shooting was not neglected. Christina Lamb records that it took the staff three days of hosing to clear the blood that had darkened the ground between the goalposts. These days, it is used every Friday for *buzkashi* games and if you are in Kabul on that day, a visit here is a must.

KABUL MUSEUM

This is certainly in better shape than in 2002, when I first saw it. Once one of the great museums of the world, with objects illustrating every period of Afghanistan's long history, much was feared destroyed by the Taliban. Now it seems that much more of the contents have survived than had been feared. Pay attention to the notices as you go in: "Speak Slowly Please. Do Not Touch the Exhibits."

CHRISTIAN CEMETERY

There are three items of interest here: the burial site of Sir Aurel Stein, the large number of British and German graves, and Rahim, the guardian, who is paid by the British Embassy to keep the place in order. His set-piece is an account of how he was beaten up by Mullah Omar, who was lodging in the Taliban guest house next door. The story has come in several versions—Dominic Medley's excellent guide records a slightly different one—but the one I recorded in 2002 is as follows:

'That house there'—he pointed to a three-story building overlooking the plot—'that was the Taliban guest house. The Taliban would come in here and hit me and ask 'Why are you keeping Christian graves? They are infidels.' ' I said it is because I am old and very poor and can do anything to earn money from Christians.' This became a regular occurrence, he said; the sort of recreational violence that the Taliban enjoyed.

He was one of the few people ever to have met the Taliban's secretive and sinister leader, Mullah Omar. 'One day I was shutting the door and about to leave and Omar's commander came over and said that he wanted to see the cemetery. He told me not to offend Omar.'

'What did he look like?' I asked, fascinated.

'He was very tall—taller than you—and very fat and very powerfully built. He was lame—his left leg was cut off at the knee and he was blind in his right eye. He looked like a bad and illiterate person,' said Rahim.

'And what happened?'

'He asked me why I worked here for infidels, and I said it is because I get a salary. He asked how much, and I said 150,000 afghanis [about four dollars] per month. He said, who gives you that and I said the International Assistance Mission.'

'He was very angry that I was taking money from infidels. Then he asked me if I was literate?'

'Why did he ask that?'

'They told me later that if I was literate he would give me a job with the Taliban. And I said, "Of course, a man who is illiterate is half blind!"'

He started laughing at the memory.

'It is a Persian proverb. And so I ran out of the graveyard and didn't come back for a week.'

I think this story might have gained something in the retelling but I was very impressed.

[B. Jenks]

'How did you get this job?' I asked.

'Fifteen years ago, when Najibullah [the communist puppet] was President, I had a shop nearby, and then the cemetery keeper died. No one was looking after it, and then one day I found the body of a murdered man here. I told the police and they took the body away and told me to look after the cemetery.'

'Who pays you now?'

He produced a much-folded piece of paper from an envelope, which turned out to be from the British Embassy. It said 'The Embassy is not making any official payment to Mr Rahim from government funds. A number of officials and military personnel have created a small fund to pay him $100 from time to time to ensure he continues to care for the few British graves at the site.' At one end mounted on the wall, and obviously recently repaired, was a plaques listing the soldiers who had died while serving in Kabul and some names freshly added, young men killed as part of the international security assistance force.

'When the British soldiers arrived in Kabul last year, one day they all came here and stood in a line and removed their hats and were very quiet.'

'I know when that would have been. That would be 11 November. It is the anniversary of the day a great war ended.'

'They passed a hat round and put money in it.' He started laughing. 'I thought it was for me!'

It is the final resting place of Sir Aurel Stein, the greatest of all the Central Asian explorers who rediscovered the Silk Road. His story is famously told in Peter Hopkirk's *Foreign Devils on the Silk Road*. He was born a Hungarian Jew but became a British citizen and died in Kabul in 1940, planning yet another expedition. The gravestone says "A Man Greatly Beloved".

Looking at the other graves is interesting and moving—the enormous number of British soldiers who are buried here, mostly from fever but also victims of the various disastrous Afghan wars. Sad also are the 1960s and 1970s graves of tourists who perished in road accidents, perhaps even hippies who died of drugs. But most interesting are the number of German graves. The Germans were active in Afghanistan in the late 1920s and 30s, trying to turn it into a German sphere of influence. It also gives me an occasion to quote a fine story recorded by Peter Levi in 1968.

[B. Jenks]

'Stranger still, we heard of a foreign company, most of the staff of which were German, all of them having left Europe in 1945 and none of them having lived since that significant date but in South America and Afghanistan. A few years ago they turned up en masse for a new year's ball at the International Club, in full SS uniform including boots and pistols. It was difficult to find these items in good condition in the Kabul bazaar, although you could certainly dress a musical comedy there for any date since 1900. There was a fight and all the ex-Nazis were thrown into the swimming bath.'[2]

BIRD MARKET (KA FARUSHI)

It sells partridges for fighting and eating, budgerigars for decoration and parrots for talking. The traditional wicker cages, covered in a purple cloth, are used for transporting decoy partridges when Afghans go shooting. Nearby one can buy 19th century British guns, apparently still used for shooting wildfowl in the Panjshir. Afghan marksmanship is amazing, as the British and Russians have also discovered.

NAQASH, ANIMAL MARKET

The camel and sheep and goat market is a 15-minute drive north of Kabul—every day but best seen in the morning when the stock is fresh. "Butchers buy their sheeps there," says Haji.

ZOO

Differential pricing means it costs 100 afs for a foreigner to enter, but 10 for an Afghan. Foreigners therefore are given ten tickets torn in half. Emergency Food Supplies provided by the Mayhew Animal Home in London.

To my mind, this is the best thing in Kabul, and Kabulis think so too judging from the men wandering around holding hands. A man with Oriental features praying in the shade, his jacket spread out in front of him as a prayer rug. Other men washing their feet and rinsing their mouths and ears prior to their afternoon prayer.

Undoubtedly, now that Marjan the battle-scarred lion has gone to a better place, the stars of the show are the pigs and the Western visitors, who get mobbed and stared at. Pigs are remarkably clean with large pink ears and straight tails and live in what looks like a cement-covered golf bunker, but to Afghans are deeply weird and exotic animals. (Åsne Seierstad's book, *The Bookseller of Kabul*, recounts how children in school are taught that Westerners are wicked because they eat these animals.)

Poor Marjan has been replaced by another lion, donated by China. Birds include bustards, including one of the few examples in captivity of Hartley's Bustard (*otis vera*), and eagles as seen in Ajar. Beautiful coloured budgerigars. Bad Ger (badger). Lots of little brown children swimming in a very dirty pool. Cute little rabbits— curious disjunction of Flopsy and Mopsy next door to a colossal brown bear, and in the background the main building destroyed by a shell burst, its skeleton of steel wires poking out. Wolf. Jackals. Go in the early morning or evening because during the heat of the day most animals hide in their dark bedrooms. Monkeys shamelessly copulating to the vast delight of the assembled Afghans.[3] Beautiful peacocks in a leafy glade.

Formerly, the monkeys would salute, Soviet-style, if you pointed a Kalashnikov at them (according to Radek Sikorski, author of *Dust of the Saints*).

NATIONAL GALLERY

The rather undistinguished collection of 430 paintings was originally in royal hands; most are painted by Afghan painters, "all Professors of Art" I was told. The Taliban got their hands on 200, which were figurative and therefore blasphemous, and tore them up. The National Gallery was re-opened by President Karzai in March 2002. Postcards can be brought here.

Entrance fee is 150 afs for foreigners. Pictures are principally by Afghan artists. Foreigners will probably be most interested in the painting of Dr Brydon, slumped over his horse, the man who—along with Flashman—was the only survivor of the Retreat to Jalalabad in 1841. Its official name is *Remnants of an Army* and is a copy of the often-reproduced painting by Lady Elizabeth Butler.

Upstairs are watercolours of the most famous sights of Afghanistan, including the Minaret of Jam and Masud's tower at Ghazni (reproduced on ATO posters). In one glass case are the shredded remnants of the Taliban's iconoclasm. Many of the paintings, naturally, depict scenes from the many defeats that the Afghans have inflicted on the British over the years. There is also a reconstruction of the workplace and bedroom of a young French woman artist who was killed by the Taliban. One room contains portraits of the royal family with a particularly interesting picture of Habibullah, dressed in a secular fashion, an attempt to portray him as an Afghan Atatürk. (His successor Amanullah, it will be remembered, came to a bad end because of his wife's bare shoulders.)

BAGH-I-BALA

This garden, just below the Intercontinental Hotel, will soon take its place again as one of Kabul's most popular places. The site is still well kept up and Afghans sit here contemplating the brown mountains beyond. To reach it, use the Intercontinental drive and turn right into an area of pine trees, passing an old summer palace (now a military base). At the end is a building—formerly the best restaurant in Kabul, (with a swimming pool), which is due for renovation.

SULTANI MUSEUM

This private museum occupies the same building as the National Gallery. The collection has been privately assembled by the collector, Mr Sultani, from auction houses and galleries in the West. It comprises three rooms. The first is full of beautiful calligraphic Korans and other manuscripts of Afghan provenance, including Sanskrit texts. In the second room are two utterly beautiful silk ikats, which he bought 25 years ago and which are no longer available on the market. There are fine wooden carved pillars that commemorate "men of influence" in Nuristan[4]—objects that are becoming rarities in Afghanistan. Notice the table—the Nuristanis (unlike the Afghans) sit on chairs and eat from tables, one of the characteristics that have led explorers to speculate that they might be descended from Alexander's Greeks.

In the third room are pre-Islamic statues, Buddhist coins and beautiful Islamic bronzework. Interestingly, in the light of the Bactrian Gold discovery, are some fine pieces of Scythian gold bought by Mr Sultani in Dubai. The museum has a fine collection of Islamic tiles, which look to me 20th century. Mr Sultani has saved for Afghanistan many pieces that were looted from national collections and appeared on the international art market. He himself wears some of the finest gold pieces.

tel. 0702 59066

GOLF COURSE

The Kabul golf course first opened in 1967 and then closed in 1978. The fairways, greens and clubhouse reopened in April 2004. *Kabul Scene* magazine have been "assured that it is safe" and a number of people have played since the opening. On offer is a 9-hole course (two nines are 18). The Club has golf clubs (2 sets), tees and balls. The professional, Afzal Abdul, was the pro in 1978 and had a handicap of zero.

ISTALIF

This village hanging on the edge of a hill gives the appearance of an Italian hill village as one approaches it. The name may derive from the Greek word for vine, *staphiloi*. The village looks out onto the Shomali plain, where grapes were grown for wine in the 1960s. They were dug up and the fields mined by the Taliban, who considered

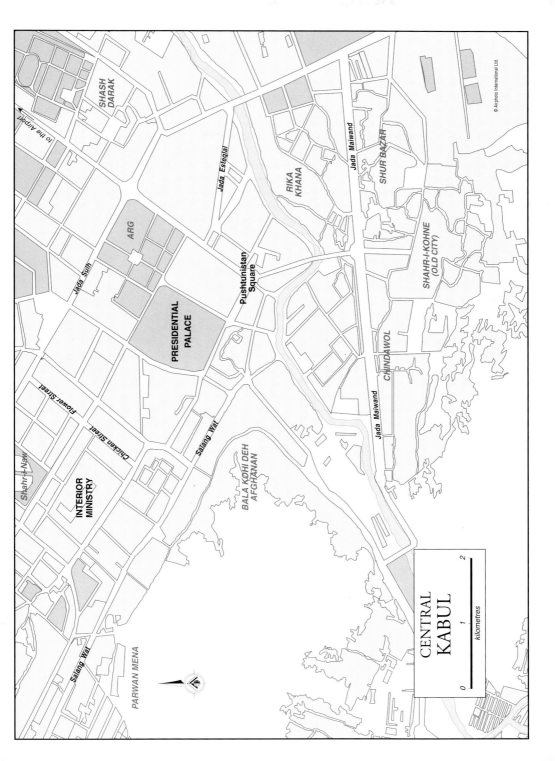

CENTRAL
KABUL

SHASH
DARAK

to the Airport

Jada Esteqlal

ARG

RIKA
KHANA

Jada Maiwand

SHUR BAZAR

Jada Suth

Pushtunistan
Square

PRESIDENTIAL
PALACE

SHAHR-I-KOHNE
(OLD CITY)

CHINDAWOL

Flower Street

Chicken Street

Salang Wat

Jada Maiwand

Shahr-i-Naw

INTERIOR
MINISTRY

BALA KOHI DEH
AFGHANAN

Salang Wat

PARWAN MENA

© Airphoto International Ltd.

kilometres

0   1   2

them un-Islamic. The village has always been famous for its pottery and it is fun to potter through the shops, which also sell some fine antique chapans (robes). Istalif pottery is turquoise and spatter-glazed and instantly recognisable.

The village was the site of a lodge belonging to Zahir Shah, now in ruins, but its gardens below make a fine place for a picnic. There is a cypress walk down to a lookout over the Shomali plain. On Fridays, the gardens are used by Kabulis for a day out from the city. The park is still in good condition, watered with tiny rills and with huge maple trees.

[1] Flashman's *Who's Who* entry reads: Flashman, Harry Paget. Brigadier-General, V.C., K.C.B., K.C.I.E.; Chevalier, Legion of Honour; Order of Maria Theresa, Austria; Order of the Elephant, Denmark (temporary); U.S. Medal of Honor; San Serafino Order of Purity and Truth, 4th Class. b May 5, 1822, s. of H. Buckley Flashman, Esq., Ashby and Hon. Alicia Paget; m. Elspeth Rennie Morrison, d. of Lord Paisley; one s., one d. educ. Rugby School. 11th Hussars, 17th Lancers. Served Afghanistan, 1841–42 (medals, thanks of Parliament) [there follows a list of many other campaigns in which he served with noteable cowardice]... Hon. mbr of numerous societies and clubs, including Sons of the Volsungs (Strackenz), Kokand Horde (Central Asia), M.C.C., Whites and United Service (London, both resigned), Blackjack (Batavia). Chmn, Flashman and Bottomley, Ltd.; dir. British Opium Trading Co.; Governor, Rugby School; Hon. Pres. Mission for Reclamation of Reduced Females. Publications: *Dawns and Departures of a Soldier's Life; 'Twixt Cossack and Cannon; The Case Against Army Reform*. Recreation: oriental studies, angling, cricket (Rugby Past and Present XI v Kent, Lord's 1842; 5 for 12). Address—Gandamack Lodge, Ashby, Leicester.

[2] Peter Levi, *The Light Garden of the Angel King*, London 2000, p 53.

[3] Which gives me an excuse to retell an old Noel Coward joke, possibly authentic, possibly traditional, arranged by David Niven: "Uncle Noel, what are those two dogs doing?" "The doggy in front has gone blind and the one behind is pushing it all the way to St Dunstan's."

[4] The title of the well-known anthropologist Schuyler Jones's book on Nuristani customs and death rituals; *Men of Influence in Nuristan*.

BABUR'S BURIAL GARDEN IN KABUL

—Deborah Dunham

Given the destruction to Afghanistan over the centuries, one is grateful that this lovely spot has been spared the worst. While a few bullet holes remain, the landmines have been swept, proper archaeological excavations have been completed and, thanks to the Historic Cities Support Programme of the Aga Khan Trust for Culture and a number of other organizations, this wonderful 500-year-old garden is being brought back to life. Situated southwest of the old city near the Kabul River at the western slope of the Koh-i-Darwaza, what one sees today is "Baghe Babur" (Babur's Garden, sometimes written as Bagh-i-Babur), a formal enclosure of 11 hectares consisting of 14 terraces, a crumbling palace, renovated pavilion, a small mosque and the grave of Babur, one of Kabul's most illustrious residents and founder of the Mughal dynasty. This early design, of Persian origins, culminated some five generations later in the famous gardens surrounding the Taj Mahal.

Shortly after conquering Kabul in 1504 at the tender age of 21, a sensitive, yet often ruthless Central Asian prince named Zahir ad-Din Muhammad, known as Babur (the Tiger), commenced the laying out of several gardens. As a descendant of both Tamerlane (Timur) and Genghis Khan, Babur created imperial gardens that marked a transition between the nomadic ways of his Timurid and Mongol forbears on the steppes, and the more settled urban existence of his offspring; these gardens would serve as places of contemplation, poetry writing, ceremonial ritual and drinking parties for local nobility and his men in arms. The uppermost terrace of Baghe Babur, as it later came to be known, was a favorite spot for the emperor to rest whilst watching the sunset after a hard day's work raiding villages, unhorsing Uzbeks and generally trying to keep his fickle warlords and cousins from defecting to neighbouring principalities.

The Baburnama, Babur's detailed and very personal diary from the year he entered Kabul (1504) until his death in 1530, describes the harsh realities of his physical hardships, military defeats and conquests (some celebrated according to Timurid traditions with towers of skulls of slain foes) which were typical of these tumultuous times of internecine warfare. Babur remained in Kabul, "a pretty little province rectangular in shape, stretching from east to west and surrounded by mountains", from 1504–1526, thoroughly enjoying its perfect climate and beautiful terrain for hunting, rafting and feasting.

Unique among memoirs of rulers of the time, the Baburnama includes aesthetic descriptions of autumn foliage, golden pomegranates and accounts of idyllic picnics and excursions (to the foothills below Parwan) to view wild flowers "Tulips of many varieties cover the foothills. Once, when I had them counted, there turned out to be thirty two or thirty three unique varieties. One sort gives off a bit of the scent of red roses, for which reason it is called the Gulboy tulip and is found in Dasht-Shaykh and nowhere else."

According to an authority on Mughal gardens, Babur's gardens provided the foundation for those of increasing grandeur made possible through his later conquest of India. "Though inspired by their Timurid antecedents, Babur's Kabul gardens evidently achieved a distinct individuality. His boldness in shaping the land and his successful treatments of space as positive volumes were entirely new. He sited and laid out these gardens himself, and whenever possible, they were dramatically located with a sweeping view. His genius for site selection was matched by his spatial sense; he preferred steeply terraced gardens, usually with a strong central axis, and he apparently never built one without water."

Following his conquest of northern India in 1526, Babur built elaborate gardens in Agra to mitigate the heat and dust which his soldiers detested as much as he did. In fact he writes: "Since the people of India had never seen such planned or regular spaces, they nicknamed the side of the Jumna on which these structures stood, 'Kabul'." While the terrain in India was flat, and much effort was required to replicate running waters of the hillsides of Afghanistan for which he pined, by the time of his death Babur had established the principles of Mughal gardens for generations to come, namely: water as an aesthetic and utilitarian element, precise formal geometry, spatial order (often using the Persian four-part chahar-baghe design) and a profusion of planting.

All of these can be seen, or at least are beginning to be seen again, as the reconstruction of Baghe Babur progresses under the watchful eye of a team of experts and local craftsmen assembled by the Aga Khan Trust for Culture, in cooperation with the Kabul Municipality and the departments of Historic Monuments and Archaeology of the Ministry of Information and Culture, among other organizations. Since 2002, work has been underway to re-build the traditional mud brick walls and to level and re-plant the terraces which have shifted over the centuries.

Preservation work on Babur's grave and the pretty marble mosque built by Shah Jahan in 1638 on the terrace below is nearing completion. A turn-of-the-century pavilion has been restored with the support of the US Embassy. The ruins of the war-damaged Queen's Palace, which dates from the 1880s are being stabilised, with a view to the central courtyard being used for public functions, pending its full reconstruction. Part of the programme is to address the intrusive modern elements in the garden; the 1960s greenhouse will be screened with trees, while the swimming pool —built on the upper northern terraces—will be demolished and replaced with a new facility, just outside of the garden perimeter.

In tandem with restoration of built structures, work proceeds on retrieving something of the character of the historic landscape, with a particular emphasis on planting of trees in the manner of the original "orchard" garden. These will be fed by a system of irrigation that combines a piped network with surface channels and small pools, which have been a characteristic of gardens in the region since the time of Babur, who wrote in 1504: "among the cold-weather fruits of Kabul and its villages are abundant grapes, pomegranates, apricots, apples, quinces, pears, peaches, plums, jujubes, almonds and nuts. I had a sour cherry sapling brought and planted. It took well and keeps getting better all the time."

With shade and water, and in the fullness of time, Baghe Babur's orchards, tall trees and grassy terraces should provide a much needed picnic area for families to enjoy on Fridays, as well as a permanent place of honour at this, the final resting place of Babur, one of Kabul's most famous and important residents. The inscription above the entrance to the mosque reads:

Only a mosque of this beauty, this temple of nobility, constructed for the prayer of saints and the epiphany of cherubs, was fit to stand in so venerable a sanctuary as this highway of archangels, this theatre of heaven, the light garden of the God-forgiven angel king whose rest is in the garden of heaven, Zahiruddin Muhammad Babur the Conqueror.

"But what a happiness to have known Babur! He had all that one seeks in a friend. His energy and ambition were touched with sensitiveness: he could act, feel, observe and remember."—E.M. Forster

Key dates in the history of Baghe Babur:

1483   Babur born at Ferghana, Uzbekistan.

1504   Babur conquers Kabul and lives there for the next 20 years.

1528   *Babur lays out Belvedere Garden (possibly Istalif?) outside of Kabul.*

1526   *Emperor Babur conquers India, establishes the Mughal Empire, and begins building many gardens along the Jumna River (across from the present Taj Mahal).*

1530   *Babur dies in Agra and is buried in a garden, called Aram-Baghe.*

1540s   *Babur's son and successor, Emperor Humayun, returns Babur's remains to Kabul.*

1607   *Emperor Jahangir makes a pilgrimage to Kabul, where he orders the following:*

- *Building of enclosure walls around all gardens of Kabul*
- *Chabutra platform in front of the tomb*
- *Erection of an inscribed headstone, still visible today*

1638   *Emperor Shah Jahan visits Kabul, ordering complete restoration of the garden*

- *Building of marble mosque on a terrace below the grave*
- *Erecting of a marble screen and improvements to water reservoirs*

1840s   *Contemporary traveller Charles Masson notes "sad havoc and disorder" in the garden, even before the earthquake of 1842 toppled the marble enclosure.*

1880s   *Abdur Rahman Khan orders renovation and improvements*

- *Building of present pavilion*
- *Building of Queen's Palace*

1920s   *Nadir Shah transforms the garden into a public park:*

- *Building of small pavilion around Babur's tomb*
- *Erection of walled platform below platform enclosing the old chenar tree*
- *Building of a swimming pool and an additional reservoir (also used as swimming pool)*
- *Central flow replaced by a series of flower gardens*
- *Building of three fountains*
- *Planting new trees*
- *Repair of terrace walls*

1930–70 Various "improvements" added, including:

- *Construction of large swimming pool to the north*
- *Construction of greenhouse close to northern perimeter wall*
- *Creation of new retaining walls and road on upper terrace*

1980s   *Garden falls into poor state of repair, as irrigation is reduced to minimal extent.*

1992–4 *Garden forms part of the no-man's land between armed factions and is heavily mined. Irrigation pumps are vandalized, buildings are burned and the remaining trees cut down for firewood.*

1995   *Remedial works by UNHS (Habitat) and Kabul Municipality, including installation of replacement pumps, repairs to pavilion and some initial re-planting.*

2002   *AKTC / HCSP signs protocol with Interim Afghan Administration for comprehensive rehabilitation programme for the garden.*

- *Relevant documentation assembled*
- *Initial clearance and repair works commence.*
- *Geomagnetical prospection by ICOMOS*
- *Initial excavations by German Archaeological Institute (GAI)*

2003–5 *AKTC / HCSP scales up clearance, conservation and rehabilitation works on site, including:*

- *Rebuilding of entire perimeter wall using traditional mud walling techniques*
- *Removal of modern additions to grave and restoration of enclosure walls*
- *Restoration of Shah Jahani marble mosque*
- *Clearance and grading of terraces*
- *Planting of 1,000 saplings (planes, walnuts, apricots, cherries, pomegranates, figs, Judas trees, etc)*
- *Excavation of upper terraces and central axis*
- *Construction of new caravanserai complex as a visitor's centre*

Deborah Dunham is a world traveller and project management consultant doing post graduate work in Islamic Art and Archaeology at the School of Oriental and African Studies, University of London. Her research has focused on Mughal court painting and the rennovation of Babur's burial garden in Kabul.

KABUL AND THE FIRST AFGHAN WAR

There are few events in history that illustrate the law of the unintended consequence quite as thoroughly as the First Afghan War. The British hoped, by the installation of a government of their choosing in Kabul, to secure at little cost the Indian borders against the threat of encroachment by the Persians and the Russians, and to obtain the friendship of the Afghan people; the result, by contrast, was the weakening of Afghanistan, the undying enmity of its people who were formerly well-disposed towards the British, and the return of the government they had endeavoured to oust, at the cost of millions of rupees and the loss of tens of thousands of lives.

One of the leading characters in this catastrophe of British foreign policy was Shah Shuja, King of the Afghan Empire, who had, in 1803, usurped the throne from his brother, Shah Mahmud. In 1809, the British government in India sent its first mission to Shah Shuja, in order to establish diplomatic relations with the government of Afghanistan. The leader of the delegation, Mountstuart Elphinstone, later described his encounter with the king in his great work *An account of the kingdom of Caubul and its dependencies in Persia, Tartary, and India*. Although Elphinstone met Shuja in Peshawar, which was then under Afghan control, his description gives a full idea as to what court life would have been like in Kabul, as well as the nature of the king and the state of his kingdom:

> "The court was oblong, and had high walls, painted with the figures of cypresses. In the middle was a pond and fountains. The walls on each side were lined with the King's guards three deep, and at various places in the court, stood the officers of state, at different distances from the King, according to their degree. At the end of the court was a high building, the lower story of which was a solid wall, ornamented with false arches, but without doors or windows; over this was another storey, the roof of which was supported by pillars and Moorish arches, highly ornamented. In the centre arch sat the King, on a very large throne or gilding. His appearance was magnificent and royal:

his crown and his dress were one blaze of jewels. He was elevated above the heads of the eunuchs who surrounded his throne, and who were the only persons in the large hall where he sat: all was silent and motionless. On coming in sight of the King, we all pulled off our hats, and made a low bow: we then held up our hands towards heaven, as if praying for the King, and afterwards advanced towards the fountain, where the Chaous Baushee repeated our names, without any title or addition of respect, ending 'They have come from Europe as ambassadors to Your Majesty. May your misfortunes be turned upon me.' The King answered in a loud and sonorous voice, 'They are welcome'; on which we prayed for him again, and repeated the ceremony once more, when he ordered for us dresses of honour. After this, some officer of the court called out something in Turkish, on which a division of the soldiers on each side filed off, and ran out of the court, with the usual noise of their boots on the pavement, accompanied by the clashing of their armour. The call was twice repeated, and at each call a division of troops ran off: at the fourth, the Khans ran off also, with the exception of a certain number, who were now ordered to come forward. The King, in the mean time, rose majestically from his throne, descended the steps, leaning on two eunuchs, and withdrew from our sight. The Khans, who were summoned, ran on as usual, while we walked on to the foot of a stair-case, covered with a very rich carpet: we paused here until the Khans had run up, and were arranged; after which we ascended, and entered the hall, where the king was now seated on a low throne opposite the door. We stood in a line, while the King of Kabul asked after the health of His Majesty and the Governor-General, inquired into the length of our journey, and expressed his wish that the friendship betwixt his nation and ours might be increased; to which I made very brief replies. The gentlemen of the embassy now retired, leaving me and Mr Strachey, who were desired to seat ourselves near His Majesty. The Imam and the Moonshee Baushee (or head secretary), stood near us, and the other Khans stood along one side of the hall. The Governor-General's Persian letter was now opened and read with striking distinctness and elegance by the moonshee baushee, and the king made a suitable answer, declaring his friendship for the English nation, his desire of an intimate alliance, and his readiness to pay the utmost attention to any communication with which I might be charged. After I had replied, His Majesty changed the subject to inquiries respecting our journey, and questions about our native country. When he understood that the climate and productions of England greatly resembled those of Kabul, he said the two kingdoms were made by nature to be united, and renewed his professions of friendship...

"The King of Kabul was a handsome man, about 30 years of age, of an olive complexion, with a thick black beard. The expression of his countenance was dignified and pleasing: his voice clear, and his address princely. We thought at first he had on armour of jewels, but, on close inspection, we found this to be a mistake, and his real dress to consist of a green tunic, with large flowers in gold, and precious stones, over which were a large breast-plate of diamonds, shaped like two flattened fleur-de-lis, an ornament of the same kind on each thigh, large emerald bracelets on the arms (above the elbow), and many other jewels in different places. In one of the bracelets was the Koh-i-Noor, known to be one of the largest diamonds in the world. There were also some strings of very large pearls, put on like cross belts, but loose. The crown was about nine inches high; not ornamented with jewels, as European crowns are, but to appearance entirely formed of those precious materials. It seemed to be radiated like ancient crowns, and behind the rays appeared peaks of purple velvet: some small branches with pendants seemed to project from the crown; but the whole was so complicated, and so dazzling, that it was difficult to understand, and impossible to describe. The throne was covered with a cloth adorned with pearls, on which lay a sword and a small mace, set with jewels. The room was open all round. The centre was supported by four high pillars, in the midst of which was a marble fountain. The floor was covered with the richest carpets, and round the edges were slips of silk, embroidered with gold, for the Khans to stand on. The view from the hall was beautiful. Immediately below was an extensive garden, full of cypress and other trees, and beyond was a plain of the richest verdure: here and there were pieces of water and shining streams; and the whole was bounded by mountains, some dark, and others covered with snow... In the above description, I have chiefly confined myself to what was splendid in the ceremony. I must however mention, before I conclude, that, although some things (the appearance of the King in particular) exceeded my expectations, others fell far short of them, and all bore less the appearance of a state in prosperity, than of a splendid monarchy in decay."

Elphinstone's impression of the decadence of Shah Shuja's government was fully justified. At the time of their meeting, Shuja's revenue was short, the tribes discontented and rebellious, and Afghan forces in Kashmir were under pressure from the Punjabi Sikhs led by Maharajah Runjit Singh. A few weeks after the departure of the British mission from Peshawar, Shah Mahmud, aided by the Vizier Fateh Khan, overthrew Shuja and reassumed power. Shuja spent time as a prisoner of Runjit Singh, losing to him the Koh-i-Noor, before escaping and throwing himself into the hands of the British, who hosted him as an exile in the town of Ludhiana. Mahmud was again king, but left the affairs of state to Fateh Khan, whilst he indulged himself in a life of luxury and depravity. This situation continued until 1818, when the two men fell out; Fateh Khan was blinded and tortured to death, at which his outraged sub-tribe, the Barakzai, rebelled and dispossessed Mahmud, forcing him to take refuge in Herat, which he held as his dominion until 1842. A period of confused civil war followed Mahmud's deposition, during which the Sikhs captured Kashmir and staked a claim to Peshawar. At the end of this strife in 1826, Runjit Singh had become overlord of Peshawar, even though the city was still administered by relatives of Fateh Khan (known as the Peshawar Sirdars); Kandahar was virtually autonomous, yet also in the hands of other relatives of the late vizier; and in Kabul (along with the smaller city of Ghazni), Dost Mohammed, Fateh Khan's favourite son, had emerged as ruler. In effect, the Afghan Empire founded by Ahmad Shah Durrani had broken apart.

In spite of the past years of trouble, the new ruler of Kabul made a positive impression on many, giving them hope that the area would recover from its convulsions. Charles Masson commented on his character:

> "The assumption of authority by Dost Mohammed Khan has been favourable to the prosperity of Kabul, which, after so long a period of commotion, required a calm. It is generally supposed that he will yet play a considerable part in the affairs of Khurasan.
>
> "He is beloved by all classes of his subjects, and the Hindu fearlessly approaches him in his rides, and addresses him with the certainty of being attended to. He administers justice with impartiality, and has proved that the lawless habits of the Afghan are to be controlled. He is very attentive to his

military; and, conscious of how much depends of the efficiency of his troops, is very particular as to their composition. His circumscribed funds and resources hardly permit him to be regular in his payments, yet his soldiers have the satisfaction to know that he neither hoards nor wastes their pay in idle expenses.

"Dost Mohammed Khan has distinguished himself, on various occasions, by acts of personal intrepidity, and has proved himself an able commander, yet he is equally well-skilled in stratagem and polity, and only employs the sword when other means fail. He is remarkably plain in attire, and would be scarcely noticed in the durbar but for his seat. His white linen raiment afforded a strange contrast to the gaudy exhibition of some of his chiefs, especially the young Habibullah Khan, who glitters with gold. In my audience of him in the camp at Ghazni, I should not have conjectured him a man of ability, either from his conversation or from his appearance; but it becomes necessary to subscribe to the general impression; and the conviction of his talent for government will be excited at every step through his country."

Dost Mohammed's first wish was to reconstruct the fractured Afghan Empire. Not only were Herat and Kandahar in the hands of others: Balkh was captured by the Amir of Bokhara; and, after a failed attempt by Shuja, in league with Runjit Singh, to retake the throne, Peshawar fell under the complete control of the Sikhs. Dost Mohammed put this desire to Alexander Burnes, who, in 1837, was sent to him as an envoy from the Governor-General of India, Lord Auckland. Burnes was sympathetic to these requests, particularly with respect to Peshawar and Herat, and advised Auckland that with not very much effort or expenditure these cities could be brought back to Dost Mohammed, who would then stand as a firm ally to the British cause. However, Auckland refused to authorise Burnes to proceed with these ideas, asserting that he did not wish to offend Runjit Singh, who had in the past supported the British. More concerned with the perceived danger of Russian expansion into Central Asia, and the threat that this would pose to the borders of the British Empire in India, Auckland pressed Burnes to make Dost Mohammed promise that he would not enter into any alliance with Russia or Persia. With nothing to offer Dost Mohammed, Burnes' mission became extremely difficult, and

Entrance to the Bolan Pass, near Quetta, through which the British army passed on their journey into Afghanistan in March 1839 [Bodleian]

after the appearance in Kabul of a Russian officer named Vitkevich, who carried what purported to be friendly letters from the Tsar, matters came to a head; Burnes could do little else but return to India.

At the same time, the Persians, with Russian encouragement, launched an attack on Herat. Although this led to a prolonged siege and a spirited defence, Auckland claimed in a notorious document—the Simlah Manifesto of 1838—that Dost Mohammed was conspiring with the Persians in this offensive, in order to allow them and the Russians to encroach on territory towards the Indian border. Moreover, asserting—without any basis in fact—that the security of India depended on the removal of Dost Mohammed, and that the Afghans wished to see the restoration of Shah Shuja, Auckland inaugurated a policy of regime change. Having made an alliance with the Sikh Army of Runjit Singh, he gathered an expeditionary force with orders to march to Kabul, depose Dost Mohammed and replace Shah Shuja on the throne. In every respect, Auckland was well-intentioned but ill-advised; he believed that this could be done without great difficulty, and that once Shuja was in place as a puppet king, Afghanistan would be content; that it would not require any great commitment of forces, and that the Indian frontier would be secure from any Russian threat.

Even initially, things did not go to plan. The Sikhs failed to provide any significant forces for the venture, and prohibited the bulk of the army from marching through Peshawar. Compelled to take a more difficult route to the south, the advancing army was seriously harassed by nomadic tribesmen. On 25 April 1839, the army reached Kandahar, and despite an initial warm welcome for Shuja, the people soon became quite indifferent, being resentful at the presence of foreign troops. Nevertheless, the army pressed northwards. Continued resistance, especially around Ghazni, was overturned, and Dost Mohammed was compelled to flee, escaping over the Hindu Kush. On 7 August, Shah Shuja entered Kabul, but it was immediately apparent that all of Auckland's claims were false; there was little popular support for Shuja, and that he would require prolonged British military support in order to hold on to power.

A permanent British garrison was stationed in Kabul, housed in cantonments outside the main city. G.R. Gleig describes the occupations of the British as they settled down in the area for a long stay, and their relations with the city's people:

"Wherever Englishmen go, they sooner or later introduce among the people whom they visit a taste for manly sports. Horse-racing and cricket were both got up in the vicinity of Kabul; and in both the chiefs and the people soon learned to take a lively interest. Shah Shuja himself gave a valuable sword to be run for, which Major Daly, of the 4th Light Dragoons, had the good fortune to win: and so infectious became the habit that several of the native gentry entered their horses, with what success no record seems to have been preserved. The game of cricket was not, however, so congenial to the taste of the Afghans. Being great gamblers in their own way, they looked on with astonishment at the bowling, batting, and fagging out of the English players; but it does not appear that they were ever tempted to lay aside their flowing robes and huge turbans and enter the field as competitors. On the other hand, our countrymen attended them to their mains of cocks, quails, and other fighting animals, and, betting freely, lost or won their rupees in the best possible humour. In like manner our people indulged them from time to time in trials of strength and feats of agility on which they much prize themselves: and to their own exceeding delight, though very much to the astonishment of their new friends, they in every instance threw the most noted of the Kabul wrestlers. The result of this frankness was to create among the Afghans a good deal of personal liking for their conquerors. Their chiefs, in consequence, invited them to their houses in town, as well as to share in their field sports when they retired to their castles in the country.

"There is a lake about five or six miles from Kabul, in the direction of Istalif, which, though partially saline, or rather metallic, in its waters, is frozen over in all winters if the weather be commonly severe. In the winter of 1839–40 it was covered with a coat of ice more than ordinarily thick, on which the Afghans used to practise the art of sliding, far more skilfully, as well as gracefully, than their European visitors. Indeed, it was the clumsy manner in which the Feringhees assayed that boyish sport which induced them to reiterate the conviction that heat, and not cold, was the white man's element. Forthwith our young gentlemen set themselves to the fabrication of skates: the artificers soon shaped the wood-work according to models given; out of old iron, smelted, and hardened afterwards, the blades were formed; and in due time a party of skaters, equipped for the exercise, appeared on the lake. The Afghans stared in mute amazement while the officers were fastening on their skates, but when they rose, dashed across the ice's surface, wheeled and turned, and cut out all manner of figures upon the ice, there was an end at once to disbelief in regard to the place of their nativity. 'Now,' cried they, 'we see that you are not like the infidel Hindus that follow you: you are men, born and bred like ourselves, where the seasons vary, and in their changes give vigour both to body and mind. We wish that you had come among us as friends, and not as enemies, for you are fine fellows one by one, though as a body we hate you.'

"Mention has been made of the hospitalities which were dispensed by Afghan chiefs to British officers. The latter were not backward to return the civility. Not only the houses of such men as the envoy, the commander-in-chief, and Sir Alexander Burnes, were thrown open to them, but the mess of the 13th received its frequent guests, most of whom ate and drank with as much good will and indiscrimination as if there had been no prohibitory clauses in the Koran or elsewhere. Among other means adopted to entertain the aristocracy of Central Asia, the British officers got up a play: a theatre was constructed, scenery painted, dresses prepared, and excellent bands in attendance; and as the pieces which they chose were chiefly broad comedies, such as the 'Irish Ambassador' and others of the same sort, great amusement was afforded to the audience. For on such occasions they changed the titles of the dramatis personae, so as to bring them and the offices of the parties bearing them to the level of the Afghan comprehension; while Burnes and others skilled in the dialect of the country, translated the speeches as they were uttered. The Afghans are a merry people, and have a keen relish of the ludicrous and the satirical; and as the interpreter never failed to bring the jokes of the actors home to them, they marked their delight by bursting into frequent peals of laughter.

"The 13th Light Infantry could boast a particularly ingenious individual among its officers. Mr Sinclair possessed a great mechanical genius, which he now applied to the construction of a boat, which he succeeded in rendering complete in all respects during the interval of the spring rains. Carriages being provided, it was conveyed, with its oars, masts, and sails, to the lake, and there launched. Now there had never been seen in all Afghanistan before that moment such a thing as a boat of any description. Individual Afghans who might have strayed as far as the Indus would possibly speak on their return of the inflated hides by means of which the dwellers on the banks of that river waft themselves from point to point; and the flying-bridges, or huge ferry-boats, which here and there cross the stream, must have had a place in their memory. But even to travellers the trim wherry in which a party of young men now embarked was entirely new, and to the multitude it became an object of astonishment indescribable. They could not comprehend the principle on which it had been fabricated. The oars, the masts, the sails, and, above all, the rudder, were marvels and mysteries to them; and when the crew, after exhibiting before them, endeavoured to explain that England possessed floating castles of the kind, capable of accommodating many hundred persons, and carrying each a hundred guns of heavy calibre, they lifted up their heads and eyes in mute amazement. It is hardly necessary to add, that of the mighty ocean it was impossible to convey to their minds any idea; for he who has not seen the sea never learns, even from books and drawings, how rightly to apprehend it; and to those who had for the first time heard of it, it was mere sound without sense."

As for Dost Mohammed, he was detained and held as a prisoner by the Amir of Bokhara. However, escaping from captivity, he raised an army of Uzbeks which clashed with British forces near Bamiyan, but was defeated. Undeterred at first, he evaded capture and collected another rebel force of Tajiks in the Kohistan region a little north of Kabul. He led these into a number of successful skirmishes against the British, but after a time he appears to have lost heart, and eventually decided to give himself up. The historian Sir John Kaye vividly describes Dost Mohammed's last battle against the British, and his surrender the next day to the resident political envoy, Sir William Macnaghten, outside the walls of Kabul:

"On the 2nd of November 1840—a day which has obtained a melancholy celebrity in the annals of the English in Afghanistan—the British force came at last in sight of the enemy. The Army of the Amir (Dost Mohammed) was posted in the valley of Purwandurrah. The Nijrow hills were bristling with the armed

PROVINDIAH AFGHAN & MAHMAND AFGHANS

Published by Smith, Elder & Co. 65, Cornhill, London 1862

From Photographs.

M & N Hanhart lith.

Pushtun tribesmen from South-east Afghanistan, 1857 [RSAA]

population of a hostile country. Unprepared for the conflict, Dost Mahommed had no design on that November morning of giving battle to the Feringhees. An unexpected movement precipitated the collision. On the first appearance of the British troops the Amir evacuated the village of Purwandurrah and the neighbouring forts; and was moving off to a position on some elevated ground commanded by a steep hill to the rearward, when, at the suggestion of Dr Lord, the British cavalry were moved to outflank the Afghan horse. What followed is one of the most exciting, as it is one of the most melancholy incidents of the Afghan war. It was a clear bright morning. The yellow foliage of autumn glittered like gold in the broad sunlight. The opposite hills were alive with the enemy. The crisp fresh air, so bracing and invigorating to the human frame, seemed to breathe confidence and courage. Dost Mohammed, who, since his defeat at Bamiyan, had been often heard of, but never seen, by the British troops, and who seemed to elude the grasp of the Army of Occupation like an *ignis fatuus*, was now actually within their reach. It ought to have been an hour of triumph. It was one of humiliation. The Afghans were on the hills skirting one side of the pass; the British troops were on the opposite declivity. Dost Mohammed saw our cavalry advancing, and from that moment cast behind him all thought of retreat. At the head of a small band of horsemen, strong, sturdy Afghans, but badly mounted, he prepared to meet his assailants. Beside him rode the bearer of the blue standard which marked his place in the battle. He pointed to it; reined in his horse; then snatching the white lunghi from his head, stood up in his stirrups uncovered before his followers, and called upon them, in the name of God and the Prophet, to drive the cursed Kafirs from the country of the faithful. 'Follow men,' he cried aloud, 'or I am a lost man.' Slowly, but steadily, the Afghan horsemen advanced. The English officers, who led our cavalry to the attack, covered themselves with glory. The native troopers fled like sheep. Emboldened by the craven conduct of the cavalry under British command, the Afghan horsemen rode forward, driving their enemy before them, and charging right up to the position of the British, until almost within reach of our guns. The Afghan sabres told, with cruel effect, upon our mounted men. Lieutenants Broadfoot and Crispin were cut to pieces. A treacherous shot from a neighbouring bastion brought Dr Lord to the ground; and the dagger of the assassin completed the work of death. Captains Fraser and Ponsonby, whose gallantry has never been surpassed even in the annals of old

The capture of Dost Mohammed. After a short spell in captivity (during which, despite his confinement, he conceived a great respect for the British) he returned to assume the throne in Kabul. [Bodleian]

Roman heroism, still live to show their honourable scars; and to tell, with mingled pride and humiliation, the story of that melancholy day.

"In front of our columns, flaunting the national standard, the Afghans stood for some time masters of the field, and then quietly withdrew from the scene of battle. Sir Alexander Burnes, awed by the disaster, wrote to Sir William Macnaghten, that there was nothing left for the force but to fall back upon Kabul, and implored the Envoy there to concentrate all our troops. Sir William received the letter on the 3rd of November, as he was taking his evening ride in the outskirts of the city. His worst forebodings seemed to be confirmed. Little did he know what thoughts were stirring in the breast of the Amir. Dost Mohammed, in the very hour of victory, felt that it was hopeless to contend against the power of the British Government. He had too much sagacity not to know that his success at Purwandurrah must eventually tend, by moving the British to redouble their exertions, rather to hasten than to retard the inevitable day of his final destruction. He quitted the field in no mood of exultation; with no bright visions of the future before him. He had won the last throw, but the final issue had ceased to be a matter of speculation. The hour in which, with dignity and grace, he might throw himself upon the protection of his enemies, now seemed to have arrived. He had met the British troops in the field, and, at the head of a little band of horsemen, had driven back the cavalry of the Feringhees. His last charge had been a noble one; he might now retire from the contest without a blot on his name.

"So thought the Amir; as he was wont, taking counsel of his saddle. None knew in the British camp the direction he had taken; none guessed the character of his thoughts. On the day after the victory of Purwandurrah he was under the walls of Kabul. He had been four-and-twenty hours in the saddle; but betrayed little symptoms of fatigue. A single horseman attended him. As they approached the residence of the British Envoy, they saw an English gentleman returning from his evening ride. The attendant galloped forward to satisfy himself of the identity of the rider, and being assured that the Envoy was before him, said the Amir was at hand. 'What Amir?' asked Macnaghten. 'Dost Mohammed Khan,' was the answer; and presently the Amir stood before him. Throwing himself from his horse, Dost Mohammed saluted the envoy, and said he was come to claim his protection. He surrendered his sword to the British chief; but Macnaghten returning it to him, desired the Amir to remount. They then rode together into the Mission compound—Dost Mohammed asking many eager questions about his family as they went. A tent having been pitched for his accommodation, he wrote letters to his sons, exhorting them to follow his example, and seek the protection of the British Government."

Despite the capture of Dost Mohammed, and the impression amongst the British that their position was generally secure, this was not at all the case. Resentment was increasing amongst the apparently tranquil Kabul population for a number of reasons, aside from the humiliation they felt at the imposition of a puppet king. The presence of foreign soldiers drove up prices for basic commodities; the Pushtuns lost a number of traditional privileges—something which, along with other poor governmental decisions, they attributed not to Shah Shuja, but to the British; and moreover, as Gleig nicely puts it, "it is much to be feared that our young countrymen did not always bear in mind that the domestic habits of any people ought to be sacred in the eyes of strangers". In other words, they formed relations with the women of the city in a manner outrageous to the traditional morals of the place.

The trouble finally surfaced towards the end of 1841. British subsidies to the Ghilzai tribesmen were cut, whereupon in protest they rose up and closed the roads connecting Kabul and Peshawar. Instead of the restoration of these funds, as officers on the ground suggested, the authorities in India reduced the payments even further. News of the disorder spread north to Kabul where, on 2 November, a mob gathered outside the house of Sir Alexander Burnes. Aid from the British and Shuja's own troops came too late; Burnes, along with his brother and several others were killed, and £17,000 was looted from a British treasury.

Reports of the weak reaction of the British were soon widespread, and Kabul began to fill with armed Afghans. Not only were the British confined to their poorly-built cantonments and unable to control the city; their ability to make strategy was paralysed by the physical weakness and senility of the senior officer, General Elphinstone (a cousin of Mountstuart Elphinstone), and the loathing for him of his second-in-command, Brigadier Shelton. As British possessions and stores were

An Afghaun of Damaun.

An Afghan of Koh Daman, in the vicinity of Istalif, 1809, R.M. Grindlay [RSAA]

"The main attack of the enemy was on the column, baggage, and rear guard; and fortunate it was for Mrs Sturt and myself that we kept with the chiefs. Would to God that Sturt had done so likewise, and not gone back.

"The ladies were mostly travelling in kajavas, and were mixed up with the baggage and column in the pass; here they were heavily fired on. Many camels were killed. On one camel were, in one kajava, Mrs Boyd and her youngest boy Hugh; and in the other Mrs Mainwaring and her infant, scarcely three months old, and Mrs Anderson's eldest child. This camel was shot. Mrs Boyd got a horse to ride; and her child was put on another behind a man, who being shortly after unfortunately killed, the child was carried off by the Afghans. Mrs Mainwaring, less fortunate, took her own baby in her arms. Mary Anderson was carried off in the confusion. Meeting with a pony laden with treasure, Mrs M. endeavoured to mount and sit on the boxes, but they upset; and in the hurry pony and treasure were left behind; and the unfortunate lady pursued her way

The Remnants of an Army, *Lady Elizabeth Butler, 1879. The work depicts the arrival of Dr Brydon—one of the few people to survive the British retreat—at Jalalabad.* [Tate Gallery]

An Afghan of Koh Daman, in the vicinity of Istalif, 1809, R.M. Grindlay [RSAA]

captured, the enmity of the two men made it impossible to decide on a plan of defence, and in the end the Afghans took control of the British supplies, while the occupying force was left short of rations. Lady Sale, the wife of a British officer, described the situation in her diary:

> "The troops had been on half rations during the whole of the siege: they consisted of half a seer [1 seer is approx. 2 lbs] of wheat per diem, with melted ghee or dhal, for fighting men; and for camp followers, for some time, of a quarter of a seer of wheat or barley. Our cattle, public and private, had long subsisted on the twigs and bark of the trees. From the commencement of negotiations with the chiefs, otta, barley, and bhoosa were brought in in considerable quantities; the former selling at from two to four seers per rupee, and the latter from seven to ten; but neither ourselves nor our servants benefited from this arrangement: it came to the commissariat for the troops. The poorer camp followers had latterly subsisted on such animals (camels, ponies, etc) as had died from starvation. The men had suffered much from overwork and bad feeding, also from want of firing; for when all the wood in store was expended, the chiefs objected to our cutting down any more of their fruit trees; and their wishes were complied with. Wood, both public and private, was stolen: when ours was gone, we broke up boxes, chests of drawers, etc; and our last dinner and breakfast at Kabul were cooked with the wood of a mahogany dining table."

In this situation, with no help coming from British troops in other parts of the country, there was little alternative but to retreat to India. Macnaghten began to negotiate a safe passage out of the country, but when it was discovered that he was secretly attempting to save the British position by fomenting dissent amongst the chiefs, he too was murdered. Nevertheless, agreement was eventually reached that in return for payments to various chiefs and the abandonment of British assets in Kabul, the British would be allowed to leave under the protection of the tribes.

Accordingly, on 6 January 1842, the 700 Europeans (including troops), 3,800 Indian soldiers and 12,000 camp followers began their march towards Jalalabad and Peshawar. Rations were short, and the weather, reports Lady Sale, was "clear and frosty; the snow nearly a foot deep on the ground; the thermometer considerably below zero". The first day's march was slowed by confusion and disorganisation; camp followers, families and soldiers were all mixed up together, making an adequate defence of the column impossible. The rear guard were attacked as they left Kabul, and already, as Lady Sale reports "the whole road was covered with men, women, and children, lying down in the snow to die". The escort promised by Mohammed Akbar, Dost Mohammed's son, had not appeared, and General Elphinstone foolishly insisted on incessant halts for negotiation, in the hope that the agreed supplies and escort would be produced. The result of this was to further deplete the British stores, and allow the Ghilzai tribesmen to take control of the heights further along the route.

On 8 January, the debilitated column entered the Khord Kabul pass. It is briefly described by Major-General Sir Vincent Eyre: "This truly formidable defile is about five miles from end to end, and is shut in on either hand by a line of lofty hills, between whose precipitous sides the sun at this season could dart but a momentary ray. Down the centre dashed a mountain torrent... with thick layers of ice on its edges, over which the snow lay consolidated in slippery masses..." Here, the column came under heavy fire from the tribesmen, despite being warned by various chiefs travelling with them to desist. Lady Sale recorded the attack on them:

> "After passing through some very sharp firing, we came upon Major Thain's horse, which had been shot through the loins. When we were supposed to be in comparative safety, poor Sturt rode back (to see after Thain I believe): his horse was shot under him, and before he could rise from the ground he received a severe wound in the abdomen. It was with great difficulty he was helped upon a pony by two people, and brought into camp at Khord Kabul.

> "The pony Mrs Sturt rode was wounded in the ear and neck. I had fortunately only one ball in my arm; three others passed through my poshteen near the shoulder without doing me any injury. The party that fired on us were not above 50 yards from us, and we owed our escape to urging our horses on as fast as they could go over a road where, at any other time, we should have walked our horses very carefully.

"The main attack of the enemy was on the column, baggage, and rear guard; and fortunate it was for Mrs Sturt and myself that we kept with the chiefs. Would to God that Sturt had done so likewise, and not gone back.

"The ladies were mostly travelling in kajavas, and were mixed up with the baggage and column in the pass; here they were heavily fired on. Many camels were killed. On one camel were, in one kajava, Mrs Boyd and her youngest boy Hugh; and in the other Mrs Mainwaring and her infant, scarcely three months old, and Mrs Anderson's eldest child. This camel was shot. Mrs Boyd got a horse to ride; and her child was put on another behind a man, who being shortly after unfortunately killed, the child was carried off by the Afghans. Mrs Mainwaring, less fortunate, took her own baby in her arms. Mary Anderson was carried off in the confusion. Meeting with a pony laden with treasure, Mrs M. endeavoured to mount and sit on the boxes, but they upset; and in the hurry pony and treasure were left behind; and the unfortunate lady pursued her way

The Remnants of an Army, *Lady Elizabeth Butler, 1879. The work depicts the arrival of Dr Brydon—one of the few people to survive the British retreat—at Jalalabad.* [Tate Gallery]

In the Khyber Pass [B. Woodburn]

on foot, until after a time an Afghan asked her if she was wounded, and told her to mount behind him. This apparently kind offer she declined, being fearful of treachery; alleging as an excuse that she could not sit behind him on account of the difficulty of holding her child when so mounted. This man shortly after snatched her shawl off her shoulders, and left her to her fate. Mrs M.'s sufferings were very great; and she deserves much credit for having preserved her child through these dreadful scenes. She not only had to walk a considerable distance with her child in her arms through the deep snow, but had also to pick her way over the bodies of the dead, dying, and wounded, both men and cattle, and constantly to cross the streams of water, wet up to the knees, pushed and shoved about by men and animals, the enemy keeping up a sharp fire, and several persons being killed close to her. She, however, got safe to camp with her child, but had no opportunity to change her clothes; and I know from experience that it was many days ere my wet habit became thawed, and can fully appreciate her discomforts."

On that day, reports Lady Sale, 500 regular troops were killed, along with 2,500 camp followers. At the end of 10 January, after four days of such conditions, it is believed that only 120 British soldiers remained, and 4,000 camp followers. Lady Sale's diary for the 11th begins:

"We marched; being necessitated to leave all the servants that could not walk, the Sirdar (Mohammed Akbar) promising that they should be fed. It would be impossible for me to describe the feelings with which we pursued our way through the dreadful scenes that awaited us. The road covered with awfully mangled bodies, all naked: 58 Europeans were counted in the Tunghee [gorge] and dip of the Nullah; the natives innumerable. Numbers of camp followers, still alive, frostbitten and starving; some perfectly out of their senses and idiotic. Major Ewart, 54th, and Major Scott, 44th, were recognised as we passed them; with some others. The sight was dreadful; the smell of the blood sickening; and the corpses lay so thick it was impossible to look from them, as it required care to guide my horse so as not to tread upon the bodies: but it is unnecessary to dwell on such a distressing and revolting subject."

Regimental Badges in the Khyber Pass, 1972. During British times, it became a custom for regiments stationed at the Khyber Pass to erect a replica of their badge. The Pakistan Army has continued this tradition. [B. Woodburn]

Aside from a number of hostages eventually taken by Mohammed Akbar, and a number of camp followers who had deserted the column, only one man, Dr Brydon, reached the British-held city of Jalalabad several days later. The remainder of the forces were cut down in various attempts to escape through the enemy territory.

In London and Delhi, unaware of the events unfolding in and around Kabul, government policy with respect to Afghanistan had changed after the election of a new Tory administration; a decision was made to withdraw all troops from the country in view of the excessive cost and poor return on the venture. However, when news of the disaster was announced, it was thought that some act of retribution was necessary in order to save the reputation of the British Army in the area. Forces were sent to relieve the garrisons still holding Jalalabad and Kandahar, which, after inflicting various defeats on the tribesmen under Mohammed Akbar, made their way towards Kabul. During this journey, they saw the aftermath of the massacres which had taken place in the various passes. The commander, General Pollock, occupied the city on 16 September; having been given discretion to act as he saw fit, he decided to destroy the 17th century main bazaar, in which the mutilated body of the envoy Macnaghten had been displayed. Pollock chose a detachment of men to ensure that the citizens were protected from plunder, but when the explosions were heard from the bazaar, a rumour began that plunder had indeed been permitted, and the troops indulged themselves without restraint.

The army of retribution left Kabul on 12 October. Shortly afterwards, Dost Mohammed was released and made his way to Kabul where he reassumed control. After the exertions of several years, the expenditure of eight million rupees, and the loss of thousands of lives, matters stood very much as they were before the British had begun their campaign in 1838, except that the goodwill the Afghans earlier felt towards them had evaporated. Nonetheless, after his time in captivity, Dost Mohammed had conceived a great respect and affection for the British, and despite the war, eventually showed himself to be a firm ally. As Burnes and Masson had asserted several years earlier, he was the only candidate capable of bringing order and stability to the region, and the abiding achievement of his reign was the reunification of Afghanistan after the ravages and collapse of the prolonged civil war.

(Following page) *Lone horseman at dawn, Khandud—Boroghil road, Wakhan Corridor [D. Grossart]*

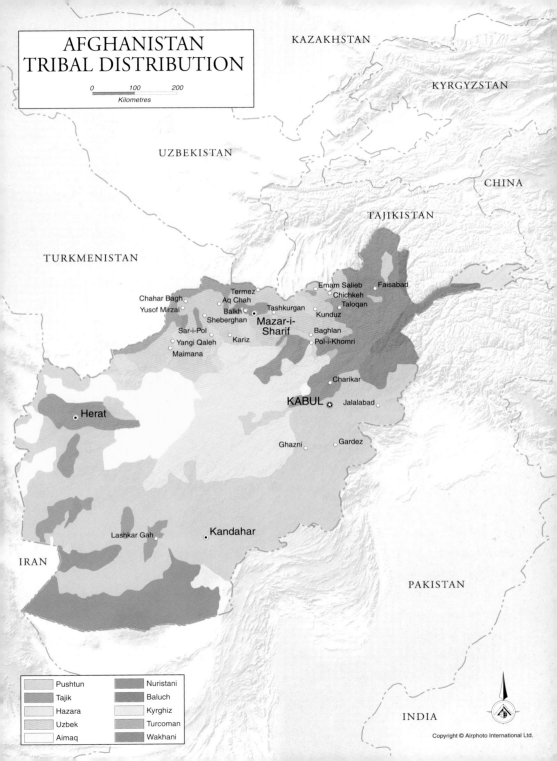

MUSIC IN AFGHANISTAN

—Veronica Doubleday

*A*fghan people love to sit and listen to live music, or get up and dance to it. During the dark days of the Taliban regime, when music was banned, people sometimes defied the authorities and hired professional musicians to go to a far-flung village for a secret music session. Hearing music was that important to them: it brought a sense of life and normality.

In Afghanistan—as in many other Islamic cultures—"music" is rather narrowly defined. It refers solely to instrumental music, or singing accompanied by instruments. Singing or chanting, such as lullabies, Sufi chants, Koranic cantillation and the Islamic call to prayer, are considered as separate. This conceptual distinction is important because it has shaped public policies and affected the status of music and musicians. Some mullahs have declared music to be sinful, so professional musicians have an ambiguous status—denigrated by religious conservatives, yet appreciated for their artistry by liberals. Zahir Shah, the ex-king of Afghanistan who returned to live there after the departure of the Taliban, is a great patron and music-lover.

In Afghan culture, music is associated with happiness, pleasure and celebration, and it should not be played when people are in mourning. The past 25 years have provided a totally hostile environment to music. Civil war, mass population movements, famines, political insecurity and other hardships made people lose the heart for it. On top of this came an increasingly powerful Islamist anti-music lobby.

From the onset of civil war, mullahs and resistance leaders put strong pressure on people not to play music, out of respect for martyred resistance fighters. After the withdrawal of Soviet troops in 1992, the coalition government cracked down heavily and very little music was broadcast on radio or television. Then, with the Taliban movement, things got worse. In one of the most serious music censorship regimes of human history, the Taliban tried to erase music from everyday life. The only melodious sounds they officially allowed were religious singing and their own chants, which were like Pushtun folksongs with new lyrics. They punished musicians, destroyed musical instruments, and at check-points and cross-roads displayed mangled audio-cassettes with tape innards strewn to the winds, as a harsh warning to passers-by. Most professional musicians from Kabul and provincial cities left Afghanistan.

After these traumas the various styles of music survive, some in better shape than others. Broadly speaking, the following types are found in Afghanistan: art music (or klasik-"classical" music), numerous styles of regional music, popular music as broadcast on the radio and ritual music and dances for weddings and male circumcision ceremonies. Emblematic of Afghan culture is the "national dance", called atan, performed in a circle by men or women on any celebratory occasion.

Afghan art music consists of two main genres: the Kabuli ghazal, which is a form of mystical or romantic sung poetry, and a style of instrumental piece known as naghma-ye chahartuk. This art music requires years of training and is mainly performed by specialist male hereditary professional musicians. The very best of these attain the honorific title of ustad ("master-musician").

Kabul's ustads look back to the 1860s, when the king, Amir Sher Ali Khan, brought a small number of North Indian vocalists and instrumentalists to his court. He gave them houses near his palace, in an area later called the Kharabat quarter. These notable musicians, their offspring and other local professional musicians worked over several decades to create and systematise a type of art music that was distinctly Afghan in style. In the 1920s the leading vocalist at King Amanullah's court was Ustad Qasem, whose fame rests principally on his creativity and excellence as a ghazal singer. He is described as the "Father of Afghan Music".

The typical art music band consists of a singer who also plays a small harmonium, accompanied by musicians on tabla drums and various stringed instruments. North Indian influence is evident in the use of tabla

Ustad Selim Bakhsh teaching ghazal singing, with harmoniums and tabla drums (Kabul 2004, AKMICA—The Aga Khan Music Initiative in Central Asia—which funds this teaching project) [V. Doubleday]

drums and harmonium (the latter originally arrived there with European missionaries). Singers perform ghazals in Persian and Pashto, often using texts from famous poets such as Maulana Jalaluddin Rumi, who was born in Balkh (northern Afghanistan) in the 12th century. Another poetic luminary, Abdur Rahman Jami, lived in Herat in the 15th century. Along with poets like Hafez (Hafiz) and Bidel, they represent the peak of Persian literature. Before the Soviet invasion of 1979, this sophisticated and beautiful music was regularly heard at weddings, concerts and on the radio. Now, due to lack of patronage and the demise of many ustads, it is somewhat in decline.

Afghanistan is rich in regional styles of music and dancing. They are quite often performed by amateurs, so in these traditions fewer musicians had to go into exile through economic need. Afghanistan is situated on a cultural crossroads, and many of its regional styles have close similarities with neighbouring ones across the borders. The main groupings are as follows: Pushtun genres, found in the south and southeast; Persian-language styles of the Tajiks (west and northeast) and Hazaras (central Afghanistan); and various types of northern music associated with Uzbeks and other Turkic-speaking peoples. Geographically and culturally distinct, Nuristan has its own particular music.

Ustad Ghulam Hossein playing rubab, with his brother on tabla (Kabul 2004) [V. Doubleday]

Pushtun music places a strong emphasis on rhythm, especially rhythmic accelerations and climaxes. Various genres include heroic epics and songs that use rhyming couplets called landai. Pushtun dances are highly dramatic, sometimes with fast spinning movements. There are close similarities with Pushtun music in the North-West Frontier Province of Pakistan. The music of Persian-speaking peoples is quite varied. A common thread is the use of quatrains (four-lined verses) about romantic and mystical love and the trials of fate. People in the remote Pamir mountains of Badakhshan share their music with similar communities across the border in Tajikistan. Across the north of Afghanistan, local styles include epics and coquettish dance pieces performed with or without a solo dancer.

Regional styles are also recognisable through their different instrumental line-ups—in particular, the type of stringed instrument playing the melody. The rubab (rebab) is especially associated with Pushtun culture, but it has spread throughout urban Afghanistan and is considered as the national instrument. It is a short-necked lute with a skin front (like a banjo), three main playing strings and numerous "sympathetic strings", which resonate and create a rich echoing sound. A prestigious instrument, the rubab is usually decorated with beautiful black and white inlay on its neck, using bone or mother-of-pearl. In Pushtun music, it is usually teamed with a singer-harmonium player, plus a barrel-shaped drum (dhol) and a bowed instrument called the sarinda.

In the west and north there are different types of long-necked lute called dutar. The name means "two strings", but, confusingly, some have more than two. In Herat instrument-makers have copied the sympathetic strings of the rubab, creating a large dutar with 14 strings. Northern players use the Uzbek dutar or an unfretted lute called dambura (which is also played in central Afghanistan). In the north and east another plucked lute, the tanbur, has sympathetic strings and a long thick hollow neck. There are also bowed instruments: in the north the ghichak, with its characteristic sound-box made from a recycled gallon can, and in the south the sarinda, which comes from Baluch and Pushtun cultures and is also played in Iran and Pakistan.

Drums are less regionally diverse. The goblet-shaped zirbaghali is played in many areas, and tabla drums have become ubiquitous in urban styles (often teamed with a harmonium).

All over the country the large frame drum called daireh is predominantly an instrument for women, except in Badakhshan, where men also play it. It is virtually the only instrument women are supposed to play. Girls and women use it to support their singing, to provide rhythms for dancing and to accompany processions connected with marriage. They play music when they socialise on happy occasions, especially parties leading up to a wedding. Some of their music is specifically connected with marriage rituals.

Another type of music, found all over the country, is played only by a particular class of low-status barber-musicians. Their instruments are a type of oboe (sorna) and a barrel-drum (dohol) played with two sticks. These ritual specialists provide music for men's processions and dances at weddings and circumcision parties. Working in pairs, they are especially active during the Afghan New Year period, which begins at the spring equinox, 21 March. Their loud outdoor music is considered auspicious, and they go around the shops and from house to house, asking for goodwill donations.

A more modern type of radio music has played an important role in creating a sense of national unity. Radio broadcasting began in the late 1940s, and through the radio many regional styles became well known across Afghanistan. The radio station in Kabul was an important focus of musical creativity, employing numerous musicians, composers and music directors. They used various elements of folk music to create a new type of Afghan popular music. The format consists of three parts: verse, chorus and instrumental section, repeated several times. In the 1970s the large official radio orchestra used many Afghan instruments, Indian instruments (including the sitar) and European instruments such as the violin, clarinet, saxophone, trumpet and guitar.

Talented vocalists made their names on the radio. One of the most famous stars was Ahmad Zahir, who died in 1979. The handsome son of a former prime minister, he helped to make the music profession more respectable. The anonymity of radio gave women a chance to perform—although some did so without their family's knowledge. Even in the more liberal atmosphere of

(Above) *Bridal procession with daireh (Herat, 1977)*;
(right) *Sorna and dohol players at a wedding (Herat, 1977) [V. Doubleday]*

Kabul, Afghan codes of modesty are strict about female public performance, almost equating it with prostitution. The female singer Mahwash was prominent in the 1960s and 1970s, and she continues to perform around the world. Mahwash lives in the United States, as does a younger star, Farhad Darya, whose band has a modern Westernised sound. In 2004 Farhad Darya gave a big concert in Kabul, playing to a huge and rapturous audience in the football stadium where the Taliban had carried out public executions.

After the traumas of Taliban rule, Afghan music is making a comeback, but increased contact with Western popular music has brought inevitable changes. In Kabul, musical instrument shops display hand-painted signs depicting keyboards, synthesisers and guitars beside traditional instruments like the rubab. People want to try out electronic instruments and to create new sounds. At weddings musicians play Westernised Afghan pop music—or people prefer to play recorded music.

Afghan classical music has suffered, but since 2001 many musicians have returned home. There are now teaching projects to support the regeneration of this music, and young musicians

Selim Khushnawaz teaching his nephew tabla (Kabul 2004) [V. Doubleday]

seem keen to learn. There are also plans to rebuild Kabul's famous musician quarter, the Kharabat, which was totally destroyed by rocket-fire in the early 1990s. If this is possible, it will be a great boost to musicians' morale.

Out in the countryside the picture is mixed. In some areas fundamentalist attitudes prevail, discouraging musical performance. There is also a dearth of instruments—the Taliban destroyed so many—and the younger generation has not picked up musical skills in the normal way. The war-torn country badly needs a period of stability in order to rebuild its vibrant, diverse and valued musical culture.

Veronica Doubleday is the author of *Three Women of Herat*. For further information and suggested reading on Afghan music, visit the website of the Afghanistan Music Unit at Goldsmith's College: www.goldsmiths.ac.uk/departments/music/amu/index.html

CULTURAL UPDATE FROM AFGHANISTAN

—Nancy Hatch Dupree

*F*ollowing the fall of the Taliban in 2001 and the subsequent establishment of an internationally recognized government in Afghanistan, there was a rush of proposals offering assistance to the Afghan cultural sector. Many donors fell by the wayside once the original euphoria had evaporated, however. Priorities were largely ignored, and there was little evidence of any desire to coordinate. Progress, therefore, may be best described as haphazard.

Much attention originally centred on the Kabul Museum, where looting andiconoclastic forays had caused severe losses. Despite this, repairs to the building are yet to be completed. Some restoration of artefacts has been undertaken and some equipment provided, but attention to the serious problem of upgrading the capacity of the staff to manage the collections lags far behind. The museum is a long way from opening.

Nevertheless, in April 2004 the authorities decided to put an end to the mystery shrouding the so-called Bactrian Hoard of 20,000 gold pieces, last put on public view in 1991 and since locked in the vaults of the National Bank within the Presidential Palace grounds. Malicious rumours that the gold had been spirited to Leningrad by the Russian excavators began circulating soon after the leftist coup d'etat in April 1978. Subsequentlyeach succeeding regime accused their predecessors of purloining the treasure. Only a few of us steadfastly defended the integrity of the Russian archaeologists and those Afghans charged with its protection.

It was therefore with considerable excitement mixed with trepidation that we joined a group of some fifty people milling about under the glare offloodlights in the foyer of the Presidential National Bank. The Minister of Finance and the Minister of Information and Culture presided. Seated quietly in the background was Victor Sarianidi, the genial head of the Russian team that had excavated the gold in 1978 at Tela Tepa (Tillya Tepe, or Golden Mound) in Jawzjan province, northern Afghanistan. The intensity of his feelings was palpable.

The atmosphere became electric as workmen attacked the keyless safe with a blowtorch and cascades of sparks exploded around us. An hour later the door swung open and the first plastic specimen bag was removed. It contained a pair of delicate five-petalled rosette hairpins with dangling discs and crescents, gleaming as brightly as they had 2,000 years ago.

Professor Sarianidi confirmed their authenticity and work on the inventory immediately began. There are six more safes with golden crowns, bracelets, earrings, rings, hairpins, pendants, belts, buckles, armlets, anklets, and even shoe soles, as well as myriad small plaquettes and discs that spangled the shrouds of five noble ladies, aged 15 to 40, and a single male warrior, buried in CE 100.

The Tela Tepa hoard is unique not only because of the high artistry of the objects, but also because it sheds light on the shadowy transitional period between the collapse of the Bactrians in the last years of the BC era and the rise of the nomadic Kushans during the early years of the Common Era.

After the Tela Tepa inventory is completed, the objects will once again be stored, although competing plans to exhibit abroad have been proposed amid considerable controversy. Security is a major concern, and expectations concerning the huge amounts of income to be gained from a travelling exhibit are clearly grossly exaggerated. One can only hope that after resting safely for so many years these incomparable objects will now not be put at risk.

The drama surrounding the unveiling of the Bactrian gold has obscured the fact that other mystery boxes in the bank will soon reveal more museum objects. Only a cursory look has yet been taken, but it would seem that much of the museum's extensive collection of 35,000 coins is safe, including the magnificent Graeco-Bactrian Kunduz Hoard dating from the 3rd and 2nd centuries BCE, as well as pieces of Bagram glass (CE 2nd century), Bamiyan mural paintings (8th century) and many familiar stuccos from the Buddhist site of Hadda (3rd–7th century). Their inventory is eagerly awaited.

While there is cause for great relief that these objects have resurfaced, it must be noted that the systematic plundering of sites continues unabated, and efforts to stem the pillaging are proving to be more dangerous than ever. The largest new site, which came to the notice of the authorities in July 2002, is a Buddhist complex spread across a valley of some 30 square kilometres at Kafir Kot in the district of Kharwar in Logar province, 160 kilometres southwest of Kabul. It dates from the 2nd to 5th centuries. A new antiquities law is about to be promulgated, but sufficient manpower and funds to apply the law are simply unavailable.

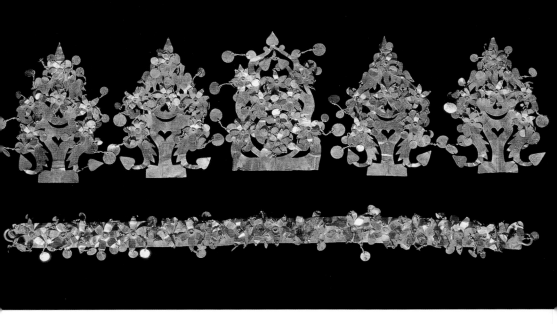

*Gold from the Kushan burial site of Tela Tepa (Tillya-Tepe),
2nd century* AD *[V. Sarianidi]*

While little headway has been made on curbing illicit excavations, several conservation projects are under way. Bamiyan, where the two colossal Buddha statues were dynamited in March 2001, predictably attracted many experts, mainly from Japan, Italy and France, with budgets of millions of dollars. They work primarily to stabilize the cliff around the Small Buddha, to preserve what is left of the mural paintings, to conserve fragments of the Large Buddha, and to conduct archaeological investigations.

The 12th century Ghorid Minaret of Jam was added to the World Monuments List in 2002 and work on its stabilization continues. At Herat the 15th century Timurid minaret that was in imminent danger of collapsing is under the care of an eminent world expert. Other monuments at risk needing immediate attention, however, have failed to attract the donors. These include the earliest Islamic monument in Afghanistan, the early 9th century Samanid Noh-i-Gumbad mosque at Balkh, with its superlative stucco decoration; as well as the late 15th century shrine of Khwaja Parsa with its sparkling blue, fluted dome, also at Balkh. Both are rapidly deteriorating because of neglect.

In Kabul, remedial conservation measures at Bagh-i-Babur, for which more millions have been allocated, progress steadily under various UN and NGO auspices, led by the Aga Khan Trust for Culture. This Mughal garden, laid out early in the 16th century, became the final resting place of the Emperor Babur, founder of India's Mughal dynasty, who died in Agra in 1530. Over 100 years later the Emperor Shah Jahan built an elegant marble-faced mosque next to Babur's tomb. And yet again, over 250 years later, the garden was still a favoured spot when the Amir Abdur Rahman built a pavilion here in 1883. During the 1990s, however, the gardens and its buildings fell victim to rockets and nearby residents scavenging for firewood. But soon it will once again become a place of enjoyment for the citizens of Kabul.

An imaginative project that complements the work at Bagh-i-Babur is the rehabilitation of an entire historic residential and commercial neighbourhood in the heart of the city, representing the traditional urban fabric of Kabul. In its midst stands the massive, octagonal double-domed mausoleum of Timur Shah who, in 1776, moved the capital of Afghanistan from Kandahar to Kabul.

These two projects in Kabul purposefully involve the communities around them, which is vital for their sustained maintenance. The expensive purely state-managed renovated properties will always require state maintenance that is often inadequate. Fostering community acceptance of shared responsibilities through imaginative awareness-raising initiatives is therefore essential. This aspect is being largely ignored. In addition, now that reconstruction is forging ahead with single-minded enthusiasm, there is a need for regular exchanges of information at the highest levels of decision-making. This is also not taking place.

Road construction, new housing schemes, industrial development, agricultural improvements and urban renewal projects are threats to archaeological sites and historic architecture. Technicians in charge of development projects, many of whom have only recently returned from years of exile, are impatient with vestiges of the past. For them it is easiest to raze the old in order to raise the new. Afghanistan is faced with many challenges on the cultural front.

This article was originally published in *Orientations Magazine*, October 2004. For further information visit www.spach.info—website of the Society for the Preservation of Afghanistan's Cultural Heritage; also in Switzerland the Biblotheca Afghanica—www.afghanistan-institut.ch

THE WILDLIFE OF AFGHANISTAN—
MAINLY CONCERNING THE LARGER MAMMALS AND PROPOSED PROTECTED RESERVES AND REFUGES

—Anthony Fitzherbert

This chapter is mainly devoted to the larger mammals that still occur in Afghanistan, but also includes an account of the proposed and 'existing' national parks and wild-life reserves. Mention is also made of the other wildlife and birds that may be encountered by the fortunate traveller. Unfortunately most are now only to be found in diminished numbers and are under serious threat. Some animals no longer found within the country are still found across Afghanistan's borders and if the rule of law is re-established might once again be re-introduced. For further and more detailed reading, some references are supplied at the end of this piece.

Afghanistan lies astride a great continental divide where the north western corner of the Indian subcontinent meets the great Eurasian plate in a jumble of relatively young mountains, plains and deserts that run westwards from Central Asia, Siberia, Mongolia and the Himalayas, through the Hindu Kush, across the mountains and deserts of the Iranian plateau to the Caucasus and the Anatolian highlands. Northwards stretch the endless steppe of Central Asia and Russia and southwards the plains of the Punjab and India. Common features are found in Afghanistan from all these regions. Geologically this region was formed towards the end of the Tertiary period and the fauna found here include elements from four biological sub-regions, the Mediterranean and Siberian (part of the Palaeoarctic region), the western Chinese and the Indian/Indonesian (Oriental). Most of the fauna found in Afghanistan belong to the Palaeoarctic region. This is separated from the Oriental region by the Sulaiman Mountains that lie along the Pakistan frontier. There are strong Oriental influences in the south and southeast corner of the country where the effects of the Indian monsoon are felt in Nuristan, Kunar, parts of Laghman, the Spingar mountains and Paktia.[1]

Altogether, 119 mammalian species are recorded in Afghanistan, about 460 species of birds[2] (of which 231 are thought to breed). Five species of frogs and toads and one salamander are recorded, but the list of reptile species (lizards and snakes) is admitted to be very incomplete, as are the species of fish, the hundreds of insects, fungi, and nonvascular plants. Some 4,500 species of vascular plant are recorded but much definitive work still remains to be done.[3]

In his comprehensive handbook "Mammals of Afghanistan",[4] (which includes mammals recently extinct and of uncertain status), the distinguished Afghan zoologist Dr. Khushal Habibi lists:

3 species of hedgehog; 4 shrew; no less than 40 species of bat; 1 monkey; 3 large cats; 6 medium to small sized cats, as well as the grey wolf, the golden jackal, 4 species of fox, 1 hyena, 2 mongoose, 2 marten, 1 polecat, the Eurasian stoat (ermine) and weasel, the ratel (honey badger), the Eurasian badger, the Eurasian otter, the Eurasian brown bear, the Asiatic black bear, the Persian wild ass (onager), 1 gazelle, 3 wild goats, 2 wild sheep, 2 deer, the Eurasian wild pig, 2 hares, 2 pika (rock rabbits), 2 flying squirrel, 2 ground squirrel, 1 marmot, 4 jerboa, 1 dormouse, 2 mice, 2 rats, 1 bandicoot, 2 hamsters, 10 gerbils, 2 mole voles and 5 true voles.

---

[1] Afghanistan is divided into three main geographic regions: The Hindu Kush highlands, the country's mountainous core; the Northern plains; the South west desert plateau. It also falls into various main and sub-biogeographic 'realms': the Palaeoarctic Realm, including the Iranian—Desert and Steppe of north west and northern Afghanistan; the Iranian—Desert of the Helmand Basin and the Rigestan; the Anatolian-Iranian Desert—Southern Steppe; the Pamir-Tienshan—north eastern Pamir Highlands; the Indo-Malayan (Oriental) Realm; the South eastern—Indus-Ganges Monsoon Forest—Lower Kabul/Kunar/Nuristan/Spingah/Pakhtya. Four main and several sub-vegetation zones are also noted: Desert vegetation; Extreme Arid, 100–150 ppt; Arid, 150–300 ppt; Steppe vegetation; Artemisia steppe; Grass steppe; Forest; Sclerophyllous Forest; Coniferous Forest; Alpine Tundra.

[2] Paludin 1959, updated by FAO 1981

[3] For further details see A Biodiversity Profile of Afghanistan: www.icimod.org/focus/biodiversity/afgbio.htm

[4] *Mammals of Afghanistan*. Dr. Khushal Habibi, 2003, Zoo Outreach Organisation/U.S. Fish and Wildlife Services; Division of International Conservation, Washington DC 20240

An account is given here of those of the larger mammals that the visitor in Afghanistan might be lucky enough to encounter, but almost certainly only if travelling in the more inaccessible parts of the country, or, unfortunately, as pelts for sale in the fur dealers shops in Kabul's Chicken Street.

Twenty five years of war, the absence of any form of law enforcement concerning hunting and the fur trade, a land awash with modern armaments as well as drought, climate change and the destruction of much of the remaining and always limited forest cover, have all taken a deadly toll of Afghanistan's once varied and interesting wild-life. The process of extermination had already started centuries ago even before the great Moghul hunts of the 16th, 17th and early 18th centuries, so vividly recorded in the memoirs of successive Moghul emperors.[5] Since the passing of the Buddhist culture in the 7th/8th centuries, there has never been any strong cultural or religious tradition for protecting and preserving wildlife in the region that is now Afghanistan. Hunting is seen as the right of any man with the inclination and the means of shooting or trapping wild animals, birds or fish.[6] However history does record that the Moghuls, following an older Mongol tradition, instituted laws that respected a 'close season' to allow game animals and birds to breed undisturbed in the interests of preservation for the hunt as well as establishing royal hunting reserves. But, it is the last 100 years, the introduction of modern firearms, increasing population pressure on limited land resources and the need to expand cultivation into fragile mountain grazing land[7] that has seen the greatest destruction. In particular the last 25 years of disorder and the break down of civil society and government controls that has lead to a rapid increase in the

[5] The Babur-nama (the memoirs of the 1st Moghul Emperor, Babur), The Humayun-nama of Gul Badan Begum, The Akbar-nama (Abul Fazl court historian to the Emperor Akhar), The Tuzuk-i-Jahangiri (the memoirs of the Emperor Jehangir); The Padshah-nama (Muhammad Amin Qazvini court historian to Shah Jehan

[6] Hawking is still a popular rural pastime in many parts of Afghanistan, usually with a goshawk (*Accipiter gentiles*) or sparrowhawk (*Accipiter nisus*) after quail (*Cotunix coturnix*, Dari *Bildirchin*) and chukar partridge (*Alectoris chukar*, Dari *kowk/kapk*). Falcons, mainly peregrine (*Falco peregrinus*) and saker (*Falco cherug*), are caught whilst on migration, but mainly for sale to Arab falconers for large prices. There is an autumn sale arranged every year by a leading hotel in Peshawar! The process is crude and almost certainly more falcons are irreparably damaged than get to the sale in good shape.

decimation of some of Afghanistan's most fragile environments and much of Afghanistan's remaining wildlife. Up until the Soviet war most local hunting was carried out with nets or with ancient muzzle loaded muskets and was comparatively sustainable.[8] Certain areas designated as royal hunting preserves helped to maintain a pool of breeding animals in comparative security. The breakdown of civil society and the rule of law, the proliferation of modern automatic rifles and cheap Iranian and Pakistan made shotguns, available in most bazaars for no more than US$20 or US$30 has put an end to more sustainable methods of hunting. Local traditions still exist in Nuristan for the sustainable use of forest resources, but these are rapidly breaking down under the pressure of outside commercial interests and most of the Kunar and almost all the Paktia coniferous forest has now succumbed to uncontrolled logging or the collection of fuel wood and the production of charcoal. In 2004 this still continues.[9] Only a remnant of the northern pistachio forest remains in Takhar and Badghis.

Starting in the 1950s and continuing through to the late 1970s, inspired by growing international concern and supported by royal patronage, international agencies[10] together with a few inspired and dedicated Afghans began a process of

[7] The ox plough and in recent years the rapid increase in mechanized agriculture has wreaked more damage to fragile mountain grazing land for unsustainable rain-fed agriculture, than over-stocking leading to increased erosion all through the central mountains and northern foot-hills. The cultivation by 'commanders/ governors' of the Dasht-i-Leyli in Jawzjan province in the winter/spring of 2003 in flagrant contravention of the law and the traditional rights of those who used the Dasht for seasonal pasturage, was just a more dramatic demonstration of a much wider problem and of the weakness of central government to impose its will.

[8] It is still possible to meet farmers in the Shomali plains, north of Kabul, during the spring migration, in March—out after duck with their home made decoys and armed with old British military muzzle loaded Tower and Enfield rifles dating from the 1850s and 60s, used as shot guns. This was also well described by Alexander Burns in his account of "Cabool," published in 1841.

[9] All through the 1990s when we were working in the Kunar valleys cedar (*Cedrus deodara*) and fir (*Abies webbiana etc*) were being extracted from the forests using mules, many of which had Pakistani army brands. The timber merchants financing the extraction were almost exclusively from Pakistan in collusion with local Afghan 'commanders'. The trade regrettably continues, ignored by the US Military occupying the valley who are even reported to be protecting the commanders who organize it in exchange for intelligence! Anthony Fitzherbert.

[10] Primarily UNDP/FAO/Afghan Ministry of Agriculture, Department of Forests and Range.

serious conservation. This was initially based on already existing royal hunting preserves to which were added a number of other locations and wetlands of special significance. By the late 1970s, serious work was in progress to establish a number of national parks and reserves to protect what remained of Afghanistan's animal and birdlife. On the eve of the Soviet intervention one national park, two wildlife reserves, and three waterfowl sanctuaries had been established under internationally recognition. In addition proposals were 'on the books' for an additional national park, three additional wildlife reserves, a game management reserve and an additional waterfowl sanctuary.[11] However, the process of establishing the official legal status of these areas was still under process in 1979. If not entirely banned, hunting in some of these reserves was carefully licensed and controlled. The 'Saur' Revolution of April 1978 and the Soviet intervention of 1979[12] brought this promising conservation programme to a halt, and any account of the present status of Afghanistan's wildlife reads more like an obituary than anything else.

Regrettably, the average traveller in Afghanistan, today, is very unlikely to see any of the large game animals that once roamed the mountains, plains and deserts of Afghanistan in their hundreds and even in their thousands or the great predators that once preyed on them. This is an opportunity open only to the most adventurous and hardy travellers in the remoter corners of Afghanistan's mountains and deserts and then only with more than a measure of good fortune and patience.

---

[11] In 1979 national parks, sanctuaries and reserves included both existing and proposed areas:

Existing: National Parks—Band-i-Amir (Bamiyan): **Wildlife Reserves:** The Pamir-i.Buzurg (Wakhan—Badakhshan); Ajar Valley (Kahmard—upper Baghlan/Bamyan). **Waterfowl Sanctuaries:** Abe-i-Estada, (Paktika); Dasht-i-Nawar (Ghazni); Kol-i-Hashmat Khan (Kabul).

Proposed: National Parks—Nuristan (Kunar, Laghman, Nuristan); **National Reserve**: Zadran (Paktya) **Wildlife Management Reserves:** Rigestan Desert (Kandahar/Nimroz); Darqand (Takhar); Imam Sahib (Kunduz).**Game Management Reserves**: Northwest Afghanistan (Herat/Badghiz); **Waterfowl Sancturies:** Hamun-i-Puzak (Seistan basin Nimroz);

[12] For instance the Darreh Ajar in the Kahmard valley in upper Baghlan, The Pamir-i-Kalan in Wakhan and the Kol-i-Hashmat Khan on the fringes of Kabul, presently almost dry.

Long gone is the Indian Rhinoceros (*Rhinoceros unicornis*—Linnaeus) from the reedbeds of the lower Kabul/Kunar river in Nangarhar.[13] Gone is the Caspian tiger (*Panthera tigris virgata*—Linnaeus) from the riparian forest along the Amu Darya river in the north, although tracks were reported from the Darqand islands from as recently as 1967.[14] Gone are the great herds of wild ass (the onager—*Equus hemionus*—Pallas) that still roamed the Dasht-i-Katawaz (Paktika) in the 16th century together with the goitered gazelle (*Gazella subgutterosa*—Guldenstaedt).[15] These were once slaughtered by the Moghul Emperor Babur (lived 1483–1530) in 1504, hunting on horseback with the compound bow and the sword, in the Mongol style of the great encirclement. Shah Jehan (lived 1592–1666) preferred the gun. Sadly the onager is also almost certainly gone from the lower valleys of the Helmand and the Harirud, where sizeable herds were still being observed by foreign travellers in the late 1800s.[16] Onager were recorded as still being hunted in Badghis, near the Turkmenistan border, as recently as 1975[17], but none have been reported in recent years. The onager still hangs on across the Afghan border in the great deserts of the Iranian plateau and possibly a few still survive in the wastes of the Kara Kum and Kyzyl Kum in Turkmenistan. Should peace and the rule of law ever permit, their reintroduction to Afghanistan might still be possible.[18] Gone too is the beautiful Asiatic cheetah (*Acinonyx jubatus venaticus*—Schreber,) that once rode to the gazelle hunt, hooded like falcons and balanced on the back of their royal owner's horses.

[13] Recorded in both the Babur Name and the memoirs of Jehangir.

[14] Khushal Habibi, Mammals of Afghanistan

[15] It is rather wonderful to imagine the Dasht-i-Katawz as it must have been in the 16th century looking rather like a Serengeti Plains in East Africa, with onager instead of zebra and goitered gazelle instead of Thompson's and Grant's gazelle and with Asiatic cheetah as their main wild predator.

[16] Connolly 1840 and Aitcheson 1889

[17] Khushal Habibi 1977

[18] The Persian wild ass, was made famous in Persian poetry as being the favourite beast for the chase of Bahram Gur—the great Sassanian hunter king, referred to in Firdousi's Shah-Nameh (Book of Kings). This gives rise to the popular punning couplet in Persian. "*Bahram ke gur shikar mikard, gur ba ru'ye gur e Bahram tambr mizad*" i.e. "Bahram who once hunted the wild ass (gur), the wild ass now stamps on Bahram's grave (gur)." Or as transliterated by Edward Fitzgerald in his rendering of the *The Rubayat of Omar Khayyam* "Bahram, that great hunter, the wild ass stamps o'er his head."

Against all odds, possibly fifty cheetah still survive[19] in the wild in Iran, in the remoter parts of the of the Dash-i-Kavir and the Dasht-i-Lut and in the aptly named Kosh Yeilagh[20] reserve in Semnan Province, east of the town of Shahrud, together with the wild ass and the goitered gazelle. Almost certainly gone are the last Bokhara red deer (*Cervus elaphus bactianus*) from their haunts they once shared with the Caspian tiger in the reed-beds and riparian forest (the *'tugai'*) along the Amu Darya river. From there they had been introduced by king Zahir Shah to the hunting reserve in the Darreh Ajar in the upper Kahmard valley in the 1960s, but none exist there now. A remnant population of Bokhara deer are thought to survive, although in great peril, in Tajikistan and Kazakhstan.

Among the most spectacular of birds, gone are the last Siberian cranes (*Grus leucogeranus*) that until recently used the alkali lake of Ab-i-Estada in Ghazni/ Paktika, as a migration stop on their way to and from the Bahratpour lakes in Rajasthan.[21] At least until water returns, gone too are the flamingos *(Phoenicopterus ruber)* from their ancient nesting grounds from Ab-i-Estada on the Paktika/Ghazni planes and the Nawar lake, high in the Ghazni mountains, dried out through drought.[22]

[19] Report on Asiatic Cheetah Surveys Conservation of Asiatic Cheetah Project (CACP) (asiaticcheetah.org)

[20] Khosh Yeilagh, i.e. the Beautiful Summer Camp. A wonderfully rich area for many wild mammal species ungulates (urial sheep, wild goats, gazelle) and wild ass as well as their predators (the leopard, Asiatic cheetah, brown bear and grey wolf) is situated among the juniper foothills, artemisia steppe and desert where the eastern Alborz mountain range drops down into the Dash-i-Kavir desert, east of the town of Shahrud (Semnan Province) The wildlife film maker John Buxton, of Horsey Hall, Norfolk, UK was probably the last person to film the Asiatic Cheetah and Wild Ass, in the Khosh Yeilagh reserve in the winter of 1977, before the Iranian Revolution made such things difficult. This was as part of a T.V. documentary on the wildlife of northwest Iran for Anglia Survival entitled "Winter at the Cross Roads" (Survival Anglia Ltd). In January 2001, Ali Reza Jourabchian captured the first images of a family of cheetah near Tabas in Khorasan Province since that time.

[21] George Archibald of the International crane Foundation, Baraboo, Wisconsin reports. *"A pair of Siberian cranes was seen in the Keoladeo National Park during the winter of 2001/2002 and these were seen on their breeding grounds in Russia in the summer f 2002. They have not been seen again since (January 2005)."*

[22] For an up date on the state of the various established and proposed national parks, wildlife reserves and wildfowl sanctuaries, see UNEP—Afghanistan Post-Conflict Environmental Assessment 2002, http:// postconflict.unep.ch or write to SMI Ltd, P.O. Box 11, Stevenage, Herefordshire G1 4TP, UK, tel +44 (0) 13438 748 844 and UNEP/FAO *Afghanistan Wakhan Mission Technical Report*, Geveva 2002.

Those of the large herbivores and their predators that do still exist within the frontiers of Afghanistan do so perilously and mostly on the verge of extinction. Yet miraculously some do still survive against all the odds of probability in remote corners of this wild and beautiful country. All is not completely lost.

What follows is an account of some of the larger mammals of Afghanistan, and where the fortunate traveller might possibly encounter them.

LARGE UNGULATES
THE SPECIES OF WILD SHEEP

The Marco Polo sheep or the Pamir Arghali—*Ovis ammon polii*; Persian/Dari *ahu-i-marco polo, qashqar*; Persian/Badakhshani *kochkor*; Pashto *marco polo gersta*; Wakhi *Rowsh War*; Kyrgyz *Arkhar*

The Marco Polo sheep is arguable the finest of all the species of wild sheep[23] widely admired for the combination of its body size, the magnificence of its great multi-curling horns and the remoteness and romantic nature of the mountain ranges it inhabits. It is the symbol of the Royal Society for Asian Affairs (formerly the Royal Central Asian Society) and is the animal for which perhaps Afghanistan is most famous. However, in Afghanistan Marco Polo's sheep inhabit only the far end of the panhandle formed by the so called Wakhan corridor,[24] where the head waters of the Amu Darya (Oxus) river rises in the south eastern ranges of the great Pamir range in what is known as the Wakhan Pamir Knot. The Knot is made up of two parts the Pamir-i-Kalan (Big Pamir) and the Pamir-i-Khord (Little Pamir). The greater extent of this species' range lies outside Afghanistan in the Tajikistan Pamir, part of western China in Xin Jiang, the northeastern Karakorum range in Pakistan and the south western Alai range and Aksu valleys in the Tien Shan mountains of the Kyrgyz Republic. Several other closely related species of large bodied, massively horned

---

[23] Although some would argue that a mature Trans Caspian Urial ram (*Ovis vignei arkal/Ovis orientalis arkal*) of north eastern Iran, with its beautiful neck ruff and finely curling horns is the most beautiful and elegant of all the world's wild sheep.

[24] The Wakhan Corridor and the Pamir Knot were 'given' to the Afghan ruler Abdur Rahman Khan by the British to act as a buffer zone between the British and Czarist Russian Empires. The boundaries were finally established in 1895/96. It was initially accepted with some reluctance but the frontiers have remained.

'Arghali' *Ovis ammon* species of wild sheep range eastwards through the Tien Shan, Altai and Himalayan ranges all the way to eastern Siberia and Mongolia.[25] Although some have more massive horns, none quite match the wide spiralling horn formation of *Ovis ammon polii,* which can exceptionally measure up to almost 200 cm in length down the outer curve although few 'trophy' rams exceed 150 cm today and most are between 120 and 140 cm [26]. Mature rams are larger than most other species of wild sheep, with a shoulder height of 110 cm and a body weight that may reach 115 kg. However, recent missions to the Pamir report seeing few animals of real trophy quality and it can be surmised from observations of the herds and the measurement of horns found lying about in herding camps that fewer animals are reaching either the maturity, age, or the horn size presented in the 1970s data presented by Petocz et al.

The ewes are half the size and have only short curved horns of about 15 cm. The summer coat is short, sandy reddish in colour while the winter coat is thicker and of a greyish white colour. The legs and belly are creamy white with a short tail.

Knowledge of this wonderful animal was first reported back to Europe by the Venetian merchant adventurer Marco Polo in his famous "Travels" which he dictated whilst in a Genoese prison some time after 1295, after his return from 24 years of adventure and travel in the orient. When writing about the Wakhan and the Pamir (*Bam-i-Duniah*—literally 'Roof of the World' in Persian) Marco Polo describes how "*Wild game of every sort abounds. There are great quantities of wild sheep*

---

[25] In addition to *Ovis ammon polii* other closely related sub-species are: *Ovis ammon ammon* (The Altai Arghali, seen as the archetype of its race—Mongolia, Siberia and Xin Jiang, China), *Ovis ammon humei* (western Tien Shan) *Ovis ammon karelini,* (central and N. Tien Shan, Kyrgyzstan, Kazakhstan); *Ovis ammon littledalei* (E. Tien Shan, Kyrgyzstan); *Ovis ammon sairensis* (Tarbagatay Mts., E. Kazakhstan), *Ovis ammon darwini* (Mongolia), *Ovis ammon hodgsoni* (Tibet, N. India, Nepal, Bhutan). Several as can be seen are named after British explorers, sporting naturalists, Hume, Littledale, Hodgson and Darwin.

[26] The largest recorded *Ovis ammon polii* head is said to have been a 'pick up' given to the Amir Abdur Rahman Khan of Afghanistan. According to Rowland Ward's Sportsman's Handbook of 1998 the record head 'hunted' was shot by Field Marshal Earl Roberts in 1895 in what is now the Tajikistan Pamir, which measured 190.5 cm and the next largest being shot by Colonel H.C.B Tanner in 1995 in the Afghan Pamir, measuring 185.4 cm. A wonderful set of horns hung in the old British Embassy in Kabul until they moved to new premises in 2004. There are undoubtedly larger heads unrecorded.

of huge size. Their horns grown to as much as six palms in length and are never less than three or four... There are also innumerable wolves, which devour many of the wild rams. The horns and bones of the sheep are fund in such numbers that men build cairns of them beside the tracks as landmarks to travellers in the snowy season." [27] Cairns made up from the horns and skulls of Marco Polo sheep and Siberian Ibex are still set up by Wakhi and Kyrgyz herdsmen to mark the way and places of special significance such as the graves of local holy men. [28]

Mature rams maintain smaller bachelor groups of between 5 and 20 separate from the immature males, ewes and lambs until the time of the rut which is rather late—from mid November through to early January, and lambs are born in May early June. They tend to graze at a higher altitude than the ewes, up to 5,000 metres in the summer, favouring the high alpine pastures and rich sedge meadows that are a feature of the high Pamir. These rams also travel greater distances commonly crossing frontiers in their seasonal migrations. [29] The ewes and lambs graze at a lower altitude in herds of up to fifty or more. The Marco Polo sheep is a mainly crepuscular grazer favouring the early morning and late evening.

Prior to the start of the civil war in Afghanistan in 1978 the species was well protected in the Big Pamir, where they are reported to have concentrated in the Tulibai, Sargaz and Abe Khan valleys and the eastern valleys draining into Zor Kol (Lake Victoria) the source of the Pamir river. [30] Licences to take a maximum of twelve mature rams were issued each year to trophy hunters in order to maintain sustainability. In the Little Pamir, mainly north of the Aksu and the Waghjir, rivers,

[27] And so they still do as was found on the UNEP/ FAO post-conflict Environmental assessment Mission to the Pamir-i-Kalan, September/October 2002—See Fitzherbert & Mishra *Afghanistan Wakhan Mission Technical Report*, UNEP/FAO, Geneva, published July 2003.

[28] These cairns of horns are composed of skulls and horns resulting from both local hunting and of winter wolf and snow leopard kills picked up by herders after the spring thaw.

[29] Fitzherbert & Mishra (UNEP/FAO environmental assessment mission) in Wakhan and the Pamir-i-Kalan (September 23 to October 9 2002) spied a group of 28 *Ovis ammon polii* ewes and lambs grazing at about 4,400 metres altitude (September 28) in the upper Ishtemich/Shikargah valley and the next day (September 29) spied 6 mature rams in the upper Shikargah valley near Chap Kol lake on the sedge meadows at just below the 5,000 metres contour line.

[30] See K. Habibi and R.Petocz 1978–2003

the local Kyrgyz were permitted to hunt and it is reported that hunting by the Kyrgyz was maintained at sustainable levels. It has to be noted, however, that high-powered rifles were at that time limited to the few.[31] There were estimated to be about 2,500 animals of all ages and sexes inhabiting the two Pamirs in the late 1970s. But, this was admitted to be an estimate based on more or less doubling the actual number of animals observed to take account of herds that had been overlooked or were across the frontier at the time of the surveys.[32] Seasonal migration across the frontiers with Tajikistan, Pakistan and China is well recorded.[33]

The total number of Marco Polo inhabiting the Afghan Pamir is not at present accurately known. The UNEP post conflict environmental mission in late September/early October was too brief to be able to make any accurate assessment, but observed both mature rams and ewes and lambs in the upper Ishtemich/Shikargah valley in early October 2002. A mission lead by Dr George Schaller in between August and October 2004, supported by the National Geographic and Wildlife Conservation Societies of the USA, mainly to the Little Pamir, confirmed that there are probably several hundred animals of all ages and sexes still surviving. These and other recent reports from travellers in the area confirm the continuing presence of Marco Polo in the Afghan Pamir, but that numbers are almost certainly much

---

[31] Up until 1990/91 the USSR maintained tight controls on hunting in the Tajikistan Pamir (The Autonomous Oblast of Gorno Badakhshan). Hay was even air-dropped to the wild sheep and ibex in the winter by helicopter. Although a population of *Ovis ammon polii* still survives in Tajikistan, these former USSR controls are reported to have broken down under the present independent Tajikistan regime. A concession for trophy hunting has been issued by the Tajikistan Government, but how well this is being managed is open to question. It is reported that the greatly impoverished local Kyrgyz population are hunting more or less at will. The author (Anthony Fitzherbert) has been fed on Marco Polo meat staying with Kyrgyz, in their yurts, near Murghab in the Tajik Pamir — 1998 and was given the impression that this was a regular feature of their diet. The situation is thought to be a little better in the Kyrgyz Republic. Protection and strictly controlled hunting is maintained on the Pakistan side of the frontier in the north western Karakorum/Pamir near Kunjarab. Across the frontier in China hunting is also reported to be rather strictly controlled by the authorities.

[32] Dr R. Petocz 1973

[33] Cross border migration is reported to have been impeded in places by fences constructed by the Soviets, but enough 'open' frontier exists to permit the Marco Polo to cross from one country to the other without too much difficulty.

reduced and likely to be less than half what they were in the late 1970s. Fewer animals are living longer than five to six years.[34]

The extreme shyness of the Marco Polo herds recently observed by a number of visitors to the Little Pamir, in particular, indicates, rather severe levels of local disturbance and hunting, by the local Kyrgyz and to a lesser extent by the Wakhi herders. Competition for grazing between the domestics flocks and herds and the wild ungulates is also a serious issue in many parts of the range.

In 2002 the Afghan Government of Mr. Hamid Karzai issued a complete hunting ban, which still holds although almost impossible to enforce in present circumstances.[35] Despite active hunting, particularly by the Kyrgyz herders, there is now good evidence to indicate that there is still a viable, if highly vulnerable, breeding population of Marco Polo in the Afghan Pamir. However, there appears to have been an overall decline in population since the 1970s in the eastern Big Pamir and a more modest decline elsewhere.

Workable controls and a viable management programme should be established for the area without delay. Ideally this should be part of a trans-boundary programme co-ordinated with Afghanistan's neighbours. A moratorium on hunting should be maintained until a proper assessment can be made and then only instituted (if at all) under proper management controls, in such a way that it will not be corrupted by government officials and which will include and benefit the local population.

The Urial Sheep—Ovis orientalis/Ovis vignei; Persian/Dari *ahu nekhsheyr, mel*; Persian/Iranian *gooch-i-kohi* (male), *mish-i-kohi* (female); Pashto *sra gertsa*; Wakhi *kooch-i-gadi (male); mish-i-gadi (female)*

The Asiatic Urial sheep *Ovis vignei*, together with its very closely related species the European/Anatolian, Mouflon (*Ovis gmelini*) are now commonly classified

---

[34] Dr George Schaller: Informal communication.

[35] The Fitzherbert/Mishra (UNEP/FAO) mission to Wakhan and Pamir found to their surprise that Karzai's ban on hunting was well known by the local Wakhi people who appeared prepared to respect it. The Wakhi, being Ismaili, are also inclined to take notice of instructions given by the Aga Khan. The Kyrgyz of the Little Pamir are, however, reported to be hunting regularly for meat, which in view of their remoteness, isolation and poverty is perhaps understandable. Recent visitors to the Little Pamir report being regularly dined on Marco Polo meat by their Kyrgyz hosts.

together as one species *Ovis orientalis* [36]. In the many localities in which these wild sheep occur they take on a number of distinct forms in respect of size, horn formation as well as the colour and form of their pelage. Both Mouflon and Urial are now generally considered to be the genetic ancestors of all the domestic breeds of sheep (*O. aries*) though the appearance of the latter in all its forms is much altered. The Asiatic Urial has a wide geographic range stretching from Anatolia through Iran Afghanistan to the western Himalaya and through the Central Asian mountain ranges as far as Kazakhstan.

According to Dr Khushal Habibi at least four sub-species of Urial [37] are thought to occur in Afghanistan extending from the westernmost ranges in the north east and

[36] The taxonomy of the genus *Ovis* (sheep) is highly contested. Various authorities have lumped *O. aries* (the domestic sheep) with *O. gmelini*—the European and Urial—*Ovis vignei*. But, many now classify both *O. gmelini* and *O. vignei* as one species, *O. orientalis* (in its various forms) and claim that collectively this is the ancestral species from which the domestic sheep derives. Some consider that populations of wild sheep on the islands of Corsica and Sardinia are sub-species of *O. orientalis* whereas others claim that they are a separate species. There is a tendency at present to simplify the older classifications that previously differentiated the various forms of the smaller European/Anatolian/Western Iranian Mouflon (*Ovis gmelini*) from the various forms of eastern Iranian/Asiatic Urial, *O. vignei*. Both are now generally classified as *Ovis orientalis*. Discounting the generally smaller European Mouflon, the Urial has a range that stretches from Anatolia through Iran, Afghanistan to the western Himalaya. Over time there has been much re-classification and there is clearly much hybridization between different types where their ranges overlap. Genetically Urial (now usually classified as *Ovis orientalis*) and Arghali (generally classified as *Ovis ammon*) can hybridise to produce viable offspring but in the wild this does not appear to happen even in areas where their ranges overlap, as they do to some extent in the eastern Wakhan in Afghanistan. It is noteworthy, however, that the sporting trophy record keepers, Rowland Wards, still designate Mouflon and Urial separately under their older classifications of *O gmelini* (7 sub-species) and *O. vignei* (5 sub-species) with the addition of two hybrids between the two. This multitude of sub-classification is based largely on local differences in horn formation, pelage, size and colour. For the sake of simplicity we will adhere to the general classification of *O. orientalis* (ref Ovis vignei—Urial Andrew Hagen—Animal Diversity—http://animaldiversity.ummz.umich.edu/site/accounts/information/Ovis_vignei.html & *Rowland Ward's Sportsman's Handbook* XIV Edition 1998—R.W. Publications Johannesburg, Republic of South Africa

N.B. Other species of true wild sheep inhabit western North America—*Ovis canadiensis* and *Ovis dalli*!

[37] In the case of Afghanistan it is noteworthy that possibly four types of Urial are classified by sportsmen: the Transcaspian Urial *O. vignei arkal* (North western Afghanistan); the Ladakh Urial (*O. vignei vignei*, western Hindu Kush/Wakhan/Chitral); The Afghan Urial (*O. vignei cycloceros*, Central Hindu Kush through Tajikistan, Kyrgyzstan, Kazakhstan); The Punjab Urial (*O. vignei punjabiensis*, mountain ranges bordering with Pakistan.)

south / south west of the country on the borders with Pakistan, Iran and Turkmenistan to the furthest north east ranges of the Hindu Kush in Badakhshan and the Wakhan —bordering with Tajikistan and Pakistan (Chitral). The sub-species classified as the Afghan Urial (*Ovis vignei cycleros / Ovis orientalis cycleros* according to opinion on classification) has the widest distribution. The Urial was undoubtedly found in much greater numbers and was much more widespread in past centuries, than today. It is commonly mentioned in accounts of hunts by the Moghul Emperors. Even in the 1970s it was not considered to be uncommon throughout much of the Hindu Kush, in particular throughout the central Hazarajat and Ghor and along the headwaters of the Helmand, Kabul, Harirud, Kunduz, Murghab and Balkh rivers. Prior to the Soviet war this species probably numbered in thousands with concentrations where it was most carefully protected such in the Darreh Ajar royal reserve, in the upper Kahmard valley in upper Baghlan / NE Bamiyan. Local seasonal migration from higher to lower altitudes was characteristic. East of Kabul, the Urial occurred from the Paghman, Kapisa mountains through the Panjshir all the way through to Badakshan to the eastern Wakhan.

The Urial is considerably smaller than the Marco Polo with the rams standing at about 76 cm at the shoulder, with long legs and a. graceful almost deer-like conformation. Mature rams grow a magnificent chest ruff of white / black tipped hair from their chin to their chest. The coat is close and thick, especially in winter and the general colour reddish brown with a creamy white belly and rump. The tail is short. Ewes are about 1 / 3rd the size of the mature rams and only have short spiky horns. The horns of mature Urial rams may measure 128 cm round the outer curve (recorded from NE Iran) but Rowland Wards register the record Afghan Urial (*O. vignei cyclocerus*) at 105.4 cm[38]; the average is more likely to be between 65 to 75 cm. Though possibly not as magnificent as the more famous Marco Polo the Urial is a beautiful and elegant animal wonderfully designed for the rocky mountainous environment in which it lives and capable of escape at high speed. Its eyesight as well as sense of smell is incomparable.

[38] Major G. Dodd 1909 Waziristan (now Pakistan)

Mature rams form bachelor herds of up to 20 or even 30 individuals generally grazing at higher altitudes to the females. This species can be found from 2,000 metres to 4,000 metres altitude and above. The mature rams tend to go up to a higher altitude than the ewes and younger animals returning to a lower altitude with the approach of winter and the rut. When undisturbed Urial may come down to graze amongst in the cultivated land and hay meadows of mountain villages,[39] but human and hunting pressure has tended to drive it to remoter and higher locations; those with the largest horns take a dominant position. The rams join the ewes at the rut which occurs from October through to November. Gestation is about 160 days and the lambs are born already very active. Urial may graze throughout the day in cool weather, prefer before and after dawn and at dusk when the weather is hot.

Very little is know of the Urial's present status in Afghanistan[40] except that numbers have been seriously reduced over the last 25 years by uncontrolled hunting and proliferation of automatic rifles. Undoubtedly conflict and bombing must have created serious disturbance. Some may still occur in the Hazarajat mountains and the author (Fitzherbert) has heard reports of this animal's continuous existence in the remoter least accessible valleys of Ghor (Lal wa Sarjangal) and Bamiyan. The Fitzherbert/Mishra (UNEP /FAO) mission to Wakhan and Pamir in September/ October 2002 heard reports from local hunters of Urial still being seen in the Wakhan corridor, in the mountains that form the Pakistan frontier. They observed Urial horns (not fresh) decorating the grave of a local '*Pir*' (holy man) at the Shah Kanda *ziyarat* near Ghaz Khan. No doubt, in view of the original wide range of this species it may be still found surviving in remote corners of the mountains in a number of different locations. Should peace and security and the rule of law return to Afghanistan this could make the nucleus of a revived population. In Afghanistan village mosques and the graves of local *Pir*s are often decorated with the horns of Urial, Ibex and Wild Goats but these are often of uncertain age. Until the status and geographical status of this beautiful animal is properly known, hunting should be

[39] As observed by the author (Fitzherbert) in the eastern Alborz mountain in Iran in the mid 1960s and early 1970s

[40] The Urial, is still thought to be reasonably plentiful in Iran.

banned and as far as possible controlled. The Urial is classified as being a vulnerable species

The Siberian Ibex—*Capra ibex sibirica;* Persian/Dari *ahu-i-rung*; Pashto *mugley*; Wakhi *yuksh;* Kyrgyz *tekke (male)*

This is the largest of all the ibexes. The mature males are thick set animals with massively curved and heavily serrated horns, standing between 67 and 110 cm at the shoulder and weighing up to 130 kg. The colour of the pelage is variable, but is generally a light tan with lighter belly hair. Mature 'billies' become darker with age with distinct patches of white on the neck and back. The females are about a third the size of the males and a have short curved spiky horns. Both sexes have a short chin beard. Rowland Ward record the record Siberian ibex head at 151.1 cm round the outer curve, shot by Kermit Roosevelt in the Tien Shan in what is now the Kyrgyz Republic, in 1927.[41] No doubt there are larger. Afghanistan marks the westernmost extent of this wild goat's range and it occurs from the central Hindu Kush all the way through the Panjshir, northern Nuristan and Badakhshan to the Wakhan and the Pamir. From Afghanistan this species is found all through the Pamir, Karakorum, Western Himalaya, Tien Shan and Altai ranges to Siberia, Mongolia and Chinese Turkestan. The Siberian ibex inhabits high rocky mountains between 3,000 metres up to 5,000 metres altitude[42] moving to the higher mountains in the high summer returning to lower altitudes in the winter. The inaccessibility of much of this animal's habitat has provided its own protection. The ibex is predominantly a diurnal grazer.

In earlier times ibex must have existed all through these mountains in great numbers and judging by the numerous petraglyphs in which they feature, this animal must have been a favourite quarry for hunters from the earliest times. Under

[41] A.Fitzherbert out with Kyrgyz shepherds in late October in the Southern Tien Shan (Atbashi region of Naryn Oblast) in 1999 saw a massive 'wolf kill' head picked up by herders on the mountain, which must have almost equalled this record. The Fitzherbert/Mishra mission to the Pamir-i-Kalan in 2002 observed some impressive sets of horns decorating these cairns and lying discarded about old herding and hunting camps in the Big Pamir in 2002 (Fitzherbert & Mishra).

[42] The ibex observed by Fitzherbert and Mishra in the Big Pamir in September/October 2002 where all between 4,000 and 4,500 metres altitude, mainly among rather inaccessible rock faces and scree.

careful protection in Pakistan's Northern Areas large herds of ibex are now being reported from parts of the Karakorum range.

Before the Soviet intervention in 1979, in Afghanistan, there were estimated to be about 5,000 ibex in the Darreh Ajar reserve alone.[43] Little is known about its present status, but due to the proliferation of high powered automatic rifles the total Afghan population is now probably numbered in the low thousands and it may well have been exterminated throughout much of its traditional range.[44] Few are now thought to still inhabit their old haunts in the Darreh Ajar although the author (Anthony Fitzherbert) has heard reports of herds of ibex still holding out in the Sar Jangal alpine valleys in northern Ghor.

Local hunters in Wakhan and Pamir indicated that ibex are still reasonably plentiful throughout this area, but in reality numbers would appear to have been much reduced since the 1970s.[45]

Several cairns of ibex and Marco Polo horns similar to those recorded by Marco Polo himself in the 13th century were observed on this mission marking the 'drove roads' and mountain trails and the graves of local *Pir*. It is not uncommon in Afghanistan to observe ibex horns decorating village mosques or the graves of local saints, harking back to a pre-Islamic tradition. The sheer inaccessibility of this wild goat's habitat mean that a scattered population may still survive throughout much of its ancient range, sufficient to build up numbers again should the rule of law and hunting controls become a reality. Experience has shown that given peace and security this resilient species can recover and build up its numbers quite rapidly if given a chance. Internationally the Siberian ibex is not classified as endangered in the 1996 IUCN list. Its status in Afghanistan must nonetheless be considered as being

[43] Shank et al., 1977

[44] A journalist acquaintance of Fitzherbert travelling in the upper Panjshir valley with Ahmad Shah Massoud's *mujahedin* fighters some time in the early 1990s, claims that when dining one evening on ibex meat his hosts boasted that it was probably the last one in the valley.

[45] The Fitzherbert/Mishra (UNEP/FAO) mission to the Big Pamir in September/October 2002 saw a total of 58 ibex of all ages and sexes in small scattered groups over a period of about ten days and spied ibex almost every day travelling in the high mountains, but no large herds. Other missions have also observed scattered groups of ibex, but not in large numbers.

highly vulnerable. For the time being, at least until more is known about its numbers and location, an official moratorium on hunting should remain in force as far as it is possible to enforce it or persuade people to honour it.

The Wild Goat (Bezoar)—*Capra aegagrus*; Persian/Dari *ahu-i-trey*; Persian/Iranian *tekke (male), boz-i-kohi (female);* Pashto *trey*

This is the archetypal wild goat from which the domestic goat *Capra hircus* was originally domesticated. This species is geographically very widespread from the Mediterranean littoral—Crete, the Greek Islands, through Anatolia (both the Taurus and Black Sea ranges and the Kurdish highlands), Iran (both the Alborz, Zagros ranges and most of the desert outcrops), Afghanistan, Pakistan and Turkmenistan. In Afghanistan this species's main range is in the southern and southwestern mountains from Farah through upper Helmand, Uruzgan, the mountainous districts of Kandahar and Zabol down to the Pakistan frontier and Waziristan and Balochistan. Its habitat is similar to the ibex preferring craggy mountains, with cliff faces and screen in environments that vary from arid desert to moist arboreal (as in northern Iran). The social habits are similar to ibex and the dominant males bearing the largest horns do most of the breeding. The gestation period is 150 to 155 days[46] with the kids being born in about April. Twins are common and given protection and peace numbers can recover quite quickly. The species is gregarious. Grazing during the summer tends to be in the early morning and late evening but more during the main part of the day in winter.

The mature males can weigh up to 136 kg and stand up to 100 cm at the shoulder. Females are about one third the size of the males. The mature 'billies' have scimitar shaped horns, which are oval in profile and keeled along the frontal edge, unlike the horns of true ibex, which are more sharply triangular in profile and more regularly and deeply serrated. The horns of *Capra aegagrus* show annual growth rings marked by knobbly protuberances. The females have short curved horns, which never exceed much more than 15 cm. Rowland Ward's records show the largest wild goat heads as coming from Iran—the biggest at 151.8 cm. was shot in 1977 by

---

[46] Dr George Schaller, 1977

Prince Abdorreza of Iran. This was exceptional, but good heads from Iran and Afghanistan have commonly measured 130 cm. The older 'billies' become silvery grey with a sooty chest, throat and face and a very distinct black dorsal and shoulder stripe. The typical goat chin beard is black. The tail is short and bristly. Younger animals and females tend to be more reddish brown in colour.

Once common in Afghanistan this species is now seriously threatened and its present status is uncertain. The hope is that the inaccessibility f its favoured terrain may mean that some scattered groups still survive which might make the basis for a future breeding population once law and order prevail. It is still reasonably secure in Iran and in the black Sea mountain in Turkey but is listed as 'Vulnerable' in the IUCN 1996 Red List of endangered species. Hunting should not be permitted in Afghanistan.

The Markhor—*Capra falconeri;* Persian/Dari *ahu-i-markhor;* Pashto *mar khura*

The third and arguably the most magnificent wild goat to be found in Afghanistan is the Markhor, which, on account of an old myth that this animal devours snakes, derives its name from the Persian *mar khor*, meaning 'snake eater'.

The markhor is a sturdy animal with relatively short legs and broad hooves. The males have distinctive corkscrew twisted horns. Mature males acquire massive long hairy beards from their chins to their chests. The body colour is reddish grey with a short tail. The belly and legs are creamy white. This wild goat lives in small groups of from five up to twenty. The geographical spread of the markhor includes southern Russia and the Central Asian Republics of Tajikistan and the south western Tien Shan ranges in the Kyrgyz Republic. It occurs (or occurred) in Afghanistan, from the northeastern Hindu Kush mountains to Pakistan; also through the western Himalaya and Karakorum ranges astride the upper Indus valley—Chitral, Hunza, Baltistan, Astor and the Pir Panjal range in Kashmir. The species extends down the Pakistan/Afghanistan border through the Suleiman range (Punjab/Balochistan) as far as Quetta.

Once numbered in thousands, this species was brought to the point of extinction by the 1930s, but careful protection measures in Pakistan since that time mean that it is holding its own, at least in certain parts of its range, although still extremely vulnerable. There may be between 1,000 and 2,000 still alive in the wild throughout its range. Its current status in Afghanistan is unknown. Although almost certainly seriously endangered Markhor have been reported to be hanging on in the remoter corners of the Spingar[47] Mountains in Nangarhar/Paktia and in upper Kunar and Nuristan. Also a few possibly still exist in the remoter corners of Badakhshan, where it once spread as far north as the Amu Darya river and what is known as the Darwaz peninsular and a small population is reported to still exist in upper Laghman along the head waters of the Alishang and Alingar rivers[48]. In the 1970s seasonal concentrations were reported for other parts of Nuristan (Kamu, Kamdesh, Barge Matal, upper Darreh Peche, Parun and Waygal) and in one survey as many as 56 were seen in one day.[49] But its status in these locations today with a heavily armed population and after the years of bombing, fighting and destruction of the forest is very uncertain. Competition with domestic stock will be another reason for the decline of this fine animal in its former range.

Four distinct sub-species of markhor are classified of which three were originally found in Afghanistan, their most distinct differences being the shape and formation of their corkscrew horns. The sub-species thought to have been most widely distributed in Afghanistan was the Kabul or Straight horned markhor (*Capra falconeri megaceros*), but the Chiltan markhor (*Capra falconeri megaceros x Capra aegragrus*) of Quetta/Baluchistan may also occur (or have occurred) across the frontier in Kandahar/Zabol provinces;[50] also Bokharan markhor (*Capra falconeri heptnerni*),

[47] The author (Anthony Fitzherbert), whilst staying in villages in the high Spingar valleys of Azro district—Mangal—of Logar, in July /August 2000, was given good accounts by local farmers and hunters of the '*ahu*'—almost certainly markhor—still surviving in the higher alpine pastures, ravines and forested cliffs and gorges. These villagers described how during the Soviet War, the Soviet bombing had seriously disturbed the animals, who at first rushed hither and thither not knowing which way to run but eventually they became almost used to it. The US bombing of the Al Qa'eda positions in the Toro Boro caves in the Spingar in October/November 2001 must have again seriously disturbed these remaining groups of '*ahu*'.

[48] R.Petocz 1973

[49] K.Habibi/R. Petocz, 1977

[50] Thought to be the result of hybridisation of the Kabul Markhor and the Bezoar Wild Goat. (*Rowland Ward's*, XIV Edition, 1998.

which occurs (or occurred) in northern Badakhshan in the mountains bordering Tajikistan and the Amu Darya River. Some markhor may still survive in the eastern Hindu Kush ranges bordering Pakistan/Chitral along the Wakhan frontier as a few well-protected herds still survive in Chitral. Hunting of Markhor should not be permitted in Afghanistan and indeed much work needs to be done to ascertain its present status.

The Goitered Gazelle—*Gazella subgutturosa*; Arabic/Persian/Dari *ghazal*; Persian/Iranian *ahu;* Pashtoo *seye*

This elegant little gazelle of between 20 and 30 cm at the shoulder once roamed in their thousands across the open plains, steppe and deserts from the Arabian peninsular, through Mesopotamia, Syria, Anatolia, Iran, Afghanistan, Central Asia as far as the Tibetan plateau and the deserts of the northern Indian sub-continent and Balochistan. For centuries it was a favourite beast of the chase by hunters using both Persian greyhounds—*saluki*, known as *tazi*—and hunting leopards—*Tazi palang* or *Yuz palang*, i.e. domesticated cheetah. With the advent of modern firearms in the late 19th century it continued to be hunted from horseback.[51] Many accounts of such hunts appear in the various memoirs and official accounts of the lives of the great Moghul emperors. It was once widespread and common across the plains of southern, western and northern Afghanistan. Sadly, with the advent of the automatic rifle and the four-wheel drive pickup this charming animal has vanished almost completely from much its former range. The once sizeable herds had already been decimated before the Soviet war (1979 to 1989). The last twenty-five years since 1979 have seen the almost complete extermination of this species in Afghanistan. Nonetheless, occasional observations are still made and A. Fitzherbert saw a kid in the possession of villagers in Balkh province near Tashkurgan in 2002, and in Mammals of Afghanistan *Khushal Habibi* reports a personal communication that related recent observations from the Rigestan in Kandahar.[52]

[51] The author (Anthony Fitzherbert) possesses a lively painting by a Qashghai tribesman from southern Iran, painted in the 1960s, of a gazelle hunt on horseback with shot guns and rifles. Clearly reflecting personal experience.

[52] K. Habibi, Mammals of Afghanistan 2003—Personal communication with Barakhzai, 2002.

The Goitered Gazelle is a smallish gazelle of reddish brown pelage with the belly and throat pure white. The rams have elegant lyre shaped horns. Rowland Wards record a record of 43.8 cm shot near Bokhara, Uzbekistan, by N. Karimov in 1967, with the next largest a 'pick up' in the possession of the Iranian Game and Fish Museum in Tehran, which is 42.8 cm. The average is clearly rather less than these. The rump is white and marked by a black tail which gives rise to its name as referred to in the Babur-nameh (written in Chaghatai Turkish) of '*kara kuyuruq*' although it is also confusingly also often referred to as '*kiyik*', a generic term for 'deer'. The winter coat is quite thick and luxuriant especially in those regions in northern Iran, Afghanistan and Central Asia where winters are extremely cold and snow falls are often heavy. In winter a distinct band of dark brown hair runs all along the flank separating the white belly hair from the upper part of the body. This line is not so distinct in summer. The goitered gazelle derives its name from the throat swelling that occurs in the rams at time of the rut. Rams are highly territorial and vocal during the rut which occurs in the late Autumn. The kids are born in March/April depending somewhat on the location. Twins are not uncommon.

Given proper protection this beautiful animal can recover its numbers remarkably quickly as was demonstrated in Iran under the strict hunting controls enforced during the late 1960s and 1970s when it was illegal to hunt gazelle. This ban remained in force, at least up until the Ayatollah's revolution in 1978 and is reported to be in force at the present time. In Iran, as the result of the controls and the establishment of well managed wildlife reserves, during the 1960s and '70s, under royal patronage, gazelle increased in numbers and this helped to support a (then) flourishing population of Asiatic cheetah for which the goitered gazelle made up the main prey of choice. The situation in Iran is thought to be much better than in Afghanistan as hunting and the possession of firearms by the rural population is controlled. There is still hope for this animal in Afghanistan should law and order and strict controls be re-established, but in prevailing circumstances this beautiful animal's future looks bleak.[53]

[53] In the late 1960s and early 1970s Anthony Fitzherbert managed private farms near Shahroud in north eastern Iran, when a herd of goitered gazelle multiplied happily to about 30 or 35, on the farms belonging to the Iranian family he was working for. They became remarkably tame and had their young in the Lucerne (alf alfa—*Medicago sativa*) fields being cultivated for hay.

THE FELINES

The Asiatic Leopard—*Panthera pardus*; Persian *palang*; Pashto *praang*; Wakhi *palang*

The Asiatic leopard is in fact the same species that extends throughout the African continent, parts of the Middle East, Arabia, Anatolia, the Caucasus, Iran, through Afghanistan, the Indian Subcontinent as far as Indo China as well as parts of Central Asia, Siberia, China and Mongolia and formally parts of southern and eastern Europe and the Balkans. Different environments and sources of prey have resulted in different sizes, colour patterns and shades and conformity, but the animal is genetically the same throughout. The form found in Afghanistan is very similar to that found in Iran and the western Himalaya (Pakistan and India), which tends to be larger and heavier than the forms found in Africa. Because of the harsh winters occurring in many of the areas in which it still occurs these leopards grow a thick and more luxuriant winter coat, making the pelts especially sought after.

A description of this beautiful big cat needs no introduction. The general impression is of wonderfully controlled power and muscle. The beauty of its tawny multi-rosetted skin is familiar to all. The cunning and versatility of the leopard means that against all odds it has survived remarkably well even in quite close proximity to man, even in quite populated areas of the Indian sub-continent and Africa. Being nocturnal and solitary, except briefly when mating, the leopard is seldom seen even by the human population with which it may live in close proximity. Internationally the common leopard is found in very different environments from dry desert to rain forest, from rocky mountains to lowland plains and savannah. The leopard's diet can include both small and large mammals as well as domestic stock, domestic dogs and even carrion.

It may come as a surprise to most people that any leopards at all still survive in Afghanistan. There are not many, but still there are more than might be expected, judging by the skins that still regularly find their way to the fur and pelt dealers in Chicken Street in Kabul. Continuing reports of Snow Leopards occasionally seen and hunted, from the area of Darreh Ajar may well refer to common leopard as many Afghan leopards are of very pale colour. Although the snow leopard is reported to have occurred in the Ajar Park prior to the Soviet war there is often confusion in the minds of the uninitiated. The Chicken Street pelts come from distantly separated locations such as Nuristan, Badakhshan and the Paropamisus Mountains that separate Herat and the northern plains and foothills of Badghis and Faryab provinces.[54] Little is known about the current status of this fine animal in Afghanistan, but it is undoubtedly under great pressure and is officially and correctly designated as endangered. It is possible that there is a scattered thinly-spread population across the whole of Afghanistan, but the locations that still appear to maintain the most viable populations are probably the Nuristan forests, Badakhshan (incuding the Wakhan), possibly parts of the Spin Garh mountains and Paktia; also the area of surviving juniper forest across the Sabzak Pass between Herat and Badghis. This geographical distribution has been assessed from the reported locations of origin of Chicken Street pelts.[55]

The Snow Leopard or Ounce—*Uncia uncia;* Persian/Dari *palang-i-barfie;* in Wakhan *khar palang*, lit. 'donkey leopard'[56]; Pashto *gharanie prang*; Kyrgyz *jylbyz*

Afghanistan marks the westernmost end of the geographical range of this handsome cat which is found through all the high mountainous regions of central Asia from the Altai (Siberian Russia and Mongolia) through China and the Tibetan plateau, the Himalayan range from Burma, Bhutan, Nepal, India to Pakistan as well as the Karakorum, the Tien Shan, Pamir and western Hindu Kush. Two distinct races of the snow leopard are classified—*Uncia uncia uncia* in the northern part of the range. and *Uncia uncia uncoides* in the southern part.

The snow leopard is wonderfully suited to its high rocky and snowy environment, with its beautifully marked coat of thick fur that perfectly matches the country in

---

[54] The author (Anthony Fitzherbert) in discussion with Chicken Street fur traders.

[55] The author ibid.

[56] Fitzherbert & Mishra (UNEP/FAO mission 2002) found the snow leopard so referred to by the Wakhi inhabitants of the Wakhan because they consider it to be 'stupid' as compared to the common leopard—particularly because of its habit of getting into stock corrals exhausting itself as the result of panic mass killing and then itself being easily dispatched by the villagers. The common leopard, on the other hand, will quietly take a single goat or sheep and escape undetected.

which it lives. The coat is thick with long guard hairs and a dense woolly under fur. The colour is greyish with a yellowish tinge and widely scattered black spots changing to large black rosettes. The tail is long (80 to 100 cm) and furry and almost equal to its body length, which when mature is between 900 and 1,350 cm. The paws are large, the legs relatively short for the body length, the nose is broad with powerful jaws and the ears are short and rounded. The snow leopard is a generally lighter framed animal than the Asiatic leopard weighing on average, when mature, about 50 kg. This big cat is not considered to be closely related to the Pantherine group having certain quite unique characteristics, and thus has its own classification of *Uncia* rather than *Panthera*.[57] Its natural prey are the wild mountain ungulates of the ranges in which it lives. It is a powerful predator capable of bringing down prey two or three times its own body weight, but it also hunts smaller prey such as marmots, hares and pikas as well as birds such as chukar partridge (*Alectoris chukar*) and snow-cock (*Tetrogallus himalayensis*). The snow leopard can live for up to about 18 years, but probably few do in the wild. It is generally a solitary hunter preferring the night early morning and evening, but may on occasions hunt as a pair, possibly when breeding and on occasions in daylight.[58] Two to three young are born. Unfortunately, the snow leopard has a bad reputation for predating on domestic livestock, when living in proximity to herding communities, especially when the domestic livestock are corralled in the winter and this is how many meet their end. On such occasions this animal has the tendency to go in for panic mass killings, a habit that was confirmed to Fitzherbert & Mishra (UNEP Post Conflict Assessment, 2002) by many local anecdotes.[59] The snow leopard is endangered throughout its range, and although internationally protected suffers everywhere from illegal hunting and trapping, for pelts, body parts and even live animals. Unfortunately, snow leopard pelts are openly sold by fur and skin traders in Chicken Street in Kabul despite the internationally illegal nature of this trade. The International Snow

[57] The Snow Leopard—Facts: http://dspace.dial.pipex.com/agarman/snowlep.htm

[58] Stockley, 1928; Habibi, 1977, and as reported to Fitzherbert & Mishra 2002

[59] This was confirmed by Dr. Mishra as a common trait from his experiences with Snow Leopard behaviour elsewhere in the western Himalaya.

Leopard Trust and other international conservation organisations are actively engaged in encouraging international awareness and supporting the conservation of this beautiful animal.

In Afghanistan the snow leopard occurs in the Pamir Knot and all through the high ranges of the Wakhan, Badakhshan and Nuristan, westwards in a corridor of high mountain country as far as the central Hindu Kush where it is reported to have previously occurred in the Darreh Ajar reserve.[60] Although its present status in the central Hindu Kush is uncertain the Fitzherbert & Mishra (UNEP/FAO) mission in September/October 2002 confirmed that there is still a surviving, if highly vulnerable, population of snow leopard inhabiting the eastern Wakhan Corridor and the western Pamir. They observed fresh tracks in the snow in two places—once in the western valleys of the Big Pamir, and also near the Dalriz Pass on the track leading from Sarhad to the Little Pamir. In addition this mission was able record a wealth of local anecdote, in particular stories of snow leopards predating on domestic livestock. This is where many meet their end.[61] This unfortunate characteristic appears to be the main cause of snow leopard deaths at present in Wakhan and Pamir, rather than deliberate hunting for live animals, pelts or body parts as is he case in other parts of its range. There are fewer reports of this animal from the eastern Little Pamir region. .

An alarming number of snow leopard as well as common leopard pelts are still finding their way to the fur traders shops in Kabul, which is a matter of grave concern indicating the extreme vulnerability of this species and the continuation of illicit hunting. The large presence of foreigners of all nationalities including foreign military make this trend particularly disturbing in spite of international customs agreements banning such trade (CITES). The Afghan Government has confirmed its support for the protection of this endangered animal, but with so many other responsibilities and problems it unfortunately hardly a priority. Even in the 1970s

[60] Dr Khushal Habibi, *Mammals of Afghanistan*

[61] A.Fitzherbert & C. Mishra UNEP/FAO—Afghanistan—Wakhan Mission Technical Report, Geneva, July 2003; see http://postconflict.unep.ch. Also ref: Oryx—Mishra & Fitzherbert, 2004

between 50 and 80 snow leopard are thought to have been killed and their pelts sold or exported.[62] The present figure can only be guessed at as is the exact status of this animal in the different parts of its original range in Afghanistan.

THE MEDIUM AND SMALL CATS:

The Jungle Cat—*Felis chaus;* The Caracal—*Caracal caracal;* The Isabelline (Himalayan) Lynx—*Lynx lynx isabellina;* The Leopard Cat—*Prionailurus bengalensis;* the Asiatic wild cat—*Felis lybica;* The Manul (Pallas's) Cat—*Otocolobus manul*

All these wild cats are under serious pressure from the fur trade that flourishes uncontrolled in Afghanistan and which has had an unfortunate boost from the influx of foreigners from many nations after the Coalition victory in 2002 and revival of a flourishing trade out of Chicken Street. Foreigners working or visiting Afghanistan are urged not to encourage this trade still further and the extermination of many of these interesting animals by purchasing furs and garments made from wild animal furs, which in any-case are almost certainly prohibited under international law.

Many of these animals were already under serious pressure even before 1979. Rodenburg reports in a survey of the Afghan fur trade undertaken in 1977 that skins of the jungle cat were amongst the most numerous.

The **jungle cat's** present status is unknown, but in earlier times it had been recorded from a number of locations from the south western/north western provinces to the south and east. It is a strictly nocturnal medium sized 60 to 70 cm) predator, yellowish grey to tawny red in colour, with a medium long ringed tail and a dark dorsal stripe. The legs are also faintly striped and the belly hair light brown to pale cream. The jungle cat inhabits semi-desert steppe, favouring watercourses and reed beds as well as cultivated land up to about 1,000 metres altitude. It preys on small rodents, bids and lizards. It can run very fast and has been recorded running up to 32 km an hour.[63]

The **caracal** is a medium sized long legged cat with a shoulder height of between 40 to 46 cm. It has a wide geographic range occurring from central and

[62] Rodenberg, 1977

[63] Hatt, 1959

northern India through Pakistan, Iran and Afghanistan to central Asia and westwards to Anatolia, Mesopotamia and Arabia. It gets its name from the Turkish Kara Kol from the black marks above each eye. The body colour is brick red and the belly creamy white. It has distinct black ear tufts, which lead it sometimes to being mistaken for a lynx. The tail is medium long at about 25 cm. The caracal inhabits semi-desert and steppe and dry hilly terrain up to about 1,000 m. altitude and preys upon game birds, rodents, ground squirrels, hares, lizards and young gazelle. In Afghanistan it has been mainly recorded from the northern foothills and plains and river valleys of the Harirud and Murghab. Even before 1979 the caracal is reported to have been very scarce. Its present status is unknown although pelts do from time to time find their way to the shops in Chicken Street.

The Isabelline (Himalayan) lynx is the Asiatic race of a very widespread palaeoarctic species, which includes the Eurasian (*Lynx lynx*) and North American lynx *(Lynx lynx canadiensis)*. Its traditional range extended across the entire northern boreal zone as well as the central Asian mountain ranges and the Himalaya. This sub-species is paler than its northern cousins and lacks a distinct pattern of spots although some of the pelts observed for sale in Chicken Street do show distinct spots, possibly indicating an intermediate form. The ears end in the characteristic Lynx tufts of black hair, which give rise to its name in Persian—*siah gosh* (lit. 'black ears'). This medium sized cat is compact and strongly built with a short stubby tail. Body length is about 100 cm and when adult stands at about 50 cm at the shoulder.

The lynx favours habitat is high mountain country, alpine meadows and forest up to 4,500 metres. The lynx is a strong and clever hunter preying on young ibex, urial and Marco Polo as well as marmots, hares, pica and game birds such as chukar partridges and snow cock. Fitzherbert & Mishra (UNEP/FAO 2002 mission) heard no stories from herdsmen in the Wakhan and Pamir of lynx taking domestic stock and they did not consider the *siah gosh* as a threat in the same way as they consider wolves, snow and common leopards. Dr George Schaller heard tell of lynx in the Little Pamir on his 2004 expedition, but observed no traces of the animal.

As recorded by Habibi the traditional range of the animal in Afghanistan from the Wakhan westwards through Badakhshan, Nuristan, Kunar, Nangarhar into the central Hazarajat. Its present range and status is unknown, but judging from information provided by the Chicken Street fur traders most of the pelts in their shops had originated from Badakhshan, upper Kunar/Laghman and Nuristan, and also possibly from the upper Panjshir.

Rodenburg records that between 200 and 250 pelts were traded annually before the civil war.[64] Fitzherbert & Mishra found lynx pelts to be second only in quantity to the grey wolf and red fox as the most plentiful skins being traded in Kabul's Chicken Street in October 2002.[65] This means that the animal is still present in Afghanistan but clearly under considerable hunting pressure and very vulnerable.

The leopard cat is a very beautiful smallish cat measuring 55 cm that inhabits mountain scrub forest and jungle up to 3,000 metres altitude. It occurs widely through Asia from China and Korea, India, parts of central Asia and Afghanistan as far as Iran. The pelage is tawny and the body beautifully marked with black spots (hence its name). The face and forehead are marked with narrow vertical black stripes. In Afghanistan it is mainly reported from the more forested areas of the east and southeast, but as it is mainly nocturnal it is seldom seen. Habibi reports live specimens brought in to the Kabul zoo in the 1970s. Fitzherbert & Mishra (UNEP/FAO 2002) were the told the story by one of their guides who had spotted what must clearly have been a leopard cat through his binoculars some years earlier in the eastern Wakhan, on a scrubby mountainside near Khandud.[66] Its present status in Afghanistan is unknown, but it is certainly very vulnerable and in danger from the flourishing fur trade.

The wild cat is another species threatened by the fur trade. This is nothing new and Rodenburg in his survey (197) estimates having seen over 1,200 pelts in the

---

[64] Rodenburg, 1977

[65] Fitzherbert & Mishra—UNEP/FAO Wakhan Technical Report July 2003

[66] The species was well known (if not frequently seen) by the local Wakhi farmers who referred to it as an *azada palang* (literally a 'free leopard' or possibly after Azada, a heroine in Ferdousi's *Shah-nameh*, associated with Bahram Gur.) Local Wakhi myth maintains that the azada palang has an extra claw in its tail! Fitzherbert & Mishra, UNEP/FAO Technical Report of 2002 mission, July 2003.

shops of Kabur furriers. Its present status is unknown. Fitzherbert and Mishra saw wild cat pelts in the fur shops in Chicken Street, Kabul in October 2002, but not in such quantities as Rodenburg.

The manul (Pallas's) cat, is a small long tailed cat with dense silvery buff fur, was formerly common throughout the alpine and sub-alpine valleys of the central Hindu Kush mountains through Panjshir, Takhar to Badakhshan and Wakhan as well as through Nangahar, Laghman through Kunar to Nuristan. Trapping for furs had already seriously reduced numbers by the late 1970s and driven the species to refuges in the remoter valleys. In the 1970s most of the pelts coming to the Kabul furriers were from Salang and Panjshir.[67] Its present status is no known but is thought to be seriously endangered in Afghanistan.

The species occurs in India, Pakistan through the Himalayas as well as Iran and central Asia.

THE MUSTELAE AND MONGOOSES (HERPESTES)

Among the members of these orders occurring in Afghanistan are the Eurasian Badger—(*Meles meles*) mainly Northern Afghanistan; the Ratel or Honey Badger (*Mellivora capensis*) mainly north east and Khost, Paktia; the Eurasian Otter (*Lutra lutra*), all major rivers, but in uncertain numbers; the Stone Marten (*Martes foina*), central and eastern Hindu Kush; the Yellow-Throated Marten (*Martes flavigula*), Kunar, Laghman and Nuristan; the Marbled Polecat (*Vormela peregusna*), mainly lowland foothills and steppe; the Eurasian stoat (or Ermine) (*Mustela erminea*), mainly north east and Paktia, Khost); the Eurasian weasel (*Mustela nivalis*), mainly eastern Hindu Kush; Common Grey Mongoose (*Herpenses edwardsii*) status uncertain but south east; The Small Indian mongoose (*Herpestes auropunctatus*), mainly western Afghanistan as well as Nangarhar, Kunar, Laghman and Nuristan.

THE CANINES

The Grey Wolf—*Canis lupus;* Persian *gorkh*; Pashto *shormos*; Wakhi *shapt*; Kyrgyz *karyshke;* Turki *boz kurt*

---

[67] K.Habibi—Mammals of Afghanistan

The grey wolf of Afghanistan is genetically the same species as found throughout Eurasia and North America and although now endangered or extinct throughout much of its historical range has been, in its time, one of the most successful predators. It is the ancestor of the domestic dog.

Despite every man's hand being against the wolf and an apparently ready market for wolf pelts, the grey wolf still survives in Afghanistan, against all odds. The wolf is still widespread throughout Afghanistan particularly in the Central Highlands, upper Kunar and Nuristan and from Panjshir through Takhar, Badakhshan to Wakhan and Pamir. Less frequently seen in the summer months when they are breeding in the remoter less disturbed mountains and valleys, winter forces wolves down to the villages and into frequent conflict with man. It is in the winter that most wolves are killed and this is the time when their fur is thickest and most luxuriant. Various colour variations are found in Afghanistan from light sandy coloured to a variegated coat of grey with black and white hairs and shading. Dark to black wolves are rare in this region. Mature male wolves in Afghanistan stand between 60 and 70 cm at the shoulder with a body length of between 100-130 cm. The tail, which is between 30 and 45 cm long, is bushy and darker towards the tip. Together with the pelts of red fox, wolf pets comprise the commonest animal furs to be found with the Chicken Street furriers.

More often seen in Afghanistan as single animals or pairs or in small family groups, larger packs numbering a dozen or more animals do on occasions gather together for hunting purposes especially in the winter time. Traditionally the wolf's main prey has been the wild ungulates that inhabit the high mountains (the wild sheep and goats) as well as smaller animals, such as hares, marmots and pica; however, human pressure and a shortage of wild game lead to frequent confrontations with man and the domestic livestock. When travelling in the Wakhan and the Pamir-i-Kalan in September/October 2002 Fitzherbert & Mishra (UNEP/FAO 2002) were regaled with numerous stories of wolves taking livestock of all kinds, some of very recent occurrence. In the Pamir it seems that wolves are frequently encountered by herdsmen when up on the summer pastures (*aylaq*). Although stock losses have been assumed to be most common in the winter when the natural prey such as marmots are not available, Fitzherbert and Mishra were told stories by herders of loosing stock even during the summer and autumn months, possibly when there were cubs to feed.[68] Hard winters, do undoubtedly bring wolves down close to the villages and winter encampments in search of food and in previous times even into the outskirts of Kabul where they have been known to take stray 'pye' dogs. The large native shepherd dogs and *sag-i-chupani and sag-i-jangi* used to guard the herdsmen's flocks are usually a match for marauding wolves. Stories of packs of wolves killing stray travellers in the winter abound, but seldom stand up to close investigation. Any enquiries on the subject of wolves in mountain villages in Afghanistan will elicit numerous stories and anecdotes. Some caution is required as not all of these stories are plausible!

Despite somehow holding its own against all odds, the grey wolf is officially considered to be endangered in Afghanistan and the continuing demand for wolf pelts does not help. Yet undoubtedly wolves to pose a problem for herdsmen in the remoter mountains, and the human/wolf conflict continues.

OTHER CANINES

Of other wild canines the commonest by far is the **Golden Jackal** (*Canis aureus*, Persian/Pashto *chakal, shogal*) which is widespread and very resilience usually living in close proximity to man sustained by cunning and a completely omnivorous diet that includes small animals and birds, carrion of all kinds and even fruit and grapes. Some jackal pelts find their way to Chicken Street, but are not as well regarded as wolf or fox pelts. The Jackal is likely to continue to manage to do better than survive.

The **striped hyena** (*Hyaena hyaena*, Persian *kaftaar*) occurs throughout the zones of semi-desert and steppe and the lower altitudes up to about 1,500 metres. A nocturnal animal more frequently heard than seen, although they frequently live in close proximity to man because of the carrion and rubbish they can pick up. They

---

[68] See Fitzherbert & Mishra UNEP/FAO Technical Report, September/October 2002, published Geneva July 2003

are not hunted on a regular basis as their pelts have little value.[69] However, they are occasionally caught to be used in dog fights, a sport popular in Kandahar. The striped hyena is widely spread through India, Central Asia, Iran, Anatolia, Mesopotamia, and the Arabian peninsular to Africa.

Of the four foxes recorded for Afghanistan, only the Eurasian red fox (*Vulpes vulpes*) can be said to be common. The other three—the Corsac fox (*Vulpes corsac*, recorded from northern Afghanistan), the Sand fox (*Vulpes rueppellii*, recorded from south west Afghanistan) and Blandford's fox (*Vulpes cana*, of questionable verification from the Rigestan and Lower Helmand) were recorded as being very scarce even in the 1970s.[70]

The red fox (Persian *rubha*; Pashto *sra geydara*; Turki *tulku/tilki*) particularly in its fine winter coat is much sought after for its pelts, which are the most commonly seen in the shops of the Chicken Street furriers. It is widespread throughout Afghanistan and at all altitudes. The cunning and versatility of the red-fox will almost certainly ensure its continuing survival in Afghanistan, and should un-controlled fur hunting continue it could well be placed under undue pressure. Internationally, however, this remains one of the most successful small to medium sized predators in the world.

The Asiatic Brown Bear—*Ursus actos isabellinus*; Persian/Dari *khers nasvary*; Pashto *kher yezh*; Wakhi *noghordum*; Turki/Kyrgyz *ayi/ayu*

In Afghanistan the brown bear is confined to Nuristan and parts of Badakhshan, Wakhan and the Pamir knot. The Asiatic race that inhabits this region is a reddish brown in colour and a little smaller than the brown bears found further north, and considerably smaller than those found in north America. It is none the less a fine animal measuring between 150 to 220 cm in body length. Against all odds the brown bear still survives in Afghanistan, although seriously threatened.

During their mission in Wakhan and the Pamir-i-Kalan for UNEP/FAO in September/October 2002 Fitzherbert & Mishra came across signs of bear in several

[69] Fitzherbert & Mishra were, however, shown one hyena pelt by a furrier in Chicken Street. October 2002

[70] K. Habibi, *Mammals of Afghanistan*

places in the Big Pamir, including scats and claw marks. In addition the mission were provided with a wealth of first hand stories by the local villagers and herdsmen, who consider sightings of bears as a not infrequent occurrence, whilst out herding on the high mountains or encountered whilst hunting ibex or Marco Polo sheep. It was reported that one of the local district Governors had shot a bear only a week or two before the mission's arrival somewhere near the 'drove road' between Sarhad and Langar in the Little Pamir ranges in the upper Wakhan river valley. As reported by Wakhi herders, sightings of brown bear are as often as not of female bears with cubs, usually twins. In this region bears seldom if ever appear to predate on the domestic flocks, although they may forage in the fields of wheat, barley, and millet on occasions. Fewer bears are reported from the Little Pamir and like the Snow Leopard the main population, such as it is may be concentrated in the eastern Wakhan Corridor and the Big Pamir.

The brown bear's diet in the Pamir appears to consist of roots, berries as well as small mammals such as marmots and voles as well as carrion. Bears do not seem to be deliberately hunted as such for their own sake, but hunters out after meat do not seem to be able to resist shooting at a bear if they see one, and in the process often ending up wounding it. For a long time brown bears have been officially protected in Afghanistan and against all expectations they appear to be hanging on in the remoter corners of the Wakhan and Pamir, but the widespread presence of lethal firearms undoubtedly places this species at special risk.

The present status of the brown bear in the rest of Badakhshan and Nuristan is not known. The animal must be considered as seriously endangered in Afghanistan, but still hanging on and worthy of protection in parts of the Wakhan and possibly elsewhere.

The Asiatic Black Bear—*Ursus thibetanus;* Persian *khers-i-siah*; Pashto *thour yezh*

The coniferous forests of Nuristan, upper Kunar and Laghman are the westernmost habitation for the Asiatic Black bear. Already seriously threatened by the late 1970s there are nonetheless still a few surviving against all odds in the remoter corners of Nuristan. The journalist and travel reporter Edward Girardet reports being shown the body of a freshly killed Asiatic black bear by local hunters when he was travelling in Nuristan in the summer of 2002.[71]

Gipsy street performers in Pakistan often have a dancing black bear as well as a performing monkey and other animals, but these bears are more likely to come from the forests of the western Himalaya.

The Asiatic black bear is a forest dwelling animal so that the destruction of its habitat must remain as much a threat as hunting. Like all bears it is omnivorous in its habits eating mainly vegetable matter, roots and berries, but also fresh meat as well as carrion, when they can obtain it. In Nuristan the people complain of bears raiding their plots of millet and maize. Although there is evidence that a remnant population of Asiatic bears still survive in the Nuristan forests, they must be considered extremely vulnerable.

The Eurasian Wild Boar—*Sus scrofa;* Pashto *sarkuzy*; Persian *khugh* or *goraz*

This animal was formerly common in all the main riverine basins of Afghanistan where water and cover, especially reed-beds and riparian scrub, give the animal cover. The proliferation of automatic weapons has lead to its decline in recent years. Wild boar are possibly still commonest in the *tugai* riparian scrub and forest along the Amu Darya river. The meat of wild boar being forbidden to practicing Moslems this animal is not hunted for its meat, but it does damage villagers' crops and is often shot for the sake of it.

Afghanistan's one Monkey: The Rhesus Macaque—*Macaca mulatto;* Pashto *bezow;* Persian/Dari *shadey*; Persian/Iranian *maymoon*

It may come as a surprise to many that any monkeys are found in Afghanistan, but the Rhesus Macaque, which is common in parts of the north of India and Pakistan, is a forest species that overlaps into the forested provinces of south east Afghanistan. It is still reasonably common in parts of Nuristan but destruction of its habitat elsewhere in Kunar, the Spingar Mountains and Paktia where it was once common has lead to its decline in recent years. This species can cause damage in the crops of mountain villagers.

---

[71] Edward Girardet, personal communication to A. Fitzherbert

PROFILE OF THE PROPOSED NATIONAL PARKS AND RESERVES

Afghanistan has never had the benefit of an effective protected area system although in the 1970s some progress was made and attention directed towards the conservation of Afghanistan's wild-life. Initially the areas designated were mainly based on already existing royal hunting preserves, but these were later extended to include a number of other locations of particular interest and significance. By 1978 just before Afghanistan entered more than two decades of war and political confusion a number of national parks, wild life reserves and waterfowl sanctuaries had been established or were proposed for international recognition. They have still not been provided with formal legal status. Everything was brought to an end by the events of 1978/1979 and it is only since 2002 that the subject is once again receiving serious international attention.

In 2002 UNEP supported a comprehensive nationwide post-conflict environmental assessment, which included teams of specialists visiting most of the designated locations.[72] Since then international interest in the conservation of Afghanistan's remaining wildlife and damaged environment has been revived. This includes the reinstatement and establishment of international as well as national status for the country's proposed national wildlife reserves. In the Wakhan and Pamir the ultimate goal is of combining this endeavour with Afghanistan's neighbours, Tajikistan, Pakistan and China. Funding is being sought and proposed and further studies and follow up missions have been undertaken and are planned.

However, continuing lack of funding as well as lack of security in much of Afghanistan still hampers the process of environmental assessment and the development of practical and effective conservation policy and well managed programmes. However, there is now a revival of international as well as national interest in conservation and for the first time in a quarter of a century there is a glimmer hope for the preservation and protection of Afghanistan's remaining unique wild-life and what remains of their habitat. What follows is a profile

---

[72] UNEP Afghanistan, Post-Conflict Environmental Assessment & UNEP/FAO *Wakhan Mission Technical Report*, 2002/2003

summary of Afghanistan's national parks and wild life reserves, where they exist at least as proposals.

A. NATIONAL PARKS

BAND-I-AMIR—BAMIYAN PROVINCE

Band-i-Amir was the first National Park established in Afghanistan, declared in 1973. It is situated in Bamiyan Province in the central mountains. By some oversight, however, it was never officially gazetted by the Ministry of Justice at that time and a management proposal by FAO in 1977 was swept away by the political events of 1978 and thereafter. The park includes the six famous Ban-i-Amir lakes (the Amir's dams)[73] of crystal-clear deep blue water, separated by white travertine dams and surrounded by spectacular red sand-stone and conglomerate cliffs. Local Hazara Shi'a mythical tradition recounts how the lakes were formed, miraculously by the prophet Mohammed's son-in-law Hazrat Ali on his way through to Balkh. The park includes a wide area of catchment on all sides of the lakes, which form part of the headwaters of the Balkh river. The particular geological formation that forms the Band-i-Amir lakes is found in a few other locations in the World, and no where in so spectacular a form. Band-i-Amir is recognised as containing a unique combination of features that meet the formal criteria for acceptance as a UNESCO World Heritage Natural Site. The lakes are home to several species of fish and has long been a place of local (Hazara Shi'a) devotion and pilgrimage to the shrine of Hazrat Ali on the shores of Zufiqar lake.

The 2002 environmental mission found evidence of increasing pollution from visiting local tourists in the form of picnic litter, orange and banana skins, plastic bags etc. Some of the local tracks and roads were infested with land mines and wild game (ibex and urial sheep) in the surrounding mountains were reported to be being severely hunted. A visit by A.Fitzherbert in late July 2004 found the 'tourist' pollution round lake Zulfiqar to be unimproved and possibly worse. Certain local entrepreneurial tour agencies had brought up boats with outboard engines and gaudy plastic 'pedalloes' from a children's park in Pakistan ! However, catching fish

---

[73] Gholaman; Qambar; Haibat; Panir; Pudina and Zulfiqar (the name of Hazrat Ali's sword)

to feed the 'tourists' appeared to be being controlled. A tented tourist camp has developed and a car park established at the foot of the Zulfiqar lake 'dam'. Some progress has been on clearing land-mines from the access roads, but the '*dasht*' above the lake is still unsafe. Hunting is still uncontrolled and the status of wild-life is unknown. A systematic environmental assessment still remains to be undertaken.

PROPOSED NURISTAN NATIONAL PARK

Prior to the Saur Revolution in 1978 and the Soviet Intervention in 1979 a proposal was 'on the books' to create a large National Park in Nuristan and the forest areas of the upper Kunar and Laghman valleys. Nothing had been formally agreed or gazetted before the outbreak of civil war. In the years that have intervened more than 75 % the forests in the Kunar and Laghman valleys have been destroyed by uncontrolled logging. The situation in Nuristan proper is better but under serious threat. The higher forest is mostly coniferous: *(Cedrus deodara; Pinus gerardiana; P. excelsa; P. morinda; Abies webbiana; Taxus baccata, Juniperus communis etc)*with deciduous forest dominating the lower to middle elevation slopes: (evergreen oak- *Quercus balut,Q. semicarpifolia and Q.dilatata,* wild olive—*Oleo ferruginea* and Walnut—*Juglans regia*, and others) Walnut is generally of planted origin and often preserved because of its economic value as are *Pinus geradiana*—the jalghozeh pine—for its edible kernels. Much of the logging is financed by Pakistani timber merchants.

Satellite imagery clearly illustrates the scale of the attrition both in Kunar and Laghman as well as in the Spingar (Nangarhar) and Paktia forests, where the situation is if anything worse. What remains of the once wonderful forests is confined to the remoter valleys, mainly in central Nuristan and the less accessible valleys elsewhere. A detailed assessment of the situation on the ground has still to be made. Unfortunately, since the Coalition victory over the Taliban and Al Qa'ida in 2001 / 2002 access has been made more difficult by continuing military action by the U.S. Coalition forces pursuing insurgents said to be opposed to the Government in Kabul. Destruction of the forests is only one aspect of the attrition wrought by the last twenty five years, which includes the destruction of traditional Nuristani buildings, architecture and culture. Wild life has undoubtedly suffered serious attrition. A systematic environmental ground assessment of the region still remains to be carried out and secure access continues to be very difficult. The proposal for a Nuristan National Park still remains and should be strongly encouraged as soon as the situation permits.

Wild Life Reserves

The Pamir-i-Kalan (Buzurg) The Big Pamir Wildlife Reserve

The Big Pamir Wild Life Reserve was formally gazetted in 1978, primarily to protect the Marco Polo sheep and other large game animals—Siberian ibex and the large predators such as the snow leopard and the brown bear. This still, however, requires formal legal recognition. The area of the reserve was based on what had originally been a royal hunting preserve established by King Zahir Shah. The area was very carefully studied during the 1970s mainly funded by UNDP and implemented by the FAO. The Park was managed as a carefully controlled hunting reserve. Twelve trophy licences were issued annually for selected mature Marco Polo rams plus others for mature male Ibex. At that time this was considered to be a sustainable off-take from a total population of Marco Polo of all ages and sexes estimated at about 2,500. Seasonal migration across frontiers was recognised.

The environmental assessment mission managed by UNEP, that visited the area of the Big Pamir Reserve in September/October 2002 confirmed the continuing presence of Marco Polo sheep, Siberian Ibex and Snow Leopard plus grey wolves, brown bears and other animals and birds, but had insufficient time or scope to undertake a detailed assessment. The activities of local hunters was confirmed as was competition for grazing with local herders in certain critical parts of the range. This still remains to be undertaken and the mission recommended a complete bio-diversity study be undertaken as soon as funds are obtained to include the whole of the Wakhan corridor and both the Big and Little Pamir be included.

In August/September/October 2004 a small mission lead by the distinguished conservationist, Dr George Schaller, sponsored by the National Geographic Society and the Wildlife Conservation Society USA spent 52 days—mainly in the Little Pamir—undertaking a field study primarily focused on the status of Marco Polo sheep in that area. This mission was able to confirm the presence of a reduced, but still viable population of Marco Polo under pressure from both local hunters and competition with herders for grazing.[74]

In view of the entirely artificial nature of the political frontiers in this area, developed as the result of 19th century imperial rivalries between Great Britain and Czarist Russia,[75] which ignore the natural movement of wildlife across frontiers. Both of these missions strongly recommend the development of a protected area in co-operation with Afghanistan's neighbouring countries Pakistan, Tajikistan and China with a view of eventually establishing a trans-boundary Peace Park.

The UNEP mission recommended that in view of the presence of a number of endangered species outside the confines of the original Big Pamir reserve both in the main Wakhan Corridor and in the Little Pamir that the whole of the Wakhan should be considered for special protected status. Both missions strongly recommended the full participation and inclusion of the local population in its development. The present hunting ban should be maintained as far as possible at least until the situation is better assessed and proper management controls instituted. There seems to be some hope that this might be possible in this area of comparative security and political stability if inaccessibility.

The Darreh Ajar Wildlife Reserve

Like the Pamir Reserve, the Darreh Ajar Wildlife reserve was based on an existing Royal Hunting Reserve established by the Afghan Kings. Amir Habibullah established a hunting lodge at the top of the Kahmard valley in southern Baghlan Province in the early 1900s. The Darreh Ajar lies at the end of 50 miles (80 km) of spectacular multi-hued sandstone gorges and canyon.

The valley is entered from the old Baghlan to Bamiyan of the valley of the Surkhab , from the bazaar of Do-Ab-i-Mikh Zarin (The Two Waters of the Golden Nail). This is where the Kahmard river joins the Bamiyan to form the Surkhab. The

---

[74] Dr. George Schaller informal communication. January 2005

[75] The national boundaries of the Wakhan were finally fixed by a joint Anglo/Russian boundary commission in 1895 /1896.

Kahmard river rises from perennial springs fed by deep underground streams, which surface in the caves of the Cheshmeh (spring) Chiltern in the Darreh Ajar. Tradition has it that the water originates in the Band-i-Amir Lakes. This remains to be proven. The river continues to flow strongly even in the worst of droughts and irrigates an interesting irrigated mixed agriculture all down its length. The geological formation is however very unstable and the valley is subject to dramatic landslides that regularly and dangerously dam up the river. In the late 1970s this area and its surrounding mountains were home to several thousand Siberian Ibex and Urial Sheep as well as their predators—notably the common leopard and (it is reported) the snow leopard and lynx. The royal family also introduced Bokharan (Bactrian) red deer to the riparian scrub forest along the Kahmard river as well as feral yaks to the surrounding mountains. The river was well stocked with trout.[76] Lake Chiltan and the upper Kahmard (Ajar) river is a migration 'bus stop' for duck and other wildfowl.

At the time of the UNEP 2002 mission the valley was very insecure with different groups fighting over land claims so that a detailed environmental ground assessment was not possible at that time. The political situation in the valley is still uncertain with simmering rivalries over land between the Tajik/Tartar and Hazara populations. The security problem has been intensified by the introduction of opium poppy cultivation to the valley in 2002 with local rivalries over control of the opium crop. At the end of 2004 a thorough environmental assessment still remains to be undertaken, but reports indicate that the wild-life of the area has been decimated over the last twenty five years. Little is known of the present numbers of urial or ibex nor of their predators the leopard and snow leopard (if existing). Ajar is reported as being the westernmost range of the snow leopard, but the very pale colour, characteristic of many Afghan as well as Iranian leopards often causes confusion and some uncertainty exists in this respect. The Bokhara deer have all gone as have the feral yaks. Recent visitors to the valley tell of uncontrolled hunting of both birds and animals both in and out of the breeding season, including song

---

[76] There are still trout in the upper Darreh Ajar and the author (Anthony Fitzherbert) on mission to the area in July/August 2001 was dined on trout by the villagers with whom he stayed in Ajar.

birds.[77] As soon as possible a systematic environmental assessment of the area should be undertaken. The whole of the Kahmard valley has considerable tourist potential which should be developed based on a sound conservation practices and a workable management plan. This must include the local population who are rather poor. The whole of the Kahmard valley is an area of outstanding natural beauty.

PROPOSED: IMAM SAHIB AND DARQAND WILDLIFE MANAGED RESERVE

This area consists of the riparian woodlands and reed beds—known as the '*tugai*'— fringing the Amu Darya (Oxus) and its islands in the districts of Imam Sahib in Kunduz Province and Darqand in Takhar Province, where the river forms the frontier with Tajikistan. This area had been designated as a Royal Hunting reserve in the 19th century with restrictions placed on settlement, hunting, cultivation and fuel-wood collection. In recent years, these restrictions have no longer been observed.

The area is important for its birdlife especially waterfowl, raptors and species associated with wetlands as well as the endangered Bokhara (Bactrian) deer *(Cervus elaphus bactrianus)*. Wild boar *(Sus scrofus)*, the Eurasian otter *(Lutra lutra)* and other animals are also found. This was the last home of the Caspian tiger *(Pantherus tigris virgata)* in Afghanistan.[78] However, the status of Imam Sahib / Darqand as a protected area was never gazetted before the Soviet conflict. Because of its uniqueness especially the two island chains and their *tugai* forest FAO recommended in 1981 that both Imam Sahib and Darqand be considered for protected area status. In recent times there has been some human settlement on the islands and for a time they were also 'settled' by refugees from civil strife across the river in Tajikistan. Much of the island *tugai* forest survives, but is threatened. The Imam Sahib island is estimated

---

[77] The decimation of local wild-life was reported by the author (Anthony Fitzherbert)—on mission to this area for the Aga Khan Aid Agency—FOCUS Humanitarian—in July/August 2001. Further reports on Kahmard, by journalist—Jonathan Ledgard in 2002 and by tourists visiting the Kahmard valley and Ajar in May 2004 confirmed this unhappy state of affairs.

[78] The Caspian tiger may have survived longer in the Mazandran forests in the eastern Alborz mountains, but this is also uncertain.

to be 100 km long and between 1 and 10 km wide while the islands of Darqand stretch for about 50 km and are thought to be up to 5 km wide. The status of wild-life is not very precisely known and hunting is almost certainly taking place. On a recent visit to Imam Sahib in December 2004, the author (Anthony Fitzherbert) was informed that local officials and 'commanders' regularly cross to the island to go 'hunting'. Smuggling of narcotics across the river to Tajikistan is also an issue in this area. Local people familiar with the islands report that there are wild boar, fox, jackal, hare, and porcupine and even possibly a few Bokhara deer and pheasant (*Phasianus colchicus*) still surviving but no proper assessment has yet been made.

Imam Sahib district is interesting in other respects—with its rich and varied irrigated agriculture growing wheat and rice and local fishing industry for sale in Kunduz and the regional bazaars. The district derives its name from an historic mosque and *ziarat* (place of local religious veneration) reputed to contain the severed head of the Prophet Mohammed's grandson Hazrat Imam Hussein,[79] which is reputed to have been brought there by Arab missionaries. The Dasht-i-Abdan and Dasht-i-Aklu plains that separate Kunduz from Imam Sahib are used by Persian speaking 'Arab' and Pashto speaking Kandari nomads (*kuchi*) as winter/spring pasturage during which time their flocks of fine 'arab' sheep and encampments of black goat-hair tents (*siah chador/khaima*) can be seen scattered across the *dasht*. They migrate to the highlands of north eastern Badakhshan in the summer.

PROPOSED: THE NORTHWEST AFGHANISTAN GAME MANAGEMENT RESERVE

This area roughly corresponds to the far north western corner of Afghanistan bordering Turkmenistan. It incorporates parts of Herat and Badghis provinces straddling the watershed and includes areas of interesting mountain and plain. As a reserve it was never gazetted and remained only as a proposal. This was the area in which wild ass/onager (*Equus hemonius*) were reported as being hunted in Afghanistan as late as 1975. The wild ass almost certainly does not exist in this area

[79] Hussein is of special veneration for Shi'a Moslems who consider him to be the 3rd Imam, or rightful leader, of the Moslem Community, killed at the battle of Kerbala (10th Muharram AH 61, Oct 10th AD 680) by the forces of Yazid son of the Umayyad (Sunni) Kalifa Mu'awiya.

any more although some small and scattered herds still hang on in the deserts of Iran and possibly in Turkmenistan. Little is really known in any detail about the present status of wild-life in this area. Urial sheep (*Ovis orientalis*) and wild goats (*Capra aegagrus*) and goitered gazelle (*Gazella subgutterosa*) used to be reasonably plentiful, but their exact status at present is not known. Leopard are still reported from the area of the Kotal-i-Sabzak on the watershed between Herat and Qala-i-Naw, and pelts on sale in Chicken Street in Kabul are often reported to come from this area. This region is also of interest for its juniper forests (*Juniperus excelsa*) of which 50% is thought to have been lost in the last 30 years, and wild pistachio forest (*Pistacia vera)* of which only a remnant remains compared to what existed prior to the Soviet war.

PROPOSED: THE RIGESTAN DESERT—WILDLIFE MANAGED RESERVE

The Rigestan desert comprises a large expanse of solidified sand-dunes in southern Kandahar. It was proposed as a wildlife managed reserve in the 1970s, but was never gazetted. The Rigestan is the traditional 'home' for several groups of Baloch nomads (*kuchi*) now mostly living in IDP camps near Kandahar having lost their flocks as a result of the drought. The environment is very fragile and has suffered seriously in the last seven or eight years of drought. The ancient, traditional wells have either dried up or fallen into disrepair, and the desert plant life—especially the larger woody species such as *Tamarisk*—are reported to have been cut for fuel-wood. The desert wildlife has also suffered severely from a population in arms as well as more organised motorised hunting. During the Taliban years large hunting parties of wealthy Arabs came to the region every winter and even had a special airstrip built for the purpose. Gazelle (*Gazella subguterosa*) and the once common Hubara bustard (*Chalmydotis macqueen*, formerly *Chalmydotis undulata*), the favourite quarry of the Arabs, are now rarely seen. Some initial study of the vegetation and state of the range land grazing was undertaken in 2004 under the auspices of the Central Asian Development Group by a rangeland specialist from Tashkent University, Uzbekistan, Dr. K.N. Toderich. However, a systematic environmental assessment has still to be carried out in the Rigestan and continuing insecurity in the region makes this a difficult undertaking.

Proposed: The Zadran National Reserve, Paktia

This area was never gazetted. Its main interest derives from the coniferous (*Cedrus deodara, Pinus geradiana, Abies webbiana, Picea morinda*) and deciduous forests (*Quercus baloot, Q. dilatata, Juglans regia* etc) of the area and the wild-life that once flourished there, including wild sheep and wild goats. Satellite imagery indicates that less than 30% of the pre-Soviet war forest cover of Nangarhar, Paktia, Khost and Pakitika provinces remains, and much of the rest has been seriously damaged. The whole of this area was seriously bombed and fought over during ten years of the Soviet war (1979 to 1989). Fighting continued until 1991 and then the area was bombed again in the winter of 2001 / 2002. Coalition forces are active in the area and meeting resistance from local insurgents. Insecurity continues in this region and a systematic environmental assessment still remains difficult to carry out.

Wetlands and Waterfowl Sanctuaries

Kol-i-Hashmat Khan Waterfowl Sanctuary

Kol-i-Hashmat Khan Waterfowl Sanctuary is (or more precisely was) a shallow, reed-covered lake situated on the outskirts of Kabul in the shadow of the ancient citadel, the Bala Hissar. Historically it was reserved for shooting wild-fowl by the Royal Family but was designated as a wildfowl reserve by the King in the 1930s, although this was never legalised. It was traditionally an important recreational area for the citizens of Kabul—then a much smaller city—and certain families had the right to cut reeds for roofing. The area and its surrounds contain various historical sites including the shrine (*ziyarat*) of Jabur Ansar built in the 1st century of the Hijra (AD 645) Since the drought of the last eight years, which started in 1999 and continues not helped by the digging of a drainage ditch around the lake, Kol-i-Heshmat Khan is presently little more than a dry clay pan. Efforts are now being made to restore the lake but drought and encroaching housing development remain a threat and its future seems uncertain. During times when water is standing in the lake bed, wild ducks and other migrating water fowl can be observed on Kol-i-Hashmat Khan, but not in the numbers that once regularly visited the place. The loss of the reed-beds has meant that the reed loving birds that once nested here no longer do so.

THE DASHT-I-NAWAR NATIONAL WATERFOWL AND FLAMINGO SANCTUARY

The Dasht-i-Nawar is an extensive high-altitude plain in highland Ghazni at an elevation of about 3,350 m elevation. It is surrounded by high mountains with peaks rising to 4,800 m that once gave home to sizeable populations of ibex and urial sheep. The plain forms an inward draining basin holding a brackish lake of variable size about 10 km long. The last eight years of drought

Since 1999, have meant that the lake bed has been virtually dry. In previous years of better precipitation and winter snowfall, Nawar provided not only a significant autumn and spring 'bus stop' for migrating waterfowl of many species, but also an almost unique high altitude breeding ground for a number of interesting species, including the Greater Flamingo (*Phoenicopterus ruber roseus*), avocets (*Recurvirosta avocetta*) and various other wading birds and plovers. The years of drought have forced the flamingo population and most of the wading birds and ducks to go elsewhere. Some migrating waterfowl still use the scattered pools that remain. A return to seasons of higher precipitation especially winter snowfall are needed to return the Nawar Lake to its former condition. If this happens it will be interesting to see if the flamingos will return. Historically this is not the first time that this situation has occurred although previous periods of drought seem to have generally been of shorter duration.

Ibex and urial are reported to be still found in the surrounding mountains, but as no systematic assessment has been made in the last 28 years and the true status of these animals in the region is not known.

The Ab-i-Estada National Waterfowl and Flamingo Sanctuary

The Ab-i-Estada is a large saline lake located on the borders of Ghazni and Paktika provinces in the inland drainage basin of the Gardez, Ghazni and Nahara rivers. The name in Persian means the 'Standing Water'. The drought of the last years has meant that the water in the lake has been seriously reduced. In 2002 when visited by the team from UNEP as part of their Post Conflict Environmental assessment it was almost completely dry. There was some water in the lake in 2003 but 2004 found it almost completely dry again.

Until the drought that started in 1999 and which has not yet abated, the Ab-i-Estada was remarkable for the numbers of greater flamingos that nested on the various islands. The flamingos arrive at high water levels in late March or April and depart when water levels decline in late September or early October. Over the years numbers have fluctuated enormously from 9,000 to none. The low to none existent water levels in recent years has meant that it is some years since flamingos have successfully bred on the Ab-i-Estada. The damming of the inflow rivers (the Band-i-Sardeh dam in particular) and the uncontrolled drilling of tube wells and increased water extraction up stream by water pump, increased agriculture as well as drought mean that the Ab-i-Estada no longer seems to have the stability of water levels it once had. This is seriously effecting the area as an exceptional site for both breeding and migrating water fowl. Among the rare species that until recent years used the Ab-i-Estada as a migration 'bus stop' was the beautiful Siberian crane (*Grus leucogeranus*) that paused here on their annual migration between their nesting grounds in Northern Russia and their wintering grounds in India—in particular the famous Bahratpur lakes in Rajasthan and the Keoladeo National Park.

All through the 1990s a rapidly diminishing number of Siberian Cranes negotiated the migration across Afghanistan. According to George Archibald of the International Crane Foundation (Wisconscin, USA) a pair of Siberian Cranes were observed in the Keoladeo National Park during the winter of 2001–02. The same pair were seen during the summer of 2002 in their breeding grounds in northern

Russia. None have been since then. It is feared that this particular group has finally been exterminated. A small group still winter on the Caspian shores in Iran and some larger flocks survive under strict preservation and winter in China.

In 1993 with a small amount of funding provided jointly by Birdlife International (UK) and the International Crane Foundation (Baraboo Wisconsin, USA) an Afghan ornithologist Abdul Jamil covered part of the autumn migration. At that time the Ab was full of water. Although Jamil failed to see any Siberian Cranes, he nonetheless brought back an interesting report on other waterfowl, flamingo, common and demoiselle cranes, pelicans, ducks, geese, waders and plovers that he did observe. The report included observations on agricultural encroachment and on local hunters who preferred hunting the larger but less palatable species such as pelicans and flamingo—size rather than the flavour of their meat being the main criteria! By 1999 the lake was dry and the wealth of waterfowl had departed elsewhere. The Ab was visited during this time by the Pakistani ornithologist and conservationist Ashiq Ahmad Khan WWF Pakistan, who also visited the area in 2002 as part of the UNEP Post Conflict Environmental Mission.

The UNEP mission that visited the lake in September 2002 found it dry with only the memory of nesting flamingo. Local youths were catching falcons for sale to rich Arabs with the aid of captive kestrels festooned with nylon snares. Some water was reported in 2003 but in 2004 the lake was once again dry.

The International Crane Foundation (Baraboo Wisconsin) is currently supporting an awareness programme through a grant to the Kabul Zoo for a crane exhibit. It is being tested initially with Eurasian (*Grus grus*) and Demoiselle cranes (*Anthropoides virgo*). If successful, a pair of Siberian cranes may be imported from Russia.

THE HAMOUN-I-PUZAK WATERFOWL SANCTUARY

The Helmand River which rises in the central Hindu Kush in the southern ranges of the Koh-i-Baba range flows south west from the mountains and across the deserts of Helmand and Nimroz, cuting through the Rigestan of Helmand as well as the well named Dasht-i-Margo (Desert of Death) and the Dasht-i-Jehannum (Desert of Hell) until turning northwards to drain into the inland Seistan Basin on the frontier with Iran. Here the Helmand River ends in a series of shallow reed filled lakes and overflow 'sumps' known as Hamoun. There are four of these, some of which are entirely in Iran like the Hamoun-i-Helmand, others shared between the two countries, like the Hamoun-i-Sabiri and the Hamoun-i-Puzak while the Ishini Am lies within the borders of Afghanistan. An enormous salt pan, the Gaud-i-Zireh (the Lower Sump), lies to the south of the Helmand river, at the point where the river turns north to the Hamoun. Irrigated agriculture has been supported here for at least 3,000 years, and until the Emir Temur-i-Lang (Tamerlane) destroyed the irrigation systems in the 14th century, a rich civilisation flourished in the area, based on caravan trading and irrigated agriculture. The ruins of palaces, mosques and fortifications dating from ancient Seistan still litter the desert. The use of the waters of the Helmand remain a matter of dispute between Afghanistan and Iran intensified by the recent years of drought when little and sometimes no water has reached the end of the Helmand river for many months of the year.

This area has much of interest to offer. Historically the Hamouns have been one of the great wintering grounds in the World for migrating as well as resident water-fowl and in the 1970s half a million waterfowl were counted on the Hamoun-i-Puzak alone representing 150 species. The Hamoun was dry when visited by the UNEP mission in September 2002. Better precipitation and snow fall in the mountains in 2003 filled the lakes again and the reed-beds are reported to have miraculously recovered, but in 2004 the Hamoun was once again dry. The human population of Nimroz province are reported to be suffering seriously both from the effects of drought and from refugees forced back across the frontier by the Iranian Government. There have been no hunting controls—at least on the Afghan side for the past 28 years.

The area has much of interest both historically and from the point of view of the environment and wildlife especially for the ornithologist, but a more sustained improvement in precipitation is required for the Hamoun to recover its former place as an area of special ornithological interest.

N.B. It should be noted that a 'National Park' indicates protection for all wildlife. A 'Reserve' indicates protection, but also holds out the possibility of limited hunting under strict controls and licence. A 'Sanctuary' (for wild-fowl and other birds) indicates a complete protection and a ban on shooting. There is little doubt that the designations originally proposed in the 1970s require some serious revision especially in the case of areas classified as potential Reserves, where a complete ban on hunting may now be more appropriate.

SOME REFERENCE READING

Afghanistan (Draft) Directory of Protected Areas (November 1988)—World Conservation Monitoring Centre—Protected Areas Data Unit

Afghanistan Post-Conflict Environmental Assessment United Nations Environmental Programme Geneva, 2002

Fitzherbert, A.R. and Mishra, C. July 2003 *Wakhan Mission Technical Report* (of September/October 2002 mission to Wakhan and the Big Pamir)—UNEP/FAO—July 2003 Contribution to UNEP Post Conflict Environmental Assessment

Habibi, Khushal. Revised 2003. *Mammals of Afghanistan*, Zoo Outreach Organisation/US Fish and Wildlife Service

Larsson, J.Y. (1978) *Status of Alpine Rangelands in Central Afghanistan with special reference to the Ajar Valley Wildlife Reserve.* UNDP & FAO with the Ministry of Agriculture Department of Forests and Range, Kabul

McCartny, H.J. (1979) *Forest Inventory Handbook—Afghanistan*, Kunar Forest Development UNDP & FAO

Mishra, C. and Fitzherbert, A. *War and Wildlife: a postconflict assessment of Afghanistan's Wakhan Corridor*—The International Journal of Conservation - Oryx Vol. 38 No. 1 January 2004

Fauna and Flora International

Petocz, R.G. (1973a) *Marco Polo Sheep (Ovis ammon polii) of the Afghan Pamir 1972–1973*, a report of biological investigations; Report to the Government of Afghanistan

Petocz, R.G. (1973b) *Background Information on fluctuations in animal population sizes with comments on the expanding rodent population in northern Afghanistan*. FAO Wildlife Conservation Project, 7pp

Petocz, R.G. (1978a) *Report on the Afghan Pamir*. Part 1: ecological reconnaissance. FAO Report

Petocz, R.G. (1978b) *Report on the Afghan Pamir*. Part 3: A management plan for the Big Pamir Wildlife Reserve. FAO report

Petocz, R.G., Habibi, K, Jamil, A, & Wassey, A. (1978). *Report on the Afghan Pamir*. Part 2: Biology of Marco Polo Sheep (*Ovis ammon polii*). FAO Report

Petocz, R.G. and Larsson, J.Y. (1977) FAO Department of Forests and Range Ministry of Agriculture, Kabul : Ecological Reconnaissance of Western Nuristan——

Schaller, G.B. (1977) *Mountain monarchs: wild sheep and goats in the Himalaya*. University of Chicago Press, Chicago and London.

Shahrani, M. Nasif (Updated September 2002). *The Kyrgyz and Wakhi of Afghanistan: Adaption to Closed Frontiers and War*. University of Washington Press. Seattle.

Shank, C.C. & Rodenberg, W.F. (1977) *Management Plan for Ab-i-Estada and Dasht-i-Nawa Flamingo and Waterfowl Sanctuaries*, UNDP & FAO with Ministry of Agriculture, Department of Forests and Range, Kabul

Shank, C.C., Petocz R.G. & Habibi, K. (1977) *A Preliminary Management Plan For the Ajar Valley Wildlife Reserve*, UNDP & FAO with the Ministry of Agriculture Department of Forests and Range Kabul.

Skogland, T and Petocz, R.G. (1975) *Ecology and behaviour of Marco Polo sheep (Ovis ammon polii) in the Pamir during winter*. Report to the Government of Afghanistan.

N.B. For information on the IUCN international classification of endangered species, see www.redlist.org

NGOs in Afghanistan

—Sandy Gall, C.B.E.

For more than 25 years—since 1978—Afghanistan has endured an almost unparalleled series of disasters: a Communist coup, a 10-year bloody war of resistance against the Soviet Union, a civil war and five years of tyranny under the Taliban. It is only since it was liberated in 2001 by American bombing and the fighters of the Northern Alliance that the country has begun to return to some semblance of normality, culminating in the election of President Hamid Karzai in October, 2004. The high voter registration and turnout, especially among women voters, impressed virtually every observer and augur well for the future.

[B. Jenks]

Not only were millions of Afghans killed, wounded and displaced in the years of fighting, but almost the entire infrastructure of the country was demolished: roads, bridges, hospitals, schools, above all people's houses, and even the countryside itself. The Russians and the Taliban both carried out scorched earth policies, deliberately destroying irrigation systems and cutting down trees.

During this entire period most essential services such as health and education either were kept going by mainly Western NGOs, or did not function at all. Without them the plight of the Afghans would have been immeasurably worse. During the darkest days of the Soviet occupation, few NGOs were able to operate at all inside Afghanistan, with the praiseworthy exception of the ICRC [International Committee of the Red Cross]. After the Russians left in 1989, Western NGOs started to pour in and have given service of inestimable value in health, education, food, agriculture, construction and many other fields. Although sometimes maligned unfairly, it is hard to see how Afghanistan could have avoided plunging into even greater misery if it had not been for the NGOs.

There follows a by no means exhaustive list of NGOs currently working in Afghanistan, beginning with some of the organizations with which my NGO, Sandy Gall's Afghanistan Appeal (SGAA), which looks after the disabled, has worked most closely. Since 1986 we have treated about 70,000 mainly mine and polio victims and trained an entire workforce of more than 100 Afghan prosthetists, orthotists and physiotherapists, male and female.

Sandy Gall's Afghanistan Appeal
www.sandygallsafghanistanappeal.org

Afghan Connection
www.afghanconnection.org

Afghanaid
www.afghanaid.org.uk

Norwegian Afghan Committee
http://afghanistan.no

Swedish Committee for Afghanistan
www.swedishcommittee.org

Aide Médicale Internationale
www.amifrance.org

The HALO Trust
www.halotrust.org

EMERGENCY
www.emergency.it

Jacob's Well Appeal
www.thejacobswell.org

Oxfam
www.oxfam.org.uk

Save the Children Fund
www.savethechildren.org.uk

International Assistance Mission (IAM)
Email: iampwr@pactac.net

Parsa
www.parsa-afghanistan.org

Afghan Institute of Learning
www.creatinghope.org/ail.htm

World Health Organisation
www.who.int/countries/afg/en/

World Food Programme
www.wfp.org

UNICEF
www.unicef.org/emerg/afghanistan

International Committee of the Red Cross
www.icrc.org

British Agencies Afghanistan Group
www.baag.org.uk

Afghanistan Assistance Co-ordination Authority (AACA)
www.af/aaca

Agency Co-ordinating Body for Afghan Relief (ACBAR)
www.acbar.org

Action Contre La Faim
www.acf-fr.org

ACTED
www.acted.org

Afghan Development Association (ADA)
www.afgdevas.org

Asia Foundation (AF)
www.asiafoundation.org

AFRANE
www.afrane.org

Afghan Health and Development Services (AHDS)
www.ahds.org

Aide Medicale International (AMI)
www.amifrance.org

CARE International (CI)
www.care.org

Co-ordination of Afghan Relief (CoAR)
www.coar-ngo.org

Danish Afghan Committee (DAC)
www.afghan.dk

DACAAR
www.dacaar.org

Goal
www.goal.ie

HELP Germany
www.help-ev.de

Ibn Sina
www.ibnsina.net

International Foundation of Hope
www.ifhope.org

International Medical Corps (IMC)
www.imcworldwide.org

International Rescue Committee (IRC)
www.theirc.org

Islamic Co-ordination Council (ICC)
email: iccpsh@brain.net.pk

Mercy Corps International
www.mercycorps.org

Médecins du Monde (MDM)
www.medecinsdumonde.org

Medair
www.medair.org

Medical Emergency Relief International
www.merlin.org.uk

Ockenden International (OI)
www.ockenden.org.uk

Organisation for Mine Clearance and Afghan Rehabilitation (OMAR)
email: omarinti@liwal.com

Shelter Now International (SNI/P-A)
www.shelternow.org

Solidarités
www.solidarites.org

Tearfund
www.tearfund.org

Terre des Hommes (TdH)
www.tdh.ch

Trocaire
www.trocaire.org

UNHCR
www.unhcr.ch

UNICEF
www.unicef.org

World Food Programme
www.wfp.org

ZOA Refugee Care/CORD
www.zoaweb.org

The Summit of Mir Samir from the Chamar Pass [W. Thesiger]

DIRECTORY AND BIBLIOGRAPHY

This directory and bibliography is intended as no more than an introductory list to aid understanding of this work, and to furnish suggestions for further reading. For full directories and bibliographies of Afghanistan, readers are referred to the authoritative works by L.W. Adamec, and D.N. Wilber (see below). For those who wish to follow contemporary events in Afghanistan, the following news, information, and current affairs websites are suggested:

Afgha.com	www.afgha.com
Afghan Daily	www.afghandaily.com
Afghan News.net	www.afghannews.net
Afghan News Network	www.myafghan.com
Radio Free Afghanistan	www.rferl.org/bd/af

Afghanistan Information Management Service (AIMS)   www.aims.org.af

A

ABBOTT, SIR JAMES *Narrative of a journey from Heraut to Khiva, Moscow and St. Petersburgh*, 2 vols, (London, 1843).

ABDULLAH, MORAG MURRAY *My Khyber marriage: experiences of a Scotswoman as the wife of a Pathan chieftain's son*, (London, 1934); *Valley of the giant Buddhas: memoirs and travels*, (London, 1993).

ABDUR RAHMAN Amir of Afghanistan, 1880–1901. Autobiography: *The Life of Amir Abdur Rahman, Amir of Afghanistan*, 2 vols, (London, 1900).

ADAMEC, LUDWIG W. *A Biographical dictionary of contemporary Afghanistan*, (Graz: Akademische Druck-u. Verlagsanstalt, 1987); *Historical dictionary of Afghanistan*, (London, 1991); *Historical and political gazetteer of Afghanistan* (Graz, Austria: Akademische Druck-u. Verlagsanstalt, 1972-1985).

AHMAD SHAH DURRANI (formerly Abdali) Founder of the modern Kingdom of Afghanistan. Ruled 1747–73. Also known as a Pashto poet. *Selections from the poetry of the Afghans, from the sixteenth to the nineteenth century*, tr. H.G. Raverty, (London, 1862).

ALLCHIN, F.R. *The Archaeology of Afghanistan from earliest times to the Timurid period*, (London, 1978).

ALI SHIR NEVAI, MIR (Also Alisher Navoii) Scholar and Vizier to Sultan Husayn Bayqara (q.v.) in Herat, (1441–1501). Writer of various Persian and Turkish texts, and leading patron of the arts. *A Century of Princes: Sources on Timurid History and Art*, ed. W.M. Thackston, (Aga Khan Program for Islamic Architecture, 1989).

ALPTIGIN Turkish slave general and Samanid Governor of Nishapur.In 961, he revolted against the ruler in Bokhara, marched to Balkh and Ghazni, capturing the latter and ruling it as his own fief, but in the name of the Samanid Empire. His actions laid the foundation of the Ghaznavid Empire. Died 963. Succeeded by Subuktigin (q.v.).

AMANULLAH KHAN King of Afghanistan, 1919-29. Having obtained power after the death of his father Habibullah (q.v.), he launched a brief attack on British India, but following air raids on Kabul and Jalalabad, he was forced to sue for peace. He later adopted a number of modernising reforms which found little favour amongst a great deal of the Afghan population, and, after his grand European tour of 1927, he was compelled to flee to Italy, where he died in 1960. *The Tragedy of Amanullah*, Sirdar Ikbal Ali Shah, (London, 1933); *Amanullah, ex-king of Afghanistan*, Roland Wild, (London, 1932).

ARNOLD, MATTHEW *Sohrab and Rustum*, (Oxford, 1916).

ANSARI OF HERAT, KHWAJA ABDULLAH ANSARI, writer and mystic (1006–89). *Intimate Conversations*, introduction, translation and notes by Wheeler M. Thackston, in *The Book of Wisdom*, int. Annemarie Schimmel, (London, 1978).

APOLLONIUS OF TYANA Neo-Pythagorean Philosopher, fl. 1st century AD. Reputed to have walked to India over the 'Caucuses', i.e. the Hindu Kush in Afghanistan. *Life of Apollonius* by Flavius Philostratus, tr. F.C. Conybeare, Loeb Classical Library.

ARRIAN Greek historian, fl. 2nd century AD. Consul in Rome and also governor of Cappadocia during the time of the Emperor Hadrian. Wrote a valuable history in eight books of Alexander's campaigns—the *Anabasis*—based on first-hand accounts by Ptolemy and Aristobulus. The last book, also known as the *Indica*, contains a description of India based on the reports of Megasthenes, Seleucid Greek ambassador to the Mauryan kings, c. 300 BC. *Anabasis of Alexander*, tr. E.I. Robson, Loeb Classical Library.

ASADI TUSI   Poet, fl. 11th century. Writer of the *Garshaspname* and the oldest known Persian lexicon. Son of Abu Nasr Ahmed bin Mansur of Tus, the teacher of Firdousi. *Le livre de Gerchâsp*, tr. Clément Huart, (Paris 1926).

ASOKA Grandson of Chandragupta (q.v.) and ruler of the Indian Mauryan Empire, (c.273–232 BC). Converted to Buddhism c. 250 BC and undertook a large missionary effort to spread the doctrine. The news of his conversion was published on a large number of inscriptions—rock edicts—two of which were located in Kandahar. *Asoka the Great*, D.C. Ahir, (Dehli, 1995); *Asoka and the decline of the Mauryas*, R. Thapar, (Dehli, 1997); *The moral edicts of King Asoka*, eds P.H.L. Eggermont and J. Hoftijzer, (Brill, 1962).

ATKINSON, JAMES *The expedition into Affghanistan, notes and sketches, during the campaign of 1839 & 1840*, (London, 1842).

AUCKLAND (George Eden, 2nd Earl) (1784–1849) Governor-general of India, 1836–42. His refusal to support Dost Mohammed's (q.v.) claim to Peshawar against Runjit Singh (q.v.), and his fear of Russian infiltration of Afghanistan, led to the British invasion and the First Afghan War.

B

EMPEROR BABUR Zahiruddin Muhammad Babur (1483–1530), Prince of Ferghana and later founder of the Mughal Empire of India, 1526. *The Baburnama in English* (Memoirs of Babur), tr. A.S. Beveridge, (London, 1921); *The Baburnama: memoirs of Babur, prince and emperor*, tr. W.M. Thackston, (OUP, 1996).

BACHA-I-SAQAO (Also Habibullah Ghazi) Tajik bandit who briefly seized the throne of Afghanistan in 1929 following an uprising against Amanullah Khan (q.v.), before being deposed and executed by Nadir Shah (q.v.) *My life from brigand to king: Autobiography of Amir Habibullah*, (London, 1936).

IBN BATTUTA Arab traveller and geographer, (1304–77). Born in Morocco, he made the Hajj pilgrimage to Mecca at the age of 21, after which he proceeded to travel widely throughout the Islamic world, reaching Constantinople, India and China. His writings give a valuable picture of Afghanistan 100 years after its devastation by Genghis Khan. *Travels*, tr. H.A.R. Gibb, 4 vols, Hakluyt Society ed.

BEALBY, J. *For a Pagan Song: In the Footsteps of the Man Who Would Be King - Travels in India, Pakistan and Afghanistan*, (Arrow, 1999)

BELL, EVANS *The Oxus and the Indus*, (London, 1869).

BELLEW, H.W. British doctor and ethnographer (1834–92). First entered Afghanistan in 1857 as doctor attached to Lumsden's (q.v.) diplomatic mission to Kandahar; became a leading authority on matters related to Afghan tribes and Pushtun history, as well as an excellent but now neglected travel writer. *Journal of a Political Mission into Afghanistan in 1857* (London, 1862); *An inquiry into the ethnography of Afghanistan*, (London, 1891); *From the Indus to the Tigris: a narrative of a journey through the countries of Balochistan, Afghanistan, Khorassan and Iran*, (London, 1874).

BERNARD, P. *Aï Khanoum en Afghanistan*, Comptes Rendus de l'Académie des Inscriptions et Belles-Lettres, 2001, pp. 971–1029.

BIHZAD (Also Behzad) Herati miniaturist (1450–1535). Court painter to Sultan Husayn Bayqara (q.v.) and later to Shah Ismail of Persia. See *The miniature painting and painters of Persia, India and Turkey, from the 8th to the 18th century*, F.R. Martin, (London, 1968); *Bihzad: Master of Persian painting*, E. Bahari, (London, 1966).

AL-BIRUNI Abu'l-Rayhan Muhammad, Muslim scholar and polymath, (973–1051). A native of Khwarazm, he completed his first major work—*al-Athar al-Baqiya* 'The Chronology of Ancient Nations'—before his city fell to Mahmud the Great, at which point he was taken to Ghazni with a number of other learned men. From there, he accompanied Mahmud on his conquests of India, the experience of which led him in 1030 to write the important *Tarikh al-Hind*, or History of India. He also wrote other scientific, mathematic and literary works. *Alberuni's India*, tr. E. Sachau, 2 vols, (London, 1888).

BOSWORTH, C.E. *The Ghaznavids: their empire in Afghanistan and eastern Iran*, (Edinburgh, 1963); *The later Ghaznavids: splendour and decay: the dynasty in Afghanistan and Northern India 1040–1186*, (Edinburgh, 1977).

BOWERSOX, GARY American gem expert. *Gemstones of Afghanistan*, (Geoscience Press, 1995); *The Gem Hunter*, (Geovision Inc, 2004) http://www.gems-afghan.com

BURNES, SIR ALEXANDER British officer and traveller, (1805–41). Having become fluent in a number of native languages whilst an officer in Bombay, he was first sent on a mission to survey the Indus in 1831. The next year, he proceeded on a journey across Afghanistan and Central Asia to Bokhara, disguised in native dress. Having described the daring expedition in his first book, he was widely praised in London, receiving a knighthood for his exploits. Later, in 1836, he was sent on a mission to negotiate an alliance with Dost Mohammed in Kabul, which, failing, was followed by the British invasion. Burnes accompanied the army as a political officer, and was assassinated in Kabul on 2 November 1841. His neglected travel writings are some of the best and most entertaining works to be found on Afghanistan and Central Asia. *Travels into Bokhara; being the account of a journey from India to Cabool, Tartary, and Persia*, (London, 1834); *Cabool: being a personal narrative of a journey to, and residence in that city, in the years 1836, 7, and 8*, (London, 1842).

BUSER, MARK *Afghanistan weighs heavy on my heart: the reminiscences of Soviet soldiers who fought in Afghanistan*, tr. Mark Buser and Gail Ann Broadhead, (New Delhi, 1992).

BYRON, ROBERT Journalist, traveller and scholar. *The Road to Oxiana*, (London, 1937); *Robert Byron: a biography*, James Knox, (John Murray, 2003).

C

CAROE, SIR OLAF *The Pathans: 550 BC–AD 1957*, (London, 1958).

CAVAGNARI, MAJ. SIR LOUIS (1841–79) British agent in Afghanistan. Became British envoy in Kabul in 1879 after the British invasion and signature of the Treaty of Gandamak with Yakub Khan, but was murdered by an Afghan mob shortly after taking up residence there. *The life and career of Sir Louis Cavagnari*, K.P. Dey, (Calcutta, 1881).

CHANDRAGUPTA (Also Sandracottus) First ruler of the Mauryan Empire of India, fl. 305 BC. A treaty brokered with the Greek general Seleucus brought the Afghan regions south of the Hindu Kush under his control. *Chandragupta Maurya and his times*, R.K. Mookerji, (Dehli, 1966).

CHANG-KIEN (Also Zhang Qian) Chinese soldier and diplomat, fl. 130 BC. His discovery of the Yueh-Chih tribes in Bactria paved the way for the opening of the Silk Road. 'The story of Chang Kién, China's pioneer in western Asia', Friedrich Hirth in *Journal of the American Oriental Society*, vol. 37, pt. 2, September 1917.

CHATWIN, BRUCE *Bruce Chatwin: photographs and notebooks*, ed. Francis Wyndham, (London, 1993); see also Peter Levi.

DI CLAVIJO, RUY GONZÁLEZ Ambassador sent by King Henry III of Castile to Tamerlane, early 15th century. *Embassy to Tamerlane, 1403–1406*, tr. Guy Le Strange, (London, 1928).

COLL, STEVE *Ghost Wars: The Secret History of the CIA, Afghanistan, and Bin Laden, from the Soviet Invasion to September 10, 2001*, (Penguin Putnam Inc USA, 2004)

CONOLLY, CAPTAIN ARTHUR British army officer and traveller, (1807–42). Journeyed overland from Britain to India via Russia and Kandahar, 1829–30. After serving in Kabul during the First Afghan War, he travelled through the Central Asian khanates on a mission to secure the release of a British officer—Colonel Stoddart (q.v.)—from captivity in Bokhara, hoping also to persuade the Islamic rulers to renounce slavery. Executed by the Amir of Bokhara, 1842. *Journey to the north of India overland from England through Russia, Persia, and Affghaunistaun*, (London, 1834).

COSMAS MONACHUS (Also Cosmas Indicopleustes) *The Christian Topography of Cosmas, an Egyptian monk*, tr. J.W. McCrindle, (Hakluyt Society, 1897).

CRILE, GEORGE *My enemy's enemy: the story of the largest covert operation in history—the arming of the Mujahideen by the CIA*, (London, 2003).

CURTIUS Quintus Curtius Rufus, Roman historian, fl. AD 50. His description of Alexander's conquests—*The History of Alexander the Great*—is perhaps less reliable than other accounts, but it nonetheless draws from primary sources, and is highly readable. *The History of Alexander the Great*, tr. J.C. Rolfe, 2 vols, Loeb Classical Library.

CURZON, GEORGE NATHANIEL Traveller and statesman, (1859–1925). Viceroy of India, 1899. 'The Pamirs and the source of the Oxus', from *The Geographical Journal*, 1896.

D

DIODORUS OF SICILY   Greek historian, fl. 60–30 BC. *The Library of History*, tr. C.H. Oldfather, 12 vols, Loeb Classical Library.

DIODOTUS First king of the independent Graeco-Bactrian state in northern Afghanistan, c.250 BC. See Holt, F.L.; Tarn, W.W.

DOST MOHAMMED Ruler of Kabul and later Amir of Afghanistan, 1826–38 and 1842–63. Son of the Vizier Painda Khan from the Mohammadzai branch of the Barakzai Pushtuns, he founded the line of Afghan monarchs that ruled until 1928. Another branch of the same family, springing from Painda Khan, came to the throne in 1929. *Life of Amir Dost Mohammed*, Mohan Lal, (London, 1846).

DOUBLEDAY, VERONICA *Three Women of Herat*, (London, 1988).

DUPAIGNE, BERNARD, see Pavia, Roland.

DUPREE, LOUIS (1925–89) Anthropologist, archaeologist and authority on Afghanistan. His book *Afghanistan*, (Princeton, 1973) is recognised as a standard work; see also *A guide to the Kabul Museum*, (Kabul, 1968).

DUPREE, NANCY HATCH Author of the latest and most authoritative guidebook to Afghanistan before the Russian invasion: *An Historical Guide to Afghanistan*, (Kabul, 1970), which is now available online at www.zharov.com/dupree; also *The Valley of Bamiyan*, (Kabul, 1967); *An historical guide to Kabul*, (Kabul, 1965)

DURAND, SIR HENRY MORTIMER (1850–1924) Indian Foreign Secretary, and later responsible for the establishment of the troublesome Durand Line on the southern border of Afghanistan.

E

ELLENBOROUGH (Edward Law, 1st Earl) Governor-General of India, 1842–44. Took over from Lord Auckland and presided over the attacks inflicted on the Afghans in retaliation for the 1842 massacre of the British on the retreat to Jalalabad.

ELPHINSTONE, MOUNTSTUART British diplomat, (1779–1859). Sent as an envoy to the ruler of Afghanistan, Shah Shuja, whom he met in Peshawar in 1809. With the help of several agents, he wrote a renowned and pioneering account of the land and people of Afghanistan. It should be noted that he never proceeded further into the country than

Peshawar. Later Lieutenant-Governor of Bombay. *An account of the kingdom of Caubul and its dependencies in Persia, Tartary, and India*, (London, 1815).

ELPHINSTONE, MAJOR-GENERAL WILLIAM (1782–1842) Commander of British troops in Kabul after the 1839 occupation during the First Afghan War. Although a successful commander many years earlier at Waterloo, he was by that time almost senile, and without knowledge of the situation in Afghanistan. This, coupled with his inimical relationship with his deputy, Brigadier Shelton, was a major factor leading to the disastrous retreat from Kabul in 1842. General Elphinstone was taken prisoner on this march and died in captivity that same year.

EPSTEIN, MARC *Ils ont assassiné Massoud*, with Jean-Marie Pontaut, (Laffont, 2002).

EWANS, SIR MARTIN *Afghanistan: a new history*, (Curzon, 2001).

EYRE, SIR VINCENT (1811–81) British Lieutenant taken prisoner on the 1842 retreat from Kabul, but later released. His journal, along with Lady Sale's (q.v.), forms one of the most important sources for the First Afghan War. *The military operations at Cabul: which ended in the retreat and destruction of the British army, January 1842; with a journal of imprisonment in Affghanistan*, (London, 1843).

F

FATEH KHAN (1778–1818) Head of the Durrani Barakzai Pushtuns, and Vizier to the ruler of Kabul in 1810. His murder by the Afghan king, Shah Mahmud in 1818 led to a civil war in which Fateh's youngest brother, Dost Mohammed (q.v.), eventually assumed control of Kabul.

FAZL HUQ Pushtun convert to Christianity who went on a missionary trip to Kafiristan in 1864. He recorded his experiences in a secret diary, excerpts of which were published the following year in the *Church Missionary Intelligencer*.

FERGUSSON, JAMES *Kandahar Cockney: A Tale of Two Worlds,* (London, 2004)

FERISHTA (Also Muhammad Qasim Hindu Shah) Historian writing at the Moghul Court, fl. early 17th century. *History of the rise of the Mahomedan power in India till the year AD 1612*, tr. John Briggs, 4 vols, (London, 1829).

FERRIER, J.P. French soldier and mercenary. Served in Africa, and then sent as a military adviser to Persia in the 1830s. He was expelled from this post after opposing the increasing influence of Russia, after which he set out to travel to Lahore to serve under the Sikh ruler Runjit Singh (q.v.). His memoirs contain much important data, particularly with reference to Herat. *Caravan journeys and wanderings in Persia, Afghanistan, Turkistan, and Beloochistan:*

with historical notices of the countries lying between Russia and India, tr. W. Jesse, (London, 1857).

FLETCHER, ARNOLD *Afghanistan: Highway of Conquest*, (Cornell University Press, 1965).

FIRDOUSI ABU'L-QASIM HASAN BIN ALI OF TUS. Persian poet (d. 1025). Served at the Court of Mahmud the Great of Ghazni (q.v.), where he wrote the *Shahnameh* (Book of Kings) which, preserving much of the mythology of Ancient Persia, is still regarded as the Iranian national epic. *The epic of the kings: Shah-nama, the national epic of Persia*, tr. Reuben Levy, (London, 1967).

FOUCHER, ALFRED (1865–1952) Founder of the Délégation Archéologique Française en Afghanistan (DAFA). *La vieille route de l'Inde de Bactres à Taxila*, (Paris, 1942).

FRASER-TYTLER, W.K. *Afghanistan: a study of political developments in Central Asia*, (London, 1950).

G

GALL, SANDY British war correspondent, noted for his documentary reports on Ahmed Shah Massoud and the Mujaheddin. *Behind Russian lines: an Afghan journal*, (London, 1983); *Afghanistan: agony of a nation*, (London, 1988); *Afghanistan: travels with the Mujahideen*, (London, 1988).

GARDNER, ALEXANDER HAUGHTON American adventurer, (1785–1877). Born on the shores of Lake Superior of a Scottish father who fought in the War of Independence, Col. Gardner proceeded to Afghanistan, where, in the 1830s, he fought under Habibullah Khan, one of the opponents of Dost Mohammed. He later sought service under the Sikh ruler of the Punjab, Runjit Singh, and continued to live in India until his death in Srinagar. *Soldier and Traveller, Memoirs of A. Gardner*, ed. by H. Pearse, (Edinburgh 1898).

GAWHAR SHAD Wife of the Timurid Emperor, Shah Rukh, and patroness of the arts (d. 1457). See *A Century of Princes: Sources on Timurid History and Art*, ed. W.M. Thackston, (Aga Khan Program for Islamic Architecture, 1989).

GENGHIS KHAN (Also Temuchin) Mongol leader and conqueror (1162–1226). Originally leader of a confederation of 40,000 Mongol families, he captured large areas of northern China before invading and devastating Central Asia and, in 1219, Herat and other parts of Afghanistan. *The History of the World-conqueror*, Ala-ad-Din 'Ata-Malik Juvaini, tr. J.A. Boyle, (Manchester, 1958); *Genghis Khan: Life, death and resurrection*, J. Man, (London, 2004); *Genghis Khan: his life and legacy*, P. Ratchnevsky, (Oxford, 1991).

GIRARDET, E. *Crosslines Essential Field Guide: Afghanistan* (Geneva, 1998)

GLEIG, G. *Sale's brigade in Afghanistan, with an account of the seizure and defence of Jellalabad*, (London, 1879).

GREY, J.A. British doctor attached to the court of Amir Abdur Rahman in the last decade of the 19th century. His excellent memoirs leave a vivid and amusing picture of Kabul and northern Afghanistan at this time. *At the court of the Amir*, (London, 1895).

GRINDLAY, ROBERT MELVILLE (1786–1877). Lieutennant, 7th Bombay Native Infantry, he accompanied the 1809 expedition of Mountstuart Elphinstone (q.v.) to Peshawar, and made a selection of paintings of local subjects, which were later first published in Elphinstone's seminal work on Afghanistan. The three reproduced in this book are in the collection of the Royal Society for Asian Affairs. Grindlay later went on to found Grindlay's Bank.

GÖES, BENEDICT Portuguese Jesuit missionary (1562–1607). Set off from Agra in India to search for Christian communities in China. Passing though Afghanistan in 1602, he heard of the Kafir communities in Nuristan which he suspected to be Christian. *Cathay and the way thither: being a collection of medieval notices of China*, ed. H. Yule, Hakluyt Society Publication.

GORDON, T.E. British surveyor (1832–1914). *The roof of the world: a narrative of a journey over the high plateau of Tibet to the Russian frontier*, (Edinburgh, 1876).

GRODEKOFF, COL. *Colonel Grodekoff's ride from Samarcand to Herat*, tr. C. Marvin, (London, 1880).

H

AMIR HABIBULLAH Ruler of Afghanistan, 1901–19. Managed to maintain Afghanistan in peace and isolation during the First World War by a policy of neutrality, but his refusal to launch a jihad against the weakened British Empire in India led to his assassination.

HACKIN, JOSEPH (1886–1941) Director of the Délégation Archéologique Française en Afghanistan. *Diverses recherches archéologiques en Afghanistan (1933–1940)*, (Paris, 1959); *Nouvelles recherches archéologiques à Bamiyan*, (Paris, 1933).

HACKIN, R.P. *Légendes et Coutumes Afghans*, with A.A. Kohzad, (Paris, 1953).

HAMILTON, DR LILLIAS British doctor resident in Kabul during the 1890s. Her account of Amir Abdur Rahman's invasion of Kafiristan was published in *The Times*, 4 April 1896.

HANNA, H.B. *The Second Afghan War*, (London, 1895).

HARLAN, JOSIAH American adventurer born in Pennsylvania (1799–1871). Serving for a time under Runjit Singh (q.v.), he is reputed to have been the first American to visit Afghanistan. *A memoir of India and Avghanistaun*, (Philadelphia, 1842); *Central Asia: personal narrative of General Josiah Harlan*, ed. F.E. Ross, (London, 1939); An extraordinary cache of documents relating to him were recently rediscovered and are described in *The Man Who Would Be King: The First American in Afghanistan*, B. Macintyre, (New York, 2004).

IBN HAWQAL ABU AL-QASIM MUHAMMAD, Arab traveller and merchant, fl. 943–977. *The Oriental Geography of Ebn Haukal*, tr. William Ouseley, (London, 1800).

HENTY, G.A. *To Herat and Cabul*, (London, 1902).

D'HERBELOT, B. *Bibliotheque Orientale*, (Paris, 1697).

HODSON, P. *Under a Sickle Moon: A Journey through Afghanistan* (London, 1986)

HOLDICH, SIR THOMAS Surveyor and soldier. Served in the Second Afghan War. Worked for 20 years on the north-western frontier; later Surveyor-General of India and President of the Royal Geographical Society. *The gates of India*, (London, 1910).

HOLT, FRANK, (M.B.E.), Diplomat and artist, 1907–1997. Born in Essex, son of a ship's carpenter; educated as a scholar at Loughton. Served at the headquaters of the Indian army in Agra as a *subadar* (Regimental Sergeant Major). Joined the Foreign office in 1956, and served in postings at Warsaw (where he met his wife Anne), Istanbul, Brussels, Khartoum, and Ankara. After retirement in 1967, he travelled through Afghanistan with his wife and Freya Stark (q.v.) from May 1968 to March 1969. His dawings of Afghanistan, published in this book, were sketched on the ground, and worked up at a later date. He also travelled and sketched in Poland and Turkey. His drawings of Afghanistan and Turkey were given to the Royal Society of Asian Affairs, and are reproduced here by kind permission of his wife.

HOLT, PROFESSOR F.L. Specialist in Graeco-Bactrian coins, University of Houston. *Thundering Zeus: the making of Hellenistic Bactria*, (Berkeley, 1999).

HOPKIRK, PETER *The Great Game: On Secret Service in High Asia*, (OUP, 2001).

HOSSEINI, KHALED *The Kite Runner*, (Bloomsbury, 2003)

HUSAYN BAYQARA, Sultan, Man of letters, final Timurid emperor and ruler of Herat (r. 1469–1506). *A Century of Princes: Sources on Timurid History and Art*, ed. W.M. Thackston, (Aga Khan Program for Islamic Architecture, 1989).

HUI-CH'AO (Hye Ch'o) Korean Buddhist pilgrim, fl. 8th century AD. *The Hye Ch'o diary: memoir of the pilgrimage to the five regions of India*, (Berkeley, 1984).

HSUEN-TSANG (Also Xuanzang) Chinese Buddhist traveller and translator, (AD 603–664). Between 629–45, he made a pilgrimage from Central China to Northern

India in order to collect Buddhist texts. He left behind a hugely valuable account of the cities which he visited in Afghanistan shortly before the Islamic conquest. *Buddhist records of the Western World, translated from the Chinese of Hiuen Tsiang*, tr. Samuel Beal, 2 vols, (London, 1906).

I

AL-IDRISI Abu 'Abd Allah Muhammad ibn Muhammad. Arab geographer, (1100–1166). *India and the neighbouring territories in the Kitab nuzhat al-mushtaq fi'khtiraq al-'afaq*, tr. S. Maqbul Ahmad, (Brill, 1960).

INAYATULLAH KHAN Brother of Amanullah Khan (q.v.). Came to the throne during the rebellion of Habibullah Kalakani (Bacha-i Saqao, q.v.) after the flight of his brother, but abdicated after three days.

J

JAMI Nuruddin Abd-al Rahman Jami, (1414–92). Herati poet and mystic. *Lawa'ih: a treatise on Sufism*, tr. E.H. Whinfield and M.M. Kazvini, (London, 1928). *Yusuf and Zulaikha: an allegorical romance*, tr. David Pendlebury, (London, 1980).

JONES, SCHUYLER *Nuristan*, with Edelberg, L., (Graz, 1979); *Men of influence in Nuristan*, (London, 1974).

JUZJANI MAULANA MINHAJ-UD-DIN, Historian (b. 1211?). Fought against the Mongol armies of Genghis Khan in the region of Afghanistan before migrating to India. Eventually appointed the Kazi (Chief Judge) of Dehli in 1261. *Tabakat-i-Nasiri: a general history of the Muhammadan dynasties of Asia*, tr. by H.G. Raverty, (London, 1881)

K

KAMRAN MIRZA See 'Mahmud Shah'

KANISHKA Greatest king of the Kushan dynasty, fl, c. AD 130. *Papers on the date of Kaniska: submitted to the Conference on the Date of Kaniska. London, 20–22 April, 1960*, ed. A. L. Basham, (Brill, 1968). *The early Kusanas: a history of the rise and progress of the Kusana power under the early Kusana rulers—from Kujula Kadphises to Vasudeva*, B. Kumar, (New Dehli, 1973); *The rise and fall of the Kushana Empire*, B.N. Mukherjee, (Calcutta, 1988).

KAYE, SIR JOHN *History of the war in Afghanistan*, 2 vols, (London, 1851).

KHUSHAL KHAN KHATTAK Warrior and poet, (1613–39). Chief of the Khattak tribe, writer of a wide range of poetry in Pashto, often exhorting his fellow tribesmen to revolt against the Moghul Empire. *The poems of Khushhal Khan Khatak*, tr. Evelyn

Howell and Olaf Caroe, (Peshawar, 1963); *Afghan poetry of the seventeenth century: selections from the poems of Khush Hal Khan Khatak*, tr. C. Biddulph, (London, 1890).

KHWANDAMIR Historian (1475–1535). Served under Mir Ali Shir Nevai (q.v.), the Vizier to Sultan Husayn Bayqara of Herat (q.v.). Joined the court of Shah Ismail of Persia after the fall of Herat (1508), and then the Mughal court of the Emperor Babur. *Habibu's-siyar, Tome three: The reign of the Mongol and the Turk*, tr. W.M. Thackston (Harvard, 1994).

KLASS, ROSEANNE *Afghanistan: land of the high flags*, (New York, 1964).

KLIMBURG, MAX *The Kafirs of the Hindu Kush*, (London, 1999).

KNOX, JAMES See Byron, Robert.

L

LAMB, CHRISTINA Journalist for the *Sunday Times*. *The sewing circles of Herat: my Afghan years*, (London, 2002).

LANE FOX, PROFESSOR ROBIN *The search for Alexander*, (London, Allen Lane, 1980); *Alexander the Great*, (London, Allen Lane, 1974); *The making of Alexander* (foreword by Oliver Stone), (Oxford, 2004)

LEVI, PETER Jesuit priest and later Oxford Professor of Poetry; travelled in Afghanistan with Bruce Chatwin in the 1970s. *Light Garden of the Angel King: Journeys in Afghanistan*, (London, 1972). See also Chatwin, Bruce.

LIGABUE, G. *Bactria: an ancient oasis civilization from the sands of Afghanistan*, (Venice, 1988).

LUMSDEN, LT-GEN. SIR HARRY (1821–96) Anglo-Indian officer present at the forcing of the Khyber Pass in 1842, and later appointed leader of a diplomatic mission to Kandahar in 1857, of which H.W. Bellew (q.v.) was also a member. *The mission to Kandahar*, (Calcutta, 1860).

LYTTON, LORD EDWARD (1831–91) British diplomat and Viceroy of India (1876–80). His strong advocacy of the 'Forward policy' and his refusal to allow Afghanistan to have any direct dealings with Russia was one of the causes of the Second Afghan War.

M

MACNAGHTEN, SIR WILLIAM (1793–1841) British civil servant in India. As head of the Foreign and Political Department, he was instrumental in bringing about the policy of installing Shah Shuja (q.v.) on the Afghan throne as a British puppet ruler. He accompanied the Army of the Indus during the Afghan invasion in 1839 as a political officer, and was murdered in Kabul during the uprising at the end of 1841.

MACINTYRE, B. *The Man Who Would Be King: The First American in Afghanistan*, (New York, 2004). See also Harlan, Josiah.

MACRORY, PATRICK *Kabul catastrophe: the invasion and retreat 1839–1842*, (London, 2002).

MAHMUD ARIFI Herati poet (d. 1449). *The ball and polo stick, or, The Book of Ecstacy* ('Halnama') ed. and tr. W.M. Thackston and H. Ziai, (Mazda, 1999)

MAHMUD THE GREAT (971–1030) Successor to Subuktigin (q.v.) as ruler of the Ghaznavid Empire and patron of the Arts. Staged a number of expeditions of conquest in Transoxiana and India, as well as into Persia. Received the title of *Yamin-ud-Dowlah*, 'Right arm of the State', from the Caliph in Baghdad. *Ghaznin, and its environs*, H.G. Raverty, Rev. A.N. Khan, (Lahore, 1995); see also Ferishta; Juzjani; C.E. Bosworth.

MAHMUD SHAH Ruler of Afghanistan 1800–1803 and 1809–1818. After great unrest and civil strife against the Barakzai Pushtuns, he was eventually driven back into Herat, which he ruled as an autonomous entity with his son, Kamran Mirza, and his vizier, Yar Muhammad. Died 1829.

MALLESON, G. B. *History of Afghanistan from the earliest period to the outbreak of the war of 1878*, (London, 1879).

MARCO POLO Venetian merchant and traveller (1254?–1324?). In 1271 travelled with his father and uncle via northern Afghanistan to Cambuluc (Beijing), and was for a time resident at the court of Kublai Khan, returning to Venice by 1295. *The book of Ser Marco Polo, the Venetian, concerning the kingdoms and marvels of the East*, tr. H. Yule, 2 vols, (London, 1926).

MASSON, CHARLES British adventurer (1800–1853). Originally a private in the Bengal Artillery named James Lewis, he deserted in 1827 with a fellow soldier, Richard Potter, and travelled extensively throughout the Punjab and Afghanistan. Wearing native dress and fluent in the local languages, he was eventually pardoned by the British authorities and re-employed by them as a spy; he was notable for his opposition to the British invasion in 1838. He also began to excavate many archaeological sites in the vicinity of Kabul, collecting Buddhist artefacts and thousands of coins, thereby paving the way for the study of the ancient Graeco-Bactrian and Indo-Greek kingdoms of Afghanistan. His travel narratives make excellent reading. *Narrative of various journeys in Balochistan, Afghanistan, and the Panjab: including a residence in those countries from 1826 to 1838*, 3 vols, (London, 1842); *Legends of the Afghan countries* (London, 1848); *Charles Masson of Afghanistan: explorer, archaeologist, numismatist, and intelligence agent*, G. Whitteridge (Aris & Phillips, 1986).

MICHAUD, ROLAND AND SABRINA, Travellers and photographers. Their pictures, taken on journies throughout Afghanistan, particularly in the 1970s, are widely regarded as a classic record of the country, especially before the period of the Soviet invasion and civil war. *Caravans to Tartary*, (London, Thames and Hudson, 1978); *Afghanistan*, (London, Thames and Hudson, 1980); *Horsemen of Afghanistan*, (London, Thames and Hudson, 1988).

MILLER, CHARLES *Khyber, British India's north west frontier: the story of an imperial migraine*, (London, 1977).

MIRKHOND (Also Mir Khwand) Muhammad bin Khawand Shah (1433–98). Herati historian writing at the court of Sultan Husayn Bayqara (q.v.). *The Rauzat-us-safa, or Garden of purity*, tr. E. Rehatsek, 5 vols, (London, 1891–94).

MOHUN LAL Kashmiri assistant to Sir Alexander Burnes (q.v.) (1812–77). Present in Kabul during the First Afghan War. *Travels in the Panjab, Afghanistan, & Turkistan; and a visit to Great Britain and Germany*, (London, 1846). *Life of Amir Dost Mohammed*, (London, 1846).

MOORCROFT, WILLIAM British traveller (1767–1825). Moorcroft was England's first fully-qualified veterinary surgeon. Having followed a course of training at Lyons, he set up a successful practice in London, before being commissioned to work on horse breeding for the British army in Bengal. After the failure of some of his schemes, he became disillusioned with his career and began to undertake perilous yet pioneering journeys in Afghanistan and Central Asia, where eventually he died as a prisoner of the Amir of Bokhara. *Travels in the Himalayan provinces of Hindustan and the Panjab; in Ladakh and Kashmir; in Peshawar, Kabul, Kunduz and Bokhara*, ed. H.H. Wilson, (London 1841).

MORGENSTIERNE, PROF. GEORG Professor of Indo-Iranian languages, University of Oslo, (1892–1978). Authority on the languages and culture in Nuristan. *Report on a linguistic mission to Afghanistan*, (Olso, 1926); *The language of the Prasun Kafirs*, (Olso, 1949)

MOUSAVI, DR SAYED ASKAR *The Hazaras of Afghanistan: an historical, cultural, economic, and political study*, (Curzon, 1998).

N

NADIR QULI KHAN AFSHAR (1688–1747); later Nadir Shah, not to be confused with the 20th-century Nadir Shah). Ruler of Afghanistan and Persia 1736–47. Originally a Turkomen slave, he rose to become commander of the Safavid Persian army, after which he deposed the weak Shah Tahmasp and ruled the country in his own name. For the last ten years of his life, he campaigned throughout Central Asia and India, waging wars primarily for plunder. He was murdered by his officers in 1747. *Nadir Shah; a critical study based mainly upon contemporary sources*, L. Lockhart, (London, 1938); *The history of Nadir Shah*, James Fraser, (London, 1742).

NADIR SHAH King of Afghanistan, 1929–33. Regained control of the country after the uprising by Bacha-i-Saqao (q.v.) and maintained the peace whilst repealing modernising legislation of his predecessor, Amanullah (q.v.). Assassinated in 1933; succeeded by his son Zahir Shah.

MULLAH NAJEEB   Fl. early 19th century. One of Mountstuart Elphinstone's (q.v.) agents, who contributed information for the Kafiristan/Nuristan chapter of *An account of the kingdom of Caubul*.

NARAIN, A. K. *The Indo-Greeks*, (Oxford, 1957).

NASIR KHUSRAW Ismaili traveller, poet and mystic (1003–c.1088). Born near Balkh, he became an Ismaili in Cairo c. 1047 and travelled extensively throughout the Islamic world, working as a missionary for Ismailism in Badakhshan. *Naser-e Khosraw's book of travels—Safarnama*, tr. W.M. Thackston, (Bibliotheca Persica, 1986); *Make a shield from wisdom: selected verses from Nasir-i Khusraw's divan*, tr. Annemarie Schimmel, (London, 1993); *Forty poems from the Divan*, tr. Peter Lamborn Wilson and Gholam Reza Aavani, (Tehran, 1977); *Nasir Khusraw, the ruby of Badakhshan: a portrait of the Persian poet, traveller and philosopher*, Alice Hunsberger, (London, 2000).

NEWBY, ERIC *A Short Walk in the Hindu Kush*, (London, 1958).

NIZAMI Poet and physician, fl. 12th century in Herat and Khurasan. *The Chahár maqála or 'Four discourses'*, tr. E.G. Browne, (London, 1900).

NONNOS OF PANOPOLIS *Dionysiaca*, tr. W.H.D. Rouse, 3 vols, Loeb Classical Library.

NOTT, GENERAL SIR WILLIAM British officer (1782–1845). During the First Afghan War, he inflicted a heavy defeat on the Afghans at Kandahar following the British retreat from Kabul. Later, in conjunction with General Pollock (q.v.), he led his troops in a retaliatory attack on Kabul. *Memoirs and correspondence of major-general Sir William Nott*, J.H. Stocqueler, (London, 1854).

O

OLUFSEN, OLAF Danish traveller and geographer (1865–1929). Led two expeditions to the Pamir region in 1896 and 1898, and was later appointed Honorary Professor of Geography in Copenhagen University. *Through the unknown Pamirs, the second Danish Pamir expedition, 1898–99*, (London, 1904).

P

PALMER, LOUIS *Adventures in Afghanistan*, (London, 1990).

PANDEY, D.B. *The Shahis of Afghanistan and the Punjab*, (Delhi, 1973).

PAVIA, ROLAND *Afghan Embroidery*, with Bernard Dupaigne, (Lahore, 1996)

POLLOCK, SIR GEORGE British officer (1786–1872). Led a relief column to Jalalabad in 1842, having forced the Khyber Pass. Later went on to capture Kabul and destroy the bazaar as an act of retribution. *The life and correspondence of field marshal Sir George Pollock*, C.R. Low, (London, 1873).

POTTINGER, MAJ. ELDRED British soldier and spy, (1811–43). Travelled in western Afghanistan disguised as a horse-trader; present at the 1837–38 siege of Herat, where he used his military expertise to play a leading role in the city's defence. Present during the First Afghan War, surviving the destruction of the British post in Charikar, he spent a period of time as a hostage. Denied medals and back pay by a court of enquiry in 1843 for acting beyond authorisation, he emigrated to Hong Kong. His life has been the subject of adventure stories, including *To Herat and Cabul*, G.A. Henty (London, 1902); and *The Hero of Herat*, Maud Diver, (London, 1912).

R

RABIA BALKHI (Also Rabi'a Qozdari) First poetess known to have written in Persian, c. 9th century, Balkh. See article in *Yádnáme-ye Jan Rypka*, (Prague, 1967).

RATTRAY, J. *The costumes of the various tribes, portraits of ladies of rank, celebrated princes and chiefs, views of the principal fortresses and cities, and interior of the cities and temples of Afghaunistaun*, (London, 1848).

RAPIN, CLAUDE *Fouilles d'Aï Khanoum*, in Mémoires de la Délégation Archéologique Française en Afghanistan, (Paris, 1973).

RASHID, AHMED *Taliban: Islam, oil and the new great game in Central Asia*, (London, 2000).

RIPON, GEORGE ROBINSON (1st Marquess) (1827–1909) Viceroy of India, 1880–84, during the latter part of the Second Afghan War. Presided over the reversal of the forward policy, the withdrawal of British troops from the lands south of the Hindu Kush and the recognition of Abdur Rahman (q.v.) as ruler of Afghanistan.

ROBERTSON, SIR GEORGE SCOTT Medical officer and British agent at Gilgit (1852–1916). In 1890 he visited Kafiristan (Nuristan) shortly before its invasion by Amir Abdur Rahman (q.v.) and wrote the final and most complete picture of its pagan culture before the forcible conversion to Islam. *The Kafirs of the Hindu-Kush*, (London, 1896).

RUDAGI Early Persian poet attached to the court of the Samanid emperors, c. 9th century, fragments of whose poetry are quoted by Nizami (q.v.).

ROBERTS, FIELD-MARSHAL EARL FREDERICK (1832–1914) British commander during the Second Afghan War. Led British forces to Kabul in 1879 following the murder of Sir Louis Cavagnari (q.v.) and took control of the city. His execution of the perpetrators caused great resentment, but his forces were able to put down the resistance. Later, after the disastrous defeat of the British garrison at Maiwand, he marched to Kandahar within 20 days and managed to rescue the situation. *Forty-one years in India*, 2 vols, (London, 1898).

S

SALE, LADY FLORENTINA Wife of Gen. Sir Robert Sale, (q.v.) (1790–1853). Resident in Kabul during the British occupation (1841), she accompanied the forces during the retreat of January 1842 until being taken hostage and released later that year. Her journal is an extraordinary first-hand account of one of the worst catastrophes to be suffered by the British Army. *A Journal of the Disasters in Affghanistan*, (London, 1843).

SALE, GENERAL SIR ROBERT (1782–1845) British officer during the First Afghan War, and husband of Lady Florentina Sale (q.v.).

SANA'I OF GHAZNI Abu'l Majd Majdud bin Adam, writer and mystic (d. 1131), lived under the Ghaznavid ruler Bahram Shah. *The first book of the Hadiqatu'l-haqiqat, or, The enclosed garden of the truth*, tr. by J. Stephenson, (Calcutta 1910).

SARIANIDI, V.I. *The golden hoard of Bactria: from the Tillya-tepe excavations in northern Afghanistan*, (New York, 1985).

SAYF IBN MUHAMMAD HARAWI Poet and historian, (1282–?). Writer of a history of Herat, composed during the reign of the Kurt Maliks, c.1310. *Tarikh nama-i-Harat*, ed. Muhammad Zubayr as-Siddiqi, (Calcutta, 1944).

SCHLUMBERGER, DANIEL *The excavations at Surkh Kotal and the problem of Hellenism in Bactria and India*, Proceedings of the British Academy, 1961; *Surkh Kotal en Bactriane*, (Paris, 1983).

SCOTT, G.B. *Afghan and Pathan: a sketch*, (London, 1929).

SEIERSTAD, ÅSNE *The Bookseller of Kabul*, (Virago, 2004).

SHAH, SAFIA *Afghan caravan*, (London, 1990).

SHAH, SAIRA *The storyteller's daughter*, (London, 2003).

SHAH RUKH (1377–1447) Fourth son of Tamerlane (q.v.) and ruler of the Timurid Empire from Herat, 1409–1447.

SHAH SHUJA (1780–1842) Ruler of Afghanistan 1803–1809 and, after a period of exile in Ludhiana and British intervention, again in 1838–42. Murdered after the retreat of British forces in Afghanistan, 5 April 1842.

SHER ALI KHAN Son of Dost Mohammed (q.v.); ruler of Afghanistan 1863–68 and 1868–79. Fled from Kabul after the British occupation of the city and died in Mazar-i-Sharif whilst attempting to seek Russian support against the invasion.

SIDKY, H. *The Greek kingdom of Bactria*, (University Press of America, 2000).

SIKORSKI, RADEK *Dust of the Saints: Journey to Herat in Time of War*, (London, 1989)

SIMS-WILLIAMS, N. *Bactrian documents from Northern Afghanistan*, (Oxford, 2000).

SINGH, MAHARAJAH RUNJIT Sikh ruler in the Punjab (1780–1839). Became governor of Lahore in 1798 as a vassal of the Afghan King Zaman Shah (q.v.), but with the waning of the Afghan Empire, he gained independence, capturing Jammu, Kashmir and Peshawar. A close ally of the British, they refused to seek that he return Peshawar to Afghan rule under Dost Mohammed, an act almost certainly to have averted the First Afghan War.

SIRDAR ALI IKBAL SHAH *Afghanistan of the Afghans*, (London, 1928); *The Tragedy of Amanullah,* (London, 1933).

STARK, FREYA *The Minaret of Djam: an excursion in Afghanistan*, (London, 1970).

STEWART, RORY *The Places In Between*, (Picador, 2004)

STOCQUELER, J.H. *Memorials of Affghanistan,* (Calcutta, 1843).

STODDART, COL. CHARLES British Army officer (d. 1842). Present at the siege of Herat with Eldred Pottinger (q.v.), and later sent on a diplomatic mission to the Emir of Bokhara, by whom he was imprisoned. Despite the efforts of Arthur Conolly (q.v.) to release him, he was beheaded in 1842.

STRABO Greek geographer, 1st century BC. His work contains descriptions based on earlier authorities of Bactria and Ariana. *Geography*, tr. H.L. Jones, Loeb Classical Library.

SUBUKTIGIN (942–977) Successor to Alptigin (q.v.) as ruler of Ghazni 963–977. Presided over the increase of Ghazni's power towards the end of the 10th century at the expense of the Samanid Empire. Followed by his son Mahmud the Great (q.v.).

SYKES, SIR PERCY *A History of Afghanistan*, 2 vols, (London, 1940).

T

TANNER, STEPHEN *Afghanistan: a military history from Alexander the Great to the fall of the Taliban*, (New York, 2002).

TARN, W.W. *The Greeks in Bactria and India*, (Cambridge, 1938).

THACKSTON, W.M. *See* Husayn Bayqara, Khwandamir, Ansari of Herat

THESIGER, WILFRED. (1910–2003) Explorer. He visited Afghanistan on several occasions, leading expeditions to Nuristan and the Hazarajat. His photographic collection is held by the Pitt-Rivers Museum, Oxford. *Among the Mountains: Travels through Asia*, (HarperCollins, 1998)

THOMAS, LOWELL Pioneering American radio journalist and traveller, (1892–1981). *Beyond Khyber pass*, (London, 1927).

TIMUR SHAH Second King of Afghanistan, r. 1773–1793. Transferred the capital from Kandahar to Kabul after suffering hostility from a number of Pushtun tribal chiefs.

TIMUR (Tamerlane) (1336–1405). Founder of the Timurid Empire. Born in Kesh near Samarkand, claiming descent from Genghis Khan, he spent time as a provincial governor before being forced from his position by court intrigues. Timur was a privateer in Seistan before manoeuvring himself into a position of power in Balkh and Transoxiana in 1369, from which he was able to build a great empire through endless military campaigns. *Political and military institutes of Tamerlane*, Sharfuddin Ali Yezdi, tr. Major Davy, (Dehli, 1972); *The Mulfuzat Timury, or, Autobiographical memoirs of the Moghul Emperor Timur*, tr. C. Stewart, (London, 1830); *The rise and rule of Tamerlane*, B.F. Manz, (Cambridge, 1999); *Tamerlane: Sword of Islam, Conqueror of the World*, J. Marozzi, (London, 2004); see also Khwandamir.

TRAUTMAN, KATHLEEN *Spies Behind the Pillars, Bandits at the Pass*, (New York, 1972).

TREBECK, GEORGE Traveller, d.1825. Companion of William Moorcroft (q.v.).

U

ULUGH BEG (1394–1449). Grandson of Timur (Tamerlane) (q.v.). Viceroy of Samarkand and later ruler of the Timurid Empire after the death of Shah Rukh (q.v.). Particularly noted for astronomical work conducted from his observatory in Samarkand; the results of his work were published in England in 1650. *Epochae celebriores, astronomis, historicis, chronologis, Chataiorvm, Syro-Graecorvm, Arabvm, Persarvm, Chorasmiorvm, usitatae, ex traditione Ulug Beigi, Indiae citra extraque Gangem principis*, (London, 1650). *Ulugh Beg's Catalogue of Stars*, ed. E.B. Knobel, (Washintgton, 1917).

UNSURI Early Persian poet (d. 1040–50?), resident at the court of Mahmud of Ghazni. *The virgin and her lover: fragments of an ancient Greek novel and a Persian epic poem*, ed. T. Hägg and B. Utas, (Brill, 2003).

UPASAK, C.S. *History of Buddhism in Afghanistan*, (Central Institute of Higher Tibetan Studies, 1990).

URBAN, MARK *War in Afghanistan*, (Macmillan, 1988).

V

VAMBERY, ARMIN Hungarian traveller and linguist, (1832–1913). From an early age, Armin Vambery showed a prodigious capacity for the learning of languages. Having studied at Bratislava, supporting himself by working as a servant, he proceeded to Constantinople in 1857. Although lame and penniless, his disadvantages did not overcome his wanderlust; at first supporting himself in Turkey as a reciter of poetry, he proceeded to travel widely in the Middle East and Central Asia before returning to Europe to settle down as a professor of languages and writer on Eastern affairs. *Arminius Vambery: His Life and Adventures* (London, 1886); *Travels in Central Asia* (repub. Cambridge Scholars Press, 2002).

VIGNE, G.T. *A personal narrative of a vist to Ghuzni, Kabul, and Afghanistan, and of a residence at the court of Dost Mohamed*, (London, 1840).

VITKEVICH, CAPT. YAN Enigmatic Russian envoy whose presence in Kabul in 1837 led the British to believe that the ruler of Kabul, Dost Mohammed (q.v.), was in league with Persia and Russia against Britain, and the consequent breakdown of diplomatic relations between British India and Afghanistan. Committed suicide, 1838.

VOGELSANG, W. J. *The Afghans*, (Oxford, 2002).

W

WALLER, J.H. *Beyond the Khyber Pass: the road to British disaster in the first Afghan War*, (Austin, 1990).

MIR WAIS HOTAK Ghilzai Pushtun chief (d. 1715) who led a revolt against Persian rule in Kandahar. His actions laid the foundation for the eventual establishment of an independent Afghan state in 1747.

WHEELER, SIR MORTIMER *Flames over Persepolis: Turning-point in history*, (London, 1968).

WILBER, D.N. *Annotated bibliography of Afghanistan* (New Haven: Human Relations Area Files Press, 1968).

WOOD, LT JOHN British naval officer and explorer, (d. 1871). Ordered to Kabul with Sir Alexander Burnes (q.v.) in 1836, the next year he proceeded to Badakhshan and the

Wakhan Corridor in an attempt to reach the source of the Oxus, a journey recorded in his own highly readable account. Disillusioned after the catastrophe of the First Afghan War, he left British government service and worked on engineering projects in Australia and Hong Kong. *A Journey to the Source of the River Oxus*, (London, 1841).

X

XUANZANG See Hsuen-Tsang

Y

YAKUB BIN LAIS Son of a copper-smith, he rose to command the army of Seistan which conquered areas of Afghanistan and Persia, and hence founded the short-lived Saffarid Empire (d. 879). His descendants, however, continued to have influence in the region until the 16th century.

YAKUB KHAN Briefly ruler of Afghanistan after the abdication of his father Shir Ali Khan (q.v.) in 1879.

YAR MUHAMMAD Vizier of Mahmud Shah (q.v.) in Herat; assumed power there in his own name after the murder of Mahmud's son, Kamran Mirza, in 1842. Notable for his role during the Persian siege of 1837–38 and his involvement with Eldred Pottinger (q.v.).

YAQUT AL-HAMAWI Arab geographer and traveller, (1179–1229). *Dictionnaire géographique, historique et littéraire de la Perse et des contrées adjacentes*, tr. C. Barbier de Meynard, (Paris, 1861).

YATE, MAJOR C.E. British officer employed on the Anglo-Russian boundary commission in 1884. Present in Herat during the Panjdeh Oasis incident, 1885. *Northern Afghanistan, or Letters from the Afghan Boundary Commission*, (London, 1888).

Z

ZAMAN SHAH (1770–1844) Ruler of Afghanistan 1793–1800. Presided over a decline in the Afghan empire established by Ahmad Shah Durrani (q.v.). Was eventually overthrown by his brother Mahmud Shah (q.v.), blinded, and granted asylum by the British.

ZHANG QIAN see Chang-Kien

ZOROASTER (Also Zardusht, Zarathustra) Reforming Prophet preaching in Balkh sometime between 1400–600 BC; founder of the eponymous religion. *The Gathas of Zarathustra*, tr. S. Insler, (Leiden, 1975); *In search of Zarathustra: the first prophet and the ideas that changed the world*, P. Kriwaczek, (London, 2003); *Zoroastrians: their religious beliefs and practices*, M. Boyce, (London, 1979); *Zoroaster's time and homeland: a study on the origins of Mazdeism and related problems*, G. Gnoli, (Naples, 1980).

GLOSSARY

A

Abbasid	Ruling dynasty holding the office of Caliph in Baghdad 749–1258.
Abdali	See 'Durrani'
Achaemenid	Dynasty ruling Persian Empire 550–331 BC. Named after Hakhamanish, or Achaemenes (700–675 BC), reputed founder of the dynasty.
Achakzai	A sub-tribe of the Pushtun Durranis (q.v.)
Afghan	Originally signifying just the Pushtuns, but now applied to all inhabitants of the modern territory of Afghanistan.
Ahriman	See 'Angra Mainyu'
Ahura Mazda	Avestan 'Wise Lord'. In Zoroastrianism, the beneficent creator of the world and the cosmic order.
Aimaq	Ethnic grouping, numbering under 800,000, living in the western Hazarajat. The Aimaq are semi-sedentary Sunni Muslims, and speak dialects either of Hazaragi, or Dari.
Aksakal	Wakhan village elder
Ali	Cousin and son-in-law of the Prophet. Regarded by Sunni Muslims as the fourth and final of the Rightly-guided Caliphs, and by Shia Muslims as the first true and lawful successor of Mohammed.
Amir	Commander, ruler, nobleman or chief. The title of *Amir al-Mu'minin*, 'Commander of the Faithful', was assumed by Dost Mohammed in 1826 and retained by Afghan monarchs until 1926.
Amu Darya	The River Oxus
Angra Mainyu	In Zoroastrianism, the god of evil and darkness in opposition to Ahura Mazda.
Arachosia	Greek name of the satrapy around modern-day Kandahar
Arg	Citadel
Arghassan River	Also Arghastan River, part of the Helmand River System.
Ariana	Name of the satrapy around modern-day Herat. Cognate with 'Aryan' (q.v.)

Aryan	Name of the Indo-Iranian tribes which crossed into Afghanistan from Central Asia after 1500 BC; from Sanskrit *Aryas*, 'noble'.
Asharite	Islamic school of philosophy named after al-Ashari (d. 945).
Attari	Perfume trader
Aukhoondzadeh	Son of a mullah
Avesta	Sacred writings of the Zoroastrians; also the name of the language in which the scriptures were composed.
Azdha	Persian 'dragon'; referring to geological features in Bamiyan, which legends hold to be the petrified remains of these creatures.

B

Bactra	Balkh; capital of Bactria (q.v.)
Bactria	Classical name of satrapy which now constitutes modern-day Afghan Turkestan.
Badakhshan	Province in the northeast of Afghanistan, whose capital is Faisabad.
Bagh	Garden
Bai	Lord, chief, petty nobleman
Bala Hissar	Citadel within a town, usually on a mound or hill
Baluch	Semi-nomadic ethinic group living generally in the south of Afghanistan. Their language is Baluchi, an Indo-Iranian tonuge, with words from Arabic and Sindhi. Their numbers in Afghanistan are no more than 300,000; many more live over the border in Pakistan.
Band	Dam
Barakzai	Branch of the Durrani tribe of the Pushtuns (q.v.) which held the Kingship of Afghanistan from 1818–1973
Bashi	Head, chief, leader
Bei	See 'Bey'
Bhoosa	Husks, straw, fodder for cattle.
Bodhisattva	In Buddhism, a being who voluntarily forgoes Nirvana in order to help others.
Brahmin	In Hinduism, the highest of the four castes; the priestly caste.

Burj	Tower
Burqa	All-enveloping veil for women.
Buzkashi	A game not dissimilar to polo, played with a goat or calf, usually decapitated.

C

Caliph	Arabic 'deputy'. The successor to the Prophet, and leader of the faithful.
Chaous Baushee	Messenger, caravan leader
Charah	Long knife or dagger
Chillim	A smoking pipe; a hookah or 'hubble bubble'.
Chupkun	Long frock-like tunic worn as ordinary men's dress.

D

Dari	One of the main official languages of Afghanistan; an Indo-Iranian tongue closely related to Farsi (the language of Iran) and Tajik. Dari is generally spoken by the Afghan Tajik population (q.v.).
Darwish	Also 'dervish'. A religious mendicant, or member of an Islamic religious order. See also 'fakir'.
Dasht	Plain, or valley floor.
Deva	In Hinduism, spirit or god; also refers to spirit in Zoroastrianism.
Dinar	From Latin *denarius*; gold coin.
Dirham	From Greek *drachma*; small silver coin.
Durrani	Major tribe of the Pushtuns; originally the Abdali, it was renamed the Durrani by one of its members, Ahmed Shah, first King of Afghanistan, after one of his honorific titles, *dur-i-durran*, 'Pearl of Pearls'.

F

Fakir	An ascetic, or religious mendicant.
Farsang	Measurement of distance, approx. 6.25 km.
Fatimid	Ismaili Caliphate based in Cairo, 909–1171.
Feringhee	European; a corruption of the word 'Frankish'.

G

Ghazi	In Islam, a champion against infidels; a title used of any Muslim who devotes himself to the destruction of infidels.
Ghayrat	Personal honour in the Pushtunwali code
Ghaznavid	Empire founded by Subuktigin from the city of Ghazni (977–1155).
Ghilzai	A major Pushtun tribe, now predominantly in the vicinity of Herat.
Ghorid	Dynasty which overcame the Ghaznavids (q.v.) to rule territory from eastern Iran to Bengal, 1150–1217.
	Graeco-Bactrian Empire Independent empire ruled by Greeks in the north of Afghanistan, c. 250–130 BC.

H

Hadiths	In Islam, the traditions relating to the Prophet or his companions.
Hanafi	Islamic legal tradition or school of thought, prevalent in Afghanistan.
Hazaragi	The language of the Hazara people, close to Dari, but with a great deal of Mongol vocabulary.
Hazrat Ali	See 'Ali'
Hephthalites	Also 'White Huns'. A Central Asian tribe which invaded Afghanistan c. AD 400.
Hijra, Hegira	The flight of the Prophet from Mecca to Medina in AD 622, from which the Islamic era is dated.
Hindu Kush	Principal mountain range of Afghanistan, stretching southwest from the Pamirs; the name, according to Ibn Battuta, means 'Killer of Indians'.
Hindu Shahi	Indian dynasty which ruled Kabul from AD 870–987

I

Id-i-Kurban	Muslim festival of sacrifice.
Imam	The leader of prayer in a mosque; title belonging to various Islamic leaders, including the Caliph; in Shia Islam, title belonging to the leader of the community—a descendant of the Prophet—who is held to be infallible. In some branches of Shiism, the Imam is held to be in hiding (occultation), until the end of time.
Imam Medhi	A saviour, of the progeny of the Prophet, whom Muslims hold will re-appear at the end of time.

Iran	In Firdousi's *Shahnameh*, the land south of the Oxus including Afghanistan, opposed to the Central Asian Kingdom of Turan (q.v.). Now only refers to the present-day Islamic Republic.
Ismaili	A Shia sect, which holds HH The Aga Khan to be the true Imam (q.v.).
Iwan	In architecture, a vaulted recess opening off a courtyard.

J

Jihun	River Oxus, or Amu Darya.
Jaji	Smaller Pushtun tribe, predominantly in the southwest.
Jaxartes	Greek name for the modern river Syr Darya.
Jezail	Heavy musket
Jui	Stream, canal

K

Ka'ba, Kaaba	Holiest shrine of the Islamic faith, at Mecca.
Kafila	Caravan or convoy
Kafir	Unbeliever. Particularly applied to the inhabitants in the mountainous region of northeast Afghanistan—Kafiristan—before their forcible conversion to Islam in the 19th century.
Karar	Bearer, servant
Kajavas	A camel litter for women travellers.
Karaiz	Also *qadat*; underground water irrigation channels.
Kasa	Cassia tree
Kash-gow	Yak
Khakan	Turkish title of rank; king.
Khan	Lord; title of honour or respect.
Khanaqah	Meetinghouse of a Sufi order.
Khatib	Islamic preacher
Khojeh	Professor; teacher in an Islamic college
Khurasan	Formerly a great province of the Persian Empire, including the cities of Herat, Balkh, Nishapur and Merv; it now refers only to a northeastern province of modern-day Iran. The name means 'Land of the Sun'.

Khwarazm Shahs	Short-lived dynasty controlling Central Asia and much of Afghanistan in the 12th century, until its obliteration by Genghis Khan in 1220.
Kinbob	Brocade, gold embroidery.
Kirgah	Nomadic tent
Kirghiz, Kyrgyz	A Turkic-speaking Sunni Muslim people living in the Pamirs. Many of them left for Turkey after the Russian invasion, leaving only a small population behind in Afghanistan.
Kishlak	Village
Kismut	Service, duty
Kiyik	Deer
Kizilbash	Lit. 'Red-heads'. One of the Shia tribes originally in the service of the 16th-century rulers of Iran; a number of them settled in Kabul in the 18th century as servants of the Afghan kings.
Kobba	Lantern in the Wakhi language; not to be confused with Persian *kobba*, 'news'.
Koh-i Baba	Mountain range in the centre of Afghanistan.
Koorgeen	A type of woven bag.
Kos	Indian measure of distance, varying between 1.6 miles and 2.3 miles.
Kotal	Hill
Kourut	Dried yoghurt
Kshatriya	In Hinduism, the second or military caste.
Kufic	A heavy variety of Arabic or Persian script, suitable for stone carving.
Kurt Maliks	Dynasty ruling Herat, 1245–1381.
Kushan	Empire ruling Afghanistan, parts of Central Asia and northwest India, c. AD 50–4th century.

L

Layla	See Majnun
Li	Chinese measurement of distance; 3 li equal approximately 1 mile.
Little Vehicle	Also *Hinayana (Theravada)—an early variety of Buddhism.*

Ludhiana	Indian city in the Punjab.
Lunghi	Turban
M	
Maharajah	Indian princely title
Mahayana	Also 'Greater Vehicle'; a major school of Buddhism, inaugurated c. 2nd century AD; Mahayana Buddhism spread from northwest India to China, Tibet and East Asia. It was prominent under the Kushan ruler King Kanishka.
Majnun	Legendary Iranian character, not dissimilar to the European Romeo, with Layla as Juliet.
Malik	King
Mamluk	Slave-soldiers, usually Turkish.
Maurya	Name of an Indian empire founded by Chandragupta, c. 300 BC.
Mazar	Tomb, sanctuary
Mehrab	Niche in the qibla wall (q.v.)
Mihrgan	Autumn equinox
Milmastia	Hospitality in the Pushtun honour code.
Mir	Honorific title; originally 'son of a prince'.
Mirza	See 'Mir'
Molamma	Poem composed of alternate Arabic and Persian couplets.
Moohtussib	Chief of Police
Moonshee	Baushee Chief secretary
Motwullee	Religious custodian or administrator.
Mullah	Muslim cleric or teacher.
Musalman	Muslim
Myrobalan	Variety of astringent fruit, particularly rich in tannin.
N	
No Roz	New Year's Day
Nullah	Dry watercourse

O

Oolose	Pushtun tribal court
Otta	Flour, meal
Oxus	Greek name of the Amu Darya or Jihun; the river forming the northern border of Afghanistan.

P

Pahlevi	Ancient Iranian dialect.
Pamir Range	Mountainous area in northeast Afghanistan.
Parthian	Dynasty ruling in Iran from c. 250 BC–AD 250.
Pashto	One of the main languages of Afghanistan; an Indo-Iranian tongue spoken by the Pushtuns (q.v.)
Pice	Coin equivalent to .01 of a rupee.
Pilau	Dish of rice and meat, flavoured with spices.
Poshteen	Afghan sheepskin coat
Pul	Bridge
Purana	Ancient Hindu text.
Pushtun	Also 'Pathan'. Major ethnic group—both nomadic and sedentary—predominantly in the south of Afghanistan.

Q

Qibla	In Islam, the direction of prayer, facing Mecca.

R

Ramadan	The ninth month of the Islamic calendar, during which a fast is observed from dawn until dusk.
Roghan	Vegetable oil
Rud	River
Rum	The Byzantine Empire
Rustam	From Firdousi's *Shahnameh*, legendary hero of ancient Iran.
Ruttul	Measure of weight.

S

Sakae	Central Asian tribe that invaded Afghanistan c. 150 BC.
Samanid	Central Asian empire with its capital at Bokhara; ruled Afghanistan during the 10th century AD.
Sangharama	Buddhist monastery, convent.
Sassanian	Dynasty ruling Persia from 3rd to 7th century AD.
Sastra	Hindu sacred text
Satrap	Governor or viceroy in the Persian empire, his province being known as a satrapy.
Sayyid	A descendant of the Prophet.
Seljuk	Turkish dynasty that flourished in northern and western Afghanistan during the 11th century AD.
Shah	King
Shahr	City
Shahna	Royal representative
Shaitan	In Islam, the devil, or Satan.
Shias, Shiites	Muslims who believe Ali, the son-in-law and cousin of the Prophet, to have been, along with his descendents, the only legitimate successor to Mohammed.
Simoom	Dust-laden hot desert wind.
Sirdar	Honorific title of rank; originally 'commander of the army'.
Soghdia	Name of the Persian satrapy north of the Oxus.
Sohrab	From Firdousi's *Shahnameh*, a legendary Iranian hero, the son of Rustam.
Stupa	Earthen mound or domed structure, generally used to contain Buddhist relics.

T

Tahirid	Short-lived dynasty in northwest Afghanistan, 9th century AD.
Tajik	Persian (Dari) speaking sedentary ethnic group of ancient Iranian stock, forming perhaps 20–25% of the Afghan population.
Teppe	Hill

Tillah	Small Indian coin.
Tirthaka	Title given to a Brahmin priest who has been on pilgrimage.
Turan	The land of Central Asia, north of the River Oxus.
Turcoman	Turkic tribal group living in Northern Afghanistan, numbering in Afghanistan less than 300,000. Their language is Turkmeni, which is closely related to the tongue of the Uzbeks.
Turki Shahi	Buddhist dynasty that ruled over Kabul, c. 6th century–870 AD.

U

Uzbeks	A Turkic tribal group inhabiting the northern areas of Afghanistan. They form around 10% of the Afghan population.

V

Vizier	A leading officer in government, generally equivalent to a chief minister.

W

White Huns	See 'Hephthalites'
Wuzeer	See 'Vizier'

Y

Yaksha	A demigod attending on the deity Kuvera.
Yueh-Chih	(also Yuezhi) Central Asian tribal group which passed into the land of Afghanistan c. 1st century BC; their leading clan founded the Kushan Empire (q.v.).
Yusufzaie	Pushtun tribe.

Z

Ziarat	Place of pilgrimage; tomb, shrine.

INDEX

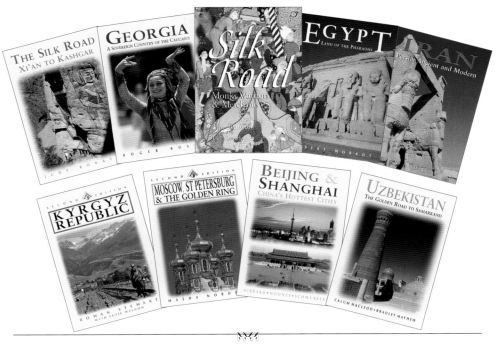

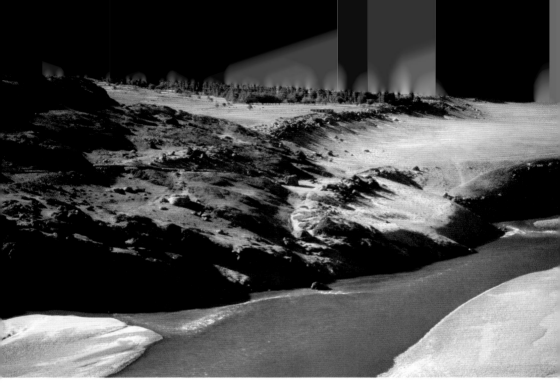

The Oxus in the Wakhan; (bottom) The Oxus near Eshkashem [J. Renouf]

THE AFGHAN TRAVEL CENTRE

107 Great Portland Street
London W1W 6QG
Telephone: (44) 20 7580 7020
Fax: (44) 20 7580 7101
Email: abdul@afghantravelcenter.co.uk

In Kabul:
1 Mohammad Jaankhan Watt
Kabul
Afghanistan
Telephone (93) 793 88901

Gandamack Lodge Hotel

Probably the finest, and certainly the most famous, guest house in Kabul. Run by Afghan veteran Peter Jouvenal, the Lodge has a garden and fine restaurant.

6 Passport Lane, Shahr-i-Naw, Kabul
Email: pjouvenal@aol.com
Telephone: 00 93 (0)702 76937
Email reservations: Gandamacklodge@yahoo.com

AFGHANLOGISTICS

- We supply cars, drivers and translators both in Kabul and for travel around the country to a wide variety of clients

- We provide lodging in our own guesthouse, managed by a hotelier who has four top-class guesthouses in Kabul

- Our clients include NGOs, companies, news organisations, journalists and Travel Afghanistan—the first tour operator to establish itself successfully in our country since 1979

- We provide security analysis by working with ANSO (Afghanistan NGO Security Organisation)

- We provide translators who speak English, Pashto and Dari

- Our fixers get what you need done time and time again

- All servicing is done by our sister company, Jamshady Trading—a company with twenty years' experience of the automobile business

- We can source and supply equipment necessary for the establishment of an office or private house—most recently a generator for the German Press Centre

Afghan Logistics, Insaf Car Seller, Khair Khana Pass, North of Kabul, Afghanistan
CEO: Muqim Jamshady Email: muqim@afghan-logistics.com
www.afghan-logistics.com
Kabul mobile: 00 93 (0)702 77408 or 00 93 (0)793 91462
International satellite phone: 00 88216 2116 4294

The Gem Hunter

(www.gems-afghan.com)

Mr. Gary

Mr. Gary

Dear Readers,

Since 1972 I have enjoyed exploring Afghanistan with my many Afghan friends. Assuming that you have purchased this comprehensive and informative guidebook on your personal quest for knowledge of Afghanistan, we personally invite you to visit our website. For further information on exploration, gems, books, films, and adventure tours to add to your experience, please contact me directly.

169 ct.
Aquamarine

$29.95 Book

Looking forward to hearing from you.

32.32 ct.
Ruby & Diamond

Mr. Gary
Gary W. Bowersox - "The Gem Hunter"
President
GeoVision, Inc.
P.O. Box 89646
Honolulu, HI 96830 USA
808-277-2543
mrgary77@aol.com
www.gems-afghan.com

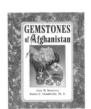

$60.00 Book

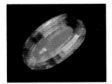

Tourmaline

$29.95 DVD

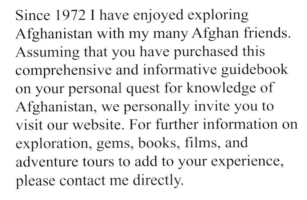

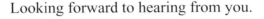

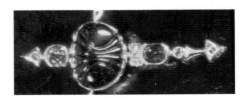

Uzbek child's cap, Balkh, c. 1920 [Paiva]

The Voice of Afghan Business in the United States

The Afghan-American Chamber of Commerce is the leading advocate for the development of trade between the United States and Afghanistan. We also work with the U.S. government and international organizations to promote investment in the Afghan marketplace and to encourage development of Afghanistan's economy.

We offer a range of member assistance programs, informational meetings and seminars to help businesses find rewarding opportunities in Afghanistan.

Please visit our website at **www.a-acc.org** to learn more about the benefits of membership.

Member of
U.S. Chamber of Commerce

In Partnership with

CIPE Center for International Private Enterprise

www.A-ACC.org

Geographic Expeditions

Specialists in Travel to Central Asia since 1982

Geographic Expeditions offers a sensationally varied roster of outstanding tours and treks across the breadth of Central Asia. We feature unique itineraries which explore the rich history and stunning natural beauty of the region. As a consistent leader in travel to challenging destinations we are delighted to introduce our travelers to the fabled Khyber Pass and the rugged beauty of Afghanistan.

In addition to group tours, Geographic Expeditions develops custom trips for individuals, academic institutions and non-profit organizations.

For a copy of our astute, amusing and award-winning catalog of adventures, please call us at 800-777-8183.

GEOGRAPHIC
EXPEDITIONS

www.geoex.com

Photos: Roland and Sabrina Michaud/Woodfin Camp

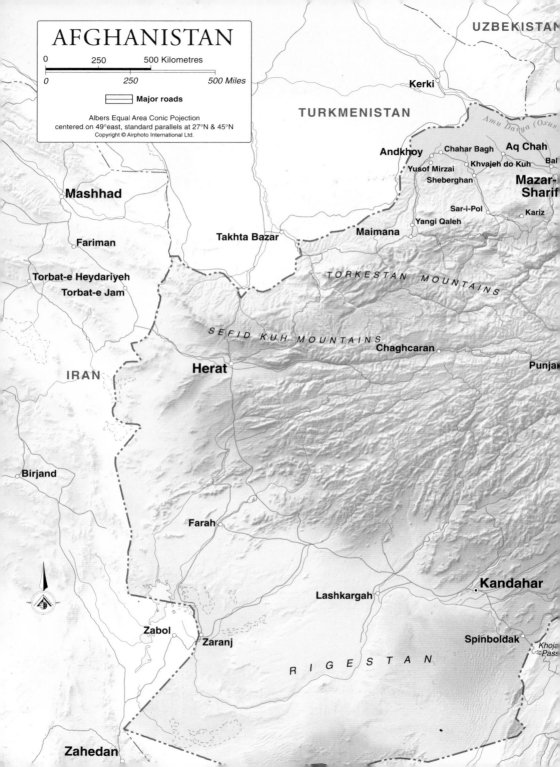